NUMBER ONE
IN
WAR AND PEACE

The History of No.1 Squadron 1912-2000

Norman Franks and Mike O'Connor

GRUB STREET · LONDON

Published by
Grub Street
The Basement
10 Chivalry Road
London SW11 1HT

British Library Cataloguing in Publication Data
Franks, Norman L. R. (Norman Leslie Robert), 1940-
Number One Squadron in war and peace: the history of
No. 1 Squadron, 1912-2000
1. Great Britain, Royal Air Force. Squadron, No. 1 – history
I. Title II. O'Connor, Mike
358.4'00941

ISBN 1-902304-55-1

Typeset by Pearl Graphics, Hemel Hempstead

Printed and bound in Great Britain by
Biddles Ltd, Guildford and King's Lynn

CONTENTS

Acknowledgements

The authors wish to thank all members of the Squadron, past and present, who have generously contributed to this work. In the main these contributions are to be found within the pages of the book. A few stand out; Air Commodore H E C Boxer CB OBE, Group Captain G A Bolland CBE, Air Chief Marshal Sir Peter Squire KCB DFC AFC, Air Chief Marshal Sir Patrick Hine GBE GBE, Air Marshal Sir Ken Hayr KCB KBE AFC, Squadron Leader C Huckstep DFC, Flight Lieutenant A R Pollock, and of course Squadron Leader D P F 'Mac' McCaig MBE AFC, until recently the Squadron Association's Hon. Sec.

Others who have helped with information and/or photographs need to be mentioned, they are: Peter Arnold, Flight Lieutenant Chris Averty, Paul Baillie, Brenda Halahan-Bartholomew, Jim Davies, Graham Day of the Air Historical Branch, Barry Gray, Tony Henniker, Peter Holloway, Christopher John, Anne Kelsey, Paul Leaman, Stuart Leslie, Simon Moody of the RAF Museum, Richard Owen, Andy Saunders, Joe Warne, Luce Wilson.

Thanks are also due to the Imperial War Museum Sound Archives for permission to quote from the taped interviews with AVM John Worrall (4757/04) ACM Sir Theodore McEvoy (3183/04) and Mr Edward Bolt (3/7). Also the staff of the Public Record Office at Kew, Surrey.

Select Bibliography

My Life, by Dermot Boyle, unpublished manuscript, courtesy of the RAF Museum.
Flying Fever, by AVM S F Vincent, Jarrolds, 1972.
Time and Chance, by Peter Townsend, Collins & Sons, 1978.
Ventures and Visions, by G Garro-Jones, Hutchinson & Co, 1935.
Fighter Pilot, by Paul Richey, Jane's Pub Co, 1980.
Fighter Pilot's Summer, Norman Franks & Paul Richey, Grub Street, 1993.
The Flying Sailor, by André Jubelin, Hurst & Blackett, 1953.
No.1 Squadron, by Michael Shaw, Ian Allan Ltd, 1986.
Aces High, Vols 1 and 2, by C F Shores and C Williams, Grub Street, 1994 and 1998.
Spitfire Patrol, by Colin Gray, Hutchinson & Co, 1990.
Spitfire RCW, by Ken Nelson, K J Nelson CD, 1994.
RAF Tangmere Revisited, by Andy Saunders, Sutton Pub Ltd, 1998.
Falklands, The Air War, Messrs Burden, Draper, Rough, Smith & Wilton, Arms & Armour Press, 1986.
Mnozí nedoleteli, by Frantiek Loucký, Nase Vojsko, 1989.
To Fly No More, by Colin Cummings, Nimbus Pub.
Lost to Service, by Colin Cummings, Nimbus Pub.

PART ONE

Chapter One

THE BEGINNING

The historic first flight by a powered heavier than air machine was by the Wright brothers in 1903 but aviation had begun long before that in the form of hot air and hydrogen filled balloons.

The Montgolfier brothers in France first flew their hot air balloon in 1783 and the first manned ascent in Britain occurred in August 1784. The Channel was crossed for the first time in January 1785. In September 1862 James Glaisher and Henry Coxwell exceeded 30,000 feet in a hydrogen balloon but their actual height achieved could not be established as both men collapsed due to lack of oxygen and were lucky to survive.

In Britain the Royal Engineers began military experiments with balloons at Woolwich in 1878 and by the following year they were able to report that they had five balloons and a small group of officers and men who were competent to use them. In 1880 and 1882 a balloon section was present at the manoeuvres at Aldershot and as a result of this encouraging start the Royal Engineers department in charge of them, the Balloon Equipment Store, was transferred from Woolwich. The move to the School of Military Engineering at Chatham, where a balloon factory, depot and school of instruction were established, gave the balloon sections a more permanent place. In 1884 a balloon detachment consisting of three balloons, two officers and fifteen other ranks accompanied Sir Charles Warriner's expedition to Bechuanaland. There was no fighting and due to the height of the terrain only the largest of the three balloons could raise a man in the air. That the white man could ascend into the sky, however, made a great psychological effect on the native population. The following year another smaller detachment accompanied an expedition to the Sudan, where a few useful reconnaissances were made.

In the 1899 Aldershot manoeuvres information gained from an observation late in the day by Lieutenant B R Ward enabled Lieutenant General Sir Evelyn Wood to make a night attack on his enemy, which was a complete success. Wood reported favourably on the balloons and in the following year a balloon section was formally set up as part of the Royal Engineers, with a base at South Farnborough, where the balloon factory had moved to in 1894.

In 1899 four balloon sections took part in the Boer War in South Africa with one of the sections caught in the Siege of Ladysmith. Despite various problems, not least prejudice against this new form of warfare from traditionalists, a lot of useful work was carried out. In 1905 a new factory was built and under Colonel J E Capper, a far-sighted officer, experiments were carried out in a variety of areas including man-lifting kites and airships. He also encouraged the aeroplane experiments of Lieutenant J W Dunne and the colourful Sam Cody, despite a very tight budget.

Edward Bolt, a fitter and storeman at Farnborough, recalled in an interview for the Imperial War Museum (Interview with Edward Bolt, Imperial War Museum Sound Archives, reference 3/7), an incident concerning Capper:

> 'I remember one Saturday: Colonel Capper before he made his general inspection, he always inspected the officers first: he came to Lieutenant Waterlow and he told him to lift his foot. He lifted his foot; we couldn't hear what he said but we could see that he told him in front of all the parade to go and change his shoes because his heels was right down on one shoe. He stood the parade at ease and gave them permission for the officers to smoke and the parade would form up as soon as Lieutenant Waterlow returned wearing a proper pair of shoes. The parade carried on as usual.' [1]

The Royal Flying Corps
In September 1907 the first British army airship, *Nulli Secundus*, flew and the next month it carried out a flight of over three hours from Farnborough to Buckingham Palace before landing at the Crystal Palace.

In 1911 the Air Battalion of the Royal Engineers was formed and the Balloon School at

---

[1] Capper had little to do with the day-to-day running and experimenting of the unit, which was left to Waterlow as chief instructor. Several officers were taught to fly the airships including J T C Moore-Brabazon (later Lord Brabazon of Tara and the holder of Royal Aero Club certificate No.1).

Farnborough became No. 1 Company and No. 2 Company with aeroplanes moved to Larkhill in Wiltshire. The total strength of the Air Battalion was to consist of only 14 officers and 150 other ranks.

Britain was far behind both France and Germany, but in November 1911 a sub committee of the Committee for Imperial Defence considered the whole matter of military flying and the result of their deliberations was the recommendation to set up a British Aeronautical Service to be known as 'The Flying Corps', consisting of a Military Wing, a Naval Wing and a Central Flying School. The Royal Flying Corps was constituted on 13 May 1912 by a Royal warrant and on 13 May the Air Battalion was absorbed by the new organization. The cavalry term squadron was adopted for the service's basic unit and thus No. 1 Company became No. 1 Squadron.

E M Maitland – the first CO

The commander of the airship company, Captain E M Maitland, became the first commanding officer of 1 Squadron. He had been educated at Haileybury and Trinity College, Cambridge and joined the Essex Regiment in 1900. After service in South Africa he became interested in balloons in 1908. Though his interest was airships he did fly aeroplanes and pioneered parachuting, including one descent from beneath a spherical balloon in 1915, when he dropped from 10,500 feet. He was a well-liked officer and had a more relaxed attitude to discipline than most. Edward Bolt was going out for the evening with some chums on their bicycles:

> 'The road by the side of the Farnborough area was very bad and the new road was being made, and it was left open, there were no lights or anything because it was a private road, and I went out with 2 or 3 others to Camberley or Frimley for a night out and we'd had one or two and coming back none of us noticed this road but I, anxious to get back to sign in before midnight (otherwise we'd have been on an absentee charge) went straight over this road dip and went in Cambridge hospital for a day or two and when I came back Captain Maitland said "Bolt you either give up your bicycle or the Flying Corps; choose which!"'

Bolt had failed to see the roadworks in the dark as he had no lights. He gave up his bicycle when Maitland added, '*bicycle or dismiss the service!*' However, Bolt recommenced riding his bicycle within a very short time and Maitland turned the 'Nelsonian' blind eye.

Maitland was considered 'the Father of Airships' and in 1919 crossed the Atlantic both ways in the airship R34. As an Air Commodore he was killed in the crash of the airship R38 in 1921.

Much important experimentation was carried out on the airships and in the 1913 Army manoeuvres the airships *Delta* and *Eta* were both wireless equipped, with *Delta* sending sixty-six messages in seven flights.

One of the airships bought was the French Lebaurdy, which was tested at Farnborough before acceptance. After one flight it suffered a serious accident as related by Bolt:

> 'When coming into land the engines were cut off and the towrope was dropped. It was going at such a speed that when coming in towards the aerodrome, the trail rope caught on house roofs, and broke down quite a number of chimneys; eventually the towrope got tangled up in the railings of the Aircraft Establishment at Farnborough; it was then manhandled by the groundcrew who were waiting for it to be able to bring it safely down back to the aerodrome. When trying to enter the airship shed, some mistake must have been made in the height of the airship shed or the Lebaurdy airship. When entering the balloon caught a bolt that was sticking down from the catwalk, it ripped a very great hole in the top of the airship that caused it to collapse. I was one of the groundcrew guiding the airship into the shed. When it collapsed, I was covered with the balloon dropping, I got scratched badly by the wiring of the fuselage of the Lebaurdy. Eventually I crawled out bleeding very badly – my face and arms were cut. When I eventually got out and got clean someone standing close by with Captain Maitland asked me if I was hurt. I said "Can't you see I'm hurt, you bloody fool!", to my astonishment, it was Field Marshal Lord Roberts, who was dressed in mufti.
>
> Captain Maitland, who was standing by the side of him, ordered me to be placed under arrest. Lord Roberts said "No, No I asked a silly question and I got the right answer".'

Opinion was divided on the military use of the airship; however the navy was clear in their use of them. Before aeroplanes had a worthwhile range and payload the airship offered both, which were essential for the navy's protection of Britain's trade routes. Thus at the end of 1913 the airships were handed over to the Royal Navy, leaving 1 Squadron without any machines or purpose. On 1 May 1914 the unit was re-organized as an aeroplane squadron but this had not been completed by the outbreak of war four months later and therefore the senior squadrons of the RFC, much to the chagrin of 1 Squadron, were 2, 3 and 4 Squadrons.

Chapter Two

TO WAR – EVENTUALLY

The outbreak of war in August 1914 found 1 Squadron at Farnborough and mere bystanders as the other squadrons were caught up in the heady atmosphere and preparations for mobilization. A number of their officers were poached to make up the numbers of the other units.

Command of the Squadron passed through the temporary hands of a number of officers such as C A H Longcroft and F V Holt before they too went off to France. As the RFC participated in the retreat from Mons and then the Battle of the Marne, 1 Squadron busied itself with training replacements for the Expeditionary Force. Using a motley collection of Henri Farmans, Maurice Farmans and Blériots a number of pilots were trained. This was despite some of their machines being taken away to bolster 6 Squadron forming for service in Belgium.

On 28 January 1915, Major W G H Salmond arrived to take command and he was destined to lead the Squadron to war. He had been serving on the staff of RFC Headquarters in France since the original embarkation of the RFC in August and brought with him all the latest news and tactics.

The Squadron received orders on 1 March to proceed to France, with seven officers going by air from Netheravon to Folkestone, under the command of Captain E R Ludlow-Hewitt, and another five by air from Farnborough to Folkestone under the command of Second Lieutenant J C Joubert de la Ferté. Each machine carried a mechanic, rather than an observer, in order to attend to any technical problems en-route. One officer was left behind after he broke his arm swinging a propeller and had to be replaced. Due to weather and technical problems the aeroplanes did not come together at Folkestone until 5 March and then were held up by fog in the Channel. This cleared two days later and a successful crossing was made. Considering the frail construction of aeroplanes and the unreliability of engines of the day, it was a considerable achievement that the first machine left Folkestone at 1400 hours and all twelve machines had arrived safely at St Omer by 1630 hours. Many squadrons, even much later in the war, would only arrive with a fraction of their number, the rest having become lost or crashed en-route. The rest of the Squadron proceeded by road under the command of Major Salmond. The transport with thirty men left Avonmouth on the SS *Twickenham* on 3 March, and the remainder of the personnel embarked at Southampton on the SS *Balmoral* two days later.

With the arrival of the transport at St Omer in the afternoon of 8 March the Squadron was now complete. 'A' Flight was equipped with Avros,' B' Flight with BE8's and 'C' Flight with a mixture of BE8's and Moranes. The unloved BE8 was known disparagingly as 'the Bloater'. It was only later in the war that squadrons were equipped with a single type of machine. Together with No. 4 Squadron they formed 3 Wing under Lieutenant Colonel H R M Brooke-Popham. Immediately practice in reconnaissance commenced, with crews familiarising themselves with the area in which they were to operate.

The Battle of Neuve Chapelle
The Squadron had no time to settle in, as their arrival coincided with a major new ground offensive. For the spring 1915 campaign the British Commander-in-Chief, Sir John French, due to lack of guns and ammunition, chose to attack in an area where there was a small tactical advantage and if successful would leave the Germans at a greater disadvantage. The opening of the battle at 0730 hours on 10 March went well, and as part of the campaign to prevent German reinforcements arriving the RFC bombed railway bridges, junctions and stations. On the final day of the battle the BE8s of 1 Squadron bombed the railway bridge at Douai and the junction at Don, during which they suffered their first casualty, when Lieutenant Oswald Mansell-Moullin failed to return. About two weeks later a message was received from him saying that he had been forced to land due to engine failure and had been taken prisoner of war, but had managed to burn his machine, despite the presence of a number of Germans.

On 21 March another machine went missing and it was later learned that the crew had been interned. Second Lieutenant J C Joubert de la Ferté and Lieutenant D M V Veitch had been hit in the engine by anti-aircraft fire on a patrol in the Ghent-Bruges area and, rather than become prisoner of war, had forced landed in neutral Holland. Their machine, Avro No. 740, was purchased by the Dutch and used by their Air Service (Joubert, the brother of P B Joubert, later CO of 1 Squadron, was repatriated in February 1918. Veitch escaped in October 1915 but was then killed in action with 70 Squadron on 8 July 1916).

At the end of March the Squadron moved to the Asylum Ground at Bailleul, as part of 2 Wing, where they were to remain for the next three years – almost a record stay in one place, when most squadrons were moved around fairly frequently. The aeroplanes that were not on patrol left at 0900 hours, with each machine again carrying a mechanic, whilst the advanced party had left at 0730 hours under the care of Sergeant Major J W Waddington. He was commissioned in September as a Lieutenant Quartermaster, together with Sergeant Major John Mead. Both remained in the peacetime RAF and later became Squadron Leader and Wing Commander respectively.

Bailleul

The aerodrome had previously been occupied by 6 Squadron. Permanent wooden-framed, corrugated-iron-roofed sheds for the aeroplanes had been built against the back wall of the enormous Asylum, with some of the personnel billeted in the hospital and others in private houses throughout the town. In the early days the mechanics and the airmen gunners slept in the back of the hangars. The officers eventually had their own compound on the other side of the Bailleul to Armentières road, where they had a bathhouse and tennis courts. The NCOs and men were able to use the Asylum bath, being detailed a Flight at a time, until in December they too built their own bathhouse. However, on match-days, the Squadron football team had priority. Over the next three years they were to make themselves very comfortable, until forced to evacuate their aerodrome in the face of the big German offensive of March 1918.

One of the distinctive features of the aerodrome was the large pond right in the middle. During 6 Squadron's tenure of the Asylum Ground the Wing Commander, during a visit to the unit, took a dim view of it and ordered the Squadron Commander to get rid of it. Lanoe Hawker (later to earn a Victoria Cross) was given the unenviable task by his CO due to the fact he was a Royal Engineer. Realizing that it would require a colossal amount of earth, plus good drains, he decided to board it over. Submitting a rough drawing to the army's Chief Royal Engineer he then left them to carry the job out. It remained a landmark right up until evacuation and subsequently disappeared among the countless shell-holes when the area was bombarded in August 1918.

Hill 60

The enemy had a good view of the British positions around Ypres from a small hummock to the south at Zillebeke, known as Hill 60. Sir John French therefore decided to capture this important position. The RFC very carefully reconnoitred it and took a good selection of photographs. 1 Squadron was given the task of keeping the German aeroplanes away from the hill to prevent them from seeing reinforcements being brought up for the attack. The first patrol took off at 0430 hours on 16 April and with quarter of an hour overlaps there were continuous patrols until 1915 hours. No hostile machines broke through, and the attack the following morning took the Germans by surprise and was a complete success. In addition the Squadron ranged British artillery down on the enemy. On 18 April 1915 after much bitter fighting the British had been forced back off the crest of the hill but this was retaken later that evening. At one point 1 Squadron had eight machines over the hill enabling British artillery to keep the enemy batteries down while British infantry retook the summit.

During the day the Squadron made their first claim of an enemy machine when Captain E R Ludlow-Hewitt and his observer, Corporal M B Fitzgerald, drove off two Aviatiks and then had a combat with a Fokker. They were flying a Morane and manoeuvred themselves above and to the east of the Hun to cut off his line of retreat. After firing at very close range he went down in a steep dive, which the Morane could not follow and they saw him 'wobble' considerably near the ground where the pilot turned and appeared to restart his engine. He was lost sight of in mist. Ludlow-Hewitt had a distinguished career, retiring in 1945 as Air Chief Marshal Sir Edgar Ludlow-Hewitt GCB, GBE, CMG, DSO, MC. Fitzgerald later became the Squadron's Technical Sergeant Major and was subsequently commissioned. He retired from the RAF as a Flight Lieutenant in 1923.

Five days later on 23 April, Captain R A Saunders and his observer Lieutenant C Court-Treatt, while flying one of the Squadron's Avros over Passchendaele, espied an enemy two-seater flying towards them. It flew beneath and Court-Treatt fired four bursts of thirty rounds in all, while the pilot spiralled down and around the target. The enemy aeroplane dived very steeply and landed in a field one mile east of Passchendaele. It was difficult to see if it was damaged or not. The Avro, fitted with only an 80 horsepower engine, was very underpowered with two men and a Lewis gun, and they were only used if there was nothing else. An 110 h.p. Le Rhône engine was sent as an experiment from the depot and the groundcrew fitted it to one of the Avros. This improved the performance though it was prone to overheating.

The flat out operations against the enemy batteries continued until 5 May when the attempt to wrest the hill from the Germans was abandoned.

The Second Battle of Ypres

While still engaged in the bitter fighting on Hill 60 the Germans surprised the Allies by attacking north of Ypres in what became known as the Second Battle of Ypres, using poisonous gas for the first time. The Allies had some inkling that gas might be used, but this was largely ignored and the shock of the new weapon knocked a great gap in the Allied line. The depth of advance was as big a surprise to the Germans who had no reserves and failed to exploit the situation. Desperate defence saved the day but great numbers of troops choked to death in the poisonous gas clouds that crept across the front. The RFC, including 1 Squadron, flew hundreds of hours desperately keeping the Army Command in touch with the Germans' new positions. They directed artillery fire onto them, as well as hampering the enemy's attempts to do the same.

The first award

On 25 May the Squadron was notified of their first gallantry award, a Distinguished Conduct Medal, which surprisingly was not for aerial activities, but for an incident on the ground. This occurred on the very first day of the Battle of Neuve Chapelle and only two days after their arrival in France. On the night of 10/11 March Corporal S C Griggs, under heavy shellfire, had assisted in the repair of an aeroplane that had forced landed in the front line trenches. It was able to fly off at first light. Griggs had enlisted in September 1909 and transferred from the Royal Engineers to the newly formed Royal Flying Corps in 1912, where he was posted initially to No.2 Squadron. Later, in August 1915, he was awarded the Russian Medal of St George Third Class and was still serving in the RAF as a Flight Sergeant in 1927.

The growth of aerial fighting

Up to the middle of 1915 air combat remained fairly insignificant primarily because neither side had suitable armament. The few combats that had taken place had employed rifles, pistols and grenades operated by a gunner but as machines ranged further afield and adopted a more aggressive attitude, two-seaters now carried a machine gun. However this all changed with the introduction of the single-seater Fokker E1 or Eindekker, which had a forward firing machine gun synchronised to fire through the propeller arc. Allied losses began to mount until they reached a peak with the so-called 'Fokker Scourge' of early 1916.

Very early in the morning of 5 July Captain D E Stodart and Second Lieutenant M S Stewart were flying south east of Menin at 7,000 feet in the Avro when they sighted a new type of enemy machine. By virtue of the courses the two aeroplanes were flying it was obvious that the German would cross the bows of the British but about 1,500 feet higher. Stewart unstowed his machine gun and the German descended 800 feet to do battle. The machines circled each other for twenty-five minutes or so exchanging fire, with Stewart loosing off about 100 rounds before his gun jammed. Eventually the German machine flew off in a northerly direction apparently undamaged. An intelligence bulletin later revealed that a German machine had come down after a combat in the locality of their action and at exactly 0430 hours. Both officers had been killed and the wreckage was taken in to Courtrai at 0913 hours.

On 6 July 1 Squadron suffered another loss, this time due to enemy fire when Lieutenant Lambert Playfair was killed. Playfair had attended the Royal Military Academy at Sandhurst on a prize cadetship in 1912 and then served with the First Battalion Royal Scots in January 1913. He had then joined the RFC and been posted to B Flight of No. 1 Squadron as an observer on 10 March 1915, just in time for the Battle of Neuve Chapelle.

On 6 July 1915, he and his pilot Lieutenant O D Filley, took off in Avro 504 No. 4223 from Bailleul for a reconnaissance. In his report Major Geoffrey Salmond, Commanding Officer of 1 Squadron, wrote to the OC 2 Wing:

> 'I herewith attach Lieut. C O (sic) Filley's report on the series of combats in the air yesterday which culminated in the death of Lieut. Playfair.
>
> I wish to bring to your notice the great gallantry of both pilot and observer.
>
> Their duty was to watch an area in order that 11th. Inf. Brigade HQ should have early information of any counter-attack. In addition they were to report any hostile batteries observed firing.
>
> Whilst they were carrying out this task a hostile aeroplane appeared over the area.
>
> It was obvious that this aeroplane would be able to direct artillery fire and report upon our dispositions unless driven off.
>
> Lieut. Playfair therefore ordered the attack and drove the German down to Roulers.
>
> He then resumed his duty, sending down tactical information and position of batteries firing to 11th Bde. H.Q. and to our supporting artillery.

The German machine re-appeared and was again driven off. And this process was repeated a third time.

Finally two German machines appeared and although Lt Playfair had only 5 rounds left and knew that the German aeroplanes were faster than the Avro he attacked.

During this encounter he was mortally wounded, the bullet passing through his heart.

During the whole of these operations they were being heavily shelled by Anti-aircraft fire, one shell bursting at the very moment that Lieut. Playfair was killed, disabling the engine. The pilot therefore landed near VLAMERTINGHE.

I think that these two officers carried out their duty bravely and zealously.

They were called upon to face a situation which was really beyond what their actual duty was. Their instructions were to report hostile movements. When the German aeroplane appeared they rightly appreciated that it was more important that he should not observe our movements than they should continue to look for a possible hostile counter-attack. Finally when they were alone they did not hesitate to engage both German machines rather than surrender the air to them at such a time.

I would also like to bring to your notice the very excellent work as an observer which Lieut. Playfair has consistently carried out. During the 4 months that he was with No. 1 Squadron he was hit by Anti-aircraft fire 3 times.

He was actually firing at the moment he met his death, with the result that the Lewis gun went overboard.

The bullet that killed him came I think from the left rear, i.e. from the aeroplane that was not being engaged by Lieut. Playfair at the time.

I would urge that Lieut. L. Playfair although dead should receive some recognition for his exemplary work and great gallantry.'

Lieutenant Colonel C J Burke, Commanding 2 Wing, wrote to Headquarters RFC on 7 July:

'I beg to enclose a report of the action in which Lieut. L. Playfair so gallantly lost his life.

The fight for the mastery of the air will be a grim one, but with examples like Lieut. Playfair's, one can look with confidence to the future.

Lieut. Playfair was ever a daring officer, and I most warmly recommend him for the highest award. I would also draw your attention to the conduct of Lieut. Filley (the pilot of the machine) whose modest report is to my mind written in a splendid spirit, and is a striking tribute to a fallen comrade.'

The General Officer Commanding 4th Division, with reference to the events of 6 July, wrote:

'I cannot speak too highly of the cooperation of the RFC on that occasion and I deeply regret that it should have resulted in the death of this gallant officer.'

The inference in the first two reports is unambiguous, considering that at the time the only two awards that could be made posthumously were a Mention in Despatches and the highest award of all, the Victoria Cross. In the event Playfair received nothing, though his pilot received a Military Cross. Oliver Dwight Filley, an American from Boston, and probably the first American to serve with the RFC, later flew with 27 Squadron, even surviving a mid-air collision. He died in 1961.

Later in the month Captain J D G Sanders and Lieutenant Thomas McKenny Hughes, a new observer, were sent to range artillery on an ammunition dump that had been reported in a farm by an agent. Taking off at 0610 hours on 28 July in their Avro they ranged a few rounds of Lyddite from 115 Heavy Battery Royal Artillery and then the order to fire was given. Almost immediately they were rewarded for their efforts with a tremendous explosion and the dump began to burn.

Very early in the morning of 2 August Eustace Grenfell and his observer Whitaker in a Morane and Captain Bell-Irving flying another Morane joined in a scrap between an FE2 of No.6 Squadron and two German Albatros types. The FE2 was more than capable of looking after itself and saw off both of the enemy, one of whom probably crashed near Wulverghem. The pilot of the FE was the formidable Captain Lanoe Hawker of 6 Squadron who earlier in the month had received the first Victoria Cross for aerial fighting.

The war was not without its humorous moments, as the C Flight diarist noted on Sunday 15 August:

'A bright little service was held in the mess at 9.45 when the men were told all about sex & electricity, and the confusion liable to arise in either case owing to inadequate control'.

Three days later he had more events to report:

> 'Meanwhile another thrill was in store for us. A rumour got about that Lord Kitchener, of Khartoum
> & the War Office, London is to inspect us today. Later it leaked out that he was to arrive about
> 12.45. He did however actually come about 12.15, but only those in the know & and a few who
> happened to be by were prepared. The squadron was drawn up in a double line with a thin brown
> line of officers as a screen in front, flying officers on the right, observers in a position of less honour
> on the left, but only a few knew of this. 2 aeroplanes, an Avro (by kind permission of C Flight) and
> a Morane (B Flight) stood on the right to give tone to the gathering.
>
> The squadron went through the drill which is so peculiarly its own with aplomb and the Great
> Man arrived with M. Millerand and a galaxy of British and French gallantry. The Major was
> introduced and took very well the question as to "his section."
>
> Capt Bell-Irving gave a blood curdling exhibition of spirals on a Morane which however
> escaped the notice of the visitors who with a few muffled words from Lord Kitchener on
> "congratulations on your work – one of the best services we have had" moved slowly off, and
> heavily upholstered cars received them out of our sight.'

The visit of the Minister for War however had a postscript some three weeks later:

> 'Today is a proud day in the annals of the flight for it appears that K of K was more observant than
> we had supposed during his short visit to us and he singled out our Mr Steinbach-Mealing as
> showing promise above the ordinary and has this morning appointed him a FULL LIEUTENANT.
> General rejoicings.'

As a result of the anti-German sentiment that swept through Britain in the First War many people with
Germanic sounding names changed them – for example the Royal Family changed their name to
Windsor. Steinbach-Mealing was one of these and he subsequently dropped Steinbach as a surname.

On 19 August Geoffrey Salmond handed over command to P B Joubert and returned to the UK. He
was destined to have a meteoric career. At the end of 1915 he took 5 Wing to Egypt as a Lieutenant
Colonel and by October the following year was commanding Middle East Brigade as a Brigadier
General. On 3 January 1918 he became General Officer Commanding RFC Middle East; he had risen
from Captain to Major General in a little over three years. In 1933 he succeeded his brother John as
Chief of the Air Staff but tragically died shortly after. If he had not 'died in harness' there would have
been on his retirement the unique situation of two brothers both being Marshals of the Royal Air Force.

New tactics
Houthulst Forest, a large wooded area well over the German side, was not only a distinctive landmark
for airmen of both sides but was also a useful place for the Germans to conceal troop reinforcements,
ammunition dumps and other supplies. One of the more fanciful schemes for dealing with it, and
winning the war, took place in August. Our diarist recorded thus:

> 'A quiet afternoon of preparation for a rather special exhibition of frightfulness. Houthulst Wood is
> to be destroyed; an ambitious scheme involving 70 Allied aeroplanes, 30 English & 40 French.
> They are to drop incendiary bombs, with just a judicious admixture of high explosive ones to give
> added piquancy.
>
> Lt Parker of ours, together with Lt Gossage & Lt Grenfell of B Flight represented the squadron.
> The whole outburst was a glorious fiasco. Not one fire was started.'

Gossage was another individual who went on to greater things and retired as Air Marshal Sir Leslie
Gossage KCB, CVO, DSO, MC and died in 1949.

In September a 1 Squadron crew demonstrated unusual initiative while being chased by four
enemy machines. Second Lieutenant R Balcombe Brown and his observer Thomas McKenny Hughes
were pursued and overtaken by four Albatros machines well over the enemy side of the lines near
Courtrai. Their only armament was a fixed forward-firing Lewis machine gun, which the pilot in
desperation fired into the air. Hughes pointed his telescope in a war-like fashion at the enemy who
sheered off and kept their distance! Balcombe Brown earned an MC while with 1 Squadron but was
fated to be killed commanding 56 Squadron in 1917. Hughes also failed to survive the war and was
killed with 53 Squadron in 1918.

One of the Squadron's jobs was the regular patrolling of the Courtrai to Depuze line and on 8 September the diary recorded, a little tetchily, a patrol of it thus:

> 'It seems the British government intend to bring out a handy ABC railway timetable of this line,for we have been sent to note trains at all hours of day light, but as not a single train has so far been observed the book will probably take the form of those pretty little Tom Thumb editions with probably just one page. "Courtrai-Depuze fares 1st class.... 2nd class.... 3rd class.... Service as between Paris & Berlin".'

The Avros and other assorted machines were steadily replaced through the latter part of the year until by late October the Squadron was standardized on Moranes, though even these were a variety of biplanes, high-winged parasols and mid-wing monoplanes.

> 'Friday October 1915. A gorgeous day. Thick fog from dawn to dusk. Aviation impossible'.

The first week in November was a period of very poor weather with howling gales,low cloud and rain. On 10 November C C Miles and L J Bayly attempted to carry out a tactical reconnaissance but were being thrown around in such heavy turbulence that they returned. Just as the machine was descending over the trees on the aerodrome boundary a particularly heavy bump caused them to drop. In the ensuing attempt to correct this the rudder appeared to give way, swinging them round and catching the propeller on a tree. The right wing came off and they plummeted to the ground on the right side of the nose. Both were removed and taken to hospital unconscious, though they survived.

Miles was wounded again as a Flight Commander in 3 Squadron and finished the war in command of 43 Squadron. He died in 1949 as a Wing Commander.

Christmas 1915, being the Squadron's first on active service, was celebrated in style. R E Neale, who was one of 1 Squadron's unsung hardworking other ranks, recorded:

> 'Christmas puddings were received from the national newspapers, which had run subscription funds for this purpose. Chocolates, sweets and cigarettes also rolled up from the same source.... Flights ran a scratch concert party in the evening, and there was plenty of beer and, of course, the rum ration.
>
> My bunk mate – one named Pulford – was very partial to rum, and used to gather quite a quantity by swapping candles for it. I had to put him to bed that night. We slept, at this time, at the back of the hangar in cubby holes which we had constructed from the mainplanes of crashed aircraft.
>
> The great disciplinarian at this time was Sergt./Major Darke. Captain Stodart, regarded as a bit of a mad blighter, had departed by the end of 1915, and my pilot, Lieut C C Miles, was struck off strength after being wounded early in 1916'.

D E Stodart later had the unique distinction of earning the only DSO and DFC awarded in Aden during the First War.

The winter of 1915/16 was quite hard, as was the following one, and the groundcrew found a novel way of entertaining themselves, as Neale again records:

> 'Around March the weather was very severe and the aerodrome was covered with snow. Light sledges were constructed from main spars and damaged wings were used as sails. Inter-flight competitions were quickly arranged and some very good speeds attained across the 'drome.
>
> Throughout this cold spell most of us slept on the floor of an old barn on the outskirts of the town, and the confined space, lack of ventilation and closely packed bodies supplied the warmth. We were on parade at 06.00 hours in the narrow alley by the door, ready to march to the aerodrome for breakfast'.

Malcolm McBean Bell-Irving

Shortly before Christmas Malcolm Bell-Irving was wounded during another of his scraps with the enemy and was invalided back to the UK.

Mick Bell-Irving was one of ten children of H O Bell-Irving of Vancouver and the fourth of six sons, all of whom served in the armed forces during the First World War. He had been working at a remote cannery in Alaska on the outbreak of war in early August and had left immediately to join up. By the end of December 1914 he had already learned to fly and joined 1 Squadron. The Bell-Irvings were a remarkable family and of the six sons, three served in the RFC, one in the navy and two in the army. Between them they were awarded four MCs, two DSOs, two DSCs, an OBE and a French Croix de Guerre. Such was the size of the Bell-Irving clan that Malcolm's brother Richard served for a short time in 1 Squadron as did two cousins, Robert Bell-Irving and Ken Creery. Another cousin, Angus Bell-Irving, won an MC in 66 Squadron.

Robert seemed a little accident-prone as he was injured twice during his time in the Squadron – the first when he picked up a Rankin Dart which had fallen off an aeroplane and it went off in his hand, and the second time when a glass soda siphon also exploded in his hand.

Malcolm went out to France with the Squadron and soon demonstrated his aggressive spirit in a number of combats and other duties. Flying both the Bristol Scout and Morane Bullet he had a number of engagements with the enemy.

On 24 May 1915 he left at 0400 hours in a BE8 on a reconnaissance but returned after only fifty-five minutes as his observer, H F Boles, had been seriously wounded by anti-aircraft fire. Boles died shortly after. Half an hour after his return Bell-Irving took off in a Martinsyde and completed the mission on his own. He was promoted to command B Flight in July 1915.

Hastings Fortescue Boles was the eldest son of Lieutenant Colonel D F Boles, who was commanding the 3rd Battalion of the Devonshire Regiment and was also Member of Parliament for the Wellington Division of Somerset. After Eton he had passed out of Sandhurst into the 17th Lancers in January 1915 and joined the RFC two months later.

On 19 December Bell-Irving was flying a Morane scout when he encountered a number of enemy machines, and despite being out-numbered, attacked them aggressively. On 30 December it was announced he had been awarded the Squadron's first Distinguished Service Order, not just for this gallant action but for all his activities since arriving in France. The citation read:

'For conspicuous and consistent gallantry during a period of nine months in France notably on December 19, 1915 between Lille and Ypres when he successfully engaged three hostile machines. The first he drove off, the second he sent to the ground in flames, and the third nose dived and disappeared. He was then attacked by three other hostile machines from above but he flew off towards Ypres and chased a machine he saw in that direction. He overhauled and had got to within 100 yards when he was wounded by a shell and had to return'.

The citation omitted to mention that the shrapnel wound to his hand was caused by a British shell! It was a well-deserved award and a high honour and was the first of only *five* such awards to 1 Squadron between 1912 and the present day, with the last one being awarded to Wing Commander Andy Golledge for the Kosovo operations in 1999.

Malcolm was transferred to Lady Ridley's Hospital in central London, where he occupied the bed next to his younger brother Duncan, who had been shot down and seriously wounded in 7 Squadron only five days before him. Their sister Isabel became a volunteer nurse in the hospital, as did yet another cousin.

Bell-Irving returned to 1 Squadron on 27 May 1916 but only three weeks later was badly wounded. On 17 June he and his observer A W Smith departed on a photography mission to Houthulst Forest in a Morane biplane. The machine was hit by anti-aircraft fire and both men wounded. Bell-Irving attempted to return to base but with a very serious head wound was forced to land in a very rough field just south west of Poperinghe. Despite his terrible injuries he pulled off a good landing and only the right lower plane and some undercarriage fittings were damaged. During the next few months he suffered seizures, blackouts and severe headaches until he was operated on in Baltimore, USA in June 1917 to have a chunk of metal removed from his brain. Once recovered he organised a flying instructor's course at the Special School of Flying at Gosport, where one of his tutors was his brother Duncan, who was commanding the unit. Unfortunately Mick had a serious crash shortly afterwards which resulted in the amputation of a leg above the knee and brought his flying to an end. After the war he was unemployable and died at a comparatively early age in 1958.

A change in command

At the end of November, after only a few months in command, Major Joubert had to enter hospital for treatment to an eye and his place was taken by Major G F Pretyman. Joubert went on to greater things and was AOC Coastal Command from 1941 to 1943 during the desperate Battle of the Atlantic in which Hitler's U-boats very nearly brought Britain to her knees. He retired as Air Chief Marshal Sir Philip Joubert de la Ferté KCB, CMG, DSO in 1941 and died in 1965.

Throughout its history the Royal Air Force always seems to have had well-known pairs of brothers, the best known being the Salmonds and another pair were the Pretymans. Sons of a General they both rose to the rank of Wing Commander. George had landed with the BEF in August 1914 as a member of 3 Squadron with Philip Joubert, who he was now replacing. He was destined to remain in command of 1 Squadron until the changeover from a two-seater unit to a scout squadron at the end of 1916.

Pretyman had only been in charge of the Squadron for a little over a month when he was involved in a bizarre incident. On 29 December he flew to St Omer to pick up a new machine and took with him a new pilot, Second Lieutenant D C Cleaver, who had only joined them four days before. The intention was for Pretyman to fly the new machine back while Cleaver returned in the machine in which they had flown out. Over Hazebrouck the CO took the opportunity to show the new man the area. Cleaver was leaning out over each side of the Morane pointing to features on the ground. Suddenly the machine dived and the stick was wrenched out of Pretyman's hand and went fast forward. Before he could grab the controls they were right over on their back. The aeroplane suddenly righted itself and Pretyman looked round laughing to make a remark to Cleaver. There was nobody in the rear cockpit and almost down in the trees he saw Cleaver above him, plummeting to earth. On landing immediately he found that Cleaver had been killed. He was only seventeen years old. Pretyman was taken to St Omer by car and General Trenchard offered him leave, which he declined. The machine was returned to the depot.

1916, the calm before the storm
For the Allies, 1916 was dominated by the Battles of the Somme for the British and Verdun for the French, both of which resulted in enormous casualties.

A J Capel, who served in the Squadron from June 1916 until March 1917 and became C Flight Commander, wrote in 1977 of this time:

> 'We carried out fairly local reconnaissance, and cooperation with artillery and photography, in fact normal Army Co-op duties as understood at that time.
> It was a singularly uneventful time in the sqn's history. The Somme Battle broke out on July 1st 1916, and we were almost the only sqn left up north, when all other sqns went to the Somme. As the Germans had more or less done the same and as ammunition for the guns was strictly limited we had a very quiet time, only responsible for seeing that, over a wide front, nothing untoward was brewing.'

The new year started badly when Captain Sanders was killed in a flying accident on Morane 5126 on 2 January. He had taken off at 0924 hours to test and to learn to fly the Morane Biplane. He evidently had engine failure and in the subsequent forced landing hit a telegraph pole with his left wing, with his undercarriage catching the wires. This threw the machine over, killing Sanders. This was a sad loss for the Squadron as he had joined it before the war and had been one of the original members who had arrived with the Squadron in France in March 1915. He had been born in August 1888 and was commissioned into the Royal Artillery in 1906. From 1911 he had spent three years attached to the West African Frontier Force and joined the RFC as a Captain in October 1914.

On 10 January Second Lieutenants J G McEwan and F Adams became prisoners of war after being shot down by a German two-seater and two days later R Barton and E S Wilkinson were killed, also in combat with enemy aircraft. Wilkinson, born in 1890, had attended Marlborough College and Manchester University and in 1911 became an engineering student at McGill University in Montreal. On the outbreak of war he obtained a commission with the 1st London Territorial Battalion and served with them in Malta and France.

The run of bad luck continued with Second Lieutenants W Watts and C O Hayward being brought down and killed near Dadizeele by anti-aircraft fire on 17 January. Wilfrid Watts, another pre-war aviator, had taken his ticket, No.633, in September 1913 and been awarded a French Croix de Guerre in September 1915.

Hayward, educated at Repton and Pembroke College, Cambridge had served with the 7th Battalion Lincolnshire Regiment at the front and had only been with 1 Squadron for three weeks. However, on the day that Watts and Hayward were lost, Eustace Grenfell was involved in a combat with a number of enemy machines and scored a notable victory. He was patrolling in one of the Squadron's single-seat Morane Type N or, as they were known in the RFC, the Morane 'Bullet'. They were considered difficult to fly, being very light in pitch but very heavy in roll, and were not popular machines. In addition they were not equipped with synchronising gear for the single forward-firing machine gun and relied on heavy deflector plates to prevent the bullets shooting the propeller off. When bullets ricocheted off these deflectors it was both spectacular and disconcerting. Despite these difficulties, Grenfell sent one of two Fokkers that attacked him into a dive and then damaged the second one sufficiently for it to have to land near Moorslede. Shortly afterwards he attacked an enemy two-seater without result and then a third Fokker and saw it go down. Grenfell was advised he had been awarded the Military Cross on 22 January but was invalided out of the Squadron the following month. His connection with 1 Squadron was not finished however, as he would command the Squadron twice during the 1920s.

The tempo of the air war was accelerating and combats were now becoming a common occurrence. On 5 February Lieutenant W V Strugnell, while flying one of the Squadron's tricky Morane monoplanes, attacked and drove off an LVG near Armentières. Later in the same patrol he spotted an Aviatik returning to the German side of the front line and slowly overtook it until he was able to fire at very close range. Tracer bullets were seen to hit the wings and fuselage and probably the pilot as well, as he was seen to fall forward. The machine nose-dived steeply and disappeared into the clouds below. Strugnell had learned to fly in 1912 and was one of the RFC's earliest NCO pilots, having joined the RFC before the First War. He was also awarded an MC while in the Squadron and subsequently won a Bar to it when a Flight Commander in 54 Squadron during 1917. He retired from the RAF as a Group Captain in 1945.

The weather was particularly bitter during this period and there were a number of cases of sickness due to the cold and frostbite. Lieutenants Plenty and McKelvie on a short recce were noted as 'came down in a semi congealed condition with their masks frozen to what they are pleased to call their moustaches'.

The first clear-cut victory over the enemy finally came on 29 February 1916 with the almost certain destruction of a two-seater. Captain R A Saunders and his observer Second Lieutenant C A B Joske were patrolling in a Morane Parasol when they joined in a fight between an FE8 of 41 Squadron and an enemy machine near Ypres. Pursuing the enemy from 7,000 feet down to 5,000 they were able to get to within fifty yards of the Hun. Tracer bullets splattered the fuselage of the machine with the observer collapsing in the rear cockpit and ceasing to fire. After another burst of machine-gun fire, smoke and flames came from the engine and when last seen it was still burning and diving near Passchendaele. Joske, an Australian from Melbourne, later learned to fly and also distinguished himself, earning an MC with 46 Squadron in 1917. He died in Fiji in 1947.

Accidental casualties

Saturday 4 March was a day off for Lieutenants C C Godwin and H A Johnston and they decided to spend it in Armentières. They obtained a lift on the tender that was doing the regular run round the various wireless operators attached to artillery batteries in the area. Having had tea they then did a little shopping for various necessities. Standing outside a shop Johnston gave Godwin a cigarette and as he did so a shrapnel shell landed ten yards away, wounding both officers. Godwin dragged his companion under cover into a cellar and after considerable effort obtained an ambulance but unfortunately, the RAMC doctor found that Johnston had died. Godwin returned to the Squadron in September but he was not so lucky the second time and was shot down and killed with his observer P C Ellis.

On 12 March Captain R A Saunders of A Flight had just completed a photography mission, escorted by Sergeant T F B Carlisle and Lieutenant J A McKelvie, as a formation of three enemy machines crossed the lines. Carlisle and McKelvie saw Saunders fire a green flare and found he had turned to engage the enemy. From the ground his tracers were seen to strike the Hun and then clouds of smoke billowed out. Almost immediately Saunders himself commenced a steep left hand spiral, which continued right down to the ground where the Morane crashed on its left wing. After removal from the wreck it was found that he had been hit in the stomach by machine-gun fire and was probably unconscious before hitting the ground. He died a few minutes later, without regaining consciousness.

An observer's experience

In the early days observers were attached directly to squadrons from army units in the field, without any training. If found suitable they were retained but if not, were returned to their units. Only later in the war was there a formal UK training set-up and with observers arriving fully trained. Alf Koch wrote of his arrival at 1 Squadron:

'I was only a colonial non-commissioned officer (and the lowest species of that order) and was given no briefing by the Adjutant (or anyone else!) as to my testing (not a word as to what my tests would consist of beyond the injunction to keep myself in readiness for calls by pilots on instant notice but not a word as to what I should do with myself while waiting – nothing but that I would be issued with two blankets (used and not very thick) with which to make myself comfortable on the wooden floor of the Nissen-Hut of the airmen mechanics with whom I was to sleep and eat. Not a single introduction to anyone N.C.O. or officer or even airmen – and it was a week before a call came to report to Captain Somebody or other on the aerodrome. Somebody did take pity on me and provided me with a flying coat, mitts, helmet and goggles and the pilot, standing beside the machine was the first man to take notice of me as a human being!! He showed me a map of our area – gave me a copy and told me that he was doing a shoot with a 15 inch naval gun assigned to the RFC for the purpose of trying to knock out the most annoying and accurate AA (Archie) gun along the front: my job (and evidently the first of my tests) was to watch out and spot the exact location of the No.2 gun of the battery which would open up on us as soon as our first shell landed. Believe it or not that was the total briefing, 3 or 4 minutes, and then into the wild blue yonder for the first time. The speed with which the sky filled with the menacing black explosions explained why that particular battery's demise was so earnestly sought. Also the finding of a shrapnel hole dead centre in my windshield from a burst 30 yards in front was a lively introduction to the joys available to an Observer in No.1 Squadron.'

Koch did as he was ordered and spotted the second gun opening up, with the success of their operation appearing in 'Comic Cuts', the official intelligence summary circulated within the RFC. He continued:

'If the pilot experienced any surprise at my success he managed to suppress any evidence beyond a brief… "Good show" and that was my last flight with him.'

The Squadron had just received their first Nieuport two-seaters and Koch relates an embarrassing episode with it:

'Assigned to do an ordinary artillery shoot on some newly discovered trench diggings by our industrious foe, I was called on to occupy the rear seat, to man our "stern" defences, the wireless signalling being still done by the pilot, who had flown over the Battery which was awaiting our signals. Code letters laid out on the ground by the Battery to indicate readiness to shoot were hastily withdrawn when we flew back from the lines to see why they hadn't answered our signals (we had no voice tube between pilot and observer) and I did not learn until we landed that the Nieuport plane – with its swept-back appearance to the upper wing hadn't been seen before or identified by the Battery, and we were mistaken for a German "Taube"!'

Koch had come to France with the first Canadian contingent as a trumpeter with the 19th Alberta Dragoons and on his transfer to the RFC had arrived at Bailleul still wearing his Stetson and spurs! Following his commissioning he was badly wounded in the back as an observer with 6 Squadron. After convalescence in Canada he returned as a pilot with 70 Squadron flying Camels and won an MC. His successful time in 70 Squadron was brought to an end when he was wounded yet again. Despite his injuries he lived well into his 90s.

The Nieuport Scout
In early 1916, 1 Squadron got a taste of things to come with the arrival of a handful of the new Nieuport single-seat scouts. The Type 16 Nieuport had been developed from the earlier Type 11 and had been ordered by the Royal Naval Air Service as soon as it became available. Just prior to the Battle of the Somme the RFC was desperately short of fighters and following a request from General Hugh Trenchard, commanding the RFC in the Field, the RNAS very generously diverted their entire order of seventeen machines to the RFC. 1 Squadron received their first one on 24 March, when W V Strugnell went to the depot at St Omer to ferry 5171 back to Bailleul. He had in fact been at St Omer the previous day for some practice on the type before bringing it back. The Nieuports were allocated in small numbers to two-seater units, notably 1, 3 and 11 Squadrons and it was not until later in the year that a squadron (No. 60) had a full complement of them. By the end of April 1 Squadron had a total of five.

Despite the rather clumsy over-wing mounted machine gun, designed to fire over the arc of the propeller, the type soon showed what an improvement it was over existing single-seat machines. On 27 April C E Foggin had taken off from Bailleul to pursue an enemy machine that had been spotted from the ground. He quickly overhauled it and fired a burst of tracer from close range, scoring hits on the fuselage. However, the superior speed of the Nieuport meant that he quickly began to overtake it and had to perform some delaying S-turns. This gave the enemy gunner the chance to get a few shots off at close range and one of these struck a centre section strut, with the result that a wood splinter flew off and hit Foggin in the face injuring his left eye. He had to break off the fight, though the enemy aeroplane was observed by anti-aircraft personnel to be still going down. Foggin had been one of the earliest fliers in Britain and had been apprenticed to Borel Morane in France during 1911. He had obtained Royal Aero Club aviators certificate No. 349 in October 1912 at Eastbourne and bought his own machine, a Blackburn monoplane, the same year. In 1913 he had joined the Aviation Department of Armstrong Whitworth. Some of his military flying training was done with 1 Squadron in 1914 and he had progressed from airman via Sergeant to a commission while with them. He was fated to be killed in a simple road accident in July 1918 when commanding 41 Squadron.

German night bombing of Allied rear areas became a constant and escalating problem as the war carried on. Not only did night raiding reduce German flying casualties, as the Allies had no dedicated night fighters but apart from destroying or damaging strategic targets it also disturbed the sleep of weary troops. The bombers ranged as far back as the large base hospitals on the coast at places like Etaples and eventually resulted in the formation of specialist night-fighter squadrons, Nos 151 and 152, by the RAF. On the night of 24 April Bailleul was attacked.

'Sqn awakened rudely about 4 a.m by violent explosions which seemed very close & which on investigation were caused by bombs dropped by a large Hun biplane which seemed to be about 2500 feet. General stampede for dug out in weird and wonderful garments. Lieut Joske's pyjamas causing many people to temporarily forget even their safety in stopping to admire & wonder, with result that he was easily first man under cover.

Some 20 bombs dropped, one setting on fire 7 ambulances at hospital, one in station & a few in No 7's aerodrome but no casualties'.

A kite balloon assault

On 25 June a concerted effort was made to cripple the German observation balloons on the entire British front. Balloons were an important target for the fighter pilots of both sides throughout the war, as they had the ability to 'see over the hill' and observe everything that the other side was doing. They had excellent telephonic communication with headquarters and all the nearby artillery batteries and could bring down an artillery barrage at very short notice on anything that presented a suitable target. They were difficult to destroy, and presented formidable objectives, as they were always surrounded by heavy anti-aircraft defences and occasionally defending fighters. The Nieuport scout could be equipped with Le Prieur rockets for the task of balloon attack. These missiles were installed in tubes, with four on each side secured to the interplane wing struts, and employing a special sight. They were not particularly accurate nor had a great range but were effective against the hydrogen-filled kite balloons. For a few days before the attack the pilots allotted to the new Nieuport scouts had carried out a number of practice sorties test firing the rockets. The practice paid off as of the twenty-three balloons up, fifteen were attacked and six brought down – two of them by 1 Squadron.

For this mission the 1 Squadron pilots had flown down south the previous day to 3 Squadron's aerodrome at Lahoussoye, some miles south of Albert on the Somme. B J W M 'Granny' Moore took off just before 1600 hours in the company of two BE2c two-seater machines. Leaving the other machines at 8,000 feet he descended and then dived steeply on the plump gasbag near Flers from 6,000 feet. The balloon was swaying violently due to the great speed with which it was being winched in. At a range of sixty yards Moore fired and then banked steeply to avoid colliding with the target. After about ten seconds, flames and smoke appeared at various places in the balloon and then in another moment or two the whole thing collapsed and fell in one huge flaming mass. Turning his machine Moore was just in time to see it hit the ground. He then returned at 4,000 feet.

J D Latta, after a quick thirty-minute familiarisation trip of the area, had a similar experience. Firing his eight missiles from 100 yards he saw several strike the target and after a few seconds it too fell in flames. The importance of bringing these balloons down is shown by the fact that one of the Nieuports that brought another balloon down was flown by Lieutenant May, a non-operational pilot on the staff of No.2 Aircraft Depot. The Germans were temporarily blinded and were unable to observe the preparations for the Battle of the Somme, which commenced six days later.

James Latta had served in 5 Squadron and after a period in 60 Squadron as a Flight Commander, returned to the UK. In 1917 he was a Flight Commander in 66 Squadron flying Sopwith Pups until wounded in action.

The following day 2 Brigade repeated the operation in their area and another three were brought down in flames – all by 1 Squadron pilots. Latta, Moore and Balcombe Brown were escorted by a

Morane biplane, crewed by T A Oliver and Corporal Alf Koch, together with A W Dore and Robert Bell-Irving in another. Oliver and Koch had to land at a Royal Naval Air Service aerodrome due to a storm and were unable to return for two days. Balcombe Brown wrote in his combat report:

'I came out of the clouds at 7,000 feet about 3 miles N.E. of Quesnoy and dived straight down on to the sausage balloon. Before firing the torpedoes black crosses were visible on the balloon. As I approached the balloon from the N.E. it began to descend and turn sideways on to the wind so that when I fired the torpedoes it was broadside on to me. The majority of the torpedoes struck the balloon about two thirds of the way up. My machine just missed the balloon and on looking back I saw one man descending in a white parachute. There was still something black, probably an occupant, in the basket as the balloon collapsed. When I hit the balloon it was 2,300 feet high.'

Lieutenant W H Dore wrote home about his part in this operation:

'When out on one of the "strafes" three scout pilots "did in" three balloons. Another pilot and I were to escort them each in a fast biplane. We left the ground with orders to wait a certain distance above the aerodrome until the scouts came up, then we were to dash across together, and, while they made for the balloons we were to see that they were not attacked by hostile aircraft. As the escorts were hovering over the aerodrome , a large rain cloud came over, so we tried to fly over it; but there were other clouds around and above it, so we went around it and to the north until we were over the coast. I flew around there at about 9,000 ft., waiting for the rain storm to blow over, flying in clouds most of the time, until it got quite late and dark, when I decided to come home in spite of the storm. I cut the engine off, pointed it where I thought home was, and glided 7,000 ft. before I saw the earth, and I was then at 2,000 ft. For a few moments I wondered whether the ground below was Hun land or British, but I soon recognised it to be behind our lines and near the aerodrome, so was soon safely home.'

Dore from Cape Breton, Nova Scotia later instructed in Canada and then returned to the Western Front as a Flight Commander in 107 Squadron, flying DH9s. He was killed in action on 9 August 1918.

Practice with Le Prieur rockets continued in July, even employing Morane Biplanes, which would seem to be a totally unsuitable machine for kite balloon attacks, but the mass attack on enemy balloons, despite its success, was for some reason not repeated.

On 8 August 'Granny' Moore was flying Nieuport Scout A136 at 17,000 feet over Lille when he spotted an enemy machine patrolling the front line trenches in a circuit from Armentières-Wytschaete-Hollebeke-Polygon Wood. Having watched the Albatros reconnaissance machine fly two such circuits Moore waited until it was flying north east again and dived at it. He zoomed under its tail and fired from only twenty-five yards. Immediately a long shaft of flame shot back past the Nieuport and the heat was felt on Moore's face. Quickly turning to avoid the flames, he did a complete circle and observed one of the poor occupants falling through the air, having jumped out rather than be burned to death. The falling, burning wreckage was followed down until it hit the ground in a huge burst of flame near Frelinghem.

George Garro-Jones, an observer in 1 Squadron, recorded his impression of Moore in his autobiography, *Ventures and Visions*:

'In this squadron there was one amazing young fellow who was not gay like the rest. He was, on the outside slow and melancholy, spoke with an old man's cracked voice, with a longer drawl than ever came out of Oxford. He moved, on the ground, even more slowly than he spoke, and his face was rather wizened and very cynical. Added to this, he was four or five years older than the rest of us, and it is not surprising that he was universally known as Granny Moore – Granny for short. And a grandmother he was in all externals. But had you been a German airman, it would have cost you dear to judge by appearances. For this was a dangerous and unique type of grandmother – one with the heart and sinew, eye and nerve of a young eagle.

I was in the orderly-room giving a report on an observation flight, when he came in with his leather coat on and demanded another observer. "Young— can't keep his nose dry," he drawled, "and it annoys me." Another observer came in, and the rejected one appeared a little later, looking rather downcast. We were naturally curious, and asked him what had happened, and he confessed his nose was apt to be a little troublesome up in the cold air.

"Did Granny say anything?" we asked.

"Yes, he kept on switching off the engine and asking me to wipe my nose. I couldn't hear what he was talking about at first; then he passed me a handkerchief: by this time we had lost height, and he came in to land."

Nobody could understand Granny, but he was allowed his idiosyncrasies even by the squadron-commander.'

Granny was a member of the Institute of Electric Engineers and when war broke out was working on a project in Canada. Refused a commission on medical grounds, he joined the RFC as an airman and within a short time had obtained a commission and learned to fly. He earned himself a Military Cross in 1 Squadron but was killed in a flying accident in the UK in June 1917.

In the middle of August the three remaining Nieuports were transferred to 60 Squadron and J D Latta, A M Walters and S E Parker went with them. Vernon Castle, a pilot in the Squadron, recorded the departure 'thrash' thus:

'Last night we had quite a rough night. Three of our pilots are joining another squadron, and we gave them a sort of farewell party, which ended with their breaking up most of the furniture and drinking all the drinks in the place. One of our guests got his face walked on by a hob-nailed boot, and it was altogether a jolly evening'.

Thus finished 1 Squadron's brief experience of true fighter aircraft and for the next few months they continued with their usual task of reconnaissance and artillery observation until early 1917 would see them return to fighters and this time permanently.

Last days as a Corps squadron

Whilst the glamour and glory undoubtedly went to the elegant Nieuport Scout, 1 Squadron still continued the mundane tasks of artillery co-operation, bombing and reconnaissance. On 3 July Lieutenant T A Oliver and his observer Sergeant R B Mumford ran into five enemy aircraft and despite the odds drove off four of them with little difficulty. After engaging the remaining machine it was seen diving vertically at full power and was believed to have been destroyed. Garro-Jones also recorded his impression of Tom Oliver:

'Now Tom was a great fighter – the most bloodthirsty pilot in the squadron, except Granny; he would spend hours flying solo, searching for enemy machines, and had already a good record. We used to joke about this in the mess, where, for some reason nobody knew, he was known as "Om" instead of "Tom". On one occasion he flew into a flight of three or four slow enemy machines which refused combat, and after one had fired a Very light, they all dived down – a very unusual reaction by German airmen to the sight of their enemy. But one of the other pilots of No.1, who saw this incident, vowed that the Very light was a code for "Om's on us!" That night one of the squadron wags painted on "Om's" machine the word Omsonus – just as the young blood of today will paint some romantic and mystic word on his car.'

Oliver returned to the UK shortly after Christmas 1916, his tour of duty complete. In August 1917 he returned to France as a Flight Commander with 29 Squadron but was shot down and killed after just four days with the unit.

A Zeppelin raid

On 2 August 1 Squadron were given the job of escorting six BE2c's to bomb the Zeppelin sheds at Brussels. The Zeppelin raids on Britain were causing considerable public alarm and much embarrassment to the government. The British flying services expended a lot of resources in countering this menace, to the detriment of the war on the Western Front. Brussels was far behind the German lines and involved a long flight both ways. Garro-Jones again:

'Just before we reached Brussels one of the Moranes was hit by anti-aircraft fire and brought down, but the rest of the machines reached Brussels, and there the whole formation broke up as each descended to drop its bombs. We went down to about 5,000 feet with ours – not, by present-day standards, a very heroic performance – but it must be remembered that with slow-climbing machines having a long way to get home, and petrol for $3^1/_4$ hours, it was necessary to keep a certain amount of height for the protection of the escorted machines. Nor could the barrage of anti-aircraft shells be ignored.

The Zeppelins, it proved, were out – had not returned from one of their raids. But we went for the sheds all the same, knowing that a Zepp is dependent for safety on its prepared base. Brand had the job of dropping our 20-pounders. They were, as I have said, very small and supplementary to the main attack. I saw one explode on the edge of one of the sheds, and another among the houses attached – a couple of hundred yards away. But one of the B.E.'s heavier bombs found its billet and destroyed one of the sheds. Then we flew over to look at the city. We could see groups of people in the streets of the occupied city, watching us, their friends.

One by one we started home, and Brand and I fell behind. To add to our difficulties, one of the cylinders stopped firing, and we had to limp home the whole sixty miles against the wind with one cylinder missing. It was a most trying thought that, any moment, the engine might fail and deposit us in Germany for the rest of the war. We saw one enemy below, but he made no attempt to intercept us – about this time the crack German machines were on the Somme. One of the B.E.s was not so fortunate. Wandering to the north, he fell in with an enemy and was brought down. However, all but two of the machines reached home safely, and we landed three hours one minute (logged time) after starting, with fourteen minutes' petrol to spare.'

In fact only one machine, a BE2 from No. 5 Squadron, was lost and the Zeppelin hangars were not hit, but it was a bold and courageous operation, which deserved more success. The air war was fought mainly on the German side of the lines due to the aggressive way the RFC conducted their operations. Consequently, there was always the danger of technical failures or combat damage resulting in a landing in enemy territory. In addition the prevailing westerly winds meant long flights back with the problem of possibly running out of fuel. Garro-Jones was a Labour MP from 1924 until 1945 and from 1946 to 1949 was Chairman of the Television Advisory Committee. He was made Lord Trefgarne in 1947 and died in 1960.

In early September the Squadron drove down three enemy machines in one day. In the evening of 8 September, Second Lieutenant T M B Newton and his observer First Class Airman Percy O'Lieff engaged a Fokker monoplane over Ypres. Despite flying a much slower and less manoeuvrable aeroplane they forced the Fokker down in a series of vertical dives with its engine stopped until it was lost from sight below. O'Lieff later learned to fly and was commissioned. Flying De Havilland DH4s with 55 Squadron he and his observers brought down several enemy machines, until he became a prisoner of war on 5 April 1918.

On 22 September V H Collins, a South African from Kimberley, and his observer Captain Thomas Gibbons flying a Morane Parasol had to range the heavy guns of the 4th and 117th Siege Batteries onto a German grenade store. The shoot was conducted by Gibbons in the rear seat and with one of the earliest shots the target blew up with a large satisfying explosion. 'Fluffy' Gibbons had been a dentist in Manchester before the war and as a result of a very bad dose of frostbite later in the year was off flying for some time. When the Squadron converted to fighters in early 1917, with all of the observers being posted away, he remained and became the Recording Officer (or Adjutant). Within the Squadron the officers had nicknames and Collins, for reasons unknown, was called José, after a character in a popular London show.

Less than a week later three machines were involved in a bizarre episode when they were sent up to investigate an enemy balloon over British lines. The observation balloon had obviously broken free and the wind, being easterly for once had, unluckily for the observer, carried the balloon in the wrong direction. Why the German had not parachuted into his own lines while he had the chance remains a mystery but he was halfway up the rigging between the basket and the envelope waving a white handkerchief, as Captain G D Hill of 40 Squadron arrived on the scene in his FE8. Hill held his fire and signalled the German to descend but whilst everyone was behaving in a humanitarian fashion by escorting the poor German further into Allied territory, a DH2 nipped in and shot it down in flames. It fell from 1,200 feet near Mount Kemmel but miraculously the German officer appears to have survived. A week later the C Flight Commander, Captain A J Capel, and his observer Frank Sharpe of 1 Squadron dropped a message bag over the German side advising them of the fate of their missing kite balloon observer. Capel had served as an observer in No. 4 Squadron during 1915 and after training appointments in the UK returned to France in November 1918 as Commanding Officer of 94 Squadron. During a tour in India between the wars he was awarded the DSO and DFC, retiring as an Air Vice-Marshal in 1945. He died in 1979.

On 16 October 1 Squadron were ordered to carry out a Special Reconnaissance of a dump near Courtrai. This was some distance into enemy territory and had the additional problem that there were a number of German aerodromes situated around the town. The days of single machines carrying out this sort of duty were long gone and the photographic machine, flown by Lieutenant E D Atkinson and Second Lieutenant D M Murdoch, was escorted by another three machines. Ten photographs were taken of the objective but one of the escort, flown by Lieutenant C M Kelly and Second Lieutenant T G G Sturrock, failed to return. Kelly was made prisoner of war but the unfortunate Sturrock was killed.

At the beginning of November Lieutenant J M E Shepherd and Second Lieutenant G F Bishop scored a rare confirmed victory over the enemy. Flying a Morane biplane they were at 6,500 feet over Messines, just south east of Ypres when they first spotted an enemy machine, identified as a Roland scout, on their right-hand side. Shepherd fired a long-range burst at it, which caused the opposing scout to turn with the obvious intention of diving on them. For whatever reason, perhaps a gun failure, he levelled off and passed over them in the opposite direction. It flew by only fifty feet above them and Bishop in the rear seat was able to give it a good burst from below. It went into a steep dive, billowing clouds of smoke and was then observed by Bishop to catch fire and crash in a field.

At the end of the month an enemy machine was claimed by a crew flying one of the Squadron's few Nieuport type 20 two-seaters. Vernon Castle and First Class Airman Percy O'Lieff were patrolling at 8,000 feet over Wytschaete (known as Whitesheet to the British Tommy) when two enemy machines were spotted. Setting off in pursuit they got close enough to one to be able to fire at it. O'Lieff fired five drums at it, upon which it turned for the safety of its own lines. The Hun observer had returned fire for a while but was then either hit or his gun jammed, as he ceased firing. After a few minutes the enemy machine, which had been above the British machine, dived steeply and came within range of Castle's fixed forward-firing gun. He commenced firing and eventually was so close he had to take avoiding action to prevent a collision. Tracers were seen entering the fuselage of the hostile machine and it apparently fell away out of control. While trying to clear the jam in his gun Castle lost sight of it in the clouds. Another pilot in the Squadron saw the machine falling below the clouds still in a spinning dive.

December 1916 was plagued with bad weather and the winter of 1916/17 was a particularly hard one. At the end of November and the beginning of December there was no flying for virtually a week, with another thirteen days lost during December itself. Flying at altitude in open cockpits was trying at the best of times and particularly so when there was bitter weather. The inactivity, however, allowed a little light relief from the strains of flying:

> 'For days we had stood by at dawn. This was not unusual. On such occasions we used to become bored and began to frolic, instead of returning to bed, on receiving the bad visibility report from the bombing squadron. On one later occasion we had been teased by one of the flight-commanders and his observer for delay, though we had no say in it, and on them we decided to take revenge. They were, of course, asleep – one on each side of their small rectangular Armstrong hut.
>
> We occupied ourselves for half an hour in the preparations for a vulgar practical joke. We worked quickly and silently, and when all was ready they awoke. To their surprise, they were not alone, for a cow, full size, was between them, and half a dozen grinning faces were at each window. By locking hands behind the beast we had succeeded in stalling it between their beds. Now cows are no respecters of persons, motor-cars or places, and this one, feeling the call of nature, made, with its tail, to obey.
>
> Airmen, however, are wont to act promptly, and – , the observer (I will not give his name; he happily survived the war and is now a rising public servant in the Colonial Service) sprang to the washstand, grabbed a receptable, and with hoots of applause from us all, held it in position. Not with promptitude alone had he acted, but with circumspection and sang-froid, for the receptacle was not his own, but the flight-commander's, wash-basin! This extremely vulgar episode made us laugh for days afterwards. In wartime you cannot be too particular what you laugh at.'

At the end of December the command of the Squadron changed again with George Pretyman leaving on promotion to command 13 Wing, which was part of III Brigade, in the Somme area. His replacement was Major Guy C St P de Dombasle, who came from 27 Squadron, where he had been a Flight Commander. In 1916 he had been senior Flight Commander and instructor at Turnhouse, where a contemporary noted, 'Dear old de Dombasle, what a charming man and what an indifferent instructor'. He was a Canadian, who had served in the Royal Canadian Regiment and transferred to the RFC in December 1915.

He spent a few days at the Depot at St Omer where a Nieuport scout was put at his disposal for practice flights and a few days were spent with Pretyman learning the ropes for the handover. He officially took command on Christmas Eve 1916. However due to the ban on squadron commanders flying on operations, as the RFC could ill-afford the loss of experienced leaders, he rarely flew except for the occasional test flight or the delivery of a new machine. Nevertheless he was a popular squadron commander.

Chapter Three

NUMBER 1 (FIGHTER) SQUADRON

With the New Year came a new role for the Squadron. On 1 January 1917 the unit consisted of twelve pilots and twelve observers, with just two Flight Commanders. During the month some of the Nieuport two-seaters were ferried to 46 Squadron, with the rest being returned to the Depot, while all the Moranes were ferried to the depot at St Omer. The pilots ferried Nieuport Scouts back and the mechanics returned by road. All the observers moved across the road to the Town Ground aerodrome at Bailleul, to 53 Squadron, who had arrived from the UK on 4 January. There was much sadness at the departure of the observers, with friendships having been forged in the heat and danger of war. Sadly four of these men were to be killed in action with 53 Squadron, including 1 Squadron's old Recording Officer, Thomas McKenny Hughes, who transferred over as their Intelligence Officer.

A third Flight Commander Captain C D Danby was posted in from 6 Squadron to take over B Flight but only lasted three weeks before going off to hospital. The last two-seaters disappeared on 28 January and in keeping with its new role the Squadron was officially transferred at midnight from 2 (Corps) Wing to 11 (Army) Wing.

The Type 17 Nieuport Scout

During the middle of 1916 the Squadron had operated a few type 16 Nieuport Scouts, but the machine now being delivered was the improved type 17. This was elegant but tricky to fly, particularly on landing. The rotary engine, where the entire engine casing rotated around the pistons, produced some odd gyroscopic forces whenever engine rpm were changed. Some pilots could not get accustomed to it and preferred stationary-engined types like the SE5a, with which 1 Squadron was to be equipped in 1918.

Though it had been designed with a single Vickers belt-fed machine gun synchronised to fire through the propeller, the RFC had removed this and substituted a Lewis gun mounted on the top wing firing over the propeller. The gun had to be lowered not only to clear jams but also to change the drums of ammunition. The Lewis drums contained only 97 rounds and pulling the gun down its rail during a dogfight was a difficult, dangerous and time-consuming operation. With such a clumsy arrangement it is amazing that 1 Squadron shot down any enemy machines, let alone the enormous number they claimed during 1917. The type 17 was replaced in time by the type 23 and 27 but there was little, if any, improvement in performance.

On 5 February Lieutenant E D 'Spider' Atkinson was transferred from A Flight and took command of B Flight in place of the unfortunate Danby. Atkinson had been serving in the Squadron since June of the previous year and like most of the pilots took to the role well. There was intensive training in gunnery and formation flying and more practice with the Le Prieur rockets that had been so successful the previous year. One machine, A6644, was fitted with a vertically mounted camera in the fuselage behind the pilot and trial photographs were taken of a number of objectives behind British lines, including 2 Brigade Headquarters at Oxelaere near Cassel. Why this technique of using a fast scout to take reconnaissance photographs instead of slow two-seater machines, which usually needed an escort, was not continued with has not been recorded.

On 9 February three machines, led by P M Le Gallais, took off at 0930 hours for their first patrol in the Ypres area but little was happening and they landed after an uneventful two-hour mission. Le Gallais, who came from Jersey, had been an observer with 17 Squadron in Egypt during 1915. He left 1 Squadron on promotion to Flight Commander in 29 Squadron – another Nieuport Scout unit.

First blood and first loss

Six days later on 15 February Le Gallais was again on patrol with J A Slater at 15,000 feet in the southern area of their 'beat' near Plugstreet, when they spotted a large German reconnaissance machine coming from the Menin direction. Slater dived behind it and pulling up fired half of one of his Lewis drums into it from about sixty yards. The enemy turned and put its nose down to try and dive away. Slater fired the rest of the drum into it from a similar range and it was last seen going down vertically out of control over Frelinghem.

The RFC daily communiqués, known humorously to everyone as 'Comic Cuts', after a popular children's comic of the day, recorded Slater's action. The French and Germans had a system where victories had to be confirmed by witnesses and officially credited. They recognised and acknowledged the 'ace' system, with their most successful pilots receiving high honours and becoming household names. The British view was that pilots were doing their duty and it was invidious to single out an individual. It was only in 1917 that officialdom relented slightly and allowed publicity about people such as Albert Ball, James McCudden and Phillip Fullard. Gallantry citations would sometimes give a pilot's 'score' but 'Comic Cuts', though an intelligence record or analysis of operations, was as close as the British fighter pilots came to having their victories officially acknowledged.

While Slater and Le Gallais were on their Southern Patrol, Second Lieutenant Hugh Welch and his Flight Commander, Captain J M E Shepherd, were conducting a similar duty to the north. Three miles east of Ypres they became involved in a scrap with three enemy fighters and Shepherd was seen to descend in a vertical dive in the vicinity of Gheluvelt. He failed to return and word was later received that he had been killed. Shepherd, like many of the early war pilots, had completed a period as an observer when you could only earn your observer's wing by actually flying on operations, unlike pilots who received their wings on completion of flying training. After pilot training he had returned to France with 16 Squadron and then been posted to 1 Squadron on promotion to Flight Commander. He would appear to have been the third and last victim of Peter Glasmacher of Jasta 8. Shepherd is buried in Perth (China Wall) Cemetery. Glasmacher was himself shot down and killed in May 1917 and today lies in Railway Dugouts (Transport Farm) British Military Cemetery near Ypres.

Some shuffling was necessary after Shepherd's loss and 'Spider ' Atkinson transferred from B to A Flight as Flight Commander, with Christopher Quintin Brand being promoted to take charge of B Flight. Brand, born in Kimberley in South Africa, had served in the Squadron since June 1916 and was destined to remain in it until wounded in May 1917.

Down on our side

Jimmy Slater's encounter was officially described as an 'out of control', much as in the Second World War the RAF used the word 'probable'. However later on 15 February, 1 Squadron achieved that rare distinction of bringing a German machine down in the Allied lines. The German air service was considerably smaller than the RFC and thus they had to husband their resources carefully. Units were frequently moved along the Front to be concentrated where they were needed. It was not often, therefore, that an enemy machine was captured but when it did happen it was of great technical interest and much was learned about German construction techniques. Each captured machine was allocated a G-number and the report about it would be freely disseminated within the RFC.

Many squadrons were not fortunate enough to bring down a German aeroplane inside the British lines but 1 Squadron was to achieve this distinction within a matter of days of commencing operations in their new role.

At 1700 hours on the same day as Slater's encounter, Second Lieutenant Victor Collins was flying a lone patrol just north of Ypres. He chased one enemy machine about two miles over the other side of the lines and when coming back at about 12,000 feet saw a formation of four unidentified hostile machines. Disregarding the odds he attacked them from behind. Two of them in turn attacked him and after a few shots had been exchanged his engine was hit and then failed. The loud, rasping noise of the engine was replaced by an eerie silence, broken only by the slipstream whistling through the wires and the chatter of machine-gun fire from the sole enemy machine pursuing him. Keeping his nerve Collins pulled his machine up and executing a very tight left turn fired about half a drum of ammunition into the enemy machine at close range. The machine fell away out of control, burst into flames and crashed. Still with a dead engine Collins made a successful forced landing. A crew from 46 Squadron also became involved when two of the enemy attacked and they claimed one of them. Ironically they were flying one of 1 Squadron's old Nieuport two-seaters that had been issued to them from the depot after its return from 1 Squadron. The German scout was identified as an Albatros DIII of Jagdstaffel 27 and was allocated the captured number G11. A Jagdstaffel or hunting squadron, abbreviated to Jasta, was the German air service basic fighter unit but was somewhat smaller than an RFC squadron, consisting of usually only about ten or so pilots. The pilot was Hans von Keudell, the Jasta commanding officer. Von Keudell, who was aged twenty-four, had joined the army in 1911 and was a very experienced pilot, having been a founder member of Jasta 1 in August 1916. He had been appointed to establish Jasta 27 on 5 February 1917, as their first commanding officer and became their first casualty.

Owing to bad weather with snow on the ground there was no flying from 18 February until 24 February and very little in the week after that. Flying conditions in open cockpits, in very low temperatures with no heating other than what was thrown back by the engine, were miserable. A number of opportunities went begging when the exposed Lewis gun failed to fire or jammed due to the intense cold. At this time the Squadron was feeling its way and learning the lessons of fighter tactics. Initially patrols were mounted consisting of just one to three machines but as the enemy formations increased in size and British losses climbed, patrols became larger. By 1918 patrols could be all three flights from a squadron with eighteen or more aeroplanes.

On 4 March the weather had improved enough for two three-man patrols to be mounted over the northern end of the Ypres salient. For an hour the B Flight patrol had running battles with a variety of German reconnaissance aeroplanes. During these indecisive encounters they nonetheless achieved their aim of driving off and denying British airspace to the intruders. Near the end of the patrol Brand and Second Lieutenant V G A Bush lost the third member of the patrol, Lieutenant T F Hazell, as his engine failed but from 15,000 feet east of Ypres he was able to glide all the way back to Bailleul and make a successful dead-stick landing. Shortly after this the two remaining Nieuports attacked a hostile two-seater. The pilot was hit, following which the machine stalled, rolled on its back and fell inverted for a couple of thousand feet before entering a dive. Several large pieces fell off and after rolling over several times it crashed near a wood. Bush, who came from Edinburgh, had been in the Highland Light Infantry and then after joining the RFC had served as an observer with 10 Squadron before learning to fly in the autumn of 1916. He was rare in being one of the very few married officers in the Squadron and unfortunately was killed in a flying accident at No.1 School of Aerial Fighting in February 1918.

Also on 4 March, Captain A J Capel returned to the UK on completion of his tour of duty and his place as C Flight Commander was taken by R H Cronyn from 19 Squadron. 'Dick' Cronyn was one of three brothers, one of whom, V P Cronyn, served in 56 Squadron and the youngest is Hume Cronyn the well-known actor. Dick had attended McGill University from 1912 to 1914 and worked on a project in Barcelona as an electrical engineer from June 1914 until March 1915. After pilot training in the UK he had joined 19 Squadron in October 1916.

On 16 March Cronyn wrote home to his family in Canada:

'I am pretty well settled down now, and have, I think, established myself with the other officers, and find them a first rate lot, indeed.

Yesterday I did my first job here, and for the first time I had a real scrap. It had been fairly "dud" earlier in the day, but later it cleared, so that three of us pushed off to do a patrol. I was under the leadership of one of the other flight commanders as I wished to see how one worked on these machines and also to get a little better idea of the country.

It was fairly clear and the visibility was very good as we climbed to about X thousand feet and started on our patrol up and down, above a certain portion of the lines. The lines in this part of the country differ considerably from those on the Somme front: the ground does not look so chewed up. On the Somme front, particularly between – (erased by Censor) – one is struck by the indescribable mess and apparent chaos of the trenches; mine and shell holes spread over miles of country, with only the one colour, dark brown. Here, seen from a height, the trenches or lines stretch across the country in a smudgey fashion – thick here – thin there – as though some one had sprinkled a light trail of dark earth across the fields.

The countryside in this section is also very different. As I told you, that behind the Somme front resembled in some ways Salisbury Plain, with the exception that it was cultivated and had more villages. But the villages were all small and looked much alike, making it extremely easy to lose oneself. Here there are a great many more landmarks, canals, well-defined roads and several large-sized towns. It is not nearly so good a country for forced landings as the fields are considerably smaller and fenced in, which is not the case further south.

The forthcoming Third Battle of Ypres or Passchendaele, as it has become known, was to change all of this and became infamous for its appallingly muddy conditions, which ultimately became far worse than the Somme. Cronyn continued his letter:

'We met some of our own machines, and shortly after I saw the leader signal that he had spotted something and was about to attack. Presently down he went, followed by the next man. I followed at some distance behind and above, keeping a very keen eye on my rear. I did not catch sight of what he was after until he attacked, and then I saw it was a large, slow, two-seater machine, so I did not attempt to follow him down. I saw the two machines circling around each other, and then, glancing back over my tail to see that nothing was following I lost sight of them altogether and so returned to a pre-arranged rendezvous. Presently our two machines appeared, having downed (although, of course, I did not learn this till later) the unfortunate Hun.

Again the leader signalled, but this time I saw the enemy, and knew we were in for a real scrap.

They were three fast, single-seated scouts, and when I first saw them I must say they did look formidable, with their brown and green paint and iron crosses.

Down we went, and of the ensuing fight I have the haziest of recollections. The main idea I carried away was a regular melée of machines turning, twisting and diving. I fired about 40 shots at a machine, but when or where – or with what result – I haven't the foggiest notion. You make for one machine – fire – pass him – up again – round – at another – down on a third – and so forth and so on. When you are actually engaged it is the most exciting sport you could dream of, nothing I have ever thought of can approach it for pure excitement, but looking forward or back on it is an entirely different matter – oh very!

Finally we were joined by our third member and went after another three. These put up a much better scrap, and I feel sure I hit one. We dived on them: I picked out my machine; when he tried to get on my tail I turned and went towards him; he passed over me and beyond. I wheeled, found him turning about fifty yards away and directly across my sight, so I let him have it good and fast. Either I hit him or he did not know I was there: at any rate I distinctly saw his machine give a sudden jerk, and around he came straight for me. Luckily he was slightly above me and so could not fire, whereas I could have riddled him, but whether I did or not I haven't the slightest idea. I was so fascinated seeing him coming straight on that I believe I did not shoot. He passed about six feet above me, and I turned just in time to see him diving vertically.

I could not see the others any where, so went off and finally back to the aerodrome. It was a great day: I learned a lot, gained confidence in myself and the machine, and felt I had done a good day's work.

The CO was very pleased. We had accounted for 3 Huns, and had driven down a great many others. But the best of the whole thing was a telegram received this morning from G.O.C. a copy of which I have beside me:-

"Congratulate Patrol led by Capt. Brand on good work yesterday afternoon. General Trenchard G.H.Q".'

Cronyn was describing a patrol led by Brand who shot down an LVG two-seater machine in flames, which shed its wings and crashed near Zandvoorde. It was possibly Gefreiter Werner von Schlichting and Leutnant Friedrich Popp of FA 250(A).

Vernon Castle

On 11 March Quintin Brand was leading two members of his Flight on a patrol along the front line and was keeping a fatherly eye on an RE8 of 53 Squadron busy taking photographs. Vernon Castle, a member of the patrol, spotting a formation of four enemy two-seaters just under a layer of cloud at about 7,000 feet, dived on them and fired a burst into the rearmost one. The gunner fired back and at this moment Castle's gun jammed and he had to turn away to try and clear it. The enemy took this opportunity and dived towards the German side. Castle was unable to see what, if anything, happened but a 46 Squadron machine reported seeing a scrap between Nieuport Scouts and hostile machines and then observed the enemy fall in flames. (Lieutenants Kay and Thomas were also flying one of 1 Squadron's old Nieuport 20s.)

Castle had been born in Norwich in 1887 and moved to the United States in 1906, where he married in 1911. He was born Vernon Blyth but took the stage name of Castle. He and his wife Irene performed as a dance team in both Europe and the US and were becoming well known by the outbreak of war. Their photographs appeared in the fashionable magazines of the day, such as *Vanity Fair* and the *Tatler*. He learned to fly at his own expense at the Curtiss Flying School at Newport News in Virginia at the end of 1915 and was awarded certificate No. 407 of the Aero Club of America. He returned to England in February 1916 and had more training at the Central Flying School and Gosport. Irene arrived in England in May 1916 and shortly after her arrival the two of them performed for Queen Alexandra at the Drury Lane Theatre.

Castle arrived in 1 Squadron on 23 June 1916 and was assigned to B Flight. He was quite a celebrity and somewhat older than his fellow officers. Just a month after he arrived he was involved in organising a squadron 'bash'. In a letter to his wife he wrote:

'Last night, as I told you, we had a squadron dinner, which means that the whole squadron (consisting of 40 officers) dines at one large table and have a big champagne dinner. This was in honour of three pilots who had won military crosses (*sic*). I have the job of providing all the drinks for the squadron, and I also arranged the dinner, which was a big success.

I managed to get a block of ice from a hospital in a town near here. We'd never had ice here before and I made cocktails and champagne cup. Most of the boys got fearfully tight, but they are all very young and felt alright this morning. I suppose it does one good to have a party once in a while.'

Castle had a fondness for animals – particularly dogs and monkeys – and after much searching acquired a monkey, which was named Hallard (a pun on 'Hallowed be thy Name'). George Pretyman also had a fondness for animals and bought some pigs. Castle then acquired a dog by teaching its owner the fox-trot. Castle was also given the job of Mess President:

> 'I don't think I told you all the things I have to do now, but they include the collecting of all the money from the officers, for their mess bills, and paying for all the food, seeing that the men keep the place clean and the baths hot, and in fact, it's a sort of Stage Manager for the squadron.
>
> I've done an awful lot of things since I've been Mess President. I've had built a great big bath-room with three baths and a shower and a regular hot water system, with an American furnace so that we can get hot water at all hours. Before we could only get sponge baths and unless you got there early you had to have cold water. Now everybody has a hot bath each morning and the bathroom is one of our pet exhibits when we have guests or visitors.
>
> I've also built a big bar with running water and an ice chest, etc. etc. It's quite a lot of fun because I can get all the men I want to build and do things. I'm going to have a tennis court built soon. A hard one, for the winter. During the cold weather we have much more spare time.'

On 11 March during a patrol, Castle was hit by anti-aircraft fire, and with little control over his machine crash-landed in the British second line trenches, where the aeroplane was totally wrecked. Fortunately he was well strapped in when the machine turned over and only received a few cuts and bruises. After nine months in the Squadron he was due for a rest and on 22 March was posted home, having been awarded the French Croix de Guerre.

Posted to Canada as a flying instructor he subsequently moved with the training scheme to Fort Worth in Texas and on 15 February 1918 was killed in a flying accident. There was a large military funeral, in which his Union Jack draped coffin was transported by gun carriage to the railway station in Fort Worth, watched by hundreds of the townspeople. As a postscript, the last film Fred Astaire and Ginger Rogers starred in together was the story of the Castles. Irene later re-married and died in 1969. Today Irene and Vernon Castle lie side-by-side in Wood Lawn Cemetery, New York.

The approaching storm

Air activity in the Ypres part of the front slowly increased in tempo during the spring of 1917. General Douglas Haig, commanding the British army on the Western Front, had decided to defeat the Germans in the Flanders area. This offensive would achieve a number of aims, one of which would be to clear the Belgian coast of U-boat bases and another to divert attention from the French army who, after the massive losses at Verdun and the disastrous Nivelle offensive on the Aisne, were now suffering low morale which was leading, in some units, to mutiny.

The town of Ypres lay in a basin and was overlooked by German observers and artillery from three sides. Before the main battle it was decided to take the Messines ridge, which formed the southern end of the Ypres Salient. The attack was scheduled for 7 June 1917. The Germans, aware that something was going on in the Ypres area, also moved units north from around Arras until they had more than doubled the number of flying units opposing the British.

On 17 March 1 Squadron escorted four FE2ds of 20 Squadron on a reconnaissance of the German rear areas in the vicinity of Lille and Courtrai. The fortunes of the two squadrons were to become inextricably linked over the ensuing months and combined patrols would inevitably draw a strong response from the Germans. The FE2s had taken off from Boisdinghem, some miles west of St Omer, and joined their escort of three Nieuports led by Jimmy Slater at 11,000 feet over Bailleul. (The 20 Squadron formation leader was Lieutenant Hugh White, later an Air Vice-Marshal CB, CBE.) From their rendezvous point they were trailed by a number of Albatros scouts and twenty-five minutes later near Lille these were joined by four more. At this point Slater overtook the lumbering reconnaissance machines and fired a red signal light indicating that the enemy were about to attack. On turning round he discovered that the Germans had already pounced, and one of his patrol was spinning down and was ultimately lost to sight below. Four hostile machines now dived on the remaining two 1 Squadron machines and a fight then ensued. The Albatros scouts withdrew to regain height, rather than continue duelling with the nimble Nieuports. Slater and C C Clark then caught up with their charges, whereupon they were again dived upon by the heavy enemy machines which used their superior speed and inertia to conduct diving attacks, followed by a zooming climb away. This pattern of a running fight continued for the remaining thirty or so minutes of the patrol.

One 20 Squadron machine was lost, but this appears to have fallen foul of anti-aircraft fire and the crew were able to burn their machine before capture. The missing Nieuport was that of Second Lieutenant Alex Ivan Gilson, who was brought down by Leutnant Paul Strähle of Jasta 18. Gilson had been educated in Bulmer in Natal and after a year's service in German South West Africa (now Namibia) had been commissioned in August 1916. According to Strähle he had been hit in the head and the machine had disintegrated in the air, with the result that the engine had to be dug out of the ground. Gilson has no known grave and is commemorated on the RAF Memorial to the Missing at Arras. Strähle was a bit of a thorn in 1 Squadron's side and was to claim another two of its machines in the coming months.

Gilson had joined the Squadron on the same day as Leslie Morton Mansbridge, who wrote home:

'Gilson has come along here with me and we are in the same hut. Yesterday we went into the town and got a lot of things for our room which we are going to make quite nice.'

A few days later Mansbridge had an interesting experience as the result of being a new pilot like Gilson:

'I have had a bit of excitement. I got lost in a snowstorm and I did not want to land in Hun-land so I steered west and came rather further than I meant to. I am now near Paris and I am quite alright. I didn't damage the machine at all. Today being dud I am stopping here, until it clears up. There are one or two awfully nice officers here and it has caused great excitement in the village. There is a French Commandant here who is awfully nice and he came up yesterday to get a look at the machine. I have absolutely nothing here in the way of clothes except flying kit but I have had some things lent to me.'

No doubt he received a ragging from the other members of the Squadron on his return and everyone probably thought he had devious reasons for landing near Paris!

Kite balloon warfare

A four-machine patrol was ordered up on 25 March to investigate an unlikely report of an airship in the Wervicq area. The cloud base was about 5,000 feet and as the formation climbed through the cloud they became split up. On coming out of the cloud Atkinson spotted what he thought might be the target but had to dodge in and out of cloud to avoid anti-aircraft fire. He eventually found himself directly above what turned out to be just an ordinary kite balloon. Diving steeply out of the cloud through heavy anti-aircraft fire he fired his rockets, all of which missed. Resorting to using his gun, loaded with tracer ammunition, he eventually set the fat sausage on fire. Noticing that the balloon was being hauled down rapidly he dived on the winch and shot up the crew, seeing two of them fall over, by which time he was down to only fifty feet above the ground.

One of the duties of the RFC in the run-up to the offensive was to clear the skies of enemy observation balloons, so that the Germans could not see the intensive preparations of the Allies. There were deep mining operations underway for the preliminary Messines operation and it was difficult to hide the vast quantities of distinctive, blue clay. Four machines were sent out to knock down kite balloons on 7 April. Slater and Atkinson found their targets protected by three or four enemy scouts and, smelling a rat, decided not to attack.

The fourth machine, flown by R J Bevington, failed to return. In a letter of 30 December 1917, from the notorious prisoner of war camp at Holzminden, to his brother Colin, he wrote:

'I was asleep in bed when an orderly came in to say I was wanted at once in the aerodrome, I crawled into my clothes without buttoning them up, got into thigh boots and a coat and went out, my machine was ready, and I was told the job by the recording officer. I went off and crossed the line at the salient at about three thousand feet, just above the clouds. The clouds were numerous and low but not continuous so I was spotted and fired at by "archie", who was pretty wide.

When about seven kiloms over I emerged into an open space, I came down a bit, and started looking about, when I heard first one and then several MG's open fire. I tried to locate them on the ground, when they seemed to get louder. I looked round and found that a patrol of six scouts had dropped onto my tail. I turned sharp round and started back for the cloud I had just left. They turned and started to over haul me again. I dodged as best I could and was within what seemed a few feet of the cloud, when one coming at right angles to me hit me in the induction pipe and the foot.

The engine stopped and I started fiddling with the adjustments to coax it on again, when my left wing hit a tree and broke both planes off half way across. Then the right bottom plane hit the ground and she stood on her nose with me hanging from the belt.

Men appeared from nowhere and helped me out and I put my right foot to the ground and fell straight over. Not till then did I realise that it was not a tiny skin graze for it didn't give me more than a slight prick when it hit. A doctor came up and tied it up and offered me a morphia injection, which I foolishly refused, for the tourniquet he put on stayed on a couple of hours and was pretty painful before it was over.

I went first in a stretcher, then a motor ambulance to a dressing station, then off in another motor to a hospital. The time from getting out of bed to finding myself down this side was not more than thirty five minutes and I got breakfast about 1.0 in the hospital. The next day the six pilots came over to see me and promised to drop a note saying that I was down wounded; but I suppose it was never found.

A lot more of the squadron came on in the evening including the late Lt Sahafer (*sic*),and Bulow. I was shown the flying casualties for that part of the front and so learnt what had happened to several missing cases whom I knew.'

Bob Bevington was repatriated on 19 December 1918 and during his imprisonment had learned of his younger brother's death in a flying accident. Between the wars he owned a garage and in the Second World War rejoined the RAF as a link trainer instructor. He died in 1975. (Slater later became a Flight Commander in 64 Squadron and was their most successful pilot. He was killed in a flying accident in the 1920s.)

On 26 March, the day following Bevington's loss, Brand and Second Lieutenant E S T Cole both brought balloons down in flames. On 22 April Stuart Cole brought down yet another and only narrowly avoided becoming a casualty. By this stage patrols were much larger and Cole was part of a nine-man formation led by Captain Atkinson. One of the patrol had to return due to engine trouble and Cole escorted him back to the safety of the British lines. On his way back to the lines a balloon was spotted and despite heavy ground fire and a patrolling German machine he attacked it as it was being hauled down. It finally caught fire when only twenty feet above the ground, at which point Cole's engine was hit. He scraped over the front line trenches at only fifty feet and had actually touched down on the German side several times when his engine had cut out temporarily. He was lucky to survive, as kite balloons were dangerous targets. Some pilots specialised in 'balloon busting' but generally most gave them a wide berth, if possible.

While Cole was attacking his balloon the remainder of the patrol attacked eight Albatros scouts south of Lille and in the confused battle that followed two enemy machines were claimed shot down out of control by Atkinson and Second Lieutenant E M Wright. However one Nieuport was seen going down rolling over, and on landing Lieutenant A W Wood was missing.

Wood was a very independent-minded individual and on one occasion had been suspended from duty for disagreeing with his Flight Commander. He was unwounded but during his forced landing injured his foot when the undercarriage collapsed. Released in 1918 he served in the RAF on a Short Service commission until 1927. After a precarious existence as an inventor he rejoined the RAF in 1937. He completed a flying refresher course in 1941 but while flying a Magister in 1943 low cloud forced him lower and lower, resulting in a crash into the top of a tree and causing more damage to his leg. In 1960 he had a partial amputation of the offending limb. He died in 1977.

The following day the lightness of the Nieuport was demonstrated. Stuart McKercher was landing after a patrol and a gust of wind blew his machine over, completely wrecking it and seriously injuring him. He was removed to hospital with a broken leg and badly cut face.

T F Hazell, in company with Second Lieutenant L M Mansbridge, was flying one of their familiar Northern Line patrols at lunchtime on 24 April when they saw the familiar shape of an Albatros two-seater 4,000 feet below them in the vicinity of Armentières. Hazell dived below its tail where the gunner was unable to fire at him, and shot off a burst of thirty rounds. Smoke poured from the bottom of the fuselage and the hostile machine went into a steep dive and finally fell in flames in the German front line. At one stage it appeared that the observer was hanging over the side shooting at Hazell with a pistol. The crew would seem to have been Leutnant Heinrich Klose and Unteroffizier Otto Haberland of FA(A)227.

The following day a nine-man patrol led by Atkinson had to return early due to bad weather and as they approached the aerodrome L J Mars and V H Collins collided. Both machines locked together and fell from 2,000 feet in to an adjacent field and were completely smashed. Both officers were found unconscious in the wreckage and were removed to hospital suffering from severe concussion but miraculously survived. In the absence of parachutes mid-air collisions were virtually always fatal.

R H Cronyn related in a letter home an 'interesting' experience in the early part of May which could have had a more serious ending:

'I had a rather startling experience the night before last. I had just climbed into bed, had turned down the lamp which was slowly going out, and had rolled over and was nearly asleep. Suddenly – very – I heard a rifle go off, and at the same instant I heard a click in my hut, the lamp went completely out, and something dropped on to the end of my bed. I lay very still for about five minutes, wondering if the performance was to be repeated. Finally, I cautiously put out my hand and felt the lamp, which I fancied might be spilling oil all over the table, but it seemed O.K. Then I felt the end of my bed, but could discover nothing, so got up and lit a candle. The first thing I found was a large hole in the lamp, then I found a deep mark in the woodwork behind the lamp, and when I looked on the end of my bed I found a perfectly good 303 bullet, which was quite hot when I picked it up. Someone had let a rifle go off by accident I suppose, and apparently a good distance away, as the bullet must have been very nearly spent.

Anyway, it had come through the end of the hut, over my bed, through the lamp and sideways against the wall, bouncing back onto my bed. So I have kept it as a souvenir.

When I told the C.O. about it, the first thing he said was "I say, what a pity your arm wasn't in the way." I thought it rather lucky that something more vulnerable than my arm had not been in the way. Imagine being "done in" in bed. "The Daily Mail" would probably come out with "TRAGIC END OF VALIANT AIR MAN – MEETS HIS FATE WHILE IN BED".'

A balloonatic

One of the many tasks that 1 Squadron undertook was chasing off enemy machines when they were reported by ground stations. On Thursday 26 April, Lieutenant A V Burbury was sent on one of these Hostile Aircraft Patrols. Unable to find the offending machine, he attacked an enemy kite balloon near Wervicq and brought it down in flames. He then set off to destroy another near Quesnoy, but while flying at only 100 feet received a direct hit from an anti-aircraft battery near Comines. He was lucky to survive, albeit injured, as the aeroplane was a total wreck. Unusually, even though he did not return and therefore did not submit a combat report, the balloon was seen to fall in flames and its destruction was recorded in 'Comic Cuts'. The irony of this situation was that Burbury, before pilot training, had received an MC as a kite balloon observer, when the cable of his balloon was shot through by a shell. Remaining in the basket he had destroyed important documents and then parachuted to safety just before the errant balloon was about to cross into German held territory.

While a prisoner of war he made several escape attempts and in one of them, was shot in the right arm as he emerged from a tunnel, shattering it, which left him with a stiff arm for the rest of his life. During his imprisonment he learned Russian and became fluent in French, having a flair for languages. On his return from Germany he attended Cambridge University and joined the Foreign Office, spending two years based in Moscow. He had been awarded the French Croix de Guerre.

More captured German machines

Despite the rarity of German machines landing in Allied lines, 1 Squadron now brought down two on consecutive days. On the last day of April Quintin Brand was sent on a Hostile Aircraft Patrol but, unlike Burbury just a few days before, he made contact with the German machines which had been reported. Finding a pair of two-seaters flying west over Wytschaete, he engaged one which was painted a reddish brown. Firing from 100 yards he hit the observer, who collapsed back into his cockpit. With the gunner out of the way Brand was able to close to 70 yards and fired the remainder of a drum into it. The machine dived vertically into the ground in the British lines near Houplines. The crew of Vizefeldwebel Max Baatz and Leutnant Alexander Schleiper, from FA(A)204, were both killed. In the German air service the observer, invariably an officer as in this case, was in command of the machine and the pilot could be of quite a lowly rank. The wreckage, which was allocated the number G27, was consumed by fire and very little was worth recovering. An accepted practice through most of the war was that each side would drop messages requesting information regarding their losses. A few days later a German message was found giving the information that Burbury had survived on 26 April and requesting any information on Baatz and Schleiper who, it was noted, had been shot down by a Nieuport near Houplines between 0900 and 1000 hours.

Brand was wounded the following day and invalided to hospital. On his return to the UK he served in Home Defence squadrons against German night-flying bombers and returned to France in 1918 as part of the RAF's first dedicated night-fighter squadron, eventually becoming its Commanding Officer. Post-war he had a distinguished career and was knighted for his epic flight to Cape Town in 1920. From 1932 to 1936 he was Director General of Aviation in Egypt and then commanded No. 10 Group Fighter Command during the Battle of Britain. He retired in 1943 as Air Vice-Marshal Sir Quintin Brand KBE, DSO, MC, DFC and died in 1968.

The following day, 1 May, 'Spider' Atkinson led eight machines for a patrol in the Ypres-Roulers area. A new pilot crashed his machine on take-off, and another forced landed near Elverdinghe due to engine failure. The remainder dived on four enemy scouts at 12,000 feet to the west of Ypres and soon discovered that they had bitten off more than they could chew. All four machines were skilfully flown, particularly one that was painted brilliant red. Atkinson fought for ten minutes with this machine until his carburettor was shot away and the engine stopped. Employing a tactic the Germans used on their side of the lines he spun away and avoided being hit again, except for one moment when he stopped spinning to see where the hostile machine was. He eventually made an engine off landing at Elverdinghe without further damage. Meanwhile Stuart Cole dived several times on another machine despite being shot at by yet another. After several bursts he managed to put a whole drum of ammunition into it whilst in a dive at only 1,000 feet and the Albatros crashed through the top of a tree and fell into a pond.

In a letter to his parents two days later Cole wrote:

'The day before yesterday was the finest day I've lived so far.

I did a long patrol before breakfast & nothing special happened, at 9.45 we had a long reconnaissance & at the end of this as we were crossing the lines I spotted a brilliantly red coloured machine with three other machines with him on our side of the trenches, all of us dived on them & a general scrap followed. The Capt brought one down but he managed to get back to hunland before crashing, in turn the Capt was shot down by one of the hun, shots going right through his petrol tank. He came down in a spin but managed to right her before hitting the ground. Two more of our patrol were shot down & it left another pilot and myself to do our best, the other fellow was splendid & put up a splendid show. However after scrapping for some time two of the huns managed to get away & it left me with one fellow. He had a wonderful machine & the finest flier I've ever been up against. We each tried to better each other from 12,000 ft to 800 ft & when we got near the ground I managed to get in some good shots & down he came, burst into flames just before hitting the ground & the machine went vertically into a pond. I landed in a field next to him & rushed over, thousands of tommies & people were watching & a cheer went up from all of them. However we got the poor fellow out, the doctor found him with 5 shots through the heart so there was no chance for him. It was all frightfully exciting. Fortunately I did not have a shot in my machine. The hun machine has been brought to the aerodrome & it belongs to their crack squadron & is the very latest type most beautifully fitted up.

The pilot who was a Captain had a topping cigar case which I was having but now all his personal belongings will be sent back to his people & I'm allowed to claim any three things belonging to the machine.'

The machine, which had a large letter 'K' on the side of the fuselage, was allocated the number G30. Much interest was displayed in the radiator, which was of a much lighter design than was used on the British 160hp Beardmore engine and it was suggested that it be fitted to this engine for a trial.

The pilot, Alexander Kutscher, born on 27 September 1882 in Saarbrucken had been a pilot in FA 32 from the beginning of August 1916 until the end of October of that year, engaged in the usual work of a two-seater unit. He had been posted to Jasta 5 and then ultimately onto Jasta 28.

Jasta 28, a Württemberg unit, based at Wasquehal just north of Lille, had been formed in December 1916 and the second Commanding Officer was Karl Emil Schäfer, who had been promoted from Jasta 11. He had kept his machine painted brilliant red in memory and pride of his old unit which employed that colour scheme. 'Spider' Atkinson was his twenty-fifth official victory and he went on to score another five before he became a casualty on 5 June 1917, probably falling victim to Lieutenants H L Satchell and T A M S Lewis in their FE2d of 20 Squadron. Jasta 28 was an unlucky staffel for commanding officers, as the next two were also killed in action. Kutscher had the dubious distinction of being the unit's first casualty and, ironically, is buried in the same British cemetery (Ferme Olivier) as von Keudell of Jasta 27.

Later in the same day Cole had a nasty incident, which he also related in a letter to his parents:

'In the evening of the same day I was on another patrol when I got a direct hit with an archey (*sic*) shell, it shot away one rocker arm of the engine damaged all the cylinders snapped one of the planes and tore off all the engine covering & incidentally knocked the machine on its back & then got into a spin but after this I got her under control & glided with the whole thing vibrating & got to another aerodrome. It gave me an awful shock, but now I'm alright again but the Colonel came round & said its about time I had a rest, so within a month I should get it.'

Cole was posted home on 5 June and was awarded a well-deserved MC on 15 June. His delight at returning to the UK unscathed was nearly his undoing. One of 1 Squadron's ex-observers, who had been posted to 53 Squadron at the Town Ground over the road, noted:

'Smith and I went over to 1 Squadron to say goodbye to Cole who goes to England tomorrow. He very nearly failed to start for England owing to a blood curdling exhibition of stunting in his Nieuport this morning, part of which we saw from 53. He tried to go between the chimney and the tower of the asylum but did not notice there was a strong power cable running across that space which destroyed his propeller and undercarriage and tipped him nose down. He just managed to pull her up a few feet from the ground and landed perfectly.'

It would appear from squadron records that this incident was hushed-up as there is no mention of a Nieuport having to be repaired.

Post-war, because his family did not want him to fly in the RAF, he ran a garage for many years in Malmesbury and had the rudder from Kutscher's machine on the wall. On the outbreak of the Second World War he immediately joined up and spent most of the war on flying duties, surviving an attempt in June 1940 to fly a formation of Bristol Blenheims and Hawker Hurricanes across German occupied France to the Middle East, in which most of the machines were lost or had to return. After the war he returned to his garage business.

The aeroplanes had a hard time in service use and Nieuport Scout A6613 is a good illustration. This machine was delivered to the Squadron on 29 January 1917 by J A Slater and had the distinction of bringing down 1 Squadron's first enemy machine after becoming a fighter unit. By May it had flown a total of 80 hours, having been used as an instructional airframe for the last six weeks, due to its poor condition. It had suffered four broken wing panels, five broken axles and had one complete crash where everything was broken, except the fuselage. It was returned to the depot as unfit for further service on 5 May. Having been rebuilt, it returned on 13 July and was wrecked only three days later, having flown another ten hours. Sent to Egypt as a training machine it was involved in at least two more crashes before being written off on 21 March 1919.

In the build-up to Messines on 7 June, 1 Squadron was kept busy escorting the FE2ds of 20 Squadron as they bombed a variety of targets. These escorting jobs always seemed to have brought the enemy up in strength and running battles would be fought all the way to and from the target. On May 12 Captain F W Honnet, B Flight Commander led eight machines on an escort operation. Before the war he had farmed in South Africa and had served with 24 and 29 Squadrons flying DH2s from May to November 1916. Honnet, while watching the descent of an Albatros scout he had just sent down out of control, was pounced upon by another seven. Resisting the temptation to dive away, as an inexperienced pilot may have done, he used the agility and climbing ability of his Nieuport to get above the heavier and less manoeuvrable Albatros. At one point while he was trying to regain the safety of his flight he fired at the enemy machines with his revolver!

On 13 May 'Spider' Atkinson was posted home, having completed nearly a year with the Squadron. After instructing duties in the UK he managed to get back to France, ostensibly on a refresher course, where he flew with 56 and 64 Squadrons and shot down a number of enemy machines. He was awarded a DFC for this and an AFC in 1919. Promoted to Squadron Leader in 1924 he twice commanded 1 Squadron and retired in 1932. He died in 1954.

A disastrous kite balloon attack

Apart from flying escort missions and keeping German observation machines out of Allied airspace, the pilots were still attacking kite balloons to deny the enemy the ability to spy on British activities. The previous week there had been a number of unsuccessful attacks where even though the balloons had been well peppered they had failed to burn. It was believed that the incendiary ammunition may have been at fault. Extensive trials were conducted at St Omer in varying conditions in order to discover the problem.

On May 18 orders were issued for what was to be a disastrous attack on several kite balloons. Six aeroplanes armed with the familiar rockets set off at 0815 hours. Two balloons were brought down but at the cost of three machines missing and one pilot wounded. The moment the Nieuports crossed the line the balloons were brought down at high speed and it may be possible that the Germans were expecting the attack. Second Lieutenant T H Lines sent his objective down in flames but was brought down, hit in the engine by groundfire and captured before he could burn his machine. Lieutenant Lindsay Drummond was brought down by ground-fire and killed. A Canadian from Toronto, he had been an observer in 1 Squadron from April to October 1916 and after pilot training had returned to his old unit. Another pilot, M G Cole, was also shot down and killed. H J Duncan, who in early 1916 had won an MC for his gallantry when in charge of a group of trench mortars under heavy shellfire, returned wounded in the thigh. Apart from the MC, he had also been Mentioned in Despatches twice and spent the obligatory period as an observer – in his case with 5 Squadron. Both his balloon and Lines' were seen to descend in flames by 2nd Army AA Group.

An epic air battle

The last week of May reached a crescendo of furious activity, with a number of victories scored and a few casualties. A formation of eight FE2ds of 20 Squadron was sent to bomb Polygon racecourse, Comines railway station and Houthem dump, escorted by ten Nieuports of 1 Squadron and six Sopwith Pups from 46 Squadron. (Of the six Pups, one was flown by E P Plenty, who had already served in 1 Squadron and another by F L Luxmoore, who was to serve in the Squadron in the 1920s.)

This large operation of 26 May is described by Stewart Keith-Jopp, a member of Dick Cronyn's C Flight, in his diary:

'I'm fed up. My beautiful machine has been lost. Macintosh (a new pilot) stole it today, and has not come back. It is too sickening. We were escorting some F.E. birds and some 'Pups' were supposed to be guarding our tails. While climbing up, I passed through the F.E formation. The formation flying was wonderful and I had the greatest admiration for their observers who were wandering casually round their machines a sight that made me feel dizzy, as I hate the idea of falling out. As I came up, six Lewis guns were pointed straight at me (to put the wind up me I suppose). So I waved and they all waved back. Pretty soon we crossed the lines, and then lost the Pups who couldn't keep up. I was the hindermost in our formation and so had to keep a good look out. After 1½ hours, I was looking at my clock and saying, "Thank God, only another ½ hour", when something made me look round and behind and under my tail. There were two Albatros V strutters, about 30 yards away, one on either side and with their guns dead on me. They were painted all colours, one wing red, another blue, yellow bodies and perhaps a green tail. I was absolutely terrified, as I couldn't dive away. The only thing possible was to leave the formation and go for the blighters, which I did, turning and going straight at the chap on my right. First I'd chase Hun No.1 until Hun No.2 dived on me, and vice versa for ten minutes. All the time I was hoping the chaps would see the scrap and come and help. But they didn't. Ten other Huns did though, and suddenly the air all round was full of weirdly coloured machines buzzing around, with, as I thought all their guns going at once at me'.

In fairness, the rest of the formation had their hands full and were fighting their own battles. The FE2ds of 20 Squadron had dived on fourteen Albatros scouts climbing from below and 1 Squadron had joined in the furious battle. Keith-Jopp continues:

'It was a sticky moment. Then they all disappeared again, and I was looking round, when I heard the familiar pop – pop – pop again quite close. I looked for the beggar everywhere, but couldn't spot him, (he was probably in front in the sun), when there was a most fearful Bonk. I stood up in my belt and fairly yelled with fright, sat down again and saw petrol spurting all over my feet from the tank; so not wanting to be a nice little aerial bonfire I switched off and went down 4000 feet in a spin. On pulling out at 2000, I saw the Huns careering round above and one diving at me, so risking a fire, switched the engine on, and dug out for home nose down at 180 m.p.h. We were 15 miles over Hunland and it seemed to take an hour instead of 5 minutes to get back. Half way to the lines another Nieuport attacked my pursuer and I was left alone. The last petrol hissed out just before I crossed the lines and I glided the last 5 miles to the aerodrome and I landed down-wind. Hopping out to have a look at the damage, I found that three shots had gone through the tank and between my legs, two through the tank sideways, two through the cowling, the wings and tail, one each, and about ten through a wheel, tearing off the tyre, one bullet went through my coat and into the seat, which I kept as a souvenir.

While I was counting the holes a General came up and asked me why the blank blank, I'd left my patrol. I replied that I'd been shot down. Silly idiot!! He grunted and went away, while I carried my still warm bullet, with great delight to the mess.'

Four Albatros scouts were sent down out of control by the Nieuports plus two crashed and one out of control by the FEs. On the Britsh side Lieutenant J C C Piggott was seriously wounded. A bullet from behind had passed right through him via a lung. He was able to land near a dressing station and when his coat was removed the bullet fell out. Despite this wound he survived to the ripe old age of 79, having spent another six years in the RAF during the Second World War.

The second casualty this day was Second Lieutenant R R MacIntosh, a brand new pilot. He had taken off with Sergeant Gordon Olley to be shown around the area but had to return due to engine problems after forty minutes and then borrowed Keith-Jopp's machine, as related earlier. Now on his own he fell victim to Paul Strähle who the previous day had shot down Lieutenant J R Anthony, the replacement for Atkinson as A Flight Commander. In 1977 Robert MacIntosh recalled:

'Having collected a new machine, I set out in search of Olley, but not finding anyone, I climbed as high as I could to have a good look round on this cloudless early morning. I didn't see a plane of any description, and was flying quite straight when I must have been stalked by a group (later I was told the number was five) of Germans who had positioned themselves between me and the sun. The first thing I knew was machine-gun fire which hit neither the plane nor me. I then altered direction smartly, but failed to keep a plane in the gun-sight for more than a few seconds. My next recollection is of bullets hitting the right side of the Nieuport and I thought it wise to heed the advice for those who found themselves cut off in these circumstances – which was to simulate being disabled by spinning down apparently out of control, and then steering westwards. This I duly did, but on straightening out at an estimated 1,000 feet, I found that I had been accompanied down by three of the group who flew along on either side. I hadn't the faintest idea where I was and decided that the only sensible thing to do was to land, which I did in quite a small field, while the German planes circled round. The Nieuport was equipped with a torch-like device which I lit as I left the plane which was soon well ablaze as mentioned in Straehle's diary. It wasn't too long before I was approached by a German soldier on horse-back, presumably a spectator or attracted by the fire. And later we were overtaken on the road by one of the German pilots on a bicycle who claimed me as his victim, so I presume it was Straehle.'

For his activities as a prisoner of war MacIntosh, a New Zealander from Timaru, was Mentioned in Despatches. He had a distinguished career and for nearly thirty years was Nuffield Professor of Anaesthetics at Oxford University and was wartime Consultant in Anaesthetics to the Royal Air Force, with the rank of Air Commodore. Knighted in 1955, Sir Robert died in 1989.

Stewart Keith-Jopp did not last much longer but his exit from the Squadron was not due to enemy action but to a freak accident on the ground. As well as ordinary flare pistols 1 Squadron had a special long tripod-mounted tube affair about three and a half feet long. While trying to attract the attention of a Nieuport circling the aerodrome he and another pilot fired about twenty flares. The last one resulted in an explosion and he lost two fingers and the thumb of his left hand, with the other two fingers badly damaged. He ended up in hospital in the bed opposite Piggott. Despite his injury Keith-Jopp was flying again before the end of the war and during the Second World War flew as a pilot in the Air Transport Auxiliary delivering new aeroplanes.

Three Flight Commanders in one day
On 3 June Dick Cronyn was posted back to the UK, or Home Establishment, as it was officially known. He was repatriated to Canada in August as an instructor and passed his knowledge and expertise on to the next generation of pilots, for which he was Mentioned in Despatches in August 1919. (His son, a Squadron Leader with the RCAF, was killed together with all his crew on operations with Bomber Command in 1944.) His place as C Flight Commander was taken by Leslie Morton Mansbridge, who had been in the Squadron since February but had not yet been promoted to full Lieutenant. Mansbridge was leading a three-man patrol that evening, when five Albatros scouts dived out of the sun on them at 12,000 feet over Gheluvelt. Mansbridge was wounded in the right thigh and the machine so badly shot about that it had to be returned to the depot. He would seem to have fallen foul of Marinefeldjasta 1 which, as its title suggests, was a German navy fighter unit. 1 Squadron was to have a scrap with them later in the year with a completely different result. Mansbridge returned to France in 1918 and completed a full tour of duty as a Flight Commander in 23 Squadron flying Sopwith Dolphins. He died in 1992 at the grand age of 95.

Mansbridge's place was taken by Lieutenant Frank Sharpe. He was another individual who had served in the Squadron before, having been an observer from June until November 1916, prior to pilot training.

Chapter Four

THE THIRD BATTLE OF YPRES

The big bang

The preliminary artillery barrage for the Messines operation began on 26 May 1917 and, by 6 June 3,500,000 shells had been fired by over 2,000 guns of various calibres. The stillness of the early morning of 7 June was broken by a series of gigantic explosions that caused panic in Lille fifteen miles away and was even heard in London. Nineteen mines totalling over 1,000,000 pounds of ammonal were set off beneath the ridge shattering the German defences and stunning the survivors. The ridge was taken with, by First War standards, a relatively low number of casualties. Two mines were not used and their positions subsequently lost. One exploded during one night in 1955, fortunately without causing any casualties but the other is still out there…..

Herman Göring and Jasta 27

No.1 Squadron were up early that morning and carried out a variety of patrols, including ground strafing of enemy troops, chasing off observation machines and attacking balloons. Sharpe celebrated his promotion by leading a three-man patrol at 0940 hours and he and Lieutenant L F Jenkin shot down an Albatros scout, which crashed near Zandvoorde. Later in the day he attacked a kite balloon, which was seen to go down in flames by British anti-aircraft personnel.

Very early the following morning Lieutenant T F Hazell was leading four of his A Flight machines on a Northern Offensive Patrol. At 0640 hours a formation of five enemy machines approached from the west about 2,000 feet higher. Hazell attacked one that had a black painted fuselage with a white band round it, firing half a drum from very close range in a head on approach. The Albatros rolled over and over and then went down in a vertical dive, which the Nieuport was unable to follow. In the midst of the scrap a Nieuport was seen going down with an Albatros on its tail but Hazell was unable to catch up with it. After landing Second Lieutenant F D Slee was missing.

The patrol had tangled with the Albatros scouts of Jasta 27, whose markings consisted of a black fuselage with a broad white band around the fuselage aft of the cockpit, on which individual pilots had their personal number. Göring, the staffel leader, had his machine painted with a black fuselage and a white tail and rudder. He later wrote an account of this action that bares little relation to the facts:

'Ten machines of my youthful staffel were flying behind me in squadron order. We were about 4,000 metres up when we crossed the Lys to reach our hunting ground, which lay about 60 kilometres from our aerodrome. Over our heads a Nieuport squadron – twelve strong – made its appearance. The little silver-grey scouts were difficult to see when they dived out of the sun, in which they had so skilfully concealed themselves. The attack was opened. All too quickly my staffel was dispersed, so that it could no longer fight as a team. Just as I am snatching a moment's respite from the crazy round of turns I suddenly see an opponent above me. He dives warily out of the sun, with intent to spring a surprise and shoot me down from behind.

A mad series of turns begins. Round to the right, round to the left, loops, turns, zooms, sideslips – we try every trick and stunt. We often whirl so close by one another that we look certain to collide. The Englishman is a brilliant, skilled and dashing flier. I slip down in a turn; my opponent promptly sees his chance and hammers away at me furiously with both his guns. Several bullets find billets close behind me.

Once more I pull my machine straight up and fire at the Englishman; he too has been hit several times. Now we are barely 2,000 metres up. Again he joins battle furiously and tries to attack me.

I hurl myself at him with one last desperate effort and put my bullets into his machine at close range. He goes down, turning over and over; his engine stops – shot to pieces.

He catches his machine when close above the ground and attempts to make a landing, but fails and crashes. He is thrown out of the machine, but remains uninjured. But all my strength has gone; my knees tremble, my pulse beats furiously and my whole body is wet through the hard work I had to put into this fight.

This exhausting bout lasted ten minutes. A telephone message from the front reported the capture of my opponent, an experienced scout pilot who had shot down five German machines.'

The truth of the matter was that Slee, an Australian from Perth, had come direct from a training unit and had been in 1 Squadron for only four days when he became a prisoner of war! Like most inexperienced pilots he stood little chance on his own against an experienced fighter and it was largely luck that enabled him to escape with his life.

The following afternoon four machines from A Flight and another four from C Flight, led by Frank Sharpe, had a fight with fifteen German machines in various formations. Sharpe attacked a two-seater, which crashed and was then set upon by three Albatros scouts. Second Lieutenant R W L Anderson dived on these machines endeavouring to distract them, but the Nieuport went spinning down with all three latched onto its tail. Anderson tried to get in a shot at the scouts who were circling the luckless 1 Squadron machine but to no avail. Eventually Anderson was down to only 700 feet over the Houthem sidings and had to change a drum, during which he lost sight of the Nieuport. It was last seen zooming over trees and houses pursued by the enemy machines. Sharpe regained consciousness four days later in a German hospital with no recollection of how he had been brought down.

The Squadron were to lose twelve pilots missing or killed in June and half of these went in the first week. With an establishment of eighteen it did not require a mathematics degree to work out how long you were going to last, but despite the losses, morale did not slump. Throughout 1917 the Squadron were blessed with a number of excellent flight commanders, who were shrewd tacticians and themselves led by example, claiming a considerable number of German aircraft. There were still losses but they were never to be as bad as those suffered that June.

There were three flight commanders who were exceptional.

Phillip Fletcher Fullard

The first of these was P F Fullard, who claimed some 40 victories between April and November 1917 and remains 1 Squadron's most successful pilot.

Born in 1897, he had been commissioned into the Royal Irish Fusiliers from the Inns of Court OTC. After joining the RFC he trained at Netheravon, then the Central Flying School at Upavon where he was then retained as a flying instructor. On 26 April 1917 he was posted to France with a total of 115 hours flying – a not inconsiderable amount by the standards of the day. He was an accomplished pilot and had been noted at CFS for his flying skill. After two days at the Pilot's Pool at St Omer, despite his efforts to get himself posted to 40 Squadron where his old CO at CFS was in command, he was sent to 1 Squadron. Due to the fact that there were no Nieuport Scouts in the UK, most pilots' first experience of the type was when they arrived at their operational unit, though some lucky souls were able to fly an hour or so on them at the depot. Even pilots as skilled as Fullard found that the Nieuport was not an easy machine to fly, as he noted in his diary:

'Had my first flip on a Nieuport this evening. Frightfully heavy handed. Not a bit like a Pup. Shall probably like them better later on. Did a little practice flying. Stall turns and spins. Machine seems very unwieldy.'

Fullard grew to love the Nieuport and in later years when asked which machine he would have preferred to fly he said that he would still favour it but his second choice would be the Albatros scout! (Later in the UK he had the opportunity to fly a captured example of his adversary.)

There is little doubt that Fullard had wisdom beyond his years. He believed in reducing the odds in every situation and not taking foolhardy risks. He practised dismantling and putting his Lewis gun back together again. Each round of ammunition was checked with a gauge before loading it into a drum and he kept his drums, whereas a lot of pilots just threw them over the side when empty. He attributed his success to straight forward flying and did not consider himself a particularly brilliant marksman.

He joined A Flight under the tutelage of that experienced fighter, 'Spider' Atkinson and took time to settle in. Experience was everything and the first objective of a raw pilot was to avoid being shot down. On 4 May he participated in his first patrol and was a member of a number of escorts to 20 Squadron. On 18 May he had been involved in the disastrous balloon strafe but had not pressed home his attack as he suspected, probably quite rightly, that it was a trap. Just before the operation he had noted in his diary:

'I had to practice contour chasing to Ypres and back. This means balloon strafing, a damn rotten prospect. Go over trenches at 25 or so feet and return the same way.'

Fullard was not a great fan of kite balloon attacks and only ever attacked three, of which only one was decisive. As far as he was concerned the risks involved were not worth it. He had his first combat on 25 May, albeit an indecisive one.

On 4 June he was involved in an epic dogfight near Roulers, during a Northern Offensive Patrol led by Tom Hazell, the A Flight Commander, and with Second Lieutenant W G Milliship they ran into fifteen to twenty German machines. Together with a patrol of ten Sopwith Triplanes from No.1 Naval Squadron, some SE5as from 56 Squadron and a Spad from 19 Squadron, they fought for over twenty minutes between 18,000 and 14,000 feet. A red Albatros latched onto Fullard's tail but by turning tightly, which the less manoeuvrable Albatros was unable to emulate, he was able to avoid all the fire it was directing at him. While engaged in this turning engagement Second Lieutenant A P F Rhys-Davids of 56 Squadron swooped and shot the Albatros down.

An enemy scout, with a black fuselage and a white band, wounded Flight Sub Lieutenant Cockey in the foot but was then attacked by Fullard from above and another Triplane from below. Each pilot fired thirty rounds at it following which it went down in a slow spin and was seen to crash. Hazell claimed four German machines crashed or driven down. One SE5a was lost and as well as the injury to Cockey and the Spad pilot who was also wounded, several machines were shot about. 1 Naval had taken off about the same time as 1 Squadron and was based on the other side of the Asylum aerodrome. The black and white machine was a familiar opponent to the pilots of 1 Naval and had been given the nickname 'Mr. Buchanan', after the current popular 'Black and White' whisky of the time.

Fullard acquitted himself well, and had survived the early stages. He was appointed acting flight commander of C Flight following the loss of Sharpe, though he was shortly transferred to A Flight. He was the fourth C Flight Commander in a week and at only nineteen years of age had tremendous responsibility thrust upon him. With the new responsibility and experience he now began to score steadily.

William Charles Campbell

The second of 1 Squadron's stars of this period was the complete antithesis of Fullard and was to have a meteoric career in the Squadron. Campbell was born in 1887 and at thirty was considerably older than his contemporaries. He had a Scottish father and French mother and spoke English with a marked French accent. Before the war he worked in Bordeaux and played rugby for the Stade Bordelais, and was a stocky, well built, larger than life character. He arrived at 1 Squadron the day after Fullard on 30 April.

He wasted little time and shot his first enemy machine down two weeks after joining and demonstrated his aggressive approach to aerial combat. Having been sent off on his own to deal with an observation machine he found one at 12,000 feet over Ypres. Diving on it he fired half a drum with the observer returning his fire. It suddenly went into a vertical dive with Campbell following down to 4,000 feet. He discovered it lying in a field close to a small wood, then proceeded to fly round the crash for ten minutes, but seeing no sign of movement came home.

Unlike Fullard, Campbell had a penchant for enemy kite balloons. On 19 May the two of them were on patrol together when Campbell saw a couple. He made two feints at one of them, each time turning away, until on the third approach he dived on it from about 2,000 feet above. Closing to within thirty feet he fired off a whole drum of incendiary ammunition. The two observers jumped out and as the balloon was being hauled down rapidly it burst into flames. On 21 May he sent an Albatros scout down to crash, and the following day had an unsuccessful attack on another balloon.

He sent down another machine, which crashed, on 2 June and two days later sent an LVG two-seater down in flames. On 9 June, in two separate patrols he destroyed two Albatros scouts and claimed another down out of control. The same day he was promoted to command B Flight. Two days later he was notified that he had been awarded a Military Cross. In a little over five weeks he had claimed eight victories, been promoted and earned a decoration! His career in the Squadron was to continue in the same manner, as we shall see.

Louis Fleeming Jenkin

Jenkin was the third of the high scoring pilots in 1 Squadron that summer and another exceptional character. He had been born in Kensington, London and was named Louis after Robert Louis Stevenson, who was a close friend of his grandfather. His father was a barrister and he was educated privately until sent to Dulwich, where he ultimately became a boarder. His younger sister wrote about him:

> 'As a small boy he had a violent temper but learnt to control it completely. He had a strong will and a strong character, which knew no compromise between right and wrong. But he also had a great sense of fun and was very popular.'

He had been badly wounded in the right shoulder when serving with the Loyal North Lancashire Regiment. After learning to fly he joined 1 Squadron on 5 May 1917 just a few days after Fullard and Campbell. Initially he was posted to the Headquarters Flight but was then transferred to the unlucky C Flight under Dick Cronyn.

On 23 May in company with Keith-Jopp, he sent an Albatros scout down out of control, another on 25 May, and yet a third on 2 June. He was ultimately to claim twenty-three enemy machines.

An anti-aircraft casualty

We left the general account of the Squadron's activities on 8 June with the loss of Frank Sharpe and his temporary replacement by P F Fullard.

One of the features of the air war that was heartily disliked was anti-aircraft fire, or 'Archie', as it was known to British aircrews. Most risks were accepted as a fact of life but anti-aircraft fire was impersonal and could bring down the most skilful pilot. The light wire-braced construction of these early machines meant that even a near miss could be potentially fatal. On 11 June Fullard was leading a late evening patrol of four machines at 8,000 feet over Pilkem when they came under 'Archie' fire. To their horror R W L Anderson was hit and both his right planes collapsed and came off. The wreckage spun the mile or so to earth with Anderson powerless to avoid his fate because there were no parachutes. Anderson, a South African from Cape Town, today lies in Perth (China Wall) British Military Cemetery – just one grave away from J M E Shepherd, who was 1 Squadron's first casualty after becoming a fighter unit.

Three days later Fullard was again leading a patrol, again a late evening one consisting of six machines drawn from all three flights. He sent one enemy machine down out of control, as did Louis Jenkin, who described his experiences in a letter home the following day:

'We were up the other night, or rather evening about 8 o'clock looking for Hun birds, and there they were:- flocks of them:- painted the most gorgeous colours, some with scarlet bodies & blue wings; some with green bodies & blue & yellow wings; some all black with red markings; some a delicate slate grey with their black crosses very conspicuous; some all mottled with brown & green.

I chose some nice looking ones, & dived on eight of them, firing busily. Suddenly from out of the sky appeared six of the black fellows. I emptied my drum of ammunition into one of them, & then went down in a spinning nose dive to try & get away. The whole fourteen followed me down. However I looped & I spun & I rolled on my back & generally upset myself until I was within ten feet of the ground, about 5 miles over Hun land. I then turned for home, & flew along over 100 miles an hour just clearing hedges & trees & telegraph wires.

The Hun birds were afraid of hitting the trees or running into the ground, & so did not follow very close. I crossed the trenches at about 20 feet, & when just this side my engine cut out; however it had lasted long enough & I landed like a bird quite safely.

My flying coat ripped in two places by bullets, one of my boots slit up by another; one of my gloves slit right across by a third. My throttle & oil pipe shot away. About 20 bullets through the office where I was sitting, & about 100 through the machine.'

It has to be wondered what effect letters like this must have had upon his parents!

On 14 June it was announced that Lieutenant T F Hazell had been awarded the MC. Hazell had joined the Squadron in December 1916 and been promoted to command A Flight when J R Anthony fell victim to Strähle of Jasta 18. Hazell came from County Galway and attended Tonbridge School. He joined the army on the outbreak of war with a commission in the 7th Battalion Royal Inniskilling Fusiliers. After service in France he had transferred to the RFC in the summer of 1916.

Having occupied the Messines ridge, the British army was now able to prepare itself for the big offensive in July. In order to keep prying German observation machines away special patrols were ordered. These patrols, termed Enemy Aircraft Patrols, were mounted regularly. Fullard prided himself on not losing any members of his flight. However on the morning of 18 June he led two of his machines on one of these patrols and on the German side saw two enemy formations of seven and four each. The British formation re-crossed its own lines and at that moment Second Lieutenant R S Lloyd chose to turn back and attack one of the enemy formations. It was a foolish act, and needless to say he was shot down and killed. His victor would seem to have been Leutnant Karl Allmenröder of Manfred von Richthofen's Jasta 11. Allmenröder was a formidable opponent and Lloyd was his twenty-seventh victim. Only four days before he had been awarded the coveted *Pour le Mérite* or Blue Max, as it was also known. A later EA Patrol consisting of Jenkin, H G Reeves and C S T Lavers evened the score as they attacked four red-coloured Albatros scouts with black wings, and were then pounced on by another four with the same markings. After a five-minute scrap, despite being outnumbered, they shot one down near Oostaverne and were able to return safely. The red scout was seen to crash by 2nd Army AA and was almost certainly Leutnant Walter Bordfeld of Jasta 11.

G C Atkins, a new pilot, found out the perils of flying on the German side of the lines with an unreliable machine on 19 June. The aeroplane he was flying had been 'snagged' the previous day by another pilot for having poor throttle control. Atkins was unable to keep up with the rest of his patrol and lost them. Returning on his own he encountered a storm; spending two hours in cloud until completely lost, he ran out of fuel and came down on the wrong side of the lines.

A new CO

On 20 June Major de Dombasle was transferred to Home Establishment after only six months in command, when he could reasonably have expected to have had at least a year. It was felt within the Squadron that he did not see eye-to-eye with senior officers at Brigade HQ, having deplored the sending of inexperienced pilots into action with the attendant losses. Perhaps Brigade felt he was a little too soft. He was later commandant of the School of Aeronautics at Reading, where his Chief Instructor was Carlo Campbell. At the end of the war the Canadians were attempting to set up their own air force and de Dombasle was appointed its head with the rank of Lieutenant Colonel. His title was later changed to Director of the Air Service and under him he had two squadrons that formed No.1 Canadian Wing. A political decision was made not to proceed with a separate Canadian Air Force and a number of the officers involved accepted permanent commissions in the RAF, de Dombasle being one of them. He was made a Wing Commander from April 1918 and whilst still in that rank sadly died of cancer in London in 1929, aged only 47.

His replacement was Major A B Adams, an Australian from Sydney, who had great experience, having joined the RFC in mid-1915. Before the war he had been an engineer in the UK and had worked for Vickers in Sheffield, and Parsons in Newcastle-on-Tyne. After pilot training, he had gone out to France with 15 Squadron as a Flight Commander and been Mentioned in Despatches. After training appointments in the UK he once more returned to France as a Flight Commander flying De Havilland DH4s with 55 Squadron. It seems a curious appointment promoting an officer from a two-seat day bomber squadron to command a scout squadron. He was not a popular CO and there was a certain amount of friction.

On 26 June a patrol ran into Allmenröder again when six Nieuports dived on six variously coloured Albatros scouts. Second Lieutenant Harry Reeves sent one down out of control whilst Sergeant Gordon Olley of C Flight sent down a red coloured one as well. Unfortunately Cyril Street, an A Flight member, was seen to spin into the British second line trenches, after a combat with enemy aircraft. He would appear to have been the thirtieth and last victim of Allmenröder, who was fated to be shot down and killed himself the following morning in exactly the same area. Street had spent two months as an observer in 21 Squadron on the ghastly RE7 and then was posted to 25 Squadron for four months flying the FE2b. On 22 September 1916 he and his pilot, Sergeant Thomas Mottershead, were bombing Samain railway station and were attacked by a Fokker but by skilful manoeuvring Street was able to shoot it down. For this and other actions, Mottershead was awarded the DCM. A few months later whilst serving in 20 Squadron he was awarded a posthumous Victoria Cross, the only flying VC awarded to an NCO or other rank in the RFC/RAF. Street arrived in 1 Squadron in April 1917 after pilot training but had a month off due to sickness and re-joined on June 20. He was buried in the trenches where he fell and his grave was subsequently lost. His name, together with a number of other 1 Squadron casualties, appears on the Arras Memorial to the Missing.

A tragic error

Inevitably with the confusion that occurs in war mistakes will be made, and during a patrol on 3 July such an incident occurred. Tom Littler, from Brixham in Devon, was only nineteen and had joined the Squadron on 12 June. He had been posted to C Flight under Phillip Fullard's watchful eye and only four days after his arrival had shot down an enemy two-seater out of control. He appeared to be settling in nicely.

C Flight took off at 1000 hours on 3 July 1917 for a patrol of the northern area of the Ypres salient, returning about 1215 hours. Major Adams, heard, then saw one of his machines spinning down, pursued by another machine, which was firing periodic bursts at it. The Nieuport continued its dive and spun into the ground at 42 Squadron's airfield on the Town Ground and by the time Adams reached the wreckage Littler was dead. The other machine, with a streamer on its tail, denoting a deputy Flight Commander, flattened out and flew away. Adams could see it was a Sopwith Pup and subsequent investigation proved it was from 46 Squadron, based at La Gorgue south west of Bailleul. From some angles the V-wing struts of the Nieuport Scout looked very similar to those of the Albatros scout, though the colours of the aircraft were completely different. It seems improbable that this mistake could have been made. As occasionally happened a quick passing shot at a friendly machine flashing by is understandable but to follow an aeroplane down firing at it where the red, white and blue roundels must have been clearly visible a number of times seems difficult to comprehend.

The inquiry went to the very highest level (i.e General Trenchard, in command of the RFC in the Field) and three days later 46 Squadron were swiftly moved down south to Bruay, whilst the offending 46 Squadron pilot, Lloyd Fleming, a Canadian, was posted to the Middle East. Fleming, during his time with 111 Squadron in Palestine, did very well and as a result of shooting down several German machines, was awarded an MC. In fact he was considered the 'star' of the RFC in Palestine. Though Canadian, he lived for many years in the UK and died in the 1950s in Majorca. Littler is buried in Bailleul British Military Cemetery, together with nearly twenty other 1 Squadron casualties.

On 12 July a patrol of twelve machines led by T F Hazell set off on an Offensive Patrol to bring the Germans up to fight; an aim they certainly achieved. Over a period of thirty minutes they tackled a total of thirty-four enemy scouts in three different formations, claiming four sent down out of control. At 0830 hours they had attacked a group of ten scouts and Hazell and Second Lieutenant R E Money-Kyrle jumped a black one, painted with yellow bands, firing at close range and sending it down rolling over and over. All machines returned safely though Money-Kyrle smashed his on landing as he had been wounded in the right leg. He later wrote of his experiences:

> 'When I did fly on patrols I was at first always getting lost & once joined a German Patrol by mistake – but luckily I was well above them. However, I then never took my eyes off our leader Bill (*sic*) Hazell & was soon promoted to flying on his inside right. We were a big patrol (2 flights) when I got that Hun. Hazell had dived at something (artillery observation plane) & I dived too – found I had a German in my sight, pulled the trigger & was told afterwards that I had got it. It was when we were climbing that I heard shooting from behind, turned round & at first thought it was a Baby Nieuport – not a 1917 Albatros as it turned out to be. I then turned towards him & was shot in the leg in the middle of the split arse turn. But I got back to Bailleul, was the best part of a year in hospital & only got back to France again with 94 Squadron (Major, now AVM Capel) on November 1st 1918 – so never got into action again.'

Roger Money-Kyrle had joined the Squadron in June, during the heavy losses and recalled a visit they had from the 'top brass':

> 'I remember Trenchard lunched with us & was very agreeable. Presumably it was thought we needed some pep; but we had our tails up all the time in spite of heavy casualties.'

Phillip Kelsey, who had joined the Squadron three weeks before and shared a hut with Money-Kyrle, wrote in a letter home:

> 'Money-Kyrle the boy who shared my room was wounded in the leg & has gone home. It broke the shin bone. I expect it will be a six to nine month job. He was very happy about it nevertheless. We had a devil of a scrap that day. It is better now that we go out in twelves at a time, in formation.
> Last night the clouds gathered round when we were up. It is really a very wonderful sight. Of course the sun is shining above the clouds & they are perfectly white. We were archied coming back but nothing to speak of & then the job was to get through this cloud. It was probably 7 miles long & two miles thick and very high. I just managed to find a little opening, it would be just about above the trenches. Very fortunate I got through it without getting into the cloud. In a thick cloud of that sort, one does not know whether one is flying upside down sideways or any old way. Your compass starts swinging & you have no sense of direction at all.'

On 13 July Fullard led a large combined patrol and while returning joined a patrol of SE5as from 56 Squadron. Diving on a formation of EA he fired half a drum at one, sending it down smoking but was unable to watch its descent as the other five set about him. At this moment his engine faded and he had to dive away west, just managing to stretch the glide past the front line. The ground was a mass of shell holes and he turned over into one smashing the aeroplane and finished hanging upside down above the murky water. Before he could be rescued some Allied troops had looted his automatic pistol and the aircraft watch. During the same patrol Second Lieutenant W C Smith was seen to go down with the obligatory three hostile machines on his tail. The machine Smith was flying when he went missing, B3483, was an unlucky one. On 7 July Second Lieutenant J M S G Stevens had returned from a patrol wounded in the leg and hand but made a normal landing at Bailleul. He died of his wounds a week later. Smith was taken prisoner of war but was repatriated in early 1918 and died of tuberculosis in the UK shortly after.

On 27 July a telegram was received announcing the news that Campbell had been awarded the Squadron's second DSO. The citation appeared in the *London Gazette* on 14 September and said:

> 'For conspicuous gallantry and devotion to duty on numerous occasions, whilst on offensive patrols. He has displayed the greatest courage and skill in attacking enemy aircraft at close range, destroying some and driving others down out of control. He has proved himself to be a scout leader of the highest class and has destroyed 12 hostile machines and 2 balloons, besides taking part in many other combats during the last 3 months. By his fearlessness and offensive spirit he has set a splendid example to all ranks.'

The Battle of Ypres

At dawn, 0350 hours, on 31July the great Flanders offensive was launched. It was a dull morning with a cloud base of 500 to 800 feet, and as a consequence the plans made by RFC High Command had to be modified. The weather became worse as the day wore on.

No.1 Squadron was primarily engaged on attacking ground targets behind the German lines. L F Jenkin attacked Herseaux aerodrome, diving on a line of Albatros scouts and setting one of them on fire. He zoomed, making another three attacks and then shot up a machine-gun team, which was firing at him.

Fullard left at 1250 hours in company with W S Mansell, but lost him in the clouds before crossing the lines. Near the Forest of Houthulst he fired at a balloon and sent it down deflated. He then found an aerodrome and dived on fourteen Albatros scouts nicely lined up and fired a complete drum into them. While flying along the Roulers – Menin road he discovered a convoy of lorries, firing into them and causing the leader to stop so violently that the vehicle behind collided. Another balloon was found on the ground east of Houthulst Forest but despite repeated attacks it refused to catch fire. At one spot an AA battery was firing at him at point blank range and tracer was coming from various directions. Later he fired at a locomotive, which then raced off east. After this Fullard became lost in cloud and upon emerging from it found to his dismay that he was over the sea with no fuel left. In a desperate effort to save weight he threw both pistols, his Lewis drums and all his spare ammunition over the side. Fortunately he was able to make a safe landing at No. 2 Naval Squadron's base near Dunkirk. It had been a hectic two hours and fifteen minutes. Due to worsening weather he was unable to return to Bailleul until 4 August.

Campbell wounded

In the afternoon Campbell led out a patrol, but this was abandoned in less than an hour because of bad weather, two of the machines having already dropped out. Campbell dived on a line of enemy two-seaters on Mouveaux aerodrome, at times coming down to only seventy feet and expended 194 rounds of incendiary ammunition. While engaged in this he was attacked by three enemy scouts and slightly wounded in the right thigh.

In only three months (which included two weeks leave) he had claimed twenty-three German aeroplanes or balloons and been awarded the DSO, MC and Bar – a remarkable record. Promoted to Major he spent the rest of the war training in the UK. Post-war he led a very successful business life, including chairmanship of Cross and Blackwell and Sarsons Vinegars and was responsible for the survival of Brighton and Hove Albion Football Clubs, by amalgamating them during his period as chairman. He died in 1958 at the age of 72 and at the funeral his coffin was carried by players from Brighton Football Club.

His place as B Flight Commander was taken by Louis Jenkin who was notified two days later of the award of a Bar to his Military Cross. On 8 August Phillip Fullard was advised that he had been awarded the MC. Fullard's steady approach to combat was like the 'tortoise and hare' story and though others had started after him and been awarded decorations before him he ultimately exceeded them all.

It was to be a day of mixed fortunes on 10 August. In the early afternoon T F Hazell led his A Flight on an escort to eight FE2s of 20 Squadron, who were on a photographic mission. A number of Albatros scouts attacked the rear of the formation of escorting Nieuports and in the short scrap that ensued Hazell and R A Birkbeck each shot down one out of control. Unfortunately two of A Flight were lost as well, but the FE2s all returned safely, together with 108 photographs, which was the object of the operation. Photographing enemy positions and targets was an essential part of the RFC's job, as the army depended on them for a variety of purposes. They were used for intelligence analysis, by the artillery for shelling targets and for the production of trench maps by the Royal Engineers, which were vital for all front line units of the army. Thousands were taken every week and hundreds of thousands of prints made from them. As an example, during the night of 14 October 1918, No.35 Squadron's own Photographic Section produced 3,000 prints from 136 plates and in the four months July to October had made 102,170 prints from nearly 2,000 negatives.

The two missing pilots were Captain A B Jarvis and Second Lieutenant J F Henderson. Jarvis, despite being a Captain was not a Flight Commander but had achieved his rank with the Middlesex Regiment. He had served at Suvla Bay in the grim Gallipoli campaign and after six months as an observer with 14 Squadron in Palestine had learned to fly in Egypt. He was buried initially in Ledeghem German Cemetery but now rests in Harlebeke British Cemetery. Henderson was luckier as he survived as a POW. He had dropped out of formation with a defective engine and was then pounced on by two EA. After firing about half a drum at them his engine cut out and fuel poured into the cockpit. He crashed and turned over and had to be released by German soldiers.

In the evening four aircraft from C Flight were sent up to chase off an enemy reconnaissance machine that had been reported. At 1845 hours they ran into a DFW CV, coloured black and white, flying at 3,000 feet over Haubordin and after three quarters of a drum from Fullard it went straight down and crashed. The crew of Unteroffizier Alfred Kind and Leutnant Gottried von Langen of KG1, were killed.

The run of casualties continued with another two lost on 12 August. A lunchtime patrol led by Fullard carried out an Offensive Patrol deep in the German lines and both Second Lieutenants F M McLaren and L Read failed to return. The well known phenomenon in air combat where one moment the sky is full of aeroplanes and the next there is not a single one in sight, plus the fact there was no way of communicating between machines in the air other than hand signals or flare pistols, could explain these losses. A new pilot might see an enemy aeroplane and decide to quickly attack it believing his patrol leader must have seen it as well, or thought his signal must have been observed. Many losses could have been avoided if inexperienced members had stuck strictly to instructions and stayed with the formation. Fullard's patrol returned, having not engaged the enemy and despite his eagle eye lost two men. McLaren was killed but Read had left the formation to attack a kite balloon and been jumped by six Albatros scouts. They had shot half his rudder bar away and sent him down out of control, despite which he was captured uninjured. It was almost certainly a trap. A few days later the Germans dropped a message bag on the British side containing a letter from Read and another from Henderson who had gone missing on 10 August. Read and McLaren would appear to have fallen victim to Göring's Jasta 27.

More escorts

The weather during the Third Battle of Ypres was terrible, setting a record for the wettest summer in years and for the flying services there were many days when flying was impossible. The British 5th Army recommenced its offensive on 16 August in what is now known as the Battle of Langemarck, twice having been postponed due to bad weather. As before the aim of the RFC was maximum disruption of supplies and reinforcements, but again they were hampered by low cloud and mist, made worse by smoke drifting across the battlefield. The air fighting was confused, but during the day Fullard claimed three enemy machines. In the morning he joined with a Spad from 19 Squadron who was fighting with two Albatros scouts and shot down one that was about to pounce on the Spad. A little later he went to the aid of a group of 29 Squadron Nieuport Scouts which, while engaged on ground strafing of German troops, had been attacked by seven or eight Albatros scouts. Fullard fired seventy rounds into one which went down and crashed, but Second Lieutenant W H T Williams was brought down and killed by Manfred von Richthofen. For von Richthofen this was his first patrol since being wounded in the head during a scrap with 20 Squadron some weeks before and he was still suffering from headaches.

In one of the other early morning patrols J H C Nixon, an Australian, was wounded in the head during a scrap. When he landed back at Bailleul his machine was a mess. The slipstream had whipped the blood from his wound and spattered it all down the fuselage with the bright red on the silver-doped fuselage looking a horrific sight. Amazingly his injury was not serious and he survived. All 1 Squadron's early Nieuport Scouts were painted in an overall silver scheme with a narrow red band round the rear fuselage and individual numbers. With the introduction of the type 27 later in 1917 the aeroplanes retained the French camouflage scheme.

Apart from their normal duties of offensive patrols throughout this period 1 Squadron continued with the 20 Squadron escort. On 19 August six Nieuports led by Fullard accompanied six FE2ds in the usual circuit from Polygon Wood round Menin and then Lille photographing German positions and targets. While engaged in taking pictures just east of Wervicq they were attacked by six Albatros scouts, which approached from the north. The FE2s closed up formation and during the fight that followed several enemy machines were either driven off or sent down out of control by them. One FE dropped out of formation with an Albatros on its tail so another FE dived on it, driving it off though the 20 Squadron machine continued to lose height and subsequently failed to return. Fullard spotted an Albatros cruising around between him and the FEs, closed on it and fired three quarters of a drum into it at very close range. It went straight down and crashed. The machine was painted yellow with black stripes, the markings used by Jasta 28. One FE was claimed by Leutnant Hetz of Jasta 28 and 1 Squadron lost H E A Waters, who was claimed by Max Müller, also of Jasta 28. Waters had been fighting for about five minutes when his engine slowed and the throttle refused to work. In this situation he was a sitting duck and at 2,000 feet he had his petrol tank shot up and he was wounded. Waters managed to land his machine intact and was taken prisoner of war.

Müller, a Bavarian, had been born in 1887 and before the war had been a driver in the army. After learning to fly he had joined Jasta 28 in January 1917 as an NCO pilot. He was the Jasta's most successful ace and was awarded the *Pour le Mérite* in November 1917. Waters was his twenty-fourth victim and he was to claim another dozen before being shot down and killed on 9 January 1918 attacking an RE8 of 21 Squadron. After the war he was awarded the Knight's Cross of the Military Max-Joseph Order which conferred a posthumous Knighthood on Bavaria's most successful pilot.

On 24 August T F Hazell was posted to Home Establishment, and his replacement as A Flight Commander was W V T Rooper. Hazell had joined the Squadron just before Christmas 1916, at about the time it commenced flying the Nieuport Scout. Over a period of five months he had brought down twenty enemy aircraft and been awarded the MC. Perhaps he did not score at the rate as the other successful pilots in the Squadron but he survived the heavy losses in the early summer and was undoubtedly a steadying influence. It seems curious that he did not receive a Bar to his MC, considering the number of German machines he had brought down. He instructed at CFS for some months and then returned to France as a Flight Commander with 24 Squadron flying SE5as. In the next four months he made another twenty-three claims, including ten balloons and was awarded the DSO, DFC and Bar and at the end of the war was commanding 203 Squadron. Granted a Permanent Commission in the RAF in 1919, he retired as a Squadron Leader in 1927 and died in 1946. It took the RAF some time to catch up with his demise, as his name was still appearing in the RAF Retired List as late as the early 1980s!

Fullard out of action

The Squadron suffered two losses on 3 September; Second Lieutenant C Pickstone, a new pilot, failed to return from a patrol and was later reported killed in action. It was the depressingly familiar story of his being last seen going down during a dogfight with enemy scouts on his tail. The other loss was Fullard, due to a totally non-combat related incident. He had been sent out solo to chase off a reported German machine, but after twenty fruitless minutes he decided to return. For whatever reason, perhaps to descend quickly from his height of 19,000 feet, he chose to see what happened if you put a Nieuport Scout out of control with the engine going full out. He had great faith in the strength of the design and this was amply demonstrated as he lost 12,000 feet in a high-speed spinning dive. Suddenly he felt an intense pain in his head and found he had gone blind. Thinking he had been shot he managed to make his machine fly straight and level and after what seemed a long time was able to see the outline of white objects faintly with one eye. He made a safe landing at base still suffering from great pain in his eyes and still blind in one of them. He saw a specialist in Boulogne the next day who diagnosed a burst blood vessel due to the rapid change in pressure during the descent. Fullard returned a month later but now had to wear goggles, something he had not done before.

Phil Kelsey wrote home about this time:

'We have been having a very strenuous time lately. There seems to be a deuce of a lot of Huns up on our front. Eight of us the other morning drove about a dozen Albatros over East of ----- about twelve miles over. They would not scrap. So we turned round & dived on a formation of Huns. My flight commander got one down. I often wonder what the Huns must think from the ground when they see us chasing their machines so far over. I don't think I have been up in the last six weeks almost without exchanging salutations with the Hun. We always have a scrap. Had my machine shot up by one of our own by mistake. He put two or three through the tail & several through the wings. Had to have a new tail on. I may say he phoned up & apologised.'

During an afternoon show on 9 September, a four-man patrol was about to dive on a hostile two-seater but were in turn pounced upon by five Albatros scouts. One passed W S Mansell to get on the tail of a Nieuport, and he quickly slipped on its tail and let off forty rounds at a range of thirty yards. The hostile machine nosed over then rolled and was last seen still rolling as it disappeared into cloud. However, the machine of W E le B Diamond was seen diving through cloud pursued by enemy machines and was then observed to land under control behind enemy lines by 30th Divisional artillery. Diamond was not a great fan of either the rotary engine or the Nieuport Scout and considered them 'wretched things to fly'. Compared to the Sopwith Pup that he had trained on they were heavy on the controls, particularly the rudder. He was, quite rightly, critical of the clumsy Lewis gun arrangement. While spinning down to avoid his tormentors he was continually fired at and wounded. He saw a nice open green space surrounded by gun-pits and was able to pull off a good landing. Only being slightly wounded, he was able to get out before the Germans arrived and burned his aeroplane. A couple of days later while in hospital the German pilot, almost certainly Leutnant Julius Schmidt of Jasta 3, visited him and asked for the wings off his tunic (Both of Diamond's brothers also served in the RFC and survived.)

Louis Jenkin lost

During an early Northern Offensive Patrol on 11 September B Flight led by Jenkin had dived on a lone green-coloured Albatros and sent it down out of control after he had fired forty-eight rounds at it. The Southern Offensive Patrol that left an hour after B Flight returned saw various groups of enemy aircraft that were too far away to engage. At 1120 hours near Houthem, W S Mansell's machine received a direct hit by anti-aircraft fire and the right wings were shattered. The wreckage went down out of control but was not seen to crash.

Worse was to follow when at 1545 hours Jenkin left with his five B Flight members for yet another NOP. Seven scouts and a pair of two-seaters were engaged by the patrol over Westroosebeke and driven east. One of the pair latched onto Jenkin's tail but was driven off and about five minutes later he was seen low down but under control. His arrival was anxiously awaited at Bailleul but he failed to return and moreover there was no news from the Germans. Perhaps he was wounded and crashed into the morass that Passchendaele had become. He has no known grave and his name is commemorated on the Memorial at Arras. The same day the great French ace Guynemer also went missing in the same area. In four months Jenkin had claimed some twenty-three victories and been awarded a Military Cross and Bar. Perhaps the last word should be left to his sister who wrote in 1977:

'Louis was a real all-rounder. He had splendid health and physique and enjoyed all games and sports. Cricket was probably his best game. He was also a good swimmer, a gymnast and a fine shot. He was in the Highlands, fishing and deer-stalking, at the outbreak of war. Although his subject was mathematics, he had wide interests and was a voracious reader, particularly of the English classics. He won a prize, at Dulwich, for reading poetry aloud. It has always saddened me that he did not live to follow his father to Trinity College (for which he had won an Exhibition). He, of all people, would have wrung the last ounce of value out of Cambridge life.'

Louis Jenkin's place was taken by Captain C L Bath, a Canadian, with lots of experience. He had attended Toronto and McGill Universities from 1910 to 1914 and after service in the Canadian Machine Gun Brigade had joined the RFC at the end of 1915. Six months were spent flying the De Havilland DH2 pusher scout with 32 Squadron, and after training jobs in the UK he had spent six weeks flying Nieuports with 40 Squadron.

More ground strafing

On 20 September the next phase of the Battle of Ypres commenced and was referred to as the Battle of the Menin Road Ridge. The task of the RFC once more was the dislocation of the German rear areas. During the previous night the FE2s of the night bombing squadrons had attacked the enemy rest areas and the German airfields around Courtrai were bombed during the day. The other squadrons, including No.1, were engaged on the familiar and dangerous duty of ground strafing. The biggest danger, in addition to German ground fire, was being caught at low level behind enemy lines by marauding fighters and having no room for manoeuvre. All through the First War whenever the

Squadron was engaged in ground attack there were heavy casualties, and this day was no exception. Three machines were lost and nobody knew what had happened, or had seen them go. Two of the pilots were killed and therefore their loss is still a mystery, though it would seem they were brought down by German scouts, probably whilst engaged on ground strafing. The third pilot, Second Lieutenant C G D Gray, had left at 0825 hours in company with Sergeant Gordon Olley and was reported to have landed at 40 Squadron's aerodrome. It was also reported he had left there after refuelling but failed to reach Bailleul. It later transpired that he had gone strafing in the Passchendaele area at 150 feet but then rather unwisely had climbed to 1,500 feet where his machine had been riddled by ground fire. His engine had cut out and he had been shot through a lung. Despite this serious wound he survived.

The first day of October proved a good one. A Flight under the leadership of Rooper came across a new type of German two-seater over Passchendaele and Lumsden Cummings fired a whole drum into it at very close range. It went down steeply and crashed. From the description of it, the aeroplane would appear to have been one of the new Junkers J1s coming into service and if so Cummings' marksmanship was excellent. The J1 was a large all metal biplane, with an armoured tub for the crew, engine and fuel tank, and was designed for low level co-operation with infantry. There were many instances of this type of machine taking scores of hits and still carrying on flying.

The run of successes continued through the first week in October, as seventeen enemy machines were claimed without loss. However this good spell was interrupted on 9 October. Six machines attacked nine enemy scouts and in the ensuing fight Second Lieutenant G B Moore shot one enemy machine off Wendell Rogers' tail, but M A Peacock was brought down. He became separated from the formation by cloud and having run out of ammunition with his magneto put out of action he was unable to reach allied lines, owing to the attentions of the enemy and a very strong headwind.

The mystery of Rooper
In the next patrol at 1450 hours disaster struck. A Flight went to the rescue of two RE8 artillery machines that were being pursued back to British lines by five Albatros scouts. H G Reeves dived on a black and white one and fired a burst of incendiary ammunition into it upon which it burst into flames and crashed adjacent to Polygon Wood. The unfortunate pilot jumped out at 2,500 feet. R A Birkbeck had another Albatros pass him in the other direction at a distance of only ten feet. Both pilots turned and raced towards each other and as the enemy machine flew fifteen feet over his head he was able to give it a short burst. It began to smoke and then went down in flames. The pilot fell out about 1,000 feet below him. However, in the confusion of the action, it was probably the same machine brought down by Reeves (it being unlikely that two German pilots would fall or leap to their deaths in one dogfight). One of the RE8s, from No. 6 Squadron, also fired at this machine and probably assisted in its destruction. The pilot was Leutnant Richard Wagner of Jasta 26, as the markings of this Jasta were black and white stripes. Captain Rooper, leading the patrol, was reported to have come down in the British trenches after a fight with five enemy machines. Three patrols were flown to try and locate his machine and two attempts made by a ground breakdown party. He was reported to have a broken leg and the Squadron records state that he was taken to hospital. Keith-Jopp recorded in his diary that Rooper's body was found fifteen miles from where he fell, unwounded and wearing only one boot but the source of this information is unknown and it must be remembered that Keith-Jopp was no longer in the Squadron and his story could have been hearsay. Rooper must have been retrieved and died later as he lies today with the other 1 Squadron casualties buried at Bailleul. Leutnant Xavier Dannhuber, also of Jasta 26, claimed a Spad in the same area and at the same time so he may have shot Rooper down – misidentification of aeroplane types was common on both sides. (Another of Rooper's brothers was killed in action in May 1918.)

200 victories
The Squadron's success was noted in the RFC Communiqués where it was stated that 200 victories had been claimed since converting to scouts on 15 February.

One of the stalwarts of 1 Squadron was posted home on 19 October. Sergeant Gordon Olley had joined the unit in 1916 as a despatch rider and had graduated to observer's duties. Posted home to learn to fly he had returned to the Squadron in May 1917 and in the next five months claimed ten German aeroplanes and was awarded the Military Medal. He was the pilot Keith-Jopp had been trying to signal when he had his accident. Sergeant pilots were not common in the First War, particularly in fighter units. Commissioned in 1918 he spent the rest of the war on ferrying duties. A distinguished career in civil aviation followed flying for KLM and Imperial Airways. He established Olley Air Services and in 1934 wrote an autobiography entitled *A Million Miles in the Air*. He died in 1958.

October saw the gradual winding down of the Ypres battle. After horrendous casualties in the appalling mud, the village of Passchendaele was taken and the British were no longer overlooked from the ridge. The whole lot was to be lost only five months later in the German offensive of April 1918. On 28 October Fullard was told of the award of his DSO, the third for the Squadron. The citation was gazetted on 5 April 1918 (such was the number of awards, citations were lagging severely behind the official notification) It read:

'For conspicuous gallantry and devotion to duty. As a patrol leader and scout pilot he is without equal. The moral effect of his presence in a patrol is most marked. He has now accounted for 14 machines destroyed and 18 driven down out of control in a little over 4 months.'

On 30 October 1 Squadron again ran into their old adversary Jasta 26, when C Flight led by Fullard dived on three enemy aircraft painted with black fuselages and white bands. Fullard fired half a drum into the leader, who rolled over, went down and crashed just north of Westroosebeke. Unfortunately E D Scott was brought down and killed by Jasta 26's commanding officer Oberleutnant Bruno Loerzer. This was the second 1 Squadron machine he had claimed, having shot down and killed C A Moody of A Flight on 21 August. Loerzer had learned to fly just before the war and for some months, while with a two-seater unit, his observer had been Hermann Göring. He had claimed his first victory in March 1916 and after service in Jastas 5 and 17 was appointed to command Jasta 26 on 18 January 1917. By the end of the war he had claimed forty-four victories and had been awarded the *Pour le Mérite*. He later rose to high rank in the Luftwaffe, probably from his great friendship with Göring, and finished the Second World War as a General. He died in 1960.

Another Flight Commander was lost on 3 November in an unfortunate manner. C L Bath was returning from an uneventful patrol with two of his flight when they were fired at from the ground by machine guns on the British side and he was wounded in the foot.

Nieuport wing problems

One of the design faults that had plagued the Nieuport Scout in its early days and which still occasionally reared its ugly head was the design of the lower wing. The machine was a sesquiplane – the lower wings were of a much smaller area and secured to the top wings by two V-shaped struts. At the bottom of the strut was a circular collar that clamped round the square mainspar of the lower wing. In order for the collar to grip the spar, packing pieces were inserted. These needed checking regularly as the wood would shrink and make the fitting loose. Occasionally, particularly in high-speed dives, if the collar was slack the wing would rotate around the spar and then the airflow would break the plane in an upward direction. Sometimes the wing would come off completely and if you were lucky the flying wires would keep the upper wing in place. There were a number of cases of machines landing with one of the lower planes missing – there were also many cases of the whole structure collapsing. There were also incidences of poor manufacture, which is not surprising considering the rate they were produced. Often there were too many screws in a component (thus weakening rather than strengthening it). On 11 November a new pilot, C S Fuller, was diving at the raft moored in Dickebusch Lake for target practice, when the machine broke up and he was drowned. Fuller, from Tasmania, was quite old at age 33 and had won an MC earlier in the year with the Manchester Regiment. Wounded twice, he had bravely defended his position until reinforcements arrived. Fuller had arrived back from a patrol and taken the opportunity for some practice. Whether he had suffered combat damage or fallen foul of the Nieuport wing problem was impossible to say but the wreckage was very difficult to recover and his body was not retrieved for a couple of days.

Phillip Fullard had his swansong on 15 November destroying two Albatros scouts. He was leading ten machines from A and C Flights as they were preparing to dive on two enemy two-seaters when three Albatros scouts dived on them. These three were then joined by five more. Fullard used the superior climbing ability of the Nieuport to get above them, and then seeing an enemy machine on a Nieuport's tail, stalled and fired a drum into it. The Albatros went down in a vertical dive and crashed near Zandvoorde. Another Albatros dived past him and manoeuvring himself on its tail he fired three-quarters of a drum from close range, whereupon it dived for 1,000 feet at which point a wing fell off and the machine folded up. One of his victims would appear to have been Leutnant Hans Hoyer of Jasta 36 – an eight-victory ace himself. With his experience and skill Fullard had now become a deadly opponent.

Fullard invalided home

The level of activity was now much reduced partly because of weather but also because the Battle of

Ypres had ended. On 16 November there was hardly any flying due to poor conditions and on 17 November only one flight, an engine test by Major Adams. However this was Fullard's last day in the squadron. While playing football against a battalion in rest nearby, he suffered a very badly broken leg and was invalided to the UK. After seven attempts to set it a plate was eventually fitted – more than a month after the accident. Fullard was off flying until September 1918 and was unable to fly operationally before the war ended. It is tempting to speculate what might have happened if he had not had a month off flying due to his eye incident and not lost more time with his broken leg. After an instructing tour he would undoubtedly have returned to France in command of a squadron. He may well have become the most successful Allied pilot of the war in terms of combat victories.

At this time the *Daily Mail*, which had conducted a campaign to publicise Britain's airmen, produced a number of articles, one of which was entitled 'Tell Us His Name'. The last paragraph was as follows:

> 'We have fighters better than Immelman or Boelcke or Richthofen, and need we hide their light under a bushel?'

Their persistence was rewarded and resulted in a short piece on 5 January 1918 entitled 'British Air Stars' and subtitled 'McCudden and Fullard'. Two days later a more detailed article appeared and the front page had two large photographs with the caption 'Our Wonderful Airmen – Names at Last'. On 16 January Fullard had the cover of *The Tatler* all to himself with a caption that read:

> 'A boy who has strafed forty-two Boches' planes.'

Fullard was recommended for a Bar to his DSO on 21 November 1917 but this was not awarded and post-war he received the Belgian Croix de Guerre and the AFC. After service in India and Iraq he was Senior Air Staff Officer No. 10 (Fighter) Group. He retired as an Air Commodore in 1947 and became a successful businessman in engineering. He died on 24 April 1984.

Fullard's place as C Flight Commander, and his aeroplane, was taken by William Wendell Rogers, a tall rangy Canadian from Prince Edward Island. He had been a student at the University of Toronto at the end of 1914 and had joined the RFC in late 1916. His introduction to 1 Squadron was not auspicious as he had arrived on the day of the disastrous balloon raid on 18 May. Under Fullard's careful protection he had claimed some half a dozen German machines and become a very useful member of the Flight. He was coming to the end of his tour and may well have not become a flight commander if it had not been for his leader's accident.

Enemy activity at this time was at a low level with the winter weather and short days. On 29 November Rogers sent a two-seater down out of control flying Fullard's trusty Nieuport B6789. During this quiet period the opportunity was taken to send the pilots six or so a time down to the Gunnery Range at Berck sur Mer to polish up their skills.

A small flurry occurred on 5 December when nine machines unsuccessfully attacked a two-seater and lost a pilot. C E Ogden was last seen low down only 1,000 yards east of the British lines but failed to return. He was captured near Passchendaele when his engine failed for reasons unknown. The next day in Ingelmünster he met the pilot of the German machine they had attacked and who was suffering from two scalp wounds.

A week later Rogers earned himself a place in the record books.

German strategic bombing

German aircraft had bombed the English coast in the Channel area intermittently since the war began, Dover and Folkestone being favoured targets. However, London was not bombed for the first time until November 1916, by a single machine that dropped six bombs, causing little damage. By late 1916 the Gothaer Waggonfabrik AG had developed their GIV twin-engined aeroplane, which could carry a bomb load of 300 kgs as far as London. A new unit, Kaghol 3, was formed and in March 1917 the first of the new type were delivered to them at their aerodromes at Gontrode and St Denis-Westrem near Ghent. On 13 June the Gothas raided London causing much damage and generating considerable outrage. The day after this raid the Commanding Officer of Kagohl 3 (the so-called *Englandgeschwader* or England Squadron), Hauptmann Ernst Brandenburg, flew to Kreuznach near Mainz in southern Germany to receive the *Pour le Mérite* from the hands of the Kaiser. Taking off the following day to return to his unit the machine crashed and Brandenburg was severely injured. His replacement as CO was Hauptmann Rudolf Kleine, who had already served in another bomber unit. The bad weather in August

1917 which was to cause so much trouble to the British in the Third Battle of Ypres also prevented operations by Gotha units. Improving defence methods eventually forced Kleine to turn to night bombing, and London was bombed regularly thus forcing the inhabitants to take to the Underground stations, much as they were to do twenty years later. These operations were fraught with difficulty and many Gothas were lost, primarily in landing accidents and engine failure. The Gothas were also used, in conjunction with Kaghol 1, to bomb British docks, dumps and other targets in France to hamper the flow of supplies to the army engaged in the bloody struggle in Flanders.

Kleine was a rather severe and reserved officer who was certainly not as popular as his predecessor. He was viewed with caution by the men of Kaghol 3, who felt he took unnecessary risks, particularly in sending them out in dubious weather conditions. A number of missions resulted in large casualties. On 4 October Kleine received the much coveted *Pour le Mérite* for his leadership of the *Englandgeschwader*.

A Gotha brought down

On 12 December Kleine and his men undertook a disastrous daylight raid on British installations in the Ypres area. It was a day of low cloud and rain. At Bailleul a C Flight patrol of five machines lifted off for a patrol of the southern part of the Ypres salient led by Rogers. One pilot returned due to plug trouble, but rejoined the others using a replacement aeroplane. Near Armentières the formation climbed through the dull, gloomy overcast and emerged into brilliant sunshine at about 7,000 feet. Just after having come out from the tops of the clouds Rogers saw seventeen specks approaching, which soon turned out to be two formations of German machines heading west and at first he thought they were enemy scouts. Despite now only having three in the patrol, having lost two of his formation climbing through the cloud, Rogers pressed on towards the enemy. As the two formations approached he realized that they were twin-engined Gotha bombers and not scouts. The Gothas had been encountered before by the British in the Ypres area, but none had been brought down. Two days previously the pilots of 1 Squadron had a discussion in the squadron office about a recently received technical report on the Gotha and were well aware of the combined fire-power of a formation of this size. They were also aware of the rear gunner's ability to fire over the top of his tailplane and, more importantly, protect the vulnerable underside of the machine by firing down an ingenious tunnel that exited from the bottom of the fuselage. The Gotha was an intimidating target with a wingspan of over three times the size of the Nieuport. Keeping out of range of the Gotha's guns, Rogers reached a position above and behind the rear of the formation and then dived on the centre machine of the rear trio. Keeping in the blind spot right behind the Gotha's tail, he saw the gunner's fire going over his head from the upper gun position and below from the floor opening. He fired three quarters of a drum from his Lewis gun from only twenty yards. The Gotha banked to the left and began a steep dive with Rogers following. Black smoke began to appear, then large flames, and as it crossed the front line at 4,000 feet Rogers dived on it again. He had just got to within 100 yards when two of the occupants jumped out, unable to bear the heat, and then a moment later the Gotha exploded and the smoking wreckage fell into No-Man's-Land north of Frelinghem. The three Nieuports attempted to pursue the remaining Gothas but were too low and too far away to catch them.

A week later a Colonel commanding an Australian battalion dropped in on 1 Squadron hoping to see the Commanding Officer, Major Adams, a fellow Australian. Adams was away on leave and Rogers, as senior Flight Commander, was temporarily commanding the Squadron. He invited the Colonel to dinner and during the meal it transpired that some of his men had crawled out into No-Man's-Land to collect souvenirs. Two wing tips were intact and the large fabric crosses were retrieved. On discovering that Rogers had been the victorious pilot he promised him one of the crosses. The following day Rogers went to the Colonel's billets and was given both the crosses. Rogers took one home with him to Canada where it still survives. When the cadre of the Squadron was disbanded in early 1919 the other cross, and two German rudders from machines captured in 1918, were on the inventory. The rudders still adorn the wall of 1 Squadron's museum but the fabric cross has been lost.

When the Gothas landed back at their base, to everyone's dismay it was discovered the missing machine was that of the Kommandeur. Killed with Kleine were Leutnants Günter von der Nahmer and Werner Bülowis, popular officers better known as 'Rabatz' and 'Matz'. The gunner who was also killed was Gefreiter Michael Weber.The England Squadron never really recovered from this loss.

Kleine's Gotha was allocated the number G99 though very little was recovered – half the wreckage landing in the British lines and the other half containing the crew ending up on the German side.

Another German machine our side!

There was little activity in the next few days, and remarkably the next German machine to come down in the British lines (G100) was also brought down by 1 Squadron and Rogers was leading again! On 17 December snow had fallen heavily on most of the front except that occupied by Second Army. About two o'clock in the afternoon 1 Squadron mounted a ten-man patrol led by Rogers. They climbed in the bitterly cold air, with the air blasting round their open cockpits and the desolate winter landscape sliding past below them. At 8,000 feet just south west of Moorsele two of the flight dived on a pair of enemy two-seaters and, while engrossed in this they were in turn attacked by six Albatros scouts. Phil Kelsey dived on one that was being harrassed by two Sopwith Camels of 65 Squadron.

Three Sopwith Camels of 65 Squadron, who were also based at Bailleul, had taken off about a quarter of an hour before 1 Squadron. Lieutenant Godfrey Bremridge and Second Lieutenant Guy Knocker had lost the third pilot, Second Lieutenant D M Sage, and spotting the six enemy machines, had dived to the attack. Bremridge fired thirty rounds at one machine and then Kelsey had joined in and fought it down from 5,000 to 3,000 feet. The fight drifted across the battlefield from over Passchendaele towards the British lines. Kelsey managed to get on its tail and after firing about thirty rounds into the enemy machine at less than twenty yards it burst into flames and the wings came off. The wingless fuselage, marked with a large letter 'V', smashed into the ground, south of Pilkem, on the British side of the lines.

The pilot of the German machine was Leutnant Karl-Heinrich Voss of Marinefeldjasta 1, a German navy fighter unit. Born in Usedom in May 1895 he had claimed a Sopwith Camel of No.10 Naval Squadron five days previously. Before his burial by 2/Wessex Field Ambulance a letter was found in a pocket addressed to Flugmeister Otto Napp, another pilot in MFJ 1, who had been killed in a flying accident on 30 November. Today he rests in Ferme Olivier British Military Cemetery, a lone German amongst his former enemies.

The following night Kelsey and Guy Moore, who had also been in the scrap, went over to 65 Squadron's Mess, on the other side of the Asylum Ground, carrying their trophies from the wrecked German machine, and were entertained to dinner. Kelsey finished his spell in the Squadron and spent the rest of the war on Home Defence duties, principally with 141 Squadron. He died in 1966. Two days before Christmas Rogers was informed he had been awarded the Military Cross.

The last event of 1917 was a patrol on 28 December when twelve Nieuports carried out an OP and James Brydone failed to return. Brydone from Edinburgh was only eighteen years old and had joined the RFC earlier in the year and the Squadron on 6 December. He had been hit by anti-aircraft fire, which struck his control stick and caused the machine to fall out of control. He was concussed in the crash and spent a year as a prisoner of war.

Wendell Rogers was posted back to the UK on 4 January 1918 for a well-earned rest, having completed eight months and survived the long summer of 1917. He returned to Canada at the end of January, spending the rest of 1918 instructing and was demobilized on 19 April 1919. He rejoined the Royal Canadian Air Force in 1940.

Final days of the Nieuport

For some time there had been a rumour that the Squadron were going to re-equip – a much anticipated event. The Nieuport had been obsolescent at the beginning of the year and though the initial type 17 had developed through the type 23 to the 27, there was little discernible improvement.

Rogers was replaced as C Flight Commander by W D Patrick and the same day the first SE5a, B643, was delivered by a depot pilot. However the last few days of the dear old Nieuport still had a few dramas. On 4 January G B Moore claimed a brightly coloured Albatros scout. Painted with a red fuselage, white tail and black and white wingtips it was shot down, crashing just south of Terband. The new C Flight Commander sent a two-seater down out of control on 9 January but two pilots were lost. Lieutenants R C Sotham and E K Skelton had been seen with the patrol at 1025 hours but H Battery AA saw two machines collide at 9,000 feet one mile east of Comines and crash. They thought that an enemy machine had collided with a Nieuport but it soon became evident it had been the two 1 Squadron Nieuport Scouts. Another pilot saw them collide while diving on a German machine. Sotham had worked in both Germany and Belgium before the war and was articled to a firm of accountants. At the outbreak of war he had been seriously ill and had undergone two operations. In the spring of 1916 he had been posted to India with his regiment but anxious to get into action had volunteered duty with the RFC and had undergone training in Egypt. Patrick wrote:

'He was easily the most reliable man in our Flight. If one went into any kind of trouble, one could rely on his backing one through thick and thin, and I know that Capt Rogers who had this Flight before I did shared this view with me.'

Major Adams when writing to his parents said:

'Your son was one of the best officers I have ever had, and one of the most popular, and he will be greatly missed.'

The Germans buried them in the same grave with one identified as Shelton and the other just as Ralph (surname unknown) and sadly their grave was subsequently lost. Both are now commemorated on the Arras Memorial.

Over the next three weeks the Nieuports were slowly handed in and exchanged for SE5as, with the last patrol on that trusty type on 13 January 1918. The honour fell to Patrick who on a lone patrol chased several two-seaters at various locations without result.

There was one final sad incident before the last one departed. On 24 January Captain Harry Reeves was ostensibly flying a test flight but gave an aerobatic display over the aerodrome – allegedly for visiting dignitaries. From a very steep dive he pulled up into a climbing right hand turn and as he did so a part of the lower left wing came off with possibly the interplane strut as well. This was followed by the complete collapse of all the wings and the remains smashed to the ground on the north side of the aerodrome. The casualty report contained the statement by Flight Sergeant Halstead, responsible for the machine, that it had been subjected to very severe strains for half an hour due to stunting. On the report someone has written: 'Surely machine is supposed to do this?' It was noted that this was the first case of a Nieuport collapsing for a very long time – a piece of information of little help to Reeves. He was another who had survived the summer battles, claiming a dozen or so German machines which must have merited an award of some sort. It was a tragic end and more so in that he had completed seven months in the Squadron and was due for posting to the UK.

The 2 Brigade Commander, Brigadier General T I Webb-Bowen, was not a popular officer and it was felt that it was difficult to gain awards in his command. Reeves had been recommended for a gallantry award some months before but in a letter on 26 September to Adams, the OC 11 Wing had written:

'Apparently Brigade require a little more picturesque detail before temporary 2/Lt H G Reeves name is submitted for an award.'

Goodbye old girl

There was now no place in the RFC in France for the Nieuport Scout. Some of 1 Squadron's type 27s were transferred to 29 Squadron, who struggled through to April 1918, until they too re-equipped with SE5s. The remainder were reduced to produce or crated up and transferred to training units in Egypt. Students at the training fields in the Nile Delta would not have realized what illustrious machines they were flying (and crashing). Fullard's B1549, Campbell's B3474, Billy Bishop's B1566 and Albert Ball's B1522 all ended their days there. However, 1 Squadron had a reminder of their glory days. Kelsey's machine, B6818, flown in the Voss action, was kept and maintained by them until June 1918 for the use of the Wing Commander, until it too disappeared – one of only a tiny handful transferred to the UK.

Chapter Five

A NEW ERA – 1918

The action in 1918 was to be completely different from that of the previous year for a variety of reasons. Firstly the Third Battle of Ypres was finished and the scene of action moved south with a new offensive, later called the Battle of Cambrai. Secondly the German spring offensive, designed to finish the war before the industrial might and hordes of fresh troops from the US became effective, commenced in March. Thirdly, later in the year the role of the Squadron changed from purely offensive fighting to that of bomber escort as well.

The SE5a was what the Squadron had been praying for for some time. It was faster, easier to fly, had a roomier cockpit and was a stable gun platform. However it had one big disadvantage. It was still equipped with the cumbersome over-wing Lewis. Why such a fitting was still used seems incredible – the drag alone must have reduced the performance of the aeroplane considerably. Francis P Magoun, an American serving in the RFC wrote in 1977:

> 'In our squadron at least we were equipped with one Vickers and one Lewis gun. Our Vickers was driven by a not altogether satisfactory device known as the Constantinescu oil-compression gear. We used to wonder why we didn't have two Vickers with fire converging at a hundred yards as was the case of the German spandaus. Our Lewis gun working on a ratchet so that it could be fired vertically upwards was reputed to be an invention of some one who had some success at shooting down big (e.g. Gothas) German planes.'

The first SE5 patrol of seven machines was flown on 3 February and included Patrick and R A Birkbeck. The formation had been sent off to intercept an enemy observation but the only one sighted stayed firmly on its own side of the lines. The same day Second Lieutenant V F S Dunton was posted out of the unit having become an 'ace'. His 'score' was seven, consisting of six Nieuports completely crashed and one SE5 badly damaged! Dunton had joined the Squadron on 4 November 1917 and after two months it was obvious he was never really going to be satisfactory as a scout pilot. His posting to 57 Squadron as an observer probably saved his life, as he happily survived the war.

An unusual pilot

Another pilot who did not remain very long had arrived on 28 January and by his presence possibly made the Squadron unique. Sergeant Harry Fusdo O'Hara, sounds Irish but in fact he was probably the only Japanese pilot to have served in the British flying services. Francis Magoun remembered him:

> 'Back when we were still flying Nieuports we had curiously enough a Japanese pilot assigned to us; he was a curious case in that he could not speak English very well nor really fly competently. He was always for ever making crash landings in shell holes, completely demolishing the aircraft, yet emerging from this mess totally unscathed and quite undisturbed. After a time we had to let him go home though I don't think he ever understood what the trouble really was.'

In fairness the Squadron had a fair number of technical problems with their SEs and at least one of his crashes was the result of an engine failure. Born in Tokyo in 1891, O'Hara gave his religion as Church of England! Somewhere during his service with the 34th Sikhs, 2nd Ghurkas and Middlesex Regiment he had been awarded a Military Medal and been wounded six times. His Royal Aero Club certificate No. 4991 was issued in July 1917 after he had learned to fly near London. Despite participating in a few patrols he was posted back to the UK at the end of March for reasons unknown. He remains a mysterious figure.

A change in command of B Flight occurred on the 14th. R A Birkbeck was transferred to the UK at the end of his tour of duty and his replacement was Guy Moore. Birkbeck had completed eight months in the Squadron and brought down his fair share of enemy machines. In June 1918, months after he had left the squadron, he was awarded its first DFC. Why this took so long and the award was a DFC, when rightly he should have been given an MC (the DFC did not make an appearance until April 1918) is unclear. Birkbeck served in the Reserve until resigning his commission in 1931 and died at a very early age in January 1938.

The weather during the second week of February was poor, consisting of a mixture of snow, rain and low cloud, which restricted the activities of the flying services. However the weather was better on 16 February and Lieutenant Percy Clayson opened the Squadron's account with the SE5. His combat report went:

> 'Saw EA at 4000' over Mont Rouge being Archied and climbed above him whereupon EA put his nose down and proceeded to shoot up Bailleul. I dived on him and opened fire at close range, after 3 short bursts EA went down and turned over in a ploughed field at approximately 27 x 22 Central. Pilot observed walking round machine.'

The pilot, Leutnant Bastgen of Jasta 30, was taken prisoner of war and his machine allocated the number G134. Bastgen had only been in Jasta 30 a short time and his lack of experience almost certainly led him into undertaking what was a foolhardy action. The Albatros had a yellow fuselage with a black diagonal line across it. The fin, rudder and elevator were also yellow with black markings. The bottom right mainplane was camouflaged in a different scheme to the rest and was obviously a replacement.

Clayson had joined 1 Squadron at the end of October 1917 but this was his first claim. He was another pilot who could not get on with the Nieuport Scout but once flying the SE5 was in his element. Not the most popular of people, he was nevertheless an outstanding patrol leader and became the Squadron's 'star' of 1918.

On the last day of February a twelve-man patrol with all three flight commanders were cruising at 7,000 feet near Gheluvelt when an Albatros foolishly dived past them towards the safety of the German lines. The whole formation turned and followed him with Magoun and Patrick getting in to a position to fire. From 100 yards they fired in all some 300 rounds from their four guns after which the EA toppled over the vertical and dived straight down. He was last seen still in a vertical dive only 500 feet from the ground.

Unsuccessful balloon attacks

For three days in March, the 9th, 10th and 11th the Squadron was employed on balloon attacks but with little success. Operations started with Captain H J Hamilton leading six SEs down onto a gasbag near Lomme. He worked the patrol round into the sun and in a dive opened fire from 400 yards. His gun jammed and he had to pull clear leaving the rest of the patrol to dive at it. After clearing his stoppage he dived again getting to within fifty yards. The balloon was last seen descending in a crumpled fashion. The following day was a similarly disappointing story; four balloons were attacked without a single one burning. Magoun put 580 rounds into one and a patrol fired a total of 700 rounds into another, with no obvious result. All the balloons went down deflated and some of the observers took to their parachutes. On the third day Hamilton and Clayson pressed home their attack on a balloon through heavy AA fire and tracer, firing in all 450 rounds down to a range of only forty yards, but still it would not burn. It is difficult not to believe that the incendiary ammunition was faulty.

Herbert James Hamilton had joined the Artist's Rifles in 1913 and arrived in France during October 1914. Commissioned into the Duke of Cornwall's Light Infantry in late 1915 he transferred to the RFC in February 1916 and spent several months as an observer with 20 Squadron. Back in the UK he learned to fly and was then held back as an instructor at three training units during which he accumulated a large number of flying hours. His first operational posting was to 1 Squadron on 22 August 1917 where he joined Louis Jenkin's B Flight. On 23 November he was posted to 29 Squadron as a flight commander and while with them claimed additional victories. He arrived back at 1 Squadron on 24 February 1918 as a flight commander.

On 12 March the Squadron suffered its first combat loss since James Brydone became a POW on 28 December, two and a half months before. W D Patrick, the C Flight Commander, led three of his flight plus three from the other flights in a mid-morning patrol. Two returned early due to technical problems. Just north of Staden, Denovan and A H Fitzmaurice dived on a two-seater, which then dived east to escape. Denovan closed to within ten yards firing both guns and then had to zoom to avoid a collision. After diving on it again and following it down to 5,000 feet he had to break off due to the approach of ten enemy scouts. They all dived on Fitzmaurice with Denovan driving one off his tail before having to spin down to avoid the attentions of another five. Hedgehopping his way back pursued by the Germans he was eventually forced to land on the Allied side with his ailerons shot away. Fitzmaurice was not so lucky and failed to return. Jasta 46 claimed three SE5s in this area at about this time but who brought down Fitzmaurice is difficult to say.

An incident on 16 March produced a little interest in the Squadron and some embarrassment to

Major Adams. Sergeant Cade in the pay office had been found defrauding the Squadron and when discovered had spirited away the sum of 12,000 Francs. At his court martial he was sentenced to twelve months hard labour. Adams engaged in a lively correspondence with higher authority over the issue of why he had not been found out before, particularly as he had signed for everything on taking command of the Squadron.

The German offensive of March 1918

The German army, bolstered by all the divisions from the eastern front where the Russians had signed a separate peace treaty, were attempting to break through in the west before the arrival of the Americans swung the balance permanently in favour of the Allies. The Allies were well aware of the German preparations but were not sure where the blow would fall. The RFC, expecting that the Somme area would be the place, started building up their forces for the defence of Amiens. German dumps and supply lines were bombed and patrols sent up to try and draw out the German fighters, as they were endeavouring to conceal their actual numbers. In the days before the assault, thick clouds and rain made reconnaissance difficult. The battle opened on 21 March 1918 with a massive artillery barrage ranging on targets as far back as twenty miles. Sixty-two German divisions attacked thirty weakened British divisions. Fog in the morning aided the Germans but in the afternoon it cleared and the air battle commenced in earnest. Over the next few days the RFC engaged in a desperate defence, with every machine being involved in ground strafing or bombing in order to slow the German advance. Further squadrons were drafted in from other brigades to stem the tide and on the 26 March, the most crucial day of the battle, 1 Squadron flew down south to 40 Squadron's aerodrome at Bruay.

Ground strafing casualties

They had been dragged out of bed at 0500 hours and, unwashed and unshaven, pilots were sent off. Every machine was thrown into the fray, bombing and strafing – many crews repeatedly returning to the battle. It was an expensive first day for 1 Squadron with three pilots missing. Arthur Hollis, of C Flight, had already done two patrols totalling four hours of intense flying when he took off for his third at 1540 hours. The great disadvantage was that the Squadron was flying over unfamiliar territory and on his first patrol Hollis became lost and had to land to ask directions back to Bruay. On his second patrol he was flying with W M R Gray and saw him hit, strike the ground, then turn over. Gray became a prisoner of war. He took off on his third patrol with Captain Harry Rigby, B Flight Commander, and a pilot from 40 Squadron. Hollis later recounted his last flight thus:

> 'I had just begun a long dive on to the German infantry on the road and had both guns going right into them when I heard Hun machines on my tail and saw tracer coming all round me – as it is fatal to fly straight under these circumstances I immediately began a left-hand climbing turn to try and get above them, and had just seen that they were black and white Albatross (*sic*) scouts, when my elevator control wires were shot away and I realised with a sickening feeling that I was out of control; the nose of my machine of course dropped and I lost height, enabling three of them to get on my tail. I was quite powerless and suddenly the control lever jumped from my hand because my bottom right wing had buckled up, having been hit by an explosive bullet, which by the way, it is against international laws to use. My machine immediately began a terrific uncontrolled spin towards the ground. I knew it meant certain death, but shut off my engine and waited for it. I remember noticing my instruments and seeing that my altimeter read 2,500 ft. and my speed 180 m.p.h. My childhood did not flit before my mind. I wish it had done – as it was I simply sat for those few seconds with a sickening feeling at the pit of my stomach each time the machine rushed into a fresh turn. What made it so bad was that I was absolutely powerless. I don't remember hitting the ground.'

Hollis was unconscious for four days and when he came round found himself in a German Field Dressing Station located in an old wooden hut. He had a broken nose and various other head injuries and a slight bullet wound in the foot. After the war Hollis rejoined his company of Chartered Surveyors and Estate Agents and became senior partner in 1939. He became a director of the Leeds Permanent Building Society in 1933 and was president from 1944 until 1948. He died in 1964. Harry Rigby had been unable to go to Hollis' assistance as he was scrapping furiously with three enemy machines. He managed to shoot one down in flames using both his Lewis and Vickers guns.

The third pilot lost was Allan McNab Denovan, a Canadian, who had previously served in 3 Squadron.

The German air service played a very small part during the first few days and the work of the

British went largely unhindered, a fact that was not lost on the harassed German troops. There seemed a marked reluctance to fight with the Allies at low level and German regimental histories testify to the effectiveness and demoralizing effect of the bombing and strafing. In the ensuing days the Jastas finally put in an appearance and British machines were forced to defend themselves, thereby distracting them from the job in hand.

The work was made more tiring for 1 Squadron as they were ferrying back and forth between Bailleul and Bruay each morning and evening – some thirty-five kilometres each way. This was on top of three or four fraught sorties each day. On 28 March their harassment of German troops continued unabated. Magoun dropped bombs on trenches around Arras and then he and G B Moore attacked a two-seater. The observer stopped firing and the enemy machine crashed in a field. Magoun then attacked an Albatros scout east of Arras. He had to pursue it east for some time before he worked his way into a favourable position under its tail. Firing five long bursts he saw it turn, fire a yellow flare and then go down, crashing in a field. For some reason neither of these combats appeared in 'Comic Cuts' though they both clearly crashed. They were probably left out because of the volume of reports available. On 30 March the Squadron, while conducting yet another bombing operation, engaged four Pfalz and three Fokker Triplanes without a decisive result but Second Lieutenant A E Sweeting was wounded in the foot by very heavy ground fire. By this stage the Squadron was down to only nine serviceable aeroplanes.

The first day of April 1918 was a truly historic day with the formation of the Royal Air Force – the Royal Flying Corps and Royal Naval Air Service being merged. This event went largely unnoticed as another day of bombing and ground strafing began. 1 Squadron were still operating from 40 Squadron's aerodrome and during the day smashed two precious machines. Lieutenant D M Bisset had a Lewis drum fall to the cockpit floor, jamming the rudder on landing, though he walked away uninjured. In the other incident Percy Clayson had his engine cut out at 2,000 feet and he hit an embankment short of the aerodrome, though he also walked away uninjured.

A new German offensive

Just as the Germans looked as if they were about to break through in the Amiens area they started moving their forces north to begin an offensive in Flanders. At first this was believed to be a diversionary tactic and valuable time was lost in responding to it. On 3 April 1 Squadron ceased their to-ing and fro-ing to Bruay. The return to normal routine enabled machines to be replaced, pilots to recuperate and losses to be made up.

On 7 April the Squadron suffered a particularly sad loss with Guy Moore, commanding B Flight, being killed. His flight had taken off at 1245 hours on an OP and had chased a two-seater, then fired into trenches east of Armentières. They were cruising at only 2,000 feet over Hollebeke when disaster struck. Francis Magoun was a member of the patrol:

> 'Of all the episodes which occurred during my stay with No.1 perhaps the most extraordinary was the one which surrounded the last flight of Capt Guy Moore of Vancouver, BC, Canada. Moore had finished up his full stint of six months or so and had received leave to go home. On the afternoon preceding the day of departure the whim overcame him to take his flight out for the last peek at the front. At 10,000 feet there wasn't a German in sight above or below us, so he fired off a Verey light and we started for home. All of a sudden he simply disappeared, vanished as if by magic. The effect on us was terrifying and curiously eerie. Back home we reported all this and explained what point in the line this happened. Major Adams instituted some enquiries but found nothing, after dinner word came from an RFA battery. They had been in the process of firing at some target or other when our flight dived down right into their range. They tried to hold off their fire but could not quite manage it. A tragic way to begin ones leave.'

For many years there was a theory that Moore had been a victim of Manfred von Richthofen but his combat on this day was miles away and at a different time. Moore had done nearly eight months in the Squadron and had claimed seven enemy machines on Nieuports and another three on SE5s. His well-deserved MC was awarded in May. Nothing of Moore or his aeroplane was ever found.

The resumption of the normal duties of a fighter squadron was rudely interrupted when the German attack started on the Lys on the morning of 9 April. In mist and rain, which precluded any air operations, and with extensive use of gas shells, the Germans punched through the Portuguese-held part of the line. The first day 1 Squadron suffered two casualties. Six SEs set off late in the afternoon to attack road crossings and trenches with bombs and guns. Lieutenant Howard McKeague, a

Canadian, returned wounded and was carried off to 15 CCS. The second machine, flown by Lieutenant G A Mercer, failed to return. Mercer, also a Canadian, had arrived in the UK in April 1915 and in August 1917 had transferred to the RFC from 2nd Division Cyclists. His primary flying training was done at the RNAS school at Vendome in France.

Joining 1 Squadron on 28 March he had been with them only two weeks before becoming a POW. In August 1914 he had been on a canoeing trip in northern Canada and was unaware the war had begun until mid September and it took him until the beginning of November to reach home in Toronto. In 1931, as a Royal Canadian Air Force officer, he attended the RAF Staff College at Andover and wrote of his experiences that day:

> 'On 9th April 1918 I was ordered to carry out a ground strafe, in formation, with two other aircraft of the Sqdn over the lines in front of Armentières to assist the Portuguese who were breaking up at this point. The clouds were down to 200 feet and visibility was very poor.
>
> When we were about four miles behind the German lines my petrol tanks were hit by machine gun fire and in a moment or so my engine stopped. I put the nose of the aircraft down towards our lines but owing to lack of height I could not glide very far and so was forced to land. When the aircraft stopped running I found myself surrounded by a company of German infantry who were bristling with bayonets and in a rather bad humour as I had been firing at them a few moments before. I was rescued by one of their officers before any harm befell me and taken to interview the Battalion Commander.'

During his captivity he was involved in a tunnel escape at Graudenz where seventeen officers got away. Mercer and his companion walked 200 miles in seventeen days and were caught just before reaching the Baltic.

April 10 – three losses

The weather was marginally better the following day and 1 Squadron found themselves attacking ground targets again but this time in their own back yard. Matters became worse as three more pilots were put out of action. Lieutenant K C Mills and Magoun set off, led by Captain Patrick on a low flying and EA patrol. Magoun recorded what happened:

> 'On that very foggy morning with the ceiling of about 300 feet, the C.O. asked for volunteers to try in perfect safety to discover, if possible, just where the front actually was. Three of us readily volunteered. It was a Monday so everything I had on was clean, including a brand new uniform which had just arrived from London. All this was very helpful later in preventing my wound getting infected. The Germans had obviously lost no time in filling the gap and were all ready for us innocents when we came swooping about. I caught it at once in the right shoulder and immediately zoomed up into the fog and saw nothing more of the action until by the merest chance the fog cleared a bit so that I was able to see a stretch of the road between Armentières and our flying field where luckily there were two or three men stationed to help out persons in need. It was long after in 1930 that Patrick told me his engine was shot out of business and he made a landing, ending up in an officers prison camp at Karlsruhe. I was extremely fond of Patrick, a bit older than I and thoroughly intelligent; he insisted on my learning to play bridge to my great satisfaction for many years.'

Both Magoun and Patrick were to have distinguished careers. Magoun, born in New York in 1895, had obtained a Ph.D. from Harvard University in 1916 and then joined the American Ambulance in Paris. A chance meeting in the city with an RFC pilot delivering a Spad fighter made the idea of joining the RFC attractive. Travelling to London he joined up in March 1917, arriving at 1 Squadron in November 1917. While in hospital he was advised by Major Adams that he had been awarded the MC. Interestingly enough his recommendation had been put forward by Roderick Dallas, the great RNAS 'ace' and CO of 40 Squadron. It was not only for all the excellent work he had done while on the Somme front but also for a number of other incidents. After convalescence in the US, Magoun returned to the Squadron before the end of the war.

Patrick, born in 1889, had been educated at Glasgow University and became a member of the Faculty of Advocates in 1913. Joining 1 Squadron in September 1917 he had replaced Wendell Rogers in charge of C Flight on 4 January 1918. Before his unfortunate capture he had been involved in the shooting down of seven enemy machines. Returning to the legal profession on his release from captivity he became a QC in 1933, a Dean of the Faculty of Advocates in 1937 and was a Senator of the College of Justice in Scotland from 1939 until 1963. The Rt. Hon. Lord Patrick died in 1967.

The third casualty this day was D M Bissett, from Aberdeen, who was wounded in the thigh during ground strafing but brought his machine back to the aerodrome.

The Squadron moves

The fighting to the south of Ypres reached a peak on 12 April despite poor weather. It was on this day that Haig issued his special Order of the Day with the famous 'backs to the wall' message to the troops. The following day 1 Squadron sadly had to evacuate the comfort of the Asylum aerodrome, after almost exactly three years of occupation. They moved back to Clairmarais, just north of the depot at St Omer. Despite the move the patrols continued unabated. At this time there were a number of rapid changes in command of flights, from a variety of causes. On the day of the move Captain W L Harrison crashed on landing and was removed to hospital. He had been flying Nieuports, then SE5as with 40 Squadron since July the previous year and had just been awarded an MC. After only two days in the Squadron, having arrived to replace H J Hamilton who had gone to hospital, he had himself become a casualty.

There were two more casualties on 16 April, one of whom was another flight commander. During a Low Flying and Bombing Patrol of their old stamping ground at Bailleul led by Captain J S Windsor, F R Knapp failed to return. They had been engaged on bombing troops and horses and Knapp's machine was brought down by groundfire although he was unhurt and taken prisoner of war. Windsor returned wounded in the wrist and was removed to 15 Casualty Clearing Station. He had learned to fly in late 1915 and from July 1916 until June 1917 had served with 30 Squadron in the heat and dust of Mesopotamia (now Iraq). While with them he had been awarded an MC. After returning to England he had instructed at CFS and on his arrival at 1 Squadron had over 500 flying hours. All this massive experience was not enough to save him from an anonymous bullet from the ground and he left the Squadron after only four days.

Windsor's replacement in charge of C Flight was another old 1 Squadron hand, Cecil Christian Clark. Clark had been a member of Quintin Brand's B Flight in early 1917 until he was hospitalised in April. On 21 April, only three days after his arrival he was in action. Together with K C Mills he attacked a Pfalz scout in the Lille area:

'While on OP we observed the EA at 16,000' and dived on him shooting him to earth. We closed to within 50 yards range firing all the time. We followed him right down and observed him to dive straight into the ground almost vertically somewhere in the neighbourhood of Lompret. EA was followed down to 400'.'

Ten minutes later in the Laventie area he had another combat:

'I was returning from the direction of Lille towards the Forest de Nieppe after diving on to EA and was flying at about 500 feet. I climbed up to 3 KB's who were about 3000-4000'. The 3 balloons were arranged in a triangle. I attacked from below and from the East, and fired a complete drum from about 200 yards range closing to 20 yards. Observer jumped out and balloon appeared to be in flames. I attacked the remaining balloons and in all saw 4 parachutes.'

For some reason, probably space, this was not mentioned in 'Comic Cuts'. While another patrol was taking off one of its members collided with an RE8 on the ground and crashed in flames on the edge of the aerodrome. The pilot, H B Winton, was killed and the machine totally destroyed.

Two days later flying a solo Roving Commission sortie Clark spotted a formation of eight Fokker triplanes 15,000 feet over Plugstreet Wood. Following them east he waited for a favourable opportunity to dive on them. Over Mouscron they turned north and he was able to dive on one, firing a good burst at seventy yards. The triplane caught fire and went down south of Courtrai. Over the next few days Clark claimed two more enemy aircraft.

The huge German offensive finally ground to a halt at the end of April, without the hoped for breakthrough, and the Flanders area calmed down. Though 1 Squadron was a fighter unit the scale of their ground-attack activities, and the desperate nature of the battle, can be judged by the fact that between 28 March and 19 May they dropped 1,110 bombs. On 2 May a six-man patrol had the dubious task of bombing their former aerodrome. Lieutenants J C Bateman and W M Chowne dropped four bombs each on 65 Squadron's old hangars at Bailleul.

The appearance of a welcome face occurred on 4 May when C S T Lavers returned to the

Squadron. This was his third tour of operations, having spent from September 1916 until March 1917 as an observer in 23 Squadron and then arrived back in France less than three months later as a pilot with 1 Squadron. A bad crash on 26 July due to engine failure left him with a cut eye and knee but he remained with the Squadron. Serving in C Flight under such leaders as Fullard he claimed five German machines, before being sent home in November 1917 on the completion of his tour of duty. He was destined to remain with the Squadron until it was reduced to cadre in March 1919.

On 7 May K C Mills fired 500 rounds into a two-seater over Dickebusch and followed it down to just fifty feet then finally seeing it crash vertically into some trees. However at that low altitude he was a sitting duck for enemy ground fire and he received a wound in the thigh. Returning to the aerodrome he too was carried off to the familiar 15 CCS.

C C Clark POW

Clark's run of victories came to an end on 8 May. Nine machines from A and B Flights left at 0612 hours on an OP. J C Wood, a member of the patrol, wrote of his experiences:

> 'Attached to No.1 Squadron on SE5 and did not last too long as on an early patrol was shot down and landed in enemy territory not far from our front line. Had two wounds in leg, one ordinary other explosive bullet making a large hole and the bullet case was in my leg for some months before the doctors found it and had it for years on a watchchain as a charm.
>
> I had a plane in my sights and pumping the lead into it and must have been excited on getting my first but slipped up on watching my tail when they started pumping shells into me. They got a strut wire and petrol tank. Thought it was best to head for near ground and perhaps could get over our lines which were near but apparently passed out and came to in a shell hole near their gunpit facing two rifles. They took me in the pit and one got the flying suit and another the gloves when the officer came and spotted CANADA on my shoulders (against regulations) and in perfect English asked me how things were in America. I said "Damn fine". He had a good laugh and told me he was in USA and often visited Canada. He ordered his men to go to the plane to get cotton bandage and said to hang on to it as I would never get another except paper.'

C C Clark, another member of the patrol, was brought down slightly wounded by Leutnant Harry von Bülow of Jasta 3 and Wood by Leutnant Karl Bolle of Jasta Boelcke. Clark served in the Reserve later and died as a Squadron Leader in November 1939.

Clark's place in charge of C Flight was taken by P J Clayson, who was promoted to Captain. Six days later in a twelve-man patrol he attacked an Albatros scout pursuing it down through the clouds. On emerging from the cloud he saw another, which he also attacked. Opening fire from long range he closed to 150 yards. After 110 rounds the right hand wings folded back and the EA began to spin. Smoke started coming from the fuselage, then the machine broke up and crashed near Dickebusch.

The American contingent

During 1918, after the entry of the USA into the war, large numbers of their airmen were seconded to RAF squadrons to gain experience before joining newly formed US Air Service units. Throughout the latter part of the year 1 Squadron had a number of them.

Duerson Knight, born in January 1893 in Chicago, joined on 12 May. In an engagement on 28 May a two-seater was attacked by a large patrol, which included Knight, and sent down to crash. At the end of an OP on 31 May he was chased by three Albatros scouts and with his main petrol tank shot through the engine stopped. He glided over the trenches and crashed 200 yards on the right side of the lines. The machine was abandoned as unsalvageable, but Knight was unhurt.

Harold Kullberg joined 1 Squadron three days before Knight, and though American, was actually serving in the RFC. Born at Somerville, Massachusetts in 1896 he joined the RFC in Canada, having been rejected by the US Air Service as too short! After training in both Canada and Fort Worth, Texas, he sailed for the UK in January 1918 and after a period at various training units was posted to 1 Squadron. He had been a member of the patrol on 28 May with Knight. His career was rapid and he was to participate in the destruction of nineteen German machines between May and September. Throughout most of the latter part of 1918 the claims made by the Squadron are less attributable to individuals than they were in 1917. Much larger formations, with the emphasis on teamwork, meant that many victories were accredited to patrols as a whole and not to one person. A typical example of this was on 1 June during a large scrap over Plugstreet Wood between ten of 1 Squadron's SE5s and a formation of eighteen Albatros and Pfalz scouts. The wings were seen to fall off one of the Pfalz' but it was not certain who had shot it down, so this was credited to Clayson's C Flight as a whole.

A total of thirteen SE5s led by Clayson and Captain K S Henderson brought down two enemy machines on 29 May. In company with Lieutenant A F Scroggs, Clayson attacked a two-seater, possibly of FA9.

> 'Lt Scroggs and self dived on the EA and opened fire at close range. The EA turned over on its back and pieces fell off. It continued gliding upside down until it crashed and burst into flames at about a mile NW of Vieux Berquin.'

Henderson was not destined to last much longer as on 2 June a small patrol of four machines scrapped with five Albatros and Pfalz scouts and he failed to return. He was last seen over Bailleul and is presumed to have fallen victim to Oberleutnant Hans-Eberhardt Gandert CO of Jasta 51. He has no known grave. It was a double tragedy for the Henderson family in Queensland, Australia, as another older son had been the J F Henderson who had become a POW with 1 Squadron in August the previous year. Gandert was shot down wounded and taken POW on 29 September. During the Second World War he reached the rank of Major General in the Luftwaffe. For some reason Henderson was not replaced until 14 June, when Captain H M Sison took over his B Flight.

Three days later Scroggs also became a casualty. For whatever reason only Scroggs and H S Hennessey were sent up on a patrol. In a fight Hennessey failed to return and Scroggs got back to the aerodrome wounded. He had joined the Squadron at the end of March and in 1919 was given a Permanent Commission, retiring as a Group Captain in October 1946. Hennessey like Henderson has no known grave.

A captured Fokker Triplane

In the absence of a B Flight commander, Percy Clayson led his men plus some from B Flight on a late afternoon OP on 9 June. At 10,000 feet over Dickebusch three of the SEs were dived on by three Fokker Triplanes. One of the enemy foolishly followed the 1 Squadron machines and was shot down by the patrol. After landing it tipped up on its nose. The formation of the RAF had resulted in a new system for numbering captured machines and this example was numbered G/2Bde/15. The pilot, Gefreiter Reinhold Preiss of Jasta 14, was taken POW. The machine was the subject of a full technical report but ultimately was dismantled. The propeller and rudder were given to 1 Squadron and the engine sent to London for exhibition with other captured material. The propeller has disappeared but today the rudder is proudly displayed in 1 Squadron's museum.

On 15 June it was announced that Clayson had been awarded the DFC. He had received the MC already and thus became the only member of the Squadron to receive both decorations.

Through July the Squadron took a steady toll of German machines, particularly two-seaters, and nearly all of them fell to Clayson's C Flight. It was a superb finalé, as he left on 29 July and returned to the UK at the end of his time in France.

His place was taken by Captain G W D Allen, yet another pilot of great experience. After pilot training he had spent from June 1916 until May 1917 with 19 Squadron and on his return to Home Establishment had instructed at 56 Reserve Squadron, 73 Training Squadron and 81 Squadron. Back in France he was a Flight Commander with 23 Squadron until hospitalised three months later. He arrived just in time for the Squadron's move from Clairmarais to Fienvillers, south west of Doullens.

The last wartime CO

On 3 August A B Adams was posted away after over a year in command. His tenure covered the busiest time in the Squadron's First War career, and it could not have been an easy task keeping morale up during the periods of heavy casualties. Nor a very pleasant task, writing the many letters to families of the missing. He had been Mentioned in Despatches in June 1916 and was to receive another for his time in 1 Squadron.

His replacement was Captain W E Young of the Dorset Regiment, who also arrived just in time for the move to the new aerodrome. Young later recorded:

> 'I took over the command of No.1 Squadron RAF on Aug 4th 1918 from Major A Barton Adams, who was proceeding to Home Establishment.
>
> The squadron was then based at Clairmarais South aerodrome and was in the 11th Wing (Lt Col H van Ryneveld MC) 2nd Brigade (Brig. Gen T. I. Webb-Bowen C.M.G.) The following day the squadron moved to Fienvillers, where we came under the 51st Wing (Lt Col. R. P. Mills MC) 9th

Brigade (Brig. Gen R.E.T.Hogg C.I.E.) At first we were in the orchard on the western side of the aerodrome, but after about a week we were able to move into the better quarters on the northern side. The squadron remained in the 9th Brigade from this time right up to the Armistice.'

Young had been a planter at Perak, in the Federated Malay States in 1913, and had even more experience than most in the RFC. After service as an observer in 6 and 11 Squadrons, he had trained as a pilot in the summer of 1916. Flying Spad fighters with 19 Squadron in 1917, he had been wounded and after recuperation had joined 74 Squadron at London Colney. Having helped train the new pilots in this unit he went back to France with it as a Flight Commander. Another flight commander was the great ace Mick Mannock, who was to be awarded the last flying VC of the war. Young was awarded a much-deserved DFC in 74 Squadron before his promotion to command 1 Squadron.

The Battle of Amiens

The German army had attempted one last great thrust, which was aimed at the French around Rheims. Although it went well initially a devastating counter-attack recovered all the lost territory within days and took the important German rail centre at Soissons. The initiative was firmly in the hands of the Allies and the German army was on the edge of disarray. The Allied assault was planned to take place around Amiens.

8 August was a momentous day and signalled the beginning of the end for the German army. At 0420 that morning a huge barrage started and shortly after there was a combined infantry and tank assault. By the end of the day the Germans had been pushed back seven or eight miles in places. The use of air power was now a science and the RAF was used in every conceivable role from ground strafing to tank cooperation. The RAF losses on this first day were probably the worst of the war. During ground-support patrols 210 Squadron suffered the worst casualties of all as seven of their aircraft failed to return.

For these few days 1 Squadron was temporarily attached to 13 Wing and on the afternoon of the first day they joined 43 and 98 Squadrons in bombing the bridges at Péronne. They were not escorting the day bombers because their primary job was also bombing, with each machine carrying eight bombs under the wings. 43 Squadron lost three machines and 98 Squadron lost four. The Germans, well aware of the importance of these targets, threw their fighters into the battle almost recklessly.

During these operations 1 Squadron lost two machines. H M Sison had been admitted to hospital on 28 July, and his place in command of B Flight was taken by K C Mills, back after being wounded in May. Two flights of seven SEs had departed at 1700 hours to bomb the bridges again and in conditions of low thick cloud had a scrap with five Fokkers. Mills was last seen between Cappy and Péronne. His body was never found. C G Pegg in the same flight spotted an enemy machine below through a gap in the clouds and managed to close to point-blank range before firing. After thirty rounds it rolled over and burst into flames. The other flight involved in this operation also lost a machine. Grady Russell Touchstone, an American from Laurel, Mississippi, was another of the USAS contingent and had arrived in the Squadron on 19 July. His loss was not observed but it later transpired that he had been taken POW and treated badly by the Germans. After the Armistice, and a short period in hospital for the treatment of a broken jaw, he joined the US 25th Pursuit Squadron.

The replacement B Flight Commander, Percy Bernard Tabernacle, arrived on 17 August. Tabernacle, despite the fact he came from Prince Albert, Saskatchewan, was British and had served with Princess Patricia's Canadian Light Infantry. For reasons unknown he only remained a week before returning to the UK. His replacement was Captain William Pallister, a Yorkshireman, who after service as an observer with 3 Squadron, had learned to fly and spent over a year instructing.

During an OP on 22 August two enemy machines were shot down, the second a two-seater by C G Pegg. Duerson Knight brought the first down and his combat report read as follows:

'When on OP I dived on one of a formation of Fokker biplanes which was on the tail of an SE5, and firing 150 rounds at point blank range. The EA burst into intermittent flames and crashed just west of railway at Achiet le Grand. Height at termination of engagement 2500'.'

The machine landed just inside the British lines but too near to get to it. Three days later as Knight flew by, he noticed that it had been removed. Young wrote to HQ requesting a souvenir from the wreck. A letter from Barfoot-Saunt, in charge of the technical assessment of these captured aircraft, elicited the information that it had been allocated the number G/3 Bde/12 but had been exposed for too long before salvage and all the fabric had been souvenired. Orders were given to the depot to forward the control lever and plate off the fuel tank to Knight.

Two days later another of the USAS group was lost and again like Touchstone the circumstances are unknown. Roland H Ritter, who was born in 1890 and came from Pennsylvania, had completed his training at Northolt and Croydon during which he had been injured. He had joined 1 Squadron on the same day as Touchstone and was last seen east of the lines with a Sopwith Camel and another unidentified SE5a. Due to the confused nature of the battle and the fact that aeroplanes would become split up during all the strafing of ground targets machines would go missing and nobody would know why. Unlike Touchstone, Ritter did not survive. After the war the families of US servicemen were given the option of having the remains of their loved ones repatriated and approximately 60% chose to. The remainder were concentrated into six cemeteries in Europe and Ritter is now buried at the US Military Cemetery at Bony, south of Cambrai.

Bomber escort

A lot of time was now taken in escorting the De Havilland DH9s on bombing raids – a task that gave little scope for chasing and engaging enemy machines as on OPs. W E Young wrote of this work:

> 'The squadrons we escorted were Nos. 98 and 107, both DH9s and at first we experienced some difficulty in meeting at the rendezvous – the trouble being that the DH9s could not do a small enough circle over the rendezvous when in a big formation. The result was that unless the DH9s timed their arrival at the rendezvous to the exact second, the SE5s failed to pick them up when they were doing their wide circuit round the rendezvous. Another little trouble was that the DH9s rather liked returning to the lines from their objectives "all out" with noses slightly down, making it quite impossible for the SE5s to do any fighting if necessary. However, these little difficulties were soon overcome, thanks to the meticulous care Lt. Col Blomfield made all squadrons concerned apply to the most minute details, and the work proceeded successfully and to the mutual satisfaction of escort and escorted.
>
> The longest raid done by the squadron was on Oct. 30th, when it escorted DH9s to MARIEMBURG, a distance of 39½ miles over the lines. It was fortunate that no Huns were encountered, as the petrol supply would not have allowed time to stay and fight – as it was, practically all machines scraped back on their emergency tanks.
>
> The escort work, however, was carried out very successfully, only one escorted machine being lost in over 20 raids, and that went down either hit by A.A. fire or through engine trouble. Captain C.S.T. Lavers led practically all these escort formations and it would be hard to find a better leader for this class of work. He was awarded a very well earned D.F.C. at the Armistice.'

On the penultimate day of August sixteen SE5s were on an escort when the formation was attacked by a formation of Fokkers. Harold Kullberg dived on three that were harassing a straggling DH9 and fired a burst from both guns at close range. The machine spun away and when pulling out both wings fell off. Later another pair of Fokkers attacked a DH9 from below and Kullberg fired a burst at this from close range. The EA went down out of control and was seen to crash by C G Pegg.

Four days later on 3 September another sixteen SEs, including Major Young, were engaged on the same task, but the DH9s failed to turn up. After twenty minutes the formation went off on an OP. Kullberg lost the formation and seeing some Bristol Fighters escorting some DH9s he joined in. On the way back from the target enemy machines dived on them and Kullberg fired about 100 rounds into one, which went down and crashed. As it hit the ground he saw a burst of smoke.

Another OP was flown on 15 September, again with Major Young, that resulted in another captured machine. Seventeen SEs attacked a mixed formation of Fokkers and other enemy aircraft. D E Cameron reported:

> 5.05 pm 12000' D E Cameron
> Single seater (type unknown)
> 'At 5.05 pm our patrol attacked a number of Fokker and other EA scouts at 12000'. I observed one diving on the tail of an SE and I turned and followed EA down. The EA attempted to shake me off by half rolls and turns but I got in half a dozen good bursts until within 100 feet of the ground.
> I then observed the EA strike the ground and turn on its back near Recourt. I fired 120 rounds.'

William Newby from the 1 Squadron patrol had to land within 500 yards of the crashed enemy machine due to engine trouble. The enemy machine had also been shot at by a Bristol Fighter of 62 Squadron flown by Captain W E Staton and his observer Lieutenant L E Mitchell. The Bristol landed near the crash and Staton and Newby walked across to see it. The following day Young wrote a letter to Headquarters 9 Brigade:

> 'Although they arrived within 10 minutes of the EA crashing they found that the infantry had removed all the instruments, black crosses, magnetos and a large portion of the fabric and 3-ply. Lt. Newby was able to secure the parachute.
>
> No units were identified except the 93rd Battery R.F.A. 56th Division, who looked after Lt. Newby till a tender from here reached him. The infantry appeared to be mostly Canadian – officers and men.
>
> The E.A. was of an unknown type and the parts cut away by the infantry would probably be of the utmost value in determining details of the design.
>
> Can steps be taken, please to try and recover some of these parts?
>
> If the machine had been left untouched, it could have been salved practically intact.'

Apart from the items listed by Young the troops had also taken the undercarriage and both guns. The report was published only nine days later and included several photographs illustrating how much damage had occurred in only ten minutes. The report also commented on the accuracy of the 1 Squadron gunnery:

> 'It is interesting to note that our pilots made some excellent shooting during the combat, there being a group of shots about 12″ in diameter through the 3-ply at the back of the pilot's seat, and a similar group on the starboard side of the fuselage about 18″ behind the pilot's seat. There were no signs of bullet holes in the fabric of the planes.'

Staton admitted his guns had jammed and at that time the unidentified machine was still under control, so he therefore made no claim for it. However he later changed his story and it was credited to both squadrons. The unidentified aeroplane was a Pfalz DXII, the only one to fall into British hands before the war ended, and thus of great technical interest. Allocated the number G/HQ/6, it was delivered from 1 Squadron to No.2 Salvage Dump a week later. The German pilot, Leutnant Paul Vogel of the Bavarian Jasta 23b, died of his wounds. Vogel had joined his unit in May and had led a charmed life. On 12 July he had been wounded and sent to hospital. He was shot down in flames on 25 and 30 July but parachuted to safety both times. Parachutes were just coming into service in the German air service before the war ended and they saved a significant number of lives. Newby retrieved the parachute from the Pfalz and, as some parachutes were used more than once, it may very well have been the one that had saved Vogel on the two previous occasions. By a little stroke of irony Vogel lies today in the Faubourg D'Amiens British Military Cemetery in Arras, only yards from the Royal Air Force Memorial to the Missing. The rudder from his machine is in 1 Squadron's museum alongside that taken from the Fokker Triplane captured on 9 June.

The following day, 16 September, fifteen SEs led by Captain C S T Lavers, escorted DH9s of 98 Squadron to bomb the railway station at Valenciènnes and had a running battle all the way to the target and back. Despite this, only one bomber was lost and the crew taken POW. Harold Kullberg brought down his last enemy machine:

> 'Lt Kullberg is in hospital wounded and unable to write the combat report.
>
> He states that while over Valenciennes with his patrol he saw an SE going down with 2 EA scouts on his tail. He drove them off the SE and getting on the tail of one, followed him down. After a long burst EA went down in flames.
>
> Lt Kullberg then found 5 EA on his tail and was forced to spin down to the ground and contour chase. The EA followed him all the way to the lines and he was wounded in three places in the leg.'

In the four months he had been in the Squadron he had destroyed or shared in the destruction of nineteen enemy machines. His DFC citation described him as 'A bold and keen officer who possesses a fine fighting spirit.' After several months in hospital in the UK he was demobilized in July 1919. Cameras were not allowed in the RAF and whilst in hospital his was confiscated by the Military Police. Both he and Major Young had to write letters of explanation.

On 29 September on yet another bomber escort, D M Bisset returned with his machine badly shot about but Lieutenant L M Elworthy was lost and became a POW. However all the bombers returned. The escort on 1 October resulted in the loss of William Joffe, a South African from Kimberley. He had served in the ranks from October 1914 until August 1917 including a spell in the Middle East and had unusually, for a junior officer, been awarded a DSO in the infantry.

The Squadron moved aerodromes on 6 October to Senlis to be nearer the advancing British army. Three days later Francis P Magoun returned to the Squadron, just in time to see the end of the war. Asked many years later why he had come back to 1 Squadron and not a US Pursuit unit he wrote:

> 'I have never regretted that step and indeed the time spent with No. 1 Squadron, B Flight, was amongst the pleasantest of my life. I should never for a moment have considered leaving the RFC for the American Army.'

After the war Magoun spent a period at Trinity College, Cambridge and then returned to Harvard. His distinguished career included Professor of English at Harvard and exchange professor at the Universities of Paris and Strasbourg. He received a number of honours from other universities.

Major Young wrote of the new aerodrome:

> 'As it seemed probable that we should be at Senlis for some time, we built a Nissen hut camp for the men, but they were only able to enjoy this for three weeks as we moved to Bouvincourt on Oct 26th. The camp there was not so comfortable for the officers, who were in small dugouts, but the men had very good huts.'

During the move from Senlis to Bouvincourt a pilot was lost. H H Hunt left Senlis at 1030 hours with two others and was last seen east of Péronne. It was later learned he had been killed and is buried in Tincourt Military Cemetery east of Péronne.

Nat Trembath – the last POW

Another escort on 28 October resulted in a dogfight in which one EA was seen to crash by Magoun but Nat Trembath went missing. Trembath, an American from Easton, Pennsylvania, had joined the Canadian forces after failing his US Air Service medical and had learned to fly in Canada. He arrived in England in January 1918 and after further training was posted to 1 Squadron on 15 June. His combat report for this day was not written until Boxing Day, on his return from captivity:

> 'While leading an Offensive patrol I observed five Fokkers leaving their aerodrome near Hirson. I circled into the sun and attacked them at ten thousand feet. During the course of the engagement, I attacked one machine and shot it down in flames. I was then attacked by four others, who punctured my petrol tank and shot my elevator controls away, sending me down out of control. I regained control in about a thousand feet. The Fokkers followed me down and continued firing. About 100 feet from the ground, I stalled and shot at another machine, which crashed, I myself crashing very close to him.
>
> I was subsequently informed by the German Squadron Commander who visited me in Hospital, that the second man had been shot through the head.'

At the foot of this report, before the signature of Major Young, were two additional items:

> 'Lt. Bellin pilot of this squadron, saw a machine, which he feared was that of Lt. Trembath, go down in flames during this combat. This machine was obviously the EA secured by Lt. Trembath.
>
> The German Squadron Commander also informed Lt. Trembath that the pilot of the second machine, had brought down 22 British machines.'

Major Young later wrote of an incident in which Trembath was involved:

> 'Lt Trembath was in Liege on Nov 11th and was at once liberated by the Germans. He was walking through the town that day when a Hun officer coming in the opposite direction deliberately crossed from one side of the pavement to the other and tried to force him into the gutter. Trembath rose to the occasion and received the Hun with a neat upper-cut on the point of the jaw. The Hun got up and they started scrapping but were separated by Belgians.'

The final fling

On 29 October the Squadron carried out an OP – a change from bomber escort and in this patrol claimed their last victories and suffered their last loss of the war. During a dogfight with a large number of enemy machines W A Smart shot one down, firing a series of bursts from 200 yards to point-blank range. However Newby was seen going down in a steep dive after fighting with a Fokker and he was later found to have been killed – just less than two weeks before the war ended. Newby, another South African from Kimberley, had been in the ranks of the sappers and served in German South West Africa in 1915. He was the last casualty of 1 Squadron and is buried at Le Rejet-de-Beaulieu Cemetery south of Le Cateau.

Captain R T C Hoidge MC and Bar, who had taken over C Flight from G W D Allen on 31 July spotted some white AA bursts near Le Cateau. Observing a Fokker attacking a British balloon he dived at it from the east and fired a burst of some 50 rounds before suffering a gun stoppage. Having cleared this, he followed the EA for some distance until he was within 50 yards of it. After firing a short burst it sideslipped and then dived before flattening out. Hoidge then witnessed the unusual sight of the German parachuting out but was unable to see the machine crash as four Fokkers were approaching him. Reg Hoidge, from Toronto, had previously been with 56 Squadron and although this was his only victory with 1 Squadron, it was his 28th overall.

After several uneventful patrols the Armistice came into effect at 1100 hours on 11 November bringing an end to the Great War. There were wild scenes of joy everywhere. F P Magoun wrote of this day:

> 'One event I remember which will redound forever to Major Young's credit. On the day of the Armistice he wisely had our hangars closed up and forbad any flying on our part.'

Young wrote a note to A J Capel, commanding 94 Squadron, who were about to commence their first operational patrol:

> 'The WAR is over from 11 o'clock today that is to say the Armistice starts then and we are all moving up to the Rhine in a day or two.
>   I believe our destination is COLOGNE!!! Seems too amazing to be true, doesn't it?'

Major Young again:

> 'A few days later the squadron moved to LE HAMEAU, where we had very comfortable quarters. We had a very good theatre, and a few concerts were given here by the Wing concert party, organised by Captain the Rev. C.T. Newcombe M.C., the 89th Wing Padre, and cinematograph shows were given regularly. This cinematograph had been in the Squadron for some time and we always fixed it up at each aerodrome in some hangar or suitable building and it was always very popular.'

In the anticlimax of peace the Squadron were kept busy ferrying the SE5s of other squadrons as these were disbanded, to the airfield at Marquise on the French coast, for transfer to the UK for disposal.

During late February 1919 1 Squadron's personnel were posted out for demobilization and as the cadre of the squadron, under Captain Lavers, left for England, Major Young departed to command 216 Squadron. The cadre proceeded to London Colney on 1 March 1919 and after handing over the squadron records and trophies Lavers left in late March. The unit moved to Uxbridge in September 1919 and here lingered in name only until disbanded in January 1920.

A little under four years had passed between 1 Squadron crossing the Channel to go to war and the Armistice. In that very short time span they had progressed from a motley collection of underpowered, fragile and unarmed machines to the sleek, powerful, twin-machine-gunned SE5a. Techniques had improved from basic aerial observation to all aspects of modern mechanized warfare, involving bombing, ground-strafing, infantry cooperation, bomber escort and fighter tactics.

The Squadron had a proud record and had established a great tradition. The cost was high with 52 men killed in action, 8 killed in flying accidents, 36 taken prisoner of war and 33 wounded in action. However, on the credit side they had claimed over 310 enemy machines, and were probably the most successful fighter squadron in the RAF during the Great War.

Chapter Six

THE GOLDEN YEARS

The Squadron reborn
Despite the euphoria of the Armistice, peace brought a host of problems for the senior officers of the newly formed Royal Air Force. Within a very short period a force of 25,000 officers and 250,000 other ranks had to be reduced to a fraction of that size. Next there was the unenviable task of deciding which officers would be the lucky recipients of one of the few Permanent Commissions. Also there was the question of which squadrons, most of which had fine wartime records, would be retained in the small peacetime RAF. It was unthinkable that the premier squadron could be left out.

No.1 Squadron had been technically disbanded on 20 January 1920 but then officially re-established at Risalpur in the far north-west of India (now Pakistan) on the following day and was initially designated as B Flight. However, the cadre was actually formed two months earlier, as Squadron Leader J O Andrews recalled in 1926:

'In September 1919 I proceeded to India and was employed as S.O.III on H.Qrs. Staff at Delhi. The condition of the R.A.F. in India after the War is too well known to need much further description. In January 1920 I was given command of No.1 Squadron, to be formed at Risalpur and equipped with Snipes. The personnel, both officers and men, was in part drawn from existing squadrons in India.

Since "P" Staff had little or no knowledge of the R.A.F. officers or units it was a heaven sent opportunity for Squadrons to unload undesirables, and to refuse to part with experienced scout pilots who were desirous of coming to the squadron. In such circumstances training on a new type of aircraft without a spare of any sort, axle or tail skid, was a ticklish matter.

We were fortunate in procuring the ubiquitous Avro to take the roughness off some of the ex F.E. and seaplane pilots. After having reconnoitred a camp and aerodrome at Parachinar in the Kurram Valley and started the necessary ground work, the squadron was moved to the peaceful station of Bangalore, where in September 1920 I left them to return to the Home Establishment.'

Andrews had a distinguished career during the First World War. He began as an observer with 5 Squadron in 1915, and after learning to fly had served under Lanoe Hawker VC in 24 Squadron. A posting as a flight commander in 66 Squadron was followed by command of 209 Squadron. By the end of the war he had been awarded an MC and Bar and the DSO. He retired in 1945 as an Air Vice-Marshal CB, DSO, MC and Bar. His replacement was Squadron Leader J B Graham MC AFC who travelled out from England. The Sopwith Snipe was not the best fighter the RAF had at the end of the war, but in such financially stringent times there were lots of them and they were cheap.

Tribal unrest on the northwest frontier of India had resulted in a limited expansion of the RAF. The Indian Group, though initially commanded by a Wing Commander, now warranted a more senior officer and Air Commodore T I Webb-Bowen was appointed in September 1919. Webb-Bowen was no stranger to 1 Squadron, having been their Brigade Commander during much of the First War. He very quickly made himself unpopular by reducing all officer's pay and allowances, as he considered many of them were running up too high bar bills in their messes. This move was not conducive to good morale, particularly when his salary was raised at the same time!

Morale was also affected by the fact that the Squadron had no operational role and the pilots were flying very few hours. The situation was not helped by a lack of spares for the aeroplanes, and William Bowden, the stores officer, was forced to buy some basic items such as nuts and bolts in the local bazaar. After the move to Bangalore in May 1920 the Squadron kicked its heels for the better part of a year, with the personnel endeavouring to entertain themselves as best as possible. Events in distant Iraq, however, were about to bring their salvation and give them a meaningful task.

The situation in Iraq
At the end of the First World War the League of Nations gave the various Allied governments parts of the German and Ottoman (Turkish) empire to govern as mandated territories. Britain was allotted Jordan, Palestine and Mesopotamia, or 'Mespot', as it was known to the British. Mesopotamia was officially re-named Iraq in September 1921 in anticipation of the country's independence. The arbitrary establishment of a new country created all sorts of tensions among the many tribes and

factions in the region, not least from the Turks in the north, and what would eventually become Saudi Arabia in the south. The repercussions of this still rumble on to the present day.

At the Cairo Conference of 1921, which was convened to address the growing problem, Trenchard, as Chief of the Air Staff, proposed the unique solution of having the RAF police this vast area, thus saving the enormous expense of maintaining a large army to control the country. (At this time the army had about 150,000 troops in Iraq.) With Churchill's approval this proposal was implemented, and command of all British forces came under the aegis of the RAF. To have the right man in charge was essential and the task was given to Air Vice-Marshal Sir John Salmond, who took over as GOC Iraq on 1 October 1922. The responsibility on Salmond was enormous and it was a make or break situation for the RAF. Salmond had to demonstrate that air power could be the decisive factor, despite the misgivings of the army, who undoubtedly were hoping they would fail. Salmond's command was doubled to eight squadrons and one of the new units was No.1 Squadron, the only one with Snipes. The other units were equipped with DH9as, Bristol Fighters and Vickers Vernons.

Posted to Iraq
No.1 Squadron left Bombay on 27 April 1921, and on arrival at Basra transferred to a river steamer for the journey up the Tigris to Baghdad. The river was the lifeline of the country, and in the absence of decent roads was the primary supply route and means of communication. The Squadron were established at Hinaidi, ten miles from Baghdad, which was ultimately to become a huge station and the centre of RAF operations in Iraq. One of the pilots at this time was Cecil Bouchier (later Air Vice-Marshal Sir Cecil Bouchier KBE, CB, DFC) who recorded:

> '1921 was spent with No. 1 Squadron at Hinaidi. The squadron did no active operational work during the period I was with them. Most of the time was spent in preparing the surface of the aerodrome, and in endeavouring to get off solo many of the pilots in the squadron who had not flown Snipes before. No.1 Squadron was the first squadron to be stationed at Hinaidi, which at this period possessed an aerodrome barely large enough for a Snipe to land in; the whole being enclosed by a barbed wire perimeter and sentry posts. The conditions during the hot weather were very bad, as we were practically the whole summer under canvas without fans, the temperature registering 128 degrees in the shade.'

The climate ensured a steady turnover of personnel due to medical problems, with dysentery and sandfly fever being the most common diseases. In November 1922 Squadron Leader Graham was replaced by Squadron Leader G G A Williams, who remained for just under a year. His replacement, Eustace Grenfell, was no stranger to the Squadron having served in Number One during 1915 and 1916. But he too only lasted a few months before handing over to another ex-member, 'Spider' Atkinson. His tour of duty lasted for two years but for some of the time the command fell to the senior flight commander while Atkinson was in hospital with the DTs!

The rest of 1921 and most of 1922 was spent in training and establishing the aerodrome at Hinaidi but things were about to change. Shortly before Christmas 1922 the Squadron were informed that one of the flight commanders, Flight Lieutenant Frank Soden, had been awarded the DFC for initial skirmishes against the Turks in Kurdistan. For Soden this was in fact his second DFC, as he had earned the first as a flight commander with 41 Squadron during 1918. His was the first of four DFCs awarded to Number One for gallantry in Iraq.

In early 1923 Sheikh Mahmud, governor of the Sulaimania district in northern Iraq, planned to attack Kirkuk and generate an uprising of the Kurdish tribes in the region. The RAF bombed his quarters in Sulaimania, forcing him to take refuge in caves nearby, but despite this he continued his plans for the campaign. A combined air and ground operation was mounted, with two columns of troops supported by RAF detachments at Mosul, Kirkuk and Erbil. 1 Squadron moved their headquarters and two flights to Mosul to support the two columns, named Koicol and Frontiercol.

A new pilot in the Squadron, Flying Officer A P Davidson, recalled:

> 'My advent in the midst of these operations gave little time for me to obtain any grasp of the situation and for some time even after the conclusion of operations I was still hazy as to what had been happening. A few days were spent in flying practice, and I went on my first flight of co-operation with Frontiercol on 18th March with my Flight Commander. The column was approaching the foot of the Spillik Dagh, and both intelligence and air reports had disclosed the Turkish intention of opposing the advance at this position, which was of great strength and ideally

Top left: Major E M Maitland, the first Commanding Officer of No. 1 Squadron.

Top right: The car of *Nulli Secundus*, the first British Army airship. On the left is Samuel Cody and on the right Colonel J E Capper.

Middle left: Major C A H Longcroft, Commanding Officer of 1 Squadron in 1914. He retired in 1930 as Air Vice-Marshal Sir Charles Longcroft KCB, CMG, DSO, AFC.

Middle right: *Gamma 11* at the Army manoeuvres of 1912. On the right are Capt J T C Moore-Brabazon and Capt E M Maitland.

Above: Left to right: Lt Bell-Irving, Lt E O Grenfell and Lt F F Minchin. The aeroplane behind is a Caudron G3. Further in the background can be seen the Bailleul Asylum.

Left: Major P B Joubert de la Ferté, Commanding Officer from August to November 1915.

Top left: A Morane Type L or Parasol of No. 1 Squadron with two unidentified mechanics.

Top right: The Morane Type BB biplane, which served 1 Squadron well during 1916.

Middle left: Nieuport Type 20 A154 served with 1 Squadron from June 1916 until January 1917 and was then passed on to 46 Squadron.

Middle right: Morane Biplane A137 in which Lt C M Kelly and Lt T G G Sturrock failed to return on 16 October 1916.   *(S/L D W Warne)*

Bottom left: Capt D E Stodart. After service in

1 Squadron he commanded 3 and 114 Squadrons. He retired in 1931 and died at an early age in 1938. His heart was buried in the corner of the aerodrome at Shaibah in Iraq.

Bottom right: The Squadron rugby team late 1916. Standing (l to r): Lt W H Dore, Lt W W Lang, Lt H M Gibbs, Lt J S Beatty, 2/Lt V H Collins, Lt P M Le Gallais, 2/Lt J E S P Bradford, Lt L B Williams; middl row: Capt Ferguson, Lt T L F Burnett, Major G F Pretyman, Capt A J Capel, Lt E D Atkinson; front row: Lt R M Collingwood, B D Willoughby. Out of fifteen matches they drew one and won fourteen.

Top left: 1 Squadron early 1917 (l to r): 2/Lt R J Bevington, 2/Lt L J Mars, Lt J A Slater, unknown, Lt E S T Cole.

Top right: Nieuport Type 17 A6605 after landing on the German side of the lines on 7 April 1917. 2/Lt R J Bevington became a prisoner of war. The upper left wing had been damaged when he collided with a tree.

Middle: 1 Squadron photographed in front of B Flight's hangars at Bailleul on 3 April 1917 (l to r); back row: Lt L J Mars, Lt J A Slater, Lt P M Le Gallais, unknown; third row: unknown, unknown, Lt A W Wood, unknown, unknown, Lt R J Bevington; second row: 2/Lt V H Collins, Capt R H Cronyn, Lt E D Atkinson, Major G St P de Dombasle, Lt C J Q Brand, unknown, Lt T F Hazell; front row: 2/Lt E M Wright, 2/Lt M G Cole, Lt S McKercher, 2/Lt E S T Cole, Lt J R Anthony, 2/Lt D J Macdonald, 2/Lt L M Mansbridge.

Bottom left: Major A Barton Adams, who commanded the Squadron from June 1917 to August 1918 – the most difficult part of the First World War.

Bottom right: 2/Lt P G Kelsey in his Type 17 Nieuport Scout. Note the worn state of the machine. The Squadron marking of a red vertical bar has been painted over the earlier flight marking of a number '2'.

Top left: Sgt G P Olley, one of the few sergeant pilots to serve in 1 Squadron, wearing the ribbon of his Military Medal.

Top right: The pilots of B Flight in the summer of 1917 (l to r): 2/Lt R S Davies, Lt W V T Rooper, Capt W C Campbell, Lt W W Rogers, 2/Lt P Wilson, 2/Lt P G Kelsey. Campbell was one of 1 Squadron's most successful pilots in the First World War.

Middle left: Capt T F Hazell in his Nieuport Scout B3455. Hazell scored eleven victories in this machine. The distinctive red stripes on the cowling were probably introduced, for identification purposes, after the accidental shooting down of Tom Litter on 3 July 1917.

Middle right: 2/Lt W S Mansell, killed on 11 September 1917 when his Nieuport's wings collapsed.

Bottom: A group of prisoners of war at Karlsruhe in late summer 1917; (l to r) back: 2/Lt R S L Boote, 2/Lt W J Mussared, 2/Lt R R Macintosh, Lt R J Bevington, 2/Lt T H Lines, unknown, unknown; front row sitting: Lt A W Wood, Lt A V Burbury. All named pilots were from 1 Squadron and were taken prisoner during the summer of 1917.

Top left: 1 Squadron pilots in the summer of 1917 (l to r): 2/Lt P F Fullard, 2/Lt H G Reeves, 2/Lt W W Rogers, 2/Lt J B Maudsley, 2/Lt H S Preston, Capt T Gibbons. 2/Lt C S T Lavers is sitting on 2/Lt F M Maclaren's shoulders. These pilots claimed a total of 67 victories. Fullard remains 1 Squadron's highest scoring ace with 40 victories.

Top right: Left to right: 2/Lt G B Moore, Lt L Cummings, 2/Lt W H Robinson, 2/Lt F E Bond. Bond was injured in an accident on 27 October 1917. Returning to France, he was taken prisoner of war on 5 October 1918 while with 74 Squadron. He retired from the RAF in 1942 as a Group Captain.

Middle left: A group in the officer's compound (l to r): 2/Lt P Wilson, 2/Lt G A Wood, 2/Lt P G Kelsey, 2/Lt R H Garratt, Capt C L Bath, 2/Lt F G Baker. Garratt was killed on 20 September and has no known grave.

Middle right: A patrol prepares to leave the Asylum aerodrome in the autumn of 1917. These Type 27s have retained the standard green and brown French camouflage. The second machine, marked 'X', was lost

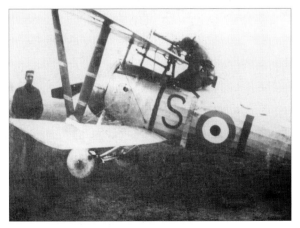

on 9 January 1918 when Lt R C Sotham collided with Lt E K Skelton and both men were killed.

Above: Nieuport Scout 'S' showing 1 Squadron's markings of a vertical bar applied over the three-bar markings of its previous owners, 40 Squadron.

Top left: Lt Lumsden Cummings climbing into his Nieuport Scout 'F' (almost certainly B6815) on 28 December 1917. The tube below the upper wing is the Aldis sight for the Lewis machine gun.

Top right: Capt P J Clayson leaning on the wing of an SE5a. Clayson was the only man to earn a Military Cross and a Distinguished Flying Cross in 1 Squadron.

Above left: Captain Harry Rigby, who was involved in the combat in which Arthur Hollis was shot down. Rigby, an Australian, won an MC in 1 Squadron.

Middle right: SE5a C8841 'K' lost on 29 September 1918. Lt L M Elworthy was shot down flying this machine during a bomber escort mission.

(W Warmoes via Bruce/Leslie collection)

Bottom right: Lt Ernest Owen in his SE5a. He has the Lewis machine gun pulled down as if for reloading the pan of ammunition. During the early period of the SE5a the Squadron marking consisted of a sloping white bar either side of the fuselage roundel. Part of this can be seen in the photograph.

Top left: Left to right: Lt W M R Gray, Lt A Hollis, Padre Bankes, Lt A E Sweeting, Lt F P Magoun, Lt L W Mawbey. Mawbey completed a seven-month tour in 1 Squadron and won an MC. Sweeting was later killed in a flying accident.

Top right: SE5a D6973 had a long career in 1 Squadron. Despite this accident it served from August 1918 until shortly before 1 Squadron was reduced to cadre in 1919.

Middle left: SE5a C1835 'T' flown by Harold Kullberg in which he scored seven of his nineteen victories.

Above right: Capt K C Mills, killed in action on 8 August 1918.

Left: Lt H A Kullberg (left) and Lt Duerson Knight, two of the United States Air Service pilots attached to 1 Squadron to gain experience. Kullberg won a British DFC while with the Squadron.

Top left: Lt Nat Trembath in SE5a E6009 'B'. This was Lt C S Dickinson's machine and the picture was taken one week before Trembath became a prisoner of war.

Top right: SE5a E5799 photographed after it had left 1 Squadron. It was while flying this machine that Capt R T C Hoidge shot down the Squadron's last victory of the First World War. The pilot of the Fokker baled out.

(Bruce/Leslie collection)

Middle left: Major J O Andrews, the first Commanding Officer when the Squadron reformed in India.

Middle right: A 1 Squadron Snipe with its engine running at Risalpur.

(Bruce/Leslie collection)

Bottom: 1 Squadron photographed shortly after the end of the war. Major Young (centre, with socks and shoes) is flanked on his left by Capt C S T Lavers and on his right by Capt R T C Hoidge. Second from the right, sitting down, is Lt Francis Peabody Magoun.

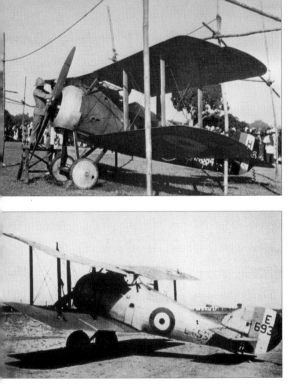

Top left: F/L F O Soden was awarded the first post-war DFC for operations in Iraq.

Top right: The Sopwith Snipes of 1 Squadron in formation near Hinaidi in 1923.　　*(Bruce/Leslie collection)*

Middle left: Sopwith Snipe H4884 being repaired after a forced landing by F/L F O Soden. *(Bruce/Leslie collection).*

Middle right: The Nieuport Nighthawk was produced in very small numbers and in 1923 four were sent to Iraq for testing under tropical conditions. Two were

allocated to 1 Squadron, of which J6927 was one.

(Paul Baillie)

Bottom left: Sopwith Snipe E6939 at Hinaidi in Iraq.

Bottom right: Armstrong Whitworth Siskin J7000. Most fighter squadrons had a two-seat Siskin and 1 Squadron had at least four. They were used for the conversion of new pilots and for check flights.
(Bruce/Leslie collection)

Top: The officers of 1 Squadron at Hinaidi in May 1926. Standing (l to r): F/O C V Lock, F/O K C Garvie, F/O A T S Studdert, F/O L S Burt, F/O D A Boyle, F/O L N Sargent, F/O H A Murton, F/O F G Jennings; middle row: F/O G A F Bucknall, F/L O R Gayford, S/L C N Lowe, F/L K E Ward, F/L N C Saward; front row: F/O Rogenhagen, F/O H S Dawe. Sargent was the Stores Officer and Murton the Accounts Officer.

Middle left: Three-pointer!! J9887, Tangmere, summer 1929. Note 1 Squadron marking on top wing.   *(via A Saunders)*

Middle right: The Air Exercises at Hornchurch during 1936 (l to r): unknown, Sgt Peskett, F/O H E C Boxer, F/O F H Dixon, F/O R J C Nedwill.   *(A/C H E C Boxer)*

Right: S/Ldr C B S Spackman DFC, CO 1931.

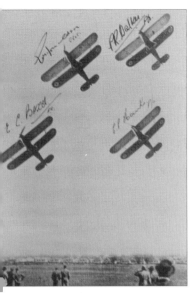

Top left: The display at Mousehold aerodrome, Norwich in 1937, with the team members in autographed positions. This team also flew at Zurich. *(A/C H E C Boxer)*

Top right: The party that flew to Zurich (l to r): P/O P P Hanks, F/L E M Donaldson, F/O H E C Boxer, P/O A C Douglas, W/C W C Hill, P/O P R Walker, S/L C E Horrex AFC, F/L J P Selby. Horrex and Selby from the Aeroplane and Armament Experimental Establishment at Martlesham Heath, flew the ground party out in a Bristol Bombay. *(A/C H E C Boxer)*

Middle left: The unofficial Squadron badge on the fin of Fury K2043. In 1936 a new standardised form of badge was introduced for all units of the RAF. After some negotiation with the College of Heralds an official badge was approved and is used to the present day. *(A/C H E C Boxer)*

Middle right: The finale of the Zurich week was a banquet, which went on until the small hours. This picture was taken at 0700 the following morning. The three Squadron officers in mess dress are Prosser Hanks, Johnny Walker and A C Douglas. *(A/C H E C Boxer)*

Left: Patrick Halahan on his wedding day to Cecily Powell, 1933. *(B Halahan-Bartholomew)*

Top left: Hawker Hurricanes of 1 Squadron at the Empire Air Day display at Tangmere, July 1939, with their pre-war code letters of NA.

Top right: S W Baldie, C G H Crusoe, C D Palmer and P R Walker, 1939.

Middle left: Relaxing on the beach late summer 1939, probably at West Wittering. Hilly Brown, Prosser Hanks, Bill Stratten and David Blomeley.

Middle right: 1 Squadron dispersal, France. Note code now changed to JX.

Bottom left: Billy Drake at Bar-le-Duc, November 1939. Moments later he fell off this bike.

Bottom right: Killy Kilmartin, Boy Mould, Leak Crus~ and P/O Mitchell (KiA 2 March 1940) at Vassincourt.
(A Hennik

op left: Boy Mould, Les Clisby, Prosser Hanks and
ll Stratton, France 1940.   *(A Henniker)*

op right: Leak Crusoe and Hanks play chess, Richey
d Kilmartin give advice. Note German machine gun
nging from the ceiling, taken from one of the
orniers shot down on 23 November 1939.

iddle left: Relaxéz vous! Bull Halahan and Johnny
alker, with Hilly Brown and Boy Mould behind.

Bottom left: Outside the Mess at Pontavert, May 1940;
(l to r): Peter Boot, Hilly Brown, F J Soper, Pussy
Palmer, Les Clisby (partly hidden), Lorry Lorimer,
Johnny Walker and Killy Kilmartin.   *(A Henniker)*

Bottom right: Scramble! Billy Drake, Lorry Lorimer,
Pussy Palmer, Prosser Hanks, Les Clisby.

Top left: Flying Officer Pete Matthews DFC, flew in France and in the Battle of Britain.

Top centre: S/Ldr D A Pemberton DFC and F/Lt Hilly Brown DFC in the Battle of Britain. Pemberton was killed in a crash on 2 November 1940, Hilly died operating from Malta a year later.

Top right: S/Ldr R E P Booker DFC, OC 1 Squadron April to November 1941, awarded a Bar to his DFC.

(via C Thomas)

Bottom left: F/Lt A V Clowes won the DFC and DFM with the Squadron, serving with it from pre-war to April 1941.

Middle right: S/Ldr J A F MacLachlan DSO DFC, OC the Squadron November 1941 to July 1942.

Bottom right: 1 Squadron in 1942. F/O Alexander, F/L Crabb, S/L MacLachlan, P/O G H Corbett, F/O W McConnell, Sgt Travis, Sgt Prideaux-Brune and Sgt Dennis.

Top left: F/L K M Kuttelwascher DFC & Bar, night intruder 'par excallance'.

Top right: Ernie Glover, Kuttelwascher and George Pearson relax at Tangmere, 1942. *(N Crowley)*

Middle left: P/O J R Campbell at Acklington. KIFA with 84 GSU, June 1944. *(N Crowley)*

Middle right: Acklington 1942, W/O Hicks, F/Sgt Sandy Sandman and F/Sgt George McIntosh VC, the latter being i/c discipline with the Squadron. *(N Crowley)*

Left: P/O Ernie Glover, RCAF, Acklington, 1942. *(N Crowley)*

Top: Some of the stalwart ground crew, Lympne, 1943.   *(N Crowley)*

Middle left: S/Ldr R C Wilkinson OBE DFM, CO 1 Squadron July 1942 to May 1943.   *(K Nelson)*

Middle centre: P/O Des Perrin (in Mae West) after downing a Me210 on 6 September 1942, with the bent propeller blade from his Typhoon. Foreground is Ted Warman.   *(FME)*

Middle right: Cpl Norman 'Doc' Gouldin GM BEM, won his George Medal while with the Squadron.

Right: Doc Gouldin's medals.

suited for the purpose. I merely followed my leader and we bombed a village named Batns with 20 lb. bombs rather ineffectually, owing to low clouds and rain. The village was deserted and we returned without having seen any hostile forces, after having communicated with the Column H.Q. by means of Popham Panel and dropped messages.

I had been given a map for this flight but found that it had little or no resemblance to the country, having been compiled from the written reports of various individuals who had passed through the area at different times.'

Ground fire from the rifles of the tribesmen was both heavy and accurate. The big fear for all crews was that of having to force land and thus falling into the hands of the tribesmen or even worse, the tribeswomen. All aircrew carried 'goolie' chits, which for the safe return of the British airman (in one piece) promised a reward. However this did not guarantee protection from torture, mutilation and death at the hands of the Kurds.

A well-known RAF song, which has numerous bawdy verses, originated at this time in this part of Iraq and one verse goes:

'There once were two pilots who went to bomb Sul
Their bombs were OK but their tanks were half-full
Then came from the back seat an agonised call
"If the engine cuts out we'll have no balls at all!"

This nightmare nearly became a reality for Davidson on only his second sortie:

'The following morning I was on the first patrol with the Flight Commander, our object being to locate the column and reconnoitre the line of march ahead, and attack hostile forces or positions. Weather conditions were again bad and hail and thunderstorms were frequent. On passing over the Jebel Makzub some 25 miles east of Mosul, my oil pressure failed and I had to make a forced landing. I thought I was over friendly country and, therefore, did not care to drop my bombs before landing. I made a landing not without a little apprehension.

About forty wild-looking Kurds at once surrounded me and the crowd gradually grew. I was relieved that I had not dropped the bombs as the situation might otherwise have been strained, and I was uncertain whether the Kurds were friendly or not. They were generally armed, carrying .45 automatics, and some field-glasses (Zeiss) presumably obtained from Turks during the war. They evinced keen interest in the bombs and from sundry signs and noises which they made, appeared to realize their use.

Further patrols passed overhead at hourly intervals and later began to return. The situation in view of my ignorance of the exact conditions was made a little difficult by a Snipe of my squadron dropping four bombs less than 3/4 mile away. I returned to Mosul after a new oil pump had been fitted, to hear the pilot of this Snipe giving a graphic description of the havoc he had wrought with his bombs.'

The same thing happened again only two days later! While circling over the column while his Flight Commander was communicating with their HQ, Davidson had an engine failure.

'My engine failed completely with a loud report and refused to function again. I was only about 200 ft. above the Spillik which was a mass of boulders and trees, and was forced to land in a valley to the East with a surface little better, I glided as slowly as possible and, hitting a ridge at about 45 degrees, tore off the undercarriage and finished up on my back. After extricating myself with difficulty from the wreckage, owing to numbness from the cold and the petrol which had literally dropped on to me from the burst tank, I found to my surprise that I was unhurt. I set off for the column armed with an automatic and, after climbing two steep ridges about 400 ft high and slipping down the other side, I reached H.Q. after a three hour journey in blinding hail and rain. Several small encampments were passed on the way with signs of very recent habitation and many empty cartridge cases observed on the ground were later identified as Turkish.

The reception by the outposts of the column was anything but friendly as I was wearing tartan trews which at a distance were not unlike the trousers worn by the Kurds. One night was spent with the column and I returned by horse the following day to Abil with an escort, and then by air to Mosul.

While with the column I was able to appreciate the value of air co-operation and the constant communication which it provided. Aircraft appeared regularly in spite of low clouds and rain and dropped large supplies on the column which were necessary owing to the unexpected weather conditions. One pilot either with a perverted sense of humour, or very bad marksmanship, dropped a heavy bag in the middle of the camp which landed quite near me, which was found on subsequent investigation to consist of 24 horse shoes.'

Davidson survived another two forced landings during his short four-month tour with No.1 Squadron. He had rejoined the RAF in 1923, having served in it during the First World War. In 1944 he was AOC Iraq and Persia and retired in 1951 as Air Vice-Marshal Sir Alexander Davidson KBE, CB.

By April 1923 the ground forces had forced the Turks, together with Mahmud and his followers, across the border into Persia. However, within a matter of months he was back in Sulaimania creating more trouble. Each year the pattern was the same with summer operations against Mahmud forcing him back to Persia, followed by a winter rest. 1 Squadron sent a detachment to Sulaimania, Kirkuk or Mosul each summer, rotating the pilots every six weeks or so.

Bombing and strafing of villages had to be carried out carefully to prevent alienating friendly tribesmen. Villages that were to be bombed were warned by leaflets being dropped beforehand, in order to reduce loss of life.

Some duties were more popular than others, as Flight Lieutenant Oswald Gayford recalled:

> 'A more domestic duty in which we interested ourselves was ensuring the regular supply of snow from the caves on the hillside behind Sulaimaniyah to the bazaar. The snow was essential to our comfort for cooling our lunch-time beer and sundown whisky and soda. It was the practice of bandits to seize the snow caves and endeavour to force the men who had gone to collect the snow to pay exorbitant prices for it. On hearing of a hold up of this nature, the Political Officer informed us and we dashed into the air and drove off the bandits. It was only a 15 minutes job, and even in the middle of the afternoon siesta volunteers to carry out a "snow patrol" were never lacking.'

Gayford served in 1 Squadron from late 1924 until September 1926 and during the summer months was in command of the detachment at Sulaimania. In 1933 he earned an AFC when flying the Fairey Long-Range Monoplane from Cranwell to Walvis Bay in West Africa setting a new world distance record of 5,341 miles. He retired as Air Commodore O R Gayford CBE, DFC, AFC and died in 1945.

Technical problems
Forced landings were fairly common in the early days as during the summer months dust caused considerable damage to the rotary engines. The Bentley BR2s had to be overhauled every thirty hours and the depot was incapable of keeping up with the overhaul schedule. In order to solve the problem the Squadron established its own Engine Repair Section by reducing each Flight to only two fitters and borrowing another six from the depot. A proper system was organised, laid out on a task basis and the engine failure rate dropped dramatically.

The climate also played havoc with the wood and fabric airframes and these had to be overhauled every 100 hours. Machines had to be left in the open and the hot sun shrank the wood, though for reasons unknown, the fabric still remained taught. Rubber perished quicker, and tyres were punctured by the persistent camel thorn. Dermot Boyle, who served in the Squadron during 1926, made a number of observations in his unpublished autobiography, *My Life*:

> 'The first of which was that everybody tried to scare me about doing aerobatics in the aeroplanes we had out there, the argument being that they were old, that the country had got them down, that they were weak and there might be a disaster if any additional strain was put on them. However I made some enquiries and found that the beautiful aeroplane I had been given, E6655, had come out from England only a couple of months before and seemed in the most perfect condition. I knew a little about these things by then, so I took no notice of the grim warnings and went on as I would have done in England. I must make the point that the aeroplanes at Hinaidi were most beautifully maintained. The ground crews kept the Snipes in the finest condition you could possibly imagine and this in spite of all the heat and dust and, at times the torrential rain. It really should be noted how good they were.'

Later in the year Boyle had to force land when his engine cowling came off and stopped the engine. Unable to fly it out, he removed all the ammunition and important parts of the machine guns and then had to burn his beloved Snipe.

Apart from the engine problems the all-pervading dust created other difficulties. On 11 July 1924 the Squadron were taking off in formation at the beginning of an operation. The large dust cloud created did not clear due to the lack of wind. Flying Officer A E Rogenhagen in Snipe H8692, lost his bearings in the murk and swung into two of the other Snipes. His machine and another were written off and a third damaged. Rogenhagen was injured but on recovery returned to No. 1 and subsequently served with them in England.

Off duty

Life at Hinaidi was not unpleasant, with all the flying being done in the cool of the morning and the machines back in their hangars by lunchtime. Dermot Boyle again:

'I played a lot of tennis and squash at Hinaidi where there were seven or eight Officer's Messes and consequently plenty of talent. The tennis courts were of mud and unusable during the rainy season but otherwise they were very true and good to play on. There was also a very good social club half way between the airfield and Baghdad. It was a combined service and civilian club where we could meet the few white ladies who were in Iraq at the time. But the young girls were so few and consequently so spoilt that it was much more trouble than it was worth to have anything to do with them.'

In April 1926 Squadron Leader C N Lowe MC DFC took command of the Squadron from 'Spider' Atkinson. He was one of the great England rugby players, having also represented the RAF. Number One improved considerably under his firm leadership. Lowe had served in No.11 Squadron during 1916 with J B Graham and in 1918 had been a flight commander with No.24 Squadron flying SE5as.

Lowe was keen on shooting and organised shooting parties as Boyle relates:

'There was some good shooting in Iraq: the flocks of sand grouse provided particularly good sport and were excellent eating and a welcome alternative to the large amount of tinned food which was our normal diet. The sand grouse used to fly round the place in large flocks and their habits were well known so it was not difficult to get in amongst them.

We used to have competitions between the messes as to which Mess could shoot the most grouse in a given time with a given number of guns. Sometimes the transport squadron equipped with Vickers Vernons distributed the various mess shooting parties to the places of their choice, in the desert near the river, and called back for them after the agreed time had elapsed. On one occasion when the Vernon had departed after dropping us, we found large numbers of sand grouse dead or wounded where the aircraft unknowingly landed amidst a flock. We collected them all and added them to the birds which we shot. We won the competition for that day by a considerable margin.'

Dermot Boyle had a distinguished career, which culminated in his becoming Chief of the Air Staff from 1956 to 1959. He retired as Marshal of the Royal Air Force Sir Dermot Boyle GCB, KCVO, KBE, AFC.

The end of an era

Life was not without its humorous moments. The officers had a motley collection of pets. Flight Lieutenant F L Luxmoore had a terrier and had gone as far as having a small cockpit constructed in his Snipe to transport 'Raggis' around. 'Raggis' had a very important secondary task in that he carried a bottle opener (or 'desert spanner') on his collar – an essential piece of kit in the climate of Iraq. Air Vice-Marshal J F A Higgins, who had replaced Salmond as AOC in Iraq, noticed the officer's pets during a visit to 1 Squadron. Higgins, known as 'Josh', also had the nickname of 'Bum and Eyeglass' due to his monocle and profile. Another of the officers had a fat turkey, which he had christened 'Bum and Eyeglass', for obvious reasons. Higgins enquired what the turkey was called. The embarrassed silence was broken by the quick-thinking officer replying, 'Fred'!

During 1926 it was decided to disband 1 Squadron in Iraq. The Snipe did not have the range for the type of operation needed against hill tribes, and it was pointless having a fighter squadron where there was no aerial opposition. Consequently, on 1 November the Squadron was withdrawn from the Iraq Command. All the airmen were posted to No. 8 Squadron pending re-distribution amongst the other units in the country. Lowe went to 6 Squadron to command, taking Dermot Boyle with him. Flying Officer G A F Bucknall was chosen as the connecting link with the re-formation of the

Squadron in England and on 2 January 1927 he embarked at Basra on HMT *Derbyshire* for England. The much-loved Snipes, being of no further use, were burnt.

Tangmere
Bucknall reported at Tangmere for duty with the Squadron cadre on 1 February 1927 and the next month Francis Luxmoore arrived to take temporary command. During the First War Luxmoore had served with 46 Squadron on Sopwith Pups and in his second tour had been a flight commander with 54 Squadron on Sopwith Camels. He had become a prisoner of war because his gun synchronisation had gone awry and he had shot off his own propeller. While with Number One in Iraq he had earned their last DFC awarded there. Tangmere almost became the spiritual home of 1 Squadron, as they were based here until the outbreak of the Second World War and returned at various times during the war. Another eleven years were spent here during the 1940s and 1950s. After the climate of Iraq it was an idyllic posting.

Peter Townsend, in his autobiography *Time and Chance*, described Tangmere;

> 'The airfield at Tangmere was a broad meadow. The slender spire of Chichester Cathedral pointed the way there; another landmark, more rustic, was the old windmill on the Downs to the north. In summertime the wheels of our Furies swished through the long grass as we landed; soon after my arrival they took a second crop of hay off the airfield and a herd of sheep was set to graze the herb. Slothful sheep and flying Furies were not meant to co-exist; both they and we had some alarming moments.
>
> Aircraft hangars, with their massive bulk, do not normally fit easily into the rustic scene. Ours did, with their wooden beams and uprights and their gently curving roofs. German prisoners of war built them in 1917, and German airmen were later to demolish them with their bombs. Meanwhile life at Tangmere was peaceful, pastoral. I loved the place; it was my home from home.'

John Worrall, later an Air Vice-Marshal, said of his time here:

> 'It was a wonderful place to be because it had the best weather in southern England and we used to be able to fly there when other people were on the ground. And it was a very good life indeed although it wasn't very well paid, I think we got sixteen and six a day which included what they said was an element for flying pay. But we got twenty pounds a month and we were looked upon as well off because there was a lot of unemployment outside in those days. We used to get about ten hours flying a month which was very little really, but we used to pack in all our training that we had to do during that time and I think most of us remained in reasonable practice.'

The reason for the lack of flying was that there were many more pilots than machines. The establishment was three aeroplanes per flight with one reserve plus the CO's own aeroplane. There were six or seven pilots in each flight including one or two NCO pilots.

During a recent interview with Guy Bolland, who served in the Squadron during 1931, he recalled a typical day:

> 'We'd report to the flight in the morning and try and get a flight. That was the first priority, always, and having summed up the situation you would try and get permission to take it to another station for lunchtime, to have lunch with your friends and come back in the afternoon. This didn't happen very often. If you failed to do that you were promptly given a task, if you were flying. You had to do what was called a battle climb or do some dummy forced landing practices – we were always very conscious of engines cutting out.'

Having spent four years with the Royal Mail Line, before joining the RAF, Guy had qualified for a Second Mate's certificate. However, his sojourn in 1 Squadron was brief, as a result of a sense of humour failure on behalf of authority:

> 'A lot of us went for an evenings outing, and I suppose we had quite a few beers but enjoyed ourselves. And on the way home, I don't know who started it, but we started collecting notices which people were advertising "teas in the garden", "fallers tuppence a pound" and all the sort of country notices which were quite common. Just outside the Mess at Tangmere, on the road to the church, was a solicitor that we didn't like very much – he was a bit pompous. Very foolishly we

stuck these notices between his gate and his fence, which was a very nicely kept garden, and just went to bed and thought nothing about it. The next day being Sunday we then marched off to church in Tangmere village church which we did every Sunday. As we passed this gentleman's house there was quite a lot of laughter going through the ranks and we suspected that we'd done something which wasn't quite correct. When we got back from church, who should be standing in the ante room warming his backside with the CO, but this solicitor, and obviously he was grumbling about our unbelievably bad behaviour sticking these notices. Well, the next morning, G B Keily, who was our adjutant, sent for me and said, "Did I know anything about it?" And I said, "Well, I did because it was my car and I helped put the stuff on the roof and we were very sorry about it – realised what a mess we had made". Well, eventually I was given Orderly Officer over Christmas and a week's extra Orderly Officer. I thought that's very fair, very fair, didn't grumble and I considered the matter closed. Come the New Year, January, I found that I was on the boat and I was posted to Iraq. That was the end of my life in 1 Squadron!'

Despite this setback, Guy Bolland went onto greater things and after an 'interesting' career, retired in 1959 as a Group Captain CBE.

On 1 April 1927 the cadre was expanded to include an HQ flight and another flight. On 13 April three Armstrong Whitworth Siskins arrived as initial equipment. The Siskin was a very different bird from the Snipe. The Mark IIIA Siskin was an metal-framed fabric-covered machine with a supercharged Armstrong Siddeley Jaguar radial engine, and was really the first new fighter the RAF had received since the end of the war.

The delivery of the aeroplanes also coincided with the arrival of 'Spider' Atkinson to take command again. Unfortunately the pattern in Iraq was repeated and the Squadron was commanded at various times by Francis Luxmoore. In early 1928 Stanley Vincent arrived as a flight commander and he took over the responsibility from Luxmoore. The situation was finally resolved when Eustace Grenfell arrived in March 1928 for his second spell in command.

Peacetime regime

Number One quickly fell into a routine and intensive training began. Pinpointing exercises, to locate objects of all shapes and sizes, ensured all the pilots were completely familiar with the area they would have to defend in time of war. For new pilots the first exercise involved them navigating to a map position and reporting what they found. The object was the Old Man at Cerne Abbas – a huge figure cut out of the chalk hillside in ancient times. The proof that the new boy had found his target was that he only had to mention the Old Man's most distinctive feature – an enormous erect phallus!

The daily routine started early in the morning with all the flying completed by lunchtime, allowing the afternoons for recreation. With the south coast so near and many delightful pubs in the area there was no shortage of entertainment. Peter Townsend again:

'Our day's duty done, we immediately discarded our uniform. Once a month, we dressed up in our tight-fitting mess-kit of "overalls" and "bum-freezers" for a guest night. After honour had been done to the guests and the royal toast drunk, squadron then pitted itself against squadron in a rowdy, good-natured debauch, which relaxed our nerves, tautened by weeks of flying. In an atmosphere charged with smoke and beer, we sang bawdy songs and recent hits, like Harry Roy's "I blow through here and the music goes round and round" or Hutch's "Get that old hunch again, champagne for lunch again. Back to those happy, happy days". Hi cock o'lorum, mess rugger and billiard-fives put a bursting strain on the tight seams of our mess-kit. For the guests, irrespective of their station, gallant air marshals, crusty admirals, lord bishops or the local mayor or peer, there was a kind of crossing-the-line ceremony, only they had to cross the ceiling, on foot. The soles of their shoes were blackened and willing hands helped them up the wall and across the ceiling where, like Man Friday, they left their footmarks. Among the distinguished ceiling-walkers was the Bishop of Chichester.'

There was no flying at the weekend, and the Squadron shut down completely from approximately mid-August to mid-September when everyone went on leave.

'We flew off to lunch with friends at other fighter stations or away for the week-end, our suitcase squeezed into the space where the oxygen bottle and the radio set were normally housed – or simply strapped on to the lower wing.'

Little wonder that the RAF was considered the best flying club in the world!

In 1929 1 Squadron, together with 43 and 25 Squadrons, combined to form No. 3 (Fighter) Wing. The Siskin equipped all three squadrons, with 1 and 43 sharing Tangmere, while 25 Squadron were based at Kenley. 'A keen and sometimes reckless rivalry united rather than opposed No. 1 and its sister squadron' is how the battle between the two Tangmere squadrons was described. The friendly competition between the two produced the very highest standards. Tangmere became probably the best-known RAF station in the UK.

The Hendon Air Display

The showcase for the RAF was the annual Air Pageant at Hendon, where the public could watch crazy flying, aerobatics and bombing attacks on mock forts or ships. The Squadron had participated in 1928 but in the 1929 event No. 3 Wing performed together for the first time. At the display itself the sight of 27 Siskins with their precision formation drew much praise, but the practice beforehand was not without its problems! Lowe had been a very active squadron commander and had made sure his pilots flew as many hours as possible. Eustace Grenfell, however, flew very little and left that side of operations to his flight commanders. Stanley Vincent wrote of the Hendon practice in his autobiography *Flying Fever* :

> 'A disconcerting incident did occur when we were practising for one of the Hendon displays. With 43 Squadron, who shared Tangmere with us, and No. 25 Squadron from Hawkinge, we were to carry out Wing manoeuvres including aerobatics of a fairly mild but showy type. One exercise entailed the Wing in line astern, diving down in succession followed by a climb into a half-loop off the top, so that the line snaked back over itself. This was a reasonably safe manoeuvre as the climb into the half-loop would take the leader and those following well above those still diving at a fairly gentle angle, and the half-roll would take them slightly out of line to those following.
>
> Eustace Grenfell, leading our squadron which led the whole wing, was over-anxious that when he pulled over he would be well above those down the line. So as he started his half-loop, he kept going up and up before pulling over at the top. Leading the second flight of three, I was No. 4 in line close behind No. 3 of the leading flight. When I got into the vertical position, the other two ahead were still going vertically themselves, straining to follow No.1 and I realised that No.1 himself would not be able to carry out his half roll, and would be bound to lose too much speed and fall out of it to the danger of all below. No.2 also realising this, pulled over with his half-loop, but already having lost speed did a sloppy twist: No.3, overtaking him, hit his tail with his propeller. I could see all this happening in front of me and decided to complete my half-loop and half-roll while I had full control, so over I went, thus avoiding what was happening above.
>
> Those behind followed me according to plan, so I found myself leading a long line of Siskins which I proceeded to re-form into squadrons by signals and break up the party.
>
> Grenfell, "waffling" out of the top of his half-loop, came out at 90 degrees to that desired entirely on his own. No.3, with a smashed propeller, was fortunately over the aerodrome and so could shut off his engine and landed successfully. No.2 having lost part of his tailplane, contemplated taking to his parachute, but realising he could maintain level flight, climbed to a safe height for parachuting to find out if there was sufficient control to attempt landing. Finding the minimum safe speed that he could use down to ground level, he very ably brought his aeroplane down to a safe landing. Grenfell then decided he would not try to lead the formation, and it fell upon "old Joe" and I led from then on.'

Stanley Vincent had been one of the original flight commanders at Major Robert Smith-Barry's School of Special Flying at Gosport in 1917, where the principles of flying training were established – principles which form the basis of all flying training to this day. He left 1 Squadron to command 41 Squadron and retired in 1950 as Air Vice-Marshal S F Vincent CB, DFC, AFC.

Mid-air collisions were to be a major cause of aircraft losses in the inter-war years, though fortunately, most pilots were able to parachute to safety, unlike their First War predecessors. In April 1930 Flying Officer K S Brake of 1 Squadron and Pilot Officer J Heber-Percy of 43 Squadron took the inter-squadron rivalry a little too far. During a practice air-fighting sortie they collided at 3,000 feet. Brake was injured as his machine broke up, losing its top wing, though both pilots escaped successfully by parachute. Brake was flying J9682, the only Hawker Hornet built and the prototype of the Hawker Fury. Heber-Percy was to serve with Number One in 1936.

Annual exercises

Apart from day-to-day training, each year there was a fortnight's practice camp, and at the end of the year the annual Air Exercises. In addition there was competition for a number of trophies. Sir Phillip Sassoon, the popular Under-Secretary of State for Air, who was passionately interested in aviation matters, had donated several trophies for a variety of different tasks, including map reading and flight attack. One trophy was the Map Reading Cup. This involved four pilots from each squadron attending one of the Fighting Area stations. Each pilot was given a sealed envelope containing four six-figure map references and the average wind speed and direction. Fifteen minutes was allowed to plot the four legs and calculate the estimated time of arrival at each point to the nearest minute before setting off on the exercise. At each point a message bag had to be dropped to a judge containing the pilot's name. However there was a certain amount of gamesmanship in that each point tended to coincide with a notable landmark, such as a crossroad or haystack, and frequently the judge or his car could be spotted hidden under a tree.

John Worrall described the annual camp:

> 'Then once a year we would be taken off to what was called a practice camp, an armament practice camp – we went to Sutton Bridge – then you would actually fire with live ammunition on the ground targets and on virtually a windsock towed by some unfortunate specialist for the purpose. Air to ground one achieved fairly high scores but air to air very, very, very poor. This I think was largely due to the lack of a sight, you only had a ring and bead and you had no deflection, or built in electrical sight or anything like that which came later.'

When Flight Lieutenant H G Lock left the Squadron in May 1930 he presented a silver model of a Vickers machine gun and it was decided that it should be competed for at Sutton Bridge. It was to be presented to the pilot with the highest aggregate score in individual and flight classification. The first person to win the Lock Trophy was Stanley Vincent, in June 1931.

The Fury

In 1932 1 Squadron received their first Hawker Furies, which were a quantum leap from the Siskin. An elegant design, and arguably the most beautiful biplane ever built. It had a liquid-cooled Rolls-Royce Kestrel engine and was the first RAF fighter capable of flying at 200 miles per hour. John Worrall recorded his impression of it:

> 'Well the Fury of course was a great improvement on the Siskin which had no performance at all really, it was just a little flying machine which was rather tricky to fly, you had to fly it all the time. It was oh I suppose rather like trying to fly a motor car that didn't want to fly, whereas the Fury was a real aeroplane, it was the first of the real fast aeroplanes. But of course it was streamlined, you had your cowling on the aeroplane whereas the Siskin was just stick and string with a radial stuck out in front which set up a lot of drag. Each of them had a fixed undercarriage but you could really pull the Fury through all the manoeuvres very smoothly, it wanted to fly and you felt that you were with it. But the Siskin – perhaps it was because of inexperience – I always felt I was riding a horse which wanted to throw me.'

Theodore McEvoy (later Air Chief Marshal Sir Theodore McEvoy KCB, CBE), who commanded the Squadron during 1936, had a less sanguine impression however:

> 'It would fly faster and higher but I don't think very much of an advance. It had exactly the same armament – the same almost useless two Vickers guns that had been in use since 1916. Absolutely no advance in armament from 1916 to 1937. And it wasn't until we got the Hurricanes and Spitfires that there was any advance.
>
> It had a water cooled engine, which was rather a disadvantage: it was subject to internal water leaks which caused trouble. I never had an engine failure I must say. They were very reliable but they did give a bit of maintenance trouble and you had to remember your radiator shutters, which you didn't have on air cooled engines'.

Aerobatics

Though there had been considerable practice in formation flying during the Siskin era there had been little in the way of formation aerobatics. However the speed and agility of the Fury lent itself to this artform. Theodore McEvoy again:

> 'Well 25 Squadron had invented the flight roll where the whole flight went round as a unit. And we had always been able to loop as a flight but this idea of rolling as a flight was a new thing. And 25 Squadron came over and showed us how it was done and we were amazed and within about half an hour the whole of the air was filled with 1 Squadron and 43 Squadron flights falling out of the air trying to do this barrel roll. And eventually, of course, everybody did button it up. And then to add zest to it for the display it was done with two flights with their aerobatics synchronised. It wasn't very spectacular because we were not allowed to come below two thousand feet and we unfortunately observed that regulation. So it all looked a bit out of reach but it was quite an enterprising affair.'

For the 1932 Hendon display 1 Squadron's arch-rivals, 43 Squadron, were performing with their machines tied together. Number One decided to enter two teams, consisting of a synchronised pair and a trio. All three teams performed flawless manoeuvres, entertaining the crowd enormously and receiving ecstatic reviews from the aviation press. This event set the trend for the inter-squadron rivalry.

One technical feature of the Fury lent itself to a trick that could be played on the unwary, as described by Peter Townsend:

> 'You lowered your seat fully so that your head was no longer visible in the cockpit. Then, looking through the gun-inspection panel in the cockpit side, you sidled up beside some unsuspecting pilot, who, terrified at being pursued by an apparently pilotless aircraft, would panic and flee, with the phantom aircraft on his tail.'

The Air Defence of Great Britain Exercises
At the end of each year came the Air Exercises. An imaginary line was drawn a few miles inland from the coast and the bomber squadrons would attack in flights or single machines from the sea. The Observer Corps would spot them and pass their position and course to the nearest available fighter squadron who would scramble to intercept. The great drawback in the days before radio was that once airborne there was virtually no way of re-directing them or passing on more up-to-date information except by sending another machine after them. This happened to John Worrall:

> 'But on one occasion I was told that I was the standby pilot who was to go down and find the squadron if necessary and try head them on to the new course on latest information from the Observer Corps. And much to my amazement I was sent off on one of these sorties, and I pushed off at full throttle to whatever height it was and even much more to my astonishment I found them and I then had to head the squadron off by waggling my wings and turning in the new direction and my squadron commander, one Spackman, squadron leader, chose not to pay any attention so I charged past him again, waggled my wings and turned in the new direction, not a blink, so realising on two occasions I'd been beaten I fell in behind. And eventually they got back to Northolt and landed and I awaited the inevitable summons. And I was marched in by the adjutant and the customary question "Were you flying that aeroplane which shot up the squadron when I was leading it? "Yes, sir" "What do you think you were doing?" Well, of course in those days you didn't answer, I knew damned well what I was doing and so did he but he wasn't to be diverted. So I got considerable stick, I forget what it was, I don't think I flew for a month or something. But discipline was like that and you didn't answer, you didn't explain, you didn't apologise, you just stood there like the Guardsmen and said nothing.'

Charles Spackman was CO of 1 Squadron from July 1931 until November 1933 and was another officer to reach high rank. He retired in 1950 as Air Vice-Marshal C B S Spackman CB, CBE, DFC and Bar. During the Great War he had been a fighter pilot and had won a DFC flying in Macedonia, earning a Bar to it after the war serving in Iraq. When Spackman left No. 1 in November 1933, he was replaced by another First War fighter pilot, Squadron Leader Roy Chappell MC. Chappell, a South African, had flown with 27 and 41 Squadrons and subsequently had also served in Iraq – flying DH9s with 84 Squadron.

War clouds gather
From 1934 through to 1937 was the golden age of 1 Squadron. During this period they made virtually

a clean sweep of all the trophies and competitions, including the important Annual Air Firing. In 1934 they were given the great honour of appearing at the Canadian Centennial celebrations in Toronto. Five Furies were shipped over to Canada, together with four pilots and twelve airmen. The four pilots were Flight Lieutenant E G H Russell-Stracey and Flying Officers G J S Chatterton, E M Donaldson and F H Dixon. As well as the Toronto display they also demonstrated at a number of other venues and were well received. It was the first time an RAF unit had performed in North America.

All these activities were conducted against a background of increasing international tension. Belatedly, the government had woken up to the threat of German expansion and ordered re-armament. At the end of 1936 there was a virtual clearout of the Squadron, as officers were posted to positions in newly re-formed squadrons. In March 1937 B Flight was closed down for flying, prior to being detached to re-form 72 Squadron. The pilots had the novel experience of having to travel to Gloster's works at Brockworth and ferry fourteen Gloster Gladiators back for the new squadron. Six officers, two NCO pilots and twenty-two other ranks were posted away.

The Zurich Air Meeting
In April 1937 B Flight reformed with three machines and the same month A Flight was selected to give the formation aerobatics display at the Hendon Air Display, as it was now known.

Pilot Officer H E C Boxer (later Air Commodore H E C Boxer CB, OBE) had joined 1 Squadron directly from Cranwell, having won the Sword of Honour and chosen the Squadron as his first posting. He joined with Peter Townsend and both of them felt shy and nervous, with their brand-new wings and uniforms, adorned with only the thin ring of a Pilot Officer. They crept in to camp late at night and went straight to bed. Braving breakfast the following morning, they were greeted with 'Why didn't you let us know last night? We'd have given you a party!'

Boxer recalled the team:

'I was in "A" Flight and my Flight Commander was Flight Lieutenant Teddy Donaldson. We knew of the tied together flight aerobatics of a year or two earlier but Donaldson thought we should try using four aircraft and changing position during the display. The No. 4 slid into box formation immediately after take off. We practiced formation loops and rolls in box position and changed to line astern and echelon formation. The names of the Flight were Flight Lieutenant Teddy Donaldson, Flying Officer "Top" Boxer (No 2), Pilot Officer Johnny Walker (No 3) and Flying Officer Prosser Hanks (No 4).'

The team had been selected after a demonstration at Northolt in front of the officer organising the display. During the summer they gave displays throughout the UK, including the Hendon Air Display, where they were honoured by being presented to the King. At the end of August the same four pilots were chosen to represent the RAF at the International Air Meeting at Zurich. They flew out via Hawkinge, Le Bourget and Dijon. Reserve machines were flown out by Pilot Officer A C Saunders and the Tangmere station commander, Wing Commander C W Hill, who had been promoted to that position from command of 1 Squadron. Three displays were given and there was much competition from the Germans and Italians. No.1 drew tremendous applause from huge crowds, particularly on the last day. The weather was very poor with a low cloud base and rain. However, due to Donaldson's intense practice and insistence on flying in all weathers, they were able to skilfully put on a show despite the conditions. Crichton Boxer described what happened on the last day:

'The Italian aerobatic team asked if we would change places with them, because they wanted to be in the last position of the show. We agreed and took to the air earlier in the show. The weather deteriorated and we were in cloud at the top of each loop and the authorities cancelled the show as soon as we landed. So the Italians lost out!'

The week was a great success and as well as the displays there were opportunities for sightseeing. The team were guests of the Swiss Air Force and each member was allocated an attractive female guide. On the final night there was a banquet that went on until the early hours. The whole event reflected great credit on the RAF and increased British prestige.

Donaldson went on to greater things and regained the world speed record for Britain flying a Gloster Meteor in September 1946. He retired as an Air Commodore and for many years was the aviation correspondent for the *Daily Telegraph*.

The end of 1937 saw both triumph and tragedy. In October Flight Lieutenant H H Peck and Pilot

Officer M H Brown won the Sassoon Pin Pointing Trophy. Just two months later, on 17 December, Peck was killed in a mid-air collision. He was leading an air drill near Chichester when he collided with the machine on his right, flown by Sergeant R E Patten. Both men baled out, but with insufficient height for their parachutes to deploy they were killed.

In January 1938 Squadron Leader I A Bertram assumed command of the Squadron. This was his second tour with them, having been a flight commander during 1931-1932.

On 22 February another pilot was killed near Lewes Race Course. Pilot Officer M V Baxter broke formation without permission, and losing height struck a high voltage electricity line. The leader saw a flash, though the wreckage did not catch fire. The visibility was poor and the cable difficult to see, as there was a 500 feet interval between pylons.

The experience level at this time was quite low, with the influx of new pilots, but by the time war was declared many of these pilots had progressed from being new boys to the flight commanders who would fight the Battle of France and the Battle of Britain. Three of the Squadron's pre-war pilots – Prosser Hanks, 'Johnny' Walker and M H 'Hilly' Brown – were to bring more glory to the Squadron in the coming conflict.

The end of the Fury
When introduced into RAF service in May 1931 the Fury had been the fastest fighter in the world. Eight years later it was considerably slower than the new breed of monoplane bomber, such as the Bristol Blenheim and Fairey Battle. From being the premier fighter squadron of the RAF, 1 Squadron now had to watch with envy, as other units were equipped with the new, sleek, Hawker Hurricanes and Supermarine Spitfires. Even worse their gleaming brightly coloured machines had to be painted in drab green and brown camouflage! Gone were the highly polished cowlings on which much elbow grease had been employed and also gone were the brilliant, distinctive squadron markings.

After the Munich fiasco of September 1938 the whole atmosphere at Tangmere changed. Not only were the aeroplanes camouflaged but so too were the hangars and other buildings. Air raid shelters were built. The halcyon, golden days of the 1920s and 1930s and 'the best flying club in the world' were gone – never to return.

PART TWO

Chapter Seven

HURRICANE SQUADRON

The RAF's expansion plans were for both more squadrons and more modern aeroplanes. At Fighter Command, the latter meant a final goodbye to the biplane, planning its future on the new and exciting Supermarine Spitfire and Hawker Hurricane monoplanes – more commonly referred to as the new eight-gun fighters.

The Hurricane had entered service with 111 Squadron at RAF Northolt at the end of 1937 and 19 Squadron got the first Spitfires in the summer of 1938. Both squadrons put their and the RAF's new fighters through their paces, flying them almost to destruction in order to discover their strengths and weaknesses in front line operations. Neither were found wanting and soon more squadrons were beginning to re-equip with these types.

No.1 Squadron were ordered to send three pilots to the Hawker works at Brooklands on 15 October 1938 and after being shown to 'knobs and tits' flew three new Hurricanes back to Tangmere. In this they beat 43 Squadron by a couple of months much to 1 Squadron's delight and 43's chagrin.

There was a lot to get used to with the new aeroplane, not least the clean lines and powerful Merlin engine which gave it far more speed than had been achieved with the Fury. In addition there was a retractable undercarriage, a sliding cockpit cover (hood), good upwards visibility without that top wing, and a variable two-speed (and initially two-bladed) propeller.

Just two days following the arrival of the first three machines, the Squadron's Annual Inspection took place, the inspecting officer being Air Vice-Marshal Ernest L Gossage CB CVO DSO MC, the AOC of No. 11 (Fighter) Group. Not only did this go off without a hitch, but by the end of the first week in November, the Squadron had fully equipped with Hurricanes.

Accidents were bound to occur. A pilot overshot on landing on 24 November, badly damaging L1677 while another pilot crash-landed L1691 on the airfield on 5 January. The next prang in the new year of 1939 occurred on 14 January, but this time it was in the Squadron Magister. Flying Officer A C Douglas flew into high ground in very bad visibility during a flight down from Martlesham Heath and was killed. Sergeant A V Hancock hit the ground at night in a Hurricane just to the south-east of Debden on 7 February during a night cross-country, writing-off L1682, while Sergeant W A Cuthbert died trying to force-land in L1692 just outside the airfield on 13 March.

Pilot Officer Paul Richey was the first to reach the dying pilot. His engine had cut out and he hadn't made the airfield. Blood was coming from the lad's ears. Not the best of sights for Richey who was about to take up a Hurricane for the first time.

A new Commanding Officer
Ian Bertram ended his long association with the Squadron in April 1939, replaced by Squadron Leader P J H Halahan. Patrick Halahan was a larger than life character, not only in looks but in personality. To family and friends he was known as Pat but to colleagues and associates in the Service, he was referred to as 'Bull'. As one might suspect, the Halahan family originated from Ireland and many of the male line were fighting men. Pat had an uncle who died at Zeebrugge in WW1 (DSO), another (Frederick) also served in the Navy and later the RNAS (1915) and RAF (and whose flight lieutenant son was killed in a flying accident with the RAF in 1941). This uncle rose to Air Vice-Marshal CMG CBE DSO MVO and, as Commandant at Cranwell, it was he who gave permission for the legless Douglas Bader to fly again in WW2. Yet another uncle commanded the Essex Regiment in WW1 (OBE).

Pat's father John had been in the Royal Dublin Fusiliers, saw action in the Boer War and later served in the Royal Flying Corps and RAF. He learnt to fly in 1912 and was later a Group Captain CBE AFC. Yet another Navy uncle learnt to fly in 1913 but later died in the submarine *E18* in the Baltic in 1916.

Patrick was born in 1908 and with so many flying influences in his life it was natural he should join the RAF. He gradually made his way up the ladder of command, often deathly slow in the peacetime air force, so it was no surprise that he was in his late 20s when considered for squadron commander. When he took over No.1 Squadron, he was 31, and previous to this appointment he had been at AHQ in Iraq from October 1936 and before that, adjutant at the RAF College, since 1932.

Halahan's job was to continue to bring his squadron to operational readiness on the new aeroplanes. There seemed little doubt now that Britain and her Empire would soon be at war again with Germany. The Squadron then had a visit from a chap from Air Ministry who had been assistant air attaché in Berlin. As he described the equipment and the numbers of Luftwaffe aircraft it was a sobering moment, and all felt glad they had not gone to war at the time of Munich.

As that summer of 1939 began and then blazed, tension began to mount at Tangmere. The young pilots of course saw it as a great adventure. If war did come they would be in it from day one, and like their counterparts in 1914, they would head the British forces into France again but this time they had very modern fighters and were well trained. Unfortunately, the RAF bomber arm was not so well equipped, and they would go to France with an already out-moded three-man single-engined bomber, the Fairey Battle, plus some Blenheims, which, if unescorted, only had a little fairer chance of survival against Germany's equally modern fighter, the Messerschmitt 109E. Meantime, a crash during a night flying exercise on 26 June cost the life of Flying Officer W O C Hemmings.

The C-in-C Fighter Command, Air Marshal Sir Hugh Dowding, was well aware that his command was under strength and was not best pleased to accede to the political decision that four of his fighter squadrons were to be sent to France if war began. Nos. 85 and 87 were to form the Air Component, attached to support the British Army, while 1 and 73 would form the Advanced Air Striking Force's fighter element.

War

On Friday 1 September Hitler invaded Poland. Just a few days earlier the Squadron was told it was to become a mobile unit. This came a few days after a load of mobilised reservists descended upon them. As the Squadron was full to establishment, these men were given the responsibility for the unit's mobility and equipment *in the field*. With no rankers in this bunch, Halahan got them to select their own NCOs and then a number were sent off to acquire vehicles from an MT park at Wembley. They did this with a flourish, returning with more vehicles than allowed, and Halahan was so pleased he did them the service of making sure the excess were well concealed until needed. The Squadron diary records that the unit had been sent no less than 42 vehicles of all descriptions, but what is not recorded is how many were assigned and how many 'acquired'. This reminds the author of a story he was told about a bomber squadron, whose CO, as war was declared, ordered all vehicles out of the station and dispersed around the countryside. This was fine except that large numbers appeared to congregate around local pubs at lunchtimes, and if the Germans had really attacked and had known this, they could have wiped out all RAF vehicles simply by attacking all public houses around airfields.

By now the Squadron had received orders from Air Ministry that a Special Advanced Party of 16 Hurricanes must be ready to move off for France at one hour's notice. Total support personnel should not exceed 100 and they must take 30 tons of stores to cover a two-week period.

On Saturday the 2nd, 1 Squadron was ordered to standby for France. The next day, while the sun shone, the British Prime Minister announced in sombre tones that Britain was once again at war with Germany. The following morning the ground party left by train under Squadron Leader D A Pemberton, of 67 Wing, for an unknown destination. Meanwhile the aircraft were dispersed around the airfield, and three tents were pitched for use by the pilots and crews on standby.

News then came that not all was well with the advance party in France so Squadron Leader Halahan took off to sort out the problems, leaving Flight Lieutenant P R Walker in charge of the air party. On the morning of the 8th came the order to depart.

To France

According to the Squadron diary it was led to France by the senior flight commander, P R 'Johnny' Walker, taking off from Tangmere some time after 1130 am and landing at Octeville, Le Havre, France at 1245. Meantime the transport section and vehicles left Southampton by ship under the command of Pilot Officer D H Blomeley. However, the list of those flying out includes the CO, so either he did not 'lead' or at the last moment – perhaps having arrived suddenly back from France himself – did lead. Otherwise he was just listed as a courtesy, with the Hurricane he flew to France in on the 7th. We don't know for sure.

Squadron Leader P J H Halahan L1905

A Flight		B Flight	
F/L P R Walker	L1676	F/L G H F Plinston	L1960
Sgt F J Soper	L1681	Sgt F G Berry	L1686

F/O S W Baldie	L1943	F/O B Drake	L1687
Sgt New	L1944	Sgt A V Clowes	L1689
F/O P P Hanks	L1969	Sgt R A Albonico	L1927
F/O M H Brown	L1925	F/O L R Clisby	L1693
P/O R H M Richey	L1971	P/O P W E Mould	L1842
P/O W H Stratton	L1685		

Pilots who went by sea were Pilot Officers C D Palmer, G P H Matthews, C N Birch, C G H Crusoe and Blomeley. However, from the recollections of A T M 'Knackers' Henniker it is more likely that the CO remained in France and is merely listed as a courtesy, having already 'gone over' in L1905. Henniker held a unique post with the Squadron at this time being the civilian Rolls-Royce Rep, tasked with looking after the RAF's Merlin engines, until September, working with the Battle squadrons.

Given the choice of going to Biggin Hill or France, Henniker chose France and would be attached to 67 Wing – 1 and 73 Squadrons – and duly arrived at Tangmere for the move. He recalls:

'Tangmere became the arena for a unique and unforgettable spectacle. As No.1 took off for France in sections of three and formed up circling the aerodrome, watched by No.43 Squadron, No.73 arrived and had just time to land and disperse around the aerodrome as two other Hurricane squadrons appeared, also to refuel before crossing the Channel. The aerodrome and sky seemed full of Hurricanes – five squadrons – an amazing sight and it all looked a little hectic. No.1's CO was already in Le Havre and I was to go with F/O "Leak" Crusoe bringing the rear party of ground personnel.

We mustered at 5 am the following morning to commence the train-boat-train journey via Southampton, Cherbourg and Rouen to Le Havre. That night we spent zig-zagging across the Channel and 16½ hours later we were met at Le Havre by the CO and the Equipment Officer, F/O Donald Hills (later Air-Vice Marshal) at 0200 hours and taken to a monastery which had been commandeered for the officer's mess.'

While 'Mr' Henniker awaited his commission into the RAF, he wore his civilian clothes but this later upset the French so he was kitted out with borrowed bits and pieces, the tunic being one of Johnny Walker's spares, so for a while he wandered about with flight lieutenant tapes up. The day after the aircraft arrived, the Squadron took off at 1135 to fly over Le Havre on a demo flight for the local inhabitants but in the late afternoon orders were received to move to Cherbourg and the aircraft landed there shortly after 7 pm. The Wing was required to give air cover to the port as several ships were about to arrive from England, not least among which was that bringing 1 Squadron's ground party. That evening their ship docked in the port of Brest. Commencing the next morning the Squadron were tasked to fly continual three-man patrols from dawn till 1500 hours, at which time another 60 Wing squadron took over. 1 Squadron continued patrols from 1900 till sunset. It was all very dull but there was a certain amount of excitement. They were in France, flying patrols and were part of the great adventure. The anti-climax was not long in coming.

On the 11th the Squadron flew back to Octeville where over the next few days the officers and airmen busied themselves by digging slit trenches in case of air raids. This done the pilots flew gun tests over the sea, and then in the air. On the 19th the CO led the pilots on a recce patrol to Rouen, Beauvais, Amiens and Dieppe, the same day Flying Officer Harris, the adjutant, arrived by air.

Nobody was surprised after all the hard work with the trenches that the Squadron received orders to move base to Norrent Fontes, near St Omer, on the 26th. Everyone had arrived by the last day of September, all being housed under canvas. As might be expected it rained for two weeks. 'Knackers' Henniker:

'With no regrets at leaving Le Havre I went ahead in No.1's "Maggie" with Billy Stratton. Landing at our new aerodrome – a large field – I met Squadron Leader Pemberton, the Ops Officer for the Wing. Stratton returned to Le Havre leaving me and "Pembers" to start organising the camp. We chose a site to pitch our tents in a small field at the edge of the aerodrome near the St Omer road, from where on a clear day one could see Vimy Ridge.

We acquired two large French mess tents to supplement the Squadron's normal issue. Aircraft and engine maintenance was going to be carried out in the open, tools and equipment remaining in the Crossley lorries. Warrant Officer Lee had a very competent and keen maintenance team seldom requiring my assistance. As the others arrived we dug trenches, made furniture from four-gallon petrol tins and their boxes, and soon found that sleeping in tents in early October was quite chilly without mattresses.

The Doc's ambulance was borrowed to visit Lille for extra provisions, blankets and dangerous-looking petrol stoves, and to have a hot bath. There was no enemy activity so we began to feel settled again. The only excitement was when the DeHavilland Dragon Rapide arrived from Tangmere with the mail from home. A little bartering was done with the pilot who brought cigarettes in exchange for Champagne, and posted our letters in England, thus avoiding delay and censoring.'

* * *

Two or three of the Squadron pilots were not long with the unit in France but the majority of them were to gain undying fame with it. Pat Halahan of course would always be known as its first wartime CO. Peter Walker, inevitably 'Johnny', a Suffolk man, was 25 and had been in the RAF since 1935. Peter Prosser Hanks, from York, was 22 and another 1935 entrant. A long and successful war and RAF career was ahead of him (DSO DFC AFC), retiring as a Group Captain.

John 'Killy' Kilmartin came from Eire and was 26. Most of his life had been spent in Australia and then in China, but he returned to England to join the RAF in 1936. At first he had been with 43 Squadron at Tangmere before moving to Halahan's outfit in November 1939. He retired as a Wing Commander OBE DFC in 1958. Billy Drake (Billy not William!) came from London but had been educated in Switzerland. Joining the RAF in 1936, he was not yet 22 by the time he flew to France. After France he saw much action in West and North Africa. He also retired as a Group Captain DSO DFC & Bar, DFC(US).

Paul Richey, from Chelsea, was 23, and had spent time in both Albania and Switzerland. He joined the RAF in 1937. In the Battle of Britain he was a fighter controller and in 1941 a flight commander on Spitfires. After a period on Typhoons he saw service in the Far East. Well known for his famous book *Fighter Pilot* which has not been out of print since 1941, he left the service as a Wing Commander DFC & Bar, Belgian Order of the Crown, French and Belgian Croix de Guerres, and after the war, was made a Chevalier of the Légion d'Honneur. Mark Henry Brown ('Hilly') was a Canadian and he joined the RAF in 1936. After a successful time in France and during the Battle of Britain he had received the DFC & Bar but was to die in action over Sicily from Malta as a Wing Leader.

Cyril Dampier 'Pussy' Palmer was born in America in March 1918, and also joined the RAF pre-war. He won the DFC in France but was to die in action in October 1942 as a Squadron Leader and leaving a widow. William 'Stratters' Stratton came from New Zealand and was 23, having joined the RAF in 1937. He later saw action in the Middle East and then the Far East before transferring to the RNZAF in 1944. He received the DFC & Bar and retired as an Air Vice-Marshal CB CBE.

Peter 'Boy' Mould, 22, came from Rutland, and joined the RAF as a Halton apprentice (*Boy* Entrant) in 1933, gaining a Cranwell cadetship in 1937. After a brief spell with 74 Squadron he joined 1 Squadron shortly before war began. In 1941 he took part in the first delivery of Hurricanes to the island of Malta from HMS *Ark Royal* and then saw considerable action with 185 Squadron, which he commanded. He received a Bar to his DFC but was killed in action on 1 October. Les Clisby was a 25-year-old Australian and came to the RAF via the RAAF in 1937. He joined 1 Squadron shortly before it moved to France but despite a good deal of success – and a DFC – he did not survive the French campaign.

Pete Matthews came from Cheshire and was 20. He joined the RAF in 1937 and had arrived on the Squadron a month before the war began. After France and the Battle of Britain he saw considerable action in North Africa. He received the DFC in May 1941 and rose to Wing Commander in the postwar RAF.

Of the NCO-pilots three gained a good measure of fame and success. Arthur Victor 'Darky' Clowes, from Derbyshire, joined the RAF as a Halton apprentice in 1929, later volunteering for pilot training. Gaining both the DFM and after being commissioned, the DFC, he eventually rose to Squadron Leader and also saw action in the Middle East. Francis Joseph Soper, from Devon, was 27. Another former apprentice he joined up in 1928, and he too received the DFM, and later the DFC with 257 Squadron in 1941 which he commanded. He was lost over the North Sea in October 1941. Frederick George Berry was born in India, and was 25. A Halton apprentice too since 1929, he volunteered for pilot training in 1936 and his first squadron was 1 Squadron's rivals at Tangmere, No.43. Winning the DFM he was to die in the Battle of Britain.

* * *

Things had changed a little since the pre-war plan for the four Hurricane squadrons in France. Once war came it was hoped that the French Air Force might provide protection for the Battles and

Blenheims of the AASF, but this had proved wanting, therefore all four squadrons were attached to the AASF and two Gladiator squadrons had been sent from England to operate with the Air Component. Air Marshal A S Barrett CMG MC (known to everyone as 'Ugly') commanded the BAFF – British Air Forces in France – while Air Vice-Marshal C H B Blount OBE MC was in charge of 60 Wing. Paul Richey remembered the moment 1 Squadron got the change of job:

'One day the Fairey Battles that were down in the east of France – the AASF – were shot up by Messerschmitts over the Maginot Line. Our CO, Squadron Leader Bull Halahan, was very quick off the mark, flew down there and saw the AOC, Air Vice-Marshal Patrick Playfair, and said we ought to be here looking after you. We've got four Hurricane squadrons up in the north doing little except convoy patrols and generally stooging around so why don't you have our Hurricane Wing with you?'

Vassincourt

It was obviously going to be a war of movement, for at the start of October the Squadron was again uprooted, this time going to Neuville (Vassincourt), near Bar-le-Duc, which was 40 miles east of Nancy. Billets were found in the nearby village. It was not lost on anyone that this was bang in the middle of an area which had seen much action in WW1, by the French and Americans. 'Knackers' Henniker:

'The move started badly and proved to be quite eventful. The weather was not good and threatened to worsen. The camp was aroused at 5 am, Billy Stratton and I climbing into the "Maggie" feeling dirty and cold. We were flying at 900 feet and within ten minutes the Squadron's Hurricanes had caught up with us, flying in open formation. I then saw what seemed, in the grey light, to be four balls of fire rising from the ground into the midst of the Hurricanes. As the Squadron broke formation and scattered I realised they were being fired on.

This seemed to be a signal for other trigger-happy gentlemen, whose orders were not to fire on anything below 1,000 feet! Then our little Maggie suddenly dropped its port wing as several puffs of black smoke blossomed around us. We were now at 800 feet and my mouth was very dry. Tracer shells were also coming up, but Stratton was doing unusual things with the aeroplane and losing height rapidly, then suddenly the shooting stopped.

However, the rear party were flying up in four Air France aircraft – Wibault three-engined passenger aircraft that could possibly be mistaken for Ju52s. Firing began again and one aircraft received a shell through the rear fuselage and tailplane but managed to continue. The fourth one had one wing badly damaged and had to force-land, luckily without casualties. Nothing official was ever heard about this incident and it was soon forgotten.

We were now heading south from the Luxembourg border to Vassincourt. Stratton landed at 88 Squadron's base to check for damage, although our real reason was to scrounge breakfast, and because of our dishevelled appearance accepted the offer of a bath.

Finally arriving at the new base, Doc Cross had organised accommodation in Neuville-sur-Marne, our dormitory village a mile from the aerodrome. The room he acquired in the village Marie for a mess was small and cold, but his real "find" in the nearest town of Bar-le-Duc, some ten miles away, was the Hotel de Metz et Commerce where the Squadron were having the first of many meals. Stratton and I meantime arrived at the gloomy and empty mess. This was the room in which we were to spend long winter evenings, and days, when it rained or snowed incessantly. Where combat reports and letters home were written; where a captured German airman, ENSA concert parties and Sir Cyril Newall (CAS) were all entertained. A room in which Lord Londonderry, Billy Cotton and his Band and other visitors shared our rations, where darts, shove-ha'penny and cards were played and where it sometimes became a little alcoholic. Today the room looks much the same; perhaps it's just as well the walls can't talk.'

As the autumn chill arrived everyone was awaiting the start of the war for real. The first clashes in the air had already taken place, although not involving No.1 Squadron. Then on the 15th the CO led aircraft to Etain from where patrols were flown to Saarlautern to 40 miles east – inside the German frontier. Some desultry AA fire came up from Saarbrucken and Saarlautern and then four enemy fighters were spotted but seeing a superior number of Hurricanes, quickly dived eastwards before they could be engaged. Yet however fleeting, some of the pilots had seen the enemy for the first time.

No.73 Squadron now moved into Rouvres, 20 miles to the north, near Etain. Wing Commander C Walter commanded the Wing, No.67, assisted by Squadron Leader D A Pemberton. 1 and 73 were now only about 70 miles from the French Maginot Line, that vast defensive system built in the 1930s and deemed impregnable. Whether it was or not was never put to the test.

On 22 October a conference was convened at 67 Wing HQ at Reims, where Wing Commander Walter made it clear to Halahan and Squadron Leader B W 'Red' Knox, the CO of 73, that their squadrons' primary tasks if any invasion should come was to escort RAF bombers and fly patrols to counter enemy raids. 1 Squadron was given the area between Metz and Nancy to protect, while 73 would look after the area Thionville to Verdun.

First encounters

Action with the German Luftwaffe finally came on 30 October 1939. At two-thirty in the afternoon three enemy aircraft were seen from the airfield flying at high altitude and the Readiness Section took off. The German formation split but one of the bombers was overtaken at 18,000 feet, ten miles south-west of Toul and shot down by Boy Mould. It was the Squadron's first victory since 1918 and the first German aircraft shot down by the RAF in France in WW2. The Dornier 17P (Wk.No.4144) of 2(F)/123 (coded 4U+BK) dived into the ground one mile north of the village of Sauvigny, near the hamlet of Traveron, 15 km west of Toul. The Dornier captain had been Hauptmann Baldwin von Normann und Audenhove, the Group CO, his crew being Oberleutnant Hermann Heisterbergh and Feldwebel Freidrich Pfeiffer. Part of the aircraft was excavated in 1999.

The Squadron, quite naturally, was overwhelmed by the press and reporters proved very tiresome to everyone after a while. Halahan eventually banned any from coming into the Officers' Mess. Billy Drake had been airborne during this combat and remembers:

> 'We had all been a bit excited about the first Hun. We'd all had a bit of a dabble and I had a go at one. Mostly in the early days, all you'd see was a contrail, then we'd take off and try to find it. We'd just had a radar organisation set up but it never seemed to work, so we were just following these trails all over the place.'

The radar Billy Drake refers to was under the direction of Flying Officer T C 'Toby' Carter. Toby Carter had learnt to fly with the Cambridge University Air Squadron and commissioned into the RAFVR. In 1939, whilst reading Physics at Cambridge, he was approached by Air Ministry, and asked if he would help with scientific work of great national importance. He agreed and so entered the secret world of RDF (radar). Soon after war was declared he took his section to France. The radar used was a type GM1 which had two 70-foot timer lattice towers, a transmitter and receiver each in a trailer, powered by a generator. Only six were built and their performance very poor. Toby Carter set up his unit near the Luxembourg border but was later ordered to get as far away from the border as he could, so chose a spot 51 miles away, at Vassincourt. In all he had a complement of 20, half radio mechanics and operators who were all young regulars, the rest drivers and aircraft hands, mostly reservists, including some old WW1 soldier veterans. Toby recalls:

> 'Mine was the first GM unit to go to France, The instructions I received from AM was that radar was terribly secret and we must not breathe a word to anybody, but that I must supply information about enemy aircraft movements to No.1 and 73 Squadrons. At Vassincourt almost all our needs were met by No.1 Squadron which had its own adjutant, equipment and engineer officers. The French were supposed to handle security but I do not recall ever seeing any. Furthermore, the local population was by no means entirely friendly; more than one of the Squadron officers was shot at while going to or from the Mess to his billet on a dark night.
>
> Close proximity of the radar site to the Squadron fostered a collaboration that made up, to some extent, for the loss of 50 miles range, but several German aircraft were shot down by the two squadrons. Soon much of Europe was gripped by appalling weather that froze everything and curtailed flying. Even a crate of beer left in the Mess overnight froze solid and the bottles burst.
>
> I did get 1 Squadron to fly some calibration for me, but their main effect was to demonstrate the appallingly poor performance of the GM1. Later GM sets all went to the north of France and my association with the Squadon came to an end. I knew Halahan as Pat rather than Bull, as his family and mine were friends in the early 1920s.'

In the oft-used picture of Prosser Hanks landing at Vassincourt one can just make out the radar unit's two 70-foot poles to the right of the trees.

* * *

Bull Halahan and his flight commanders were more than aware of some of the shortcomings with current RAF tactics. Already they had discarded the approved firing spread of the Hurricane's eight .303 machine guns. This had been devised, more or less, to help the average pilot put the maximum number of bullets into a target, but the experienced 1 Squadron pilots had argued that by harmonising the guns so that the mass of bullets converged at a more concentrated point ahead of the aeroplane, if a target was there it would be severely hit. Paul Richey told me (NF):

'The substitution of spot harmonisation of our Hurricane's guns at 250 yards for the Dowding Spread at 400 yards was our idea. Others may have started this in 1940 but we had already done it secretly at our annual squadron armament camp at Sutton Bridge as early as April 1939 and without telling anyone, and had kept it. It undoubtedly accounted for our marksmanship in France and became the subject of a special investigation by the Air Ministry in the spring of 1940 and subsequent adoption by all RAF fighters.'

This helped again on 23 November. At 1030 an enemy aircraft was plotted flying west towards Commercy at 20,000 feet. Flying Officer Pussy Palmer, already in the air, was told of the bandit and two other pilots who had just left the ground were also informed. The bandit was now over Bar-le-Duc going south-west, then exploding AA shells were seen. The three Hurricane pilots quickly picked out a Dornier 17 and each attacked, the Dornier being forced down. Two parachutes were seen to open, so victory seemed assured.

Palmer throttled back and flew alongside the Dornier, but it seems the German pilot too throttled back and Palmer overshot. The records state the German pilot, Unteroffizier Arno Fassberger of recce unit 4(F)/122, then went forward and manned the front machine gun, fired into the Hurricane, knocked out its engine and forced Palmer to make a forced landing. However, as Palmer was looking for a place to put down, the Dornier's engines stopped. Fassberger put his machine down near Moiremont, west of Verdun, where he was taken prisoner. That evening he was dined by the Squadron before going off to a PoW camp.

Not long after this another German machine was spotted, this time by a patrol led by Flight Lieutenant George Plinston patrolling Verdun to Metz. It was ahead and above them, heading towards German territory. The three Hurricane pilots gave chase and caught it up over the frontier. Most of Plinston's and all of his No.2's guns froze up but Sergeant Clowes attacked successfully and the Heinkel 111, from 2(F)/122, went down over Saarbrucken and crashed near Königsmacher on the east bank of the Moselle, near Thionville. Four crewmen were taken prisoner, and one gunner died.

Far from being any help, six French Hawk 75 fighters now appeared on the scene and attacked Clowes and smashed up his tailplane. The Squadron diary notes that their fire shot away half of the rudder and one of the elevators, but it appears in reality that one of the eager Hawk pilots actually collided with the Hurricane. Palmer managed to get back to Vassincourt where he made a creditable crash landing without injury to himself. In the event, this kill was shared by Palmer, Flying Officer N Orton from 73 Squadron who had also made a pass, and three French Hawk pilots of GC II/5, each of whom said they had attacked too. 1 Squadron probably wondered if their French allies wanted to claim a Hurricane as well!

It was proving a busy day. At 1400 hours Squadron Leader Halahan and Hilly Brown, on patrol between Verdun and Metz, saw AA fire and upon investigation spotted a Dornier 17. Both pilots attacked from astern individually and the German went down in flames east of Metz, although only three of Brown's guns worked. The German unit – Aufklärer 122 – had lost another aircraft to 1 Squadron, this one also from the 4th Staffel, coming down outside Haumont les Lachoussee, near Longuyon, Oberfeldwebel Baptist Schapp and his crew all being lost. From Fassberger's Dornier the Squadron salvaged a 7.9 mm machine gun as a souvenir, which was to feature in several Squadron photographs.

French fighters had tried to horn-in on this third kill too but it was rightly credited to Halahan and Brown. Paul Richey had also had a recent experience with the French. He had been heavily engaged by Morane 406 fighters while on a lone patrol and it took all of his expertise to avoid being shot down. In the event he got lost and had to put down at a French airfield. Meantime, one of the French fighter pilots had called up this same airfield and instructed them to pick up a downed German pilot in the area. They informed their French colleague they 'had' the pilot, who was British and badly wounded! The French proceeded to bandage their guest then awaited the crest-fallen French pilot as he landed. One look at the mournful face of the French NCO pilot was enough for Paul to end the charade – then it was drinks all round.

These encounters with French fighters led to RAF aircraft in France having the red, white and blue tail markings applied to the whole of the rudder of all aircraft, in the same way the French painted their rudders. It was hoped this similar marking would prevent problems in the future. The code letters JX, of course, had been obliterated some time after landing in France.

Three days later three new pilots were posted in to the Squadron, Pilot Officers J S Mitchell, Shepherd and a Canadian, R G Lewis, but they came after the recent excitement, and as winter's grip began to bite. On 7 December, Squadron Leader Halahan with four of his officers, one sergeant and two airmen went to Villeneuve to represent the Squadron during a visit by the King, who was also to bestow recently awarded medals to RAF personnel the next day.

Just over a week later the Squadron received a 32-seat coach together with a driver. Shades of 1914, but it was useful for transporting men about, especially with so many billetted some distance from the airfield. Billy Drake recalls this time:

'For us in France is was something brand new with nobody to really guide one. None of our senior officers had really fought, and then that terrible winter. It was the coldest bloody winter I think I've ever come across; we used red-hot bricks wrapped in towels as hot water bottles.

It was a sort of dream world that we lived in at Vassincourt, going into Bar-le-Duc for the odd cup of tea, perhaps laced with whisky, at the "Lion D'Or". Getting to really know your chums who you'd known for quite a long time but now it was wartime. Sometimes you saw something in people you didn't expect.

The CO was away much of the time and so Johnny Walker virtually ran the Squadron. Everyone had great affection for Johnny, and later my flight commander was Prosser Hanks – a great chap.'

The New Year – 1940
Despite the severe weather, several patrols were flown during January 1940, but these occasioned a number of engine problems due no doubt to the cold. However, the pilots concerned generally managed to land safely. After the flurry of air combat the previous autumn there was a distinct lack of contact with the Luftwaffe until 22 February. Because of the weather, the Squadron had sent three Hurricanes to Rouvres the previous day for Ops. On the 22nd, Boy Mould flew a patrol with Shepherd and Mitchell between Grandpré and Triacourt taking off at 0950.

The two new pilots lost their leader in cloud and returned to the airfield but at 1030, Mould saw a He111K flying at 19,000 feet north-west of St Menehould. He dived on it out of the sun and fired. The Heinkel dived steeply followed by the Hurricane pilot down to a mere 20-30 feet above the ground, Mould firing as his guns came to bear. Down on the deck his ammo ran out and his last sight of the German machine was as it flew on into Belgium. On landing he found that four of his guns had stopped through defective ammunition. The Heinkel, another recce machine, this time from 1(F)/122, had had a lucky escape.

March began with a flurry of activity. Patrols were flown throughout the morning of the 2nd between Nancy and Metz. Shortly before 11 am, Hilly Brown, Soper and Mitchell took their turn and within ten minutes Brown spotted an unidentified aircraft east of Pont à Mousson, but then lost it in a turn. Sergeant Soper then saw a Dornier 17 at 24,000 feet and after calling his leader, broke away to chase it, making an attack near Luneville. As Soper finished his first pass, Brown closed in and as he was about to press the gun button his engine belched smoke and he had to pull away. He lost height rapidly and finding his wheels selector had failed, had to make a belly landing on the airfield at Nancy. Inspection showed that his airscrew had vibrated loose from the propeller boss – not caused by enemy action.

Meantime, Soper and Mitchell continued to pursue and attack the Dornier, which began to trail smoke from one motor. Then Soper saw Mitchell break off with smoke pouring from his engine. Soper closed in once more and finished his ammo on the Dornier, then headed down towards Mitchell's Hurricane. Mitchell said he was having difficulty due to the smoke and Soper directed him to put down on a suitable field. Having selected one, Soper then saw Mitchell lower his wheels whereupon the experienced NCO told Mitchell to make a belly landing and to retract his undercarriage. However, Mitchell had left his radio on 'send' and did not hear the advice, and being short of fuel, Soper had to head for home. Mitchell crashed one mile south of Sarre-Union and was killed.

Soper made no immediate claim for the Dornier, but their combined fire had taken effect. The machine, from 4(F)/11, piloted by Oberleutnant Adolf Leupold, made a smooth crash-landing near La Petit Pierre, 15 miles north-east of Sarrebourg. It appears that the crew put up some resistance to their capture for all were wounded before giving themselves up, although a note in the Squadron diary records that the French told them only two had been wounded.

The following day Brown and Soper were on patrol in the same area, taking off at 1120. Within half an hour they saw a German machine dead ahead and above, some three miles distant, flying north at 26,000 feet. The two Hurricanes were 4,000 feet below but they began to climb, led by Soper, and attacked from below but were fired on by the German belly gunner. However, the RAF pilots' fire took effect and both engines of the Heinkel began to leave smoke trails, then it headed down to crash-land in a field south of Forbach. As Brown and Soper circled the spot they saw two men climb out and place a small object under the nose of the aeroplane, then run off towards their own lines. Shortly afterwards the Heinkel became enveloped in a ball of blue flame.

The aircraft was another recce machine, this time from 3(F)/121, and the radio operator and a gunner had been killed during the combat. The pilot, Unteroffizier Fredy Nagel, had also been wounded, but he and the other crew man managed to evade into No-Man's-Land where they were rescued by a German infantry patrol.

Now that the winter weather was beginning to ease, some Nissen huts were erected for an Operations Room, a crew room and for the maintenance and armament sections. The Squadron also began using an Advanced Landing Ground (ALG) at Azelot. Another innovation for the Squadron, and a welcome one, was that its Hurricanes were fitted with rear armour plate behind the pilot's seat during March. While the weight slightly altered the flying characteristics of the aircraft the installations added to the pilot's confidence. Not that any of the pilots had yet encountered the much vaunted German fighters, the single-seat Messerschmitt 109E or the twin-engined *Zerstörer* – the Me110. But other units had, including the French, and it was a comfort to know that in a surprise attack from behind by a German fighter, the heavy armour would give some protection to the pilot. Until now of course, official Air Ministry thinking was that with only bombers to contend with over Britain, rear armour had not been necessary. Actions in France forced a change of heart, which was just as well as the year progressed.

Two more pilots arrived on the 14th, Pilot Officer R H Shaw RAFVR and then Flying Officer H N E Salmon RAFO. With such an experienced crowd as 1 Squadron it was not surprising that Squadron Leader Halahan was soon moaning to HQ that these reserve-type pilots were insufficiently trained as far as he was concerned. They had had little or no training in the use of R/T and had never used oxygen. With an already busy work routine, the Bull was not keen to waste time training men he felt should be of a higher standard. While one might sympathise, there was a war on, and he was left to get on with it. 1 Squadron also lost its medical officer, Flight Lieutenant E H E Cross, replaced by a VR 'Doc' – Flight Lieutenant D M Brown. The new Doc quickly put his stamp on things, ordering an immediate clean-up of the village of Neuville, which must have upset the populace somewhat!

* * *

First contact with German fighters
Almost as if the new seat armour for the Hurricanes tempted the fates, German fighters were encountered for the first time. This came on 25 March but the skirmish with some Me110s was brief and no results came of it. Temptation of another kind came within hours. Air Marshal Barratt, BAFF's Commander-in-Chief, announced the promise of a dinner in Paris for the first RAF pilot to shoot down a Me110.

The Me110, similar to the RAF Blenheim 1f and the French Potez 63, came from the perceived idea that because of the distances from Germany to France and Britain, single-seat fighters would not have the combat ranges necessary, and therefore a heavier, twin-engined fighter would be required. What appeared not to be fully appreciated was that in such long-range operations that were envisaged, these types must inevitably run into the more agile single-seaters and be at a disadvantage. Once France fell, of course, the Luftwaffe needed the 110 to escort bombers to England, and these were often at the mercy of Spitfires and Hurricanes.

However, in the spring of 1940, the propaganda hype about the Me110 was such that it was thought this machine would create a distinct problem for any sort of French or British aircraft, so the Allied air force commanders were keen to see if, when encountered, it could be overcome. Hence Barratt's generous offer.

Four days later came not only the first success against the 110, but also against the Me109E. That morning Pussy Palmer, Paul Richey and Pete Matthews were on patrol over Metz at 20,000 feet, and Richey saw AA fire to the north. Heading towards it an aircraft was spotted and chased but they lost it. Hoping to pick it up again they continued north and climbed to 25,000 feet and at 0930 Richey's keen eyesight picked out two Me109s to their left, about 1,000 feet above but flying in the opposite direction.

The three Hurricanes climbed and turned in behind the 109s which began to circle too. There was some R/T mess-up and in those moments one Hurricane dived away but Paul banked round and one Messerschmitt attacked him; Paul shook the 109 loose and got behind it. Opening fire at 300 yards he discovered his gun button was sticking and his bursts were too long and using up precious ammo. However, his three or four long bursts produced smoke from the fuselage and the 109 began to go down in a vertical spiral, followed by Richey, still firing. As his guns finally fell silent the 109 was still going down steeply but then another 109 came onto the scene, so Richey broke away and headed back home.

Paul could not claim an immediate victory as he had not seen the 109's end but it seemed fairly certain that if it hadn't crashed, it had been severely damaged. In the event he was credited with a kill, but as was later discovered, the German pilot, Leutnant Joseph Volk of the 9th Staffel of III/JG53 had survived, although wounded, and his fighter had been severely damaged, having crash-landed behind the German frontier near Saarbrucken.

That afternoon, Johnny Walker led a patrol over Metz at 2 pm and ran into nine Me110s of V(Z)/LG1 half an hour later. In the fight that ensued the Hurricane pilot found the 110s fast and manoeuvrable but not so much that they couldn't turn inside them. Walker hit one but was attacked by another and had to take evasive action. Stratton saw Walker's 110 in trouble, leaving a trail of black smoke from one engine and went after it, and following his attack the other engine belched smoke. It was last seen gliding east still trailing smoke. Taffy Clowes attacked two 110s in rapid succession and both seemed to go down out of control.

In the event, the damaged 110 finally crashed in Allied territory with a dead gunner, its pilot, Feldwebel Friedrich Lindermann baling out to become a prisoner. This was the only loss by the German unit. However, one of the German 110 pilots claimed two Hurricanes shot down, whereas 1 Squadron did not collect so much as a bullet hole between them.

The next day, the 30th, Pilot Officer P V Boot RAFVR arrived. So too did an invitation from the C-in-C for Johnny Walker and his section to dine with him on the evening of the 31st. So, the next evening, Walker, Stratton and Clowes were picked up by car and transported to Paris where, it is recorded, a 'corking' time was had by all.

* * *

April came. Early spring was allowing more flights by both sides and patrols by No.1 Squadron between Thionville and Boulay began at 0630 on the 1st, the 22nd Anniversary of the creation of the Royal Air Force. At 1140, Prosser Hanks, Les Clisby and Boy Mould saw AA fire and then nine Me110s. A dog-fight began and each pilot claimed a 110 shot down. Hanks, in a head-on attack on one, got a cannon shell in the port wing of his Hurricane which exploded, sending pieces of metal into the oil tank, main spar, petrol tank and through the perspex of his cockpit hood. He did not break off the converging attack, but the 110 pilot did. Hanks got his machine back and down safely at 73 Squadron's base at Rouvres.

The 110s were from I/ZG26 and had been escorting a Dornier of 3(F)/11. Although HQ AASF acknowledged the claims, they did not give confirmation, which in the event was correct, for only one of the unit's 110s was damaged, and one crew member wounded.

Werner Mölders shoots down Palmer

Next day Clisby, Lorimer, Palmer, Kilmartin and Richey were up and they too were attracted by AA fire, then saw an enemy aircraft and gave chase. The German easily outclimbed them but then Palmer spotted another aircraft and reported it to Clisby. Moments later several Me109s came down on the Hurricanes and Palmer's machine was hit in the reserve fuel tank and set on fire. Palmer quickly took to his parachute but delayed pulling the rip-cord for 4-5,000 feet in order to clear the area and to make sure he did not drift into nearby German-held territory. He landed 500 feet inside the Allied line. In the fight which developed both Clisby and Kilmartin claimed a 109. The first machine was believed to have been a 110 and the pilots assumed it was a decoy which led them under the waiting single-seaters. Luckily they had been spotted by Palmer who had been flying cross-over turns behind the others as a look-out. As Billy Drake recalls, Palmer, an ardent smoker, apparently lit up a cigarette as he drifted down, while enjoying the view!

The German unit had been III Gruppe of JG53 led by the German ace, Hauptmann Werner Mölders, and it had been him who had shot down Pussy Palmer. It was the German pilot's 8th victory in WW2, not counting his 14 kills in Spain. He would go on to record more than 100 kills by 1941. JG53 suffered no casualties in return. One of the claimed Messerschmitts was seen to crash into a house, but this must have been Palmer's burning Hurricane.

Things were now starting to move. At this time the Germans occupied Denmark and then invaded Norway. It seemed as though an invasion in the west was imminent but nothing occurred. The Squadron was due for a visit on the 11th by Marshal of the RAF Viscount Trenchard, and when orders were received for an immediate move to the Reims area, there was a difficult moment, for they had to delay in order to get the visit over first.

Then at 1500 hours orders came that the Squadron had to leave by midnight. The visit over, the Hurricanes flew off at 1700 and were at Readiness at their new base at Berry-au-Bac, 30 miles north-west of Reims, at 1745. All transport vehicles were away before midnight and had arrived at the airfield by 0300. The one casualty was the unit's 32-seater coach which overturned into a ditch as its driver fell asleep at the wheel. Fortunately there were no injuries for it carried only kit and just one well-cushioned passenger. The driver only suffered a few slight facial lacerations.

The officers moved into the château at Guincourt, occupied by the officers of 142 Squadron (Battles and with whom 1 Squadron was to share the airfield), while the men were accommodated in Ville-aux-Bois and Juvincourt. The next day the Squadron made a rapid and successful set up on the airfield, erecting tents and so on. The pilots took over a windowless concrete structure, making it reasonably habitable with a stove and a gramophone. The immediate surrounding area gave graphic evidence of the battles of WW1, with old trenches, shell holes, rusting metal and war memorials. Just the thing to lift morale.

After four days the men were moved to Pontavert for better accommodation, thanks to Squadron Leader Halahan's forcefulness and with the help of the Squadron interpreter, Jean-Francois Demozay. Little did anyone realise what destiny held in store for this French Air Force officer. Pontavert was much better, its cafés were larger and grander, for the whole village had been built (rebuilt?) following WW1. The Officers' Mess was a bungalow, complete with verandah, which in peace time had been a summer house.

Having settled in nicely to their 'war station', and as the war had not started, the Squadron was ordered back to Vassincourt on the 19th. The next day, the first back on the Metz front, Killy Kilmartin was Scrambled at 0945 after a high flying aircraft reported between Reims and Chalons at 26,000 feet. The German crew spotted the Hurricane and began to dive towards home but Killy slowly overhauled it by which time both aircraft were very near the ground. Making skidding turns to throw off the British fighter, the German pilot in fact made it easier for his pursuer to keep within range. Finally the German began to fly straight and level – possibly hit.

A bullet from the rear gunner hit the Hurricane's port engine cylinder block which forced Kilmartin to brake off and land. Soon afterwards the German machine came down and it turned out to be a Ju88, which accounted for its superior speed. This aeroplane was from 4(F)/121, and came to earth in a crash-landing near Macon, north of Lyons, where Oberleutnant Klaus Pritzel and his crew were taken into captivity.

However, it seems that no sooner had Kilmartin broken away than the Ju88 was seen by a French pilot in a Bloch MB152. He finished it off, thus claiming the first success for a Bloch 152 fighter.

Meantime a four-man patrol from the Squadron found a He111 escorted by Me109s. These were attacked by Boy Mould, Prosser Hanks and Sergeants Berry and Albonico, near Charney at 23,000 feet. Hanks saw the Heinkel going down into Allied lines, Berry shot down a 109, while Albonico claimed another. Mould claimed a 109 probably destroyed which went down smoking. In fact he claimed a He112, a much publicised German fighter which (with its sister the He113) was often 'seen' by RAF pilots in the first year of the war but was never ever in action; they were always 109s.

There appears to be some question over the Heinkel, for there is no recorded loss and it seems it was confused with Kilmartin's Ju88. No fighters from the escorting III/JG2 were lost either. The black smoke seen in many such combats, as the RAF would learn later, often came from the exhaust smoke from the Daimler-Benz engine as a pilot opened the throttle. As 109s, with fuel injection, could also nose dive without losing power, unlike the Hurricanes and Spitfires which had a float carburettor which did cause the engine to cut in such a manoeuvre, together this gave the impression of a damaging hit on a 109 fighter.

At 1130 another Squadron patrol was airborne with Walker, Brown, Drake and Stratton. They met nine Me109s from 7/JG53 over Sierck-les-Bains, near the frontier. In the fight which followed, Walker claimed one crashed in British lines, and Brown another down in German lines. Billy Drake attacked two, seeing one go down out of control while the other he chased into Germany where he saw it crash onto a hillside. Of this Billy Drake remembers:

'I got close to this 109 and went into a dive and the next thing I saw a ruddy great high tension cable. The 109 pilot went under it, so I thought I'd go under it too. Then he did a stupid thing and pulled straight up, which gave me the opportunity of closing in and down he went.'

JG53 lost Leutnant Sievers to Johnny Walker, who crashed near Thionville and was killed. Drake's Me109 actually crash-landed near Gau-Bickelheim, east of Bad Kreuznach and was severely damaged.

On the last day of April, Pat Halahan became acting CO of No.67 Wing HQ, Johnny Walker taking temporary command of the Squadron. Then on 1 May Hilly Brown flew to Bricy (Orleans) to try out a captured Me109E, also getting the chance to test a Morane 315. He flew the 109 again on the 2nd, and on the 4th Hilly took it to Amiens. It was another first for the Squadron, Brown noting in his logbook that he was only the third Allied chap to fly it but the first RAF pilot. On the 4th some of the Squadron pilots also went to Amiens to look over the 109, and then Brown flew it while Prosser Hanks took off in his Hurricane and they fought a 45-minute mock combat together. To them it seemed that the Hurricane was more manoeuvrable at all heights than the 109 and slightly faster at ground level, but the 109 was faster at operational heights, and with a good rear view. This was good information for the RAF pilots who would soon be in the thick of battle.

A couple of days later Mel of the *Tatler* magazine paid a visit to the Squadron in order to sketch pilots 'who have any claim to fame.' All the 'famous' were duly drawn – Halahan, Walker, Hanks, Mould, Richey, Kilmartin, Clisby, Drake, Soper, Lewis – even J C Roberts, the Adj and Brown, the MO. Those not sketched obviously had not become famous enough – Stratton, Palmer, Matthews, Berry, Clowes, Albonico – and what about Hilly Brown? Perhaps some were absent like Hilly, who was flying the 109 from Amiens to Boscombe Down.

Some new pilots had recently arrived. Pilot Officers Roland Dibnah, Don Thom, C M 'Red' Stavert and G E 'Randy' Goodman, all of whom Halahan kept on the sidelines as it seemed certain that the real war was going to start any day now. The Squadron had been tested and tried. The Big Match was about to begin.

Chapter Eight

THE BATTLE OF FRANCE

Blitzkrieg

Whatever the thoughts had been concerning the impending attack by the Germans in the West, it still came as a surprise. On the evening and night of 9 May there was much activity. Guns could be heard in the distance and a large number of aircraft were about in the night sky, with French AA batteries firing away at them. Paul Richey had a disturbed night, constantly awaking to the sounds of aircraft and guns. When he finally fell asleep he seemed instantly to be awakened by an airman telling him he was urgently needed at the airfield. It was 3.30 am, 10 May.

Soon he and the other A Flight pilots were in the truck heading for the field. B Flight had apparently already taken off, and Walker led A Flight off at 0500 to patrol Metz, at 20,000 feet. They climbed through a thick haze which they penetrated at 5,000 feet, meeting a low watery sun. Despite the rumours no aircraft were about but then a faint radio call warned of an aircraft going east away from Rouvres.

Soon the Hurricane pilots saw it away to their right and the attack was on, Johnny leading, Hilly next, then Paul Richey. Each took turns at the Dornier which caught the full force of their fire. Next in was Kilmartin, then Frank Soper. Badly hit, the Dornier began to go down and crash landed in a field near Dun-sur-Meuse. It was a machine from 7/KG3 piloted by Unteroffizier Wolfgang Gräfe. However, Johnny Walker had been hit by return fire and he also had to find a place to put down. He bellied in east of Verdun, but was himself unharmed.

Meantime, Prosser Hanks leading B Flight had met a formation of Do17s of III/KG3 and went for a vic of three at the rear – the 8th Staffel. His steady fire brought down the machine flown by Feldwebel Helmut Hoffmann. Boy Mould went for another but overshot and got clobbered by the rear gunner. One bullet punctured a wheel while another tore through the right leg of his flying overalls.

No sooner had the Hurricanes landed than they were refuelled and rearmed and sent off to circle the airfield to protect it in case of attack. All flyable aircraft were airborne, even one with gun problems so that it wouldn't be caught on the ground. Not long afterwards came the order to move to the Squadron's war station, Berry-au-Bac. B Flight were away by 1430 but en-route they ran into a formation of Heinkel 111 bombers from 5/KG53. Boy Mould and Billy Drake each claimed one shot down, while Prosser Hanks and Richard Lewis shared a Dornier 17, which in fact may have been a third Heinkel. KG53 lost two aircraft and had a third shot-up with one crewman wounded. Lorry Lorimer's machine was hit by return fire and he had to bale out near Châlons, but he and Walker were soon back by car.

Bull Halahan led off A Flight not long afterwards and landed safely at Berry. Half an hour later the base was attacked by a German bomber and three French labourers, including two young lads, who had been ploughing next to the airfield, were almost blown to bits and five of their horses badly injured; they had later to be shot. It gave the pilots added incentive for the coming sorties.

News began to filter through that this was the real thing at last. It was not just a case of the Luftwaffe having a go. German troops were streaming across the Belgian border, thereby by-passing the Maginot Line, and heading through the Ardennes. Holland and Luxembourg too were under threat. Elite parachute troops were also landing at key points in Belgium and any number of RAF and French airfields had already come under air attack. In England the Prime Minister resigned, his place taken by Winston Churchill.

The pilots were roused at 0245 the next morning and were on the airfield before first light. They decided to abandon their concrete hut and instead, put up a tent on the fringe of a nearby wood. They then rigged up a telephone line and stashed their flying kit inside. They were pleased to find a couple of shallow trenches nearby.

Prosser Hanks was sent off at 0540 as a raider was seen approaching. Climbing to 15,000 feet they saw a Heinkel, chased it but failed to get close. News of more German aircraft about soon came in and by 0800 the pilots were sitting in their cockpits, watching the eastern sky as the sun began to blaze down. They did not have long to wait. Keen eyes picked out hostile aircraft and engines began to burst into life. Then the Hurricanes were trundling out to take off, led by the CO.

There was no time to form up once in the air and it was suddenly every man for himself. A bunch of Heinkels were heading east in open formation going flat out and Richey and Drake gave chase. It was obvious they had turned back on seeing the Hurricanes climbing up but they had too good a start and Halahan had to order a recall. However, Richey delayed a bit and then spotted a lone Dornier 17P of 3(F)/10 and attacked.

He chased the Dornier for a long way, smoke coming from both engines but by the time his ammunition ran out the German was still going strong. However, the Hurricane's windscreen was being splattered with oil, so the enemy pilot was in trouble. Richey had finally to break off, but the Dornier, although it got back into German territory, had one engine then catch fire and the crew had to bale out. Having become lost, Richey landed at a French airfield at Mézières but damaged a wing tip as he ran into a bomb crater. The base was the home of Escadrille GAO 547 (Potez 63s) and they courteously flew him back to his base, but his crippled Hurricane was destroyed on the ground three days later by raiding Dorniers.

After the morning excitement there was a break until 1445 pm. B Flight took off to escort Fairey Battles to north-east of Rethel and were almost at the target before spotting a gaggle of Me110s of I/ZG2 in a fight with other Hurricanes. Prosser Hanks went down on one and set its starboard engine smoking. Mould fired at another and its starboard engine jerked to a stop, then Les Clisby knocked out its other engine.

Pilot Officer Stavert knocked pieces from a third Messerschmitt. Hanks and Mould then ganged-up on the second 110 and it force landed west of Chemery, its crew being captured. Clisby and Stavert finished off the third 110 which crashed south-east of Rethel, while Clisby swung in behind the first 110 which was last seen diving with its starboard engine and wings in flames. I/ZG2 lost two aircraft.

That evening A Flight got into action at 1915 after a Scramble upon the approach of bombers heading for Reims. This was a force of 30 Dornier 17s from III/KG76 escorted by Me110s of I/ZG26. Walker led an attack on the 110s and in all the pilots put in claims for nine kills: two each to Brown, Kilmartin, Richey and Soper, with Walker getting the ninth and a probable. Local villagers later reported seeing six German aircraft falling in flames and it was later said that ten wrecks were found.

Despite the wealth of evidence, it appears that only two 110s were actually lost, two pilots being taken prisoner but both their gunners were killed. Paul Richey saw one of his go down in flames and as its tail came off a parachute appeared. He was later attacked by three other 110s. There was a loud bang and he was enveloped in black smoke and saw a flicker of flame. Time to go. He baled out and once safely on the ground had to fast talk two French soldiers who were convinced he was German until he was allowed to open his flying overalls to reveal his RAF uniform. Fortunately Richey spoke French well. From one of 'his' kills Richey and the engineering officer collected one of the tail fins which they brought home the next day. Apparently too, the Dorniers had turned back having had their escort break off to fight the Hurricanes.

The bridges at Maastricht

Despite Army orders to blow up the bridges across the River Maas, two had been left intact at Maastricht which would allow the rapidly advancing German army to cross without too much trouble. Despite two days in which they could also have been bombed from the air, it was not until the 12th that a raid was mounted to destroy them. By this time of course, they were not only in German hands but they had been surrounded by a protective mass of anti-aircraft batteries and machine guns.

No. 12 Squadron – Battles – called for volunteers to make the attack and to their credit every man stepped forward. Six crews were selected and No.1 Squadron were ordered to provide escort. Shortly before take-off one Battle became u/s and a spare machine also had a problem, so just five took to the sky shortly after 0815.

There was no doubt in anyone's mind that this was going to be a tough mission. Already the light Battle bombers had proved vulnerable to enemy fighters at height and ground fire when low down. Under-powered and under-armed, this was in any sort of terms a virtual suicide mission. And so it proved.

Equally aware of the importance of the target and the danger the bomber crews faced, Bull Halahan decided to lead the escort personally. Whether he remembered it or not, his father had helped form 12 Squadron in 1914. The plan was for the Hurricanes to arrive first and sweep away any fighters they encountered in order to give the Battles a clear run. They ran into a large force of sixteen Me109s from 2/JG27 and as the Battles came on the scene, the Hurricanes were already heavily engaged.

Hilly Brown fought five 109s and had his Hurricane hit twice so dived into some clouds and got away. Les Clisby saw Soper shoot down a 109 then attacked another and saw this crash too. Lorimer and Soper attacked a 109 and it was last seen near the ground streaming smoke. Peter Boot fired a long burst into one 109 but then his starboard wing was hit and he lost sight of his opponent. Kilmartin went after two 109s [reported as He112s] and hit one which rolled and dived vertically into some cloud. He then fought three more fighters without result. Lewis was shot down in flames and seen to bale out. Halahan shot down another 109 but was then shot in the oil tank and dived into some cloud. Coming out he found two Hs126 observation machines ahead of him and he quickly despatched one of them.

On his way back, Clisby also came through cloud to find seven, what he recorded as Arado biplanes (Hs126s?), and claimed two shot down. Getting back to base Soper had to make a forced landing. Halahan also had to make a forced landing but came down in Allied territory west of Maastricht and returned by road. On his journey he had seen a force of Seneglese troops going up to the front. They came upon the crew of a He111 which had force landed in a nearby field and a group of these black soldiers promptly dragged them off and decapitated them. Lewis had been captured by the Germans but was released following a counter attack by Belgian troops. He claimed a 109 destroyed and another as a probable!

Meantime the Battles met a wall of flak and three were shot down while the other two fell to JG27. Flying Officer Donald Garland and his observer, Sergeant Tom Gray, received posthumous VCs for their actions, although their gunner, LAC Lawrence Reynolds got nothing. In all six men were killed, seven taken prisoner and two came down in Allied territory. The German 109 pilots claimed four Hurricanes. One Me109 pilot – Leutnant Friedrich Keller – force landed near Aachen with a badly damaged aircraft. Billy Drake remembers:

'One of my recollections of those first couple of days was seeing us trying to put the bridge out at Maastricht, and all those poor buggers in Battles being shot down. As I said at the time, it was 10/10ths 109s – and there was only a handful of us. So we sort of looked and came home. It was suicide to get in there.'

Monday the 13th

Prosser Hanks led off five Hurricanes at 0640 hours the next day and ran into about 30 Heinkels of KG55 with escort fighters, south-east of Vouzières. Boy Mould and his section attacked from the rear while Les Clisby went down on a straggling fighter. His attack set the 110 on fire and it crashed in flames. Switching his attention to a bomber he saw white smoke coming from both motors but then he was attacked by a French Potez 63 and he had to break away. On his way home he found another Heinkel, attacked and saw it crash-land south-east of Vouzières. In true WW1 style he landed his Hurricane close by and took the five-man crew prisoner, later handing them over to the French at Bourcq. However, he damaged his fighter and it had to be abandoned.

Mould got his bomber and then a fighter, while Lorimer and Randy Goodman shared a bomber, but Lorry was hit too and had to force land at St Loup-Terrier, writing his fighter off in the process.

While this had been going on, Billy Drake, who had earlier left the formation with oxygen problems, heard over the radio that some bombers were near to him and upon looking around saw three aircraft right overhead – Dornier 17s. He pulled up to attack but then there was an explosion in his cockpit. Unseen by him a Me110 had dived from out of the sun and had caught him. Simultaneously he had fired up into the Dornier which erupted in flames and crashed. However, he felt a jolt in his back and one leg and with his cockpit full of smoke and fire decided to bale out. Dangling under his parachute he was attacked by the 110 but after one pass it flew off. Billy Drake relates:

'In May it was mostly banging off at anything you saw and pissing off as quickly as possible. When I was shot down I panicked a bit. A cannon shell, or two, exploded behind me and I was peppered by fragments across my back and shoulders and in the back of my legs; my left one hurt like hell. I didn't see the German as I was attacking a bomber but was told it was a Me110.

I saw my aircraft was in flames and I stank of petrol and glycol, and I tried to bale out without taking the hood off. That probably saved my life because, being upside down, all the flames went the other way. So when I suddenly realised the hood was still there, and then got rid of it, I fell straight out.'

I was picked up by some French farmers who didn't like me at all because being very blonde and only wearing a white overall, they said – "Sale Boche!" (filthy German). I said I was not, I was an officer Anglais and as soon as they realised – finally being able to show them my 'wings' – they put their pitchforks and scythes down and took me to a Casualty Clearing Station.

I was operated on by some French doctors who were pissed I think, anyway they stank of garlic, and they'd run out of anaesthetic. So they were taking great lumps of metal and pieces of flying overalls out of my back and legs, saying, does it hurt?! I told them – yes!'

French fighters also attacked these Heinkels, KG55 losing in total six of its aircraft with four others damaged. Clisby's 'capture' was at Douzy on the west bank of the Maas. However, such was the speed of the German advance that they were released the same afternoon by advancing Panzer troops.

* * *

The next day, the 14th, saw the only really big effort by the RAF in France to attack the advancing Germans and it cost them dear. The Battle crews flew valiant missions against tanks, motor transport and troops but they were always up against a mass of defensive gunfire and all too often cut to ribbons. If they climbed to any sort of height the Me109s got them. It was desperate.

Me110s overflew Berry-au-Bac at 0745 and although Hanks and his Flight scrambled they were unable to close until the 110s changed direction. At that moment Hanks dived on one, fired and saw it explode. As he pulled into a climbing turn a 110 attacked him but the German pilot did not allow enough deflection and Hanks could see all the tracer shots going behind him. Continuing a tight turn he got behind the 110 and shot it down in flames.

However, yet another 110 hit his Hurricane and he was drenched in hot glycol and not having his goggles over his eyes was completely blinded. His machine went into a spin and everything was getting hot, so he decided to bale out. He undid everything but the force of the spin pressed him down. After screaming in anger he suddenly found himself out and in his parachute.

Boy Mould claimed two Messerschmitts, one shared with Peter Boot, and Pete Matthews claimed one and a probable. The fight had been with the 2nd Staffel of ZG26 who reported the loss of two of their fighters. One fell near Chimay but the other got back to its airfield at Vogelsang before it crashed and killed its crew. The disaster, however, was that Les Clisby and Lorry Lorimer failed to make it back to base, both men being later reported killed, the French finding their wrecked Hurricanes.

The Squadron's afternoon mission was as escort – with 73 Squadron – to 23 Battles from 105 and 150 Squadrons, plus eight Blenheims from 114 and 139 Squadrons, assigned to attack bridges over the Meuse. This was the second wave, the first, of 25 Battles, having been severely mauled in the mid-afternoon. Advancing German troops and Panzers brought with them as a matter of course their formidable array of AA and machine guns, and above this were the ever present patrols of Me109s. Almost half the bombers of the first wave had been shot down.

Waiting for the second wave were 109s from III Gruppe of JG53. In the air too were 109s from I/JG53, circling to await the arrival of the Ju87 Stuka dive-bombers they were scheduled to escort. 1 Squadron ran into the latter Gruppe and the approaching Stukas and before the German fighter pilots could react, 1 Squadron had hacked down five Stukas – Kilmartin two, and one each to Stratton, Clowes and Hilly Brown. In all StG77 lost six, the leader being shot down by French AA fire.

As the 109 pilots got their act together, so had 1 Squadron and in a series of dog-fights, the Hurricane pilots claimed four – Palmer, Brown, Clowes and Soper. I/JG53 did indeed lose four plus two others damaged, although one pilot was thought to have run into debris from an exploding Blenheim he was chasing. However, it had been a tremendous victory for 1 Squadron, nine claims and virtually all accounted for in German records. One of the German pilots killed had been Oberfeldwebel Walter Grimmling who had scored JG53's first kill of the war.

With aircraft in short supply, Flying Officer Salmon was sent off to Mézières with some mechanics to see if they could get Paul Richey's aircraft, which he had been forced to leave there on the 11th, into flying condition and bring it back. As their truck arrived they discovered the base under attack from the air and could only watch as the Hurricane was destroyed in front of their eyes. Salmon and his men also found the base deserted of Frenchmen and all the aircraft under camouflage netting had been immobilised. Little wonder, they thought, that so few French fighters had been seen in the air in recent days, while the RAF knocked themselves out fighting against huge odds.

A new arrival on the Squadron was Pilot Officer N P W Hancock, sent out from 266 Squadron – which flew Spitfires! His flight commander, Ian Gleed, gave him the good news that he was going to France. Gleed had had a narrow escape from a Spitfire which had disintegrated in the air back on 18 February – after it had been flown by Pat Hancock, but Pat is sure this was not behind the reason his name came up to go to France. In any event, Gleed himself was about to depart for France – to 87 Squadron. Pat recalls his rude arrival at the war:

'The Germans were being thoroughly beastly and so they sent for Hancock to go to France. I was given two days leave to say "goodbye" to my parents, then off I went. I flew out in a Dakota, late of Sabena, that had been stolen by its Belgian pilot – Captain Vanecre – and flown to England.

Much to his chagrin he was then asked to fly it to France full of replacement pilots for the BEF, yours truly being among them. We left Hendon for Amiens, then from Amiens to Coulommiers.

No sooner had I arrived at 1 Squadron, I was ushered into the CO's office. He was in conference with one of his flight commanders and with all the action going on, he obviously had no time for me and I had appeared at a very inopportune moment. I was immediately told to "Get out!" For my part I don't think he liked the look of me, so out I went.

Shortly thereafter I found myself in a lorry heading for 501 Squadron. After a three day journey I found 501, only to be told I was going back to No.1. So I got myself back, and then began flying some Ops.'

15 May – from bad to worse

Holland was all but finished and the Netherlands Government surrendered at 11 am. In Belgium Antwerp was under direct threat, the French army was in retreat and were about to join up with British troops at Charleroi. The whole river defence was virtually lost between Namur and north of Stenay and Panzers were spear-heading fast towards Mézières, the latter forcing the AASF squadrons to fall back too. South of Sedan a huge gap had opened up in the Allied line.

So serious was the situation that the French Prime Minister telephoned Winston Churchill saying they were defeated and had all but lost the battle, confirming the front had collapsed near Sedan. Soon the French PM was asking for at least ten more RAF fighter squadrons, which considering the size of the French Air Force, confirmed everyone's worse fears that the French air arm was large in overall numbers but small (with just a few exceptions) in action.

Churchill, knowing what the fall of France would mean was reluctantly forced to agree and but for the firm intervention of Sir Hugh Dowding might well have frittered away so many fighters that Britain would have been unable to defend itself. A small compromise was made, but overall Dowding got his way, and saved this country.

These high policy developments were unknown to the airmen in France. The bomber people were too busy in any event trying to stem the steamroller that was the Wehrmacht, while the fighter pilots were endeavouring to protect them and the ground troops from an avalanche of Luftwaffe aircraft. With their numbers and equipment the bombers were but pin-pricks, while the Hurricanes were almost constantly overwhelmed.

For the AASF fighters it was a time of protecting their bases. At 0730 six aircraft of A Flight were Scrambled on the approach of a raid and they intercepted around 40 Dornier 17s from I and II Gruppen of KG53, that were heavily escorted by 110s of III/ZG26. On the approach of the Hurricanes, the 110s went into a defensive circle at which the RAF pilots began to nibble. Over the next half hour six Messerschmitts were claimed as shot down – Walker, Kilmartin, Richey, Soper and Clowes – although Walker's machine was hit and he was forced to put down.

Paul Richey shot down one and possibly another – which he shot off the tail of another Hurricane – but then a 110 got him and began to trail smoke from his engine. Time to go, Richey rolled over and dropped out, landing near Béthenville.

The German pilots thought they had been fighting French Moranes, and claimed no fewer than nine of these shot down, admitting the loss of two of their own machines with two more crash-landing seriously damaged.

Despite the action, the Dorniers managed to bomb the airfield at Berry, although 501 Squadron came onto the scene and shot down a couple of them. From one, a parachuting airmen landed in a field near a road, along which Pat Hancock was being driven by 'Sammy' Salmon, following his 'move' from 1 Squadron. They saw the man come down but also spotted some hostile looking French people converging on the spot. The two RAF pilots felt obliged to go to the German's rescue before he was lynched, then drove him to the nearest French army post. The badly injured pilot of the Dornier was later extricated from the wreck of his machine but died the next day.

Having deposited his erstwhile companion at Béthenville, Salmon was returning in his Bentley only to witness another fight, this time between 73 Squadron and some Me110s, seeing two Hurricanes go down and three 110s although in fact only two were lost. It is not too difficult to understand how pilots in a fight can believe more enemy aircraft were shot down than were actually lost, but strange how a pilot on the ground can also be misled.

Despite Dowding's reservations, more Hurricanes arrived in France on 16 May which led to his famous letter to Air Ministry stating that even if France were to fall, no more Hurricanes should be sent, otherwise Britain's defence would be under serious threat, Fighter Command already being dangerously under strength.

No.1 Squadron received orders to move shortly after midnight. Their new base would be at Vraux, near Condé-sur-Marne, which was mid-way between Reims and Paris. Pat Halahan had been grounded by the C-in-C after the Maastricht raid and so he led the ground party which set off at 0130. Soon after dawn the Hurricanes followed and although the pilots remained at cockpit Readiness all day, they were not called into action. The Squadron had been put in the direct path should the Germans make a lunge at Paris, but the enemy plan was to turn and head for the Channel ports. The rear ground party were lucky, having left just in time to cross the Marne-Aisne canal before French engineers blew up the bridge.

Squadron Leader Halahan took time that evening to pen a letter to the AOC informing him that in his opinion if the pace continued all his pilots would be either dead or exhausted within a week and asked that all those who had been in France since September be allowed to return to England, where their skill and experience would be needed once France fell.

During the night retreating French tanks and troops, informed Halahan that the Germans had reached Reims and must surely arrive at Vraux by dawn. He then found the line to 67 Wing HQ had been cut so had little choice but to get the Squadron up and away, with orders to make for an airfield at Anglure, 30-odd miles to the south-west. Leaving Johnny Walker with orders to take off at first light, he led the main party away in his Humber. Not very long after they had left, came a call from Wing to say that the French must be wrong and that Walker was to remain *in situ*. However, with little fuel, no spare ammunition and just a handful of ground crew, things were looking a bit fraught.

Trying to get some pilots rested, he waited until 0900 before leading a patrol off to see for himself where the Germans had got to and to intercept some dive-bombers reported attacking Allied troops near Sedan. He found no sign of any hostiles on the ground but ran into some Me110s. Forced to abandon any hope of intercepting dive-bombers he went for the Messerschmitts. In the action the pilots claimed five 110s plus two probables, although Pussy Palmer had to bale out after his fighter was badly hit, and Walker's machine was also damaged by a cannon shell in the wing and aileron. Soper returned with a badly ventilated Hurricane and although he got it down safely it was deemed beyond the capabilities of the Squadron to repair it. Apart from three large cannon shell hits, there were more than 30 bullet holes in it and several dents in the armour plate behind the seat.

The 110s, from V(Z)/LG1, had in fact been escorting He111s, one of the latter being spotted and then shot down by Hilly Brown. LG1 recorded the loss of three of their fighters, one pilot, Oberleutnant Werner Methfessel having gained eight combat victories before his death in this action.

Later, B Flight were Scrambled to intercept Dorniers but on the approach of the Hurricanes the Germans turned and fled in various directions northwards.

18 May
The remaining twelve serviceable Hurricanes finally left for Anglure at dawn on the 18th, leaving Soper's machine burning in a shell hole into which it had been pushed and set alight. On the way, Pilot Officer Charles Stavert, a fairly new arrival, spotted a Dornier 17 some way off and peeled away to intercept. He attacked it and it crash landed, although its crew, from 3(F)/31, survived.

Having secured his first victory he headed for the new base but in totally the wrong direction. Nearing what he thought must be the area of the new field, he was relieved to spot an aerodrome ahead of him but on the approach was un-nerved to see a Heinkel landing ahead of him. Without hesitation he shot this machine down and realising he was not where he should be headed away rapidly. He almost made it back to Vraux before his fuel gave out, forcing him to belly land in a field. On his walking arrival at Vraux he was just in time to cadge a lift with the rear party.

That afternoon, eight Hurricanes of the Squadron led by Hilly Brown, took off at 1430 hours as part of an escort to 18 Squadron Blenheims on their way to bomb German columns near Cambrai. They came under intense AA fire near St Quentin so Brown circled, waggling his wings to the French gunners but the fire did not stop. By this time the Flight had become dispersed and then Hilly spotted a Hs126 observation machine below him. In a quick fight in which the nimble two-seater put up a spirited defence, Brown got in a telling burst and did not see the Henschel again.

Sergeant R A Albonico rolled over and was seen going down, presumably to investigate some troops he had seen on the ground, but his Hurricane was hit by ground fire. He survived the encounter and the crash-landing near St Quentin but was picked up by German soldiers and taken prisoner.

That evening, in the new Mess – a small café in Pleurs – they received word that the Squadron was to take part in a major escort mission the next day. Tents had been set up in the grounds of a local château, and into these everyone huddled and tried to get some sleep.

* * *

Heinkels everywhere

Two large German mechanised columns had been spotted advancing towards the Neufchâtel-Montcornet road and Air Marshal Barratt quickly ordered a bombing attack by all available Battles from the Air Component, whose squadrons had already been decimated. They managed to assemble 33 aircraft, and were escorted by 26 Hawker Hurricanes from 1, 73 and 501 Squadrons.

Twelve Hurricanes from 1 Squadron, led in Flights by Walker and Hanks, took off from Anglure at 1015 hours. On the way to the Rethel-St Quentin area several formations of bombers and fighters were seen but were ignored. At around 11 o'clock, north-east of Rethel, they again spotted formations of twin-engined aircraft although they did not immediately recognise what types. At first they thought they were Blenheims but soon identified them as Heinkels.

They were a formation from III/KG27 assigned to attack targets in the Soissons-Compiègne-Noyon area. One Flight of Hurricanes went from echelon but a message to 'look out behind' messed up this attack, although Hilly Brown did not hear it and he left a Heinkel with both engines smoking and its wheels down. Walker also saw wheels come down from a bomber he attacked and then with smoke from both engines he saw it begin to glide earthwards. Brown made other attacks and saw one bomber dive away and later crash-land in a field where French soldiers took the crew prisoner.

Bill Stratton set another smoking and Kilmartin saw his victim drop out of formation trailing glycol smoke. He then attacked another and severely hit this one too. Soper claimed two more Heinkels and a damaged, but his fighter was hit by return fire and set ablaze. He dived and put out the flames but with a cockpit full of glycol fumes he was forced to make a landing 'blind'. In the belly landing he knocked himself out on the gunsight but came round quickly and was able to get a lift by road back to base.

Prosser Hanks and his pilots had stayed above to give cover but seeing no escorting 109s or 110s, he finally went down and attacked a straggler but only two of his guns worked. Boy Mould damaged another but his fighter's engine began to run rough so he broke away. Palmer attacked one already damaged and saw it burst into flames. Lewis also attacked one already hit then attacked another which headed down with one engine trailing smoke. Stavert's target trailed black smoke from one engine and glycol from the other before his guns seized up.

Paul Richey, in the first attack, failed to get home. He had attacked the extreme right-hand Heinkel of a rear section of three. It slowed quickly causing Richey to almost overshoot. Another attack and the bomber went down in a vertical spiral. Although hit in one wing, Richey went after another bomber and amidst heavy cross-fire from other Heinkels, set both motors of his target smoking and the undercarriage dropped down. A large hole appeared in one wing of his Hurricane but he was already after a third bomber. Dead in his sights, both engines streamed grey smoke, then smoked from the wing-roots and fuselage before becoming enveloped in it.

As he turned to break away he was hit again. Pieces of an armour-piercing bullet lodged against his spine at the base of his neck also causing a bad wound. Blood spurted down his right side and he lost all feeling in his right arm. He tried to bale out but could not manage to open the hood so glided down to make a crash-landing in a field with a dead engine. After a struggle he managed to get clear and then two French soldiers got him to a hospital near Château-Thierry, from where he was taken to hospital in Paris.

Despite claims for seven Heinkels destroyed, three probables and five damaged, KG27 lost five, but had others damaged. Most of the German crew members were taken captive by the French. Three of the losses came from the 8th Staffel, two from the 9th.

The returning pilots from this large battle landed back even more exhausted. It ended a ten-day period of intense pressure during which they had seen constant action on nine of them. They had fought against great odds and although far from unscathed they had remained a fighting unit, which says much for their training under Bull Halahan, and the two Flight Commanders, Walker and Hanks. 1 Squadron, along with others, had fought themselves to a standstill and had done much to blunt the vastly superior Luftwaffe. While the French campaign was ultimately lost, it was lost on the ground and in part by the failure of the French air force to match the heroic actions of the Royal Air Force squadrons, both fighters and light bombers.

No.1 Squadron had lost only two pilots killed, one taken prisoner and two wounded. It is difficult to assess its combat claims. Most of the records in France were lost in the retreat and the Squadron diary was only compiled later back in England from recollections of the pilots, many having also lost their flying log-books, while others had been too busy to keep their's up to date. Paul Richey managed to keep his and from it and his immediate memory, his excellent book *Fighter Pilot*, first published in 1941, not only gives us the closest account of those memorable months from September 1939 to May

1940, but also of those incredible ten days from 10 to 19th May.

Victories

As can be seen from the above combat actions, there was some over-claiming, but this is not strange or unusual in any air actions, either before or since. It is extremely difficult to be objective and these young men, often not far off being youths, faced with action and possible death, with the adrenaline pumping can be forgiven for making assumptions under these extreme conditions. The emphasis however, must be on claims. They are not saying for certain that such and such an aircraft crashed, burned or broke up in the air, although often they did. An experienced fighter pilot did not sit around to admire his work and watch a hostile aeroplane fall from 18,000 feet to the ground in order to know that it was destroyed. Nor did he rush back to base, put a note to this effect in his log-book, or paint another swastika on his aeroplane. All this is the stuff of armchair historians and would-be chroniclers of events as they see them, or would like to see them.

Nor is it unheard of that several pilots would attack and claim the same aircraft as shot down, without even seeing another brother pilot hammering away at the same target. More surprising is that more pilots did not collide in doing so. One has only to read the above account of 19 May to see that several pilots must have attacked the same aircraft or seen the same aircraft going down with 'both engines smoking and wheels down' to suspect that several pilots were seeing and reporting the same event.

Despite this – and it happens to all fighter squadrons to a lesser or greater degree – the claim figure can still give an assessment of the intense action. If there were no claims, it follows there were no actions. 1 Squadron were enveloped in action and the pilots were always closing with the enemy. I estimate that in those ten days at least 80 aircraft were claimed and a good percentage were either destroyed or returned to their bases severely damaged, and were thus out of action for periods. That the Squadron had also claimed around 20 or so victories before 10 May brings the grand total in France to the 100 figure, which still makes it a very high scoring squadron.

At the time, of course, with the RAF propaganda boys in full swing, they would read more into things than later-day readers of history. No doubt in an attempt to boost how well any unit had done in what, in reality, was a defeat, everything possible would be embraced. It is apparent that in trying to compile records after the event, claims and kills were noted wrongly for different days. Victory credits for one day are given for other days as well, and in this way, the real total becomes enlarged. Some too may decide that probables and unconfirmed claims were also, really, German losses, which they may not have been. In late 1943, as we shall see, there is a note that the Squadron victory tally was 234. Taking the known claims after the Battle of France, it is quite clear that the French campaign estimate is way too high when compared with the known facts.

But all this is really immaterial. While achievements cannot and should not be ignored, there is more to a successful squadron than notches on a tally stick. Each time a German bomber was turned away from its intended target, even if undamaged, it was a 'victory' and undoubtedly saved the lives of both soldier and civilian. Each patrol over friendly troops gave a morale boost to the men on the ground. Read any army account of actions where friendly aircraft were not overhead, and one will see how important it was to know the RAF were there.

* * *

The final days in France

If events had been happening quickly, then the next few days saw things happen just as fast. Amazingly, Pat Halahan's request that his veteran pilots be rested seemed to have been taken seriously. An order came that Halahan was to hand over command to Squadron Leader Pemberton, while Walker, Hanks, Stratton, Palmer, Kilmartin. Mould, Lewis and Soper were to return to England. Hilly Brown stayed to take command of A Flight and 'Darky' Clowes remained as senior NCO.

A new flight commander arrived for B Flight – Flight Lieutenant P E 'Fritz' Warcup together with two former Spitfire pilots from OTU. Warcup had no time to get acclimatised. Hilly Brown sent twelve Hurricanes off on a Scramble against Stuka dive-bombers attacking British forces near Arras. Bad weather forced them to fly below 2,000 feet where they met fierce ground fire. The Squadron were quickly out of touch with each other and had to return. Warcup pressed on, thinking the others would soon formate but instead he was attacked by several 109s, who proceeded to blast lumps from his fighter. Shaking loose and heading for home he found Clowes and Flying Officer Thom, and then a He111 over Rouen which they shot down. On this same day, the 23rd, Pilot Officer R H Dibnah bagged a Dornier 17.

The Germans were now heading off towards Calais and Dunkirk, so the Luftwaffe reduced their efforts towards Paris, giving 1 Squadron its first break for several days. However, on the 25th Flying Officer Thom was brought down and captured and the next day Dibnah was wounded. At dawn on the 25th a five-man patrol covered the line Bergerfs to Brienne and then Le Chateau between 10 and 11 am. In the afternoon a protection patrol covering a French recce aircraft over Chauny-Laon met heavy AA fire and three Hurricanes were hit. Thom was seen to break away with smoke or petrol pouring out of his machine and was last seen heading north into German territory. The patrol was then cut short due to flak damage and fuel shortage.

On the 26th three patrols were flown, one being an escort to Battles bombing Ochamps aerodrome at 0940. AA fire over German territory hit Dibnah's aircraft and he was wounded by shrapnel. He broke away and his leader instructed him to head towards the French lines, which he did, and eventually force landed safely near Verdun where he was hospitalised. Knackers Henniker:

'I drove back to Bar-le-Duc to pay a Squadron bill and found that Madame Jean at the Hotel Metz, had located a wounded No.1 Squadron pilot. The doctor had taken him to a local hospital. It turned out to be Pilot Officer Dibnah, one of the new pilots, who had been seen to go down but no further news of him had been received. He was in a bad way and the local doctors not being able to cope soon sent him off to the American Hospital in Paris.

A few days later, 1 June, one Flight of the "new" No.1 did a "blood bath" – flying low over enemy AA guns to draw fire away from the Fairey Battles. Shepherd's aircraft caught fire and he baled out. [Hilly Brown damaged a 109 which was later confirmed after the wreckage was found.]

The next day our stay at Anglure was to end abruptly as was now normal procedure, and we were off again, still retreating. The signal didn't come in till late afternoon and it was not until 6 pm that Moses Demozay and I got away. It was a long step to Châteaudun [code name Thelma] so we planned to spend the night in Orléans. We found the aerodrome at 7 am the next day only to find the Squadron had already landed but there was a spot of bother with the French over where the aircraft should be parked. Most of the hangars had been bombed, aircraft were burnt out, some on their backs having been parked in neat lines outside the hangars. Finally Pembers and the French CO got it sorted out.'

Although the Squadron had a château at their disposal, the CO felt it safer to use tents within nearby trees, and at dawn all the aircraft were flown off to patrol around Rouen, refuelling at Boos.

The action on the 1st started with 12 aircraft leaving at 0625, landing at Rouen 35 minutes later, where they remained at Readiness. B Flight were sent off later to patrol from St Valéry to the south-east covering British troop movements. A Flight relieved them and at 1109 nine Me 109s were reported behind. The Hurricanes, led by Hilly Brown, circled and tried to engage them but Brown himself was attacked by three 109s but got a burst at one. Pilot Officer Shepherd was shot down and took to his parachute near Dieppe and was later reported safe. Peter Boot was also hit badly but flew his Hurricane home. Another mixed A and B Flight patrol was flown in the afternoon but no enemy aircraft were seen. At 1700 the Squadron returned to base, Shepherd later being collected from Rouen by air whence he had made his way.

More action came on the 5th. Eleven serviceable aircraft took off from Thelma at 0550 to patrol west of Rouen but before reaching this area they found a mixed bunch of Heinkel and Dornier bombers (approximately 60 with more Me110s above and behind) and waded in.

Hilly Brown led A Flight towards the 110 escorts, while Fritz Warcup and B Flight went for the bombers. Brown, however, shot down a Dornier, Pilot Officer H B L Hillcoat got a Heinkel, while Pete Matthews got two, although only one was confirmed. Peter Boot claimed one of each. Most of the Hurricanes were damaged – those of Hillcoat, Lindsell and Sergeant Arbuthnot badly. Hillcoat was hit in the radiator and his machine caught fire but he force landed safely. Arbuthnot had his radiator shot away but he also force landed without injury to himself. Pilot Officer Lindsell force landed near Deauville also shot up. Three other B Flight aircraft landed at Thelma, one with petrol and oil tank shot through, another crash landing.

A Flight engaged the 110s, or to be accurate, 20 Me110s engaged them. The pilots tried to avoid combat in order to engage the bombers, at which time Brown claimed his Dornier, going down with both engines smoking and the rear gunner no longer firing. Pilot Officer J A Shepherd did not get back, seen to go down, in flames. Pilot Officer Browne damaged a Heinkel, while Pete Matthews followed his Heinkel down, seeing both engines stopped, its pilot looking for a spot to put down. He then attacked a straggling Heinkel with one engine already out and this appeared to go down too. Peter

Boot knocked the engine out of one Heinkel, then attacked again and stopped the other engine. He then went after a Dornier, disabling its starboard engine, then swung behind another Dornier but ran out of ammunition. Overtaking the first Heinkel he saw it force land in a field between Thelma and Rouen. Only two of the crew were seen to leave the machine once on the ground. Pat Hancock had been in this action and had been the pilot who crash-landed at base:

> 'We intercepted a number of He111s over the north of Rouen. There seemed to be lots of aircraft about – no 109s though – but the Heinkel gunners did a good job of peppering my Hurricane, including knocking out my ASI which was a bit inconvenient. I had some trouble keeping straight on landing at Rouen-Boos, having the choice of either hitting a hangar or a parked Blenheim; I chose the Blenheim, but got out alright although the Hurricane had had it.'

For the next several days the Squadron continued patrolling from Boos before returning to Châteaudun each evening. The Germans, following the escape of the BEF from Dunkirk, were now heading again for Paris and it became increasingly difficult to have any proper communications with Wing HQ. The Squadron was then ordered to move towards Caen, and give cover to Le Havre where more evacuations were taking place.

At dawn on the 9th, Warcup led 11 aircraft to 'Maudie' (Dreux) and after refuelling patrolled between Verdun and Point de L'Arche. Pilot Officer Mann saw a large formation of aircraft flying north up the Seine but his R/T was not working. He caught the leader's attention by waggling his wings and then dived on a straggler. After his attack the hostile aircraft began to trail smoke from one engine and as Mann began another pass he spotted ten Me110s coming for him. Mann immediately turned to face them and as one came into his sights he let fly but without result. The others then chased him away and he dived to safety. Meantime, the other Hurricane pilots failed to see the German aircraft.

Shortly after mid-day, Pete Matthews was ordered by the AOC to carry out a recce down the Seine between Nantes and Rouen to see if any bridges were still serviceable. He did this successfully at 500 feet despite French AA fire and on landing he made a personal report to the AOC.

Hostile aircraft were again met on 14 June, Brown shooting down a 109 and a Heinkel, Flight Sergeant Clowes another 109. Clowes then saw more fighters above and climbed to engage, damaging one of them. Then they were off again, this time to Nantes, which seemed full of Hurricanes, Battles, Blenheims and assorted light aircraft, many in poor shape. It seemed certain now that it was only a matter of time before they would be returning to England. Everywhere was chaos, with roads blocked with refugees, Germans advancing, rumours abounding, and German aircraft constantly in the air.

Things began to happen on the 17th, with Hurricanes flying the last patrols over St Nazaire. Ships were busy taking on troops in the dock, soldiers and airmen, and this invited reaction from the Luftwaffe. Heinkel bombers came in and Hurricanes engaged. Sergeant Berry and Pilot Officer Goodman each shot one down, Berry's victim downed as it scooted away after dropping its bombs, one of which appeared to go right down the funnel of the SS *Lancastria*, crammed full of men. It is impossible to say exactly how many were aboard her, but somewhere between 4-5,000 soldiers, sailors and airmen died. It was a graphic climax to the Squadron's Battle of France.

These last few days are recalled by LAC Frank Kennedy who had joined the Squadron in April:

> 'After the 10th of May we were always on the move to different airfields, sleeping in tents, barns, under trucks, etc. At one port, probably Brest, we watched army drivers riding brand new motor cycles along the waterfront to the end, jumping off at the last moment and letting the bikes go into the sea. At the previous airfield we were in the woods and the NAAFI trucks were opened up and airmen queued for whatever was issued free. We headed for St Nazaire maybe to board the 'Lancastria' but were turned back to head for Brest where we boarded a collier on 17 June, and landed at Plymouth the next day.'

Chapter Nine

THE BATTLE OF BRITAIN

Back from France

Numerous books could be written describing the many and varied ways soldiers and airmen got themselves out of France and back to England in 1940. Pilots lucky enough to have a serviceable aircraft might fly home, but others either did not, or were not in a place where aircraft were available. One such was Billy Drake. It will be recalled that he was wounded on 13 May. He relates:

'Having got out of a clearing hospital I was sent down to Chartres and they eventually released me. I remember one gruesome sight, that of a French officer who still had his tin helmet on, which had been hit by shrapnel which pushed the front of it into his skull so he couldn't remove it. And there was no doctor who had time to deal with anyone who wasn't yelling, or near to death. This poor chap was wandering about, taking salutes etc, with this caved-in helmet. Incredible.

Then I was picked up by a girlfriend of mine who was in the Ambulance Corps and on our way back from Chartres to Paris where I was declared an out-patient at the American Hospital – just three days before the Germans marched in – we were arrested. I was dressed only in mufti, no uniform, so the French police took me and asked Helen who I was. It took her half an hour to persuade them I was who I said I was, and not to be put up against the wall and shot as a Fifth Columnist.

Getting back to Paris I stayed with her family until, finding nobody at the Embassy, I saw an army unit and asked what they were doing. They said they had orders to blow up the telephone exchange and to pick up an army officer who had been signing a deal with the Renault people for so many hundred vehicles. At that moment he arrived saying that that had been a waste of time!

I asked where they were going and they said Le Mans, so I more or less got a lift but then Helen said I should take one of the family cars and drive down. So I did, taking this army bod too and met up with the Squadron at Le Mans. The Squadron was getting ready to evacuate via Jersey, so I got into the back of a Battle flown by an ATA type and as soon as we landed on the island, somebody rushed up and told us to get away, they were about to be invaded. So we took off and landed at Tangmere.'

Pat Hancock remembers:

'There was an air of anxiety in France because we all knew we were going the wrong way – backwards. Not a pleasant feeling. Towards the end we heard there was a French airfield not too far away on which were several Hurricanes and some fuel. The CO sent me off with two sergeant pilots and we found this place – Angers I think – and landed. There was no ground control of course.

There were indeed several abandoned aircraft there, Hurricanes and Battles, so I telephoned the CO on a land line and amazingly, because of all the panic, got through. He told me to refuel our aircraft by hand, from tin cans, and as we were doing so, up came the French Commandant and some of his officers.

He presented me with an enormous bunch of keys, which he told me were now mine and that I now owned the airfield! He then said they were all off to North Africa. We had this airfield for the day while we completed our refuelling.

Finally we ended up somewhere which was some sort of maintenance base, full of lorries, rations – much of it being of the liquid variety – and all sorts of goodies. So from here we went back to England, arriving at Tangmere, had lunch, although the officers were all very uncouth we felt, they said we smelt! This wasn't far wrong for we'd been sleeping by our fighters for the last four nights.

We were then despatched north to Wittering where we stayed until we finally moved down to RAF Northolt. When I arrived at Wittering, having lost practically all my personal gear, I looked around for, and found, a station accountant. I persuaded him that I needed lots of money to replace my goodies – and he paid me! Then I think he realised what he'd done for apparently I was the only one he paid, the others had to go through other channels. Not that it did me much good, for my father borrowed half of it and I never saw it again.'

Paul Richey had discharged himself from hospital and failing to get away by train had finally moved off by road. After a day or so he turned up at Châteaudun.

> 'Next morning I rejoined the re-formed 1 Squadron. Squadron Leader Pemberton was in command and Hilly was a flight commander. Sergeant Clowes was still there, and Knackers, as irrepressible as ever and keeping everyone's spirits up as he had done throughout the French campaign.
>
> That night three mysterious civilians arrived to collect all secret documents, which they did after Pemberton had checked with AHQ. The incredible rumour was that the French were going to throw in their hand... All non-essential documents were destroyed and our kit was packed ready to move at a moment's notice.
>
> Just before the Squadron left, Moses Demozay was ordered by his French superiors to report to a depot at Nantes. Rightly suspecting he was to be demobilised, he ignored the order and went to the airfield instead to thumb a lift to England. After being pushed off several aircraft, he found an abandoned Bristol Bombay with a broken tail-wheel and rudder. Although he had not flown for five years, had never flown a twin, and had no maps, he got a fitter to help start the engines and flew the old crate to England with fifteen jubilant RAF airmen aboard. As if this was not enough, when he couldn't find an airfield, he allowed a sergeant who lived in the Midlands to guide him by railway lines to one near the man's home town!
>
> I left in a DeHavilland Rapide mail-plane on the 14th, from an airfield littered with destroyed hangars and French aircraft blown on to their backs, then headed north-west for Normandy. Since being wounded my capacity for sleep had been prodigious and I slept now. I woke over the Channel Islands and soon we were crossing the Dorset coast. I looked down on the calm and peaceful English countryside, seeing a cricket match being played on a village pitch.
>
> We glided down on to Hendon aerodrome with mixed emotions which I had great difficulty in controlling. I was home.'

Henniker and Flight Lieutenant Barber, the IO, managed to get to the outskirts of St Nazaire on the 16th and led the main ground party into the docks. With only the kit they could carry, they sailed shortly before mid-day to Plymouth in an old tramp steamer.

Reforming

Squadron Leader David Pemberton had taken command of the Squadron on 23 May due to his rank and position rather than combat experience. Not that this was out of the ordinary. The war was still new and not too many senior officers had been able to gain this experience so the status quo remained and those who held the appropriate rank got the jobs.

Pemberton came from Stratford on Avon and was a product of Cranwell and his first squadron had been No.99 – bombers. He then saw service in the Middle East and then held a staff job with 601 Squadron RAuxAF. A spell as a Group examining officer before going to 67 Wing completed his career thus far, so 1 Squadron, having reached the age of 28, was his first real command. Nevertheless, he was popular and had been connected with the Squadron since the previous year.

Once ensconced at Northolt, Pemberton got the few old boys and the new pilots into a training routine, having been joined by returning ground crew. Some new ground crew also arrived, one being LAC John Flood, in from 25 Squadron. He recalls arriving at the maintenance hangar and being greeted by the Flight Sergeant in charge, 'Starry' Knight. John's main charge would be aircraft JX-A. One pilot he recalls during the Battle of Britain was Pilot Officer C E C Chetham. Taller than average, John wondered how he ever got the Hurricane's hood closed. He also remembers him landing on one occasion and yelling: 'The buggers won't stay and fight!' A wartime complement of 225 men (reduced from 300) began to receive replacement equipment – tools and spares – and some new Hurricanes. Time was also taken to try and reconstitute the Squadron diary, the original having been lost/destroyed in the retreat. Hilly Brown continued to lead A Flight, and Brian Hillcoat took over B Flight.

While decorations for the Squadron's activities in France were not announced until later in the year, perhaps it is fitting to mention these at this juncture. Pat Halahan, who had been promoted to Wing Commander, and Johnny Walker had already received DFCs. Halahan now had to submit recommendations for further honours and awards. Although no doubt motivated by the extreme high regard he felt for his pilots, he recommended four officers for the Distinguished Service Order – Kilmartin, Mould, Hanks and Richey. After this, DFCs should go to Palmer, Stratton and Lewis, with a DFM for Sergeant Soper. These eight names went to the AOC of 67 Wing, Wing Commander Cyril Walker, who approved them, but downgraded the DSOs to DFCs!! All the other DFCs and the DFM he also approved with the exception of one, a DFC to Dick Lewis, almost like the spendthrift trying to make a point over excessive expenditure. In any event, there were few DSOs dished out for actions in France, certainly not to ordinary squadron pilots. After all, whatever these pilots, and others, had achieved in France under appalling conditions, it had been a period of defeat.

However, in the summer of 1940 these men, plus earlier recommendations for DFCs to Hilly Brown and the late Les Clisby already having been announced, were all gazetted with their DFCs, while Sergeant Clowes and Berry also received DFMs. Tagged on somewhere too was a DFC for Peter Boot. Thus for the Battle of France, 1 Squadron had collected fourteen gallantry medals.

For the survivors 1 Squadron became a memory. Paul Richey, still unfit for operational flying, was trained to be, and during the summer of 1940, became a fighter controller, mostly at Middle Wallop. Peter Walker went to No.5 OTU, which became 55 OTU, to be an instructor. Prosser Hanks was posted here too, even managing to shoot down a Ju88 in July in one of the unit's Spitfires. Kilmartin arrived too, before going off to 43 Squadron as a flight commander; Mould turned up at the OTU as well. Pat Halahan, promoted to Wing Commander, was given command of this OTU so he soon had most of his old bunch around him. The Bull retired from the Service in 1943.

* * *

Operational

As the Squadron began to work-up to operational standard, new pilots arrived; Pilot Officers J A J Davey and J F D Elkington came from OTUs, while a retired Indian Army Major, now Pilot Officer L W Grumbley, arrived to take over from Flight Lieutenant Roberts as Adjutant. In fact is was Major Grumbley, Indian Army Retired, who had volunteered for the RAF when war came. Years later his grandson would be a pilot with 1 Squadron.

Finally the Squadron was declared operational with effect from 3 July and took its place on 11 Group's Order of Battle. Several uneventful patrols were flown as the Luftwaffe, having established its bases in France and the Low Countries, began to probe Britain's defences over the English Channel. The first clash for the Squadron of what was later termed the Battle of Britain, came on the 19th.

In the late afternoon, Squadron Leader Pemberton, Pete Matthews and Pilot Officer D O M Browne sighted a Heinkel 111 20 miles north of Brighton which they attacked. Having failed to bring it down, Browne continued the chase, he too firing off all his ammunition and continued to follow the German but was then hit in the radiator by a single bullet from the rear gunner. Moments later the Hurricane caught fire and Browne was forced to crash-land near Brighton just before it blew up. The damaged Heinkel, from III/KG55, was finished off by Hurricanes from the Squadron's old rivals, 43 Squadron.

With Northolt being somewhat north of the Channel actions, 1 Squadron sought to use Hawkinge as an advanced base during the day before returning to Northolt in the evening. This arrangement only lasted for one day, for on the 23rd, they began to use their old base at Tangmere as an advanced base during the day. Two days later the Germans raided Portland but the Squadron failed to make contact. That afternoon Blue Section were Scrambled at 1520 hours and encountered Me109s. Flying Officer Hillcoat emptied his guns without result while Flying Officer Salmon fired off half his ammo and followed his target down as it spun from 10,000 to 2,000 feet. He then blacked out and did not see if the 109 hit the water. Pilot Officer Goodman was attacked by a 109 and as it broke away, the German pilot stalled, then dived into the sea. This had been Oberleutnant Karl-Heinz Kirstein of the Stab (staff) staffel, III/JG27, who was killed.

On the last day of July, Matthews, Davey and Sergeant H J Merchant were Scrambled late morning and chased a Do17 south of St Catharine's Point. The Dornier pilot dived to sea level, heading for France flat out. Pete Matthews closed in and his fire caused one engine to trail smoke but that was all, so he could only claim a damaged. With the recent poor showing in air gunnery, David Pemberton arranged for a bomber affiliation exercise with half a dozen Blenheims from 15 Squadron on 4 August. While the Squadron pilots gained valued experience, unfortunately one of the bombers crashed near Whitchurch, Salop, whilst taking violent evasive action. All four men aboard were killed.

These opening rounds by the Germans, testing the RAF reactions, came to an end in early August with the commencement of the assault on its airfields in southern England. However, August activity began for 1 Squadron on the first day, Hilly Brown, Davey and Merchant taking off and engaging a Dornier south of Beachy Head early in the morning but without result. Hilly fired 400 rounds before the Dornier was lost in cloud.

The Squadron were starting to feel like gypsies, for not only were they using Hawkinge again, but also Manston and North Weald as ALGs, but returning to Northolt at the end of the day. It was obvious the German build up was leading to a heavy assault.

On 11 August the Squadron flew an early patrol along the south coast and at 0940 spotted German fighters. One Messerschmitt came screaming through the Hurricanes and broke up their formation and then Pilot Officer C A C Chetham, a fairly recent arrival, together with Randy Goodman went after a 110. Chetham got in first and his fire appeared to silence the rear gunner whilst also setting fire to the starboard engine. Goodman attacked, closing in to 50 yards and following a five-second burst the 110 splashed into the sea. Hilly Brown attacked another 110 and it fell away in flames, Pilot Officer H J Mann seeing its port engine explode as Brown broke away. Brown noted in his log-book:

> 'Vector 190° to point 30 miles south of St Catharine's Point. Shot down one
> Me110 – camera and pilot confirmation; landed at Tangmere.'

The Me110s from ZG2 lost several of their aircraft this day with several others returning damaged. Undoubtedly 1 Squadron accounted for two of them. Pilot Officer John Davey's machine was hit in this scrap and in attempting a forced landing on Sandown golf course, on the Isle of Wight, crashed and was killed. A former aircraft apprentice he had been awarded a Cranwell cadetship. Although this scheme was later suspended, he remustered as an airman under training at FTS Cranwell and gained a permanent commission.

Four days later, the fateful 15th, two days after the Luftwaffe had commenced their major assault code-named *Adler Tag* (Eagle Day), 1 Squadron became heavily engaged during the afternoon. The first contact came after a Scramble from North Weald against Raid 22 – sixteen bomb-carrying Me110s of ErprGr/210 escorted by nine 109s from its 3rd Staffel – heading for Martlesham Heath airfield. (Erprobungsgruppe 210 was a specialist unit flying low-level precision fighter-bomber sorties against England.) Hilly saw them over the sea but the Hurricanes were themselves attacked south of Harwich. Hilly Brown was hit and forced to bale out over the sea, but was rescued by a trawler, with slight facial and hand injuries due to burning petrol.

> 'Clacton 10,000' vectored 045° 20,000'; attacked by 16 Me109s – shell in gravity tank – face
> burned – baled out, picked up by the trawler "Kenya" six miles WNW of Clacton. P/O Browne and
> Sgt Shanahan missing.'

The two pilots mentioned in Brown's log-book were indeed shot down and lost in this action. Twenty-five-year old Martin Shanahan, from Essex, had been on the Squadron just 12 days. Dennis Browne, 21, had been with the Squadron during the retreat in France.

Later Pete Matthews saw a Ju88 aircraft attacked over Martlesham and engaged it too, damaging it. He last saw it in a steep dive with its starboard engine on fire.

At 1445, the Squadron were in action again. Pilot Officer Mann was attacked by a 110 and then a 109 with yellow wing-tips. However, he then managed to get on the tail of another 109 and his fire blew off the top of the fighter's canopy and the 109 went down in a dive. Pilot Officer Elkington was also attacked by a 109 but he got onto its tail and after several bursts the 109 turned slowly onto its back and dropped like a plummet to the sea. His Hurricane had also been hit in the fuel tank and his petrol quickly ran out but he switched to his reserve tank and got home.

Following a subdued evening at Northolt, the Squadron were sent off the next morning, just on mid-day, to patrol Tangmere at low level – 1,500 feet – where fighter pilots do not like to be. Some Me109s were engaged near Selsey Bill but the skirmish was indecisive. On the way back, Elkington's machine was hit – it was believed by British AA fire – and he had to take to his parachute near Thorney Island. Elkington was slightly injured and his fighter JX-O dived into the ground at Manor Farm, Chidham. It was excavated in 1975, with the engine, armour plate and some cockpit items being recovered. In his log-book, Elkington wrote the following, which seems to indicate a 109 got him:

> 'Ran into 100 Huns in morning raid near Portsmouth. Got split up doing cross over. Ran into eight
> 109s, went after one and three others were behind. Cannon hit starboard tank and kite burst into
> flames. Baled out and landed West Wittering on my...! Berry blew me onto land with his slipstream.'

At 1630 came the Scramble. Three waves of He111s, each consisting of 40 bombers, stepped up and with Me109s and 110s above were met and engaged in company with Hurricanes of 615 Squadron and later some Spitfires of 64 Squadron. Squadron Leader Pemberton led A Flight in an assault from the beam and front and his fire sent down one Heinkel in flames. However, his own engine was hit and caught fire but it died down so he was able to make a good landing.

Pete Matthews attacked one of five Me110s and shot it down in flames, but Peter Boot DFC (recently awarded) caught a bullet in the glycol tank and had to crash-land on the Hogsback, near Guildford.

Sergeant 'Darky' Clowes hammered another bomber and saw it go down in a vertical dive, and on climbing again, attacked another Heinkel and then a Ju88, scoring hits on one engine. Goodman shot up a Ju88 and it began to head down. Four Spitfires then joined in and the 88 dived and crash landed without waiting, apparently, for their attack to commence. It came down near Petworth, and while he circled the spot the Junkers suddenly blew up, and a fragment hit his Hurricane and damaged the oil pressure, but he got it back to base and landed safely.

Led by Hillcoat, B Flight now arrived. Flight Sergeant Berry attacked two hostile aircraft and saw one dive vertically, out of control. Sammy Salmon had straggled so climbed to 22,000 feet and came down on the bombers from their left side, and whilst closing, he also found a 110 below him. Deciding to attack this his first burst stopped its port engine and the 110 dived vertically. Electing to land at Redhill to refuel, the airfield was bombed by a Do17, so he quickly took off and returned to the comparative quiet of Northolt.

Pilot Officer C M Stavert, who had celebrated his 19th birthday five days earlier (and therefore had been only 18 during his time in France), made a frontal attack with the others. Pulling up through some cloud he met a He111 head-on, fired and the bomber dived vertically into the clouds. Following it through he came out and saw the smoking remains of a twin-engined aircraft below him.

Pat Hancock returned to base with combat damage courtesy of a 110 above the South Downs. Two longerons had been hit and severed but he got back without mishap. In all the Squadron claimed five destroyed and two proables.

The Heinkels all came from KG27 and KG55, the former losing one while the latter lost three aircraft and had another five damaged. The bomber which blew up over Upper Frithwold Farm, Northchapel, north of Petworth, was from the 4th Staffel and flown by the Staffelkapitän, Hauptmann Sabler. He and his crew were killed. The extent of the explosion can be imagined because the starboard wing from this aircraft landed in a nearby wood and was not discovered until 1973.

On 18 August they were back again at North Weald and A Flight were Scrambled in the afternoon and sent towards Southend. Climbing up through cloud they came out into sunlight at 21,000 feet to encounter about a dozen Me109s. The 109s quickly pounced on the RAF fighters but without success. Squadron Leader Pemberton followed one of them down to the ground and, having flown over the Thames, contour-chased it over Kent. The jinking fighter was hit again and it fell in flames north of Tenterden.

This Messerschmitt came from the 8th Staffel of JG3 and came down at Blue House Farm, Milebush, near Staplehurst. Its pilot, Obergefreiter Basell did not survive. In 1981 the crash site was excavated and several bits of the 109 were discovered including the complete front section of the cockpit canopy frame.

B Flight had been ordered off to patrol base, then sent south towards Shoreham, where they encountered a large formation of 60 Dornier 17s. Despite rapidly drying fuel tanks, a full beam attack was carried out and one bomber fell away in flames after some attention by Harry Hillcoat, Goodman and Stavert, some of the crew being seen to bale out. Looking with interest at one parachute, Goodman's eye caught sight of a Me110 over the sea heading for France, with one of its engines leaving a trail of smoke. He dived after it and set its other engine on fire then watched as the fighter crashed into the sea.

The Dorniers had been those of KG76 which had just raided RAF Kenley. This 8th Staffel machine went into the sea at 1.40 pm, piloted by Leutnant Leder. He and his crew did not survive. Randy Goodman's 110 was a 6th Staffel ZG26 aircraft that had been damaged earlier by 56 Squadron. It went into the water off Folkestone, the pilot being killed but the gunner was later rescued and taken prisoner.

The Squadron now experienced a slight lull in the fighting, but in anticipation of Fighter Command having eventually to engage raiders at night, night flying practise needed to be addressed. Shortly before midnight on the 19th, Pilot Officer C N Birch got himself well and truly lost and blundered into the London balloon barrage. He struck a cable at 1,500 feet and had little choice but to bale out. He landed on the roof of a house near Finchley which caused him some slight injuries, but his Hurricane crashed in Chatterton Street, Finsbury Park and caught fire. Some damage was caused to property but fortunately no one on the ground was hurt.

A few nights later Pilot Officer Chetham was on a night flight and was caught and held in a searchlight beam. Thoroughly disorientated he got into a spin from which he could not recover so he too baled out into the night sky near Amersham, landing without injury.

It was back to business on the 28th, the weather having improved. The Squadron were Scrambled from Northolt to patrol over RAF Hornchurch at 1230 hours. High over Rochford they ran into a formation of Dorniers with escorting Me109s. 1 Squadron waded in, and two bombers fell away, one to crash on Rochford aerodrome, another going into the sea near the Tongue Lightship. At least one more was severely damaged, last seen low over the water being covered by others. Fortunately the

109s – for once – did not mix it with the RAF fighters, the result of Luftwaffe orders to stay close to the bombers and not go wandering off to claim fighter kills.

The bombers were from KG3, who had two aircraft lost over England, two more which crashed in France and another which crash-landed near the French coast. 615 Squadron had again been involved in this battle and it had been so intense that as far as 1 Squadron was concerned, no individual claims could be attributed, so the Squadron merely noted two kills and left it at that. More good news was that Hilly Brown was about to return, following his bale out on the 15th.

On Friday 30 August a Squadron Scramble at 1630 led to a force of 30-40 bombers with around 30 escorting fighters. Sergeant Merchant shot down a He111 which crashed near a cemetery east of Southend, its crew taking to their parachutes. Pilot Officer Birch damaged another Heinkel, while Pat Hancock claimed a probable after leaving it spewing smoke, oil and flames. 'Darky' Clowes knocked pieces off a He111 and a Me110 and Mann also damaged two 110s. Pete Matthews damaged a straggling Heinkel which was then finished off by Hurricanes of 56 Squadron.

The bombers were from KG53 which were attacking Radlett. They lost several of their aircraft to various Hurricane attacks, and others returned home damaged. ZG26 were escorting them and they lost one fighter and had at least three more damaged. 1 Squadron returned to base without a scratch.

The next morning it was Readiness at dawn as usual at Northolt. The telephone sent seven pilots to their fighters at 0740 to patrol Chelmsford. Over the town they ran into in excess of 100 Dorniers and Junkers escorted by a mass of fighters. To 1 Squadron, the odds seemed just about right!!

Going down on the bombers, 110s came down on them. Merchant gained his second kill in two days by destroying a 110 (it exploded right in front of him), which he shot off the tail of David Pemberton, then damaged another, but he was also hit and had to bale out, receiving burns. It took a few seconds to get clear and his injuries put him in Halstead Cottage Hospital.

Pemberton hammered a Ju88. Clowes made a frontal attack on a bunch of Dorniers and saw one swing from the formation and another go spinning earthwards. Attacked then by a 110 Clowes pulled up into a loop, closed in behind a 110 and knocked out its starboard engine. The 110 headed for the deck closely followed by the RAF pilot, snapping off bursts as his sights came on. The rear gun ceased to fire back and Clowes could clearly see the pilot desperately seeking a place to put down. Peter Boot, Harry Mann and Rupert Dibnah also attacked 110s and claimed damage to each.

The Messerschmitts appear to be those of I/LG1 or ZG26 who had a number of their aircraft shot down and damaged in action with both Hurricanes and Spitfires. Dibnah, short of fuel, decided to divert to Hornchurch but with ground mist failed to locate the airfield. Putting down in a field to ask the way he was told it was just 'over there'. Taking off he was so close he did not have to bother to raise his wheels.

Serviceability was still a problem, but on 1 September the available aircraft went up to nine. While the going had been tough and several aircraft had been lost or damaged, pilot losses had been relatively few. This is probably why the Squadron was kept 'down south' while other units which had been badly mauled had been sent north for a break. However, 1 Squadron's turn would come.

Meantime, on the 1st Hillcoat led off the nine pilots at 1045 and got into a fight with Me109s which were escorting bombers to the east of Tonbridge. Four of the German fighters were claimed as shot down, one each by Hillcoat, Birch, Chetham and Boot. However, the Squadron suffered a grievous loss. Flight Sergeant Berry was shot up, crashed at Brisley Farm, Ruckinge, north of Romney Marsh, and was killed.

The pilots were probably a bit over-optimistic in their claiming as few 109s were lost this morning, and only one possibly at the right time and place. The problem with 109s was that with fuel injection the German pilots could nose down into a dive without stalling their engines. As they also tended to throttle back, this blew out a cloud of smoke from their exhausts which looked like a damaging engine hit. The RAF pilots of course could not do this due to their floating carburettors and had to take care not to flood the engine and have it cut out, so they had to try and avoid negative 'G'.

That afternoon the Squadron was Scrambled again and once more had to mix it with 109s. Hillcoat and Chetham claimed a probable and a damaged respectively. But two days later, on the first anniversary of the war, Hillcoat and Bob Shaw both failed to return after a 1010 am Scramble and the Squadron had nothing to show for their loss. They had been on a mid-morning patrol, and Shaw's Hurricane crashed at Parkhouse Farm, Chart Sutton, south of Maidstone. Hillcoat has no known grave. Shaw too was initially only remembered on the Runnymede RAF Memorial, but it has since been established that his remains were buried locally in Sittingbourne Cemetery although not formally identified. For the last 30 years there has been a memorial service held by the grave, situated on a slope overlooking the Kentish Weald.

The pilots managed to take some revenge for their recent losses on the 6th. Hilly Brown led nine aircraft away at 0845 hours to patrol Kenley at 20,000 feet, and from here they saw a large gaggle of

Ju88s and Me110s heading for Brooklands. Going into the attack, Hilly damaged one bomber, leaving it with one engine knocked out, while Stavert shot down another. Randy Goodman and 'Dib' Dibnah each blasted a Messerschmitt, although Goodman's machine took some hits from the back-seat gunner and he had to bale out near Penshurst. The bombers were probably from KG76 who lost one aircraft in the Channel, damaged by a fighter and finished off by AA fire over the coast. Another 88 came down near Tonbridge at 0915. If ZG26 had been escorting them, they lost three 110s, one of which went into the sea, another falling near Coulsdon, Surrey.

Two minutes past 1 o'clock, the Squadron were Scrambled again, nine aircraft grabbing height towards Maidstone. Vectored towards Raid 43C near Dungeness they were attacked by Me109s but shook themselves free without loss. Stavert then found a He111 and his attack produced smoke and it was last seen losing height.

Flight Lieutenant John Holderness, from Rhodesia, had joined the Squadron in August, and he had his first action on the evening of the 7th. Eleven Hurricanes were sent off to patrol over base at 1625. The Luftwaffe had now turned its attentions towards London, right in 1 Squadron's back-yard. Having gained height they soon saw a mass of Dorniers and 110s to the north-east of the city and attacked. Holderness was able to claim one Dorner shot down, 'Darky' Clowes a 110.

No sooner had they landed back and been rearmed and refuelled than they were Scrambled again and met more Dorniers. John Finnis, another Rhodesian, had come in to replace the lost Hillcoat as flight commander, and he and another new pilot, Michael Homer DFC, each damaged a bomber. Pilot Officer Homer had won his DFC with a bomber squadron for an attack on two cruisers in Kristiansand Bay. With a shortage of fighter pilots he had answered the call for volunteers. He was only with the Squadron for a couple of weeks before going to 242 Squadron on the 21st, but was killed in action six days later.

Rest

This ended the Squadron's period in the south. Orders came on the 9th to move north for a rest. Squadron Leader Pemberton led his pilots to a new base at RAF Wittering that same day, a base which the Squadron would know well in later years. It must not have been so great in 1940, for Hilly Brown, in noting the move in his flying log-book put down "rotten hole" after his arrival. However, perhaps he was referring to the Station's satellite at Collyweston, where the Squadron were dispersed. In all 15 Hurricanes flew north, while 30 NCOs and other ranks arrived by road. Three days later came the announcement of the award of the DFC to the CO. Clowes was also about to be commissioned. He had recently been awarded a Mention in Despatches, Gazetted 11 July 1940.

RAF Wittering, 12 Group

While some patrols and a few Scrambles were flown over the next weeks, the pressure was definitely off. Just as had happened after the fall of France, most of the senior pilots were now posted out, either to go to other squadrons still in the south, or to become instructors. Numbers were quickly re-established with an influx of Czechoslovakian pilots, all of whom had escaped from Europe one way or another in order to continue the fight with the French and then the RAF. Another new arrival was an old friend, 'Moses' Demozay, who had been the Squadron interpreter in France. He had now gone through the RAF training system and had become an operational fighter pilot. He had no language problems, but those first weeks with the Czechs were a testing time for everyone.

The Squadron was now officially a 'C' type unit, which meant that while being rested, it retained a few experienced pilots, was given an influx of new pilots to bring to operational standard and then had to 'feed' them to squadrons in the battle area. But there was still some action for the veterans.

On 8 October, Pete Matthews and Randy Goodman were sent off after a lone raider and found it near Bucknell at 6,000 feet. They chased it and Goodman felt sure he had knocked out the rear gunner before the 88 was lost in cloud. Elkington had returned from his shoot down in August, and this same day he took a Hurricane over to Leicester so that roof-spotters could see what one looked like. As he noted in his log-book – they saw all they wanted!

The very next day Elkington and Sergeant M P Davies were sent off after another Ju88 at 1020, which they engaged, Davies believing it had gone down into the sea. One Ju88 of 6/KG30 did fail to return and may have been this raider. Davies was posted out the next day. Elkington noted:

> 'Vectored onto Ju88 below us. Chased it through clouds 5/10ths, to coast, firing. Davies damaged starboard engine but left me at coast. Got burst in from about 20 yards, pulled away and blacked out badly. Recovered but no sign of 88 (40 miles NE of Skegness). Plot ceased and hits seen by ROC. (Claimed.) All ammo used.'

However, the day was marred by the loss of Sergeant Stan Warren, who had arrived on 21 September. He was on a training flight over the Wash and must have gone into the sea. On the 19th Brown, Clowes and Chetham chased another raider and although they found it, it quickly disappeared in cloud pursued by a number of .303 rounds.

Further success came on the 24th. Just on mid-day Brown, Clowes and Pilot Officer A Kershaw were Scrambled and were vectored onto a Dornier east of Banbury. They attacked and the Dornier was badly hit and began to reduce height. However, the German machine was then attacked by a section from 17 Squadron before it crashed near St Neots. In fact it was a Dornier 215 from 3/Aufkl/Gr.Ob.d.L – a photo-reconnaissance unit – which had been on a sortie to Coventry and Birmingham. It had started to break up shortly before hitting the ground near the Crown Inn, Eaton Socon, at 1215, on the western side of the Great West Road. The crew had attempted to bale out but only one survived. A machine gun which had either fallen or been thrown out was found at Towcaster, which had happened just before the survivor had jumped out.

It was proving a busy week. On the 27th Goodman managed to get some bursts at a Do17 before losing it in cloud, although the Hurricanes had been hindered by AA fire. Two days later another Dornier was claimed by Sergeant W T Page, Pilot Officer J C Robinson and Sergeant V Jicha in the late afternoon. Goodman's target had been a machine from 7/KG3 that had been attacked near Feltwell, and had one crewman killed. The other machine does not feature in German loss reports so must have succeeded in getting away. However, in an earlier action on the 29th, a Dornier 17 was engaged by Hurricanes and Pilot Officer E Cizek wrote off his fighter in a crash at Wittering, but he was not injured. Evzen Cizak had seen action on the Continent before France fell and later commanded 312 Squadron. By 1942 he was a Group Captain with the Czech Air Force, but was killed in a crash in November that year, his aircraft hitting a balloon cable.

The month ended with a success and a red face. A section was Scrambled at 1345 on the 30th and at 1418, near Skegness, an aircraft was spotted. Goodman, Lewis and Jicha closed in but Goodman identified it as a Blenheim and broke away. However, the other two saw it was in fact a Ju88, attacked and shot it down. This was a machine from the 8th Staffel, III/LG1 and its fall was confirmed, much to the chagrin of Randy Goodman. It had been on an armed incursion raid and came down in a belly landing at Priggs Yard, Middle Fen, Stuntney, Ely, Cambridgeshire, where Unteroffizier Arndt and his crew were taken prisoner.

Changes in command

It is unfortunate that the Squadron diary is missing for November, but the main feature of the month was the loss of David Pemberton on the 2nd. Having progressed from a wing staff officer to a successful fighter pilot and squadron commander speaks volumes. He had led the Squadron throughout the Battle of Britain, secured his share of victories and been decorated. He had personally flown more than 70 sorties during the Battle.

On the morning of the 2nd he had taken off from Collyweston just before 0730 and from some accounts poor weather at Wittering caused him to dig his starboard wing into the ground as he came in to land; he cartwheeled, the wing sheered off, the aircraft crashed and he was killed. Another version is that he, for some reason, slow rolled too near the ground and crashed. Visibility was low with a poor horizon. In any event, LAC Treffrey, driving a bowser, was the first at the scene and finding the CO lying amid the wreckage got to him just as he died. Another accident this day badly damaged P3395, Pilot Officer Cizak crash-landing in a ploughed field – Cat C.

Hilly Brown was immediately given command of the Squadron and Pete Matthews and 'Darky' Clowes were promoted to flight commanders. Clowes' rapid promotion, while well deserved, was no less than meteoric. In a little over six weeks he had risen from Sergeant to Flight Lieutenant, without having the time to hold Flying Officer rank.

On 15 December the Squadron were moved back down to Northolt to resume their place on 11 Group's Order of Battle. For all anyone knew, the New Year would see a resumption of attacks by the Luftwaffe. Everyone felt they had won the summer and autumn air battles and that once the winter weather moved on, it would all start again. The Luftwaffe, however, had other ideas, and began to use the night sky to assault London and other major towns and cities all over Britain. It found the RAF ill-prepared to combat the night raiders.

For 1 Squadron, the end of the momentous year of 1940 had confirmed their place as the RAF's premier squadron, their actions in France and in the defence of Great Britain had been second to none. 1941 would see the start of a very different air war.

Chapter Ten

NIGHT AND DAY

If the RAF were thinking that 1941 would see a resumption of the Battle of Britain they certainly did not sit back and await its re-commencement. With night raids on the increase, much thought was being given as to how to combat bombing raids in darkness with so few twin-engined night-fighter aircraft. These would have to be supported by Spitfires and Hurricanes, with all the inherent problems and dangers this posed for the pilots.

Meantime, others were taking the time to think of ways of pressing on with the war by starting to dish it out rather than just take it. Young fighter pilots seated in a fast and well armed fighting machine could see the potential for flying across the Channel and taking a swipe at anything they found marked with a cross or swastika. For their part, the chiefs at Fighter Command HQ could see nothing wrong in this. It encouraged an offensive spirit and sent a message to the Germans that Britain was not sitting around waiting for the inevitable.

Just four days before Christmas, two Spitfires of 66 Squadron had flown across the Channel and strafed the German airfield at Le Touquet. They did little damage but did get home unscathed – and it had been exciting. Once the story got around, others were keen to have a go too.

Well up in the queue was No.1 Squadron. Orders came on New Year's Eve that Flight Lieutenant Clowes should take two pilots off on the morrow and see if they could find anything to attack. He chose Dick Lewis and Tony Kershaw. Thus on the first day of 1941 these three flew out low across the sea, headed down the French coast and shot up German installations between Calais and Boulogne.

In the beginning these sorties, usually restricted to days with low cloud so that pilots could quickly hide from trouble, were called Mosquito raids; after all they were not much more than an annoyance, just like the real-life mosquito. Later, due to a new aeroplane of the same name coming into service, these raids became known by the code-name of Rhubarb. Flown mostly by a pair, or sometimes two pairs, these were flown on and off for the next couple of years whenever suitable weather prevailed. They proved exciting, but also extremely dangerous and costly and had eventually to be curtailed.

The New Year also saw the announcement in the Honour's List of an MBE to Flying Officer E D Hills, of the Squadron's ground personnel, and Mentions for former pilots, H B I Hillcoat and P E Warcup. Five NCOs were also recommended for meritous service in France (see appendix).

News came now for a transfer to RAF Kenley, although weather delayed the move until the morning of the 5th. At Kenley Number 1 became part of a Wing, with 615 Squadron, commanded by a new flying position, a wing commander flying, or wing leader. In Kenley's case this was John Peel DFC. In future these wing leaders would take Fighter Command's war to the Germans.

Winter weather rarely favours any sort of operations so the Squadron had to wait until the beginning of February to resume real actions against the enemy. On the second day of this month they were assigned to fly a Cover Patrol to Boulogne in the afternoon. There was little point in just flying over France hoping the Luftwaffe would 'come out to play' – they had no need to. Fighter Command, therefore, being keen to 'play' encouraged a reaction by escorting small formations of light bombers across to hit targets of value which they hoped the Me109 pilots would be encouraged to defend. There was quite an organisation around these operations. Not only would the bombers have close escort, but the escort would be escorted, while other squadrons would fly in support of the whole show, either going into the target area first to sweep away any 109s waiting around, or supporting the subsequent withdrawal to prevent 109s nibbling at the bombers and fighters as they flew home. Thus this first mission for 1 Squadron was to fly cover in support of the main operation.

Pat Hancock was back with the Squadron after a brief sojourn to 85 Squadron:

'In December I was sent to 85 Squadron, under Peter Townsend, which had Defiants and Hurricanes, but somehow I persuaded them that I should not stay, so soon found myself back with 1 Squadron. I was quite a good organiser for myself if nobody else. I did of course like the Hurricane. It was very nice to fly and very manoeuvrable. It saved my life frequently because they could knock holes in it and it would ignore them, whereas holes in the Spitfire tended to be more serious.

I liked Hilly Brown, he was a great chap. On one occasion he decided to take three of us to the wicked city of Nottingham. He was a very human man and a splendid pilot.'

Pat was down for this show, flying as Blue Leader. It was termed Circus No.2[1], Circus being the code word for bombers with fighter escort. Shortly before 2 pm he was weaving behind the Squadron escorting the bombers over Boulogne. Moments later JG3's Messerschmitts attacked. Pat spotted a 109 making a diving attack on the bombers and then it climbed to the left. Pat pulled up behind it and still turning fired short bursts at it from 300 yards and then got in a deflection shot. Glycol began to stream out of it but then another Hurricane cut in front of him. The last he saw of the 109 was it heading for the sea.

One of the Czech pilots also shot at (although he did not know it) the same 109 and it was claimed as a probable. The pilot's name was Sergeant Karel Kuttelwascher, and he was to become famous in the annuls of the Squadron. He had already seen action in France, flying with the French after his escape from his homeland. He had shared two kills and one probable. Pat Hancock recalls:

'Kuttelwascher was a bit of a card. Great pilot though, but then all these Czech and Polish pilots were very experienced, with hundreds of hours in the air. They seemed to have been flying their two-wing jobs for a couple of centuries, or so it seemed to me. They also had a high level of discipline.'

Circus No.3 came on the afternoon of the 5th. In his log-book Hilly Brown noted that it was a:

'Bloody cock-up – fired at a Me109 over Gravelines, no result seen. F/O Lewis came down in the sea and was not rescued – RIP.'

Canadian Ray Lewis, veteran of France and the Battle of Britain, was hit by a 109 which came sweeping through the formation. With his Hurricane on fire he had to bale out into the cold waters of the English Channel. The ASR service was still in its infancy at this stage and a man's survival in a cold sea was generally counted in minutes. RAF fighter pilots would not have dinghy packs until well into the early summer. Several RAF fighters were lost in this operation, battling with JG3.

Three days later Hilly Brown flew a Rhubarb sortie with Flying Officer Jim Robinson, taking off at 1220 from Manston. Brown's log-book is noted:

'Shot up 'drome at Quercamp and Me109 taking off – last seen gliding down wind at 200 feet.'

JG3 were using this airfield, which in fact was Arques, and the 6th Staffel reported one Me109 crash landed damaged and one 4th Staffel machine damaged on the ground.

New aeroplanes
On the last day of February the first Hurricane IIs started to arrive. These had Merlin XX supercharged engines giving more *oomph*! These Mark IIs would soon replace all the old Mark Is, and some would have 12 .303 Browning guns instead of the usual eight (Mark IIA). Later still the IICs would come with four 20 mm cannons.

Almost every RAF fighter squadron had the task of flying convoy patrols at some stage of the war, and 1 Squadron did their share. They were thankless, boring jobs, where one had to keep watch not only for German bombers, but fighters – and 'friendly fire' from trigger-happy gunners on the ships. Aircraft recognition aboard ship left much to be desired and it was sometimes a case of shoot first, ask questions later.

On one of these convoy patrols, flown in the late afternoon of 19 March, between Dungeness and Hastings, two Me109s from I/LG2 zipped in from the south and engaged the Hurricanes, and then five Spitfires from 609 Squadron joined in. However, Tony Kershaw was hit, dived, and baled out too late. His body was later picked up by a minesweeper's whaler and brought ashore. Sergeant Stefan's machine was also hit but he crash landed without injury although his Hurricane was a write-off. Both Hurricanes had been the victim of Hauptmann Herbert Ihlefeld, who had around 30 victories at this stage and would add another 100 before the war's end.

Five days later, the 24th, south east of Hastings, on another afternoon convoy patrol, Moses Demozay spotted a 109 diving down from some clouds to attack his section, which was spread out. He turned quickly to pass beneath the 109, whose pilot, seeing the danger, nipped back into the cloud. Reforming, the same, or another 109, came down and warned by his No.2, Demozay took violent evasive action. Then two 109s attacked from astern. The Frenchman throttled back and they overshot

---

[1] The very first Circus was flown on 10 January 1941.

him and went into some low cloud. Following them, he emerged right behind the two fighters and fired at one with a long 12-second burst. The 109 erupted in flames and went down.

Following Brown's strafe of Quercamp, the Squadron, led by Wing Commander Peel, flew across and shot up Berck-sur-Mer on 7 April. Some transport and Me109s were hit, and in firing his de Wilde tracers at two parked 109s, Sergeant E Goy saw two men fall. Peel claimed two 109s set on fire.

The next morning four Hurricane IIs were off to patrol near Dungeness led by Flying Officer Robinson and they spotted three Me109s off Cap Gris Nez, in a wide vic at 30,000 feet. Eager to join combat the three Czech pilots in the formation engaged the fighters and Kuttelwascher stalked a 'yellow-nosed' 109 which had just made a pass at Sergeant Jan Plasil's machine. Kut fired from 30 yards and the 109 crashed into a small wood 15 miles south of Gris Nez.

Things were certainly starting to hot up with the warmer weather. The German fighter pilots were still offensive enough to fly hunting patrols over south-east England on the look-out for RAF aircraft. On the evening of 21 April Sergeant Josef Prihoda was part of a patrol flying over the Maidstone area. Near Canterbury the Controller warned of hostile aircraft and then white contrails could be seen above. Flying Officer Robinson, leading the patrol, climbed to starboard to keep in front of the sun. Suddenly a 109 came at Prihoda and he and the 109 came at each other head-on and the Czech pilot did not give way.

The 109 pilot then pulled up before diving. Prihoda turned and followed the 109 as it went below him. Firing from 500 yards with his 12 guns he then chased the 109 over the Channel to the French coast, gradually closing to 200 yards. White and black smoke began to come from the German machine and finally it went down out of control from 7,000 feet. Meantime, Robinson had attacked another 109, observing his de Wilde ammunition hitting it and knocking pieces from the port wing root – then it dived away.

These successes were marred by the loss of Sergeant C M Stoken the next day. In poor weather he took off in the Squadron Magister without prior authority from Ops, crashed and was killed.

LAC John Flood remembers the Czech pilots, especially Dygryn and Stefan. Dygryn went to great lengths trying to get the green colour out of the service petrol – an instant giveaway if caught filching it. He used all manner of filters, even pouring some through his gas mask, but to no avail. Dygryn had a motor-bike, and getting fed up with his aircraft always being the farthest away from the flight hut, used it if ever he was Scrambled! John and Dygryn would have friendly wrestling matches, which the Czech generally won. Today, John Flood occasionally tends Dygryn's grave at Westwell, Kent. Sergeant Stefan befriended a dog, and when asked about it, would reply poignantly: 'He has got no one, and I've got no one, so we are friends.'

Frank Kennedy also recalls Sergeant Dygryn:

> 'While at Redhill in April 1941 I was talking to Sergeant Dygryn at the dispersal area, he was showing me a .22 automatic pistol that he carried with him at all times. On each side of the butt was engraved in silver the map of Czechoslovakia. We were standing about eighteen to twenty feet away from a stream that ran behind the hut, which was about three feet wide. Suddenly a rat ran along the opposite bank and Dygryn immediately fired three shots at it. When we recovered the body there were three bullets in it. His reaction time and then his accuracy were amazing.'

New Commanding Officer

It was now time for another change. Hilly Brown had been with the Squadron non-stop since before the war and was more than due for a rest. On 23 April Squadron Leader R E P Brooker arrived to take command, and two days later Flight Lieutenant W H Sizer DFC came in to replace 'Darky' Clowes, who was also being rested, moving to 55 OTU as an instructor.

Pete Brooker had been a school teacher before joining the RAF in 1937, and had been with 56 Squadron during the Battle of Britain. He came from CGS Sutton Bridge where he had also been an instructor. Wilfred Sizer was 21 and another pre-war pilot, but had seen much action with 213 Squadron in 1940. With 1 Squadron, Clowes had flown a distinctively marked Hurricane with a hornet painted on the nose (JX-B P3395). It was said that each black band on the hornet's yellow body represented a German shot down. This author is not sure about this even though the stripes numbered 8 or 9 depending on how one counts them. Clowes had around 10 victories, but if the story is true it left no more room for him to add more it he scored more kills. Probably good journalistic licence. However, his experience would be sorely missed, having risen from the ranks to flight commander and about to receive the DFC to add to his DFM. He would later command squadrons in the Middle East and be granted a permanent commission after the war. Sadly he was to die in 1949 while still in service. Hilly Brown had also received a Bar to his DFC and his score of victories totalled 18 or 19. Although he stayed around for a short while he was finally posted to a couple of OTUs before becoming a wing commander and sent to Malta later in 1941. Leading the Takali Wing, he was shot down and killed during a strafing attack against Gela airfield, Sicily, on 12 November.

* * *

The Squadron had also been moved to Croydon aerodrome on the 8th, and it was from here that four Hurricanes took off on 28 April to fly a convoy patrol over the Thames Estuary. They were later vectored to Dungeness, with Sergeant Prihoda weaving behind as look-out. Unfortunately the look-out was often the first to be attacked and so it was on this occasion. Picked off by a diving Me109 he force landed in a field near New Romney, but was unharmed. The next day came the announcements of DFCs for Clowes and Peter Matthews, the latter also leaving the Squadron, off to 52 OTU to instruct. In 1942 Matthews saw a lot of action in North Africa commanding 145 Squadron.

On 2 May, the Squadron moved again, this time to Redhill, in order to help with the nightly raids by German bombers.

The Night Blitz
German night raids had been increasing for some time, and they came to a peak in May 1941. 1 Squadron were now assigned to help with the defence of London and on the night of 10/11 May, had a field day.

Twelve pilots were put on stand-by for a Fighter Night on the evening of the 10th, and began to take off in pairs but to work singly, an hour before midnight as the raiders started to come onto the radar screens. Squadron Leader Brooker and Moses Demozay each shot down a He111. Brooker found his above the burning city of London, attacked and the German's port engine began to burn then dived into the ground. His windscreen was covered in oil making it difficult to see two other bombers he had a go at.

Demozay was at 17,200 feet over the East India Docks and saw a Heinkel caught in three search-light beams. Closing in to 30 yards it too went down with an engine on fire to explode on the ground.

The second two off were both Czechs, Josef Dygryn (actually Dygryn-Ligoticky) and Bedrich Kratkoruky. Levelling out at 17,000 feet above London, Dygryn saw a twin-engined machine parallel and just below him and attacked. Return fire zipped back at him but once he began firing into the bomber this fire ceased. The bomber began to dive and following it, firing again, watched as it dived into the ground. Kratkoruky, over the Thames, saw a bomber over Canvey Island just above him so climbed to make a beam attack. After a burst the bomber dived and after another attack he lost the German which was still going down south-west of Southend.

Third pair off, Sergeants Jaroslav Novak and Prihoda both found bombers too. Novak chased a Ju88 north but several bursts did not appear to hurt his opponent and then he lost it. Prihoda saw two Heinkels over the city and was just about to attack one as the air erupted with exploding AA shells, forcing him to break away. Also away in his Hurricane was Sergeant Frantisek Behal. It is thought he was hit by return fire from a bomber and he reported to Control that he was baling out. However, he crashed at Selsdon Park, near Croydon, and was killed.

The night was not over yet. Aircraft returned to be refuelled and rearmed and at 0115 Flying Officer Robinson took off and engaged a bomber. He fired five bursts but then lost his prey at 7,000 feet, although it was trailing smoke.

At 0135, Dygryn took off from Redhill and over Kenley he saw a He111 just above him, going south. Giving chase the Czech pilot met return fire but then his fire produced smoke from the bomber which he could see going over the top of his cockpit. The bomber then burst into flames and spun vertically.

Flight Lieutenant K C Jackman and Pilot Officer W Raymond were away at 0225. Half an hour later Jackman saw a He111 heading for London, chased it for three miles and opened fire at 250 yards. The bomber went into a steep left-hand diving turn trailing smoke. As he followed it down, he and the rear gunner exchanged fire and then he lost it still diving south of Redhill. Raymond also attacked a bomber, opened fire at close range and it dived out of control. Circling, the RAF pilot saw a large fire on the ground ten miles south of base.

Sergeant Dygryn landed and took off again at 0315, and found a Ju88 north-east of Biggin Hill at 16,000 feet. He attacked at point-blank range, firing all his ammunition in several bursts and the bomber began to descend, leaving a smoke trail. He followed it over the south coast where he saw it catch fire and dive into the sea some miles south of Hastings. In all the Squadron claimed seven destroyed and two damaged. Of these Sergeant Dygryn-Ligoticky claimed three.

This fateful night for London saw the loss of 11 German bombers, seven He111s and four Ju88s. Two of the Heinkels appear to have fallen to 29 Squadron Beaufighters, and all four 88s went into the sea, three of KG55 into the Channel, and one from the recce unit 3(F)/122 off the Dutch coast. Another He111 fell to 74 Squadron (near Ashford) and one was shot down by flak near Birmingham. Brooker and Demozay say their victims went down over London, Dygryn's first also in this area. Dygryn's next two kills – both seen as Ju88s – may well have been two of the ones that went into the Channel. Kratkoruky's may also have gone into the sea near the Thames Estuary. Jackson and Robinson's combats and times tie-up with a 9/KG55 He111P that crashed at Swift's Field, Station Road, Withyham, East Sussex at 0330. (Locations of other He111 losses were near Chelmsford, Essex at 1232 and Upchurch, near Gillingham, and close to the Thames, at 1400.)

Sergeant Dygryn's eye was obviously in. On the 16th, during a patrol over Tenterden, which was intercepted by 109s, he claimed another kill. Operating from Redhill, four Hurricanes headed for Dungeness and were then vectored towards hostile aircraft over the Channel. Due to weak radio reception, Brooker handed over the lead to Flight Lieutenant Jackman and they climbed to 26,000 feet. They found three Me109s orbiting at 32,000 feet and although they tried to get to them, they could not. Then Dygryn saw a fourth 109 diving on Jackman, went for it and fired a short burst from 250 yards, followed by a long burst from 150-200 yards.

With no visible result, he broke away and climbed back towards the original three Messerschmitts, selected one and opened fire. He could still not see any effect but later the British 'Y' Service which monitored Luftwaffe radio traffic, reported hearing that a 109 had gone into the Channel at this time and place. However, this loss was a 109 of JG3, hit by ground fire during an attack on Hawkinge. Dygryn probably hit another JG3 machine, flown by Leutnant Erich Buchholz, who crash landed at St Pol, wounded.

The next day, Squadron Leader Brooker was informed of the award of the DFC for his work with 56 Squadron and the bomber he had shot down over London. On the 19th, Dr. Edouard Benes, the President of the Czech Republic in exile, visited 1 Squadron in order to bestow upon Flight Sergeant Dygryn-Ligoticky the Czech War Cross for his recent actions.

On 21 May twelve Hurricanes took off at 1655 as part of the escort to 18 Blenheims (from 21, 82 and 110 Squadrons) on Circus No.18 to Gosnay power station. It provoked a large Luftwaffe reaction. Linking up with 258 and 302 Squadrons over Kenley, 1 Squadron had the job of Top Rear Escort at 15,000 feet. The balbo crossed the English coast at Dungeness and the French coast at Le Touquet. Halfway to the target eight Me109s were seen climbing up behind, which caught up with the RAF formation over the target where they proceeded to attack the bombers. One Blenheim was hit and began to spew flames from its port engine. Two sections were ordered to intercept but 302 Squadron got there first so they rejoined.

Two more 109s were spotted off to starboard so Green Section, Pilot Officers W Raymond and B G Collyns, were detached to see them off. As they did so, four more 109s appeared suddenly from some cloud, one coming down on Collyns' tail but it was engaged by Raymond. It was hit before it could fire and smoke began to pour from the 109 but he was unable to see more as several other 109s appeared above so he dived away, right down to sea level.

Collyns meantime joined up with White Section and a few other Hurricanes from another squadron. Eight further 109s came up astern of the RAF fighters and 1 Squadron engaged. Flying Officer Antonin Volebnovsky was attacked but he half-rolled and got behind the German, fired at it and saw pieces come away from its wings and fuselage. Squadron Leader Brooker engaged a 109 without result and Sergeant Dygryn, Yellow 2, attacked another firing at a Hurricane, fired, hitting cockpit and fuselage, and saw it stagger away, then dive steeply.

Sergeant Kuttelwascher, acting as top weaver on the way out, saw four 109s attack two Hurricanes and dived on the rearmost, firing two bursts from 50 yards. The 109 went down out of control pouring smoke. Sergeant Bedrich Kratkoruky, weaving below and in front of the formation, saw two 109s dive through the Squadron to attack the bombers and got a burst into one of them from 50 yards. He saw the 109's tail drop off and the pilot bale out. Then he saw Flying Officer J C E Robinson's Hurricane shot down, catching fire as it dived gently towards the sea. Sergeant Nasswetter, Red 2, knocked pieces off another 109's engine cowling but had to break off as another 109 came at him.

The Squadron returned with two claims for 109s destroyed, plus three damaged for the loss of Robinson, who was later reported killed. They had been in a fight with 109s from JG3, which shot down the Blenheim (110 Squadron), while they and JG51 claimed two Spitfires and four Hurricanes – exactly matching Fighter Command's losses. The Luftwaffe record no losses from this action.

Four days after this fight, on the afternoon of the 25th, Demozay was leading four Hurricane IIBs at 10,000 feet over Canterbury, but became separated in cloud near Ramsgate. He then spotted a lone Ju88 heading south, chased it as far as the French coast but then lost it in cloud. He then saw a rescue boat heading north from France towards the Goodwin Sands, escorted by eight Me109s. Unable to attack he decided to wait until they turned for home, hoping to pick off a straggler. But then he spotted three Me110s flying north just out from Dunkirk. With the odds a bit better he stalked them for some miles and then closing to 250 yards fired a four-second burst at one which turned steeply to port with one engine on fire and it dived into the sea. There were no 110s lost from operational units this date so perhaps these three were on a training flight.

To RAF Kenley

On 1 June 1941, the aircraft and pilots, together with 108 airmen with minimal equipment moved to Kenley for two weeks, relieved by 258 Squadron in connection with the moonlight period for night fighting. Pilot Officer R N G 'Bob' Allen joined the Squadron at this time:

> 'I joined the Squadron at Kenley although it was also operating from Redhill. It was divided into two Flights, one almost entirely Czech, under Flight Lieutenant Velebnovsky. I went into A Flight in order to help balance up the Squadron to stop them operating completely as a Czech unit. Kuttelwascher was one I remember well; still a sergeant pilot then. All the Czechs were very experienced and a bit older than most.
>
> I was later moved to B Flight under Colin Gray but the problem with the Czechs was that they had this awful habit of using their own language, particularly on the R/T when they got excited. Another pilot I recall was René Marcinkus, who was a Latvian, later one of the fifty men shot by the Gestapo following the Great Escape.
>
> We used a large house as a Mess, owned by the goldsmith's organisation – you can still see it from the M23 today. I shared a room with Marcinkus. He was only a Pilot Officer too but had been a colonel in the Latvian air force [bombers].
>
> We were at Redhill for the moon period because of night Ops. It was only a grass strip but I was too inexperienced to be involved. I flew on day sorties, convoy patrols, escorts and sweeps. Also Channel patrols, meeting the Blenheims as they came home.'

The Squadron returned to Redhill on the 15th and on the 16th A Flight were Scrambled to patrol off Folkestone. Colin Gray DFC, a New Zealander, had arrived to take over A Flight just two days earlier. He had had a successful period with 54 Squadron in 1940 and was one of the high-scoring pilots with the RAF at this time.

Some Lysanders were out on Air Sea Rescue patrol and 1 Squadron were to give them some cover as radar had picked up hostile interest from the Germans. It turned out that the Germans had similar ideas and had sent off one of their Heinkel 59 float-planes with a Me109 escort. The two formations met in mid-Channel and a fight instantly started.

All this activity had been generated following several actions over the Channel earlier in the day, and a number of men from both sides were believed to be in the water. Spitfires from 91 Squadron had then been covering the Lysanders but as 1 Squadron came on the scene, had flown off to engage the 109s escorting the Heinkel. After that skirmish the 109s had reformed and flown north again, running into 1 Squadron. As some pilots fought the 109s, Gray and his No.2, Bob Allen dived onto the float-plane and then as it began to fall away towards the sea, several Czech pilots took shots at it, until it finally hit the water. The machine was from Seenotflugkommando 3, piloted by Feldwebel Erich Bohrenfeld. He and one of his crew survived but wounded, the other two died.

Meantime, one of the 109s was claimed shot down by Sergeant Josef Prihoda but Sergeant Albin Nasswetter was brought down into the sea. Badly wounded, he was rescued but died of his wounds the next day. Bob Allen recalls:

> 'On 16 June we found a He59 over the Channel and shot it down. It didn't carry any Red Cross markings. I was No.2 to Colin Gray and there were also ten or a dozen Me109s about who were naturally very aggressive. I took a shot at them, more in haste than in anger I have to say.'

The next day, the 17th, the Squadron took part in a Withdrawal Support operation over the Channel, helping to cover Spitfires and Blenheims returning from France. Brooker led the Squadron and north-west of Boulogne ran into some 109s, one of which Sergeant Dygryn claimed shot down three miles off the coast. On the 18th, Moses Demozay left the Squadron, posted to 242 Squadron. He would eventually become the highest scoring French pilot flying with the RAF, only to die in a crash in late 1945.

The Hurricane was now beginning to be very 'second eleven' on day operations, and not just quick enough to stay healthy. The 12-gun IIB machines were also seriously effected by the weight of four extra guns and ammunition, and while the IIC's cannons were useful, the new 109F models were causing problems for Hurricane pilots.

The last real day combat 1 Squadron fought with its Hurricanes came on 21 June during the return flight from an escort mission to Desvres that afternoon. Four Me109Fs were claimed destroyed, three more probably destroyed and two damaged. The CO shot one off the tail of a Hurricane and saw the pilot bale out; Collyns saw his victim go down and crash, Kratkoruky saw the tail of his target also shot off and the pilot bale out (same 109?), while Marcinkus attacked one which his wingman saw fall to pieces in the air (again same 109?).

Two top cover squadrons had become separated during a turn near the French coast so 1 Squadron alone had taken the brunt of an assault by 109s from JG2 and JG26 over Boulogne. 609 Squadron came to their rescue after two Hurricanes had gone down, Pilot Officer Kopecky having to ditch just off Folkestone, while Pilot Officer Nick Morantz, an American Eagle pilot serving with the Squadron, was shot down and killed. Both had been shot down by JG26 pilots, one to Oberleutnant Gustav Sprick leader of the 8th Staffel which brought his score to 29 in this action, and the other to Leutnant Johannes Naumann of the 9th Staffel for his second kill.

Although difficult to define who may have been lost from JG26 in this fight with 1 Squadron, especially as German pilots often mistook Hurricanes for Spitfires, at least one JG26 pilot fell to a Hurricane west of Le Touquet. In all this day, in two major actions, the RAF claimed 26 Me109s destroyed and another 13 probables and damaged, against the actual loss of just nine. The Germans filed 24 claims against RAF losses of just six fighters and two pilots.

Just under a week later, the 27th, during an operation to Lille, Flight Sergeant Kuttelwascher claimed a 109 destroyed but this was the last daylight operation flown by 1 Squadron with Hurricanes that resulted in any combats. In any event, the 109 force across the Channel had now been depleted to just two Fighter Groups, JG2 and JG26, following the invasion of Russia on 22 June.

The wind of change

The Spitfire squadrons were now taking the bulk of the daylight sweeps and circuses to France, the Hurricanes relegated to night sorties and the occasional intruder operations. A new pilot, Pilot Officer B Horak, who had just arrived from 55 OTU two weeks earlier, was killed in a crash flying from Redhill to Gatwick on the 29th, and then on 1 July the Squadron flew down to Tangmere for night-fighter patrols.

Tangmere had suffered several bombing raids during 1940 and the airmen were billetted out at Goodwood racecourse. LAC John Flood remembers he, with others, slept in the old bar, now sadly emptied of liquor. There were few lights, John having to fill a Brylcreem jar with paraffin and dipping a piece of string through the lid to act as a wick. Each day they would be picked up by a coach which drove them too and from the airfield.

Little of importance followed but Flight Lieutenant Velebnovsky was killed. He was flying a searchlight co-operation sortie and radio contact was lost. Later the wreckage of his Hurricane was found near Graffham, having crashed into a wooded hillside. Flying Officer W Raymond took over command of B Flight.

Colin Gray recorded in his book [Spitfire Patrol] that over the three months July to September 1941 he never fired his guns in anger, except on one occasion, being fed-up and bored, he flew a sweep with 41 Squadron from Merston, and shot down a 109F.

Aircraft flew down to Manston on 26 August and flew to the Pas de Calais, shooting up barges and a minesweeper during a low-level strafing mission, then in the afternoon flew out with 242 and 485 (NZ) Squadrons attacking and setting on fire a ship north-east of Gravelines. This bit of excitement was short-lived for the next night Pilot Officer E Bloor crashed and was killed near Horsham in another searchlight co-operation flight. This same night Sergeant G S Metcalf crash-landed on his first night landing after a searchlight co-op., overshooting the runway.

Most of the machine-gun Hurricanes had now been flown away, replaced totally by four-cannon IIC machines. The pilots spent their evenings and nights flying alongside the Havoc Turbinlite machines, a useless and dangerous occupation, during which the Havoc would try to locate a German raider in the dark, to turn on a massive searchlight so that the Hurricanes could shoot it down. Of course, it tended to blind everyone, and the Germans never stayed around long enough for the poor

Hurricane pilot to get in a crack at them, so it became a dismal failure and total waste of effort, not to say aircraft and lives lost in trying to perfect this useless (desperate?) endeavour.

Colin Gray received a Bar to his DFC in September and was then posted to 403 Squadron on the 28th. He was to gain more honours and decorations in the Middle East later in the war.

Taking Gray's place came Flight Lieutenant J A F MacLachlan DFC, a pilot with a good deal of experience but without a left hand. He had flown Fairey Battles in France and having survived, and collected a DFC, was sent off to Malta where he claimed a number of successes against the Italians and Germans over the island, gaining a Bar to his DFC but losing his left lower arm. Once he had recovered and had an artificial hand fitted, he persuaded the 'powers' to let him not only fly again, but return to operations. He now moved to 1 Squadron, pending the job of CO which was on the horizon, those same 'powers' thinking that while the Squadron was in an operational slump, he could do little to cause a problem.

By November, the Squadron was declared fully operational as a night-fighter unit and on the 3rd MacLachlan took over from Peter Brooker, pending the latter's move to the Far East. War with Japan was still a month away, but his skill and experience came to the fore over Singapore and Java (Bar to DFC). Brooker later became a 2nd TAF Wing Leader, won the DSO and Bar, only to be shot down and killed in a Tempest by a FW190 less than a month before the war ended.

As 'Mac' (or 'Jay' as he was also known) took over, Flight Lieutenant J M Crabb arrived from 3 Squadron to command B Flight. However, November was to end badly. Sergeant E Ruppel RCAF was killed on the 18th, crashing into Bury Hill, near Arundel during night landings, and then on the 22nd, Sergeants L J Travis and D P Perrin, on a Scramble to the Isle of Wight at dusk, collided in the dark an hour later. Travis was killed but Perrin survived a bale out.

Some of the Czech pilots began to move to other units. Josef Dygryn-Ligoticky DFM, Czech War Cross, went to 310 Squadron in September. He was to return to 1 Squadron in March 1942. Josef Prihoda was commissioned and received the DFC and in early 1942 was with 111 Squadron, and then 313 Czech Squadron. He was lost during a sortie over Brest in March 1943. Bedrich Kratkoruky went to 313 Squadron too but was lost over the Channel in January 1943.

LAC Ted Warman arrived on the Squadron in November, as an FME – flight mechanic engines. He found that practically all the buildings at Tangmere had been destroyed during the Battle of Britain, though one or two were made serviceable, including the airman's mess and the NAAFI but everything else had gone. The first morning after his arrival Ted was given his first task:

> 'I shall not forget the first time I ran up the engine of a Hurricane. It had been impressed on me in training that when an engine is to be shut off, the correct way was to pull the "cut off" – a device which in effect starves the carburettor – but never to shut it down by switching off the magnetos. When I attempted to shut this engine down nothing happened when I pulled the "cut off", and although I throttled it right back the propeller was still rotating.
>
> I had just begun to wonder how I was going to stop it when up stormed Flight Sergeant Hicks, yelling for me to switch off the magnetos as I was sooting up the plugs. This I did, but when I tried to explain that this had been forbidden by our instructors, he told me in some very fruity language just what he thought of my tuition.
>
> Another thing we were taught was that when filling the petrol tanks the hose pipe was to be bonded to the mainplane by a wire attached to the hose. This was to conduct any static electricity that may have built up while the tanks were filling. The first time I had to fill the tanks after the aircraft had landed, I asked the petrol bowser attendant for the bonding wire. He looked at me in amazement and asked, "What's a bonding wire?" So much for theory.'

Frank Churchett, another member of the ground crew, recalls the occasion security at Tangmere was severely tested, and found wanting. An airman, hitching his way back to the airfield, had the delight of being picked up by a senior officer. Reaching the Guard Room, the man on duty, recognising the airman with the officer, waved the car through. Dropping off the airman the officer made a brief tour of the airfield in his car before heading for the Officers' Mess. Once inside it was finally noticed that the man was masquerading in a German uniform!

Chapter Eleven

NIGHT INTRUDER

Channel Dash

The year of 1942 was to see a marked change in 1 Squadron's recent fortunes, but it didn't start off well, due to the loss of Sergeant J Smith who crashed on landing after a Turbinlite sortie. He was caught in the Havoc's slipstream and crunched into the ground. This was followed by another tragic death on 11 February. Sergeant E G Parsons RCAF overshot the flare path on return from another Turbinlite sortie. He bounced hard on landing, opened the throttle but stalled-in due to selecting flaps up instead of wheels up. He touched a tree and some obstruction wires, then crashed with engine full on in a field by the south-east corner of the airfield and died instantly.

The following day came Operation 'Fuller'. This was the code-name for RAF reaction should ever the German battleships, bottled up in Brest, try to make an escape into the Atlantic, or even try to head back towards their northern ports round Ireland and Scotland. In the event, a well planned operation had them slip out of harbour and make a rapid, not to say audacious, dash up through the English Channel and North Sea, heading for Norway and then the Baltic.

Due to a number of unforeseen factors, the three capital ships, the *Scharnhorst*, *Prinz Eugen* and the *Gneisenau*, were way up along the Channel before they were either missed from harbour by daily recce aircraft or submarine watch, or located by the RAF or radar at sea. The story has little credit for British forces and the German Navy and Luftwaffe really pulled one off this February day.

By the time the ships had been located and 'Fuller' put in motion, it was almost too late to be really effective against them. In poor weather, bombers, torpedo bombers and fighters were rushed to the attack, but the ships were heavily defended by surface vessels and fighters. The famous attack by Eugene Esmonde and his small force of Fleet Air Arm Swordfish biplanes is a study in heroic, if suicidal, devotion to duty, which resulted in a posthumous Victoria Cross for its leader.

Among the many fighter squadrons the RAF put up in a vain attempt to escort these and other attack aircraft and motor torpedo boats, 1 Squadron put up six Hurricanes of A Flight, detailed to attack German E-boats and destroyers escorting the big ships. Flight Lieutenant W Raymond RNZAF led with Pilot Officer E S G Sweeting as his No.2. Yellow Section comprised the recently commissioned Kuttelwascher and Pilot Officer G R Halbeard, White Section were Marcinkus and Flight Sergeant E F G Blair, a South African.

They took off at 1337 hours and met up with 129 Squadron over Hawkinge at 1405, at 300 feet. Setting a course of 100° they headed out and ten minutes later the Spitfire leader reported – 'Target Ahead!' Four ships loomed out of the greyness in line astern. The Hurricanes passed to starboard, then went on for another two or three minutes. Three more ships were sighted, identified as destroyers, which immediately opened up on the Hurricanes. The fighters were already diving into the attack, approaching from the Belgian coast at 1430, height 50 feet. Raymond and his wingman were in the middle, Yellow and White Sections to his left and right, in line abreast. They met a terrific barrage but each section began firing from 100 yards, raking the decks and superstructure of the destroyers. Kuttelwascher saw his cannon shells striking beneath the bridge of his target and on his return he claimed the ship damaged – Cat III! White Section were not seen again, both clawed down by the massive gunfire. The four others landed at 1515.

B Flight took off at 1355, missed the rendezvous with their Spitfire escort and so landed at Hawkinge, from where the mission was called off. It was Raymond's last sortie with the Squadron. Two days later he was rested and sent to an OTU. Blair was never heard of again while Marcinkus, forced to ditch, was picked up by the Germans and taken prisoner. As Bob Allen mentioned in the previous chapter, he was one of those who escaped from Stalag Luft III in March 1944, was recaptured and shot. He had got as far as Danzig before recapture. He was 33 years old and in the PoW camp had been one of the main forgers, intelligence expert for the Baltic and 'pumper' of 'soft' German guards for information.

How not to win friends!

Having had such a long association with Tangmere, the Squadron had often been closely associated with the town of Brighton. Both air and ground crews had wined and dined there and pursued the fair sex. The pre-war link should, it was felt, be reforged.

So, at this time, in order to cement relations with the town and the Borough Council, the Mayor was invited to lunch in the Officers' Mess on 16 February. He also accepted an invitation to view his town from the air, the CO taking him up in the Maggie. Upon his return the Mayor asked if his (male) secretary could go too and so Pilot Officer Sweeting took him in the same aeroplane. On their return and coming in to land ten minutes later, the aircraft was in a steep left-hand turn when its nose dropped and the machine crashed in an open field just west of the airfield. Both men were killed. Ted Warman:

> 'The Squadron Engineering Officer was Chunky Chown. He wore a rather battered old cap with a very frayed peak and rode around the dispersal on an ancient motor-cycle. The senior NCO of B Flight was Flight Sergeant Hicks, who was a bit of a martinet, who the lads considered excessively "service minded". Then there was Sergeant Tupper who would eventually be replaced by Sergeant Sandham. In addition there were Corporals Jack Savage (engines) and Ernie Dearing (airframes) on one 24-hour shift, and Corporals Paddy Vandersberg (engines) and Joe Collingwood (airframes) on the other.
>
> Joe Collingwood was a bit of a character. He hailed from Morpeth and spoke with a broad Geordie accent. His heart was in the right place but sometimes became the victim of practical jokes. One day there was a tail wheel to be changed but instead of placing the tail up on a tressle he ordered some of the lads to get underneath the tailplane, lift it bodily while he effected the change. At the end of the exercise, instead of allowing him to get clear, the lads lowered the tail, trapping poor Joe in a crouching position and unable to move. He shouted for help but all this did was to send everyone into fits of laughter. Eventually they took pity on him but for a while Joe was walking around like a chimpanzee.
>
> A fitter and a rigger's chief tool was his screwdriver which for reasons I never did discover was only ever called a "G.S." – the word screwdriver was never used. In addition the fitter was armed with a key which was used for removing the petrol tank filler cap, and this was known as a "Winker". These tools were carried everywhere, being tucked in a belt round the waist ready for instant use. The G.S. was in constant use for tightening or loosening the buttons that held the panels and cowlings in place.
>
> Often on the ground we needed to push aircraft from place to place, especially for inspections. To get the aircraft in motion, the lads doing the pushing would be encouraged by shouts of "Two Six" as they strained to get it rolling. This peculiar expression was constantly used to encourage all sorts of tasks requiring strength or energy. It was so commonplace an expression that it was used by everybody whenever they required help or assistance – "Give us a two six, mate".'

Mac MacLachlan was a great pilot and leader, much admired and loved. Bill West was his fitter and would help strap him in before sorties. Bill also helped clamp his 'claw' on the throttle control.

Stan Greenwood recalls the occasion he was ordered to wheel out a Hurricane onto the grass and run up the engine. Stan duly did so but the slipstream lifted a lump off the tarmac which struck the propeller, taking a chunk out of it. He decided to own up, although he could quite easily have waited for the pilot to come out, run the engine up again, then blame him for the damage.

Having owned up, Flight Sergeant Hicks had no choice but to put Stan on a charge and he was duly marched in front of the CO. Admitting the offence he was given seven days CB and asked if he had anything to say. Mentioning that had he kept quiet he could have blamed the pilot, he then turned to march out. Mac, smiling, called to Stan, saying that perhaps it should only be three days CB. Today he was on duty anyway, next day, Mac would give him a chit for late cookhouse duty and day three he would be back on duty. Stan thought this very fair, especially as the cookhouse had been cleaned by the time he got there, and he arranged to walk one of the ladies home!!

Stan Greenwood recalls too an occasion he was taken up for a flight in the Squadron Tiger Moth. Stan noticed the pilot had a large spanner in his flying boot and enquired why. He told Stan that it was to bang him on the head if Stan messed up while in the front cockpit. Once airborne and given control, Stan had no intention of getting things wrong but he soon discovered that however much he pulled back on the stick, the Moth's nose was going down. With the stick finally back as far as it would go, and the nose still pointing earthwards, he was waiting for the bang on the 'nut' but then suddenly the nose shot up. The pilot, of course, had been slowly working the trim wheel back and had then suddenly rolled it forward again – for a laugh!

War in the dark

The following day, Kuttelwascher was promoted to flight lieutenant and became OC A Flight. A good deal of bad weather in March kept activity to a minimum but plans were afoot to put the Squadron back on to the operational map as soon as it improved. With their experience gained tortuously over the previous winter months, it was thought that rather than try to locate German raiders over England, without airborne radar and where the chances of actually finding a German bomber were never good, they'd look for them at a more likely spot.

It was thought it was far better, or at least the chances would improve, if fighters were put up over German airfields to await the return of the raiders. At least some would have on their navigation lights which would be visible, and because of the concentrated area around the field, it would not be too difficult to spot an aeroplane's exhaust flames too. There would also be runway lights to assist in the location of the airfield and these would also help illuminate the bombers. While they might have already bombed targets in England, any that were shot down would not be doing so again, and if aircraft were taking off for further raids, these at least would be brought down too, if the Hurricane pilots were on target. The matter of denting German morale would be a bonus.

The Hurricanes were fitted with long-range fuel tanks under the wings. They were already painted black underneath for night flying, all that needed to be consulted, with the help of RAF Intelligence, was which French airfield housed the Dorniers, Heinkels and Junkers bombers that raided England. Once maps and courses were studied, and arrangments made with the various defence people in order for them not to be greeted with massed gunfire upon their return to southern Britain, the scene was set for the more experienced pilots to start operating.

The night of 1/2 April 1942 saw the start of the Squadron's new role. One hour, forty minutes before midnight, Kuttelwascher trundled down the runway in his BE581 JX-E, lifted off and headed for France. He crossed the enemy coast at Le Havre, flying at 3,000 feet, heading for Evreux airfield. Seeing no activity here, he altered course for Melun, south-east of Paris, where an illuminated flare path helped fix his position.

Circling some short distance away for a couple of minutes he was rewarded by the sight of a red flare arcing into the sky and then he spotted an aircraft on the runway obviously preparing for take-off. As he headed in the bomber took off and began climbing to 1,500 feet but Kuttelwascher was right behind it and opened fire from 100 yards. A bright flash from the starboard engine and the bomber dived into the ground.

As the Hurricane flashed over the aerodrome he spotted another Ju88 on the runway. He dived down and fired five or six short bursts, seeing cannon strikes. Then a searchlight illuminated his fighter and AA fire began to explode near him. Enough. The Czech evaded quickly, climbed to 3,000 feet and then flew off. Crossing out at Fecamp he reached base and landed without mishap. One destroyed and one damaged was not a bad first night's work.

The next night MacLachlan took a turn. At 2320 he headed out for Rennes and Dinard airfields but he found no sign of activity at either. Frustrated, he spotted a goods train near Combourg so strafed it, leaving the engine enveloped in steam from its ruptured boiler and two trucks on fire. He touched down at 0250 not unhappy but not as happy as he had hoped. On the same night, Pilot Officer H Connolly had engine trouble over the Channel during a patrol and had to bale out off Selsey. Getting into his dinghy he was fortunate to spot a trawler and attracting it with his whistle, was soon rescued and returned to land.

On the 5th Sergeant Z Bachurek, on patrol over base, crashed near Fontwell by the Arundel-Chichester road and suffered severe head injuries. It seems that he forgot to switch from mains to reserve tank and lost his engine. Five days later, another of the Czechs, Sergeant Jan Vlk, crashed during a Turbinlite training sortie near Barnham, Sussex and was killed.

Kuttelwascher was out again on the 16th, taking off at 2245. Once again Evreux proved unproductive, as did St Andre and Dreux. Wandering around for a while he decided to return to Dreux, via Chartres, where he encountered some flak. Making for St Andre again (west of Paris) he saw two enemy aircraft with their nav. lights on. Undoubtedly warned, one pilot immediately switched his off, but 'Kut' attacked the other and it went down and hit the ground with a bright orange flash. He was not sure of the type but thought it looked like a Dornier 217. He was back home at 0135.

Not so lucky was Sergeant Vlastimil Machacek on the night of 24 April. Taking off at 2315 on an intruder sortie, radar plotted him till mid-Channel, but he failed to return. He was one month short of his 34th birthday.

Mac scored his first night success on the 26th. Again carrying LRTs, he left base at 2205 and crossed into France at Fecamp at 9,000 feet, then let down over the Seine, 15 miles west of Paris. He flew to Bretigny where he circled for half an hour but saw no activity. Mac then headed for Dreux at 2,000 feet but in fact spotted activity to the north, at St Andre and Evreux. Circling St Andre the airfield lights were switched off so he headed away north but nipped back five minutes later just as the runway lights came back on. He could see an aircraft just taking off but then lost it as its pilot did not have his nav. lights on. Going north to Evreux he circled at 200 feet then saw a Dornier 217 silhouetted against the sky line. Closing in to 600 yards he fired three short bursts down to 100 yards but saw no results. Another burst produced sparks from the bomber's starboard engine then it nosed down and crashed into a field. Heading back to St Andre he saw another bomber and attacked, seeing it begin to leave a smoke trail in the moonlight, but then he lost it. This may have been the Dornier 217 of I/KG which was severely damaged at Evreux that night.

Kuttelwascher was out the same night although he did not take off until 0135 on the 27th. Heading also for Evreux he crossed the coast at Fecamp where he could see a rotating white light beacon between Le Havre and Fecamp. Six white lights in two parallel rows of three on the Rouen-Boos aerodrome and red and green flashing lights east of the aerodrome also helped. Like MacLachlan, he could easily pick out the River Seine in the moonlight as it meandered east and then south-east, leading both men to the airfields they were going for. Orbiting Boos he did not have many minutes to wait before a Dornier 17 came into view between him and the moon. Closing to 100 yards he gave it a long four-second burst. Its starboard engine caught fire and it then went into a left hand dive and crashed between some hangars.

Tracer fire went over Kut's cockpit canopy and he dived as a Ju88 overshot him just 20-30 feet above. Dropping his tanks he followed the impudent 88, chasing, firing four short bursts from close range, which produced sparks. Then the 88 went into a steep left hand turn upwards before he lost it south of the airfield. Landing at 0325 he, like his CO, claimed one destroyed and one damaged. Both men received congratulations from the AOC 11 Group, Air Marshal Trafford Leigh-Mallory.

It is not always that easy to tie-up claims to losses, assuming surviving German records are accurate. However, bombers from KG40, KG4 and K.Fl.Gr.106 had raided Bristol and KG4 had a He111 damaged by fighter attack and Gr.106 lost a Ju88 with its pilot and one other crew member killed.

On the night of the 30 April/1st May, Mac was again frustrated with darkened airfield but on his way home he shot-up two trains and then a tug boat. Meantime, Kuttelwascher was having better luck. Taking off at 2330 he headed for Rennes, which, being south of St Malo, was a long way from the Squadron's recent hunting ground. Crossing over the French coast at 2,000 feet he located the airfield and began circling Rennes aerodrome two miles away. With nothing doing he flew north to the coast, then headed south again, this time to the east of the aerodrome, as he could see two white lights near the runway. Then he saw that an aircraft was taking off with a single white nav. light in the nose, but this was switched off as soon as the machine became airborne. Kut manoeuvred to bring himself between the moon and the bomber, which he could now see was a Dornier 217, closed in and fired three short bursts. After the third burst the bomber went down, crashed and exploded.

After a few minutes he headed north towards Dinard and orbitted four miles away at 2,000 feet. He saw one EA but then lost it, but five minutes later picked up a He111 as it took off with nav. lights on, but which were switched off before the bomber had left the runway. Kuttelwascher was still able to keep it in sight and as it got to 1,000 feet or so he attacked. Large lumps fell off the starboard engine and both aircraft had now reached the sea. Two more bursts of cannon fire and the Heinkel nosed down and dived into the water off Dinard. Kut returned to base, via Jersey, landing at 0220 on 1 May, having been airborne for nearly three hours.

One can never assume a pilot identifies correctly an opposing aeroplane even in daylight, far less at night. KG30 lost four Ju88s this night, although no reasons or locations are given, but one must assume Kuttelwascher's claims were for two of these losses as he was the only one operating over France to engage German aircraft – always assuming KG40 lost some of its machines to fighter attack.

Trains, and boats and 'planes

This night of 1 May, Pilot Officer D P Perrin RNZAF took off at 40 minutes past midnight, intruding for trains in the Abbeville area. He found a goods train between Etaples and Abbeville just north of Rue. Attacking the engine he was rewarded by the sight of steam from the boiler, and attacking another goods train travelling north, left this also spewing steam.

Sergeant G S M Pearson meantime, taking off at 0115, sought out trains in the Amiens area. He found one about ten miles north-west of the town, which screached to a halt as it was attacked. He then found and attacked three more trains between Amiens and Albert. Two more were found and attacked but his ammo ran out during his approach on the fifth one and he had to return home.

Pilot Officer G H Corbett took off at 0320 and also flew to the Abbeville area. He found one with steam up, in a factory siding and the engine blew up and then several trucks were strafed. Flying south of Abbevillle he now found a train entering a shed and again his fire produced a mass of steam as the 20 mm shells ripped into the boiler. He used the last of his ammo up on two more trains which were side by side north of Abbeville, both being left steaming.

Two more pilots were also out train-hunting. Flight Sergeant C F Bland attacked five trains between Airiel and Caen, all of which stopped and blew steam. Flight Lieutenant L S B Scott attacked a train near Yvetot, raking its whole length with cannon fire which set at least one truck ablaze. The next night Scott attacked a train outside Caen and 'steamed it'.

Kuttelwascher was out on the night of 2/3 May but finding no airfield activity he too searched around for trains. Near St Lô he attacked a goods train and left the engine blowing steam and later, after heading out over the coast, spotted a small motor boat and after making three strafing attacks left it stopped and trailing oil.

At 0205 on the night of 3/4 May, Squadron Leader MacLachan was off to Rennes but with nothing in sight he flew north to Dinard where he spotted a flashing red beacon. Moments later he saw a bomber landing but he was not quick enough to attack before the ground became blacked-out once more. Then another bomber, possibly a Dornier, came into view, its nav. lights burning, and he attacked it from dead astern. A spurt of flame came out of the starboard engine which then appeared to fall off. The bomber spun into the ground and blew up.

Another bomber, this time a He111, with nav. lights on, could then be seen coming in to land. Mac attacked and it went into a shallow dive with its port engine burning and hit the ground with a brilliant flash. Heading out low and fast he found a train which he shot up and left steaming.

Kuttelwascher was off at 2320 on the night of the 3/4th, returning to his old haunts of Evreux and St Andre. Three searchlights came on at Fecamp but were switched off as he flashed his nav. lights on and off twice! He then picked out four white lights in a straight line from Fecamp, pointing along his course, the first one flashing dot-dot-dash. Coming to Evreux he could see no activity so flew on to St Andre, seeing its double east to west flarepath.

Six bombers, He111s, with white tail lights could be see orbiting between 1,500 and 2,000 feet. Kuttelwascher circled for a couple of minutes and then attacked one the starboard engine of which caught fire and it dived to the ground north-east of the aerodrome. He repeated the action with the next Heinkel and it dived in flames into a wood east of the base. Attacking a third bomber, his shells began hitting it and then it went down steeply from 1,500 feet. Thirty seconds later he counted three fires burning on the ground. The airfield lights naturally went off and some machine-gun fire began to probe for his Hurricane so he quickly headed away. Seeing four searchlights just to the north he again tried his nav. light ruse, but this time it was ignored, so he lost height and headed for home.

Only one Dornier was lost this night, a 17z, piloted by Obfw Albert Heyer of IV/KG2, location and reason for loss not recorded in the German quartermaster's return. IV/KG30 lost two Ju88s, while K/Fl.Gr.506 had two of its Ju88s shot down by enemy fire. Thus five aircraft were lost this night, although as well as 1 Squadron, 23 Squadron (Havocs) damaged an aircraft over NW France too, and 3 Squadron, also intruding with Hurricanes, claimed an aircraft damaged over Gilze Reijen and a Ju88 destroyed at Venlo, both in Holland.

Sergeant J R Campbell tried his hand in the early hours of the 5th, heading for Evreux airfield. With nothing doing there, he was going towards Dreux but then saw a tanker lorry on a road and attacked, which produced burning petrol all across the road. Flying on to St Andre he began orbiting but flak fire broke out and his machine was hit and the starboard drop tank burst. His engine cut out for a moment or two but picked up as he turned on his reserve tank. On the way out he opened fire on two trains, both of which were left pouring steam, while the trucks behind the second train caught fire and began to burn furiously, lighting up the night sky like a white light. After a third attack the train was well ablaze.

In the middle of the month, Mac MacLachlan was awarded the Distinguished Service Order and Kuttelwascher the Distinguished Flying Cross. Mac's DSO was the first awarded to the Squadron since WW1, and, despite the actions which followed, it was, surprisingly, the last awarded to one of its pilots for over 50 years.

The next moon period began in late May. On the night of the 29th Pilot Officer Corbett intruded to Rouen and Paris, attacking four goods trains, each resulting in steaming engines. Sergeant B C Williams, a New Zealander, flew to Beauvais, north of Poix, attacking another goods train which blew up with a brilliant flash. Pilot Officer F W Murray went to Amiens, disabling three engines of goods trains. Flight Sergeant G C English attacked two goods trains near Rouen and Barentin, disabling both engines and setting the second train alight in two places.

The next night Sergeant Campbell attacked no less than six trains at various locations around

Lens. In each case strikes were observed and the engines stopped with clouds of steam blowing from their shattered boilers. On one train, the trucks caught fire too. Meanwhile, Sergeant G S M Pearson disabled engines of two goods trains in the Lens-La Bassée area.

Squadron Leader MacLachlan was, on the night of 30/31st, shooting up four trains, three around Péronne, the other near Soissons. Warrant Officer G Scott RCAF intruded to the night-fighter base at St Trond and claimed a Ju88 damaged. This was probably the Ju88C-6 from II/NJG2, damaged near Gilze Reijen this night with the loss of one crew member.

RAF Manston

From the start of June 1942 the night-intruder pilots began operating from Manston having first topped up their fuel tanks there. On the first night MacLachlan headed for the Evreux area but south of Le Havre he hit a bird. Thinking that the blood on the windscreen might be oil he decided to abort and got back safely.

Kuttelwascher also flew out but he spotted a convoy of 12 ships off the French coast. When he returned he telephoned Group with the information. Meantime he carried on and shot-up two trains. Flying back he again picked up the convoy, now seeing some E-boats too, weaving to the rear. Never one to let a chance slip by, Kut dived down and strafed one of the motor boats, causing it to pour smoke and as he flew off he could see a large patch of oil spreading over the water.

Sergeant J F Higham blew up the engine of a goods train east of Dieppe, and Pilot Officer Des Perrin also spotted a convoy of ships between Ostend and Blankenburge, and he too had a go at an E-boat, but saw no results of his fire.

At 0240, Flight Sergeant Pearson headed for airfields at Gilze Reijen and Eindhoven. At the former he spotted aircraft over a lit airfield, its nav. lights being switched on and off. Pearson attacked and saw strikes and debris, and then the starboard engine caught fire. The machine went into spiral dive to the right and hit the ground five miles south of the aerodrome where it exploded. It was either a Ju88 or a He111, he thought. It was in fact a Ju88C-4 night-fighter from VI/NJG2 and its crew, Oberfeldwebel Dieter Schade with Unteroffiziers Jacob Cezanne and Adolf Jensen, were all killed.

On 1/2 June, Pilot Officer Harry Connolly took off at 0050 and headed for St Trond. There he found a Ju88 clearly set against the moon glow at his same height, 1,500 feet. He attacked and saw strikes. His port guns jammed which caused him to side-slip, and then another Ju88 was seen behind. He circled, but lost it.

Flight Sergeant English headed for Venlo, Holland, at 0040. Nothing was seen at either Gilze or Eindhoven but near Venlo he attacked a train, which stopped. Returning to Eindhoven he saw a Do217 at 0215, lost it, found it again and slipped in behind it. His cannon shells smashed into the starboard engine and the bomber dived into the ground and burst into flames.

Kuttelwascher was out on the night of 2/3 June too, taking off at 0240. Flying over Canterbury he saw fires in the town so flew towards Deal in order to cut off any raiders heading back to France. Not un-naturally he caught the attention of the Dover AA batteries so he headed south towards the beacon at Nieuport. He was rewarded by the sight of a Do217 and overhauling it, closed to 150 yards and opened fire. Its starboard engine caught fire and the aircraft went into a shallow dive, then plunged into the sea five miles off the Belgian coast. Kut again headed for Nieuport but it was starting to get light now so he returned to base. His victim was probably Feldwebel Hans Koch's Do217E-4 from III/KG2 that failed to return this night.

This day also saw the first loss for some time. Flight Sergeant English was carrying out a practise interception on another 1 Squadron aeroplane but he stalled. Unable to regain control he dived into the ground and was killed.

It had now become almost a contest between MacLachlan and Kuttelwascher. Certainly they were both very practised and experienced in this specialised intruder work. It was not as easy at it might appear on paper, however. Several night fighter two-seat crews were having success over Britain, but they had airborne radar to assist them. Flight Lieutenant R P Stevens of 151 Squadron had gained much success at night over England in a Hurricane in 1941, but he also had help from searchlights and could be guided from the ground by radar and radio. Intruders had to find the enemy the hard way but once they had got the hang of it, results came.

Both men were out on the night of 3/4 June 1942. Mac was off at 0100, heading for the Evreux area. Nothing was doing at Fecamp, St Andre or Dreux, but on going back to St Andre he was amazed to find around 15 Dorniers orbiting at 1,000 feet, all preparing to land, and all continually switching the nav. lights on and off. He was like a bee around a honey pot.

Mac closed in behind one Dornier, followed it as it began making its approach, fired and it crashed in a shower of sparks just short of the runway. Six searchlights immediately came on, illuminating the Hurricane, quickly followed by flak and ground fire. Mac dived to one side and still seeing about ten aircraft orbiting, selected one and opened fire. Strikes appeared on the bomber but Mac was obliged to break away as a searchlight got him again. Climbing to 2,000 feet he found another bomber, attacked and saw sparks come from its port engine. The port wing dropped and the bomber went into a 45° dive. This was followed by a bright red flash on the ground by the side of the aerodrome. A fourth aircraft was attacked as it came into land, strikes were produced but then his cannons stopped – out of shells. He claimed two destroyed and two damaged.

Kuttelwascher went out an hour after his CO and also headed for St Andre. But over the Channel he saw a Do217 at 3,500 feet heading for France. Its crew must have seen the Hurricane's exhausts as the bomber began to weave and lose height. Kut lost sight of it near the dark sea, so on reaching the French coast, turned straight for St Andre.

Arriving over the base at 0300 a single flarepath was lit and after keeping clear for 15 minutes he saw two bombers orbiting – He111s. He attacked one and its starboard engine caught fire, then it crashed in flames. Circling round he then saw a Do217 at 1,500 feet. His attack produced strikes, but he then lost it as it dived. Circling once more he then saw four bombers three or four minutes later, at 1,000 feet. Selecting a Dornier he made two attacks and it crashed east of the airfield. Continuing to circle he failed, however, to find any more targets. The Germans had obviously got the message.

No.1 Squadron were the only unit operating over France this night and KG2 caught the full force of the two intruder pilots. I Gruppe lost one Do217E flown by Uffz Gerhard Wagner, and a Do217E-4 flown by Ltn Gerhard Besüner. II Gruppe had one Do217E-2 damaged in a crash-landing at Evreux, while III Gruppe likewise had a E-4 badly damaged at St Andre. II Gruppe also recorded four more damaged bombers at St Andre.

This night, however, was not all success. Warrant Officer Josef Dygryn-Ligoticky DFM, who had recently returned to the Squadron, failed to return from an intruder mission to the Evreux area, and was later reported as killed.

Nevertheless, thanks came from the AOC-in-C Bomber Command. His bombers were enjoying a period of light losses which he felt was due in part to the night intruding of German airfields. Sir Archibald Sinclair, Secretary of State for Air, also sent his congratulations for the night's work. There were also plaudits from Air Commodore Karel Janousek, of the Czech Inspectorate, in London, which read: "Heartiest congratulations on your Squadron's success last night. Good luck in future hunting to you and 'Old Kut' – Janousek."

Further success had to wait until the next moon period, but on 21/22 June, Kuttelwascher was out again, taking off at 0055, crossing the French coast north of Le Havre. He went to St Andre where he found a red flashing beacon and a few white lights. However, he could see no aircraft about so went to Dreux, then came back ten minutes later flying at 2,000 feet. Losing height to 1,000 feet, he saw a Ju88 with its nav. lights on pass below him on the opposite side of the aerodrome. 'Old Kut' crossed the airfield, slid in behind the 88 and opened fire at 100 yards as it went in to land.

The aircraft's starboard engine and fuselage caught fire and it crashed, spreading itself out in flaming pieces along the runway. As searchlights came on to search for the intruder, Kut saw another 88 with, incredibly, its nav. lights on. It was on the opposite side of the runway at 1,000 feet. He chased after it immediately but now fully aware of the danger, the German pilot dived away and then Kut's port guns stopped, so he could only claim a damaged. More searchlights and flak came up and although he oribited some way off for another 40 minutes, no more aircraft were seen. The only aircraft which ties in is a Ju88A-4 from K.Fl.Gr.106 which lost Ltn Walter Schleimitz and crew.

Flight Sergeant Pearson was also out to the Evreux area and at 0210 saw a twin-engined aircraft which fired a green Very Light in answer to a red from the ground. Pearson got behind the aircraft and opened fire from 30 yards. Cannon strikes appeared, then a glow and smoke from the port engine, but that was all. He claimed a probable.

Later in the month, Sergeant Campbell attacked two trains between Antwerp and Turnhout on the 26th, the engines of both blowing up, but Warrant Officer Gerry Scott RCAF failed to return from his sortie. The next night Sergeant Campbell disabled three trains of goods engines near Rouen.

This same 27th, Kuttelwascher was notified of the award of a Bar to his DFC.

* * *

At this time an unusual fighter pilot arrived on the Squadron, Commander A J M Jubelin posted in from 118 Squadron – Spitfires. André Jubelin, a Frenchman, had been a gunnery officer in the French

Navy when the war began, serving in the Far East. He had learnt to fly in his spare time. Once France had fallen, Jubelin determined to get to England, and by a series of adventures did just that. Despite his naval background he managed to get into the Fleet Air Arm and then the RAF. After some months with 118 Squadron he was posted to No.1 at Tangmere.

In his book *The Flying Sailor*, he recalls his first meeting with MacLachlan, describing him as a man with an obstinate expression with a slight reddish mustache. Mac had told him intruding was: 'A terrific job.' Having lost an arm it was obvious to Jubelin that his CO had an account to settle with the Germans. When he talked of the intruder work, Mac had said of attacking a German bomber: 'If you only knew what it feels like when he's so near that he fills my view-finder and I'm going to fire! Oh Boy!'

Soon after he arrived, a call came through to say that bombers were heading for Bristol and that the Squadron should prepare to fly over the western area of France to meet them upon their return home. Maps were spread out, plans were settled, and at 0115 on the 28/29th, Mac and Kuttelwascher were off and heading towards Rennes and Dinard.

Kuttelwascher went in west of Cherbourg but found nothing doing at Dinard so flew towards Cherbourg and at 0320 saw a Do217 three miles south of him, 500 feet below. He chased it towards Bayeux for ten minutes, closing to 150 yards. Attacking, the Dornier dived, but it was on fire. It was last seen in a steep dive well alight. III/KG2 lost a Do217E-4 near Caen; Uffz Michael Petres and his three companions died.

Heading out near Barfleur Kut spotted seven E-boats firing at another Hurricane and despite considerable return fire, Kut went down and strafed them. One began to smoke and put on a heavy list to starboard. Another was also damaged but then his ammunition gave out. The other Hurricane was being flown by Pilot Officer Corbett. Not finding any hostile aircraft he had found instead two goods trains on the Rouen-Paris line and shot them up, disabling the engines and setting fire to some trucks.

The last actions of this intense intruding period came on the night of 1/2 July 1942. Kuttelwascher, Campbell and Pearson had flown out to the Carteret and Carentan areas over the Cherbourg peninsular following another German raid to the west country. They had all found Dorniers, Kut destroying two with another damaged, the two NCOs damaging one each. On 9 July, the Squadron packed its bags and moved north to Acklington. A new era was about to begin, the old one gone forever.

Chapter Twelve

THE TYPHOON

The days of the Hurricane as a day fighter in Europe were long gone, and now that night intruding was being undertaken by twin-engined fighters with radar, Hurricane squadrons were re-equipping with Hawker's latest fighter, the Typhoon.

The Typhoon (or Tiffie as it was also called) had become operational in the summer of 1942 but had had a number of teething troubles. It initially was to have some success as a pure fighter but it was not as good as the Spitfire IX which was just starting to come into service too and in order to cash-in on its obvious low level capabilities, the Typhoon began to be used as a fighter-bomber. With four 20 mm cannon, added to either eight rockets or two bombs under the wings, it became the most versatile RAF ground-attack aeroplane and the back-bone of the future 2nd Tactical Air Force. While the Typhoon's new merits were still in the ascendency, No.1 Squadron's change of equipment was approved.

July 8th, 1942 saw the Squadron's Hurricanes take off for RAF Acklington, in formation, while the advance party and ground crews flew up in a Harrow. The rest followed in a special train. However, Flight Lieutenant Kuttelwascher and Pilot Officer Harry Connolly left, the former to go to 23 Squadron (night fighters), the latter to 32 Squadron. Kut had had his day too. He had no success with 23 Squadron's Mosquito aircraft and then became non-operational. After the war he flew with BEA, but died from a heart attack in 1959 aged only 42.

Wilkie arrives

The first Typhoons began arriving on 21 July but the following day Squadron Leader MacLachlan DSO DFC left for a training post. Flight Lieutenant E J F Harrington took over in an acting capacity, until the arrival of Squadron Leader R C Wilkinson DFM & Bar. Royce Wilkinson had seen considerable action during the Battle of France, serving with No.3 Squadron, and had won his decorations for action in May. By 1941 he had been commissioned and became a flight commander with one of the US Eagle squadrons and the following year commanded 174 Squadron. Shot down over France he successfully evaded capture and returned via Spain. In October 1942 he became an Officer of the Order of the British Empire. After a spell as a base commander he was given command of 1 Squadron to help with its conversion. 'Wilkie' was immediately accepted by all ranks.

Fighter Command was having problems with the new aeroplane, including a tendency for it to lose its tail in the air, but Wilkie and the Squadron's well-liked engineering officer, Pilot Officer J S 'Chunky' Chown (later Flt Lt), helped to overcome most of them, as did other squadrons. Chown was liked for many reasons, not least that he was usually to be found, sleeves rolled up, arms and hands covered in oil as he helped his men with their work. On the occasion Flight Sergeant Harry Bletcher crashed on take-off, fortunately being unhurt, it was found that a rigger had left the control locking gear in the bottom of the cockpit. With the pilot's agreement, Chown put the crash down to engine failure in order to save the airman from a Court Martial, as he had already learned his lesson.

The pilots found too there was no space for their maps, so Wilkie bought a mousetrap and mounted it in the cockpit of his aircraft. It worked so well he then bought a couple of dozen more and had one installed in every machine. Ken Nelson wrote and published a biography of Wilkie (*Spitfire RCW*) and recorded:

> 'Always ready for a lark he submitted a bill to Air Ministry so he could be reimbersed. Letter after letter exchanged hands and explanation after explanation followed. Once a mountain of paper had built up the Air Ministry realised they had been "had" and sent Wilkie a cheque for the mousetraps. Every letter received from the bureaucrats in the Ministry was greeted with great rounds of laughter, just what the Squadron needed to sustain high morale.'

There was also the occasion an airman inadvertently pressed the gun button of a Typhoon, sending a few rounds out into the Northumberland countryside. When the man was brought before Wilkie he said to him that as long as a bill from some irate farmer for a couple of dead cows was not received, he was willing to overlook the matter!

* * *

Operational

By the end of July most of the new Typhoons had arrived and the Squadron finally said goodbye to its Hurricanes. In early August Pearson and Higham were commissioned and Fred Murray became OC A Flight. By 1 September, twenty of the Squadron's 26 pilots were deemed operational on the new fighter.

While several minor scrapes had occurred with the Typhoon the first serious recorded problem came on 5 September. Sergeant A E Pearce RAAF, on a sector recco, was forced to belly land near RAF Longtown, Cumberland, due to a broken con.rod. Coming down in a field the Typhoon skidded through a fence, ground to a halt and burst into flames. Pearce was out in quick time with no more than shock and some bruises.

The following day two Typhoons were Scrambled at 1116 hours and vectored north to Farne Island, then south to Blyth, at 20,000 feet, before being ordered up to 30,000. Two hostile aircraft were picked out at the same height, weaving. Turning west the two Germans tried to out-run the two Tiffies and a few minutes later, jettisoned bombs and began steep turns. Pilot Officer Des Perrin chased one, closed to 250 yards and let go a two-second burst. Strikes were seen and pieces flew off its starboard engine. He then overtook the German – now identified as an Me210 – and fired another burst from 100 down to 50 yards, whereupon the 210's rudder caught fire and parts of it fell away. The German machine went over onto its back and dived vertically.

Perrin endeavoured to follow, his IAS reaching 520 mph, before he blacked out. He came to at 3,000 feet off Hartlepool, and called for a fix in case the German crew had baled out. The safety catches on the cockpit door had come loose during the dive and the door was hammering violently in the slipstream but he got home safely. His prop had also been distorted.

Pilot Officer T G Bridges followed the other Messerschmitt but despite a speed of 230 mph did not appear to be closing. Then the German turned to port, enabling Bridges to get in a burst at long range, seeing the EA turn and then dive. Bridges was not able to close in and two more bursts produced hits between port engine and fuselage, top of fuselage and cockpit. Pieces flew off and white smoke streamed from the port engine. The 210 began weaving, then caught fire as more pieces came away. Still diving, Bridges also blacked out for a while, and lost sight of his opponent. He came round at 4,000 feet and later saw an ASR launch below so returned to base. The 210 crashed into Robin Hood's Bay.

The two Me210s were from 16/KG6. Of the four men, Oberleutnant Walter Maurer and Feldwebel Rudolf Jensen survived to become prisoners, while Feldwebel Heinrich Mörgen and Obergefreiter Edouard Czerny were both killed. 266 Squadron had achieved the first combat victories with the Typhoon in August, but 1 Squadron had got victories four and five for the Tiffie. However, it would be another six months before the Squadron would add to this victory tally.

Sergeant Pearce left on the 12th, and J R Campbell was commissioned ten days later. By the end of the month the Squadron had 20 Typhoons on strength, one lone (sentimental) Hurricane and a Magister I. While the pilots continued to work-up with their new aeroplanes, there were a few more Scrambles and some patrols flown, otherwise nothing much of note occurred till the spring of 1943. Except, that is some accidents. On 21 October Pilot Officer P N Dobie and Mr P E G 'Gerry' Sayer, the famous Chief Test Pilot for the Gloster Aircraft Company, were conducting air-to-ground firing tests. Over the sea the two fighters mysteriously collided off Amble and both men were killed.

On 9 November, Pilot Officer Bridges's Typhoon was hit by another machine while on the ground and damaged beyond repair, while on the 21st, Flying Officer C H Watson had engine failure and force landed near Charterhall, writing off the machine.

*   *   *

RAF Biggin Hill

Shortly before the Squadron moved south, some pilots were having problems with the local police. The local hostelry – 'The Trap' – being a frequent watering hole, was usually visited on free evenings by bicycle. Pilots didn't bother with lights and a few were caught and arrested by the two local bobbies, and if they didn't co-operate, the pilots ended up in the local nick. This upset Wilkie who then began to accompany his pilots, ordering everyone to leave en-masse on their bikes – in formation – with him leading. These numbers overwhelmed the bobbies and they brought in reinforcements. When the two groups met, at least three of the policemen were knocked over which led to an official complaint from the Sherrif's Office. However, before things got out of hand, the Squadron were ordered south and the matter became legend rather than a court case.

On the morning of 9 February 1943, the main party moved off at what was recorded as "the un-Godly hour of 0550", and all went well until movement control at Newcastle Central railway station got a bad attack of 'finger' trouble, and did not hold the train long enough to get all the airmen on board. Twelve senior NCOs, acting as 'whippers in' were left behind. Finger touble later spread to the LNER, which managed to disperse the railway vans to various locations over the landscape. In the end it needed the use of a good deal of unlimited petrol and lorries to collect the equipment together at Biggin, but eventually it was all rescued.

Meanwhile the aircraft left Acklington during the day but had to divert to Wittering as the weather deteriorated, although some managed to press on and got as far as Southend. Cloud was thick and low and it was said that at one moment it was being contemplated that everyone should bale out rather than try to land. Sergeant E Crowley in DN241 overshot due to failure of a wheel, his flaps and brakes, turning over just off the airfield. The machine was a write-off but Ned Crowley was not hurt. He was to record:

'Somehow I had lost all my hydraulics and was left with one wheel locked down and the other up, with of course, no flaps. Wilkie was in his aircraft on the ground trying to advise me by R/T. After several circuits at practically zero feet, he ordered me to climb through cloud and bale out. Unfortunately at this point my fuel ran out and I had no alternative but to run into the airfield and slam the aircraft on the ground, hoping to crush the single wheel that was down. However, it stayed down and bounced me into the cloud again, so I stuck the nose down and hoped for the best.

The best, as it turned out, was that the aircraft flipped over and landed upside down in a swampy area just outside the aerodrome. The cockpit was completely buried in the mud but the only injury to me was a graze on my face from a rescue axe wielded by an enthusiastic recovery team member cutting a hole in the fuselage to extricate me.'

Ned had forgotten to open his canopy, usual procedure in these emergencies, which turned out fortunately as otherwise he might have drowned in the swampy mud.

One party of ground crew flew down in a Harrow but the bad weather forced it to divert to North Weald. The next day the Wittering pilots had landed at Biggin by mid-morning, followed by the Southend lot on the 11th. The reason they took longer was that there were no Coffman starter cartridges at Southend to get the engines going and they were stuck until some were flown in.

This day also saw the arrival of a new Intelligence Officer, Pilot Officer Oliver Wakefield. Oliver was a professional comedian and having 'connections' in London's theatre world, he was often able to organise shows for the boys in town, not the least of which were seats at the famous 'Windmill Theatre'.

The 13th – it had to be the 13th – Sergeant R W Hornell flew a sector recco. His Typhoon developed an engine problem and rather than bale out, he rode the machine down to a crash-landing to avoid injuries to a large body of troops he could see dispersed over the countryside below. The Typhoon (R7864) was a write off but Hornell got away with it. The Squadron received a letter of appreciation from Major-General C R Stein, GOC of the 5th Canadian Division for this effort.

Hit and run raiders
At this stage of the war, the Germans were using hit-and-run tactics by their Jabo staffels, bomb-carrying Me109 and FW190 fighters, which would nip across the Channel and bomb almost anything, military or otherwise, along coastal towns, or towns short distances inland. There was no use Scrambling fighters even if the German aircraft were spotted on radar as they came in low over the sea, for by the time Spitfires were airborne, the enemy fighters had bombed and were on their way home. Therefore Fighter Command were forced to set up standing patrols over the coast or a short way out to sea in order to combat the menace. With the Typhoon being so versatile at low altitudes, they took the brunt of these sorties – and they were around 50 mph faster low down than the Spits. While they had their successes, engine trouble put a number of Typhoon pilots into the water, although most were saved. No.1 Squadron were called to begin standing patrols on 15 February, flying their first sorties off Beachy Head. These continued over the next few weeks. To compliment these sorties, the Squadron always had two Typhoons at immediate Readiness at the end of the runway, the pilots prepared to Scramble at a moment's notice – heralded by a red Very flare fired from the watch tower.

These operations caused the first Squadron casualties on 6 March. Pilot Officer G C Whitmore RCAF and Sergeant H R Fraser RAAF went off on an evening patrol but collided in thick cloud. 'Slim' Whitmore's machine was found at Glassenbury Park, Goudhurst, Kent, scattered over 150 yards. Harris Fraser crashed at Red House Farm, Benenden, Kent, five miles away, wreckage spread over 250 yards. Both men probably died instantly. Fraser's twin brother Charles was also a pilot with the Squadron at this time.

Just over a week later, the 13th, the Squadron had better luck. At 1705 Blue Section took off to patrol south of Beachy Head under Kenley control. Ten miles south of the Eastbourne promontory they were vectored towards 'bogies'. Seen at zero feet to starboard, Blue Section came round onto the tails of two German FW190s. The German pilots saw the danger, turned south and began to climb rapidly. Flight Lieutenant L S B Scott took the right-hand machine, Sergeant Robert Hornell the other.

Les Scott opened fire from 250 yards and the 190 seemed to explode in dense black smoke and pieces flew away. Pulling round, Scott next saw the 190 in a gentle dive to port with white smoke pouring out. Attacking again from 150 yards more bits were blasted off it and although trying to evade the cannon shells, a third attack sent the fighter onto its back, then went down and crashed into the water.

Hornell opened fire on the other Focke Wulf as it reached 10-12,000 feet, from 400 yards. His oxygen tube had broken on take-off but hoping the 'low' patrol would not cause him to use oxygen, had carried on. Now in a climb he feared he would need it soon, which is why he opened fire at long range rather than lose the 190. He was lucky! To his surprise and delight, smoke began to stream from the German fighter, bits flew off and then the 190 went into a shallow dive, pouring smoke, then flicked into a spin into the sea. Both 190s had a vertical red stripe on their fins and yellow under the wings.

RAF Lympne

Two days later the Squadron moved down to Lympne on the coast to be better placed for their new job. However, according to Wilkinson, who told Ken Nelson, the real reason began with a bit of a row with Group Captain A G 'Sailor' Malan DSO DFC, OC Biggin Hill. Although Malan wrapped it up nicely, what he wanted was for the Typhoons to act as bait so that his Spitfire squadrons could come along and bounce the German fighters. Wilkie wasn't impressed, and said so. Malan then enquired what Wilkinson thought his Squadron had been sent to Biggin for? Wilkie retorted along the lines of, 'To catch the hit and run raiders which your Spitfires can't catch!' – something not designed to help the matter over much. Wilkie eventually telephoned the AOC 11 Group, Air Vice-Marshal Trafford Leigh-Mallory, to complain and requested a move to Lympne. L-M understood, but said they would not be able to land safely on Lympne's grass airfield. Wilkinson was quick to explain that he had already flown down there and landed his Typhoon on the grass with no problem, going on to say his 'seasoned' pilots would have no difficulty either. He won the day.

To add insult to injury, when Malan later organised a surprise visit to Lympne, Wilkinson, who'd got wind of it, took everyone off to Folkestone (the Squadron was on stand-down), leaving just three NCO pilots to greet him on landing. The snub complete, the non-welcome Station Commander left.

Not long after the move, Flight Sergeant Harry Bletcher was caught by an RAF police officer who accused him of not saluting, and on inspecting his I/D saw that it still carried his old rank of LAC. Convinced the man was an airman parading as a sergeant pilot he was carted off. Harry persuaded the officer to telephone his CO at Lympne, which he did, only to have Wilkie reply that he had never heard of him! After more grilling Harry was released with a charge sheet and told to report to his unit commander. Arriving at Wilkie's office, Harry handed over the sheet at which Wilkie laughed, apologised and then burned it.

*   *   *

The Officers' Mess was the large seaside house (Porte Lympne) owned by Sir Philip Sassoon, one time secretary to Sir Douglas Haig and an Honorary Air Commodore to 601 Squadron RAuxAF. He was also an Under Secretary of State for Air. It was a vast place, complete with a hidden stairway from the library, while the accommodation was superb. There was a sun lamp so the pilots were able to keep 'bronzed' during the early spring months, and also an outdoor swimming pool.

Being once more 'down south' the Squadron were approached by Brighton Council again, to renew their association. The Mayor accordingly invited the Squadron to attend their, 'Wings for Victory' week. The Squadron were not in a position to be released, so it was decided that just Wilkie, Flying Officer Tony Scope-Davies, who was the Adjutant, Pilot Officers C H Watson and Johnny McCullough should attend.

McCullough and the Adj were in London, so travelled to Brighton by train, leaving 'Zulu' Watson and the CO to drive over in Wilkie's car. Watson was given the task of driving and by a good piece of navigational skill, he managed, after driving for seven miles, to get them back to the Officers' Mess! A second try proved more successful.

Flying Officer C L R Bolster RCAF failed to return from a Channel patrol on the 29th. His wingman, Sergeant J W Sutherland returned alone at 1135. Both had been patrolling south of Beachy Head and had been given several vectors. Sutherland reported oil on his windscreen so the pair were ordered to return. However, Sutherland was not able get a reply from his leader as they continued to head south. Finally he had to break away and head north, leaving the other Typhoon still flying south, 40 miles south of Beachy Head at 300 feet. What had occurred was a mystery. Had he seen something, was his radio u/s, or what? He was later reported dead, and it seems he was shot down by a pilot from JG2.

Squadron Leader Wilkinson and Pilot Officer E A Glover were on patrol in poor weather south of Beachy Head on 3 April and received vectors, the third of which brought them to a bogey heading north-west, 15 miles ahead. Increasing speed they closed in and at five miles they were told the bogey was at 1,000 feet. Suddenly Wilkie saw something loom up and he turned steeply to the right to avoid some cliffs and passed over what he thought might be either Brighton or Worthing Pier. The weather was getting steadily worse and the bogey was now identified as definitely hostile. Wilkie asked Control if he could go further out where the weather appeared better, hoping to catch the German as he turned for home. He was given the OK so headed out to orbit but he was then told that someone else had got there before him. The 'hostile' turned out to be a Mosquito of 85 Squadron returning from a Ranger sortie, shot down by British AA fire off Hove!

Wing Commander Mac MacLachlan visited his old Squadron on the 6th, after his recent visit to America. He recounted that he had had a great time in Hollywood, and brought photos to prove it, including one with Betty Grable! Among the ground crew at this time was rigger LAC John Tack, who had failed aircrew selection due to being colour blind but he had then trained as a flight mechanic. He remembers:

'Joining the Squadron we were greeted by Flight Sergeant McIntosh, the unit's WW1 VC winner. He informed us in no uncertain terms how honoured we were to be joining 1 Squadron. He was a very strict disciplinarian and made us feel far from welcome. At this stage the Squadron was engaged in stand-by for hit and run raiders, with two aircraft at Readiness at the end of the runway, as well as bombing V1 targets in France later.

Going on stand-by the mechanics would sit on the wing, legs either side of the cannons, as the pilot taxied at 50 mph while we hung on like grim death, holding our little fire extinguishers; Typhoons were prone to catch fire when starting. If the pilot over-primed it before firing the Coffman starter, the little pellets would fall into the air intake and set the petrol alight, causing a flame. So it was the duty of the mechanic to rush forward with his extinguisher and put it out. In the early days of the Typhoon several mechanics were killed or badly injured, as the pilot, in a hurry, fired off another cartridge jerking the huge propeller into the man. To get over this the pilot had to hold both hands outside the cockpit so we knew he wasn't about to press anything.

One day on stand-by I was sitting under a wing on a warm summer evening, one pilot asleep in the cockpit, the other reading a book. Suddenly a Very flare went up from the Tower and as I yelled "Scramble!" the book came flying out and both pilots took off in a hurry. Starting to walk back to dispersal I was surprised to see both aircraft coming back to land within a short space of time. There was a lot of who-ha going on, as the Red Very light had in fact been Green, calling in the aircraft from stand-by. However, my documents said I was colour blind and they couldn't touch me!

In the next bed to me at Lympne was Max Bygraves, then unknown. He went on to win a Fighter Command talent contest [*Hayes Challenge Cup*] and we never saw him again. Up until then he used to keep us thoroughly amused in the pub telling stories and yarns, everyone enjoying his company.'

Max Bygraves, of course, was part of the Squadron's entertainment squad, called the 'Erkadians', under the direction of LACs Tom Merry and Frank Churchett. They became quite a good team, in the end being some 40 strong.

A Flight were sent off on 9 April at 1835, being vectored towards Cap Gris Nez, along with Spitfires from 611 Squadron, where they were set to bounce four FW190s. However, they in turn were bounced by ten 190s, but Sergeant J W Sutherland managed to get in a quick burst at one of them, then fought his way out. Des Perrin and Sergeant Hornell were on patrol too, and were ordered to join the scrap. Hornell spotted five 190s and he informed Perrin, then dived to attack the last 190, opening fire from 300 to 200 yards. The 190 pulled up, its undercarriage dropped and bits flew off. Turning on its side the German fighter pilot baled out as his aircraft went into the sea. Three 190s came at Hornell but he quickly pulled up steeply into some cloud and flew home. The 190 is thought to have been from JG54's Jabo staffel, piloted by Leutnant Otto-August Backhaus who was killed. 611 got tangled with the 190s and claimed two shot down and they later telephoned the Squadron and thanked them for leading them to a successful engagement.

In May the Squadron returned to some of its old ways attacking ground and surface targets. They were escorting 41 Squadron Spitfires on the 5th, on a shipping recco, and as the Spits headed for home, Pilot Officer H T Mossip dived into France, found a goods train east of Dunkirk and proceeded to shoot it up. He then saw another to the south-east and damaged this too. Heading back over Furness he strafed three barges. These had been the first trains attacked since the old Hurricane days and these two brought the Squadron's train tally to 62.

Pilot Officer Ernie Glover and Sergeant Hornell shot-up an R-boat in Boulogne's outer harbour on the 15th, seeing cannon strikes on its superstructure. Then the next day Les Scott and Pilot Officer J M Chalifour went out early on a Rhubarb. Crossing the coast at Gris Nez they flew along the Calais-St Omer rail line. On the outskirts of St Omer Chalifour attacked a goods train and south of Bethune both pilots strafed another which was left in clouds of steam. South of Lens 'Collie' attacked another successfully. South of Douai both attacked a train and saw it blow up. Crossing out at Berck, they had between them shot-up five trains. Scott had his windscreen damaged by a small calibre bullet in the last attack, unless it had been a lump of something blasted off the engine.

May's poor weather encouraged another Rhubarb on the 19th, this time Glover and Flight Sergeant S H Brown flew over the areas Lens-Lille-Roubaix. Crossing in at Gris Nez they became separated inland. Ernie Glover was not seen again, but Brown found a train near a signal box and Roubaix and shot-up both. Steam shot from the punctured boiler and the engine stopped. Glover was later reported a prisoner, poor return for one damaged locomotive.

Squadron Leader Wilkinson OBE DFM was notified of his pending move on 22 May, to take command of RAF Gravesend with the rank of wing commander. An outsize binge was organised in the Mess and Wilkie, with a tacked-on third wide stripe recalled very little of the latter half of the evening. Chunky Chown had also mysteriously disappeared and a search revealed him in his underwear lying asleep in a Roman marble bath. Everyone thought it best to leave him there! As Wilkinson left, Flight Lieutenant Scott took over temporary command.

The Germans too took advantage of some poor weather on the 23rd, resulting in a Scramble at 1300 hours for Flying Officer Watson and Flight Sergeant W H Ramsey. Within ten minutes they had a visual on a 190 south of Hastings. After a five-minute chase Ramsey got close enough for three long bursts and, as the Squadron diary records: "... the German pilot, remembering an urgent swimming engagement hurried over the side." Ramsey flew close and the German waved, Ramsey returning a V-sign, then gave a Mayday. Two ASR Spitfires flew out but could find no sign of the downed pilot. He came from II/SKG10, the unit also losing another aircraft to AA fire.

There was a Squadron dance on the 28th, Wing Commander Wilkinson sending over a Section from 245 Squadron from Gravesend to take on Readiness duty, so that everyone in 1 Squadron could attend. That was Wilkie! To ensure there would be enough female company to go around, the Adj, Tony Scope-Davies, 'phoned round at the last minute and managed to rustle up an assorted bag of WAAFs, ATS girls and nurses. Next morning most people looked as if they could easily report sick with floating kidneys! There was also another strange phenomenon – the flattening of a considerable area of crops, but in tiny sections, in the vicinity of the dance hall. It was firmly asserted that this must have been due to some freak storm which must have reached its height during the party, although apparently this had gone un-noticed by the Met boys. What else, the first recorded sighting of crop circles perhaps?!

A firmer hand arrived on the 30th with the arrival of the new CO, Squadron Leader A Zweigbergh, who came in from 118 Squadron and had been a former Swissair airline pilot. Still being part of the Biggin Hill Sector, some invitations had been received to attend the dance arranged at the Grosvenor House Hotel in London (on 9 June) to celebrate the 1,000th German aircraft to be shot down by pilots in the Sector since war began. No. 1 Squadron's few victories had helped with the total which was finally reached by Biggin's Spitfires on 15 May.

June began with a morning Rhubarb on the 2nd flown by Pilot Officer 'Moose' Mossip and Flight Sergeant Ramsey. They went after trains and Mossip found and damaged four engines and Ramsey another in the Armentières area but Ramsey had a lucky escape. His starboard wing struck a pole and one of his fuel tanks became u/s, but he got home, flying through cloud with his engine cutting all the time. He gave out three Mayday calls being convinced he would have to bale out into the Channel, and when the engine finally did die, he was over the coast and was able to put down into a field. The field was a bit short and the Typhoon slithered into the next field, one in which a farmer was growing peas. Finding himself alive and unharmed, he climbed out – and had one!!

Ned Crowley recalls an amusing story:

'I was sent to Fighter Command for a commission interview. I was shown into an office where Air Marshal Leigh-Mallory was seated, flanked by an AVM and an Air Commodore. L-M did most of the talking and finally he turned to the others to see if they had any questions. The Air Commodore felt he ought to say something so asked: "What do you do in your spare time?" I was so surprised at this that I blurted out, "Oh, I drink a lot, Sir." I thought I had blown my commission right there and then, but L-M burst into laughter and said I could go. My commission came through about a week later.'

MacLachlan made another visit to the Squadron on the 4th, this time flying a North American Mustang. He persuaded the CO to let him have three Typhoons to help create a diversion while he broke away to shoot up a training base he had pin-pointed in the Orléans-Châteaudun area. Unfortunately lack of cloud cover caused Mac to abort the mission.

Mossip was on another Rhubarb on the 11th, shooting up a train at Lumbres, which blew up. Flying on to Aire he shot up a barge which was left burning. He found a train on a depot turn-table at Lillers and his cannon fire left this in a cloud of steam.

Flight Lieutenant Les (actually Lindley Stuart Brebner) Scott with Flying Officer S P Dennis RAAF, went out on a dawn Rhubarb on the 16th, crossing into France at Gris Nez. Outside Béthune Scott shot-up a train and between here and Douai they accounted for nine more – one carrying petrol was left burning furiously. Scott claimed four, Dennis three, with the other two shared, although on the way out Dennis was hit by flak.

Keeping an eye on his No.2, Scott suddenly saw two aircraft west of Douai, at least one being immediately identified as a FW190. Warning Dennis of the danger, Scott turned and fired at the 190 and forced it away from Dennis's tail. Another 190 turned and both Typhoon pilots engaged. He last saw Dennis with two 190s on his tail, but his own aircraft had taken hits and Scott lost his boost control. His speed dropped and then the engine cut out as he climbed for cloud. Coming out the other side, he continued this hide and seek with some 190s, and during one moment out in the open was hit and wounded in one arm and leg.

He finally managed to loose the fighters in cloud, dived for the coast and crossed out at Berck, crash-landing at Lympne at 0610. Dennis failed to get back, but Scott was pretty sure his wingman had damaged a 190. He ended up as a prisoner of war. Scott's Typhoon was severely damaged and later written off. The 190s came from 4/JG26 and had Scrambled from Vitry as the alarm came that two RAF fighters were shooting up the Béthune railway yards. They located the Typhoon at the coast and Leutnant Dietrich Kehl forced one back towards France where it crashed. Leutnant Helmut Hoppe had chased Scott's machine and thought it must have come down in the Channel. Because of the missing pilot, ASR aircraft went out to search and were engaged by other JG26 fighters. They engaged Spitfires of 91 Squadron which were escorting a Walrus, and shot down two, although they claimed four. Dennis was Kehl's first victory, Scott almost Hoppe's tenth. For his actions, Scott was awarded the DFC.

*   *   *

Mac goes down

MacLachlan again organised 1 Squadron to act as a diversion for one of his forays into France on 29 June. This time Mac took Flight Lieutenant A G Page DFC as wingman. Page had been with 56 Squadron in the Battle of Britain and been badly burned when shot down in August. Having returned to operational flying Geoff Page too was at AFDU (Air Fighting Development Unit) at Wittering, testing all sorts of aircraft including the Mustang. Mac and Page had decided an intruder sortie would be good sport.

They headed out with the Typhoons but over France the two Mustangs broke away and darted towards the Paris area where they located a number of training aircraft and some Ju88s flying around near the airfield at Bretigny. Their surprise arrival cost the Luftwaffe two Hs126s and two Ju88s.

Meanwhile, Squadron Leader Zweigbergh found and shot-up a trawler off the French coast. Later in the afternoon, Mossip went out on a Rhubarb and shot up six trains in the St Omer, Lillers, Lumbres and Desvres areas, bringing the Squadron's score of trains to 92. He then shot up a canal barge near Lillers which was left burning, although he very nearly hit some chimneys by the canal bank.

Up until now the Squadron had not been affected by the Typhoon's problems to any great degree, but on 15 July, Pilot Officer Chalifour and Sergeant P L Grey were Scrambled. There was no contact, and on their way down from 10,000 feet, the tail of Chalifour's Typhoon suddenly snapped off. He was killed in the resultant crash. More bad news came four days later. MacLachlan had flown another intruder sortie but this time he must have caught some ground fire as they headed in over the coast at low level. Mac tried to crash-land his burning aircraft but did not do too good a job of it. Geoff Page orbited the site but could see no sign of life. In the event Mac was badly injured and died before the month was out in a German hospital.

On the 23rd Mossip and Jim Campbell flew a late afternoon Rhubarb under 10/10th cloud at 700 feet and between them they shot up six trains. This brought the score to 98.

* * *

At the end of July, 1 Squadron were beginning to feel a bit miffed that they were flying a defensive role with so many others constantly taking the war to the enemy. They deemed it unworthy for such a great and distinguished Squadron. During a visit to them on the 28th by the AOC, Air Vice-Marshal Hugh Saunders CB CBE MC DFC MM, the CO mentioned this point to him and he promised to give the Squadron some more offensive work. As a matter of record, the Squadron flying personnel as at 1 August 1943 were as follows:

S/L A Zweigbergh

A Flight:	B Flight:
F/L F W Murray	A/F/L D P Perrin
P/O J F Higham	F/O R G Baker
F/O J R Campbell	P/O R A Miller
P/O H T Mossip	F/O H J Wilkinson
P/O J H McCullough	F/O J W Wiley
F/O H T Jackson	W/O W H Dunwoodie DFM
P/O G J King	W/O G Hardie
F/O L J Wood	W/O T Y Wallace DFM
F/S W H Ramsey	F/S R W Hornell
Sgt J W Sutherland	F/S J D Fairbairn
Sgt S D Cunningham	F/S H Bletcher
Sgt W A Booker	Sgt A R H Browne
	Sgt P L Gray

Flight Leiutenant L S B Scott DFC returned on 5 August to resume his place as OC B Flight which had been looked after by Des Perrin. On the 16th, Flying Officer Wood on an early morning Scramble developed engine trouble and had to force land on the beach near Lydd. He sustained severe head injuries and died the next day.

On the 18th the Squadron went on a different sort of 'intruder' mission. That evening seven pilots made a mass sortie into Hythe, with determined faces and a kitty! The beer went down well, songs were roared out and the local 'rozzer' (policeman) was seen beating it down the road desperately hanging on to his helmet. This 'avalanche' of men finally descended onto the Squadron Mess where a splendid game of rugger was enjoyed by all.

The following day the Typhoons of 609 Squadron arrived to join them on the airfield. 609's first Typhoon CO back in 1942 had been Paul Richey DFC, one of 1 Squadron's famous 'old boys'. A few days later, Flight Lieutenant Scott was posted to 198 Squadron, and within days, Chunky Chown the EO was posted to Station HQ. On the 23rd Murray flew to Tangmere, followed by Pilot Officer Gray in the Squadron Hurricane, in order for Gray to make his first Typhoon trip. Gray made two successful circuits and landings, then took off again. He seemed to attempt a slow role at low level and dived into the ground, being killed instantly.

Again there was more bad news a few days later. Flight Lieutenant Scott had been shot down over Holland, together with his CO, on one of his first sorties with 198 Squadron. Fortunately both were later reported as German prisoners.

Sergeant Browne was in the 'wars' at the beginning of September. On the 5th he hit the runway on take-off, bending back eight inches of each propeller blade but continued to fly a one hour, 20 minute patrol – 'without noticing anything unusual!' Then on the 7th Browne failed to change fuel tanks soon enough and very nearly went into the sea, but his engine picked up just in time.

King's Standard

Better news came on the 8th. In the newspapers the Squadron read that the King had approved the award of a King's Standard for 25 years of continuous service, an honour the Squadron could be, and was, justly proud of. The news came at the same time as the announcement that Italy had surrendered to the Allies.

As if to celebrate, Mossip and Davey went down to Manston on the night of 14/15th September and flew a night intruder. Between St Omer and Hazebrouck they shot up two trains, to bring the Squadron tally to 100. The next night Mossip was at it again, but this time, as a first, he flew a Typhoon which had been fitted with bomb racks under the wings, and stuck on two 500 lb bombs. Then he latched onto a raid flown by 16 rocket-armed Hurricane IVs and seven other Bombphoons on an attack on Abbeville fighter base. His two bombs were seen to explode in the dispersal area.

This heralded a new phase in the history of 1 Squadron. Obviously AVM Saunders' promise of more offensive action was taking effect, and the new role appeared to be as a fighter-bomber. However, this made Lympne's grass runway unsuitable to operations, so aircraft would fly to either Tangmere or Manston, bomb-up and operate from there.

More good news came on 14 October with the announcement of the DFC for Flight Lieutenant Des Perrin. This was to be followed on the 23rd with the news that Moose Mossip too had won the DFC.

Before that, however, Moose had another fighter bomber sortie on the 15th, escorted by Flying Officer Jimmy Wiley RCAF. This time it was a Rhubarb, the bombs going down on Tingry transformer station, near Samer, then both pilots strafed the place with 20 mm cannon. Six days later, Wiley and Flight Sergeant J D Fairbairn RCAF were Scrambled at 0800 following a report of enemy aircraft over the Channel. They spotted the bandit 15 miles off St Aubin and Wiley went into the attack.

Closing right in he found his gunsight had worked loose (much basic English used!) but holding it in place with one hand he closed in again and opened fire. Strikes appeared on the German's port wing root. Breaking away, Fairbairn attacked as the Focke Wulf fell apart and hit the sea. This brought the Squadron's score to 234, or so it was thought at the time. As the diary records this was "... a figure which the pilots could easily enlarge if only Jerry would play – which he won't."

Jerry did make an effort to play on 1 November. Hornell and Wilkinson were Scrambled in the afternoon to assist some Spitfires near Calais and ran into a fight with half a dozen Me109G fighters. Hornell damaged one before breaking off to avoid being rammed by another. Wilkinson chased one down but could not close before it went into cloud at 2,000 feet – still going down.

Mossip and Davey were out on an evening intruder on the 6th, and succeeded in shooting up a train and two motor cars near Le Touquet but in the process Mossip was hit in the port wing. A shell had entered the ammunition box but the machine was only slightly damaged.

There were a number of strange looking emplacements being built along the northern coast of France as the year came to a close. Obviously Intelligence knew all about them but for some while their purpose was kept under wraps. These turned out to be V1 launching ramps being built in readiness for the launching of hundreds of V1 rockets against Britain in the early summer of 1944. A good deal of effort was made against these sites, which were little more than a sort of ski-ramp and a hut to house the men who would fire the things off. They were protected by a good deal of flak and machine guns, and over the next few months they became deadly targets to attack. This coupled with the fact that they could be quickly repaired if knocked out made Fighter Command's task a hard one. As Second TAF was also formed in readiness for an invasion of mainland Europe in 1944, its squadrons too were tasked with helping to knock out these targets – known as 'Noball' sites.

The Squadron began operating against these targets during late November, and carrying two bombs was fast becoming the norm. On the second of two shows flown on 25 November, a Noball target was attacked mid-afternoon near Cherbourg, and a good deal of flak had been met. Heading back to England Flying Officer Wiley called to report that he'd been hit. He pulled up to around 500 feet and was hit again. His Typhoon burst into flames, turned over and dived into the ground where it exploded.

The next day the Squadron escorted American B26 Marauders, following which they went down and shot-up 19 gun positions. One blew up in spectacular fashion, covering Moose Mossip's aircraft with mud and filled it full of holes. He almost had more holes than aircraft, but it was soon back on the line, thanks to the ground crews.

The first operation of note in December was on the 7th. Warrant Officer Fairbairn and Flight Sergeant L E Watson were Scrambled just on mid-day but made no contact with the reported bogey. The weather them clamped and the two pilots were diverted to nearby Hawkinge. Watson got down but Fairbairn crashed into hills three miles away and was killed. Tragically his fiancée was at Hawkinge, so probably he had been pleased about the chance to see her.

A week later 609 left Lympne for Manston, while their replacement was 137 Squadron, equipped with rocket-firing Hurricane IVs. Mossip and Flight Sergeant S D Cunningham flew an ASR patrol on the 21st, the latter flying the now repaired JN144 which had been so badly damaged on 26 November. Cunningham reported a rough engine and was told to return home but he was not seen again.

The next day, Flight Lieutenant Murray led an attack against a V1 site at 0905. There was some good and accurate bombing but at the cost of two Typhoons. Jack Sutherland and Warrant Officer F J Wyatt RAAF were both shot down, fortunately surviving as prisoners. This same afternoon they went back to the same target. Des Perrin had a bomb hang-up and when he shot at a gun position, the vibration from the cannons shook it off. The explosion blew off his trim tabs, made a large hole in the starboard wing plus some smaller ones, not to mention frightening the New Zealander witless! The only consolation for him was that the German gunners must have been frightened too.

George Medal

An event in August led to one of the Squadron's Corporals winning the George Medal. Corporal Norman Gouldin, who already had the BEM to his name, together with two other men, Corporal Frank North, RAF Regiment, and LAC Frederick Withers of RAF Lympne, rescued a badly injured soldier. All three were decorated; the citation for their awards read as follows.

> In August 1943, four soldiers entered a minefield; three were killed instantly and the fourth was seriously wounded. Corporals Gouldin and North, who are nursing orderlies, and LAC Withers, who is a motor driver, immediately proceeded to the scene of the accident. To reach the injured soldier it was necessary to cross a canal and pass through barbed wire. Corporal Gouldin although unable to swim, entered the canal and with his two companions waded across. After crossing the barbed wire the rescuers penetrated about 16 feet into the minefield and reached the soldier to whom they rendered first aid. Afterwards, carrying him on a stretcher these airmen recrossed the canal, with water up to their armpits and insecure footholds, and brought the soldier to safety. Throughout they showed great fortitude and initiative and complete disregard of their own safety.

Chapter Thirteen

1944 – YEAR OF INVASION

Following a good Christmas, the new year opened with Ramrod 407 on New Year's Day. Eight aircraft took off to attack 'constructional' targets at Hesdin – Noball sites – escorting 184 Squadron's Hurricane IVs. The slow speed of the Hurricanes made it necessary to hang about over 'Indian Territory' much longer than considered healthy.

Flying Officers D V McIntosh and G J King both caused considerable excitement on landing. Mac dropped a wing and opening up decided to go round again. However, the starboard wing dug into the ground, throwing up clouds of earth and making a most unpleasant noise. The aircraft swung through 90° and finally became airborne again – to everyone's surprise. Mac went round again and made a good landing with his wing tip bent up and the aileron jammed.

At the same time, Jimmy King was seen to have a hang-up but as his radio appeared u/s it was impossible to warn him. On landing he became amused, wondering why everybody was running like mad in every direction except towards him. He then saw that the bomb had dropped off at the end of his landing run. Only then did he stop laughing.

On the evening of the 6th, at the local pub, the last of the Christmas decorations were tossed onto a dying fire and soon a merry blaze was under way. A knock on the door heralded the arrival of the police, taking an interest, and saying that the chimney was on fire. A discreet withdrawal was made into a back room whilst the police worked on the fire with a stirrup pump, but then the local fire brigade turned up, getting wind of the blaze and deciding a fire in a public house was too good to ignore. It all ended in farce.

The more shy and retiring members of the Squadron in the back room decided on a strategic retreat out the rear door, leaving the police and firemen in full possession. All that seemed to be missing by that time was a fire! Later, Bob Hornell's Austin Seven car was found under the stairs in the Mess so someone was having a great time. Mention of Gremlins was made but it wasn't very convincing.

Next day the CO led eight Typhoons to the Cherbourg peninsular. Over the sea his aircraft engine began cutting so he turned back with his No.2, handing over the lead to Des Perrin. But he was having problems with his undercarriage doors, so he too had to abort with his wingman. R A 'Dusty' Miller took the lead but then he developed an oil leak so turned back too taking his wingman with him. The remaining two pilots were fed up by this time and didn't really fancy a solo trip, so they turned back also.

Flight Sergeant Bletcher – the Squadron artist – had a lucky escape on the 26th. On take-off his engine failed as he had reached the dizzy height of just twelve feet! He immediately whipped his wheels up and put the aircraft down. Slithering and screeching across the ground he struck a concrete pill box, crushed the Tiffie's port wing, then charged into a wood on the north-east corner of the airfield. The machine dug its nose into a bank, cartwheeled and finished up on its nose with the remaining wing in the air. Bletcher got away with just a tear in his trousers but his machine (EK139) was Cat E!

Ramrod 495 mounted on 29 January cost the life of Flight Seargeant L E 'Spike' Watson. The Squadron was escorting 164's R/P Hurricanes, and Spike was last seen just before bombing. There had been no flak and no fighters. Another Op to Cherbourg on 3 February saw everyone at least get there despite cloudy weather. Bombs were dropped on an estimated target position – never very satisfactory – but Moose Mossip had both his bombs hang-up. He then discovered that due, no doubt, to pre-occupation twitch, etc, he had omitted to turn on his bomb selection switches. He quickly rectified this and turned back, bombing a fort on the coast thus acquiring more satisfaction than everybody else.

Rangers

If the Squadron was still in need of more offensive sorties, it came on 15 February. The pilots flew up to Martlesham Heath where they were briefed by 198 Squadron, whose pilots operated a good deal on deep penetration sorties over Holland, using Ranger tactics. The aircraft were also fitted with long-range drop-tanks. LAC John Tack recalls Martlesham:

> 'We shared Martlesham with an American Thunderbolt Group. When we arrived we were amazed at the food we were given. At meal times the Americans sat with their hats on, forks in one hand, peanut butter sandwiches in the other, and we noticed very different behaviour from ours. Within a week the Americans, most of them, sat down without a hat and their behaviour had changed

considerably. The cigarettes were cheap too.

Soon after arriving there, one of our Typhoons took off on an air test and proceeded to fly quite a display. Not to be out-done a P47 took off and tried to do likewise but it hit the runway on a low pass and its engine ended up two miles away.'

Phil Williamson, LAC armourer, also recalls Martlesham:

'It was freezing cold, that I do remember. We were billeted in requisitioned houses just off the perimeter. At one stage the boys resorted to burning fences in order to keep warm. However, some of us discovered the US Red Cross hut where we would go to keep warm and have hot drinks. The US PX hut and the chow line had to be seen to be believed – we'd not seen food like it for years. In the Mess Hall there was unlimited sugar and tins full of free cigarettes. Unfortunately some of the lads began taking the sugar and filling their pockets with cigarettes as they left, which the US commander took a dim view of and we were threatened with "jankers" if caught. But the Yanks certainly organised things when dances were arranged, sending US Liberty buses into Ipswich to collect local girls, airmen for the use of.'

The first Op from Martlesham came on 24 February, an escort to Bostons attacking Hesdin – a V1 site – but this was in France, so the Typhoons needed to land at Lympne, where they had recently been, to refuel. Who organises such things? This was followed by an escort mission to Mosquito aircraft to Neufchâtel. It was the final operation for Flying Officer Mossip DFC, who now went on rest – to an OTU!

On the 29th, Des Perrin led an Op in support of American 8th Air Force B17 bombers to Holland. During this they spotted an 800-ton ship and an R-boat on the Zuider Zee and attacking, damaged both. The trip took two hours, five minutes, a record for the Squadron.

This record was almost immediately broken on 2 March. Perrin led eight aircraft on Rodeo 612, escorting Marauders to the marshalling yards at Tergnier which had them airborne for two hours, 25! However, they lost Warrant Officer Neil Howard RAAF who had engine trouble over the target but was seen to make a good forced landing. He evaded capture and although it took him and the Resistance many months, he eventually returned. Four days later Ramrod 603 called for close escort to more B26s, together with 3 and 198 Squadrons. FW190s bounced 3 Squadron and they lost a pilot. This sortie gave 1 Squadron a further new record – three hours in the air.

On the 17th a Lancaster pilot decided to practise a flapless landing at Martlesham on the impression he was landing at Woodbridge, the 5,000 yard emergency strip five miles down the A12. The pilot overshot, ground looped and lost his undercarriage with the most expensive noise that had been heard around the airfield so far. No sooner had the dust settled on this scene than a USAF P47 Thunderbolt made a belly landing on nearby waste ground, hit a lump and turned over. Willing hands lifted up the fighter and the pilot scrambled out OK. The speed with which nearby American crash wagons, ambulances, photographers, Uncle Tom Cobley and all arrived had to be seen to be believed.

It was obviously the crash season, but an embarrassing one for Moose Mossip. He arrived back for a visit in a Spitfire on 21 March, and to attend Des Perrin's marriage. He then persuaded the Squadron to let him have a flight in his old Typhoon. Poor Moose burst a tyre on take-off and had to end up with a belly landing. He achieved this with some skill but left a little less popular than when he arrived. Harrison Mossip was killed in action in March 1945 flying with 245 Squadron, of all things, hitting high tension cables during a mission over Germany.

Two days later, flying cover for an ASR mission off Orfordness, Flying Officer H T Jackson called up with engine trouble. McIntosh turned in time to see Jacko hit the water but his Typhoon sank immediately. Shortly afterwards his body came to the surface and was later picked up by a Walrus amphibian but despite artificial respiration, they failed to revive him. Phil Williamson recalls the Squadron activities:

'When I joined the Squadron they had Typhoons. It was winter time and the flight mechanics went out first, getting up about 5 am. Our sleep was disturbed by the noise of the Coffman starters, firing up the engines. When they'd finished their D.I.s we went out, and having finished breakfast did our D.I.s. By the time we got back to our dispersal shed, in the middle of which stood one of those huge cast-iron fires, all the flight mechs. would be sat round it so we couldn't get anywhere near its warmth. So we would occasionally bring in some cellulose nitrate pellets from the starter cartridges and fling a handful into the fire – that would scatter them and we'd quickly dive in and grab the chairs.

I was the first armourer on aircraft "O". What we did, we each had three aircraft to look after, mine were "O", "P" and "Q". I was first armourer on "O", second on "P" and third on "Q", so that if anyone was on a pass, or whatever, you took over on his aeroplane too.

'We would also go down to the bomb dump and collect the bombs, manhandling them onto trollies. Once up onto the trolley you had to use a detonator gauge to see that the cavity inside the tail-end was clear, and once that was OK you'd put the detonator in. Then you'd screw the pistol into the end and that had a vane on a thread which engaged with a propeller device in the tail. The tail clipped on with a propeller at the end of it and it took 3½ turns of the prop and a tip block – like a jubilee clip – to hold it. When the trolley was taken to the aircraft the bomb would be hoisted up to the bomb rack and then the cable from the prop would fit into it so that when the bomb was released the clip was pulled off, which left the prop free to turn, and upon impact the firing pin would sheer a little brass pin, go forward, hit the detonator and explode the bomb.' *All very simple really!*

Changes were now afoot. At the end of the month the CO, together with Johnnie Higham and Bob Hornell were posted and on 3 April the Squadron moved to North Weald. Then on the 8th Des Perrin and Dusty Miller were posted. Des, a most popular New Zealander, did not survive the war either, being killed in September 1944 with 198 Squadron. He burst a tyre on take-off, crashed and died. Another loss was Chunky Chown. Despite the odd move to various places he was now permanently posted, as station EO at Northolt. He had been with the Squadron for 2½ years and was now a flight lieutenant.

The Spitfire

There were not many Typhoon squadrons that changed over to Spitfires during the war. In some way this could be the RAF hierarchy – and possibly some senior old boys – not wishing to see the *premier* squadron just becoming either a part of 2nd TAF, or just another fighter-bomber outfit.

Whatever the background, No.1 Squadron was now to be equipped with the one aircraft every schoolboy associates with the RAF in WW2 – the Supermarine Spitfire. No sooner had the move to North Weald been made than the first Spitfire Mk IXs began to arrive. During this period, as the Squadron flew Spitfire Vs and IXs, the more experienced Typhoon pilots were posted to other units and new pilots posted in. The new CO was something of a legend with the RAF, a New Zealander, Squadron Leader J M Checketts DSO DFC. There were also four Danish pilots posted in.

Johnny Checketts had commanded 485 New Zealand Squadron in 1943 but had been shot down over France on 6 September. Successfully evading capture he was picked up by the French Resistance and seven weeks later he was back in England. He received the DSO and following a period with the Central Gunnery School he was given command of 1 Squadron. His senior flight commander was Flight Lieutenant I P Maskell.

No sooner had he arrived than the Squadron was sent to Ayr in Scotland for an armament practise camp. They now had 19 Spit IXs, one Mark V, and two twin-engined Oxfords to carry the ground party. On forming up, Flying Officer R G 'Red' Ward, wingman to Flying Officer F H Cattermoul, pulled up in front of his leader as the Squadron formed up, his tail clipping the other's prop. Ward's machine flicked over and dived straight in, and he was killed instantly. Cattermoul kept control of his Spitfire and landed safely.

Johnny Checketts' period as OC was short lived, for on the 29th he was promoted to Wing Commander and given command of a Spitfire Wing in the Biggin Hill Sector. The new CO was Squadron Leader H P Lardner Burke DFC. Henry Lardner Burke (or just H P L Burke) came from South Africa and was known at 'Pat'. In 1941 he had flown off the carrier *Ark Royal* to fight from Malta. He had his successes there, was wounded but also won the DFC. In 1943 he had been a flight commander with 222 Squadron. Within a day of his arrival the Squadron moved again, this time to Predannack, Cornwall, to be part of Wing Commander D Smallwood's Wing. William Noakes arrived in April, a trained fitter from 2nd TAF. Like John Tack he came from Ilford, and when they met it began a friendship which has lasted till this day. He recalls:

'I came to the Squadron to get experience of the Typhoon in a less hectic environment than under canvas at Hurn waiting for the Invasion, and would return there in May. So as I joined the Squadron I found they had just converted to Spitfire IXs. Having been in the RAF for well over a year I felt that this was par for the course!

Everything was in a shambles so I was told to go home for the weekend. When I got back I found all my kit and everything gone – the Squadron was moving to Predannack. I had not worked on Spits before but soon got into the swing of things. We were living in double-summer time and it never seemed to get dark. At the same time as I arrived a new CO also joined – Henry Lardner

Burke. I got the feeling that the NCOs were not too keen on him and as a 'new boy' I was allocated his kite, JX-B. Sort of take it or else proposition!'

John Tack also recalls this move to the south-west. Like most airmen he had a bicycle which had to be jealously guarded, and he kept his padlocked to the end of his bed. Returning from leave he found all his stuff gone, but arriving at Predannack, discovered bed and bike safely installed in his new billet.

Back on Ops
Operations started again in May 1944, and a new flight commander for B Flight arrived on the 7th, Flight Lieutenant A A Vale DFC. Alex Vale had been in the same squadron as Lardner Burke on Malta, although not at the same time. The Squadron's first Spitfire show came on the 14th, a strafing attack upon Gael airfield. A train was also attacked after a gun on a flak wagon had had the temerity of opening up on the RAF fighters.

Also this month they began flying 'Instep' patrols. These were patrols out over the Brest peninsula or even towards the Bay of Biscay in order to give protection to Coastal Command aircraft flying anti-U-Boat sorties in the Bay. These sorts of operations were normally better suited to twin-engined Beaufighter and Mosquito aircraft, but in order to keep the long-range Ju88 fighters of V/KG40 in check, Spitfires and Mustangs were often assigned this duty, although particularly arduous for single-engined aeroplanes flying over long stretches of water.

Disaster struck on 22 May. It was obvious that the invasion of France was not far off and the RAF were being even more offensive at this period, attacking everything they could find over France, Belgium and Holland. In part this was designed to inflict the maximum hurt on road and rail traffic, as well as radar sites. They attacked everywhere, not favouring any particular area so that the Germans could only guess where the Allied armies might land.

In keeping with this strategy, Flight Lieutenant Vale led four Spitfires out on a Rhubarb to the Vannes-Châteaulin-Morlaix area, looking for trains. They found two, one being a troop train, and both were left covered in smoke, flame and steam. Sergeant E F Jacobsen, one of the Danish contingent, pulled up during this attack and was lost to sight. Vale's aircraft was hit by small arms fire on his second strafing run at the troop train. He tried to force land, hit a hedge and the Spitfire broke up. He had been due to journey up to London in order to receive his DFC from the King on the 23rd. However, luck was with him and he was later reported a prisoner, but the Dane was killed.

Flight Sergeant Ken Weller, a recent arrival following a tour with 72 Squadron in the Middle East, was on this show and remembers:

'We were on a Rhubarb and flew out right on the deck. It was a bit of a line-shoot to say we always tried to leave a slipstream trail on the sea as we headed over, but if you didn't you were too high and German radar would spot you.

It seemed at this time that the whole of the Cherbourg peninsular was one mass of anti-aircraft guns, and it certainly appeared so when we hit this railway goods yard and a troop train. Alex Vale was just off to my starboard side and he went down and blew up. Then Jake went in. Campbell and I were both hit; I could see smoke streaming from his aircraft as we turned for home. In my case a shell had come through the bottom of the cockpit, up between my legs and then blew a hole through the canopy above me. It took me some moments to realise that to have done so, the shell must also have gone right through my overload tank and that I was undoubtedly streaming petrol.

I immediately switched to the main tanks, pumping like mad to ensure the engine didn't pack up. Then I was over the sea, re-crossing the 110 miles of water back to Predannack.

When I landed I saw Campbell had also made it back although I had had to land without flaps or brakes. I taxied up to dispersal only to find my canopy wouldn't open. My Spitfire, as well as the shell which I knew about, had about ten flak holes in it and something had caused the cockpit sides to bulge out which jammed the canopy runners.

The CO was waiting for us and he saw my problem and jumped up onto the wing, and by pushing the bulging metal, managed to get the canopy to slide open. It was just as well I hadn't had to bale out on the way back. Very shaky do!'

The new B Flight commander became Flight Lieutenant P W Stewart RNZAF.

The Squadron increased their 'time in the air' record on the 24th during a shipping patrol, carrying 90 gallon slipper drop-tanks – 3 hours, 10 minutes. But on this sortie, Flying Officer R W Bridgman suffered an unusual injury. Bob decided to do some windscreen cleaning whilst travelling at around

200 mph and as he put his arm out so it was caught violently in the slipstream. His shoulder was dislocated as the arm was whisked backwards. This led to much leg-pulling, but it was noted with some relief that he was still able to log good bar hours using his other arm.

June the first saw a morning Rhubarb and another loss. The four pilots were looking for trains in the Châteaulin-Quimper-Kerlin Bastard areas and found one. It was successfully attacked but Flying Officer 'Pussy' Cattermoul's (leader) Spitfire was hit in the engine. He called his deputy that he was going to have to force land and was last seen heading for a suitable spot. He was reported as a prisoner but he later died on 9 July.

D-Day

John Tack recalls spending long hours painting black and white stripes to wings and fuselages of the Spitfires immediately before daylight, and, standing on the cliffs at Predannack, seeing huge number of ships out in the Channel. Also, that the Squadron began using 500 lb bombs and/or LRT drop tanks, and having to constantly change them over as an operation was changed. He also remembers:

'On one occasion a pilot landed complaining that when switching over to his 90 gallon drop tank the red warning light had come on and so he aborted and returned to base. I could understand his problem as he had bombs on, not a tank. What he was supposed to do with his bombs I never found out!'

D-Day arrived on 6 June 1944 but 1 Squadron were not in the main arena. Instead they flew two Roadstead operations and one Ranger. On the latter they shot-up two trains – Flying Officers T Wyllie and K M Longmuir, the latter also strafing a staff car. Strikes were seen on the windscreen and the car turned off the road and into a ditch. Several other operations were flown immediately after the Allied Invasion , giving cover to the shipping in the Channel off Normandy, but the weather was pretty poor and a lot of time was spent at Predannack waiting for it to clear. On the 7th the Squadron flew a Wing Ranger to Nantes, as recalled by Flying Officer E N W Marsh:

'The Wing was detailed to fly an eight aircraft Ranger to Nantes airfield in Brittany, just south of the River Loire, led by Wing Commander Smallwood, who for this show flew with 165 Squadron's flight of four. The other flight was led by our CO, Des Maskell as his No.2, No.3 was the other flight commander R W Stewart and I was No.4.

At the briefing we were advised by the Wingco to maintain R/T silence, if possible, and to transmit only when necessary. Smallwood's call-sign incidentally was appropriately "Splinters". The operation was to be flown at zero feet with the exception of a rapid climb to 10,000 feet when crossing the Brittany coast – both going and returning – to avoid light flak. We were advised to get permission from the Wingco if a suitable ground target presented itself as it was necessary to conserve ammunition for our primary target. Anticipation and expectations had been very high for the success of this Ranger although in the event our prime objective was never actually reached.

The English Channel from Predannack to Brittany was about 110 miles and zero feet was not an exaggeration. I occasionally observed long wakes on the water behind the aircraft similar to that made by speedboats. This phenomenon was due mainly to the prop wash so close to the water surface. After crossing the Brittany coast there was about 140 miles more to the target. At perhaps 70-80 miles along the track, a passenger train appeared directly in front of our CO. After a brief exchange on the R/T with Splinters, permission was granted to attack. My own position at that moment was on the right flank of our four. The Wingco's flight was about 200 yards to the left. In my mistaken enthusiasm I assumed that all of No.1 Squadron's Spits would converge in an attack on the loco and I commenced firing at about the same time as Squadron Leader Burke. The steam engine was truly pranged with steam hissing out from many shell hits and after about a 3-second burst from me, I noticed Stewart, my No.1, in a steep turn to port, exposing a clear view of the underside of his aircraft about 50 yards away. I immediately banked to starboard, half expecting impact with his aircraft. About four seconds later when nothing had happened I straightened out and reformed with the Flight.

The next target appeared on the River Loire. This was a type of tugboat and was slightly to my right and ahead, about 1,500 yards when I first spotted it. After another brief R/T exchange I was granted permission to attack. After a slight climb to 100 feet or so, in order to achieve a good strafing angle, I commenced firing with all guns. I was never an enthusiast for the Spitfire's selective gun button on the control column, to either use cannons only, just machine-guns, or both. It seemed to me that if something was worth shooting at you had better deliver the complete package in one go.

Anyway, my range to the target was now possibly 1,200 yards and in order to allow for shell trajectory at that long range, I put the reflector sight bead on the top of the bridge and held on to this point until shell hits could be observed bursting on the hull above the water line. Then as range was closing, I corrected to hit bridge first and then the waterline. The long burst was probably of six seconds. There was no doubt that the boat was seriously disabled judging by all the pieces flying off and the effect of the HE and incendiary shells. The combat film displayed this very well. After this attack, we had crossed the Loire and were instructed to drop our babies – release drop tanks – and prepare for the attack on Nantes airfield – fast approaching. Much to our surprise and disappointment there were no aircraft of any description on the airfield and after making one circular pass around the field we headed north for home.

Any target now presenting itself would be fair game as there was no longer any need to conserve ammunition. Several minutes later, Pat Burke was able to deliver a short attack on a German staff car with seveal black uniformed people attempting to bale out. The vehicle had stopped in front of a large French château flying a swastika flag. Pat Burke left his thumb on the button as he climbed over the building blasting off what seemed to be half the roof.

We continued on our way at zero feet for a while, Splinters calling "UP! UP! UP!" whenever trees or some other obstruction blocked our path. My duty was to scan the section of sky to the right and rear of our formations. Then, looking ahead immediately after an R/T call I found I was converging on a high tension power line to my immediate left. There was not enough time to clear them by climbing so I was committed to go under. I reduced altitude by about eight feet which put me right on the deck and I flew under the cables on a near parallel course to the powerline which had a low droop in those near the middle between the pylon towers. I think prop clearance was not much, either up or down! The impact of all this didn't hit home until later in the mess bar.

We then came upon a goods train travelling from the east, apparently towards Brest, and 165 Squadron attacked, followed by our four, with a strafing run along the length of the train.

That concluded our strafing attacks and shortly after this we crossed over the coast at 10,000 feet and then flew at zero feet for Predannack. Upon inspection of the aircraft it was found that one of the 165 Spitfires had one of the underwing radiators crammed full of tree leaves and twigs – luckily not the coolant radiator. My log-book indicates two hours and 20 minutes for this operation.'

On 14 June the Squadron flew on a Rodeo to Le Mans. Flying Officers E N W Marsh and H L Stuart landed at a forward airstrip south-east of Grandcamp to refuel, being the first 1 Squadron pilots to land in France since 1940. Eric 'Junior' Marsh also recalls another operation, this one flown on 18 June 1944:

'On this date the Squadron flew a dive-bombing operation on five German ships evacuating the Channel Islands. The ships were located in the bay to the south end of Jersey, off St Helier. Unfortunately three of the ships were flak ships. Roadsteads were never a "piece of cake" and on this occasion, although we all returned home in one piece, we didn't achieve much.

The CO was leading, I was Blue 3, and all our aircraft were armed with one 500 GP (HE) bomb mounted under the fuselage. The weather was clear and sunny without a cloud in the sky – wonderful conditions for anti-aircraft defence which on this occasion was quite incredible in its intensity.

Our approach was from west to east and well south of the bay, when we spotted the ships. The CO ordered us to form echelon starboard and no sooner had we broken battle formation than the sky around us filled with 88 mm flak bursts – lots of it! They were obviously tracking us and fired as soon as they realised our intentions.

Squadron Leader Burke then ordered us to bomb from our current positions which was not yet in echelon. Immediately commencing the dive the whole arsenal of guns from the three flak ships literally filled the air above the ships with fused light flak bursting everywhere. There was obviously a well planned system for defending the ships as the sky between 2,000 to 3,000 feet was saturated with 20 mm bursts which appeared as small red fiery explosions in a blanket layer. The sky above this, up to 6,000 or 7,000 feet, was just filled with what looked like 40 mm bursts, which appeared as greyish puffs of smoke. The large black irregular shaped bursts of 88 mm which we were receiving soon ceased after we had all entered our dive.

The angle of dive was far from ideal, it being much too shallow, probably only 30 and 40 degrees and led to pure guesswork when to release the bombs. Of course, everybody wanted to do that as quickly as possible to limit flying through that maelstrom. As Blue 3 I was the 11th aircraft to enter the dive and on the way down I noticed that all bombs were bursting well short of the target ship. In order to compensate for this error, just prior to bomb release, I raised the nose of my

Spitfire for a shallower dive angle, in order to throw the bomb. This naturally obscured the target beneath the engine and I pressed the button when I thought things were about correct. Then I broke hard left and up.

I was greeted by 88 mm flak bursts immediately in front of me (about six shells) and I banked hard to port. Just a few seconds later another group of shell bursts exploded to my right and about level. During this time I was subjected to intense light flak with tracers whistling by from all angles. My exit route was naturally to follow the rest of the Squadron and this was certainly anticipated by the flak ships, thus the accurate gunfire. I remember quite clearly changing my climb at full throttle to a shallow dive to port with throttle reduced and kicked on a lot of rudder to induce a skid hopefully to complicate all that good gunnery. The next group of 88 mm bursts were not close and also the light flak ceased about that time.

After turning to starboard and opening to maximum throttle in order to catch up with the now distant Squadron I looked around but could not see my No.2. I did notice one of our bombs had exploded in the sea on the far side of the target ship. Not very close, but may have wet down a few flak gunners. Anyway, they must have been somewhat concerned watching the bomb trajectory all the way down to impact.

I suppose one could say they won that round. After a short while I caught up to the Squadron and found my No.2 formating on Blue Leader. Apparently he had released his bomb early thinking there was not much chance of a hit anyway and got the hell out of there. He was right. And lucky us, we all arrived home safely.

I believe the term "half a crown – sixpence" originated with somebody experiencing intense flak conditions similar to this operation. This pertains to the alternating size of those coins in relation to one's anus!!'

Buzz-bomb Alley

A couple of days later the Squadron moved to Harrowbeer. However, things were changing further to the east with the arrival of the first V1 rocket bomb. The Squadron had been involved in dive-bombing the V1 sites in their Typhoons but now the Germans had begun to launch their evil 'doodlebugs' which fell indiscriminately all over the place. Preparations had been made to defend against them but it was going to be a tense and testing time. RAF fighters would attempt to intercept them over the sea, then a belt of AA guns would try, followed by more fighters and finally a string of barrage balloons on the outskirts of London for those that reached that far.

These flying bombs – which were code-named 'Divers' – had speeds of between 320 and 400 mph, could average 250 miles range and carried a 2,000 lb warhead. They were smaller in size than a fighter aircraft and it generally took a high-speed dive to get into range to fire. Even then they might explode in the pilot's face. Not all RAF fighters could close the range with them, certainly not in a horizontal tail-chase. Squadrons about to help support the D-Day landings were now withdrawn to combat the new menace, one being No.1 Squadron.

The first V1s fell on England on 13 June and within a few days 55 rocket sites in France launched 244. From then on they came over almost daily until September. The immediate danger, of course, was from those that might be directed into the areas along the south coast, particularly around Portsmouth or Plymouth, where the bulk of the invasion support forces were being held.

The Squadron were rapidly deployed to RAF Detling, Kent, on the 22nd to be right in the path of the flying bombs. Bill Noakes remembers the move:

'Having arrived at Harrowbeer we finally got to sleep in the small hours only to be rudely awakened around 5 am by the Tannoy, calling us to dispersal because our Spits were about to arrive. Having sorted that out we were released to get some sleep but having just about got our heads down the Tannoy blared again – we were off to Detling.

We airmen went by train via Paddington Station. We were a motley bunch in our scruffy oil-stained uniforms, not usually worn outside the flights, looking bedraggled and tired. We formed up in some sort of order and vaguely marched onto the Station concourse. We were suddenly greeted by loud clapping and cheers from the civilians and from nowhere cups of tea and sandwiches were thrust into our hands. We quickly realised that they had mistakenly thought that we had just returned from France! We managed not to tell anyone.

Detling was one of the old-style aerodromes. The billets and the aircraft were all side by side, but quite some way from the Station HQ – and the cookhouse. Our task at Detling was to pursue and destroy 'Doodlebugs', and for our pilots it was a new experience. Here appeared an un-manned craft flying faster than the Spitfire IX and which could explode in your face should you hit it.

About this time Rolls-Royce sent senior technical staff to increase the performance of our Merlin engines. I think the super-chargers were running at 17.5 lb per square inch. They increased this to 25 lbs and at the same time we turned over from 100 to 150 octane fuel. This all pushed the Spit IX from approx 350 to nearly 400 mph which enabled our pilots to catch the V1s and really start to shoot them down.'

The Squadron's WW1 discip. warrant officer McIntosh, was also spotted near Paddington, by a General. He called him over and Mac was not seen for three days, and when he later turned up he was a very happy person, having been on a bit of a binge. Apparently he had saved the General's life in WW1 when he'd been a young officer. Despite being AWOL, little could be done, after all, he'd last been seen being taken off by a General!

George Imlach McIntosh, from Buckie, Banff, had won his VC as a private with the 1/6th Gordan Highlanders on 31 July 1917, the first day of 3rd Ypres, later known as the Battle of Passchendaele. With his comrades under fire he rushed forward and with rifle and grenades had secured a German dug-out, then brought back two light machine guns. This action saved several of his comrades' lives and made an advance possible. He died in Aberdeen in June 1960, aged 63.

Two days after the Squadron's arrival at Detling, anti-Diver patrols began. However, it was three days before the first kill was obtained, and it fell to Bob Bridgman, Ken Weller and Iain Hastings.

They were on patrol and vectored towards a plot. They spotted the bomb near Dungeness, flying at an estimated 360-375 mph at 2,000 feet. They chased and attacked it south of Tonbridge and it crashed and exploded near Wadhurst. Later that morning Flying Officer W J Batchelor got another as it passed over Hastings and it crashed near Rye. He had closed from 500 to 300 yards dead astern. After his attack the glow from the ram-jet appeared much brighter then it went into cloud. A second attack from close range probably damaged the gyro as it changed course and then dived into some cloud going east.

Jack Batchelor was another experienced fighter pilot who had just arrived. He had been with 54 Squadron in 1941, was wounded, then flew with 64 Squadron. Later he saw action in North Africa, Malta, and during the invasion of Sicily and Salerno, with 81 Squadron. When he was posted to 1 Squadron, his CO had told him that he was going to the 'Guards Squadron'! He had arrived just after the invasion, and recalls:

'I owned an MG, PA type, four-seater car I'd bought for £50. Eric Marsh had an MG T-type. When we were posted up to Detling, my car had a burnt-out tyre following my trip down to Predannack, so Eric loaned me his spare tyre. Once at Detling, I returned it to him and I could see I had problems with at least one other tyre. I told our flight sergeant he could borrow the car provided he looked after it.

Later I noticed it had four brand new tyres of a make I didn't recognise. I asked him what they were and he said "Arthur Mitchell" tyres. I'd never heard of this make but later another pilot said they looked remarkably like the tyres used on our trolley-accs! So Arthur Mitchell must have stood for "A.M." – Air Ministry!

Just as we were leaving for Detling, Flying Officer Neville Brown suffered a silly accident. For a lark, we used to take mouth fulls of petrol and blow it out through a flame. Neville had a blow-back which slightly burnt his face. The Doc put a gauze mask over his face and he had to journey to our new base by train via London. With his RAF uniform and so on, and it being the time of D-Day, all his fellow passengers thought they had a wounded hero in their midst so really looked after him, and this continued in London. By the time he staggered into Detling he was well gone and feeling no pain.

We were now with ADGB although we'd hoped to have been with 2nd TAF on the Continent. However, our task now was to combat the V1 menace. Initially the AA guns had a circle round London and we were patrolling over the south coast and Channel, having to leave any V1s we were chasing once they neared the city. It was extremely difficult to spot them due to the summer haze over the sea and they moved exceptionally fast. Once I chased one from Eastbourne to the outskirts of London but could not narrow the gap. Now and again I'd lift the nose of my Spitfire and let go a burst but didn't hit it, and I was using 25 lbs of boost.

We were successful, but not as successful as we'd have liked. Then they brought the AA belt down to the south coast so our time of catching them was reduced. Coming in after one towards the coast one would suddenly be in the midst of AA shell bursts, leaving us no alternative but to pull up vertically.'

On the 28th the Squadron destroyed five flying bombs. Flight Lieutenant T D Williams DFC got one near Willards Hill, and was nearly hit by AA fire in the process. McIntosh was Scrambled at 1735, saw the 'Diver' approaching at 1,300 feet, fired from 200 yards and it exploded in mid-air. He had barely got his undercarriage up and the bomb exploded at 1736. Despite the time given, this appears to be the V1 which Phil Williamson remembers, but a little more vividly:

'This chap had just taken off and this V1 came over. Our pilot got round onto its tail and opened fire and it took a dive right above us. I jumped into a Nissen hut, hit the floor with my hands over my ears, but nothing happened. I came out again and the V1 had circled round the other side of the airfield and then exploded in a ball of flame. Our pilot pulled round and landed within seconds and we could see all the fabric had gone from the tailplane. A great lump of aluminium from the V1 suddenly landed near us, clanging along on the concrete.'

Ken Weller also recalls the robot bombs:

'The closest call I had with one was the day I was vectored towards one in cloud. Control kept saying our two radar plots are together, you must be right on top of it. I just said, well, I'm in cloud and can't see a bloody thing. Suddenly the V1 came 'whoosh' right by me, within feet of my Spitfire and immediately disappeared again. Scared me fart-less!

We patrolled over the Channel, sometimes as far as the French coast trying to pick them up. They would come over at speed, so we were trying to get around 2,000 feet higher than they flew so we could pick up some speed to catch them. Then we got 150 octane petrol which gave us about another 30 mph or so. But this made it necessary for our Spits to have an engine change about every 60 hours.'

* * *

On 30 June the pilots destroyed six doodlebugs and shared another with two Spitfires. All actions occurred in the late afternoon/evening. Pilot Officer K R Foskett scored a double. The first one he overshot twice but finally three strikes and the size of the jet flare increased. Then it rolled over and went in, exploding on some farm buildings. At the same time an American P47 was attacking from the port side but without apparent effect. The second one was more straightforward. Strikes seen, the V1 went down and blew up in a wood north-west of Hastings.

A few days lull followed but on 4 July three more were destroyed, two over the sea, the third north-east of Hastings. Next day Flight Lieutenant Stewart sent one into a wood east of Laughton, Sussex, while Flight Sergeant Iain Hastings chased one to the fringes of the balloon barrage before he sent it down to crash near Gatwick. However, he was unable to avoid hitting a balloon cable, which snapped off the starboard wing-tip of his Spitfire and bits off two prop blades. Hastings managed to land at Gatwick, Cat AC.

Wing Commander Peter Powell, DFC & Bar, the Wingco Flying, took up one of the Squadron's aircraft and bagged two flying bombs around noon, which brought the Squadron's total to 19.

On the 7th they got three in the afternoon, Flight Sergeant H J Vessie getting one in his first combat, Junior Marsh getting another between Eastbourne and Hailsham. Two more on the 10th and three more on the 11th brought the score to 28. Iain Hastings got two of them, bringing his personal score to four and one shared.

* * *

Another car story is recalled by J O Dalley and Reggie Brown's vehicle. He was driving Joe Dalley and Tommy Williams back to base but ran out of petrol. Having walked to the airfield to get more, they arrived back to find the car gone, but a friendly local bobby told them it had been towed to Manston police station. 'Takoradi' Brown, as he was known, who also acted as squadron adjutant, knew he was for it, as he had been using an old Guinness beer bottle label as a road fund licence for several months.

Arriving at the police station, they were ushered into the inspector's office, congratulated on their work against the V1s and offered coffee. The inspector then said he had been disturbed to find under the driver's seat an RAF file marked 'confidential' and felt that these sorts of things should not be left around. Brown promised it would not happen again, and then – much relieved – they said their farewells. As they passed the desk sergeant on their way out, the man said that he hoped the Guinness label was holding up well!

Another story involved Reggie Brown's dog (a mongrel bitch) who loved to sit behind a Spitfire on warm days as it was started up in order to have the benefit of the prop wash's cooling blast. One day a visiting 616 Squadron Meteor jet was on the airfield and as the dog spotted men obviously about to start up the aeroplane, she trotted behind it and sat to await the cooling rush of air. When the two jets burst into life the dog moved faster than it had ever been seen to move before, and never again did it sit behind any aircraft.

The Squadron now moved back to Lympne on the 12th, sharing the field with 165 and 41 Squadrons. Bill Noakes:

> 'We were off again in the middle of July, back to Lympne, which we shared with two other Spitfire squadrons. We were now right in doodlebug alley and soon experienced the weight of V1s coming over. On Romney Marshes, adjacent to the airfield, there appeared to be hundreds of AA guns which were becoming a bone of contention with the pilots. Picking up a V1 over the Channel the pilot would chase it across the coast possibly by now in firing range. Suddenly AA guns would open up despite one of our aircraft being near, thus putting him in danger. Pilots were reluctant to back-off because they felt they had a better chance of a hit.
>
> We were instructed to wear our tin helmets due to the amount of shrapnel that was falling on the airfield, sometimes damaging aircraft on the ground. At night, as we tried to sleep, the AA gunners would be pounding away at a continuous stream of flying bombs. On one occasion one of our aircraft taxied in having just blown up a V1. When we examined the skin of the machine, the after suction of the explosion had forced outwards some of the moulding that wrapped around the carburettor intake. V1s flew over the airfield regularly and it was certainly a hectic time dealing with these ghost-like flying machines plus all the ducking and weaving we seemed to do when one was suddenly shot off course and crashed down near the aerodrome.'

As John Tack also remembers, one V1 was hit by gunfire near the airfield which upset its gyro mechanism and it turned and came right back over the airfield, everybody scattering. Another apparently hit a balloon cable further towards London but instead of bringing it down merely swung it round. It later roared over the airfield with everyone cheering as it headed south, back towards France; eerily, all the nearby guns stopped firing.

On the 14th Flight Lieutenant Stewart and Junior Marsh each bagged a V1, Vessie got another the next day and Flight Lieutenant Williams one on the 16th. On the 16th, the Squadron's V1 line was put between Cap Gris Nez and about 20 miles SSW of this point. Unfortunately vectors were not always in time and aircraft got close to the gun belt just as they were about to close in, and had to break off the action.

Tom Williams had been a RAuxAF pilot and had served with 611 Squadron in the Battle of Britain and 602 Squadron in 1941. Another veteran to join the Squadron around this time was Flying Officer J O Dalley DFM. 'Joe' had begun his operational career with 603 Squadron at Hornchurch in 1941 but later became a PR (photographic reconnaissance) pilot with Malta's famous 69 Squadron, where he won the DFM. On his return from Malta he began to languish at a Spit PR OCU in Scotland. Via circumstances too long to relate here, he was able to persuade AM Sir W Sholto Douglas, former C-in-C Fighter Command, now with Coastal, to get him back onto Ops, and he arranged special treatment to get him to 1 Squadron. On 22 July, 'Joe' Dalley and Flying Officer D Davy each shot down a V1. Joe recalls:

> 'My first V1 was over farmland on the Weald. On being hit, it reared up vertically and then went straight down into a field full of cows. The cows took off like the start of the Grand National, leapt over a hedge into the next field and then started eating a growing crop within a minute or two. The farmer did not seem very pleased as he ran from his house to recover matters. We always dreaded that a V1 we might shoot down would fall on a house.'

At Detling the Squadron was right in the firing line from V1s. Joe Dalley remembers that the Station Commander, Mike Crossley DSO DFC, Battle of Britain veteran, decided to bring back the old routine of dining-in nights despite the wooden mess building being a very meagre one-story affair. One evening during an alert a V1 was heard approaching and everyone trooped outside, amazed to see a flying bomb zoom just over the roof of the building, narrowly missing the nearby water tower. Everyone was instantly happy that the building was not two-storied, otherwise that V1 would have taken out most of the Squadron's pilots.

Flight Sergeant Vessie got his third kill on the 23rd, and Davy got three in two sorties that morning. This made it five for Davy who promptly became a personality, but not with the Americans. The third one he shot down this day fell on Kingsnorth airfield, near Ashford, and damaged three

USAF Thunderbolts of the 36th Fighter Group, US 9th Air Force. There was also a damaged US B17 on the aerodrome which was damaged even further, but there were no casualties and the American ground personnel later confirmed that it had saved them up to three months hard work to repair it, so thanks. Joe Dalley recalls Davey at this time:

'We gave Davy a mock Iron Cross with Oak Leaves for his destruction of those American aircraft! He also upset the CO by really bending the wing-tip of the CO's aircraft trying to tip over a V1 after firing all his ammunition. Although perhaps worth a try the V1 could not be tipped over easily as popular myth has it – the gyro control was too powerful when in full flight. Lardner Burke told Davy to "get with it" in his shooting. Rather rough as the target was very small from the rear but good gunnery should be effective as it was a straight and level target.

One must also remember that when the guns were fired it immediately knocked 30 mph off the speed and was troublesome if the V1 and Spitfire were both at the same speed – when flat out.'

Jack Batchelor:

'I shared a room with Davy – a great chap. While I was on a 48-hour leave he shot down five V1s. We were all envious and he was soon known as "ace Davy". At Lympne we had spare time on our hands as normally we only had a few anti-V1 patrols a day. The Mess was at Porte Lympne House. One day we were lying around by the pool and a Halifax bomber with one engine on fire came over at about 12,000 feet and people started to bale out as the pilot turned back towards the sea. However, as we watched, the port undercarriage wheel fell off. It appeared that it was coming straight for us and we all started running.

The amusing thing was that a 41 Squadron pilot, who had lost a leg below the knee was with us, and on these bathing periods would naturally take off his tin leg and hobble about on crutches. What amazed us all as we ran for cover was this guy going past us like a bullet!'

Flying Officer Freddie Town spread a V1 through a wood north-east of Ashford on the 24th, while Flying Officer K R Foskett became a 'local hero'. Ken Foskett shot a V1 down west of Ashford but it fell on a railway line. As he pulled away he saw a train was approaching in the distance. Short of baling out all he could do was to race alongside it, lifting and dropping his undercarriage, and his efforts were rewarded. The driver got the message and stopped his train well short of the damaged track. Later a letter of appreciation was received by ADGB HQ from grateful passengers.

Ian Maskell got his first V1 kill on the 26th, while Davy got one and shared another with Flight Sergeant Tate. Two days later Joe Dalley got his second south-west of Gris Nez, Freddie Town bagging another. Town then went after a second one. This was under attack from two Mustangs and two Spitfires, but Freddie flew over all four, attacked it, scored hits and it glided down to crash. Although he was certain it had been his fire that had done the trick he had to share the kill with the two other squadrons. Joe Dalley:

'My second V1 was perhaps more memorable. It was dusk and over the English Channel beyond the AA belt on the coast. It was a very strange experience. The V1 had a much longer flame thrust than usual, was flying only at 140 mph and at about 2-300 feet. I seem to remember reporting it as being unusual in my combat report.

I despatched it promptly; it hit the sea right under me, exploded, and gave me a very sharp "kick up the pants". My engine stopped momentarily due to the negative 'G'. The V1 had been heading directly for Dorchester and if No.1 Squadron had not done its stuff, some of the hotels might today be of a more modern design.'

Flight Sergeant Tate's Spitfire developed engine trouble on the 30th flying near Gris Nez. Because of sea haze his leader lost sight of him but he did see a splash in the sea. No sign could be found of aircraft, parachute or dinghy and a Walrus which flew to the spot found nothing either. He had only been married a few months.

Anti-V1 sorties continued into August. Flying Officer D R Wallace got one on the 3rd near West Malling airfield, and the next day Jack Batchelor got his second near Eastwell Park – after some aerobatics. On the 9th Flight Lieutenant J J Jarman shot down his first V1 south-west of Hailsham. It brought the total score, with that strange counting method of adding halves and thirds togther, to $47^{1}/_{16}$, or in reality, the pilots had destroyed or helped destroy exactly 50 flying bombs.

The V1 menace was slackening but not yet over, but the Squadron was now moved to Detling again in order to fly escort missions. The pilots were happy with the change of role despite the importance of shooting down doddlebugs. Without wasting any time, the Squadron, together with 165 and 504 Squadron, flew escort to 120 Lancasters to the marshalling yards at Lens on the morning of the 11th, then ten more against a Noball site near Cassel in the afternoon. On the 12th came a close escort to 36 Mitchells – Ramrod 1191 – to a site north-west of Beauvais.

Wingco Powell led the Wing as escort to 36 Marauders on the evening of the 13th, bombing a bridge near Cherisy. On this show – Ramrod 1196 – the Americans seemed to have little idea where the target was and Control had to insist that Powell lead them in, which he did, going down over the target. Having now seen it, the bombers flew in but meeting heavy flak three of them were shot down. Next day the Wing escorted Bostons to Frevent in the morning, then RAF heavies to Patigny in the afternoon.

Ramrod 1211 on the afternoon of the 17th called for the Detling Wing led by Powell, to escort 36 Mitchells to fuel dumps in the Fôret de Bretonne. The B25s were in two boxes, 1 Squadron escorting the rear one. The rendezvous went to plan but during the bombing one Mitchell was hit by flak and exploded. The aircraft were all split up due to heavy flak which they flew through for some ten miles. Then the unexpected happened. Yellow Section, down to three Spitfires due to an abort, flying at the rear, was called up by the CO – in front – reporting that a gaggle of aircraft was coming in.

Yellow Section broke too late and were bounced by four FW190s. Yellow 2, Warrant Officer McKenzie, and Yellow 4, Warrant Officer Wallace-Wells RAAF were both hit. Mac force landed near Yvetot but called up to say he was down safely. Wells glided over Fecamp streaming glycol and baled out four miles off the town. Fixes were given and he was seen waving from his dinghy. It was not long before he was picked up and landed in Normandy none the worse for his dunking.

These two had been neatly picked off by pilots of III/JG26. Leader of the 8th Staffel, Leutnant Wilhelm Hofmann got one for his 28th victory, while Unteroffizier Erich Klein made his first kill. Hofmann had scored 23 kills between June and August 1944 despite the loss of his left eye earlier in the war. Before his death in March 1945 he brought his score to 44. Erich Klein was killed in September – shot down by a Canadian Spitfire. The next day Wingco Powell gave a lecture on tactics – and the importance of keeping a good look-out! German fighters were being seen less and less now and Powell obviously thought his pilots were getting slack.

Perhaps Peter Powell thought they were getting slack in other ways too, for on the 21st, during a football match between the Squadron and 165, pilots not playing were taken out in a closed van, dropped off armed with just a compass and two pennies (telephone emergency money). Rain fell heavily all afternoon and it was a very bedraggled bunch of players and hikers who invaded the messes and bathrooms later on. This exercise was no doubt due to the fact that many RAF pilots were coming down in France and having to evade capture and get across the Allied front line. As if to boost this, two pilots arrived back on 8 September. One was McKenzie from the 17 August show, the other Neil Howard who had force landed a Typhoon in France six months earlier.

Operation Market Garden

The rattling telex printer spewed out a Form 'D' (operational order) which was 12 feet long on 17 September, indicating the size of an operation code-named 'Market Garden'. No.1 Squadron was tasked to escort aircraft carrying airborne troops at low level, as well as gliders and glider tugs. As one pilot was to put it: "The sky was 10/10ths Allied aircraft." The sortie was carried out successfully and some flak positions were strafed.

Arnhem and the Rhine bridges were the target for airborne troops in an operation which, it was hoped, would help shorten the war. It was also necessary to take the Dutch ports and to get into the areas where the V2 rockets were starting to be launched against England. History tells us that despite heroic attempts by the men of the Airborne Divisions, the operation failed, but was, nevertheless, ably supported by Allied aircraft and crews. On the 18th the Squadron flew low level patrols to try and spot flak positions, and a similar sortie the next day with 90-gallon LRTs ended due to poor weather. More sorties were flown over the next few days but it seemed that the weather was always against them.

On the 27th an afternoon Sweep to the Venlo-Arnhem area was hampered over the Dutch coast by the sight of bogeys. The LRTs were dropped but then the aircraft were seen to be Spitfires. Shortly after this Blue 3 and 4 – Tommy Wylie RNZAF and Warrant Officer E R Andrews – called up Manston on Channel 'C' for a homing. They were given a course but they ran into bad weather and failed to return.

Similar operations were flown in early October as the Arnhem operation came to a pitiful conclusion, by which time the Squadron's serviceability was suffering. Joe Dalley also recalls the day

Wing Commander Powell said that support for Arnhem was so important that they would all have to go despite terrible weather, even if it meant everyone baling out if they could not get back. Luckily the mission was cancelled although engines had already been started up.

Another experienced pilot joined on the 9th, Flying Officer A J Adams DFC, who had been with 111 Squadron in Italy prior to his rest tour. For the rest of October the Squadron flew escort mission to RAF Lancasters. Of one of these missions, John Morden has a story:

'On 25 October, led by Squadron Leader Lardner Burke we were returning from a 200 Lanc escort daylight bombing raid over the Ruhr. The weather, while OK over the target, started to deteriorate as we neared the English coast. Our CO had not forgotten that there was a special "do" scheduled for that night in the Mess and was bent on "pressing on". An enquiry as to the weather states brought forth the response – ceiling 6/10ths at 1,000 feet. Now close to the coast we were obliged to reduce height to little short of wave hopping.

The next two or three minutes are something of a blur. However, I became aware that we were circling as if to land but with no sign below of anything remotely resembling an aerodrome. Suddenly two lines of what seemed like small fires penetrated the fog and in we went. One after the other of us landing between these two lines without incident. So ended our introduction to FIDO [Fog Intensive Dispersal Operation].

The sting in the tail to this story is that we learned later that the data in that weather report when put over the R/T, should have been 10/10ths at 600 feet! We had landed at Manston, about 40 miles from Detling.'

With the arrival of winter, the airfield became u/s in early November. The Wing also lost Peter Powell as OC, replaced by Wing Commander Bobby Oxspring DFC & 2 Bars, another Battle of Britain veteran. He had been in North Africa for some time and was getting used to ops in Europe again. On his first operation, he led the Squadron over Cologne, right through the flak belt! Joe Dalley, unknown to him until his flight sergeant showed him later, found out that a long sliver of shrapnel had slammed into his oil sump like a dart, but had remained in situ acting like a plug!

On Guy Fawkes' night, Batch Batchelor and Jimmy Adams were detailed to escort a VIP in a Lockheed going to a conference in Paris. In case they could not get back, they took with them their best blues. In the event (Oh, yeah!) they couldn't and with no accommodation at Buc, had to go into Paris itself, staying in Montmartre. They returned the next day but unfortunately most of the shops had been shut. But they managed a bottle of champagne apiece and somehow made a profit on the trip.

The Squadron Doc – Flight Lieutenant W S Wallace – who had been with the unit since September 1943, after nearly eight hours of dual instruction in the Tiger Moth with Flight Lieutenant Jarman, was considered by the CO to be able to go solo. Doc took off and landed back safely, which undoubtedly cost him dear in the Mess that night.

Bad weather prevented Ops till the 16th, on which day they escorted Lancasters to Duren on Ramrod 1372. Three bombers were seen to explode over the target and another go spinning down out of control. Only one parachute was seen.

At the start of December a Spitfire Mark 21 flew in and the Squadron assembled and was given all the gen. on the new aeroplane, some being able to give it a real look-over. The Squadron often played 165 Squadron at football. In October they beat them 3-0, and on 7 December, 4-1. A week later they beat 165 at rugby too.

RAF Manston

On the 18th came a move to RAF Manston, 165 Squadron going to Bentwaters. 91 Squadron was at Manston too, and the Wing consisted now of 1, 91, 124 and 504 Squadrons. Each unit provided a section for early morning weather recces, and also a Readiness Section during the hours of daylight. Meantime, bomber escorts were maintained.

Christmas Day saw Rodeo 47 to Arnhem-Bonn-Liège. A Messerschmitt 262 jet was seen at 18,000 feet over Bonn but that was the closest anyone got to it. The Christmas food at Manston was poor so on Boxing Day the pilots went to Detling for a good evening – both food and drink. Luckily for everyone, poor weather prevented flying and thus were spared numerous whiffs of oxygen from the aircrafts' supply. A clear head didn't help Warrant Officer D M Royds on the 29th during an escort to RAF heavies to Cologne marshalling yards. Well west of Coblenz he called up to say his engine was playing up and was last seen at 15,000 feet on his way down, his prop stopped. However, he got down and was later reported a guest of the Germans. He was the Squadron's last casualty in WW2.

PART THREE

Chapter Fourteen

PEACE, AND THE JET AGE

Squadron Leader Lardner Burke was posted out to become OC Coltishall Wing on the second day of January 1945. He would be awarded a Bar to his DFC for his leadership of 1 Squadron. Flight Lieutenant D G S R Cox DFC & Bar, CdG, who had arrived as a supernumerary, took over. David Cox was yet another very experienced fighter pilot, having seen action during the Battle of Britain and the North African campaign. His third operational tour had been in 1944, winning the French Croix de Guerre, and commanding a Spitfire squadron. He relates:

'I was CO of 222 Squadron but had this car crash and then, being only an acting squadron leader, you went down to flight lieutenant again. Then I was sent to Group Support Unit, testing Spitfires and things, but was then posted to 1 Squadron because I had created about not going back to Ops. TAF didn't like me very much because of my car crash, so finally, on New Year's Day, Lardner Burke, who had been in 19 Squadron in 1941 when I had still been with it, was posted out. I remember he called me into his office and said, "Two things; first you're the new CO, and second, you'll have to write a letter to the parents of a chap we lost the other day." It was a very cosmopolitan Squadron – we had every nationality under the sun.'

Another experienced pilot to leave the Squadron was Jack Batchelor, going to 229 Squadron as a flight commander, then to 603 Squadron where he received the DFC. An Indian pilot come to the unit at the beginning of February, Pilot Officer Bahadurji, but some couldn't cope with the name so he quickly became 'Barry'.

The Squadron flew some more escort missions despite the winter weather, some going some distance into Germany, as David Cox recalls:

'One of the longest penetrations we did was to Paderborn, well into Germany. Another was to Mannheim; very picturesque with snow on the ground. Of course, we had 90 gallon drop tanks but would refuel in Belgium, at either Maldeghem or Ursel, in Holland.'

Then on 2 March, David Cox was lucky to survive a nasty crash. It came at a time when the Squadron was asked to escort a number of VIPs to the continent, including Winston Churchill, the Prime Minister. It was thought that he asked for 1 Squadron because it had escorted him to France in 1940. On the morning of the 2nd, the VVIP (Churchill) was escorted across the Channel after which the CO had a crash. The story is recalled by David Cox:

'We did a couple of escorts to Winston Churchill, but the stupid part about it was that we were ordered to wear our best uniforms, which was pretty silly for the PM never saw us, but at least it got us a free trip into the West End. The US President had loaned him his Skymaster to fly across and the CO of the escort – me – had to go in and see the captain. The man said to me, "Keep your silly little fighters away from my aeroplane." I replied, "Yes, trolly-bus driver!" When we got near Venlo some P47s came close, being a bit curious. I had to weave my "silly fighter" close to the Skymaster to fend them off.

Concerning the crash. Taking off from Ursel, which had felt material on the runway, I somehow managed to damage my tail wheel. When I landed at Northolt, I quickly discovered the wheel was jammed at 90°. This resulted in a cartwheel, in which I lost a wing and smashed up the aircraft quite a bit, becoming trapped in the cockpit. Talk about the longest two minutes of my life.

The Squadron sent a two-seater for me [*an Auster, with F/O Harrison*] as there was a Squadron party that evening but Flying Control wouldn't let us take off on a night flight. I wasn't about to miss the party, so off we went. It soon got dark and my Aussie pilot started to get worried. I told him to just head south until we picked up the sea. Luckily some Mosquito aircraft were landing at

Lympne and the airfield lights were put on, so we landed amongst the Mossies and got to the party. It was quite some time later that I discovered I had been considered for a Court Martial for flying and landing against regulations.'

Flight Lieutenant Ian 'Mick' Maskill RNZAF left on 8 March, going off to command 91 Squadron. He had been a flight commander on the Squadron for a year, and for this he received the DFC. More VIP flights were flown during March but then came Operation Varsity on the 24th – the Allied crossing of the Rhine.

Massed airborne troops in Halifax, Stirling and Dakota aircraft, some pulling Horsa and Hamilcar gliders, flew across this final barrier into Germany. As they headed for an area around Wesel, 1 Squadron's Spitfires patrolled along the huge stream of aircraft. The next day David Cox was promoted to Wing Commander and posted to the Far East. His replacement was Squadron Leader R S Nash DFC, who had received his decoration while serving with 91 Squadron. McIntosh became a flight lieutenant, and the longest serving pilot still with the Squadron. He became acting CO until Ray Nash arrived in April.

A few more Germany escorts to RAF heavies were flown in April, one, on the 11th, was the longest flown, escorting 100 Lancasters to Nürnberg, from Coltishall but refuelling in Belgium. It took three hours. The last wartime sortie came on the 25th after again refuelling in Holland. 446 Lancasters were going for German defence positions on the Dutch island of Wangerooge, in the Frisians, which they bombed accurately from 14,000 feet.

Suddenly the war was over. A few more Spitfire 21s had arrived and were test-flown, but then the Squadron moved up to RAF Ludham on the 14th. Before that however, came the story of VE night, as related by Joe Dalley:

'I'd been made officer in charge of the Sergeant's Mess, and that day the senior warrant officer had suggested to me that I ask the Station Commander for £100 in order to celebrate the occasion. I did ask, but the Station CO thought this a time for reflection not celebration. I reacted strongly, but politely, in differing with his assessment, especially thinking we should thank the NCOs and airmen, and that they deserved a few hours of relaxation. Both 1 and 603 Squadrons (also resident at Coltishall) had senior warrant officers in their 50s and should be treated with the respect they were due.

I said I was sorry but I wasn't prepared to go back to this senior W/O and tell him this, and I really thought the Station should do something. So he very reluctantly agreed to £50 but on the proviso the bar be shut at midnight and that no such concession would be granted for the officers, having already ruled on this with the PMC. The W/O congratulated me when I told him, for he knew the Officer's Mess had got nothing, and their bar was to close at the normal time.

We officers were then invited to the Station Commander's house where we were given a single glass of sherry to toast absent friends, and that was that. Most of us then went off to various pubs which of course were remaining open, and we finally staggered back to base in the early hours. Back in the Mess, our old CO, Lardner Burke had turned up and as we had brought back several bottles of beer each, we began to celebrate. Then someone had the bright idea of a shooting match and I regret to say I was nominated to go first. Someone drew a sketch of Hitler's face on the clock in the ante-room and it was this that triggered the shooting, with: "Who will shoot Hitler and finally finish off the war in Europe?" We shot the clock off the mantlepiece at the fifth shot!

I also had occasion to look at the Sergeant's Mess, finding it ablaze with light and the place really jumping. I telephoned the W/O who confirmed that the Station Commander's orders had been carried out to the letter and that the bar had been closed at midnight, and they now only had another five buckets of booze left. They had collected every bucket they could find and moved gallons and gallons of drink from the bar long before midnight!

The next day I was in front of the Station CO who asked what had happened. I told him and confirmed the bar had been closed on time, but that we didn't cover the fact that they would move a little bit of drink outside it. He said he thought I should have anticipated the move. I said, I'm sorry, Sir, but I think an old fashioned regular warrant officer would beat me any day. I also had to admit I'd shot the clock and he said he knew that too. How many shots did you fire? I said three. And who fired the other two? I said I didn't know, not wanting to get our former CO into bad odour, for it had been him who had fired the other two. Anyway, he made me pay three times the cost of the clock, but the lads had a whip-round to help cover my "fine".'

On 12 May the Squadron flew from Warmwell, along with other squadrons, to cover the landings on

Jersey in case the garrison made any move in opposition, but everything went off smoothly.

In June the Australians with the Squadron received their orders to sail for home. Pete Crocker, Bridgman, Wallace-Wells and Harrison were sent up to Cranfield to await the next ship. This must have taken some while to materialise because the Squadron diary reveals that Harrison came back to the Squadron on 2 August, having missed it! Where he had been is not recorded. David Bonham was a member of the ground crew at this time, and remembers:

> 'I recall at Ludham going for a sail on the nearby Norfolk Broads for the first time and nearly the last. One of the ground crew claimed to know all about sailing so two of us went with him. We soon knew that it was a tall story and we had to take over otherwise the tale would have been of the only known shipwreck on the Broads.'
>
> At Hutton Cranswick later that year the first member to face demob. was given a great send off from his hut friends. Firstly the village hall social evening took on a new meaning and then an all-night vigil in our hut (after we had all been suitably fed and watered) to make sure the lucky guy made it during the "morning after".'

The Squadron moved to Hutton Cranswick in July. On the afternoon of 3 August, nine Spitfire IXs were bounced by two of the Mark 21s. The IXs broke to port and 30 seconds later Flight Sergeant Jeffrey's aircraft collided with that of Warrant Officer Scall's. Thomas Jeffrey's machine broke up and spun in, Henry Scall managing to parachute down with only slight injuries.

There was another mid-air collision ten days later. Flight Lieutenants Bradshaw and Jimmy Adams were involved. Brad flew home with about half his elevators and rudder chewed away, but by keeping the stick well forward managed to land safely. Adams, with all five blades damaged also managed to get down.

With VJ Day and the coming of total peace, flypasts over various towns and cities were organised, and on 28 August, 1 Squadron flew over Newcastle-upon-Tyne in celebration.

There was a temporary detachment to Bentwaters in mid-September in order to take part in the first Battle of Britain Flypast. This much publicised and photographed occasion was led by Group Captain Douglas Bader DSO DFC, recently returned from Germany. Fifteen of the Squadron's Spitfires took off at 1200 hours, including three spares, flying over London and St Paul's Cathedral on this historic 15 September 1945 – the fifth anniversary of the day the Battle of Britain was said to have turned.

No sooner had the Squadron returned to Hutton Cranswick than it was off again, this time moving to Hawkinge. On the 27th Flying Officer Tom Glaser experienced engine trouble, tried to make it to base, stalled and crashed just off the eastern end of the airfield. He was killed instantly and the aircraft destroyed by fire. The Squadron returned to Hutton Cranswick in October.

For the rest of the year the Squadron flew their few Spitfire 21s with their contra-rotating propellers. If they harboured any ideas that their old Mark IXs would be totally replaced by the 21s they were wrong. Things were about to change even more dramatically.

Jets

Heralding the first change was a BBC 6 o'clock news announcement on 6 January 1946 that the RAF were to introduce a system of green and white cards, possession of which would give pilots the right to decide whether or not they were allowed to take off in different degrees of bad weather. In other words, either they were deemed experienced enough or they were not. While this news was taken with the usual shrug of the shoulders, it only affected those pilots wanting to remain in the RAF now that hostilities had ceased. For No.1 Squadron, however, it was going to affect it quite a lot before too long.

Ray Hesselyn DFC DFM, A Flight Commander, a New Zealand Malta veteran, who whilst later operating from the UK had been shot down and captured, became an MBE – announced in the New Year's Honours List on the 8th – due to his escape attempts. This, plus it being someone's birthday, heralded a party. Someone who missed this 'do' was Squadron Leader H R Allen DFC, the new CO, who arrived on the 9th, following Nash's posting to a Mustang squadron in the Middle East. Dizzy Allen was also a Battle of Britain veteran.

The few Mark 21s were made even fewer on April Fool's Day. Warrant Officer Ross overshot in one during an 'experience on type' sortie, and it became Cat E. However, better news came at the end of the month – the Squadron was returning to RAF Tangmere. On arrival at 'home' base, celebrations continued that evening at the 'Unicorn' in Chichester.

To stamp their mark, all the stoves, doors and garden ornaments were re-painted, and a large '1' was nailed on an outside wall of the new hangar (replacing the one bombed in 1940) facing across the aerodrome. Someone also painted a large yellow band around the CO's white bull terrier, whose name was 'Crippen'! As if to fool everyone, a replacement Mark 21 flew in on 25 May, just when it was thought their recently lost machine would not be. However, that was just camouflage. No sooner had the Squadron begun to establish themseves on their old stamping ground, and also attended an APC (armament practise camp) at Acklington, than they were stood down for the first nineteen days of August.

The Squadron were selected to lead the 1946 Battle of Britain Flypast, which they did on 14 September, at the head of 300 aircraft over London and the south-east. A couple of days later came the news that the Squadron were about to convert to jets – Meteors. Upon their return from APC the previous month the pilots had found the RAF High Speed Flight had been formed at Tangmere, so the new whining of the Meteor's Derwent engines was fast becoming a familiar sound. It was commanded by Wing Commander E M Donaldson DSO AFC, who had been a pre-war flight commander with 1 Squadron.

The first Meteor IIIs arrived on 7 October, the CO taking one up that afternoon. They came from 222 Squadron, which had also just received Meteors. Five of their pilots brought them in so as to help with the conversion. The Squadron also received a twin-engined Oxford for the pilots to become used to two engines and assymetric flying, although it was then found to be u/s, so they had to borrow 222's Oxford. By the 11th the Squadron had a full complement of eight Meteors. Allen had been full of enthusiasm about the new aeroplane but then he was posted out to India on the 29th, to take command of 20 Squadron. He was later at pains to point out that he and the Squadron had great difficulty with the lack of landing aids for the new aircraft, and helped to pioneer not only jet flying but approach and landing techniques with jet aircraft.

Allen's place was taken by Squadron Leader C H MacFie DFC, who arrived from 691 Squadron. Colin MacFie (he had changed the spelling from McFie) had won his DFC in 1941 with 616 Squadron, before becoming a prisoner of war.

The first Meteor broken, if only slightly, was that flown by Flight Sergeant Foster on 18 November, stalling on his final approach which resulted in a broken undercarriage.

To Germany

By the spring of 1947 the Squadron was well advanced with their new fighter. An APC at Acklington was attended in March and in April they left for Lübeck, Germany, via Eindhoven. The CO went out first with Warrant Officer Watson on the 27th, Flight Lieutenant N D H Ramsey DFC, B Flight Commander, leading the rest out two days later. Flight Lieutenant Harris force landed near Eindhoven with wheels down, so the machine was undamaged.

For the whole of May the Squadron were engaged on the Army Close Support Course along with 222 Squadron. A mock war was laid on over Schleswig-Holstein and all flights were regarded as operational. The aircraft were flown in finger-four formations on exercises except 'Cabrank', at which time open pairs were used. Simulated attacks, armed recces, Cabrank, etc, were all flown and practised.

A week into the exercise, MacFie left to take over 3 Squadron in Germany, while Norman Ramsey took over temporary command. On 30 May, 1 and 222 Squadrons flew as a wing formation to carry out a Flypast over Army HQs at Plon, Kiel, Schleswig, Husum, Hamburg and Lübeck. During the month over 130 sorties had been flown and Squadron strength as they returned from Germany was five officers and 79 other ranks. One of the O/Rs was Corporal Jim Brown, Fitter 2E, who served with the Squadron from November 1946 until October 1947. He recalls:

'I was with the Squadron when we were detached to Acklington for air firing practice and got snowed-up twice for three days. We were turned out at 0400 to help clear the runway as Acklington was a "master" aerodrome.

Along with 222 Squadron and another unit, we went to Lübeck Blankensee for a month, for another APC. We travelled by train to Hull, to a transit camp, then by boat to Bremen, then by rail to Bad Oldeslow, and finally by road to Blankensee. I was flown to Eindhoven on one occasion to pick up an engine spare and I travelled around in Schleswig-Holstein, from one aerodrome to another, hunting for this particular engine part. I arrived back after the transport for the Squadron party had left. I hitched to Lübeck and was greeted by the Adj, with: "Where the Hell have you been?" After I had explained, a half tumbler of gin was pushed into my hand – to help me catch up!

Corporal "Bunny" Bunce was the airframe fitter to my engine fitter. Between us we just about ran the Squadron as most of the sergeants were just soldiering on after long service and had no great interest. We had to fire an annual five rounds with a service rifle on the 25 yard range. Two of the sergeants were seen to be aiming at the target alongside their position! Terrible eyes – can't send them overseas!!'

A New Role?

A new CO arrived in July; Squadron Leader T R Burne DSO AFC, a former bomber and fighter pilot and the first since Mac MacLachlan not to have a full set of limbs. He had flown Hudsons in the Far East early in the Japanese war and lost a leg during an air raid on Palembang airfield, Sumatra. Between then and joining 41 Squadron (Spitfires) in 1944 he had been awarded an AFC. Flying operations on the Continent, he was severely wounded in the chest attacking a train in February 1945 but managed to fly back to base, for which he received the DSO.

In August the blow finally fell. Those green and white cards, mentioned over the BBC 20 months earlier had now become a reality and a means of assessing RAF pilots was needed. Rather than create a special unit, for some unknown reason, No.1 Squadron were chosen for the task, which appeared to turn them into No.11 Group's ITU.

Thus from 11 August 1946 the Squadron assumed the role of an Instrument Flying Training School (Squadron). The first course began one week later after Instrument Flying practice had been carried out by the newly acquired instructors. The Meteors, of course, had departed, and in their place came some Harvards, although only three were immediately serviceable, and one Airspeed Oxford. This later became eight of each.

The instructors, or assessors, were Flight Lieutenants A F Osborne DFC, John Crampton DFC (ex bombers), and T H Hutchinson, together with Flying Officer Ruben W J Horsley. 'Sammy' Osborne had been a successful fighter pilot in the war, and he recalls:

> 'I joined the Squadron in August 1947 and until May 1948 we were equipped with Harvards and Oxfords for instrument rating work. I had been sent up to Hullavington for what was called the Empire Flying School Course, from January to March 1947. It was a hell of a course which seemed to be doing its best to kill us. It was certainly the most dangerous thing I'd done in the RAF, even having been on Malta!
>
> It was also during that terrible winter that most RAF stations shut down, certainly stopped flying, but we had to soldier on; they really kept us at it. Pilots came from all over the place, Bomber, Coastal, Transport, as well as Fighter Commands. I think I was one of the only chaps from Fighter Command. One Sunderland flying-boat man hadn't landed on land for over two years but was sent up in a Spitfire. He soon decided he'd had enough. Of the 30 pilots that began the course, only 19 finished and two were killed. Of those 19 only 16 finally passed.
>
> Having done so myself I found I was about the only Instrument Rating Examiner in 11 Group, so any pilot in the Group, from group captain ops. downwards, had to be passed by me in order to get his green or white card. Back on 1 Squadron we were a splendid bunch of chaps under Tommy Burne, although because he only had one leg, was only allowed to fly the Oxfords, as the Harvards had toe-brakes.
>
> The whole scheme was organised due to the requirement, from about 1948 onwards, that all RAF pilots had to be Instrument Rated. The only way for 11 Group people was to come down to Tangmere for the three-week course. Depending on the number of total hours someone had in his log-book, determined whether he had a green or white card. Mostly they were white, for a lower total.
>
> At this time Major Robin Olds joined us as we were converting back to Meteor IVs and when I left in February 1949, he took over from me as senior flight commander. He was a splendid chap and very well liked.'

Other instructors had arrived during this period, Flying Officer Keith M Pearch, Warrant Officer W S H Cole, and Flying Officer R A Gambier-Parry, who came in January 1948 and added the job of Adjutant to his duties. Richard Gambier-Parry recalls the CO:

> 'Tommy Burne had lost his right leg above the knee in the war but coped admirably with his "tin" replacement. I had no car at the time and so was grateful to him for a lift up to London at the weekend on more than one occasion. I remember his car was an open Morris tourer and his driving technique was to press his "knee" down into a kind of mechanised lock and steer all the way up the A3 at full throttle. When stopping was essential or desirable (eg. at the "Talbot" in Ripley), he would knock up from underneath with his fist to unlock his knee. Fortunately there was little traffic in those days.'

This period as 11 Group ITU came to an end on Tuesday 1 June 1948, after twelve courses had been completed. The Squadron then went on leave for ten days w.e.f. the 7th, although four pilots and a skeleton ground crew remained. Their time was used to carry out acceptance tests on four new Meteor IVs that arrived, while also painting and redecorating the pilots' room. As the Squadron returned to being a Squadron, the following pilots were posted in. Flight Lieutenant P J Chambers, Flying Officers M Paterson and J D Price, and PIIs A E Cover, R Volanthan, F Foster, G J Patmore and C J Howard. Crompton and Hutchinson left together with Flight Lieutenant J F P Tate, who had arrived during the Course work.

During August 1948, the Squadron did much affiliation work, being vectored onto various British and American aircraft, using cine-gun, such as Mosquitos, B29s and Avro Lincolns, and during air-to-ground firing, used Dengie Flats. Between 3-5 September exercise Dagger commenced, with 16 sorties, then flying in the Battle of Britain Flypast over central London. On 24 September Flight Lieutenant J Burls (South African) collided with a Tiger Moth from No. 24 RFS (N6927), in a Meteor III (EE461) and was killed, as was the pilot of the biplane. He crashed into a field at Rustington Farm, near Chichester. Then on 14 September, Flying Officer H W B Patterson, a New Zealander, had his port engine catch fire after landing (VT172). He was OK but the Meteor was Cat B.

Affiliations continued during the autumn, and in October Robin Olds arrived. A successful Mustang fighter pilot with the US 8th Air Force in WW2, with 13 air-to-air kills and 11 air-to-ground kills, in addition to his American decorations (Silver Star, DFC, Air Medal and French Croix de Guerre) he also held the British DFC. He became an exchange pilot with the RAF, and was assigned to 1 Squadron. He remembers his first flight:

'As the RAF would say, it was pissing with rain on that October day in 1948, and it was thoroughly damp, the sort of damp that made a mockery of a trench coat and made me wish for a fire-place and a hot glass of something. It was also cold.

I trudged toward the flight line and tried to work up some enthusiasm for the situation, not helped by my recent breakfast of a limp piece of toast on which rested twelve evil looking beans. Together with a shot of canned grapefruit juice and a small cup of bitter black liquid meant to be coffee – that had been breakfast. The hot sun of southern California seemed remote and far, far away.

I knew it would be different when I finessed this assignment. I had wriggled my way out of a lousy desk job at March Field back to a flying slot, a very special flying slot. I was assigned as an exchange officer with No.1 Squadron RAF. The RAF had been my inspiration when I was a cadet at West Point and back in 1940 it worried me that the war would be over before we could ever get into it. The smile brought me back to the challenge of the present and suddenly I didn't mind the rain and the damp. I did wonder, however, how this Squadron felt having a Yank shoved into their midst, especially a 26-year-old Major.

I had been told I would find the Boss in Squadron Ops. Feeling every bit the new kid on the block, I squared my hat and entered. Even without his rank braid anyone would have known the man by the small table was Squadron Leader Tommy Burne. I snapped a salute, immediately wondering if the RAF saluted while inside. The CO seemed somewhat taken aback and returned the salute with a casual wave of the right hand. Lesson number one: don't salute in Ops, at least not here with 1 Squadron. Lesson number two: get here earlier in future.

He welcomed me and introduced me to the chaps. Then he said I should take a look at what they called Pilot's Notes – Meteor IV. After a short study the CO said we should take a look at the kite. It was still raining. At the aircraft there was a wooden stand with stairs to the cockpit. This I guessed was for the CO and his aircraft and I was right. Up he went a step at a time and motioned me to join him.

The first thing I saw as the hood went back was the parachute already in place, looking as if it had been there for some time. He told me to get in and the parachute seemed a bit damp. The CO indicated all the various things and then he was showing me how to start the engines. A horrible suspicion swept over me as he snapped me into the harness I watched the gauges settle down and then he said, "Jolly Good," as he handed me a leather helmet, patted me on the shoulder and continued happily, "Now then old boy, off you go!"

Off I go where, for God's sake? I didn't even know where the runway might be, let alone how to close and lock the canopy, turn on the radio, what my call sign was, who to call, what kind of clearance to get, what speed to take off, where to fly in this soup, and more important, at what speed this critter landed. And how was I going to find this field again in this stinking weather?

Turning my attention to the radio I soon found the lead wire that fastened to my helmet, found it worked – a four-button VHF set similar to ours in the States. I pressed button "A" and listened and timidly said "Hello." A cheery voice came back immediately. "That you Yank? Tangmere

Flying Control here, what can we do for you?" After some minutes I discovered where the runway was, the visibility, but was foxed by something called QNH.

Hoping the wet grass and rain would suck up into the engines and stop them I taxied out and found the runway. The CO had said that one particular instrument in the centre of the panel was "quite useful" and now discovered this was the attitude indicator. What did matter and what I didn't know, was how to get this beast back on terra firma in such weather. Thinking, here goes nothing, I released the brakes. "Tangmere Control, Yank is rolling." "Rightho Yank, have a good flip." (Flip?)

I pushed the throttles forward, made sure I was aligned, glanced inside for the engine and oil gauges, couldn't find them, so peered through the heavy glass at the runway ahead. The Meteor accelerated smoothly and the stick came alive. As I lifted off I became eager to fly and I no longer gave a damn about the rain and dank clouds. We sailed into the murk and I was in a dark grey bottle of milk. But things felt good and "quite useful" was steady and level. I inched the power back a tad and eased the stick forward very slightly. Keeping my eyes over the leading edge of the left wing I watched for Mother Earth to reappear. Sure enough there she was, just where I had left her, trees and all.

I settled into a very low and slow cruise and did a 90 degree turn to my left. I knew this would soon bring me to the south coast near Bognor and about four minutes later houses appeared in the murk and I had to make a correction to avoid a large gas storage tank in the town. A port turn parelleling the beach just above the waves and I was beginning to enjoy myself. Now a turn north and there it was, the A45 and soon, there was my storage tank. I dallied along for a few minutes, put the gear and flaps down, slowed to a crawl, said a silent prayer and watched out for the end of the runway.

Suddenly, there it was! I didn't care that I was looking at the wrong end, a runway was a runway and under the circumstances, any end would do. A hard careful bank to line up, back on the throttles, and I made what would probably be my best landing for the rest of the year.

I taxied in, and the shut-down was a breeze. I trudged to Squadron Ops feeling somewhat proud of myself and secretly glad I hadn't had to bale out on my first sortie under RAF colours. I walked in, not knowing what to expect from my new Squadron mates, perhaps some joyful remark. The place was empty. Flying had been cancelled and they had all gone off to lunch.'

* * *

The Squadron continued flying numerous affiliation sorties against a host of different aircraft types that winter. New Year's Day 1949 saw the move to Acklington again for the APC, returning to Tangmere on the 28th. Not surprisingly Olds achieved the highest scores. The day after the return PIII G E T Forest went missing and later was presumed killed over the sea. Tommy Burne left in February, and Robin Olds took command. He was the first ever USAF exchange officer to command an RAF squadron.

Little of note happened until June. Flying to Manston the Squadron took part in Operation 'Foil' till the first week in July. With their camera guns the pilots scored '60 destroyed and 39 damaged', against 'hostile' aircraft, so the affiliation work was paying off.

Another wartime veteran flew with the Squadron from July to November, Flight Lieutenant J R Urwin-Mann DSO DFC. A successful Battle of Britain pilot he'd won the DFC in 1940, and later in the Western Desert had added a Bar. After a brief period on Malta he was badly injured in a collision on the ground, but was awarded the DSO.

The Squadron were scoring more camera-gun kills during Exercise 'Bulldog' at Manston in September. Ten B50s, nine Meteor IVs, six Mosquitos, three Harvards and a Spitfire 'destroyed', four Meteors, three B50s and two Mossies as 'probables' and six Meteors and eight B50s 'damaged'. The 'attacks' included head-on and high quarter passes. This was followed by the annual Battle of Britain Flypast, then demonstration flights over Odiham, West Malling, Biggin Hill and Booker during RAF open days. The Squadron's demonstration pilot at this time was usually Flying Officer H W B Patterson. Also at this time the Squadron had a Meteor VII on strength for instrument rating and training, and pilots also began flying at night. Pilot strength was now eight officers and six NCOs. Meteor VT180 had both engines flame-out on the afternoon of 4 October, but the PIII P Walden glided into a forced-landing at Heathrow airport despite bad visibility and a misted-up windscreen.

Major Olds left in September. He would later fly Phantoms in the Vietnam war and add four Mig kills to his already impressive WW2 score of combat victories, plus the American Air Force Cross. Tommy Burne returned on 1 October, as a caretaker CO, until the arrival of another USAF exchange officer, Major Donovan F Smith, who took command in January 1950.

During March 1950, on Exercise 'Morning Glory', 27 sorties were flown against attacking Royal Navy aircraft, and they were severely mauled by the RAF Meteors. The first pilot casualty for over a year, occurred on 19 April. The Squadron had entered a four-man aerobatic team in the Fighter Command Championships. Flight Lieutenant P W Speller, its leader (VT146), collided over Tangmere with PIII D C Harpham (VT243) and the tail of his Meteor was sliced off and Speller crashed right in front of spectators by the control tower. Pete Speller, aged 28, had been a fighter pilot in Burma during WW2. No blame was associated with either him or 21-year-old Harpham who got down safely. Then on 25 May Pilot Officer R W M Dixon, also 21, who had only been on the Squadron for two weeks, spun in executing a single-engine approach after one had failed, and he was killed in the crash. He had been on an air-to-ground cine-gun sortie in VT173. It was just after mid-day and Dixon allowed his speed to fall below the critical level for one-engine flying and spun in on the cross-wind turn. This was down to lack of practise and it transpired that he had had no assymetric checks or practise during his two months at 226 OCU prior to joining the Squadron.

During Major Donovan Smith's tenure as CO, RAF squadrons were allowed to re-instate their colourful pre-war markings, and although the first scheme used by 1 Squadron was deemed a little too extravagant by the powers-that-be, the red oblong diamond surrounding a winged-one, soon became standard on all aircraft. In mid-July, knowing he was soon to depart, Major Smith laid on a 'sundowner' for the Squadron personnel, also as a well-done for work during May and June. As far as the RAF men were concerned, this appeared to be a typical GI affair with iced canned beer and hot dogs. However, judging by the rapid disappearance of these items, a good time was had by all.

Smith left in August, and Squadron Leader J L W Ellacombe DFC arrived on the 18th. John Ellacombe was another wartime fighter pilot, seeing action in the Battle of Britain, having won his DFC with 151 Squadron in 1942. Later in the war he flew Mosquitos with 487 RNZAF Squadron, adding a Bar to his DFC in 1944. The day after his arrival the first Meteor VIIIs came with their uprated Derwent engines. By the end of August, ten were on strength. Within a month the Squadron were up to full strength for the first time in four years with 16 aircraft and 17 pilots. This later became 20 pilots.

Exercise 'Emporer' in October saw the Squadron move to Biggin Hill for two weeks, during which time Air Vice-Marshal Tom Pike, the AOC 11 Group came down for a couple of days and flew several sorties in one of the unit's Meteors.

All Meteors were grounded in March 1951 because of an aileron defect and while on the deck, time was taken to fit them with new 20-channel VHF radios. Then in July the Squadron visited Brussels (Beauvechain), receiving splendid hospitality and co-operation from the Belgian Air Force. On their way home again, the Squadron simulated a high level mass bomber raid in order to exercise the RAF's defence systems. The following month No.349 Squadron of the Belgian AF visited Tangmere.

A new pilot to arrive in June 1952 was Pilot Officer C P Hine. Paddy Hine was a National Serviceman who had never intended to join the RAF but at the time of being called-up there was a great expansion of the UK armed forces due to the Korean War, and he asked if there was any chance of training as a pilot. This was agreed but he was told that if they converted anyone on to jets they would have to agree to serve three years with the auxiliary air force at the end of their National Service. This seemed fair so Paddy Hine agreed. In due course he completed his training, and at OCU was one of five pilots selected to be sent direct to front line squadrons to convert onto jets. This was new and untried, but Paddy chose Tangmere as it was not that far from his home. So that same afternoon he was posted to 1 Squadron. He remembers:

'Having arrived and dumped my kit, sharing a room with Mike Chandler, I went into the bar. In came Flying Officer Frank Day who introduced himself as the Adj. He'd not heard of me, so I explained the circumstances. After a moment he said that he didn't think the Boss was going to like it, having a chap who had not completed OCU. Sure enough, about half an hour later in came Squadron Leader Ellacombe and he went absolutely "ape". He thought I would be a total liability and was going to talk to Fighter Command to get the whole thing stopped. Anyway, he failed so I survived and I remained.

Mike Chandler had been brought up in Kenya by a well-off farming aunt and uncle. He had his own aeroplane and flew in the King's Cup Air Races. I went into A Flight, Flight Lieutenant Martin Evans, who didn't like National Service people and me even less, so for the first two or three months it was not easy for me. Bunny Bunyan was B Flight commander, then John Tedder. I got on very well with John and it was he who later convinced me to stay in the RAF.

Bill Nuttall was a Cranwell Cadet, totally dedicated pilot, but quite a wild character. Great and serious beer drinker and fun to be with. Bill missed a Met briefing one day because of the night before, came in and was told to lead a formation of four – eventually just three. It was all above cloud and he headed off towards Manston and after various exercises thought he'd better check for the right steer back to Tangmere. In those days all we had was CRDF (Cathode Ray Direction Finding) to give a bearing and a thing called the DME (Distance Measuring Equipment) – which they put in during my time on 1 Squadron. This was showing that he was near enough 40 miles from Manston during their exercise but when he called for a steer they said it was a "Class Charlie" bearing – a pretty poor one – so steer 270°, which he did, but they were getting low on fuel, so called up again and was told the same course.

At this stage he thought this was not sounding good so he went over to the International Distress Frequency, 121.5, and said who he was. We had a call-sign "Endless" then, and he was Endless Black Leader, which was very appropriate. The IDF people said he was something like 30 miles east of Cambrai, so was well and truly over France and there was no way he was going to get home. Somehow the three pilots then managed to lose each other and each landed on different French aerodromes. Bill was hosted by a French escadrille and that afternoon sent the AOC a postcard, saying:

"Dear AOC, Having a super time with the French Air Force, who are marvellous

hosts – wish you were here. Yours sincerely, W F Nuttall, F/O No.1 Sqdn."

The ACO, now Sam Patch, saw the funny side but our Station Commander, Johnny Kent DSO DFC, didn't. When Bill flew back with his two companions, he was put under close arrest and I was his escort officer, because I now shared a room with him. There was the usual Board of Enquiry, and so on, and it wound its way inexorably up to the AOC and Bill was called for an interview.

When this was over Bill Nuttall saluted and turned to leave, then the AOC said, "Nuttall, come back a moment. Do you normally wear your hair that long?" Bill replied instantly, "No, Sir, I had it cut last Monday." At this point the AOC asked Bill to sit down again. He was put on a six months probation to improve – despite him being ex-Cranwell – and he did somewhat, and remained in the airforce.

But Bill had a wonderful sense of humour. I remember quite well him looking back through the Mess suggestions book, which was always around for suggestions or complaints. This night he wrote in it, "With regard to the complaint by F/O P Goodwin, dated 1 April 1929, about the burnt bacon, what has been done to address this complaint?" The PMC was not too enamoured about this.'

An entry in the Squadron diary for 10 November 1952 concerns an inboard leading edge panel breaking off in flight and a serious accident being only narrowly avoided. The panel had not been properly replaced during servicing and a formal investigation was held and three airmen were found involved. Paddy Hine was the pilot of the Meteor:

'We were in a four-ship battle formation, tail-chase sortie, and we came back, I being No.2, in echelon starboard, and broke into the circuit for landing. Not long after I'd pulled hard into the break, there was a sort of bang and the aircraft lurched round a bit. I straightened up instinctively and it became incredibly hard to handle, lots of vibration and turbulance. I called the tower and said I think I've collided with something. Bill Nuttall had followed me in the break and he had enormous difficulty in missing me.

I came down to about 150 knots, yawing all over the place, made a wide circuit and came round and landed on the grass. I climbed out half expecting to see the tail hanging off or something but couldn't see a thing wrong. Until I then noticed the leading edge section of the wing between the fuselage and starboard engine nacelle was missing.

Someone had not replaced the screws on the underside of this panel, so that as I pulled into the break the airflow got underneath it and pulled it right off. Later I heard that one or two other people in the RAF had experienced a similar problem and one chap had in fact speared-in and been killed.'

John Ellacombe left the Squadron for HQ 11 Group in November, his place taken by Squadron Leader R B Morison DFC. Brian Morison had been a wartime night-fighter pilot, winning his DFC with 89 Squadron – Beaus and Mossies. He recalls:

'As soon as I had joined No.1 we had a request from scientists to carry out low level flights over the sea towards the radar station on St Catherine's Point on the Isle of Wight. To assist in their research they fitted a few of our aircraft with a transmitter in the tail which sent out a signal every 50 seconds. This enabled the height and position of the aircraft to be plotted on their radar chart. It struck me, after one flight, that it would be suicide if we flew individually at a very low level over water as our altimeters were useless at that height. So I arranged that we should fly in pairs and we could look at the other aircraft's plume of spray coming off the belly of the fuel tank and we could warn each other if we were flying too low. It was a bit hair-raising to say the least, and I was relieved when we completed the exercise just before Christmas 1952.'

In December, Squadron Leader Morison and Sergeant C H Maynard suffered bird strike damage during an AYF run (radio altimeter trial), Brian Morison's Meteor needing a change of mainplane. In January 1953 Sergeant Wilkins had his starboard engine fail in flight during a cine-gun sortie and he experienced severe vibration, preceded by a bang and a sharp drop in rpm. He closed the fuel cocks and returned to base where it was revealed he had had blade failure, causing considerable damage to the shroud ring.

As well as piloting Meteors, Paddy Hine was something of a golfer and his prowess soon brought him to the attention of others, not the least of which was reaching the semi-finals of the RAF Golf Championships in April, against the county of Lincolnshire, the RAF winning 9 – 3. From then on he would regularly disappear as necessary to uphold the RAF's golfing reputation.

Presentation of the Squadron Standard
In the spring of 1953 plans were underway to present the Squadron with its Standard, granted by the King ten years earlier. As 1 Squadron was the first of 30 such units awaiting the presentation, it was only right that the RAF's premier Squadron get their's first. Brian Morison:

'The presentation of the Squadron Standard was originally planned to take place in early March, I think, but unfortunately Queen Mary died and we had to postpone the event. I tried to find out what procedures took place for the presentation, but as it was the first such occasion in the RAF, I was left to dream up my own procedure. I think it went quite well, even though I say so myself.'

The actual ceremony took place on 24 April 1953. It was presented by Air Vice-Marshal Sir Charles Longcroft CMG DSO AFC, the Squadron's second CO from way back in 1914. Number One was paraded in three flights, along with the Squadron band and the ASP in front of the hangar. The weather was perfect, blue sky, warm with just a light breeze. The Standard was received by Flying Officer Mike Chandler and consecrated by the RAF's Chaplain in Chief. Sir Charles addressed the Squadron, and guests included Air Chief Marshal Sir Philip Joubert de la Ferté, Air Vice-Marshal T R McEvoy, Air Commodore R W Chappell, Group Captain E O Grenfell and Wing Commander H R Allen – all former COs. The AOC-in-C Fighter Command, Air Marshal Sir Dermot Boyle, AOC 11 Group, AVM the Earl of Bandon, together with the Southern Area Commander, Air Commodore Kelly, were also in attendance.

A couple of days later the Squadron moved to Biggin Hill, where it remained until July, mainly for the coming Coronation Flypast. Rivalry with 41 Squadron, also on the Bump, was keenly felt and the slightest *faux pas* in the air was greeted with great enthusiasm by the opposite side. Paddy Hine went off to represent Fighter Command at golf. There was also a story about the Duke of Edinburgh, recalled by Brian Morison and Paddy Hine:

'We were all told that Prince Philip would be landing at Tangmere as part of his flying training with the RAF. He arrived at about 1230 and all the officers were lined up to be introduced to him. We then went in for lunch and as we went into the dining room the Prince, walking just ahead of the Station Commander, noticed a piece of paper on his chair. He scowled a bit as he read what was on it – then burst out laughing and passed it around. It had: "Psst. Do you want a good seat for the Coronation!"'

Bill Nuttall and I wanted to see who was on the top table with the Duke and Bill noticed the Mess Secretary had spelt Edinburgh as Edinborough, so he took the card to Bill Barrel, the Sec.; he gratefully typed out a new card and we took it back for him. However, Bill wrote a PTO at the bottom, and then the message. Unfortunately he also wrote: "Apply to Bill Nuttall, 1 Sqdn."

Prince Philip passed it across to Johnny Kent, saying that he'd got a couple of live wires here, but took it very well, but not so Johnny. Bill was duly called in and given a hell of a rocket and a serious warning, but again, he survived it.'

Bill Nuttall was killed before the end of the decade in a Sycamore crash in Cyprus. The tail rotor of the helicopter caught the side of a mountain and he came down. There exists a wonderful group photo of the Squadron officers, all seated very correctly, smiling at the camera, and so on. There is, however, one seated pilot in the front row, his face obscured by a pint mug pressed to his lips. No prizes for guessing the man's name.

Meteor WK908 (L-Love) which had given Sergeant Wilkins a few anxious moments back in January, was being piloted by Flying Officer C H P Anthonisz during one sortie. He felt a loud thump in the port engine, accompanied by excessively high jet pipe temperature and a sharp drop-off in rpm. The pilot cut the engine and carried out a starboard engine landing without mishap. The actual Coronation Flypast was quite impressive, as Paddy Hine remembers:

'It was a massive formation – 168 aircraft, seven boxes of 24. We were teamed up with 41 Squadron at Biggin for about two months where we did our work-up. I've never seen anything like that before or since. All those wings sort of fed in from different directions and by the time you'd got down to Dungeness they were all in position. There was one box of four and then another vic of three behind. Then all that would run-in towards Buckingham Palace from the south-east. There was a Direction Finder put on the roof of the Palace and the leader of the overall formation, a chap named Jimmy Wallace from Duxford, could check the position on the way in until he got a visual on the Palace.

That was how we trained but on the day the visibility was so bad and we could not join up the big formation, so we just flew past by wings at something like 15-second intervals. But it was that night, after a good night out in town, and the AOC of 11 Group – Paddy Bandon – was with us having a drink or two. It was a huge party, and that was when four or five of us thought it was quite a good idea to take him outside and throw him in the pool! We did so with some difficulty as he put up quite a spirited fight. But he took it all in good part and the Station Commander then took him off to get changed.'

Of the 12 officers on the Squadron, eight had flown in the Flypast and four had not, so there was some jealousy as those eight then received Coronation Medals. Paddy Hine was off again, representing Fighter Command at golf versus the Channel Islands. It was thought, however, that next year the policy should be to have two teams – one to play, the other to drink! In July came the Coronation Review at RAF Odiham.

While, at the time, the dunking of the AOC in Biggin's outdoor pool was thought a good one, Flying Officer Hine had time to reflect on this within a very short space of time, as he remembers:

'It was not much more than two weeks later that I had to appear before him on my Permanent Commission interview. It was a Monday morning and he was late. Finally he swept through the outer office – there were about three or four of us waiting – and I was the first one in. His ADC wheeled me in and announced me, but the AVM just grunted and continued to sign letters.

At last he looked up and opened the right-hand drawer of his desk and pulled out a bottle of gin. "How do you take your gin," he asked, "neat or with a little water?" "Well," I replied, "if you don't mind, I'll have a little water." "Oh, really," he said, clearly disappointed. We went over and sat down on a settee and a chair and we got talking, then he said that he thought we'd met before. This raised a few hairs on the back of my neck and I said that he was my AOC, and had probably seen me during an inspection at Tangmere. "Oh, no, no," he said, "I think it a bit more recent than that." So at that point I admitted I had been one of those indiscreet enough to throw him in the pool at Biggin. "Well, I'm glad you owned up," he said, "because if you hadn't you wouldn't get your PC. I'm not going to guarantee it now but you wouldn't have got it at all!"

Fortunately for the Squadron, and for the RAF, Paddy Hine (later Air Chief Marshal Sir Patrick Hine GCB GBE FRAeS CIMgt) got it.

Another event concerning this detachment to Biggin Hill was related by LAC M Roe, whose father had been an engine fitter with 1 Squadron in Iraq in 1924:

'Life at Biggin for the ground crew was idyllic. The Squadron occupied a hangar in the far corner of the airfield and the days were warm, and it was easy to skive-off into the adjacent woods and golf course once tasks were completed. However, this was interrupted by a CO's inspection for us and 41 Squadrons.

The current pop song had the opening line: "Number one, number one, number one, that's my darling, darling Caroline...", which we all took up, naturally. This Saturday the Station Commander inspected the assembled ranks and then mounted a chair to give a short address, which in fact, turned out to be a eulogy for 41 Squadron over 1 Squadron. It seems they were better organised, their formation flying was better, their air-to-air marksmanship was better, their air-to-ground rate superior, their 'scramble' time quicker, and overall much smarter than us, and so it went on.

The lads of 1 Squadron stood there and took all this but eventually he came to the end and the parade got ready to march off. The serried ranks of officers stood behind the Station CO, ready to take the salute. There was no band so the music was supplied by means of gramophone records. As we broke into the first steps of the march-past there came out of the loudspeaker those wonderful words: "Number one, number one, number one, that's my darling, darl..."

There was panic behind the Station boss as someone hurriedly switched the pop song for something more martial. The lads of 1 Squadron were first to pick up the fresh tempo. Heads were high, chests out, backs straight, arms swinging – bags of swank – and in unison we wiped the floor with 41 Squadron as we marched away, after all, didn't we have a pop song in our honour – well almost!

Even better was to follow. On the eve of our return to Tangmere, certain members of the ground crew, under "Dad" Buckley, appropriated 41 Squadron's treasured carved wooden squadron shield. Back at Tangmere it was photographed, suitably adorned with lavatory seat, chain and toilet paper, then returned to them with a souvenir picture!'

* * *

Brian Morison was promoted to wing commander and posted as Wingco Flying at 226 OCU, Stradishall at the end of July, Squadron Leader D I Smith coming to take over on the 27th. There was also a new A Flight Commander, Flight Lieutenant H J Irving, a Scot, who had survived a tour of Ops on Lancasters in WW2. He had been flying Meteor VIIIs at Waterbeach with 63 Squadron.

The Squadron returned to Tangmere, where 602 Auxiliary Squadron had been spending its summer camp. The officers were dined out not long after their return, but after the auxiliary boys had left, it was discovered that a treasured trophy – a doorman's topper liberated from Claridges on one historic occasion – was missing. The Scots had liberated it, but the Squadron quickly responded by grabbing one of their Vampire FB5s and painting it in Number One's colours, then using it as a centre piece to a photograph.

Chapter Fifteen

FROM METEORS TO THE HUNTER

Squadron Leader Smith's tenure did not start well. In August 1953 there was a mid-air collision between Flying Officers J M Gisborne and C H P Anthonisz (Ceylonese) over the English Channel on the 16th. They had been making a mock attack on a Lincoln at 19,000 feet and hit each other. Their wings locked and both Meteors exploded and disintegrated, falling into the sea 30 miles north-east of Barfleur.

In the same month Flying Officer Legge, on a Rat and Terrier exercise had his cockpit canopy break apart at low level while flying at 450 knots, and the following month another hood partially disintegrated. Investigations seemed to indicate a flaw in the perspex.

The missing 'topper' saga continued, now with 602 Squadron sending the Squadron a photograph of one of their pilots stepping out of a Vampire, wearing it. Then came the APC at Acklington, Paddy Hine went off to represent the RAF against Addington Golf Club, otherwise things continued as normal.

Another Meteor was damaged in November. Lieutenant Russell, on attachment, shot the banner off the tow-plane during air-to-air firing, then flew into it, causing substantial damage to N-Nan. Smith was taken ill in December, and so Squadron Leader F W Lister DSO DFC was posted in from 65 Squadron as OC. Freddie Lister was a bit older than most of his pilots, but was a very experienced fighter pilot from WW2. He had flown Hurricanes and Spitfires, and recently, Meteor VIIIs. He was also a great party man. Harry Irving remembers:

> 'Freddie lived north of the Station. Although single, he had a lady friend who was a stewardess on the "Queen Mary" so we all knew when it was due in at Southampton. Freddie would say he'd want an aircraft at 3 o'clock or so, some afternoon, so we could all guess when the boat was due. We "bounced" him one day, and sure enough, he was doing high-speed runs along the side of the liner. Great chap, great drinker!'

December saw Flight Lieutenant Tobia collide with two seabirds at low level, but they only caused some dents and grazed paint. Hitting birds was becoming an occupational hazard flying low, or even not so low, over the sea. At the end of the year the Squadron had 23 officer and three NCO pilots, eight SNCOs and 60 other ranks.

January 1954 began with Pilot Officer K W Raby colliding with a banner target during an air-firing sortie, while Flying Officer M G King and Sergeant Maynard both had arguments with seagulls on a low level battle sortie. To take off the pressure, and to foster interest in local business affairs (the diary says!) a visit was organised to Henty and Constable, the local brewery. Great interest was shown, especially in the samples (yeah, right). One assumed this did nothing to help a ground collision between Raby and Flying Officer S Greenslade who ran into the other jet whilst turning off the runway in February, but then again, as the diary also relates, a visit to Honily in March was notable for two things, the atrocious weather and the amount of beer drunk!

Flight Lieutenant Tobia was in trouble again that month losing the whole of his nose wheel assembly on take-off, the actual wheel striking his ventral tank. He carried out a very creditable wheels-up landing after dropping the tank. The reason was the fracture of the long retaining bolts in the assembly caused by excessive 'shimmying' set up by striking the built-in landing lights laid across the runway.

Taxi!!

The Squadron joined 41 Squadron again at Biggin Hill on 10 May for a Wing show to welcome home HM the Queen, returning from a Commonwealth tour. However, the most important event in mid-1954 was the purchase of a taxi for Squadron use, as Paddy Hine remembers:

> 'The other squadron at Tangmere, No.29, bought a taxi which was used as a sort of communal transport, so we decided to buy one too. The Squadron was up at Biggin for the Queen's return flypast. We were going to over-fly the Royal Yacht as it sailed up the Thames.
>
> I said to the Boss, why don't I take a day off, go up to London and buy a taxi? So, with another pilot, we headed up and after scouting around bought this thing for £50 in Brixton. In advance I had arranged to get some kind of temporary insurance cover – we weren't worried about the comprehensive bit , only third party obviously.

I drove it back to Biggin and it was the night after the flypast – being loose to celebrate – we decided to drive up to town. About six or seven of us, including Freddie Lister, climbed into the vehicle and drove to the West End. We went to the Brevet Club in Mayfair first, and coming out decided to go on a bit of a pub crawl before going to the RAF Club.

As we were leaving Mayfair, one of the chaps – it had to be Bill Nuttall – left one of the back doors open and as we pulled away it swung open and side-swiped a row of parked Rolls-Royces and Bentleys. We thought this might be a little serious so we closed the door and pushed off!

We then started our pub crawl, during which Bill managed to fall out of the taxi in Park Lane. He cut his head a bit but otherwise was, by this time, feeling no pain. At last heading back to the Club, a police car pulled up alongside and asked if we had been involved in an accident in such and such a street. We said we didn't think so but they insisted they had had reports from a couple of car owners that our door had hit them, and could they inspect our taxi. Obviously our rear door showed some scratch marks, so we all went to the scene of the "crime" and discussed it with them and the owners.

The CO, meantime, made a strategic retreat to the RAF Club – exited stage right – saying that when you've sorted it out come and pick me up. The end of a long story was that we were let off with a caution, provided we paid for the damage, but while I was negotiating with the police and the owners, Bill Nuttall came round and staggered out of the back seat of the taxi, his face all covered in blood, and tried to intervene and help me out. At this stage, one police officer took me to one side and said, "Excuse me, Sir, but I don't think your colleague 'er is 'elping your case at all! If I was you, I'd tell 'im to go and sit in the taxi and keep quiet."

When I left the Squadron they kept the taxi for some time. The record for bods inside and on, this taxi, was 17 people. It had a little sticker in the back window, which read: "Madam, don't laugh, your daughter might be inside." It was great fun to have and it had insurance which allowed three nominated drivers, of which I was one. Luckily this was all long before drink-driving was heard of. It also had one of those lovely old horns which one squeezed – great fun.'

At one stage BBC TV filmed the taxi driving into Biggin Hill, ten-up, and they were kind enough to send the Squadron a copy of the film.

* * *

Pilots flew to RAF Pembrey on 8 June 1954 for a four-day exercise with the Royal Navy, followed by four days at Chivenor the following week. To the delight of the pilots there was no accommodation available but they returned home in the best of spirits. They had been 'forced' to spend four happy nights in the bar of the Saunton Sands Hotel. During this period, Flying Officer Chandler suffered a bird strike, OK for the Meteor, fatal for the bird, while Pilot Officer D T Bryant made a good single-engine landing after the starboard engine caught fire.

In July came Bill Nuttall's experience over France, referred to earlier, a victim of a 130 knot headwind. All of which occurred just prior to Fighter Command's Annual Exercises. Tough as this might have been, tougher was the Command Aircraft Recognition Test, held at the beginning of August. For instance, a DH Comet with wheels and flaps down, head-on, five miles away, had features not normally presented to the average fighter pilot. Answers to this problem ranged from a Russian Stormovik to a Sunderland flying boat! One good feature was that the CO emerged top of the Fighter Command squadron commanders when the results were announced.

The annual Battle of Britain display had twelve 1 Squadron Meteors flying over Portsmouth, then immediately disappearing into low cloud which proved 'most exciting'. Section leaders had to split up and a rendezvous was made over Brighton, then a dash made for Tangmere, awash with Open Day visitors. One pilot had to overshoot as he had only one green undercarriage light showing. Strangely enough, the other two came on when he was right over the crowd; as a result, one person became very happy, 1,500 were disappointed.

After its recent aircraft recognition showing, the Squadron did well at the Fighter Command Competition, averaging 81-56%. This was remarkable as the presence of two officers from the School of Aircraft Recognition compelled the pilots to use their eyes, not their ears!!

It had become obvious that the jet-age had really arrived for in October, each pilot received a silver crash helmet (now known as bone-domes). A few deft strokes with a paint brush transformed them into rather exotic creations which considerably enhanced the appearance of each pilot.

The arrival of a Vampire T11 in December caused interest. This was intended for instruction and to familiarize pilots to single-engined aircraft. The promise of the Hawker Hunter was being eagerly awaited, although none had been seen so far. Meantime, the Christmas party at the Walnut Tree Inn at

Runcton proved a success and the piano was well lubricated with beer, on which it appeared to flourish. The following morning flying was somewhat restricted by severe haze – heat, sea or pilot, is not now remembered. A coal skuttle and two equally large tea pots were returned to the pub at a later date.

Jet-age technology was enhanced further in January 1955 with the arrival of G-suits, 'boots – escape', and 'domes – bone', was regarded with some delight, although the sight of even one Hunter would have been even more delightful. The down-side to all this, pending the arrival of the said Hunters, and the consequent requirement to reduce the number of pilots, was that six were posted out during the month. Paddy Hine had recently left for CFS but he returned back for a visit. Taking up a Meteor to 35,000 feet his hood disintigrated, which annoyed him somewhat, but he got down safely. One reason why the Hunters were so eagerly awaited was the simple fact that the only bomber the Meteor could now catch was the Avro Lincoln, which were rarely seen these days. Attacks on US B47s were forbidden and generally impossible anyway. The only time a Meteor could catch a Canberra was if it was in the landing circuit! Up until recently the Meteor pilots had engaged all sorts of aeroplanes, as Harry Irving remembers:

> 'During my days at Waterbeach, the skies over East Anglia seemed always full of aircraft, especially American fighters. Wherever you went, we usually ended up in a dog-fight with them. It got to the ears of the hierarchy and the practice was stopped.
>
> Derek Bryant, however, decided one day, to go up and have a look at East Anglia and got involved in a dog-fight with some Americans. So involved did it become that he forgot to monitor his jet-pipe temperatures, which became very crucial at around 700°C. The aircraft caught fire at about 1,000°, but he didn't bale out because the fire then went out. When he arrived back at Tangmere, both jet pipes, which in situ are 8-10 feet long, were both hanging out of the back of the engines at extraordinary angles, and also a lot of the wing's trailing edges had been burnt away too.'

Suddenly, at the beginning of February, a Hunter arrived, a Mark 2 (WN919). Any euphoria was extremely short-lived as hordes of little men with spanners and screwdrivers descended upon it immediately and dismantled it. It was in no state to fly for the rest of the month.

Meantime, to take their minds off things, the Squadron made an exchange visit to the Dutch airfield at Twente on 23 March, 326 Dutch Squadron flying in to Tangmere. Arriving at Twente all pilots were thoroughly briefed about local conditions and it seemed clear that when flying over Holland, unless a pilot is under radar control, he will either collide with something or be shot down by Dutch AA fire.

A large exercise was laid on with bags of Scrambles in sections of four, intercepting anything from KLM Dakotas, to Canberras and Sabres. There followed an expedition into nearby Enschede for a terrific thrash, with establishments such as the White Huis, DeGraff Hotel and the Memphis being either visited, wrecked – or both. The Squadron left on the Friday with a flypast back at Tangmere, and 'going Dutch' was definitely to be recommended!

If the pilots thought that upon their return the Hunter would have been put back into one piece and made available, they were to be disappointed. They found that a film was about to be made on servicing the Hunter so it would be staying firmly on the deck for at least another month. To get if off squadron strength it was moved to ASF 12. Then medics from RAE Farnborough decended to check the sizes of individual bone-domes. When issued they had just been allocated out and provided it went over the head, that was that, but now these medics were saying that it was dangerous for a pilot to wear an incorrect size. Several pilots were indeed found to have helmets up to two sizes too large.

Constantly trying to broaden educational and cultural horizons, a pilgrimage was made to Tamplin's Brewery on 25 May. The hospitality of the management was only equalled by the capacity to accept it. Thus the pilots got off to a good start to what proved to be the most successful 'thrash' for some considerable time [obviously overlooking the recent Dutch trip]. Whether they were still 'Brighton's Own' became a debatable point.

Hunter Squadron

Finally, on 2 June 1955, the first Hunters arrived, and by the end of the month, sixteen Mark 5s were on strength. The Squadron now ran one Hunter and one Meteor Flight as pilots converted. Flight Lieutenant C F Pickard had spent much of May at the DFSL, West Raynham, converting to the Hunter in order to pass on this knowledge to the other pilots. Freddie Pickard relates:

> 'I joined the Squadron in June 1954 while it was still flying Meteors. In March 1955 I went off to West Raynham on the Day Fighter Leaders Course (DFL School) which had just been equipped

with the Hunter Mark 1. It was pretty tough and lasted until about 5 May, giving me a total of 30 hours on the Avon-engined Hunter.

Back at Tangmere, the Squadron started to re-equip with the Sapphire-engined Hunter Mark 5 in early June. At this time I took over from John Tedder as OC B Flight. Colin Telford was appointed OC C Flight in August, to provide a technical focus for the aircraft as the Sapphire was proving troublesome. The engine had a tendency to flame-out when the guns were fired. The solution, I think, was to fit "Sabrinas" either side of the fuselage to collect the ammunition links.

We had great fun with Boscombe Down during the summer of 1955 conducting fire-out trials; low level, 600 knots over the sea from Selsey Bill to Brighton. We reckoned that if the engine did flame-out, we could climb to 20,000 feet and make it back to Tangmere for a flame out landing. Fortunately for everyone we never had to try it except in practice.

One thing we did discover was that the Hunter was not too clever at landing on a flooded runway. On one occasion an aircraft touched down at 125 knots and went off the end into a ploughed field at the same speed. This contributed in some way to the fitting of "max-arret" brakes. Otherwise, life in general was full of incident and hilarity, like for instance the 'grimmy' contests in the Mess on a Saturday night.'

Harry Irving, who was to be the Hunter solo aerobatic display pilot for the 1955-56 season, recalls his conversion and also the gun test trials with Boscombe Down:

'I was sent to Chivenor where they had Hunter 1s to do a conversion course, which lasted about a day and a half! The first evening I attended lectures on things and the next day I made six flights, each of about 30 minutes, during which I did not get out of the aircraft. Each time it was refuelled the instructor came out and ran through the next series of tests, and off I went. The next morning I did three more and then was on my way back to Tangmere, where I checked out all the pilots, including the Station Commander and CO. Everyone converted safely.

The Hunter was undergoing all its trials at Boscombe Down, and gun firing was one of them. It was all being rushed through because the Suez campaign was on the horizon and questions were being asked in the Houses of Parliament about the amount of time this aircraft was taking to get into service.

The snag was that firing all four Aden guns the gas back-fired into the intakes, in some cases stopping the engine, or perhaps stalling the impeller, so the gun firing trials were handed over to us at Tangmere. Derek Bryant, myself, Jimmy Mansell and another chap, undertook the trials and commented on them. They were carried out off Bognor Regis where we had our own air-to-air range.

It was an interesting little trial, sometimes we had to fire short bursts at various speeds, and sometimes what was called a run-out, which was at maximum speed at low level, 660-680 knots, then press the button. Looking down the line of flight seeing these huge lumps of metal going away in front of you was impressive. It was an extraordinary experience, with the "G" register on max. "neg-G", the aircraft seemed just to be shaking itself to bits! So we carried on and the trouble then was that after the flights, we discovered little cracks here and there and instead of redesigning that particular part they were strengthening them.

Of course, you strengthen one bit, you'll invariably weaken another. For example I had a nose wheel fall down when I was doing about 475 knots. By the grace of God I was pointing slightly upwards. I rolled over on my back, but if I had been level or slightly nose-down, I would not have had the strength to hold it level, but by rolling over I was able to bunt it and roll out safely again. The trials were completed successfully and we had no engine problems at all.'

There was great prestige in knowing now that the Squadron was now a 'swept wing' outfit. It was noted that the pilots were now having to part their hair in the middle as well as having it brushed well back after going solo on the Hunter.

While still working up on the new aeroplanes, the Meteor had to take part in Exercise 'Regulus', Fighter Command's part in NATO exercise 'Carte Blanche'. The Meteors acted as raiders against France on twelve occasions, being intercepted by Ouragons or Vampires, each occasion accompanied by many furious French voices over the R/T. It was also noted that nobody had been heard over the radio to exclaim: 'Vive le Numéro Une'!

Back on the Squadron, pilots were now having the experience of going through the sound barrier. The Wing Commander Flying, P J Simpson DSO DFC went first, becoming known instantly as 'Supersonic Simpson', followed soon afterwards by Flight Lieutenant C J Tedder (known as the

Thrash King, and about to leave for a 13 Group HQ post), Harry Irving and Freddie Pickard. Flying Officer C Shaw experienced engine failure in August, during a practise forced landing, ending up with Cat 4 damage. He was alright apart from a hangover the next morning.

As September arrived, so too did the Farnborough and Battle of Britain displays. The Squadron's Hunters flew as part of the mass formation of 64 Hunters at the SBAC display over Farnborough and the Tangmere Open Day began with seven Hunters in close formation, led by Freddie Lister, heading over the airfield after having done their part over London. The display team was flying so close together now, that it was said that the close formation team pilots could be easily recognised by the fact that their necks were permanently twisted either to the left or right, depending on their flight position. Presumably the CO's head was either OK or permanently facing aft. Harry Irving flew a spectacular solo aerobatic display, the first many spectators would have seen.

Squadron personnel strength at this period was 20 officers, one SNCO; ground personnel, one warrant officer, 11 SNCOs, 18 corporals and 47 airmen.

* * *

Pilot Officer Turner's Hunter sheared its port undercarriage leg during a landing on 28 October, but he was OK. However, he firmly refused to consider any laundry bills from the GCA personnel whose caravan he only narrowly missed! Two aircraft were also damaged by bird strikes; Flying Officer Bryant went into a flock of them, claiming nine confirmed! After Turner's effort, representatives from Dowty arrived at Tangmere, and upon inspection discovered six aircraft were showing cracks in their oleo legs, which was a bit disconcerting.

First Hunter ejection
Harry Irving and Flying Officer A W Ginn were on a sortie on 5 December. Over East Grinstead, Alan Ginn ran into trouble with his controls and soon had to bale out. Harry Irving:

> 'The Hunter was the first aircraft with power controls and they had a hydraulic jack on both ailerons. You could fly with these controls on or switch them to manual. One of these jacks suddenly went manual on Alan's aircraft and the other stayed in power while at very high speed. The aircraft just rolled and no force on earth could hold it. So he ejected and landed in a field.
>
> At that stage we didn't have the leg restraints that were normal later, to attach one's legs to the seat so as he went out his legs splayed right out and he damaged both knees. He passed out, then, of course, landed on them as he hit the ground. He was taken to McIndoe's place at East Grinstead and ended up with one leg shorter than the other.'

There was another ejection in February, but it was not a 1 Squadron aeroplane. The Squadron had been lending pilots to 34 Squadron, also based at Tangmere, helping them with their training. This ended on the 23rd after Derek Bryant had a flame out climbing to 37,000 feet, accompanied by much vibration and grinding noises. He tried to get into Boscombe and then Hurn but neither airports were used to the RAF's radar approach system and got it all wrong. According to Harry Irving, Bryant made a valiant effort to glide it down. Breaking cloud and seeing he was nowhere near the second airport it was time to get out and leave the aeroplane (WP193) to its own devices, at 4,500 feet. He lost his shoes and watch but once down, rang up from a pub to say he was OK, and by the time the Squadron got to him he was well away.

Flying Officer Snowdon also suffered a flame out in March but made a successful wheels-up landing. The following month Flying Officer D R M Morris had his starboard oleo leg fracture on landing but although the aircraft needed a wing change, Morris was unharmed.

Cyprus
In May the Squadron took four Hunters on a Proving Flight to Cyprus, which needed to be made in case Hunters had to be urgently moved to the Middle East. Wing Commander Peter Simpson took the lead, with the CO, Harry Irving and Derek Bryant. The flight would go via Istres (southern France), Malta and El Adem, and all went well until the final leg, at which stage Bryant's booster pumps failed 100 miles out from El Adem, necessitating (beyond question in his view!) a return by the Nos. 3 and 4. Lister and Bryant made it safely back to El Adem (inland from Tobruk) where the Hunter was fixed. The two then continued on to Cyprus and all four returned to the UK without further mishap. Total flying time for Harry and the Wingco was 5 hours, ten minutes. Harry Irving:

'I flew as No.2 to Wing Commander Simpson because, having been a wartime Lancaster pilot I was the only chap who could (be trusted) calculate a point-of-no-return, so I was charged with doing all the navigation. I had to liaise with the French, while an RAF air traffic officer from Tangmere went down to Castres, in southern France, so we could have an English-speaking chap to help us.'

Lieutenant M L Brown RN was attached to the Squadron from the Fleet Air Arm. In June Mike Brown experienced a flame-out at 45,000 feet and made a dead stick landing at Chivenor. The cloud at the time was just on the tops of the hills and he was advised to eject. But he rode it down, broke cloud at 1,200 feet and did well to line up on the short runway. Unfortunately he had to take avoiding action as he spotted a taxying Hunter on the runway and he was forced to land on the grass. Rolling on he hit a parapet which whipped off the undercarriage. Brown suffered a fractured small bone in one foot and a dislocated shoulder. One wonders why the runway was not cleared for the emergency but having been advised to eject, it is supposed the tower people did not expect him to try a landing.

Operation Quickfire
Freddie Lister departed in June, going to 2nd TAF Germany. A new CO was appointed, one who was just finishing a DFLS course at West Raynham but in the event this posting was cancelled. Instead, Squadron Leader R S Kingsford was selected to be the new boss, and he arrived in August. However, he missed a detachment to Akrotiri, Cyprus, which began on the 7th of the same month – Operation 'Quickfire'. 1 (acting CO being Harry Irving) and 34 Squadrons moved there in quick time due to the unsettled situation in the Middle East, all 25 aircraft arriving safely, covering the same route as the Proving Flight in May, with a night stop at El Adem. Wing Commander Simpson's Wing was given the responsibility of defending the main Middle East bases in Cyprus. Exercises in the role were flown from Akrotiri and then from Nicosia.

The move to Nicosia came on 1 September. On arrival Flight Lieutenant C M Telford's port oleo leg collapsed, causing Cat 4 damage to the Hunter. One of the Squadron's tasks was to check aircraft not flying in the approved air corridor over the island. In one case a French DC6 was compelled to land at Nicosia much to the crew's annoyance. The Squadron also kept a Battle Flight at Operational Readiness from dawn until dusk, until 21 October. During this operation RAF aircraft carried black and yellow identification bands on wings and fuselage.

During November the unit continued with their fighter defence of Cyprus, along with 34 Squadron, and also provided four aircraft as top cover to transport aircraft making a 'drop' on Gamil airfield in the Canal Zone. Unfortunately the Egyptian Air Force stayed on the ground. Several fighter sweeps were flown over the Nile Delta at 30,000 feet as far south as Cairo, to cover sorties for VIP aircraft into Gamil and as escort to PR Canberras checking on Syrian airfields. Eventually the Battle Flight was relaxed following the end of the Suez crisis.

All military forces on Cyprus were having trouble with EOKA terrorists, and on 10 November, Hunter WP180 was blown up and destroyed on the airfield. This resulted in much more guard duty being imposed, especially at night, and the pre-flight pilot inspections became unbelievably painstaking.

There was also the famous occasion following a Scramble, that two Squadron Hunters were vectored onto bogies at 40,000 feet, 100 miles from Cyprus. They got to within 300 yards before they were recognised as four F86Ds of the US 6th Fleet. What was noteworthy was that the American pilots did not see the Hunters until this range despite being in battle formation.

With the crisis over, the Squadron prepared to leave on 17 December, taking off on the 21st for a night stop on Malta. Then fog was reported over the UK so a second night was spent on the island. UK fog continued to be a problem but at least the pilots got to Istres on the 23rd. Everyone was anxious to be home by Christmas and fortunately the weather improved sufficiently, and Tangmere was reached on Christmas Eve morning. Of his period on Cyprus, Harry Irving recalls:

'We went to Nicosia, which had a bumpy, undulating runway, and when we landed on our narrow, very high pressure tyres, they walked over these bumps so we knew it was going to be a problem. Soon we had five or six aircraft strewn across the airfield, having landed on the bumps, causing tyre bursts. This was not helped by the heat and the extremely hot tarmac. In consequence we only flew, prior to Suez, in the evenings after the temperature had dropped.

Being the Squadron aerobatic display pilot on Meteors and then on Hunters, I carried out many displays in Britain as well as in Europe, Malta, Channel Islands, El Adem as well as Cyprus. I did one at Akrotiri shortly after we arrived and, to show just how easily accidents can happen – with the temperature being extremely high – I staggered off and gained height. The display always began with a low level run across the airfield from a high-powered dive. On the way down this day, I went supersonic and normally I'd start pulling out at somewhere between 12-16,000 feet in order to race across the airfield. So I started to pull out, as I had done many times before, but pulling back on the stick, nothing happened.

The chaps were all standing looking up at me and apparently I went down the runway at the same time as the sonic boom arrived, so it shows you I was about supersonic at very low level which was a mistake. The mistake I made, of course, was not calculating what the true airspeed would be because of the very high temperatures before I took off, which is one of the things one does normally at pre-flight planning. That I didn't do and I was very lucky.'

In mid-February 1957 the Squadron had a six-aircraft exchange visit to Cambrai, with French Mystère IVs flying in to Tangmere. Captain J Baird USMC, on exchange, had an undercarriage leg sheer on his first night landing but he was OK. It was not often that a squadron member died on active service other than due to accidents, but at the end of February, Warrant Officer V A Willis died from a cerebral haemorrhage. He had been with them for ten months in 1950 and rejoined in October 1952 till January 1957. He had done well on Cyprus and had just gone to the Station Flight at Tangmere.

The normal routine was maintained during the summer of 1957, the Squadron taking part as usual at Farnborough and, with 34 Squadron, during the Battle of Britain Open Day displays over several airfields in southern England. On 9 December, eight Hunters took off for Soesterberg for an exchange visit with 327 Squadron Royal Netherlands Air Force, returning on the 13th. Visits to Utrecht and Amsterdam were a welcome distraction especially 'window shopping' along some of the lesser known streets of Amsterdam!!

There was a 'friendship' weekend with the Squadron's 'Brighton Connection' in January 1958, just as Air Ministry announced that Tangmere would be closing down – a casualty of the 1957 White Paper from Duncan Sandys, the Defence Minister. Another shock was Sandys' revelation that the Lightning would be the last RAF fighter to have a pilot, and that missiles would replace them. More than 30 RAF squadrons were ear-marked for disbandment, and the signs seemed ominous for 1 Squadron, as it had Hunters, not Lightnings, and its base was being closed. Then their co-squadron, No.34, was disbanded only to be reformed as a Beverley transport unit.

In March 1958 came a three-week detachment to Aldergrove, Northern Ireland but tragedy struck on 5 May. Flying Officer J J Turner took off from Tangmere on an air test following a routine engine change. Shortly afterwards he 'attacked' a pair of Hunters and one of the pilots, Flying Officer M J Paxton, accepted the challenge. During the mock fight that followed, both aircraft collided and crashed into the sea. Mike Paxton and John Turner were both killed.

The Squadron was stood down from operations on 1 June with the knowledge that it was indeed to be disbanded, but the good news was that it would be reformed simultaneously at RAF Stradishall, by renumbering No.263 Squadron based there. Obviously it was never the intention to lose the RAF's premier unit. 263 Squadron had recently been equipped with the Avon-engined Hunter Mark 6. Pilots and ground crews of 1 Squadron would be dispersed upon disbandment, with just two pilots, Flying Officers Pete Highton and Bob Turner, remaining with the new formation in order to maintain continuity. The date of handover was to be 23 June. Things would not be the same again.

With the pending closure of Tangmere, the ties with a number of Squadrons, especially 1 and 43, would come to an abrupt and permanent end. 1 Squadron had been based here for long periods, and as Flying Officer Gerry English, one of the Hunter pilots, recalls, one thing that would now be a thing of the past was the 'Barnham Junction Approach', in bad weather:

'The Squadron's old Tangmere hands may recall how we found the airfield in claggy weather. Fondly known as the Barnham Junction Approach, one flew below cloud at perhaps 200 feet over the Channel and somehow found the Pier off Bognor Regis, then followed the railway line out of Bognor for four miles to Barnham Junction Station. Lowering the landing gear we then made a rate one turn left onto 250° and there you were – perfectly placed to land on Tangmere's runway 25. The procedure worked charmingly, which was just as well as fuel reserves were usually pretty minimal, although it must be said that the fuel endurance of the Hunter Mk 5 was a vast improvement on the Mks 1 and 2.'

Re-born 1958

Following a dinner/dance on Friday the 13th of June, at the Bedford Hotel in Brighton and then a dance for the airmen at the Unicorn the following Tuesday, preparations for the disbandment began.

This occurred on Monday the 23rd. 25 Squadron, also at Tangmere, were being disbanded too, and the Squadrons' Standards were handed over to 263 and 153 Squadrons. The parade was taken by the C-in-C Fighter Command, Air Chief Marshal Sir Tom Pike KCG OBE DFC, followed by a flypast of both Hunters and 25's Meteor NF11s. Captain Jesse Hughes USMC, the A Flight commander, acted as escort to the C-in-C.

On 1 July 1958, at RAF Stradishall, 1 Squadron reformed, and the Standard was paraded on the 22nd, 11 Group's SASO, Air Commodore J H McGuire DSO OBE, deputising for the AOC. Life went on but with a new twist. The Squadron had finally ended their pure fighter role, now to become a fighter-bomber outfit.

The newly appointed CO, Squadron Leader L de Garis AFC had taken over on the 5th and would command until the end of the year. Meantime the pilots began work on their Hunter 6 fighters within No.165 Wing, 65 Squadron being the other unit. The Hunter 6, as well as its uprated engine, had wings strengthened to carry extra fuel tanks and weapons, including rockets.

During August, while flying from Horsham St Faith, Flight Lieutenant J R Jackson was lining up on the runway as No.3 in a normal pairs stream take-off at which time his starboard brake partially failed. Swinging to the left he passed behind his No.1, whose jet-wash swung him back to the right. Jackson's starboard brake then failed completely and he rolled XE604 into a parked aircraft, sufficiently fast to cause Cat 3 damage to both machines.

Before the month was out, on the 22th, there was another incident. Captain T D Hassig, of the Royal Netherland Air Force, on an exchange tour, had his Hunter struck by lightning. His G4F compass started spinning and the tail trim ran away, though quickly rectified by switching off the follow-up tail. Ted Hassig got it down safely but the aircraft became u/s.

Landing at RAF Duxford three days later, Flight Lieutenant B A Weeden overshot the runway by 300 yards. The Squadron was making a stream landing ready for the Farnborough Air Show. Visibility was nil due to heavy rain and he touched down a bit too fast, at 125 knots, but with a wet runway and rain on the windscreen, he went through the boundary fence and into a field of wheat, which caused Cat 3 damage to XE614.

Over Farnborough the following month the Squadron led a formation of 45 Hawker Hunters during the SBAC display. Six squadrons supplied aircraft and as all were based around Cambridge, de Garis suggested an inter-squadron punt race on the River Cam. 1 Squadron were doing well until assailed by a wave of missiles from rival crews. Ted Hassig did not like to admit defeat even though his punt was sinking fast and paddled valiantly until the water came up over his head.

Back to Cyprus

At the end of September the unit deployed once more to Cyprus, this time to convert to the ground-attack role. Ten aircraft left on the 29th and landed at Luqa (Malta) but only eight could be refuelled so these carried on, followed by the other two on 1 October. The other pilots flew direct by DH Comet on the 7th.

One of the pilots to arrive on the 30th was Pilot Officer C P J Coulcher and he had a problem because he was not given the full picture during his landing approach. Chuck Coulcher explains:

'We came in to land at Nicosia and I'd been told that the first 200 yards of runway was sterile, but that's all I'd been told. The thought was that perhaps the threshhold was breaking up or something. What they hadn't explained was there was a six foot barbed wire fence round the airfield against the terrorists. Therefore, the reason for not landing before 200 yards was so as to miss it. Nobody had said one couldn't come in low and hold off, which is what I did. I felt I'd hit something but didn't see it of course, and managed to wrap some barbed wire round the undercarriage and scratched the aircraft a bit but it was soon repaired. A few weeks later a 66 Squadron pilot did exactly the same thing; they hadn't told them either!'

As well as the ground-attack training, the Squadron were still on standby against EOKA terrorists. A regular dawn army convoy in the south-east of the island was frequently ambushed, so frequent air support, armed recces and patrols proved useful. On one occasion Flight Lieutenant T Gribble and Flying Officer D G Brook were asked to make a couple of dummy runs at a church tower from where sniper fire had come and the terrorists made a hasty retreat. It so happened that two news reporters racing to the scene in their car, suddenly found themselves face-to-face with the two Hunters as they flashed by them, and they drove straight into a Turkish roadblock. Chuck Coulcher continues:

'We did a lot of convoy escorts, flying ahead and trying to see if any ambushes were being set up around mountain bends. Flaps down, 200 feet, trying to spot terrorists round corners proved quite interesting.

Of course, we all carried side-arms, especially when we went into places like Kyrenia on the northern coast. We would swim at a place called 'The Slab', run by an English couple, where we could get tea and cream cakes. Swimming there was pretty safe for us and we usually went there once a week. [Another watering hole was the Harbour Club.]

Mac Cameron, who was later killed doing aerobatics, was the first chap to get some proper snorkling gear, air tanks, mask, harpoon – the lot. One day he boasted that he was going deep to hunt big fish. About ten minutes later there was a huge flurry of water and up he shot. Racing ashore, ashen-faced and obviously petrified, he yelled, "There's a bloody great shark down there!" Of course, it was only a dog fish or a grouper, but I don't think he ever went in again.

We lived in tents, eight men to a tent, and we had one chap who snored terribly. We lifted him and his bed out one night and next morning he woke to find himself alone out in the scrub. We refused to let him back in again.

On another visit to the island later, Harry Davidson, one of our flight commanders, who was quite a disciplinarian, sorted us out. By this time we were using G-suits but being so hot in Cyprus we tended not to wear them and Harry knew this. So this day he took me and another chap up and as soon as we took off he pulled up into four-G and kept this up, all the time pulling hard-G. We were occasionally blacking out and when we landed we asked what that was all about. He simply reminded us to wear our G-suits in future.'

Pilot Officer E G Marshall had a trying experience on 7 October in XE625. On take-off he found his undercarriage would not come up so had to fly around to burn off fuel and in landing he dropped his speed below 130 knots and came in semi-stalled due to checking his rate of descent using the elevator rather than power, and the back end of the Hunter banged into the ground. Cat 3 damage, but he had only seven hours on Hunters and this was his first sortie with the Squadron.

Flight Lieutenant D Allison had total hydraulic failure at 42,000 feet on 30 October but he descended in manual, selected emergency flaps and undercart and landed safely, but then it was time to go home. They left on 5 November via El Adem. Flight Lieutenant J M Henderson's XE620 caught fire on the ground, made expensive noises, and half-burnt Avpin and metal filings oozed from the drain vent in the starter bay. The starter motor had seized. Seeing this, Flight Lieutenant D E Brett began to laugh, realising Henderson would be left behind in the desert, and jumping into his own aircraft began to start up. As he did so the Hunter blew a ten foot column of fuel into the air, spurting through the bleed valve louvres on the starboard upper fuselage due to PV ram failure. That stopped him laughing.

Leaving the two pilots behind the rest pressed on to Malta only to have weather problems delay departure. Then the CO's aircraft (XG207) lost all hydraulics near Orange (southern France) and he had to force-land manually. Taking over another aircraft – leaving the lad to return later by Beverley – the pilots flew on to England. The two delayed pilots finally got back next day, one flying a 65 Squadron aircraft. Apparently a coin had been tossed with a 65 Squadron pilot as to who should fly back in the first serviceable pair of aircraft to become available – and the 65 pilot lost! One can only wonder what the chap's CO said when he found out he had even taken the wager in the first place.

At Christmas, de Garis handed over command to Squadron Leader J J Phipps. There was a farewell party at the 'Bull', in Long Melford, for the CO as well as Brett and Flying Officer R M Sinclair who were also leaving. With his customary style and aplomb, Brett drove at high speed into the bundi, rolled, and crashed back onto the road. First aid and protection from inquisitive policemen was given by the Squadron and although the car was a write-off, Brett survived. One can imagine the roar that went up when it was announced he was off to Aden – as a Flight Safety Officer!

* * *

At the start of 1959 the Squadron strength was 20 officers, one warrant officer, 18 SNCOs and 76 airmen. Two Hunters were slightly damaged early on, one of the machines having been at Readiness with Flying Officer David Brook:

'We were on standby on the Operational Readiness Platform at Stradishall. The ORP was on a slope and when I was stood down from two minutes readiness the ground crew put one chock behind the nose wheel. Alas, on icy concrete, this was not enough to stop the aircraft from rolling backwards and then to one side into the other standby aircraft. As I wasn't in the aircraft I was not held to blame.'

David Brook was involved in a far more interesting occurrence on 17 February. According to the Squadron diary he crashed into a tree trying to land while some Javelins were landing on the other runway. He remained airborne and staggered off to Honington for a wheels down landing. His own story reads much better:

'I was No.2 to my flight commander and after a routine training sortie we tried to do a pairs landing from a radar GCA. We were landing into a low February sun in haze and the visibility was poor. I think Tom Gribble landed on, or anyway towards, my side of the runway and I went round again. On the next attempt to land off GCA I failed to monitor my altimeter and, when I looked up for the runway, my windscreen was full of tree. There was much banging as the aircraft flew through the top of it and by the time I had put on power I was past the runway threshold and getting short of fuel.

The engine was making a peculiar noise – perhaps it was burning wood – so I said I would eject. Squadron Leader John Phipps was by now in the Control Tower: "Don't bale out, lad, divert to Honington." I am not sure to this day whether he knew how hard I had hit that tree! Anyway, it is irrelevant as the gallant Hunter moaned its way to Honington. I landed there without using the air speed indicator because I could see the pitot tube had suffered from the tree-strike. Once on the ground the unusual moaning noise was explained by the left (I think) intake, which was, amongst other parts of the airframe, badly beaten about. I think the aircraft might have been repairable but I have some vague memory that because it was one of those paid for by the Americans (Off-shore Purchase Scheme), it was scrapped.

I don't recall any disciplinary action against me following was what, quite frankly, a major pig's ear but a few months later I did have to ask quietly why my promotion to flight lieutenant was a few months late!'

Harry Davidson, who had just been appointed as a flight commander, did know the answer to David's question about whether the CO had known he'd hit the tree, as he explains:

'When I was posted to 1 Squadron, John Phipps told me he had asked for me, so once the posting was received, he asked me over for a look round. I drove down from West Raynham and was actually sitting with John in his office when the alert call came from the Tower and could he come as quickly as possible.

It was a very foggy day and we raced up the tower steps two at a time, and as John entered, all he heard on the radio was the second part of David's call, saying "...I'm going to climb up and bale out." The CO grabbed a mike and said, "Don't bale out, go to Honington!" He didn't hear the part about hitting the tree and thought he was baling out because of the fog. David later said that he thought that if the boss felt he could make it to Honington, he'd try.

In any event, this was a good way to start my tour with 1 Squadron.'

David survived, but the tree didn't. It was chopped down. Hunter XE619 did not survive either – officially deemed beyond economic repair.

This year's APC at Acklington began on 27 February, with 11 F6s, one T7 and one Vampire T11, plus three Meteor FVIIIs headed there at intervals during the morning, where the first to arrive made a tidy run-in and break. All landed in time for the pre-lunch drinks on the CO, except the last three Hunter pilots who missed the booze. Chuck Coulcher has occasion to recall the Vampire for two reasons:

'We had a Vampire T11 prior to dual Hunters and Ted Hassig, who was very senior to me, wanted to fly in one. Having just come off Vampires in training I was told to go off with him, so assuming he'd flown all these things, I sat in the second seat. As we sat there he asked me to show him how to take it off and later he took over. As we came into land, approaching at about 180 knots, I said that we were going a bit fast and he then admitted that he'd never flown one before. It was lucky I had said something!

Going up to Acklington for our APC, I was flying the T11 and was told to take up the Squadron tea urn (very important), which we strapped to the right-hand seat. Once I arrived at Acklington I discovered that the urn must have edged forward slightly during the trip and was in the way. I couldn't get the stick back for landing. Everything was all right in level flight but I needed it right back for landing and the other stick was up against the urn.

Eventually, not wanting to say anything to Control, I landed on all three wheels, although the nose wheel got a bit scuffed. It would have been an interesting story had I been forced to eject! The

Court of Enquiry would have made interesting reading too. At least I got this important piece of equipment up there.'

The APC was a success for during March large quantities of beer were consumed. A serious 6 o'clock drinking school was established and there was hardly a sober moment at weekends. On Saturday the 7th, Flying Officer A Mumford bought a dozen bottles of champagne as a final fling before his marriage and to celebrate a £100 win on the Premium Bonds. Acklington Mess soon ran out of champagne and beer, while gin and whisky stocks became dangerously low.

During April the Squadron took part in exercises 'Buckboard', 'Halyard' and 'Ciano'. On the latter air-to-air cine attacks, claims were made on one VHF-jamming Valiant and five Canberras. This was followed by Exercise 'Topweight' and claims during this were for nine F101s, two F100s, two Super Mystères (disallowed), seven B66s, two Hunters (disallowed), 17 Canberras, two KC97 tankers and one Lincoln; total 42 'destroyed'.

The Mystères and Hunters that were disallowed were supposed to be 'friendly' aircraft but the Squadron took great delight in dealing with any apparent traitors. And it was all good experience anyway.

On 29 April there was a visit by the Persian Minister of Defence and after lunch he was flown in the T7 by Flight Lieutenant M G Tomkins. Despite some ear trouble he became the first Persian defence minister to go supersonic, and Mark Tomkins became the recipient of a silver cigarette case.

Operation 'Halyard' is recalled by Harry Davidson, whose wife was expecting their second child:

'When my second daughter was born we were on Operation Halyard, freezing our bums off at cockpit Readiness at the end of the runway during daylight hours. Early this particular morning, my wife decided the baby was coming but as duty flight commander I had to go. In fact the mid-wife and I crossed on the stairs, she coming, me going. I had no 'phone so I couldn't call the airfield, so taking my 4-year old daughter with me, drove to the base.

We got the Hunters out and Tony Chaplin was on his way, so sitting Christine on the Ops Room table, I taxied one down to the end of the runway, then Tony arrived and relieved me so that I could return home. We used to joke later that for five minutes the fate of this country was in the hands of a 4-year old girl, she being the only link between Communications and us!'

Chapter Sixteen

HUNTER DAYS

During May 1959 the Squadron began converting pilots to fly Meteors so that they could fly their own banner-dragging aircraft during air-to-air firing exercises, thus making them a little more independent of others.

There were always dangers about. Flying Officer B J Grainger had engine failure with his Hunter on 6 May flying at 570 knots at 400 feet during a 'rat and terrier' exercise. He used his momentum to pull up to 5,000 feet then managed a good force landing at Waterbeach. Ten days later a faulty temperature control unit caused Ted Hassig's engine to flame out at 40,000 feet as he was about to commence a dog-fight. Re-light failed but then the engine re-lit itself at 17,000 feet – which was nice – and he landed safely. Also this month some of the XE serial Hunters were repainted, to 'smarten them up a bit'.

More engine trouble came on 9 June, this time involving Flying Officer Anthony Mumford, the adjutant. Flying XE628 he experienced compression blade failure and his revs dropped to nothing. Later, the Station Commander, Group Captain C Foxley-Norris, wrote the following endorsement:

'After final run over target, Flying Officer Mumford turned to port and started to pull up behind his leader. At 1,500 feet, 400 knots, a loud thump from the engine and the revs dropped to zero. Informed his leader but before receiving a reply, saw Lakenheath and decided to land. Told leader and contacted Lakenheath without success. Main runway was under repair but he found enough height to turn right to runway 32 (2,200 yards). Lowered undercarriage and flaps on emergency systems, crossed the threshhold at 165 knots and stopped in 1,500 yards, having to avoid a lorry and a tractor which crossed the runway during his landing run.

Quick thinking and a successful landing from less than 7,000 feet.'

Wing Commander A D Boyle, the WingCo Flying 154 Wing, led 16 Hunters over Buckingham Palace on 13 June, a Flypast for the Queen's birthday, including Hunters from the Duxford Wing. However, there had been an initial hitch.

When word came down about the Flypast, orders were that the WingCo would lead but, being a Javelin pilot this was going to cause a problem. HQFC firmly stuck to their guns and said that the WingCo should learn to fly a Hunter in the ten days remaining. On the day of the rehearsal, 1 Squadron's CO and Harry Davidson were on his wing as they lined up on the runway but to their surprise the lead Hunter suddenly shot off four minutes early. The others quickly took off after him and on forming up he was advised that they would arrive over London early and they should make a 360° to use up the time. The Wing Commander vetoed this in case he got lost and said they would slow down and lose the time that way. A moment or so later the leader of the Duxford Wing, Charles Maughan (OC 65 Sqn) called up: 'This should be very interesting leader, your average speed to Buckingham Palace to lose four minutes will be 125 knots, which is slower than a Hunter can fly.' There was a long hush as they flew on, then the WingCo just packed it in and everyone turned and flew home, leaving their lordships to scan the London sky in vein.

After a lot of telephone calls, the next day came the real thing and the WingCo was persuaded to let John Phipps do the timing and Harry the navigation as they flew on his wing, while all he had to do was to fly his Hunter and be guided in. All went well and they hit London spot on and later, back at base, the WingCo bought champagne for everyone which began a wonderful party. HM later sent her congratulations for a superb show.

Almost two weeks later (24th) came the Annual Inspection by the AOC 11 Group. However, the Squadron had a problem. This, and how it was overcome, is described by Anthony Mumford:

'We were informed by Group that there would be no flypast this year, and the boss, who was a bit of a player, to put it mildly, said that was rubbish, we always have a flypast, and told me to sort it out!

So I rang Cardington and got hold of the WingCo there to ask it he could help, and he put me on to Jerry Long who knew all about Cardington. I spoke to him and he was hugely enthusiastic about my idea for a balloon, and to fly it past the AOC. So we did a bit of a deal, that we would collect it, while he arranged for a shipment of hydrogen gas to inflate the thing at Stradishall. It wasn't a large balloon, it wouldn't take two people, and our poor old SATCO was combing through the regulations for balloon flying, etc.

We got this silver and orange thing inflated alright on the day, with Jerry Long's help, but we had to keep hiding it behind hangars and buildings so the AOC wouldn't spot it during his inspection as he moved round the airfield in his car – so that was fun. Then we gathered eight pilots, eight ground crew and a flight sergeant, to pull it about in the direction we wanted and so, as the CO gave permission for the parade to 'March out', from around a corner of the hangar appeared this balloon – with me in the basket.'

As the balloon was hauled along, Anthony Mumford gave an 'eyes right' but his own smart salute turned into an undignified clutching of the basket as the balloon decided to dip in salute itself, just as it went by the AOC. The 17 'engines' were too worried about the unexpected manoeuvre to hear the delightful irresponsible exhortions by the AOC to 'Let go!' Later the AOC sent a signal to the Squadron:

'Your Squadron demonstrated their versatility and airmanship by the competent manner in which they handled their balloon during my inspection last Monday. But for a slight lack of control in regard to altitude, your adjutant would have been well within the limits for a Green Instrument Rating (balloons). Reconversion of Squadron to Hunter Mark 6 is now to be completed in time for transfer to 12 Group.'

This episode which linked the Squadron with its past was welcomed by Mr Jerry Long, for he had been with it way back in 1912.

RAF Stradishall became part of 12 Group on the first day of July 1959 and on the 13th, 54 Squadron moved up from Odiham to Stradishall, being given a welcome party on the 17th. Christopher Foxley-Norris left as Station Commander, replaced by Group Captain Stan B Grant DFC, a wartime fighter pilot. Anthony Mumford recalls that John Phipps knew 54's CO, Ian Warby, and so knew too that his birthday was coming up. A serruptitious question to some 54 Squadron types brought forth the information that they were not planning anything for the occasion. Phipps therefore purchased a large coffee-table colour book of fighter aircraft, and with a wonderful use of words, inscribed in it: 'From 1 Squadron to another.' 54 were always referred to as 'Fifty Plonk'.

September was, as usual, extra busy with Battle of Britain displays. The CO, Hassig, Flight Lieutenant J R Jackson and Flying Officer Tony Chaplin flew to Jersey and did a display, returning in the evening by Anson for celebrations. Next day Flight Lieutenant Harry Davidson, Flying Officers Mumford, Coulcher and F Marshall flew over Biggin Hill, Tunbridge Wells, Eastbourne, Tangmere, Andover, Benson, Halton and Bassingbourne, with Flying Officer Grainger doing some solo aerobatics. On the 20th, Flight Lieutenant Tomkins, Flying Officers Mumford, Cameron and Coulcher were part of the Whitehall flypast taken by the Prime Minister.

Cyprus Again
Anthony Mumford:

'We changed from fighter to ground attack just as we were about to go to Cyprus and none of us had ever done this. This was on the Friday and on the Monday the first inboard drop-tanks arrived. We did not have a two-seater but did have a two-seat Vampire. On Wednesday we were doing our first air-to-ground firing, which was quite exciting as we were normally at 40,000 feet. I got sent home for a low warning; what happened was that I'd been briefed that we were against a 15 foot square target and was told to start firing when the fixed "X" was slightly bigger that the target, and cease fire when it was slightly smaller. Unfortunately, it was only a ten foot target, so doing as I'd been briefed, frightened the range officer to death, so we all had to be re-briefed.

On Thursday all went well on a long cross-country with four drop tanks – two hours, 40 minutes. On the following Monday or thereabouts, we left for Orange, then on to Malta. Here the experts decided that because of a tail wind we could get from Malta to Cyprus in one go, by-passing El Adem. So we did this and got to Cyprus without further delay.'

Squadron haunts in Cyprus were 'Angelo's', and 'Chanticleer', where everyone was able to study the current belly-dancer, and 'Charlie's Bar', where the last night of the month party was held. Next morning, seven pilots were Cat 3 and three Cat 4, which was roundly attributed to an octopus dish. There was a lot of tension with the Greeks at this time and some of the pilots thought the food had been fixed! These detachments were fine but one had to keep alert. A bomb in a settee in the airmen's mess caused some casualties, and on another occasion, 54 Squadron had a bomb planted in an officer's bag which exploded just before it was loaded into a Comet. After that, departures were kept a secret until the last possible moment.

Another incident on Cyprus involved Ted Hassig. He was ordered off to do a sector recco and decided to do this off the coasts of Egypt and Libya, which almost started a war.

The final couple of days on the island were taken up with tests with the long-range tanks and then on 10 October, the Squadron set off for Malta for the two-day trip home. On this trip, they were the first single-seat squadron to get all their aircraft to Cyprus on the same day, and all back to the UK on the same day. By this time, the Squadron's role had definitely become one of ground attack, and by December the pilots were firing rockets at Holbeach range. Flying Officer B J Dimmock was the best of the novice pilots on one sortie. A snag on the Hunter's rocket rails caused two rockets to fire at once and he scored two direct hits! Chuck Coulcher recalls Barry Dimmock:

'I took Barry up on an air-to-air sortie at Acklington and told him that if he lost sight of me or the tow aircraft, to yell out. So we were flying about, firing at the flag, and the next thing I knew was that he had flown right through the tow rope between the Meteor and the flag, cutting it adrift with his wing. Of course, I got the blame – the reason escapes me now – but these things happen.'

Rocketing continued into the new year of 1960, the Squadron being kept hard at it. At the AOC's inspection this year, Air Vice-Marshal C Hartley DFC was the inspecting officer. The Squadron Standard was paraded in a 25-knot wind and later the flag bearer suggested, obviously with some feeling, putting a cross-wind limitation order on Standard parading, in the Flying Order Book!

Mark Tomkins recalls a visit by an Iranian General to the Squadron, who wanted to fly supersonic. Mark was a little concerned because the man refused to wear a flying helmet which was going to be difficult flying at height. However, Mark took him out over the Wash, going fairly fast, and informed him they were now supersonic(!). He didn't know the difference and seemed more than satisfied.

At the end of May ten aircraft were fitted with two x 230-gallon and two x 100-gallon drop tanks, took off for Malta, refuelled, then headed off to Nicosia, Cyprus. This was another first – the first Hunter squadron to fly to the island in only two legs; two hours, 40 to Malta, then two hours to Cyprus. During air-to-air practice, Flight Lieutenant Harry Davidson scored 100%. He fired 60 rounds and the flag showed more holes due to flag rippling. The Squadron diary says it was 50 rounds, but as Harry explains:

'We fired 60 rounds as ammunition came in boxes of 30 so armourers re-armed the aircraft using two boxes of 30 linked together. I scored 60 out of 60 although I wasn't totally sure myself but it was marked so, therefore I accepted it. And I received a signal of congratulations from the C-in-C, Fighter Command.'

On mid-summer day, the CO, with Chuck Coulcher, Harry Davidson with Tony Chaplin, flew a long-range sortie to a new destination while making a trial flight. Chuck Coulcher:

'We were the first Hunters to land at Diyarboukir (Turkey) and the main thing was to make sure we could restart our engines after landing. We were cleared to do all the things ourselves but we would need AVPIN to start-up. We had been told this had been delivered so off we went. The reason for the trial was to see if we could get aircraft across Africa via this route.

Having landed, no one was found who could speak English but they all seemed clear that no AVPIN was around, so we decided to hunt about. Finally, in the corner of a hangar – a pretty primitive place – we spotted some packing cases on which the local storeman slept. Underneath this chap's bedroll we found the missing AVPIN.'

Having got their aircraft going, they taxied out in single file the next morning for take-off, just before some Turkish F-84s were coming in to land. Harry Davidson takes up the story:

'The four of us taxied down the runway in line astern and began to swing round for take-off. Chuck was a little slow and I a bit quick so in order not to hit his tail with my wing I moved a bit to the left and Tony moved even further to the left and ran off the concrete onto some tarmac which did not take the weight and it sank in. Seeing his second pair were stuck, the CO told us to sort it out – we're off!

The Hunter was eventually lifted out – after the F-84s were diverted, not best pleased – by about 500 Turkish soldiers who came marching along, after we had refused some chaps trying to jack it out, which would have damaged the wing. The soldiers got underneath the Hunter and stretched their backs and heaved it out.

Next morning Tony, having left his brakes on while parked, had dissipated his accumulator, so lost his breaks and as we two started up, he rolled down an incline in a gentle curve and hit the controller's caravan. This damaged the nose cone which houses the radar, putting paid to our flight. We called Nicosia and they sent out our EO, John Griffiths, in a Hastings, bringing with him a new nose cone.

However, while this was sorted he found damage to the nose wheel was such that it would be a risk if raised, for it might not come down again. So he proposed to fly back with wheels down, but locking the nose wheel in place so that if Tony had to raise them in an emergency, the nose wheel would stay down. We headed directly for Cyprus and despite being low on fuel we got there.'

Meantime, while all this was going on, the CO and Chuck Coulcher had continued with the trip:

'The CO and I did the whole trip, which was quite exciting, really to prove that we could reinforce the Middle East quickly by going round all the staging posts to Nairobi and back.

As the boss and I were heading back across Africa, flying pretty close together, I glanced across and saw that he still had the pin in his ejector seat inserted. I wondered if I should say anything or be tactful and keep quiet. But it worried me that he may just need it so I called across. All he said was, "Oh." We were at 42,000 feet and he began wobbling about as he tried to reach behind and above to pull the pin but later I noticed he had not managed it.

As it happened we had the most hairy landing I've ever had coming into Sharjah. From 30,000 feet we could see Sharjah, the Persian Gulf, everything, but in those days we could only get contact from about 150 miles and as we did so we were advised that we were clear to come straight in. Sharjah then was just a sand strip, with a line of black barrels out into the desert pointing towards the landing centre line. We both headed down but at about 1,000 feet there was a dust/salt layer and once into that we could only see about half a mile. By then we were committed but couldn't see a thing. We came in on dead reckoning and missed it.

Going round again and this time we were coming into the sun which didn't help, and suddenly these oil barrels were beneath us. The boss began to weave over them almost like a slalom, but we got down luckily. It was so hot there you could fry an egg on the wing surface. In fact I did!'

According to Chuck Coulcher's log-book, the flight times were as follows: Nicosia to Diyarboukir (Turkey) – 1.40; to Sharjah (Saudi Arabia) 2.55; to Khormaksar (Aden) 2.35; to Embakazi (Kenya) 2.25; back to Khormaksar 2.30; to Sharjah 2.55, to Bahrein 1.10; total flying time 15 hours, 30 minutes, in Hunter FG9 XF454.

With the Navy

Before returning to the UK, the Squadron had its first link-up with HMS *Ark Royal*, in July. In a combined exercise – 'Pink gin' on the 13th – the Hunters made a simulated attack on the carrier at low level. Flying at .91 mach, none of the aircraft were intercepted by Navy Scimitars before they reached the ship, which probably made the Navy people think. The Squadron returned to home base on the 27th.

The usual Battle of Britain displays were undertaken again this year, and then November proved an embarrasing time. Twice within a week Flying Officer R C Humphreyson experienced a jammed starboard wheel causing Cat 3 damage, and then he had a tyre burst on landing in XE628.

On the first occasion, the 11th, Harry Davidson had flown lead and landed first. Climbing out he walked towards the runway with helmet in hand, in case there was a need to get to Roy Humphreyson in a hurry. However, Roy got down alright, except for the emergency landing, and so Harry began to walk back. Next thing he knew the 'blood wagon' came rushing up, and despite his protestations, he was bundled into the ambulance and taken to sick quarters where he finally managed to persuade the Doc he was not suffering from stress and it really was not him whom they should have 'rescued'!

Humphreyson's second mishap occurred on the 18th, the same day Barry Dimmock hit his leaders's jet wash during a stream landing. Dimmock overshot, leaving his port wheel behind. Coming round again he landed on the starboard wheel but this sheered off as he touched down. XE622 came to rest on just its nose wheel, one wing and belly, 20 yards off the left-hand side of the runway – Cat 4. The month ended with Mac Cameron having a bird strike on a ground attack sortie in XF519 but only suffered damage to the port leading edge.

In December John Phipps left for Staff College, Bracknell, his place taken by Squadron Leader P V Pledger. Barry Dimmock was killed in a flying accident off the Cowden Ranges on 2 March 1961, stalling his Hunter following a practice rocket attack. He had only been married the previous August. Also in March Mac Cameron left to go to 92 Squadron. He too was to die in a crash later in his career.

Record Flight to Malta

April brought another first, or in truth, a top. With preparations underway for Cyprus and exercise 'Fabulist' the record for a flight from UK to Malta was up for grabs, as Harry Davidson recalls:

'Such a flight was impractical until the Hunter Mark 6 was uprated into the Mark 9 – the essential difference being the provision of 2 x 230-gallon overload tanks which replaced the 100-gallon tanks of the 6. There were also other improvements such as the provision of a radio compass which improved navigational accuracy. The instigator of the flight was Wing Commander Harry Bennett AFC, OC Flying at Stradishall, who did the administrative work of securing the agreement of the AOC No.38 Group (the Stradishall Wing had transferred from Fighter to Transport Command at the beginning of the year) and the blessing of the Royal Aero Club.

The Royal Aero Club had rules governing record flights so it would be officially timed by them. The record which existed had been set by a RN Scimitar with a time of two hours, 12 minutes for a flight between London and Valetta. The rules required that the flight started from an airfield further away from Valetta than London and terminated at a point further away from London to Valetta. These requirements were best met by Farnborough to Luqa. Stradishall would have qualified too but the distance from there to Luqa was too great for the Hunter FGA9 flying at maximum speed. The distance from London to Valetta was 1,298 miles but Farnborough to Luqa was 1,305.33. The timing was taken from Farnborough to Luqa and then corrected to the official distance.

For reasons which are well known today, a condition of the attempt was that it had to be part of a routine deployment to Cyprus to avoid media criticism. As No.1 Squadron was due to deploy to Cyprus in April, Wing Commander Bennett invited the Squadron to provide a pair of aircraft, one of which would be flown by himself. Our CO, Squadron Leader Peter Pledger, had recently joined the Squadron and nominated me to undertake the planning and execution of the flight as neither he nor the OC Flying had experience of such a flight, whereas I had participated in four previous deployments to Malta and beyond.

The two aircraft were deployed to Farnborough on 24 April 1961 and the flight began the following day, We were exceedingly fortunate as the Farnborough Met Office provided us with a perfect forecast – a north-west jet stream of 80-100 knots over France at between 35,000 and 40,000 feet. We took off as a pair and carried out a right-hand circle to overfly the timing mark at speed – a difficult decision, as the circle consumed considerable fuel whilst a straight run meant a starting speed of zero and would thus take longer.

The flight was uneventful, the French air traffic co-operative (they didn't know the purpose of the flight) and the weather excellent, allowing us to see Malta from 100 miles away. We landed well below the official minimum fuel state of 300 lbs (approx 40 gallons) and this was our only cause for anxiety. We were met on landing by the Air Commodore Malta and the Station Commander Luqa. After refuelling we went on to Cyprus to join the detachment. We learned on arrival that Uri Gagarin had been into space for the first time on the same day, making our puny effort somewhat insignificant! My copy of the subsequent press release notes our time was two hours, three minutes, eight seconds over a distance of 1,298 miles at an average speed of 633.33 mph.'

Cyprus ended at the start of May and in June the Squadron deployed to the island of Sylt, Germany. This seaside location was 'enjoyed' by many fighter RAF squadrons over the years, to some extent due to some local beaches which allowed nude bathing, which apparently proved an attraction. Of course, the Germany squadrons did not think much of Fighter Command squadrons coming to Sylt and pinching the best summer slots.

Flying Officer Humphreyson was in bother again on the 15th – in an aeroplane. Returning to dispersal in XG253 both drop tanks were explosively jettisoned onto the taxi track. Some damage was sustained by flying debris and the suspected fault was thought to be an intermittent electrical fault in the tank circuitry.

No sooner had it returned from northern Germany than the Squadron were called to three day

Readiness – at 24 hours notice – for an operational deployment to Kuwait, which was under threat from Iraq. To bring all aircraft up to date on progressive servicing, and modify them for deployment by fitting LRTs, flying was cancelled. All guns were re-harmonised – twice – blast deflectors removed, which kept the ground crews working to 10 pm most nights. While this was going on the pilots were spending considerable time on intelligence briefings, tank recognition tests, and small arms firing. In the second week of July the state moved from 24 hours to three days and was finally cancelled.

Squadron Leader Pledger returned from a high altitude operational turn round exercise on Bempton Range on 20 July and on landing it was discovered that some damage had occurred to the drop tanks, from discarded shell cases. Although the tanks had been holed, fuel transfer failure did not happen. In August, Air Vice-Marshal R N Bateson DSO DFC was the Annual Inspecting Officer, during which he presented a Commendation to Sergeant N Biggs.

Mark Tomkins recalls a party:

> 'Together with another squadron, more than likely 54, we had a party which eventually got pretty lively as parties tend to do. At one stage the boys were burning squadron numbers into the carpet by spraying lighter fuel, then setting it alight. A young provost marshal officer arrived and decided to order everyone out because there had been a fire incident. Needless to say the only one who "went out" was him!
>
> Next day an inquiry was instigated and the mass of evidence pointed to a few pilots having a quiet drink, but who were then disturbed by the arrival of a drunken provost marshal officer! No further action was taken.'

* * *

For once September's various displays did not feature in the Squadron's program quite so much as exercise Gulf Ranger II. Flight Lieutenant D Whittaker took Flying Officer Humphreyson, Flight Lieutenant B J Scotford and Flying Officer J R Owen on this sortie flying from base to Malta, then to El Adem on the 19th. Two days later they headed for Khartoum, escorted by a 32 Squadron Canberra, where they made a night landing. The trip continued on the 23rd with a journey to Bahrein via Sharjah, and while at Bahrein they flew a recce of the Kuwait area.

The 26th saw the pilots fly to Tehran, then after refuelling, they headed for Nicosia. During this leg, Dave Whittaker experienced a single generator failure in XE584 but this was put right by 43 Squadron on Cyprus. The next day they returned to Stradishall, via Luqa, having flown a total of 101.35 hours, which reflected credit on the work of the Squadron's ground personnel.

In October, the CO, Flight Lieutenants Duncan Allison, T Page and R J Quarterman flew over the same route. Again, the leader's aircraft, Pledger's XG253, had a problem, this time with the fuel transfer pressure and then a brake unit snag at Nicosia.

During the summer the Squadron had been helping to train Forward Air Controllers with their joint ground-attack work. In October too, two Mark 9s and the T7 all sustained debris damage during live strikes on Stamford PTA although the pilots did not fly below their safety heights.

RAF Waterbeach

A move of station became scheduled for November 1961, as Number One had been at Stradishall for 3½ years now. However, before this could be fully implemented the Squadron were off on exercise 'Neuralgia', based at El Adem for one month, where it was the only ground-attack unit, except RN aircraft for one day, providing fighter support.

Back in the UK and having got themselves installed at Waterbeach, near Cambridge, they began using Cowden, and Theddlethorpe ranges off the Suffolk coast, the air-to-ground training, and it was back to the old days with increases in bird strikes and ricochet damage to the aeroplanes.

They returned to El Adem APC in May '62. Here the ranges were not affected by the English weather but the stony desert floor still helped cause ricochet damage. On the 13th the Squadron's 50th Birthday was celebrated with a huge cake and champagne. The bar at El Adem was well patronised during the deployment and frequent excursions to the beach club at Tobruk were organised, which also embraced Bar-B-Qs and bingo sessions. Great interest was also shown in water ski-ing, Duncan Allison holding the record for the longest inadvertent under-water tow! When bills were sorted out, the amount for liquid refreshment totalled £315 for the period of the detachment [and this was 1962 prices!].

More training at home in the summer, a BBC TV crew recorded a flypast by the Squadron to mark the 50th Anniversary of British Military Aviation, then in October it was off to Bahrain, relieving 43 Squadron. The situation in Kuwait was again a concern and everyone was briefed on the current situation.

The Boater tradition

It was during Peter Pledger's period of command that the tradition of wearing a straw boater appears to have been born. According to Tom Lecky-Thompson the idea stemmed from him, with the help of Podge Page and John Spencer, because it was felt that when attending any social functions with the Americans they needed suitable head-gear, but with a difference! It was decided that boaters should be taken on visits in the cockpits and arriving at the parking slots everyone would shut down engines simultaneously, open canopies together, bone-domes off and boaters on, then all stand up together. As Tom Lecky-Thompson also recorded:

'Our best arrival was into Bahrain, via El Adem, Khartoum, Aden and Masirah; 12 departed and ten arrived together. We were met by the Station Commander who was not impressed by our head-gear and said, with what he hoped was a tone of regret, that it was such a shame we would not be able to attend the evening function in the Mess as it was DJs. To this we replied in unison: "Oh, don't worry, Sir, we knew, and we all have our DJs with us!" The look on his face was but the start of a typical No.1 Squadron riotous evening.

We also introduced the golf umbrella for a heat shade over the Hunter cockpits. When I put that idea as the spec for the Harrier, the engineering branch at PE would not agree unless it was fashioned with a cranked shaft, so that the pilots would not be able to use them on the beaches at the weekends. Typical!'

The boater tradition remains and is often worn at functions, reunions and the like, although probably less likely to be taken into Harrier cockpits today.

1 Squadron's first trip to Pakistan

Flight Lieutenant P Millard and Flying Officer M Perkins had a near-miss with a USAF Globemaster whilst climbing away from base under GCA Control, which was a bit disconcerting, but then came a two-day good-will visit to Mauripur (Karachi). Flight Lieutenant M Akber of the Pakistan Air Force was on an exchange posting with 1 Squadron and he led the CO, Allison and Mike Perkins eastwards. The formation was intercepted 90 miles from their destination by five PAF Sabres and two F-104s, and escorted in. On arrival a small reception was held and later the CO and Mo Akbar attended a dinner party at the UK High Commissioner's residence while the other two were entertained at another party celebrating the anniversary of Revolution Day in Pakistan.

Meantime, one Hunter which had been left at Orange on the trip down due to engine trouble had been under repair. This seen to, Flight Lieutenant B L Scotford began to follow on on the 28th. 100 miles from Khormaksar out over the Med the aircraft had rear bearing failure. Brian Scotford turned back as his rpm dropped to 5,000 revs. He jettisoned his tanks and called a Mayday, but he was never going to make it, and had to eject 35 miles out. Although he suffered slight compression damage to a vertebrae, he was safely rescued by a helicopter crew.

While all this was happening the remaining pilots were at Sharjah firing rockets and cannon into the Jebajib range. Tom Lecky-Thompson scored the first 100 percent air-to-ground score for some considerable time.

The Royal Navy saw the Squadron again on 6 November. Four Hunters led by Duncan Allison flew a strike against the frigate *Loch Alvie*. This achieved a fair amount of success considering it was some time since anyone had flown an anti-shipping strike. Returning to the UK in early December, bad weather over England caused a diversion to Wattisham but they were finally home on the 6th. Squadron Leader Pledger was posted out soon afterwards, his replacement being Squadron Leader F L Travers-Smith.

His term of office was no doubt viewed initially with mixed feelings after the New Year. Bad weather curtailed flying so the new boss organised a team race between 1 and 54 Squadrons around the airfield with alcoholic beverages as a prize at noon, donated by himself. Needless to say with such a tempting prize, No.1 Squadron got their last man home 23 seconds before 54 Squadron.

To help the dreary month along there was a successful dining-out night for Peter Pledger, and a pilgrimage to the Sly Brewery, as well as a five-a-side soccer game. Then came a visit to an all-in wrestling event in Cambridge, followed by curry, then a house-warming by the new CO. Squadron strength now was 20 officers, one warrant officer, 17 SNCOs, 22 corporals and 35 airmen. The aircraft as February got underway were six FGA9s, three Mark 6s which had just arrived, and the T7.

This month Allison led a small detachment on a three-day visit to Gutersloh, Germany, while on the 13th and 14th, Flight Lieutenant Tom Lecky-Thompson experienced not one but two flame-outs in XG195. The engine was changed.

El Adem APC came around with grinding regularity in April, this time an emphasis being put on operational aspects. Prior to arriving at the range, a low-level cross-country flight lasting 28 minutes was completed, and as soon as each pilot had completed four such sorties he went onto a tactical operational (TACOP) pattern, firing on every pass. Once a rhythm had been established, scores were very good.

All this was marred by the loss of an USAF exchange pilot on the 24th. Captain Frank Matthews went into the sea in a Hunter, off Set Tehami, Libya, and was killed. He had been attached to the Squadron for the detachment primarily as range safety officer, but he had also achieved a considerable number of flying hours during his stay. The cause of the crash remained unknown.

To RAF West Raynham

As the summer wore on so came another move of base, this time to West Raynham in mid-August. Again, they had hardly settled in before they were off once more to El Adem APC at the beginning of September. John Phipps was now the WingCo Flying and within a short time he in turn handed over to another previous boss, Peter Pledger.

The following year restrictions were placed on the aircraft that proved unacceptable. Pilots were limited to pulling +6 'G' while it was easy to pull +7 'G' at normal operating speeds. The new order was also taking a technical inspection up to 40 hours. This also reduced rocket scores on the ranges. By the end of September 1964 100-gallon LRTs were replacing the 230-gallon ones, which were only to be used on ferry flights, but the +6 'G' limitation remained in force. Thus the Squadron were obliged to train with aircraft using an unrealistic configuration.

Nevertheless, it was back to El Adem in November for a three-week APC during which the Squadron fired 877 rockets and 15,822 rounds of cannon ammunition. El Adem threw down a sporting gauntlet, offering a Challenge Cup, open to visiting squadrons, against the Station strength. 1 Squadron rose to this patronising challenge and won in hockey, squash, tennis and volley-ball, while soccer was drawn; only basketball and badminton were lost. This made them overall winners – another first.

December and another change in command, this time an old-boy – Squadron Leader D C G Brook – arriving to take over from Travers-Smith:

'Frank Travers-Smith handed over command to me in December 1964. The organisation was agreeably simple: CO in command, A and B Flights commanded by Flight Lieutenants Tommy Thompson and Jerry Seavers (inevitably known as Tom and Jerry), 12 pilots, an engineering officer, an army ground liaison officer, a secretarial officer adjutant, a warrant officer and about 80 SNCOs and other ranks.

We had 12 Hunter FGA 9s and a T7 two-seater. The FGA 9 was a derivative of the Mark 6, strengthened for ground attack and armed with up to 12 High Explosive Semi-Armour Piercing (HE/SAP) rockets, or napalm tanks, in addition to the Hunter's standard 4 x 30 mm Aden cannon. We often flew with 2 x 230-gallon drop tanks on the inboard pylons and had the option of carrying 1 x 100-gallon drop tanks outboard to give us a ferry range of about 1,300 nautical miles. In addition a tail parachute on the Mark 9 reduced the landing run, thereby giving greater flexibility in choice of airfield.

The Squadron's concept of operations had changed markedly since my time as a junior pilot in 263 Squadron when we were re-numbered No.1 in July 1958. Then, we were, in the first place, high-level day fighter interceptors armed only with cannon. By 1964 the Raynham Wing was well established as an air mobile force, trained to deploy as required within Allied Command Europe to attack enemy armoured and other targets. We also had a national "gun-boat" role and within two months of taking command, HMG sent us to Gibraltar at the time Spain threatened to close the frontier. On 12 February 1965 we flew eight Hunters to RAF North Front, Gibraltar, with guns loaded and ready. There we stayed until 5 March, marking the British presence with training sorties including air-to-sea gunnery against a splash target towed by the Royal Navy.

Deployment to the Royal Norwegian Air Force base at Bodø followed a fortnight later [four aircraft had already been to Bodø in January, Ed.], for Nato exercise "Cold Winter", and it was indeed cold. Our Hunters had to be left in the open overnight and we needed large amounts of anti-freeze to free-up the flying controls. Taxying on the icy airfield surfaces was a skill one had to develop quickly. Against an invading "enemy" we flew pre-planned "attacks" (nothing fired or dropped but release range, dive angle etc, checked on gun-sight recorder film to assess effectiveness) on less mobile targets such as fuel dumps and, in addition, armed reconnaissance (seek and destroy) missions against tanks, armoured personnel carriers and artillery. Raw herrings for breakfast at 0530 presented British stomachs with a minor challenge and one more meal – to us equally eccentric –

was served at 1600. After my urgent plea to RAF West Raynham, each of us was awarded a modest daily cash subsidy to buy more familiar food down town. I tried to make sure that this was not spent on expensive Norwegian alcoholic refreshment but I doubt if I succeeded!

A month later we flew to El Adem for a four-week concentrated APC. The 3.5" R/P was great fun to fire. The training version had a 60 lb lump of concrete as a "warhead". Its ex-WW2 rocket motor burnt relatively slowly so the projectile was severely affected by gravity, wind velocity and any movement of the aircraft while firing. A steep dive and firing range of about 1,000 yards helped but too often the rockets impacted 20 yards or more from the target, despite the modification to our gun-sights to allow for wind effect and gravity drop. Culmination of R/P training was to fire all 12 HE warheads at a vehicle-size target in the desert. The dust, smoke and shock wave from the exploding rockets were gratifying and impressive but the target, a large rusty boiler, was depressingly resilient! Probably more lethal were our four cannon. We normally shot 30-50% of our rounds through a 15 feet square canvas target, stood up at about 45° from the vertical. When firing explosive ammunition from all four cannon we obliterated the targets. During my time in command we did not drop napalm but we trained to deliver it from a level pass 50 feet above the ground or in a 10° dive, aiming to drop a 4 lb practice bomb on a "court" in front of two canvas targets set side by side.'

Practically the whole of May was spent in the desert. The previous year, Flight Lieutenant C Boyack had organised a Squadron Museum at home base, contributions coming not only from present records, but previous squadron members, as far back as WW1. At El Adem in 1965, Museum funds were boosted following a 'casino' gaming evening, which followed a successful cocktail party.

In 1964, Mr Leslie Hunt, a well known aviation author and historian, who had himself been in the RAF until 1959, contacted the Squadron to inform them that one of their old Spitfire 21s (LA225) was rotting away at RAF Cardington. This quickly galvanised everyone and it was not long before this machine was pride of place amongst 1 Squadron's historical artefacts. LA225 had been with the Squadron in 1945 and it is still with them, non-flying, but otherwise in pristine condition.

Back in UK, a successful summer visit to Whitbread's Brewery in London kept up the dedication of squadron personnel in making sure these well-established institutions remained in the fore-front of everyday life. Whitbreads also presented them with a pub sign which had previously hung outside the 'True Briton', a hostelry patronised by former members of the Squadron when it was based at Lympne during the war. It had a painting of an ancient Briton on one side, a Battle of Britain pilot on the other. David Brook continues:

'During the summer of 1965, training from our base at West Raynham included Fighter Reconnaissance, "attacking" military targets under the direction of a ground-based Forward Air Controller (FAC) and acting as enemy "bombers" for Lightning air defence interceptors during exercise "Tiger Camp". For our own training during this exercise we 'attacked' targets such as bridges and crossroads in Scotland and north-east England. We were allowed only limited evasion against the Lightnings but, thanks to moist air causing heavy contrails, we could see the defenders in plenty of time to evade their "attacks" with air-to-air missiles. In dry air during the following summer, however, the Lightnings scored heavily against us.

Exercise "Dazzle" in October 1965 was a major joint services exercise in the Libyan desert. We had already completed an APC at El Adem in September, and we were joined there by substantial RAF detachments, including Canberras, Hunter FR 10s and an Air Control Centre plus radar. To our surprise we were occasionally tasked on air defence sorties, generally failing to catch "enemy" Vulcan bombers flying at around 45,000 feet. Most of our flying, however, was in support of ground forces under forward air control or on armed recces beyond the Forward Line of Own Troops (FLOT). I think it was before the start of exercise "Dazzle" that the GOC No.3 Division visited us, as we were to fly in support of his units. I vividly remember his initial comment on seeing our line of aircraft: "That's my anti-tank force and it's lined up like a row of soldiers waiting to be shot!" I was very embarrassed and set about trying to disperse our aircraft around the airfield. But in those days we did not have enough ground equipment to operate from dispersals, which was something that was well and truly rectified when the Harriers came into service.'

During this period, Squadron Leader Brook led six aircraft to Cyprus for an operational shoot on the range at Larnaca. They landed at Nicosia and returned the next day. 'Dazzle' involved all three services and the land battle took place west of El Adem, the latter place being used as a Forward Air

Base. Malta and Cyprus units were used for strikes against El Adem, while the Royal Navy provided aircraft for close support of the 'enemy'. No.1 Squadron's air defence work was also flown against RAF Javelins. In total they flew 157 sorties covering 141 flying hours. David Brook:

'After varied training during the winter of 1965-66, we deployed in April to the RNAS base at Yeovilton, simulating a deployment to a "bare base". We therefore lived in tents and brought our own engineering and admin/domestic support. The only official contact with the RN was to arrange air combat with their Sea Vixens as part of exercise "Lifeline". But in the first place this was a close air support exercise under FAC. The operational value of this form of support appeared to us to be dubious when, from the air, we could see concentrations of armour etc, on the other side of the hill beyond the view of the ground based FAC. (FAC from a helicopter appears to have been rare at this time.)

With training, the FACs became quite skilful at guiding us to single tanks and other targets. Coloured smoke fired by artillery and landing near the target helped – the air mobile artillery in those days probably not having the clout to disable enemy tanks. It was explained to us that timely air support could influence a land battle favourably and that aircraft with heavier war-loads, such as the Canberra, were better suited to tasks beyond the FLOT. But without a better system of target marking, such as the laser now in service, our close air support was not as effective as the army, or ourselves, would have liked.

During exercise "Lifeline" the Sea-Vixens kept our look-out sharpened. We had to fly further apart (2-3,000 yards) in line abreast formation to see them in time to evade their "Red-Top" missiles. The same applied in the case of the Lightnings, but the difference was that the Lightnings intercepted us above 20,000 feet, whereas the Sea-Vixens "attacked" us flying at 250 feet above ground level to and from the close-support missions. Within the constraints of the limited evasion allowed, some exciting situations arose and all concerned learnt some important lessons.

May and the first half of June 1966 saw us once again at El Adem for APC. During this, No.32 Squadron, flying Canberras, bet us a case of champagne that we could not fly some 300 miles out into the desert to find the wrecked US Liberator, "Lady Be Good", which crashed during WW2. Craftily using an oil firm's radio beacon, Jerry Seavers and I won the bet, bringing back gun-sight recorder film to substantiate our claim to the champagne. We got away with it by the skin of our teeth because we started to search ten miles too far to the west but fortunately realised our mistake before our fuel states became critical. I've always thanked my lucky stars that nothing went wrong. As it was an unofficial, spur of the moment bet, we never made any Search and Rescue arrangements in the event of baling out. Like the unfortunate B24 crew, we might have got a bit thirsty.

Routine training flying from our home base in July and August included the Lightning combats we had done before, and in early September we deployed to Norway, this time to Andoya, for NATO exercise "Bar-Frost". Andoya is a somewhat remote island about 70 miles south-west of Tromso and we were briefed that we would find a girl under every tree .... but, as we quickly found, there aren't any trees! Flying on the exercise was varied and interesting, including "attacks" against troops and convoy targets under FAC, recce missions, pre-planned "attacks" against buildings and fuel dumps in the Arctic Circle – close to the border with Russia – and a carefully planned and co-ordinated strike against the airfield at Bodø, as well as R/P "attacks" against Fast Patrol Boats.'

Jeremy Seavers also recalls the 'Lady Be Good' incident:

'No.32 Squadron were deployed at El Adem while Akrotiri runway was being re-surfaced. Their boss, Mike Waters, in the usual bar-room banter between squadrons stated that a Hunter outfit had no chance of finding the "Lady Be Good". Well, you do not make statements like that without a challenge – the prize being a crate of beer (no draught at El Adem). David Brooks and I worked out a plan for flying a creeping-line-ahead search with the believed position of the crashed B24 in the centre of that range. In the event we were almost at the end of the available fuel when we found the crashed aircraft. It actually proved much easier to see than we had expected, for apart from a broken fuselage and bent propellers, it was very much intact. We took gun camera film and a shot from our G90 nose cameras to prove the find and earn our beer. A good evening was had by one and all. This flight occurred on 23 May 1966 and our sortie length was two hours 15 minutes. Very sadly, Mike Waters was killed not long afterwards in a boating accident in Cyprus, run over by a ski-motor boat.

Another story of interest concerning inter-squadron rivalry was the time some of the younger pilots on 1 Squadron decided that it would be a good jape to pinch a 54 Squadron Hunter. This was secreted from their line and towed to the far side of West Raynham airfield and hidden. There was then much merriment watching an increasingly concerned 54 Squadron counting aeroplanes and searching around before slowly coming to the obvious conclusion and visiting 1 Squadron in force.'

David Brook – later Air Vice-Marshal, and after commanding 1 Squadron – left in October 1966, his place taken over by Squadron Leader G 'Spike' Jones.

Shortly before the year end, Flight Lieutenant P B Curtin ran into a problem returning from a gunnery mission to the Cowden Range. Pete's engine began to fail and although he tried to get into Leconfield had finally to eject short of the runway as the engine seized. The Hunter dived into the nearby village writing off several houses and cars, and also blew the back wall out of the rectory, much to the surprise of the vicar who was in his toilet at the time, and suffered a broken arm. Embarrassingly, the vicar was also chaplain to the airfield.

Setting the *Torrey Canyon* ablaze

After timely words by SASAO No.38 Group in a Defence Minister's ear, the Squadron was finally able to drop 'live' napalm in March 1967. The super-tanker *Torrey Canyon* of 61,000 tons, smashed into the Seven Stones Reef off Land's End and began leaking her entire cargo, 118,000 tons of crude oil. Soon the sea had broken her back and the environmental problem, especially to marine and bird life, not to mention shoreline, was going to be terrific. In the end it was decided that the best way of getting rid of the oil was for aircraft to set it all on fire. Navy aircraft bombed the ship on 28 March, set it ablaze, and although Chivenor-based Hunters tried to keep the flames going, this proved difficult. The next day, after the armourers worked all night and as the Station Commander manned the Ops Desk, 1 Squadron sent out three aircraft for the first attacks using napalm – the CO, Flight Lieutenants B K 'Wally' Walton[1] and A R Pollock – each dropping two 100-gallon napalm tanks, explosively from their outboard wing pylons, at 1215. The CO's 'attack' failed to ignite the surface oil, but Wally Walton's drop created a huge fire ball, which forced Alan Pollock to abort his run. However, Alan came round again and dropped his napalm as soon as he entered the smoke. Further attacks needed to be made in the afternoon, including rockets to open up the ship's oil compartments. A further pair were tasked under HMS *Barrosa*'s control for 1500 hours, and three more Hunter 9s, five minutes later. The following afternoon six aircraft dropped a further 12 napalm tanks. Overall the operation was not a massive success but *Torrey Canyon* was great fun and a large target which did not fire back.

The next month aircraft took part in an attack demonstration and flypast as part of HM the Queen's Review of the 16th Parachute Brigade at Aldershot. August, with Exercise Unison on Salisbury Plain, was the first occasion the Squadron's prowess operationally with the new SNEB 68 mm anti-tank rockets, far faster than the trusty 3″ R/P in RAF service for two and a half decades, was on very public display before NATO VIPs. The key targets were accurately destroyed on the first pass, further witness to the value of so many live weapons fired and simulated strike sorties practised.

It was back to Gibraltar in September that year as Spain was still sabre-rattling. This detachment, committing one fully armed pair of Hunters, would extend for three years, alternating with 54 Squadron and was later shared with the Chivenor OCU staff, having to maintain a small British presence on the Rock for moral support. 1 and 54 Squadron pilots generally liked the diversion, especially during the summer months, flying down from St Mawgen or via Decimomannu in Sardinia, depending on upper winds and arrival weather.

The Squadron won the inter-squadron shoot for the Buchanan Trophy in October, all aircraft using not only cannon but rockets and practice bombs. 54 Squadron were a massive second in these competitive single pass, operational attacks – a result. In firing practise continuity terms, even more satisfying for No.1 since they were just about to go off to their twice annual Libyan Armament Practise Camp, thus starting at an initial advantage to 54.

At El Adem in November, the aircraft again as in May, practised with SNEB, the 68 mm French anti-tank rocket pods under the wings. Night ground attack trials were also started, which was not universally welcomed, flares being dropped by Canberras. One pilot, Flight Lieutenant Paddy Hughes, suffered a black-out recovering from a standard daylight rocket dive attack on the range, regaining consciousness at low level, several miles from the range, flying towards Egypt – a quite amazing, yet terrifying occurrence.

---

[1] Brian Walton's son Ian, a Tornado pilot, was flying Mystère 2000s on exchange in 1999 and flew with the French airforce during the Kosovo crisis, winning the Croix de Guerre.

The RAF's 50th Birthday

With the 50th anniversary of the formation of the RAF on 1 April 1968, 1 Squadron felt, being themselves 57 years old, a little underwhelmed. However, some celebrations were in order and at West Raynham a Hunter flew low over 54 Squadron's dispersal dropping greetings cards and toilet paper derision out of the airbrakes. Later 1 Squadron had four aircraft doing similar sorties to other airfields. One Lightning from Binbrook retaliated in kind but unfortunately its leaflet bombload also fell on (innocent) 54 Squadron's hangar area.

Flight Lieutenant Alan Pollock had joined the Squadron in late 1966 after a period as adjutant with 43 Squadron at Aden, involved in the post-Radfan and Beihan operations up country.

'No.1's role at Raynham was really enjoyable, hardworking for all and demanding in its variety and scope. I was joining the "Fighting First" ten years exactly after first flying the Hunter F1, yet I am sure there was still plenty to do to remain master of all the Hunter FGA9 could do. Its 30 mm close support punch made us popular with the Army up-country in Aden and the Hunter also took ricochets and ground fire damage well. What intrigued me was the cachet still there in the small UK Hunter force, the pleasure and sense of achievement of the youngsters on being made operational on one of the only six Hunter FGA9 squadrons throughout most of 1967. The old Mark 1 Hunter sorties were invariably 35-45 minutes, any longer would make for Martin-Baker assisted flight. Now, our FGA9s had more than double that sortie length and greatly stretched potential for ground support, even just using the normal two 230 gallon inboard drop tanks.

During my time on the Squadron we had two splendid and popular USAF exchange pilots, firstly Billy Allfrey and then a former Thud (F-105) expert from Vietnam, who returned there later, and Pete Albrecht. Both of them at various times would give expressively wry smiles at some of the antics and tactical flying we Brits used in 1 Squadron, partly from our choice, partly from our training necessity, in European weather, in our much smaller air force.

Much had been going on pre-April 1968. With tremendous groundcrew effort in UK and detached down in Gibraltar, we caught up 54 Squadron on flying hours after the Buchanan Trophy, detachments and operational training syllabus cycle of intensive flying in Norway's Arctic Circle to Libya's desert, Cyprus, Germany, Gibraltar and elsewhere.

Then came the cancelled special events for the RAF's 50th anniversary, officially denied later in the press but known to me personally from Red Arrow colleagues. Today it is not easy to recall how desperately low both national and even international morale was before the later events that spring of 1968.

We had been expecting at least a flypast over London to celebrate the RAF's 50th birthday, a standard practice in both earlier and later eras. Nearer the day it became obvious that no formal flypast was going to take place. As senior operational flight commander of the RAF's senior and the world's oldest military air squadron, I felt a particular responsibility lay with us to honour the occasion suitably. As nothing now was going to happen from an airborne point of view, and we were scheduled for a normal training flight to Salisbury Plain, I prevailed upon the boss that we should carry out some leaflet raids to mark the occasion. We carried 57 'One in the Sun' leaflets, compressed in the flaps, one sheet for each full year of our own service, plus an adequate supply of $4^1/_2$" GP (government property) bog-rolls, loaded into and released from the airbrakes. Soon after the Parade and a flap-less take-off I made a good drop above 54 Squadron's pilots outside their crew-room, then tried with less success, the more difficult, rarely known Hunter singleton pass trick, in level, low flight, to plant a supersonic boomlet – staying just a bit higher and faster than ultra low level, since the aircraft would buck slightly at the critical moment, when one reached back with some difficulty, at the speed and altitude, to press the airbrake test switch as fast beyond .92M as one could.

The technique of ultra low level, low speed irreverent leaflet and bogroll delivery in fact was a serious, excellent flying exercise, one of about a dozen extra extensions to sharpen up our skills further in an already delightfully varied syllabus content. Into light surface winds – which one had to offset for the Hunter's airbrake – it could be amazingly accurate lobbing such items into a VIP's sofa!

Other pilots went to other airfields and some responded well while others rang to blast our Station Commander. I saw red at some of the latter. Over the next three days I asked a dozen airmen, without any response, what was significant about this week, and with precious little in the press either. Some of us – the boss, both flight commanders, plus David Ainge and Barry Horton – had been invited down to Tangmere to attend a function there after Mike Webb timed to the second, Freedom of the City flypast fourship over Chichester. Here I found one royal duke and some VIPs 100% ignorant of why they were attending this party in the Tangmere Mess. Having been getting over a heavy cold, and having drugged myself up a bit with anti-histamine tablets, I was lacking sleep, not helped by the do at Tangmere. I still felt someone should flagwave at least once over the Houses of Parliament this anniversary week, if only for 50 years of such splendid ground crew and our WW2 ex-servicemen.

London lay astride my straight-line return route to West Raynham. All I needed was to lose contact with the others after I was airborne and slip off unobserved. This I did and headed NNE low down and six minutes later entered London most quietly, throttled back at low speed. Reaching Richmond and the Thames, my aircraft swept over Wandsworth, Battersea, Albert and Chelsea Bridges, crossed Vauxhall and Lambeth Bridges and then suddenly ahead were the Houses of Parliament, in magnificent "earth hath no sight so fair" silhouette. I banked over, climbing to circle Whitehall, opened the throttle, this engine noise interrupting a debate in the House, one that day actually being on Aircraft Noise Abatement! Three times I circled, exactly as Big Ben struck 12 noon. On that brilliant, cloudless Friday, my aircraft "H" (XF442), had empty outboard tanks, which cartoonists would depict as symbolic "bombs" for a beleaguered Wilson government in No.10! With a dip past the RAF memorial and the statue of Viscount Trenchard, I carried on down the River, over Waterloo Bridge, with St Paul's Cathedral under a scaffolding lattice work over on my left, in view. Over London Bridge, then suddenly Tower Bridge was plumb ahead of me. It was easy enough to fly over it but the idea of flying through the spans struck me in a trice.

From a trained low level pilot's point of view it provided an interesting penetration problem. With less than half a mile to go I realised that it would be easy enough to fly through, but what would be the best and safest way? Three seconds on, after an inverse bombing run at and under the top span, for safety of a bus and bridge-crossing traffic, I was through and heading out downstream for Wapping, Greenwich and Hornchurch.'

Alan landed back at base, not long afterwards asking the switchboard girl to put a call through to his wife and other family members about what he'd done and that he would undoubtedly be under close arrest for a few days. He then went off to confess to the CO but found that he, the WingCo and the Station Commander already knew. For his part, the CO was at least relieved that Whitehall hadn't been showered with leaflets. Alan was put under arrest, was inspected by the MO, who found him normal. It was, however, the end of his RAF career. The Squadron had mixed feelings over the matter, but many admired the courage it took. It was another first, of course, the first jet to go through Tower Bridge, and the first pilot ever to go through it downstream. It seems too that he and the others had also flown the last 'operational' fighter sorties out of RAF Tangmere, doyenne RAF fighter base and Battle of Britain Sector 'A' Station. A dozen years later, by then an exporter, Al would half initiate the Tangmere museum project and see its charitable trust, active to this day, set up.

Perhaps significantly there is no mention of this episode in the Squadron diary, although as Alan says: '.. every recruit, ground or air, is supposed to know, from 1918 onwards, that RAF stood for *Resolution, Audacity and Fortitude*.'

*   *   *

Alan Pollock's replacement as flight commander was Ken Parry, and the Squadron were off again to El Adem and the APC. During their time in the desert they took part in exercise 'Crayon', joined by Buccaneers from 801 Squadron FAA. Then in June they sent eight Hunters as part of 38 Group's support display during HM the Queen's Review of the RAF on the 14th, at Abingdon.

Then in August came great news. The Squadron had been chosen to be the first to fly the Harrier vertical jump-jet the following year. In fact they had seen the beginnings of this back in 1964, as the Kestrel Evaluation Squadron had been at West Raynham, the Kestrel being the forerunner of the Harrier. For those who wished to make the analogy, No.1 Squadron would once again become a vertical unit; first the balloon in 1912, now the VTOL role in 1969.

Chapter Seventeen

HARRIER SQUADRON

Squadron Leader Jones ended his tour of duty in mid-September at which time Squadron Leader L A B Baker took over. A National Service u/t pilot in 1952, Bryan Baker had flown Sabres and Hunters, and been a QFI on Vampires. Subsequently he had been on a staff appointment for some time and had come back through the re-training system: refresher training on Jet Provost, then Hunters. In fact he had been preparing to go to 1 Squadron for about ten months. Even at this stage there were hints about the Harrier coming although the question of when was not being talked about.

'I took over on 20 September 1968. At that time life in 38 Group was very busy and demanding of all ranks, for it was the front line Tactical Support provider and its units were the most likely to be required to respond immediately to a variety of crisis situations whether foreseen or not. The watchwords were readiness, versatility and effectiveness, and Nos 1 and 54 Squadrons provided the teeth.

I found my Squadron in three parts. There was a detachment based at Aldergrove in Northern Ireland conducting low level target acquisition trials. Another detachment was taking its turn in Gibraltar where confrontation with the Spanish Air Force's F-104s was a daily ritual. The Squadron was stretched to maintain high serviceability in these two locations whilst maintaining an effective daily training back at West Raynham. There the most pressing and never-ending task was to train up the newest pilots to proficiency and "fully declared" operational status – a NATO requirement from which we could never be excused.

Of course, the two detachments could be conducted only by experienced operational pilots and they had to have very serviceable aircraft. Lame ducks had to be replaced immediately from main base whilst they might take a week to get back to UK in the bowels of a Hercules C-130. To train the inexperienced pilots left at West Raynham also required a core of experienced men and serviceable machines in which the sub-systems were reliable, often easier said than done when there were conflicting demands.

When I took over it was a tired unit but in good heart following a period of remarkable, some said unsustainable, pressures. Over the next six months the external pressures thankfully decreased. During this time we heard that we were to be dismantled as a unit and converted to the Harrier. In the short term I set out to find my scattered assets, visiting the team at Aldergrove on 23 September. As a need arose to fly two aircraft back from Gib in mid-October, I flew out on the weekly RAF transport flight for a couple of relaxing days where I met my senior flight commander, Mike Webb, and pilots Tim Smith and Roger Wholey for the first time. Mike and I ferried back two Hunters, staging through Sardinia to refuel.

It was all a bit of a ritual at Gib. There was a line drawn around the airport and you knew exactly where that line was to the yard. On one side of the railway we could fly, the other side they could fly. You'd make a point of flying exactly as close to the edge as permitted, but it wasn't regarded as smart to go over the line. There was no aggression or animosity, just a case of establishing territory. It was silly in the sense that it was all posturing. We were paid posturers and we did it jolly well – for months – but it was very tedious.

The most exciting thing was the occasion a Russian submarine went through the Straits. We were the first to spot it and followed it over the next several days, almost to Cyprus! We made it a recce task because you could see the thing below the water at the right angle.

Back at West Raynham, with my Squadron more or less together for the first time, we picked up the routine with an intensive weapons training phase in December, including some demanding night close formation flying. Our WingCo, Ron Wood, instigated a series of mass formation attacks with 1 and 54 Squadrons combining to test our airfield defence system, primarily Bloodhound SAMs.

By the end of March we had completed a NATO exercise from Skrydstrup in Denmark and resumed our duties in Gibraltar where we shared alternate six week stints with 54. We also exercised another of our NATO employment options – protecting the Allies' rights to Berlin during two weeks in March and April flying from Gütersloh. It didn't attract much attention and really all we had to do was our standard training job of ground attack and recce, but it was all done from Gütersloh, or somewhere near the air corridors. Again it was a lot of posturing but not an operational situation. It was all over our own territory without provoking the Russians. It was under a tri-partite banner, not NATO, so other NATO powers couldn't be involved. Keeping Berlin open was just with the US, France and Britain.

Then we were off for a month at APC in Libya. Towards the end of May most of the Raynham pilots took part in exercise 'Tracer' which held special significance in view of our planned conversion to the Harrier which would bring our first experience of flying with a head-up display (HUD). Flying very fast at low level, the pilot has to look into the cockpit every few seconds to check performance or navigational parameters. When this information is projected 'head-up' onto the windscreen, a pilot can see it against the background of the outside world which enables him to fly safer/faster/lower. 'Tracer' attempted to establish the benefits to the fast jet at low level in visual flight conditions of having a HUD. Pilots flew along a predetermined course marked by coloured balloons tethered just above treetop height. So, without having to look into the cockpit, pilots were asked to fly at 250 knots and as close to 50 feet above all obstacles as felt safe. It was exhilarating as well as interesting.

Back in UK, with scant time for preparation, we had our Annual AOC's Inspection with a Wing precision flypast of 16 Hunters for which we managed just four rehearsal flights. A month later, in July, we began pre-Harrier training at RAF Ternhill – the RAF's helicopter training school – where we each did six vertical flights to give us our first experience of the sensations which were soon to become so familiar on the Harrier.'

One notable incident occurred during the period in Northern Ireland. Flying Officer Paul Wilcox was flying low above a road and as his Hunter crested a rise he came virtually face to face with four policemen in a car, driving up the incline. At 50 feet and 450 knots, it was quite a 'head-on' for the poor coppers.

Quite suddenly there was a change of CO, just before the APC began. It was a question of rank, the 'powers' dictating that squadrons should now be commanded by wing commanders. Bryan Baker:

'Jimmy Mansell arrived to take over from me just before El Adem. From a personal standpoint I had a dilemma. The arrival of costly new Harriers meant that I would have to hand over my command to a wing commander, although my flying tour had lasted less than a year. I was offered command of another Hunter squadron but that would only delay the inevitable as it too was due to have Harriers. I could stay with 1 Squadron as senior flight commander, not an obviously attractive option, but I wanted to be amongst the first to fly the Harrier operationally, so for me it was Hobson's choice. For many months only the best new pilots out of training had been sent to 1 Squadron. There was not yet a two-seater Harrier or flight-simulator and MoD were not about to sanction un-necessary risks, so we were, in some respects, well prepared for the challenge.'

During this time, on 15 January 1969, Flight Lieutenant D J Page was seen in a dive, his head slumped forward over the controls. He had either suffered a sudden illness or anoxia, and moments later the Hunter (XF517) went into the sea. Then another loss on 21 May was that of Wing Commander J A Mansell. Flying XE616 off the Norfolk coast, he crashed into the sea during a combat manoeuvre, being killed instantly. This was the third loss to a flying family; his father had died on active service with the RAF and a brother had also been killed in a flying accident. Mansell had been the Squadron's A Flight Commander back in 1956-7. Then in July Flight Lieutenant M J Webb was promoted and posted to Bahrein. As a flight commander, Mike Webb had done much valuable work with the Squadron. Bryan Baker continues:

'Another of 1 Squadron's former flight commanders, now Wing Commander Duncan Allison, was selected to replace him. In the meantime, I was to take command again. Then came the downside of our conversion to the Harrier; we were to lose our magnificent ground crew. Whilst the pilots were to be part of the new 1 Squadron at RAF Wittering, the ground personnel, with a few exceptions, were to remain at Raynham maintaining some of the Hunters ready for war just in case of an emergency before we were proficient. Gradually they were posted out and scattered to new jobs, whilst we got to know a new body of men, and some women, on whose skills and commitment we were to become just as dependent.

We were to start converting in two waves. I would be on the second wave and would supervise the Squadron's permanent move to Wittering. Duncan Allison arrived and took command at the beginning of August and went straight into the conversion programme. It was all rather rushed and

Duncan was taken off Harrier training when he encountered difficulties, so I again assumed command whilst another wing commander was sought.

During the tedious move to Wittering there were some administrative problems. We were not supposed to take any furniture or office equipment, being assured that lots of shiny new stuff had been on order for nine months and would be there when we arrived. Each morning I rang my adjutant who had gone on ahead and I could tell by the time he took to pick up the 'phone that it was still on the floor! So we found an extra truck and loaded all our old stuff and took it with us. More difficult was the case of the Squadron's prized Spitfire 21, lovingly restored, preserved and displayed in the hangar. My discreet (I thought) enquiries of West Raynham's Station Commander, Group Captain Basil Lock, alerted me to a problem. It appeared that the RAF Museum had laid claim to it, tacitly supported by the Air Force Board no less. A request to have it moved to our new home would not be sympathetically received, so there was no point in asking. Instead I summoned Graham Eastaugh (F/O), the Squadron's young but resourceful Engineer Officer who could dismantle the Spitfire and had connections at an MU that might be prepared to lend us a "Queen Mary" low-loader.

Raynham's Station HQ was just inside the main gate and on the fateful morning chosen for the move, the Group Captain looked up from his desk at the wrong moment and spotted the "Queen Mary" coming through the gate. As these vehicles are usually associated with badly broken aeroplanes, of which we had none, he was quickly on the telephone to me and my life was threatened. So we had to leave our Spit – after reassembling it – but not too long afterwards it was delivered to us at Wittering thanks to Basil Lock's intervention and influence – via proper channels!

Our conversion timetable was re-written as a result of a number of delays caused mostly by technical problems. There were a number of excitements and dramas during conversion but thankfully no pilots were lost. The failure of critical engine components had to be taken seriously and it was. The Harrier was grounded. Engineers at Wittering and at Rolls-Royce, Bristol, worked round the clock. We pilots kept our hands-in flying Jet Provosts at Cranwell and a few remaining ex-1 Squadron Hunters which had been temporarily redeployed for our use. With the technical problems mostly resolved in a very few weeks, the delayed conversion programme was resumed.

Everyone made mistakes. For some people they were seen and were spectacular, and they had tremendous impact. Others were just little errors which you went off and thought about and hopefully learnt from them. We all had to learn new control techniques and they didn't immediately become second nature. Your hands were darting around the cockpit while operating nozzles, power, flaps, etc., on approach to land in a way that would frighten some pilots. With conventional aircraft everyone is taught to keep one's hand on the throttle as engine power is absolutely critical, to ensure the throttle doesn't slip back, and so on. But with the Harrier, you've got to take your hand off the throttle because this and the nozzle control are both on the left-hand side. So we tended to make cack-handed errors as we were learning.

I remember one day I was coming in to land and was going to do a slow landing. During a slow landing, with nozzles partly down and some of the lift provided by the engine, I was actually below the stalling speed. I wasn't doing a rolling vertical landing which is a slow forward-moving landing, which needs hover power, and I got into a mess. I made one wrong movement with one lever. At the appropriate moment you would hit the hover stop, in other words, you'd pull the nozzle lever back to the nozzle stop which held it in the vertical position. At that point the aircraft would no longer fly but sink beautifully onto the ground.

However, when I thought I was pulling down the nozzle lever, I had actually got hold of the throttle and pulled it back. Suddenly I had no power and was still 6-8 feet up, and it came down fairly hard and I recall my body disappearing below the level of the cockpit as I was hammered into the seat! Fortunately I'd hit with all the wheels at once, so the load had spread and luckily there was no damage. I only did that once.'

The two flights as at July 1969 comprised:

A Flight		B Flight	
S/L R V A Munro AFC	(Tony)	S/L L A B Baker	(Bryan)
F/L D J Sowler	(Cid)	F/L J D L Feesey	(John)
F/L J K Sim	(Joe)	F/L M P G L Shaw	(Mike)
F/L R Fowler	(Bob)	F/L D L Whiteley	
F/L J W Thorpe	(John)	Capt A W Hall III USAF	(Bud)

F/O C M Humphrey	(Chris)	F/O T R C Smith	(Tim)
F/O S G Jennings	(Steve)	F/O N J Wharton	(Neal)
F/O J B Grogan	(John)		

On 5 August 1969 Flight Lieutenant D J 'Cid' Sowler executed a cunningly inverted landing. Decelerating on the approach to a hover at West Raynham, the aircraft suddenly increased its rate of descent short of the airfield, hit the ground very hard on all fours, reared up on its nose and sank down, ending up on its back like a dead insect. Cid smartly operated his MDC (miniature detonating charge, which shatters the perspex prior to ejection) and scrambled out. XV751, Cat 4 damage.

Bryan Baker continues:

'Our first conversions were done at Raynham before Wittering was ready and this was not ideal. In particular, the very first landing we all did in a Harrier was Hunter-style – forget all about nozzles. This is fine except the Harrier does not have a brake parachute and the brakes only work below 75 knots forward speed. The brakes were only designed to absorb energy of around 19,000 lbs, from 70 knots down to zero. So if you started braking at 80 knots then they would fail at 10 knots and you'd trundle off the end of the runway at this speed, unless you cut the engine and managed to turn onto the grass. When making a conventional landing at say 160 knots, you had an awful lot of energy to get rid of before you could use the brakes. You could ruin them braking between 150-110 knots, then you'd have no brakes left.

So then we had power-nozzle braking, where the nozzles go past the vertical and then forward. You then add power to brake. But as you put the power on, 80% of it is giving you lift and only about 8% retardation. So you've got to be careful otherwise you're up on your twinkle toes and the thing starts sliding and slithering around, and you can easily lose control. So at Raynham the first thing the blokes had to do was to stop on a runway that was 1,000 yards or so shorter than Wittering, from 160-170 knots with brakes that would only stop the aircraft at 75 knots. Therefore we had to get the power nozzle braking right the first time. It frightened two or three people. The second flight was a vertical take-off and landing. So one day you're flying a conventional aircraft, then suddenly it was a "helicopter". Exciting!

Wing Commander Ken Hayr took command at the end of 1969, converted easily to the Harrier and took a firm grip on the Squadron. The pace of work to operational status was bedevilled by the sort of teething problems which are inevitable and mostly unpredictable with so much new technology to settle down and be proved. Full declaration to NATO required a very high standard of operational effectiveness and many institutions and individuals take credit for this achievement in September 1970. Ken Hayr had charged me with developing the Squadron's off-base capability – the key to exploiting the aircraft's unique features. He gave me all the rope and encouragement that I needed and a concept of off-base operation was developed through a series of unique and unforgettable exercises from sites as varied as Wymeswold, a crumbling, dis-used airfield, grass flying strips and Dhekalia, an army helicopter site on Cyprus.

We had to experiment, we had to calculate risks, we made some mistakes and had to draw back when it became apparent that some of the possible operating methods would involve an unacceptable level of risk for the long term. Having hand-picked pilots was fine but we had to reject some options which would have made sense only if exceptional skill could be taken for granted. Through a great deal of trial and error, and with generous help and advice from industry and Boscombe Down, we were well on the way to achieving our aims – without having lost an aircraft or a pilot (we didn't count aircraft bent during conversion, those were down to the Harrier Conversion Team) – when I was posted out. This was September 1970 and the Squadron had just been fully declared to NATO.

I had spent two years on the Squadron and had had four spells in command. I was the last man at squadron leader rank to command the Squadron and, after all my ups-and-downs, I was beginning to wonder in what circumstances I might be promoted. With my posting from the Squadron came the answer. I was to be the first wing commander CO of No.233 (Harrier) OCU which was to be formed and based at – yes you've guessed it – RAF Wittering, effective immediately. I was delighted and reflected at some length and with gratitude on my astonishing experience with the RAF's premier Squadron.'

* * *

Freddie Pickard, who had been a flight commander in the early Hunter days, recalls how he returned to the periphery of the Squadron's activities at this time:

'After a suitable interval (12 years, including a three-year stint as OC 6 Squadron) I was posted to Wittering as OC Operations to oversee the introduction of the Harrier into RAF service. No simulators, no two-seaters, just a very good and professional Harrier Conversion Team of four instructors and "cold turkey". No.1 Squadron arrived and began to exchange Hunters for Harriers, soon with Ken Hayr as their new boss.

I wasn't part of 1 Squadron although I did occasionally fly with them, and, of course, I was very close to everything that was going on. Very noticeable was the professional and focussed attitude of all the aircrew to mastering the complexities of the new aircraft. It was both difficult and demanding to fly (especially taking off and landing) and the new tactical role demanded unprecedented skills, discipline and concentration from both ground and aircrew. All very different from the light-hearted atmosphere of their previous existence. It brought with it a sea-change in professional attitudes, and a determination to exploit the unique features of this revolutionary aircraft to the absolute maximum. All credit must be given to the outstanding leadership of Ken Hayr.'

The HCT was under the command of Squadron Leader Richard (Dick) le Brocq, with Flight Lieutenants P Dodsworth, R Profit and B Latton. With no two-seat Harrier, the pilots hung on their every word.

Harrier ground fire

Steve Jennings (later Wg Cdr) had a problem with a Harrier in October 1969. The machine was XV745, which coincidentally was the first Harrier he had flown two months earlier. He remembers:

'The incident occurred at Wittering during a conventional take-off on runway 08 at about 100 knots on the take-off roll. At that point there was a loud bang, a lot of vibration and a succession of warning lights started to appear on the Central Warning Panel (CWP). I immediately aborted the take-off, trying to make sense of what was happening. I managed to turn off the runway at the A/B intersection before bringing the aircraft to a halt, having already shut down the engine and fired the extinguisher as a result of the "Fire" light illuminating. Prior to shut-down, there were very few warning lights on the CWP which were not illuminated!

I had called the tower to inform them that I was aborting and had received an acknowledgement. Once at rest just off the runway at the A/B, I then had to decide whether to vacate the aircraft over the side, or carry out the first Harrier 0/0 ejection. I still had the "Fire" light on along with all the other warnings although there were no other signs of fire in the cockpit. I called the tower for an external assessment of the situation, but unknown to me, my radio had already failed. At the same time I was called by one of the other pilots, Bob Fowler, I think, who was taxying in along the southern taxiway. He could see flames coming out of the nose wheel bay under the cockpit and advised that I should eject. Still with no radio, I did not hear the call.

I elected to go over the side. I did not fire the MDC (miniature detonation chord), which in those days was only around the perimeter of the canopy and not over the top as well, so if fired could still leave a very large piece of perspex to shift out of the way. It was only when I stood up in the seat having unstrapped myself and opened the canopy, that I saw the flames coming up around the cockpit on both sides. I jumped the eight or ten feet from the cockpit and hit the ground running! Fortunately there was no explosion and the fire service were quickly in action with their foam.

None of us there at the time will forget the sight of 'People-Eating' Pete Williamson, the Station Commander, standing on top of the foam-covered fuselage, covered in foam himself, directing the fire service's operation!

The problem had been caused by the loss of a front fan blade from the Pegasus 101. This resulted from a fault in the blade manufacturing process which caused a weakness in the leading edge of the blade, approximately six inches up from the root of the leading edge. I believe mine was the third occurence, but the others had happened on ground runs so we were still flying while the investigations continued.

The cure was to shave the leading edge of all the front stage blades in the area of weakness. Although this made the blade narrower at the critical point, by eliminating the inherent weakness, the problem disappeared. XV745 was declared Cat 4, it being unacceptable to lose an airframe if it could be avoided. I think it was at least 18 months before it flew again.' [1]

---

[1] XV745 was lost in a mid-air collision in January 1976.

Ken Hayr takes over:–

'I was being sent to Staff College and I thought I'd been short-changed having my time on the Phantom cut short in consequence, so this displeased me. I told my Station Commander at Coningsby, but all he said was "Tough!" All the bumph arrived about Staff College but at the last minute, the Groupie came over and said; "You remember how you were belly-aching about going to Bracknell? Well you're not going, instead you're going to Wittering on Tuesday, to command 1 Squadron."

Being slightly aware of what was going on at Wittering because we used the same ranges – we were new on Phantoms but they were newer on Harriers – I knew they were at the embryonic stage. I took over from Duncan Allison, a friend of mine, who had been axed because someone thought he wasn't handling the Harrier safely, which was sad. The Station Commander was Group Captain P G K Williamson, a very strong character, and once I'd taken over I eventually had to go to him to say, look, you run the Station and I'll run 1 Squadron, which he'd been doing between Duncan leaving and me arriving. In fact "he" hadn't actually "given" me the Squadron until I'd proved I could fly the Harrier. So it was only on New Year's Eve that he announced that Hayr was now CO of 1 Squadron.

Every dog has his day and this was the time of my life, because it was the most exhilarating, interesting, and fantastic period in the peacetime life of a squadron commander. It was all totally new and nobody could tell us what to do because nobody knew. We therefore broke new ground both literally and figuratively; we wrote our own book!

On the way a few people tried to codify certain things, such as minimum grass strip lengths we should operate into, which wasn't very easy and in the end it was all a matter of judgement. And we were pushing boundaries all the time. The ground crews were all ex-Hunter and none of them were used to servicing in the field. I was conscious that the older hands had not joined the RAF to be boy scouts as well as being engineers – and guards – because when we went out into the field we didn't have RAF Regiment guards, we did all that ourselves. This kept me awake at night because there were some odd people around who might just put something in an air-intake and walk away. So it was a combination of boy-scouting and flying the most wonderful fast jet in the world at that time.

We all had to do five hours in a helicopter because there wasn't a two-seat version of the Harrier and we had to accustom ourselves to stopping in mid-air. Some people just couldn't get used to it. We had a number of aeroplanes dented and broken because we hadn't a two-seater. There had been some early problems. For instance, when one makes a vertical take-off you bring the nozzles to the "stop" and you quite quickly rotate the nozzles and then power-up in one go. The automatics on the engine allow you to slam the throttle. But if you get it the wrong way round, if you went up with the throttle before you went down with the power, you're off forward very fast because you have more thrust than weight, by definition with vertical take-off. So the odd chap went forward, then realised, and put the nozzles down when he was on the edge of the pad; down came the nozzles and lifted the power and thwacked the back of the aeroplane. As one of our later Americans said once, "Hey, this beats sex," and it did.

We had planned for a trip to Cyprus. The route proving flight was to be done by Air Commodore (by now) Williamson, and Pete Dodworth, the most experienced Harrier pilot from the Harrier Conversion Team (HCT).[1] The Squadron would then go down to Cyprus the next month. I asked if the chap who was going to lead the push (me), shouldn't go along too. PGK didn't want to allow that because he could see that he would be the one to drop out. So in the end he argued for three aircraft, which allowed him to stay and let me in too.

When we were out there we spent a couple of days at Akrotiri and I was flying around behind Pete Dodworth when suddenly, without any input from me, the aeroplane jerked up, which when you hadn't moved the controls, quickly captures your attention. We found there was a fault and discovered there was a single failure case which should not have been allowed by design; you should never have a single failure case that will do that.

So then we were not allowed to fly below a certain height and not above a certain speed. We got the aeroplane (XV754) back to UK and then became faced with the Cyprus detachment which was going to be ground attack. So amid much sucking of teeth, wondering if we should go or not, we decided in the end to go. It was the making of the Squadron.

In March 1970 we flew 300 hours – a real total. The Squadron was away, morale was up and

---

[1] Retired as an air vice-marshal CB OBE AFC BSc.

the ground crew came together which was even more important. I had a bunch of ground crew who were good jacks. They behaved well and didn't let me down despite all the booze, etc., on the island. Upon our return the Squadron moved into its own hangar, previously having shared one with the Conversion Unit – the old Blue Steel hangar. When we came back the guys who had stayed behind, had painted the 1 Squadron marking right across the hangar. So we were back and without a doubt, a Squadron. So that was the start.'

Work in the Field

One of Ken Hayr's first parades occurred on 1 January 1970. At the end of the previous year a liaison had been formed with No.1(F) Squadron of the Air Training Corps, based in Leicester under the command of Flight Lieutenant B Lockwood RAFVR(T). During the parade to mark the event Ken Hayr took the salute during a march past.

The proving flight to Cyprus mentioned by Ken Hayr above took place on 16 February, staging through Istres and Brindisi, coming back via Souda Bay, Luqa and Istres.

Flight Lieutenant Feesey had a lucky escape on 6 April. As he become airborne from Wittering he saw a flock of birds ahead on a reciprocal course and they met at 170 knots. Unable to avoid them he sucked in several and crunched down onto the airfield seven seconds after take-off with just a slightly bent Harrier – and several bent birds.

During the summer of 1970 several short exercises were flown, at which time, out in the field, the Squadron's camouflage techniques were improved upon, much of it developed by John Grogan. Aircraft started using the Ferranti Inertial Navigation and Attack System (INAS) and the French SNEB rockets, as well as retard bombs. Using INAS did not bring the desired results and many pilots used their own 'TLAR' system (That Looks About Right) to increase personal scores. Wing Commander Hayr, however, insisted pilots persevere with INAS in order to get it right.

At Farnborough that year, four pilots thrilled the crowd (CO, Munro, Bud Hall and Stuart Penny), and after this the Squadron went to Bardufoss, in northern Norway, to experience working in the cold arctic climate. One pilot, Mike Shaw, thought it a good idea to fill the CO's tent with smoke by fixing his heating chimney, and supplying some specially doctored damp wood. For some unexplained reason, Mike then found himself whisked away on a survival course with the SAS!!

A few aircraft had minor scrapes; Porky Munro decided to plough a field during a take-off miscalculation, Joe Sim wrecked an aluminium pad during a hover, which then tried to wrap itself around his Harrier, while Mike Shaw managed to dent two Harriers in two days landing in a clearing, although there is no record of him attending another survival course. Ken Hayr:

> 'We went off into the field for the first time and our first exercise away from normal logistics. This we performed on the airfield itself, so we parked on a corner of the base and stayed out overnight trying to sleep in our tents. Then we went off to Wymeswold, landing at this place which was dis-used, setting up tents and a cook house. The next morning I had to give some coins to Porky Munro, one of my flight commanders, so he could telephone Wittering to see what the diversions and the weather was like because we didn't have radio contact or anything. We were not used to landing jets without having two diversions noted on our knee pads.
>
> So we did that for a couple of nights then moved to Bruntingthorpe and set up again with a slightly different arrangement, and finished up with a dining-in night. Our wives and girlfriends had given us Tupperware containers of food and we'd taken the Squadron silver, so that ended our first real off-base experience.
>
> After that we did several more. Usually I reckoned on about 120 chaps were needed, the Squadron having about 12 aircraft – on paper, and a two-seat Hunter – of which we'd usually got ten Harriers on deployments. Our first accident in the field happened to Neal Wharton, at Ouston (County Durham). He had an engine problem and ejected. It was interesting having a Board of Enquiry, in a tent!
>
> Then we were getting ready to go back to Cyprus via Rome, which was interesting (June 1970). We were asked to make a bit of an effort on behalf of the Company so we went to Ciampino. When we arrived all the traffic stopped on the nearby roads, never having seen Harriers before. It was an eye-catching thing, and still is. We carried out a formation routine, formation hovers, bows to the crowd – all that.'

Flight Lieutenant Neal Wharton had previously been with 20 Squadron. Suffering engine failure he had successfully ejected from Harrier GR1 XV796 on 6 October 1970 during exercise 'Gold Tint'. He later flew with the Red Arrows display team. Neal remembers it well:

'I was on a Hi-Lo-Hi to Tain range sortie on the Dornach Firth in Scotland, dropping 28 lb practice bombs. We were operating out of RAF Ouston in Northumberland on the Squadron's first off-base exercise. This gave us our first look at camouflage netting, hides and all the other paraphernalia that we were to get to know and love – but mainly know!

My wing-man was Flight Lieutenant Stu Penny. He was in trail on me as we turned finals on our return to Ouston and had a good view of the subsequent events. At about 800 feet AGL and without any warning my engine started to run down. My immediate action was to hit the re-light button, make a brief R/T call and ... check the fuel gauge (a reaction based on – "engines don't just fail, it must be something I've done, or not done"). There was plenty of fuel but no engine and by now I was descending quite rapidly. (The Harrier GR1 in landing configuration and 40° of nozzle had the gliding characteristics of a brick!) Only when I was aware of the ground coming up very fast to meet me did it occur to me that ejection might be a good option. I made another quick call (I think) and pulled the seat-pan firing handle.

I can remember an extremely violent jolt as the seat fired – rush of air – perspex confetti (as the MDC fired) and then tumbling, as the drogue stabilised the seat. At some point I looked up from my now inverted attitude, and saw the aircraft hit the ground in a spectacular orange, napalm-like swathe. Now I was in the 'chute, coming down in open countryside. I just had time to lower the PSP (personal survival pack) and adopt some sort of landing posture when I hit the ground. The reported wind speed was 25-knots and I landed going backwards. Surprisingly I suffered only a strained neck (probably due to the whip-lash effect during the ejection itself) and a few bruises. Fortunately the parachute deflated on impact with the ground and I lay for a few moments ascertaining that I was still in one piece. With a fair degree of relief I stood up and surveyed the remains of XV796 burning white hot only 50 metres away.

The first person to the scene was Margaret Dinsdale, wife of the farm manager in whose field I had landed. She appeared to be more shocked than I was and was at a complete loss for anything to say. Eventually she spoke, and I shall always remember this for its stoic Englishness: "Would you like a cup of tea?" she asked.

Meanwhile, back at Ouston someone had hit the crash button and the fire tender was on its way. Unfortunately as it scorched out of the main gate it ran head-on into a Triumph Herald car, which just happened to be passing by. No one was injured but I had to wait quite some time, chatting to Mrs Dinsdale, before another crash vehicle arrived on the scene.

The cause of the engine failure was a bearing failure in the turret drive gear box which drives the main fuel pump. The ejection was from the first Harrier to be lost in RAF service although Hawker Siddeley test pilot Duncan Simpson survived an earlier ejection from a T2 at Dunsfold. XV796 was one of only two 1 Squadron Harriers to be fitted with MDC, a device which breaks up the cockpit canopy prior to the seat going through it and undoubtedly saved me from severe neck injury. For the record, the ejection sequence was initiated at approximately 100 feet AGL with the aircraft descending at about 6,000 fpm. Impact occurred 1.1 seconds later. Time elapsed from my initial call to ejection – 12 seconds.'

Sardinia

Over the following months the Squadron continued to grow in confidence with the Harrier. A new name for the Squadron was Decimomannu (or Deci – pronounced Dechi – for short) on Sardinia. The Squadron would make regular visits to this island over the next several years for weapons training.

Meantime, in March 1971 came a full deployment to Milltown, a dis-used airfield near Lossiemouth firing SNEB rockets at Cape Wrath and lobbing 1,000 lb retard bombs on the range at Tain. On 17 June 1971 the Squadron lost its last remaining Hunter, the T7 two-seater, as Steve Jennings relates:

'In those early Harrier days we used a Hunter T7 (XL601) for our dual checks. That aircraft last flew with the Squadron on 17 June. John Feesey, the Squadron IRE, had completed my IRT and we were finishing the sortie with a few visual circuits. Downwind, we realised the engine was not performing properly, so we elected to carry out a fixed throttle landing using a medium power setting. After landing and as we had closed the throttle to idle, the engine seized. That was almost the end of the Hunter era for 1(F). On 20 July 1971 I collected the Squadron's first Harrier T2 (XW271) from Dunsfold.'

During June 1971 more international recognition was gained during the Paris Air Show. A five-man team led by the CO (Messrs Munro, Grogan, Wharton and Searle) got good press and media coverage, although Porky Munro's outrigger wheel collapsed on landing. One of the ground crew there was Arthur Hancock:

> 'This Harrier (XV776) was in the hover with the others when it ran out of water for the injection system and suffered a heavy landing, snapping the starboard outrigger. Water augmentation was used to give the extra thrust needed because of the weather and we poor sods had to manually pump fifty gallons into each kite.
>
> All went well and the show commenced. However, all the aircraft were hovering gracefully when XV776 decided to drop out of the formation and land with an equally graceful thud on its outrigger, which promptly snapped. Several of us jumped into a Land Rover and made the scene before the Gendarmes. I had a very old Kodak vest pocket camera (c.1920) and managed to take three shots before the French police began confiscating all cameras and I was the only one to keep mine hidden.
>
> Ken Hayr later flew the damaged Harrier safely back to Wittering with the undercarriage locked down where it had a mainplane change.'

A number of VIPs invaded the Squadron field sites, one being HRH Prince Philip, the Duke of Edinburgh on 9 July. He arrived at Wittering in a helicopter then moved to the site at Wakerley Oaks (Sitex 7). A pair of Harriers led by Louis Distelweg demonstrated RVLs while four more led by Squadron Leader D J Willis carried out a mock attack. Another VIP visitor was Lord Carrington, the Defence Secretary. Ground equipment began appearing in green paint while khaki working dress became the order of the day. Dave Willis was the B Flight commander, who had joined the Squadron in September 1970. He had previously served with 20 and 54 Squadrons, and IV Squadron in March 1970.

Hunter XL601 also left in July. It had been on the Squadron strength since 1959 and was used in the London-Paris Air Race that year. It was also the last Hunter on a UK-based operational squadron. An era had passed.

Ken Hayr continues with the deployment by the Squadron on the aircraft carrier, HMS *Ark Royal*, in the summer of 1971:

> 'I had spent some time with the Navy, was a Qualified Air Warfare Instructor, and had done $2\frac{1}{2}$ months on the ground at Whale Island, Portsmouth. Before that I had spent a lot of time not flying on carriers but picking up some naval weapons techniques. I had always wanted to go on a carrier but didn't really want to land with a hook and then get catapulted off, so our Harrier concept was ideal.
>
> We went aboard HMS "Ark Royal" for an overnight stop as an orientation, flying around in a helicopter. I stayed in an admiral's cabin which I thought quite commodious, and looked forward to going back into it when I arrived by jet, but needless to say, I didn't get the chance.
>
> This wasn't long after the Fleet Air Arm had been told that it had no future as a fixed-wing force, it was going to be rotary only. Naval aviators were sure that the RAF had knifed them in the back and were responsible for their demise. So our reception had been cool. The Harrier, of course, was a natural for the FAA, and we soon won them over.
>
> It all went very well, although not with my first landing. I had Dave Willis as No.2 and we'd been told the deck was full of aeroplanes but that when we arrived they would clear the whole deck. We had already been told very forcefully that we must do as we were told by the Flight Deck Officer (FDO), and that if we didn't pitch up on time, don't expect to find the ship! So we reached it on time and proceeded to beat it up. I'd briefed Dave that I would do a rolling vertical touch down on the back of the carrier, about 45 knots, and roll out to the front as it was supposed to be clear of aircraft. Dave, in the meantime, was to come to the hover and do a pure vertical.
>
> After our beat-up, the ship turned into finals and I was ordered to land on Spot Five which was about two in, but I wanted to be on Spot Seven. I knew we'd been told to do as ordered but as a compromise I thought I'd give it about Spot Six. So I did this, rolled out, put it on a day-glow strip, applied the brakes – and the aeroplane went sideways! It was as slippery as hell and once the Harrier goes, its like being on a motor-cycle on ice. Fortunately it slid right; if it had gone left I'd have gone over the side and that would have been the end of that.
>
> Instead of the deck being clear of aircraft, the front right was chocker and for a moment I had visions of sliding into them. After No.2's landing I asked if I could do a vertical take-off, but a voice

said: "I think you just stay where you are!" So after that we didn't do another rolling vertical; every landing was vertical. We also impressed the Navy types on non-flying days (deck maintenance) by persuading them to let us just use the lift area. Taking off vertically from just this spot got their attention.

One day we encountered bad weather. Two of us were coming down doing the Navy equivalent of a GCA but really just a carrier talk-down. I could hear Phantoms putting power on and going past us but couldn't see them in this fog. Eventually all aircraft were ordered to divert to land base – deck landings were cancelled. I asked, "Can't my chaps have a go?" Having prevailed my money was now on the line! Joe Sim just found the ship's wake as he was about to go round again, went into a braking stop, turned the nozzles and got down.

Towards the end of our carrier duty, several of us went ashore and those RAF left behind rigged up one of those paint hoists over the side of the ship and slipping down unseen, painted in large letters on the "Ark's" side: FLY RAF, FLY VSTOL. Some time later the duty officer discovered this. On the day we finally left, the Captain suggested that when I flew by I should operate my camera to take a shot of the signal flags that were going to be flown. I duly did this and later, when we developed the film and had the flags interpreted, they read the same – FLY RAF, FLY VSTOL.'

The Squadron lost their distinguished American exchange officer on 3 August, Captain Louis Distelweg Jr. This occurred shortly after their first reunion and open day, at which many former members attended, including the first war ace, Air Commodore Philip Fullard. There was also an 80-year-old airman who had actually been on the Squadron the day it was formed in 1912.

Distelweg had flown 318 missions in Vietnam in F-100s, winning a Silver Star and four DFCs, so was an experienced pilot. On this day he suffered a malfunction and the nozzles would not respond to the lever. They sometimes were inclined to go their own way and didn't respond to changes in airspeed so as a pilot went faster the nozzles tended to go further aft. As Distelweg, leading a four-man strike sortie to Wales, slowed up and called saying he might not be able to land, he was told not to hesitate and eject.

While jettisoning fuel prior to landing three minutes later, the nozzles appeared to run away to a vertical position and control was lost. He finally called to say he'd have to eject and pulled the handle. Nothing happened. He had forgotten to take all the pins out of his seat and he was killed in the crash. The cause of the problem was due to swarf in the air motor servo unit that controlled the position of the nozzles. It was also discovered that Distelweg had managed to remove the main firing pins before ejecting, but valuable time was lost and he was killed when the seat hit the ground during separation.

During October the Squadron was introduced to air-to-air refuelling (AAR) which was now added to their training tasks. A one-day course was held at the School of Air-to-Air Refuelling at RAF Marham on the 8th. By the end of the month, Wing Commander Hayr had set up a new airborne flight record of three hours, 20 minutes.

Then came an exchange with 725 Squadron of the Royal Danish Air Force at Karup led by Squadron Leader Willis, who took four jets and seven pilots, a similar number coming to Wittering from the Danish. Ken Hayr:

'On Cyprus we were on the weapon ranges. I had dug out all the old Squadron silver, some never used for many years, so we had a trophy for each of the events – strafing, rocketing, bombing, and so on. Then upon our return we were straight in for Farnborough, then off to Norway.

There was a lot of snow I recall, and we had another accident. Steve Jennings had the nose wheel steering system freeze up on the way. After landing the only way to steer is by the nose wheel, the outrigger wheels don't have brakes, and he just bounced into a snow bank and was very lucky because he went upside-down. The canopy had to be smashed to get him out.'

Of this incident, Steve Jennings says:

'The nose wheel incident occurred on 24 November 1971 in XV792 while landing at Gardermoen in Norway. I was one of the flight arriving from Wittering at the start of a two-week detachment. The ground temperature at Gardermoen was sub-zero, around —13°C – and the runway was covered in packed snow, so we were carrying out RVLs, touching down at 50-60 knots. My landing was quite normal but on the roll out, the aircraft started steering to the left and I was unable to control it. Unfortunately, instead of leaving the side of the runway, where there were no snow banks, my aircraft left at an intersection, ploughing into the high bank alongside it.

By this stage, my speed could not have been more than 40 knots and I braced myself for a sharp stop. Instead, the world went white and I was knocked around, becoming completely disorientated. When everything settled, I was still strapped into the aircraft, but was buried in snow. Only after digging with my hands, still strapped in, did I see daylight and realised that I was upside-down and there was no canopy – it had been broken on impact with the ground. My immediate fear was fire, but when I saw a Norwegian running towards me, I guessed my fears were unfounded. The Norwegian confirmed this and I relaxed a little.

The next problem was to extricate myself from the cockpit. I was able to unstrap, but the seat pack had come free from the seat and had fallen onto the back of my legs, trapping them under the coaming. I was unable to make the seat safe, so refused all offers of assistance until a qualified Harrier person arrived on the scene. This was Joe Sim, who had been duty pilot in the tower for our arrival. He attempted to make the seat safe by inserting pins into the main sears on top of the seat. After several minutes trying, he had to give up because the sears were coated with solid ice resulting from the ground impact. The fear was that breaking away the ice, the sears could be withdrawn inadvertently.

The only course of action left was for Joe to squeeze into the cockpit with me to lift the seat pack away from my legs. Having done this, two burly Norwegians pulled on my arms to drag me clear; Joe ensured that neither of my feet nor any of my equipment snagged on the ejection seat handle during the process. All went well and twenty minutes after the crash, I was free, none the worse for wear.

The problem had been caused by the grease in the nose wheel leg which could not handle sub-zero temperatures. Normally, the grease would have a chance to thaw after a high level flight, but not at Gardermoen's temperatures. Once again, this was not the first time this had happened. I think it was Mike Shaw who had a problem when taxying, but investigations had proved inconclusive. After my incident, and thanks to the perspicacity of Hoof Proudfoot, a member of the Board of Enquiry, Dowty were able to reproduce the fault with XV792's nose leg in their cold chamber and a new formula grease was substituted. As before, I think the airframe eventually came back into RAF service, but a long time later.' [1]

Hawker Siddeley invited the officers and their ladies to a dinner party at the Café Royal in London's Regent Street on 17 December, and then laid on a factory visit to Kingston, Surrey, with a magnificent lunch for 130 of the Squadron at a local hostelry. The party was then conveyed by HQ Air Strike Command 'Britannia' aircraft to Dunsfold and returned to Wittering in high spirits. The outing for the ground crew was a 'well done' for two years of dedicated work on the Harrier.

---

[1] XV792 was destroyed in a crash at Gütersloh with 3 Squadron in October 1980.

Chapter Eighteen

HARRIERS HOME AND AWAY

By the time Ken Hayr left the Squadron, in January 1972, the Harrier concept had been firmly established. No.IV Squadron had been the second RAF unit to receive Harriers, in March 1970, and would be commanded by former 1 Squadron CO, Bryan Baker, between August 1972 and October 1974. In early 1972 No.3 Squadron at Wildenrath, would begin to equip with the Harrier, where IV Squadron were also based.

As 1972 came so too did air-to-air refuelling for 1 Squadron, from Victor tankers in preparation for deployments further afield in the world. Mike Shaw, who also left the Squadron at this time, records that his final flight with it was a 3½ hour scenic trip round Scotland and Northumberland during which he twice refuelled from Victors. Mike went off to 3 Squadron in Germany.

The new boss of the Squadron was Wing Commander E J E Smith, formally of IV Squadron, on low level reconnaissance, where he had had '... great fun thrashing around at 250 feet looking for needles in haystacks.' Flying Officer Chas Cairns, the adjutant, also left, replaced by Pilot Officer Makin. The Senior Engineering Officer, Derek Brinsden left too, his place taken by Squadron Leader Richard Kyle.

In March 1972 the Squadron went to Kinloss on exercise 'Snowy Owl' with six aircraft, with another six at Milltown. It was the first time two dispersed sites had been used simultaneously. By this date the Squadron had received their two-seat Harrier T2. Eric Smith recalls:

'The T2 was already in service at the OCU when I arrived there in July 1971. In advance of my posting, I had been very cheeky and had flown down to Dunsfold in April 1970 for a "test flight" with Tony Hawkes, then followed this up with a Dunsfold flight with the late Don Riches in 1971.

When the Squadron got its T2 I'm not sure, but it was certainly there when I arrived in December. From personal experience, any two-seat ride before bashing off solo was always welcome.'

Another Harrier was lost on 26 April. XV749 had been the CO's aircraft for around two years but on this date was being flown by Flight Lieutenant C Marshall. Shortly before mid-day he was at Theddlethorpe Range and was running in at 350 feet prior to strafing. Suddenly he ran into a flock of sea birds which caused considerable damage to the engine and Marshall had no choice but to eject.

He landed in the sea half a mile off the coast but luckily there was a 72 Squadron helicopter crew working at nearby RAF Strubby and hearing the Mayday call they came to the rescue. Chris Marshall was only in his dinghy ten minutes before he was being winched aboard.

More tanker work came along before the unit headed off to Cyprus in May, prior to another ejection. Flying Officer Kit Adams, in XV777 'W' – the usual aircraft of Squadron Leader Willis, OC B Flight – was attempting a cross-wind deceleration to the pad to do a vertical landing. The aircraft developed an uncontrollable yaw and Adams banged-out from 100 feet, although suffering some facial and eye damage from MDC particles. The aircraft was one of those carrying an in-flight refuelling probe and it was subsequently established that this could cause adverse roll and yaw characteristics during slow speed flight. Later all in-flight probes were altered to allow them to be folded flat against the airframe.

Later that summer, two pilots, Flight Lieutenants N J Wharton and D J Fisher were chosen to fly a display at the Toronto Air Show, giving the Squadron its first chance at a trans-Atlantic flight which would test their air-to-air refuelling training. Neal Wharton relates:

'The trans-Atlantic flight to Canada took place on 29 August 1972. I led a pair of Harrier GR1As with Dave Fisher as my No.2. We took off from Wittering at 0900 hours and landed at Downsview Airport, Toronto, after eight hours, 24 minutes – a Harrier record at the time. This feat was surpassed by an even more impressive one – the fact that both pilots managed to complete the flight without resorting to use the "piddle pack", a difficult operation at the best of times with immersion suit and no auto-pilot!!

The flight involved three tankers from Marham in Norfolk and two from Goose Bay, Labrador. We planned about four "prods" from the tankers but Dave needed considerably more. Due to an unserviceability he discovered that he could only refuel on one side. What we should have done is to throw it away at that point and land back at Wittering. What we actually did was to carry on, with Dave running max out-of-balance on one side before topping up to max on the other side!

The displays for the CIAS took place off the shore of Lake Ontario using Toronto Island Airport as an operating base for the display itself. We carried out one rehearsal and three displays between 1-4 September, the final one being viewed live by 300,000+ spectators along Lakeside Boulevard, including the Prime Minister, Pierre Trudeau.

The boss gave us a very free hand in the format for the display and we produced, I think, a pretty impressive combination of pairs hovering and high-speed fly-bys. After much pleading and technical argument we were allowed to hover over the Lake with undercarriage retracted, a clearance which, as far as I know, is unique. The display concluded with me executing a steep climbing acceleration from the hover with Dave flashing by below at 550 knots.

On 4 September we were given special authority to fly low level over Niagara Falls with "Daily Telegraph" photographer, Anthony Marshal, snapping away from a light aircraft. We tried it a couple of times at low level right over the edge of the Falls – great fun but there was too much spray for a good picture. The best shot, which was published, was taken with us in close echelon at about 500 feet with the Falls a couple of miles away in the background.

Our return flight home took a mere seven hours. My only excitement to report is that on this occasion I finally resorted to using the dreaded "piddle pack". In doing so in the rapidly failing light and halfway across the Atlantic, I succeeded in losing visual contact with the Victor. The white light I then pursued fortunately turned out to be its tail light and not a planet!'

Tromso came next, the autumn NATO exercise. Eric Smith:

'Exercise "Strong Express" was played in September. This may have been the deployment when our young adjutant was standing behind the drivers' seats in the Hercules transport delivery flight and it slid off the runway at Tromso, pinning his hand to the roof. The aircraft in question had all the booze for the deployment too, so a very valuable cargo was nearly lost!

During one of our Tromso deployments the ground crew had to defuel a Harrier and over-filled the receiving tanker and fuel spilled out all over the brand new asphalted parking area, causing £££s worth of damage. I recall dealing with the problem very quickly and summarily, in a bid to avoid the individual responsible getting into trouble with our Norwegian hosts.'

More changes came. Squadron Leader M A P Pugh, known as Jack, arrived to take over B Flight from Dave Willis, who later went to 38 Group HQ, where he was able to look after the Squadron's interests as the Harrier Staff Officer. He was to receive the AFC for his enthusiastic leadership in the 1973 New Year's Honours List.

The annual APC in November took place at Decimomannu. Eric Smith remembers that the Squadron had no less than three pipers at this time – one being Squadron Leader H W 'Jock' Beaton. They took great delight in parading around – in full regalia whenever possible – and giving everyone a full blast on their pipes. Eric also recalls that after one detachment to Cyprus, the Squadron 'primed' the local Customs Officials, inviting them to a return party so that the boys could 'import' a fair gallon or two of the famous Cyprus wine. It was a huge success and something that was sadly – and surprisingly – never repeated.

There was a return to Milltown (one of their favourite dispersal sites) in February 1973 – exercise 'Sky Mist'. Squadron Leader Jack Pugh suffered a bird-strike on the 12th flying over the Cairngorms. As he crested a ridge he came face-to-face with a flock of birds with no chance to avoid them. Several birds were sucked into the engine and it began to surge, then lost power. As the Harrier began to drop, he decided to eject but then the engine picked up. He managed to re-light it whilst heading over another ridge at 200 knots, and fortunately found Kinloss right ahead of him. He went straight in making a fixed throttle landing thereby saving the aeroplane. He was later awarded the AFC.

Captain Tom Plank USAF arrived on an exchange posting, not long after returning from Vietnam. During his tour there he had flown 173 combat missions in Phantom F-4s. He converted onto the Hunter and then moved towards the Harrier. Tom recalls:

'I was on the Squadron longer than most exchange officers because I requested a one-year extension to the normal two-year exchange tour. This added to my eight months of lead-in training, made my RAF assignment almost four years in total. My justification (I needed strong rationale to

Top left: Ned Crowley, J W Sutherland and Kelly Wright. Wright was an American who was later killed flying P47s with the USAAF.

(N Crowley)

Top right: F/O E N W Marsh. After 1 Squadron, Eric flew in the Far East.

Above left: John Morden.

Middle right: W/O Neil Howard RAAF; shot down 2 March 1944 he evaded capture and got back a year later via Spain.

Bottom right: F/O Duncan McIntosh, Lympne 1944.

Top left: F/O D H Davy, top-scorer against V1s.

(K Weller)

Top right: F/O Ken Weller.

Bottom: 1 Squadron summer 1944. Front, l to r: F/O E G Hutchin, F/O W J Batchelor, F/L K Green DFC, F/L T D Williams DFC, F/L I P Maskill, S/L H P L Burke DFC, F/O T Wyllie, F/L J J Jarman, F/O Petersen, F/L W S 'Doc' Wallace; Rear: F/O F M Startup (EO), unknown, W/O Wallace-Wells, F/L J O Dalley DFM, F/O D R Wallace, F/Sgt H J Vassie, P/O K R Foskett, F/O K C Weller, F/O F Townsend, F/L K M Langmuir, F/L K C Pedersen, P/O I Hastings: On prop – F/O E N Marsh.

Top left: John Tack and William Noakes, ground crew. They looked after S/L Lardner Burke's aircraft.

(J Tack)

Top right: S/Ldr David Cox DFC, OC 1 Squadron January to April 1945. *(D Cox)*

Middle left: David Cox's Spitfire (MK644) after his crash at Manston, 2 March 1945. *(D Cox)*

Middle right: Spitfire LA 255 in 1945. This machine is still with the Squadron today! *(K Weller)*

Bottom: Spitfire JX-B (ML119) used by Lardner Burke and David Cox. *(D Cox)*

Top left: Spitfire ML119 later served with the Czech and Israeli airforces, then became the aircraft of Col. Tin Maung Aye, CO No. 1 Squadron of the Burmese Air Force. Shown here as gate-guardian to Mingaladon aerodrome, Burma in May 1997.

(Peter Arnold)

Top right: Meteor JX-B being refuelled. *(J Brown)*

Middle: 1 Squadron on 10 May 1945. Front, l to r: W/O J W McKenzie, F/L D H Davy, F/O W R Harrison, F/L R Brown, S/L R Nash, F/L P D'A Stewart, F/L J O Dalley DFM, F/L P E Crocker, F/L D Mackintosh;

Rear: F/O K C Weller, F/O J W Still, unknown, F/O R W Bridgeman, unknown, P/O R C Bahadurji, W/O H G Wallace-Wells, unknown, unknown, Sgt Richardson.

Bottom left: S/Ldr C G McFie DFC and pilots, 1946-7.

Bottom right: 1 Sqn as No. 11 Group's Instrument Rating unit, August 1947 – February 1949. Front, l to r: John Carpenter AFC, Tommy Burne DSO AFC (CO), Sammy Osborne DFC, Hutch Hutchinson; Rear: Johnny Tate, Keith Pearch, Eng Off, Richard Gambier-Parry, Ruben Horsley. *(A Osborne)*

Top left: One of the North American Harvards used by the Squadron. *(A Saunders)*

Top right: ACI Dick Humphries on a Harvard used by the Squadron for blind flying, Tangmere 1948; probably one of those painted yellow. *(R Humphries)*

Middle left: Tommy Burne, centre. Extreme left is Maj Robin Olds, who later became the first USAAF officer to command the Squadron. *(A Saunders)*

Middle right: S/Ldr F W Lister DSO DFC, OC December 1953 to August 1956.

Bottom left: Airmen, Bates, Cpl Jim Brown, Crossley, Nixon and Cpl Southall, 1947. *(J Brown)*

Bottom right: A Flight ground crew RAF Honily 1954. From left, Alan Easter, Den Firman; behind cockpit, Mich Timms, George Whitehouse, Pete Masterson; astride the engine – Norman Izzard. *(P Masterson)*

Top left: Longest man on 1 Squadron! Den Firman and Norm Izzard provide the illusion. *(P Masterson)*

Top right: Flying Officers Paddy Hine and Alan Ginn.

Middle left: Flight Lieutenants Harry Irving and Peter Pledger. Pledger became CO in January 1961.

Middle right: F/O Mike Chandler receiving the Squadron Standard from AVM Sir Charles Longcroft, 24 April 1953. *(via A Saunders)*

Bottom left: Squadron pilots, Tangmere 1958. Back row l to r: F/L Ken Hunter, F/L Cliff Lake, F/L Don Norris, F/L Potter, S/L R S Kingsford, F/L Ray Martin, F/O Jim Blackford, P/O John Turner, F/L Mike Paxton, F/O Pete Self, F/O Gerry English. Front: F/L Ian Madelin, F/O Roy Booth, F/O Browne, F/O Tony Gordon, Capt Jessie Baird USMC, F/O Mike Dodd. Paxton and Turner were killed in a collision in May, the last operational losses from RAF Tangmere. Aircraft is Hunter F.5 WP188 'X'.

Right: Flying Officer Bill Nuttall, as he was often seen!

Top left: Harbour Club, Kyrenia, Sept 1958. Front three from left – Chuck Coulcher, Roly Jackson, Frank Grimshaw; next table up – Jack Henderson & John Griffiths (with lager glass); third table, Channing Biss, unknown, Barry Grainger; Tom Gribble, fourth table, extreme left.
(C P Coulcher)

Top right: AOC's balloon 'fly-past' 24 June 1959, Stradishall, with F/O Mumford in the basket. The Hunter far right, XE628, was lost off Libya 24 April 1963.

Middle left: David Brook's Hunter XE619 after colliding with a tree 17 February 1959.

Middle right: El Adem October 1959: Mark Tomkins, Anthony Mumford and John Griffiths. Note the two 'dark' flying overalls, died red, but which came out maroon.
(A Mumford)

Bottom: Squadron pilots June 1959. Standing from left: Frank Marshall, Mac Cameron, Tony Chaplin, Chuck Coulcher, Anthony Mumford, Pete Little, Dave Brook, John Griffiths, Barrie Dimmock, John Smith; Seated: Ted Hassig, Harry Davidson, Mr Long, S/L J J Phipps, Roly Jackson, Mark Tomkins, Kit Netherton; Front: Barry Grainger.

Top left: 1 Squadron, Stradishall, (l to r): B J Dimmock, R C Humphreyson, J Smith, Oswell, M Tompkins, D Whittaker; front: F Marshall, H J Davidson and G/Capt H Bennett (Stn Cdr).

Top right: Harry Davidson on Malta after his record-breaking flight 23 April 1961.

Middle left: Queen's Birthday Flypast 13 June 1959. From left, F/L Jackson, F/L Gribble, S/L John Phipps (OC), F/L Harry Davidson and W/Cdr Boyle.

Middle right: W/Cdr J A Mansell, OC 1 Squadron in 1969 but killed in flying accident 21 May.

Right: S/Ldr D C G Brook, showing former CO Maj W E Young DFC (1918) the cockpit of a Hunter FGA.9, summer 1965. *(D C G Brook)*

Top left: F/Lt 'Cid' Sowler's effort, 5 August 1969.

Top right: Landing at Ciampino, Rome, 24 June 1970. The two wing-ships are XV754 and XV753.

Middle: Formation RVL – Rolling Vertical Landing.

Bottom left: XV776 slightly 'sick' – Paris Air Show June 1971.   *(A L Hancock)*

Bottom right: Duke of Edinburgh's visit, July 1971; (l to r): G/C Alan Merriman, Stn Cdr Wittering, C-in-C, Prince Phillip, W/Cdr Ken Hayr, (CO), AOC 38 Gp, AVM D Crowley-Milling.

Top left: MP shaking hands with Capt Louis Distelweg USAF, KIFA 3 August 1971 while on attachment. John Grogen (left) and Ken Hayr (right). *(K Hayr)*

Top right: Operation White Tent, Norway. *(K Hayr)*

Centre: HMS *Ark Royal*. Note Harrier doing a low fly-by. *(K Hayr)*

Bottom left: Capt J O Roberts RN, commanding *Ark Royal*; his father had been in 1 Squadron in 1940. W/Cdr Ken Hayr AFC swapping plaques. *(K Hayr)*

Bottom right: W/Cdr E J E Smith OBE, (left) OC 1 Squadron 1972-3. *(E J E Smith)*

Top left: W/Cdr P P W Taylor AFC, OC 1 Squadron 1973-76. *(P P W Taylor)*

Top right: Exchange visit with 2° Stormo, 103° Gruppo, July 1973, Treviso, Italy. RAF l to r: Tom Plank USAF, Keith Grumbley, F/L Reggie Wargent; 6th from left, F/L Allen.

Middle left: 19,000 lbs of thrust was too much for the Belize airfield steel planking.

(via Saye)

Middle right: W/Cdr J G Saye, OC 1 Squadron 1976-8.

Left: F/L B M Brookford's GR3 'spread' landing at RAF Lyneham, 28 June 1973 (XW919).

Top left: 1 Squadron 'boater-hatted' just before Dijon exchange trip, October 1976.

Middle left: Peter Squire and some of his pilots prior to the Falklands campaign, from left: Squire, Nick Gilchrist, Tony Harper, Bob Iveson, John Rochfort, Mark Hare and Jerry Pook.

Middle right: W/Cdr P T Squire DFC AFC, OC 1 Squadron 1981-83.

(P T Squire)

Right: W/Cdr Squire landing on HMS *Hermes*, 18 May 1982. *(P T Squire)*

Top left: RAF GR3 and Navy Sea Harriers ranged on *Hermes* in the South Atlantic. *(P T Squire)*

Top right: S/Ldr Bob Iveson in front of his wrecked Harrier after the war.

Middle left: W/Cdr I R Harvey MBE, with Princess Diana, Honorary Air Commodore of RAF Wittering.

Middle right: W/Cdr Harvey hands over to W/Cdr C C N Burwell MBE, May 1991. Pilots, l to r: S/L Les Garside-Beattie, S/L Chris Benn (Exec), W/C Chris Burwell, W/C Ian Harvey, F/L Tony Norris.

Left: W/Cdr I M Stewart, OC 1 Squadron 1986-88.

Top left: F/L Sean Perrett, F/L Chris Huckstep, F/L Simon Turner and W/C Chris Burwell.

Top right: Kate Saunders and Ashley Stevenson after their ejection, 25 September 1991.

Above: F/O 'Spike' Jepson loosing off the Squadron's first Sidewinder air-to-air missile.

Right: S/L Benny Ball about to take off from Gioia del Colle for Kosovo, April 1999.

Top: W/Cdr David Walker in his Harrier GR7 'cabriolet' after being hit by small arms fire 2 February 1995. *(D Walker)*

Middle left: F/Lts Dave Kane, Chris Averty and Myles Garland after their first sorties over Kosovo.

Bottom left: Chris Averty taking off for Kosovo.

Above right: Bomb markings on a Squadron GR7. Three LGBs (laser-guided bombs), 14 cluster bombs and seven 1,000 pounders.

Top left: W/Cdr Andy Golledge DSO, OC 1 Squadron 1998-2000.

Top right: S/Ldr Chris Huckstep DFC, 1 Squadron Exec.

Bottom left: S/Ldr Chris Norton DFC, B Flight Commander 1 Squadron.

Bottom right: W/Cdr Sean Bell, OC 1 Squadron, 2000-.

convince the USAF personnel system to extend my tour) was that being a graduate of the USAF Fighter Weapons School, the Squadron selected me to complete the ground portion of the Harrier Pilot Attack Instructor (PAI) course, and therefore, the Squadron deserved a reasonable return on the investment. Having flown 173 missions in Vietnam as well as a PAI, put me in a position to pass on lessons learned from my combat experience.

After the Hunter I linked up with other members of my Harrier class for the five-sortie Whirlwind training course. The purpose of the course was to show a fighter pilot that you don't necessarily crash and burn if your machine comes to a stop in mid-air.

One of the reasons I joined the USAF was so I didn't have to live in tents during deployments. I soon discovered this didn't apply in the RAF Harrier world. During "Sky Mist" at Milltown in February 1973 it got so cold that the CO decided that if he didn't lodge his pilots into Lossiemouth Officer's Mess each night, he wouldn't have anyone well enough to fly. We "reluctantly" obeyed his order; who would want to give up a tent for a warm room and clean sheets?

During the May 1973 APC in Cyprus, my close friend Flight Lieutenant Keith Grumbley ("Gum"), somehow was able to beat me for the Hilly Brown trophy. I would have won had it not been for the Kokkinelli wine he plied me with the night before. This apparently affected my depth perception, because fellow PAI Flight Lieutenant Geoff Hulley, with much bell-ringing fanfare, disqualified my incredibly high strafe score (which would have clinched the trophy for me) for firing inside the 600 yard foul line. Anyway, that's my story and I'm sticking to it. Awful stuff that Kokkinelli – I actually saw it eat through a styrofoam cup!

Cyprus was a great APC. Not only did we go to the range once or twice a day, each weekend many of us would squeeze into a rented VW Bug and head north for Kyrenia by the sea. It just didn't get any better than renting a chug-chug boat, anchoring off shore for a lunch of roasted chicken and wine, and having the pre-arranged ski-boat come to where we were anchored for an afternoon of water skiing. Our nights were spent on the harbour with the Squadron band playing the oldies, much to the delight of the tourists who would buy us rounds of drinks all night long. Geoff Hulley stayed in Cyprus for a few days after the APC to perform a demo and had to eject during a steep climbing accelerating transition from the hover. A photographer got a picture of this and it made the cover of "Aviation Week".'

Geoff Hulley broke his left ankle as he landed. Corporal Doyle, a PTI at Episkopi, rushed into the flaming wreckage of XV739, (24 Sep 1973) to help him get clear, thereby saving him from further injury.

Flight Lieutenant Keith Grumbley, from Kenya, had arrived following a tour with 8 Squadron in Bahrain earlier in the year. His grandfather, Major Lawrence Grumbley, a retired Indian Army officer (ex-Lancashire Regt) had been 1 Squadron's adjutant at Tangmere in 1940. Gum's father had also been a Blenheim pilot in WW2. Of Tom Plank's accusation, Keith comments:

'I recall winning the trophy on 8 June 1973. We were operating the Mark 1 Harrier which had no laser rangefinder. The inertial weapon aiming system was in something of a development stage and we were having a lot of trouble with it. My friend Tom Plank knew that because he was one of our weapons instructors. I doubt if a professional like him would have let Kokkinelli interfere with his performance! However, I do not recall what we got up to the evening before the shoot, but I remember that I had not had a particularly successful APC. We seemed to be plagued with weapon-aiming problems and I suspect that success on 8 June was more to do with getting an aircraft that worked as advertised. There was a skill required in assessing that it was working correctly though.

While on Cyprus we had a sort of Squadron impromptu cabaret act. Kit Adams was an accomplished guitar player, Plank would do some crazy thing from an American TV show with a handkerchief in front of his lower leg so that it apparently disappeared, and I was going through my glass eating phase! Eating glass is not harmful if done properly but it is not recommended because in later years the erosion of teeth plagues one a bit. The Squadron was enlisted by Hawkers and Ferranti to entertain clients from time to time and that year we looked after some Jordanians. After the "cabaret" one of them tried my glass-eating trick, without any prompting or tutelage from me and succeeded in embedding a shard in the roof of his mouth. It was late and I recall the doctor, whose name was (would you believe) Livingstone, being unimpressed at dealing with this. In the morning it turned out that he was an old mate of the boss, Eric Smith, so that was all right – or sort of!'

On 27 June Flight Lieutenants J R Lloyd and B M Blackford flew to Lyneham to give a display the next day for the Chief of Staff to the Italian Air Force. Unfortunately during a practice on the morning of the 28th Brook Blackford suffered some kind of engine malfunction which caused the Harrier (XW919) to descend very rapidly from the hover and on striking the ground sustained Cat 4 damage. Parts of the undercarriage were scattered over a large area, and Blackford suffered injuries to back and head. Another pilot and aircraft were quickly despatched from base and John Lloyd led the display that afternoon without further mishap.

* * *

Following Cyprus, the Squadron had a NATO exchange in July with the Italian 103° Gruppo, based at St Angelo, Treviso, which flew Fiat G-91s. In July too, three pilots landed on HMS *Bulwark* for a short exercise. This was not the first encounter with this carrier, as Eric Smith recalls:

'During our APC at Akrotiri in May, we heard that HMS "Bulwark" was in the area. Somehow we made contact, and then after a family arrival by Wessex helicopter, a couple of us made several hovers over the "wooden deck" before returning to Akrotiri. I did this twice, so it was obviously fun and very enjoyable.'

Then came a trip to Vandel, in central Denmark. All support equipment had to be flown in as part of the exercise, and gas masks were worn. Ken Hayr came on a visit in early August, Eric Smith flying him in the T2 for a recce of the airfields for possible deployment. As 1973 came to an end, Eric Smith prepared to hand over to Wing Commander P P W Taylor AFC. Peter Taylor had been a pilot with both 92 and Treble One Squadrons' aerobatic teams earlier in his career, then in Aden with No.8, and now he came from IV Squadron. He had also been with Air Support Command as the Harrier policy guy and therefore involved in Harrier policy since the beginning. He remembers how he found the Squadron:

'It was recognised by Group that the Squadron had been just too busy; the programme they'd been given was just phenomenal. During Eric's time as CO they had hardly ever been back at base and never had a real opportunity to work people up.

When I got to the Squadron it was realised that the pressure had to come off. Over December and January we pulled ourselves together, then went off to Deci, which was my first opportunity to get the Squadron by itself, and it proved a very successful detachment. We had a good Squadron, good people and especially good ground crew who were very experienced. As soon as we got back we had to prepare for exercise "Big Tree". This was a very large exercise for the time, designed to show how many sorties a Harrier squadron could generate over a very short period of time, while detached away from base, so we went off to RAF Watton, a disused airfield, using some of the old buildings for sleeping. We built "hides" for the aircraft around the field and flew 364 sorties in three days, which is a lot of flying. The concept behind "Big Tree" was to get right up behind a supposed front line and fly ten minute sorties.

We had 12 aircraft and having borrowed a couple of extra bods we had 18 pilots, but the idea was for each man to fly five consecutive sorties. Later, after my time, it was thought the ideal was six sorties, three in succession, take a break, then fly three more. At this stage my flight commanders were Squadron Leaders Bob Holliday, Jack Pugh and Dave Lott[1]. We had one responsible for deployments and setting them up, while the other two concentrated on training and so on.

After "Big Tree" we were involved in Sky Watch, which was a BBC programme on air power, which took place over a day, a lot of it based at Wittering. Vulcans were brought in, Jaguars, Lightnings, and ourselves. Broadcast live on television, this was a tremendous event at the time. There is a good anecdote worth recording.

Part of what we had to do was to send five aircraft off on an attack sortie, which I led. We landed at Cottesmore to refuel and then Jack Pugh, who is the archetypal British gentleman, the most proper officer you could imagine, was sent off to make a recce of the "target". Then, while the commentator – who was Raymond Baxter – was talking through the sortie, he said that Squadron Leader Pugh, carrying the recce pod and taking photos, would be coming back to report. Then the idea was that Jack would go to him and Baxter would ask him questions. So we did all this; Jack landed, the photos were developed and printed in no time, then Jack was standing in front of the TV camera. Over to Jack, who was standing like a wax-works dummy, and doesn't move at all. We, of course, were all looking at this on a TV monitor. The producer then hissed: "Say hello to Raymond!" Jack looks across at him, off camera, and says: "But I can't; we haven't been introduced."'

---

[1] Dave Lott's father George, who retired as an AVM, commanded 43 Squadron at Tangmere in 1940, winning the DSO and DFC.

Keith Grumbley also recalls this Sky Watch programme:

'Raymond Baxter was the commentator for this high visibility production which involved just about every RAF aircraft type, flying out of Wittering. The Squadron occupied a field location at the western end of the airfield. I was flying out of an inflatable hangarette thing – an appaling invention. The first time I started the engine, the whole thing imploded inwards and threatened to be sucked down the engine intakes. There was a great urgency to get this thing to go right for the TV cameras and to make "good TV", things had to happen quickly. Several of us had excursions across the bundu. I recall on one occasion I had just about reached flying speed when I heard a radio call: "Gum, don't take off!" I thought it must be one of Neal Wharton's pranks but aborted the take-off and brought the jet under control somewhere in the Collyweston salient. It turned out that in the confusion over the imploding hangarette and re-starting engines, the undercarriage ground locks had not been removed. As this was the umpteenth "take" of a co-ordinated field site take-off for eight Harriers, the boss was not impressed. Eventually it did go right and was good TV.'

Farnborough '74

That September 1 Squadron was required to produce an eight-man team for Farnborough in which a complicated sequence, including formation hovers, high-speed passes and simulated attacks had to be demonstrated. Dave Lott remembered how it was all a bit of a shambles on the first rehearsal. The CO took a four-ship in close formation over the President's tent very low. Group Captain George Black, in charge of the RAF team, was angry at this, and showed it at the debrief. Peter Taylor:

'We did a work-up with eight Harriers. We were to go down to Farnborough and make a simulated attack using two four-ship formations, then do some VSTOL and land. I don't think in rehearsals we ever did the same thing twice. I remember George Black, Group Captain Ops at 38 Group, who had also been Station Commander at Wildenrath when I'd been there with the Harrier Wing (so I knew him quite well), came across. I've never had a bollocking like it in my entire life – he really laid into me. The funny thing was that this seemed to work and we then got it together.

The weather, however, was dreadful. Every day saw high winds, never less than 25 knots, and mostly 40-50. However, we flew on all eight days and it all worked really well. Then, on Press Day, we were all lined up on a particular stretch of the airfield from where we'd taken off to do our thing, but the evening before the organisers said that we shouldn't really be there, as some of the bigger aircraft couldn't get by. So we were moved to another spot.

Day one dawned, and it was really blowing. The Blackhawk helicopter flown by an American civilian pilot, who'd already given us quite a spirited display in practice, part of which was to roll the helicopter twice as he progressed down the runway, came into view. Rolling a helicopter, especially in 1974, was quite an unusual manoeuvre. None of us will ever know why he did it, but he had done his two rolls, while the wind was still blasting down the runway, and he came along much faster than he thought and suddenly decided to throw in a third roll. As he came out of this extra roll, he dug a blade in and the helicopter crashed exactly where our Harriers had been parked the previous day.

The thing blew up and there was a terrible fire. The poor chap, although he survived, was very badly burned and died some days later. We, of course, were all lined up waiting to go on next and each of us knew how lucky it was that we'd been moved away from that spot.

About half way through the week, Jack Pugh had an electrical failure and one of his undercarriage legs didn't indicate it was down and locked. In fact it was OK, but he didn't know that. We were all trying to get the aircraft on the ground and there was Jack hovering in front of us all, shouting to everyone: "I've got a starboard out-rigger red!" We didn't know he couldn't hear us because he'd gone over to the emergency frequency, so we could hear him, while I was yelling for him to land.'

Tom Plank was also at Farnborough:

'The 1 Squadron tactical display at Farnborough (two four-ship and a singleton) was the top attraction at the air show. I flew as the singleton, flying 100 feet (the minimum allowed), 400 knots (the maximum allowed) recce pass followed by a tactical break to 1,000 feet for a very steep, 50 knot rolling vertical landing (RVL). Group Captain Black had already threatened to send me back to Wittering, if not the USA, if I made any more passes at 35 feet and 500 knots! Well, at least I had impressed the Squadron's ground crews, who had gathered on the infield grass to watch our performances. After the display, my crew chief said, "That was a super low pass, Sir. Your vortices left a whirling trail of grass clippings!"

The ironic thing about all this was that I was quite comfortable as a Harrier pilot flying the pass at that altitude and airspeed. But I was very uncomfortable hearing the Group Captain tell me to steepen-up my RVL, which wasn't a normal profile and which was made all the more challenging by having to fight the 30 to 50 knot shearing cross-winds that accompanied the bad weather during the first part of the show. I also remember on Press Day watching the Blackhawk attack helicopter dish-out of a barrel roll attempt and crash in front of our nine Harriers while we waited with engines running in the drizzling rain, to take the runway for our display. Witnessing the fiery crash was a little off-putting, especially when the Tower allowed the show to continue and cleared us to move onto the runway. I will never forget Boss Taylor's comforting words on the flight frequency; "Let's put that out of our minds and put on a super show ... wipers on, Go!" And we did.'

Keith Grumbley remembers these or similar words from the boss:

'I recall pretty poor weather in which we flew nine Harriers on every day of the show. The radio call which summed it up came from the boss on about day four: "We're doing the full, good-weather show; windscreen wipers on, Go!"'

Belize
Peter Taylor continues:

'We thought we were in for a comparatively quiet time thereafter, but in November, Shirley Bassey came to Wittering. Her producer was working on a series of shows with spectacular backgrounds, one of which was going to be the Harrier, filmed for a Christmas special. One scene was Shirley seated in the two-seater being flown next to an Argosy, with a camera man almost hanging out of it, and she'd then be filmed singing away with lots of shots of Harriers being cut into the song and so on.

Down she came and we kitted her out with a bone-dome clamped over her huge wig, flying suit, mae-west, etc., but finally MoD decided she could not be flown in the T-bird. So we filmed it all on the ground, me in the cockpit, Shirley in the back, and a camera mounted on a sort of gantry going up and down to simulate the aircraft flying. To get actual airborne sequences we got a WAAF and with some make-up and a wig, flew her up by the Argosy so the camera guy could take his shots. It all worked and came out very well.

In early 1975 we went out to Tromso once again, exercising the Squadron deployment concept. It really is a magnificent part of the world and we had the most marvellous time. Then it was back to Deci but then, right out of the blue we received a signal to get ourselves ready to go to Belize. I had to confess, when I got Bob and Jack in, none of us knew where Belize was. Of course, on our maps, it was still marked as British Honduras. It seemed an incredible distance away.

We would have to air-to-air refuel across the Atlantic to Canada, then fly down to Bermuda and finally across to Belize. It really necessitated us to put on the ferry wing-tips, which one very very rarely put on and it was going to take forever and more importantly, a long job to get them off again once we arrived.

I had to go to 38 Group to see if we could dispense with them and this was finally agreed. My main concern, if going into a possible operational area, I didn't want to be buggering about taking off these wing-tips. I wanted to land, drop the 330-gallon tanks and be ready to operate immediately. It would, of course, be the first operational Harrier deployment and we left on 5 November 1975. Bob Holliday led the aeroplanes, while I and the reserve crews went to Bermuda direct to wait for them.

The weather across the Atlantic for those flying the Harriers was pretty awful and they had their work cut out to refuel. Bob led quite an epic journey, refuelling something like six or eight times. It was also bad for the four-hour trip from Bermuda to Belize – me leading this time – and absolutely glued to our Victor tanker; we just didn't take our eyes off it for a moment. We flew out over the Turks and Caicos islands, skirted Cuba – all very exciting.

We landed at Belize airport. The dispersal we set up was primitive, putting our aircraft all round the airfield. We built bridges over storm drains in order to taxi the aircraft about; handling them on the ground was almost as difficult as flying them. We were met by the politicians, because we were helping to stop the war with the Guatemalans, who were threatening to invade Belize. It was an enormous experience for us to be there. A country no bigger than the size of Wales, Belize had quite a well developed coastal strip but inland it was all jungle. It seemed clear that anyone ejecting over the dense jungle wouldn't get out so we kept very much to the coastal region, only over-flying the jungle if absolutely necessary.

The value of that decision came as Bernie Scott hit a bird and had to bale out over the coastal plain. Within minutes we had him back with the Squadron, despite his lower face being peppered with perspex, because he'd not had his face visor all the way down. By December it seemed very unlikely there was going to be a war but politically we had to remain there to provide morale-boosting and military clout. We did a good deal of flying, although limited in what we could do.

It all seemed a bit endless so we began to gradually re-cycle all those back at Wittering through to Belize on rotation, including ground crews and pilots from the OCU. Then, of course, the aircraft began to suffer, with serviceability becoming a major problem – not least fuel leaks. The detachment just about petered out about Easter 1976, when all the aeroplanes had to be taken home – we didn't fly a single one back – for at that stage they were in quite a bad state.

We ourselves had had a phenomenal time, having been there the best part of five months. It had been a long time with some family problems at home too. One guy had his wife's wedding ring appear in an envelope on Christmas Day, which didn't help a great deal. The social life had been tremendous and we'd all been taken out to some of the Keys – similar to the Florida Keys, but less developed. While there a big earthquake rocked Guatemala. At the time we were in the officer's mess watching the film "Earthquake"! Somebody noticed that their glass was rattling but it wasn't until the next day the news came through.

There was also the time, while sailing some boats, that a young American civilian came rushing down the beach, imploring us to hide him and get him away, as some chap was after him with a knife. Apparently he'd been caught with the man's girlfriend. So we got him away and he was very grateful, especially as, some minutes later, a guy with a huge knife did appear on the scene. Later, our American said that if ever I was in Montgomery, Alabama, I should look up his daddy, who owned one of the largest Cadillac dealerships in that State. Oddly enough, I was later posted to Montgomery for a tour of duty with the USAF. And I did look up "Daddy" and got an amazing deal on a huge Cadillac, so it does show how a helping hand can sometimes pay dividends!'

Belize had been named Operation 'Nucha' and the Harrier was the only RAF aircraft which could operate from the short single runway that was Belize airport. As Fidel Castro on Cuba had expressed his support for Belize, the RAF were unable to use any USAF bases during this period. Some of the taxi-ways were just strips of PSP (Pierced Steel Planking) which were often lifted by the blast from the Harrier's VTO.

Dave Lott and John Buckler had been the first two pilots to land on Belize. Ground crews quickly took off the external tanks and within twenty minutes they were airborne on a flag-waving sortie over Belize city. All the Squadron personnel obviously had a great welcome from the local populace. Sorties flown over the coming weeks gave the pilots some wonderful views of jungle-covered mountains and tropical sea. Any number of aircraft were intercepted, all being innocent civilian airlines flying along unaware of the tension in the area, but it was all good practice.

At least one pilot, Flight Lieutenant Henry de Courcier, found his future wife on Belize. Just before they left, the Squadron was asked to 'beat up' the city, which it was more than happy to do.

Fred Welsh was to spend 13 years with 1 Squadron, ending up as Chief Technician airframes. He recalls the spartan existence on Belize and the heat. The airmen began wearing just the bare essentials, little more than shorts and flip-flops. One day Peter Taylor called Fred over and referred to the dress code, saying that this wasn't a M.A.S.H. unit as seen on TV, and at the very least they should wear their boots rather than flip-flops. The CO's call-sign was 'Lupin' and, airmen being airmen, they soon organised a warning system with a radio, calling Lupin as a code word. Whenever the CO was seen approaching, the airmen, duly warned, would dive into an aircraft shelter and change their flip-flops for bundu boots, changing back again once he had cleared the area!

Fred also recalls a young airman who had a distinct dislike of rifles, so during his turn on guard, Fred gave him the gun but kept the ammunition in his own pocket. He thought this would be safer for everyone concerned.

The water table on the airstrip was high and there were occasions during engine testing that aircraft would begin to lift on the throttle and up too came the metal strips, pulling out the huge pins from the sodden earth. Airmen were kept busy hammering them back into the ground before they were blasted away – not always successfully.

There was also the 'Big C' bar, frequented by the airmen, but more commonly known as the 'Bamboo'. Fred recalls the beer was pretty awful and on his first visit there couldn't understand why those in first were appearing to run to the bar. However, he soon discovered that while the front of the building was on firm ground, the back was on stilts over a river and it had begun to sink down. So the distinct slope 'encouraged' one to get to the bar, but was rather a hindrance when staggering back up later in the evening.

Harrier losses

Shortly after Peter Taylor had taken over the Squadron, Harrier XV776 was lost on 9 April at Wittering. Flight Lieutenant John Buckler ejected from it after the engine flamed out. Over Belize Flight Lieutenant Bernard Scott had ejected from a GR3, XV788 on 1 December 1975. Then back in the UK, meantime, Wittering lost XV745 and XV754 on 19 January 1976. This had followed a mid-air collision near Crewe, Cheshire. These two had been part of a four-man sortie on a ground-attack exercise. They failed to maintain separation attacking a target from different angles, colliding with each other as they crossed over. Flight Lieutenant John K Roberts and Flight Lieutenant James E Downey BSc were both killed. Downey had already ejected from another Harrier, as well as handling several other emergencies extremely well; now his luck had run out.

* * *

Tom Plank:

> 'Wing Commander "boss" Taylor was a great squadron commander, the best I ever had. He could do it all, in the air and on the ground, working or playing, with great style and professionalism. I remember him getting back at me for having served him the blood, disguised as wine, from some steaks I had cooked at one of my "Yank barbecues" during an APC at Deci. Several months later, I went with him in the back seat of the Squadron's rarely serviceable two-seater on a site-survey trip to Denmark in advance of the Squadron's deployment to Vandel.
>
> He told me that he would load his own travel bag in the Harrier's internal cargo net – an awkward and often dirty procedure – and that I could use the more convenient nosewheel well compartment. This well was much better so long as you planned no VSTOL manoeuvres during the sortie, since the hot air pipe for the nose puffer duct is located there. I thought, "what a mate" the boss is. Well the boss somehow "forgot" about my bag when arriving at Vandel he couldn't resist a hover and "bow" to the tower. So it was no surprise on landing to find the contour of the hot pipe burned into the side of my bag. It didn't appear to have burned through, but later, at a social event with the Danes that night, he asked me how I had got a burn mark across the back of my lounge suit jacket!
>
> Another of the boss's tricks was to plant a raw egg in a bottle of beer for some unsuspecting newcomer to arrive and be challenged by him to a "down in one" contest. Yuck!
>
> Exercise "Cold Winter" to Tromso offered especially challenging cold weather flying experience. We would fly the entire close air support mission, navigating up and down the fjords with the clouds well below the mountain tops, leaving only 1-2,000 feet of airspace in which to manoeuvre. It was while returning from one such sortie that I was asked, upon checking in with the Squadron Ops, to do the first vertical landing of the deployment, since a good bit of snow at the airfield had melted.
>
> As I recall, the procedure was to manoeuvre the Harrier to a hover at 70 feet over the pad, higher than the usual 50 feet, in order to blow away the remaining snow without becoming engulfed in a blinding cloud of Harrier-made precipitation. After doing this, I descended to the standard 50 feet hover, picked up the 12 and 9 o'clock cueing markers, and started to descend for landing. Unfortunately, the ground was so wet that at about 20 feet I found myself inside a self-made rain storm and unable to see the ground markers. Judgement told me I was committed and, somehow, I was able to complete the landing without bending the jet.'

Peter Taylor's reign came to an end in July 1976, his final months organising intensive training and maintenance, desperately needed before the Squadron could once more resume its place as part of NATO's front line. Deci was his last deployment just before he handed over to Wing Commander J G Saye, and Flight Lieutenant Peter Bennett got his hands on the Hilly Brown Trophy.

That autumn the Squadron went to Oerland, on Norway's west coast, for exercise 'Teamwork'. They were joined by air units of the US Marine Corps, who had their AV-8B Harriers on board the

USS *John F Kennedy*. They also had their F-4 Phantoms and A-6s. According to Dave Lott, the Yanks didn't have a clue and had all their aircraft and vehicles bogged down in the mud which caused them some excitement. Their Admiral was particularly incensed to learn that 1 Squadron's 12 Harriers had flown more sorties that the entire Marine Air Group, which had more than 80 jets, on land and on the carrier. As Jeremy Saye remembers:

'This was a US Marine-led exercise and the only aircraft I recall were their F-4s and A-6s. We did not see any AV-8s, although these may have remained on the USS JFK. The 4-star general was the archetypal "grunt": gung-ho, dynamic, crew-cut, sleeves rolled for action, no tolerance for wimps camping, all in favour of "stamping-out our skivvies" (personal laundry)! and was so happy with us he could, "... pee ma pants!" Alternatively, he was just as likely to "... cloud over and piss on ya!" A real character.'

French mustard (Dijon)

November and another exchange visit, this time with the French Air Force and its GC12 Cigognes outfit, equipped with the Mirage, and based at Dijon. Jeremy Saye:

'We approached the forthcoming Squadron exchange to the French Air Force's Mirage squadron at Dijon with a mixture of excitement and apprehension. Excitement because such exchanges are always a highlight on the annual calendar, and apprehension because we were not entirely sure, with France's political detachment from NATO, how far the FAF would be able to co-operate with us. In the event, our fears were groundless. Our hosts were extremely hospitable, and proved themselves to be extremely competent professionally.

We enjoyed some very exciting composite attack sorties involving ourselves, Mirages and Jaguars. As was to be expected, the French displayed a traditional "joie de vivre". We certainly envied their approach to a quality of life for which our own commitments never seemed to allow enough time. Their working day, at least during our visit, was to start early, and to finish flying in time for a late and leisurely, Nuits-St-Georges assisted, lunch. The afternoons, or what was left of them, were given to less-essential tasks, including a little administration.

As is so often the case, the Devil creates mischief for idle hands, and one of our chief technicians – a notable cartoonist – took it upon himself to embellish our host squadron's badge – a flying stork – with another more lascivious stork mounted in flagrante, so to speak! We all thought this a jolly jape, until, on the morning of departure, our own T-bird was discovered covered in garish pink and purple. A wash-paint would have been OK, but the oil-based paint took hours to remove, and somewhat took the "gloss" off our return (if the pun can be excused).'

The new year of 1977 began with continued training which led to a Taceval (Tactical Evaluation), in which RAF Leeming took on the guise of a Turkish airfield. No sooner had this ended than more rumblings from Belize put the Squadron on Readiness again, although this time there was a little more warning, allowing for some air-to-air firing for the new boys. Again the INAS results were poor, the pilots resorting to fixed sighting.

Squadron Leader Lott, with Flight Lieutenants Scott and Watts flew to Belize in a VC10 a day before the first pair of Harriers arrived, finding the locals in more than a panic about the Guatemalan invasion threat, although they also found the local soldiers in a more relaxed mood. The SAS had also arrived and were preparing to move into the jungle to await the arrival of Guatemalan troops without waiting for local army support. Wing Commander Saye with Squadron Leaders Peter W Day and John S Finlayson landed later. Jeremy Saye reports:

'Our hopes of a short break after the pressure of the Taceval were immediately dashed as we were told to gear-up for a return to Belize, which was again being threatened by the Guatamalans. The principal threat, apart from the obvious ground forces, appeared to be from the Guat Air Force's US-supplied A-37s, basically a two-seat jet trainer in the Jet Provost class [Strikemasters], but certainly capable of carrying 4 x 500 lb bombs. As it was to be our job to ensure they would be shot down before they reached Belize Airport, we immediately set about honing our air-firing skills.

'A few of us older hands with previous Air Defence experience, mindful of our earlier abilities in the Hunter to score at least 50% of the "flag" on a good day, thought this would be a piece-of-cake. We were all humbled to witness almost totally virgin flags being returned to the ground. Despite the best efforts of our Qualified Weapons Instructors (QWIs), John West and Chris Bain, burning midnight oil, along with a Ferranti team, we never did get the gun and gunsight in line. I noted at the time that it was somewhat ironic that we were preparing to go into a potential air-air shooting war using a fixed-sighting technique not much different from that used by our predecessors in WW2!

The build-up prior to deployment was notable for two other events. Aware of our own limited air-air expertise, we sought to exploit any known weakness in the enemy's capabilities; his equipment, his training, his tactics, etc. Presumably, we felt, some Intel team from on high would come to brief us. I recall no such briefing, and in the end it was fortunate that my predecessor, Peter Taylor, was at that time on exchange duty at USAF HQ Tactical Air Command. He was able to convey certain essential information to us via his "sources". I suspect this was highly illegal, given that the US had supplied the Guats with their arsenal, but we both understood the importance of it for the honour of the Squadron.

During the preparations, we were also aware of the consequences of a possible bale out over the Belizean jungle. Those of us with previous experience of operating over the jungles of Borneo and Malaysia remembered the value of the "tree-scape", which we had all carried. Consequently we invited a team from IAM [Institute of Aviation Medicine] Farnborough up to Wittering to brief us (and equip us). It was not comforting to hear from these august gentlemen that the "tree-scape" could no longer be released to the Service, because tests had shown that the nylon rope could melt if it were subjected to the weight of a gorilla descending at 20 mph – or some such figure. The fact that aircrew had successfully used this device in the Far East throughout the 1960s was ignored!

In the end, and on the principle that it was better to try than to die, we devised our own. Sometimes one has to go with one's own initiatives when faced with the inherent resistance of those for whom, in this case, the "best was the enemy of the good enough."'

Return to Belize

'At 0130 hours on Friday 8 July 1977, with less than three hours sleep after the long ferry flight, I was awakened by the Air Commander, Wing Commander Derek Hine, to be told that, on the best intelligence information, the Guat A-37s were sitting on the end of Guatamala City Airport runway, bombed-up in readiness for a presumed dawn attack on Belize. Galvanising dog-tired air and ground crew into action was helped by the adrenalin-rush which always accompanies fear and expectation. Needless to say, we launched three armed Harriers at 0500, keeping the remaining two at cockpit readiness and we continued patrols throughout the day until dusk (1800).

We kept up this 13-hour flying day for a week, with the ground crew on their knees, operating from primitive conditions, in steaming tropical heat with Mosquitos everywhere. In the end, the Guats never came, and whilst we were relieved, I believe we, the aircrew, felt cheated that we had been denied the opportunity to fire our guns in anger. No praise can be too high for the way in which the whole detachment had operated under very difficult and tiring conditions. Our ground crew, particularly, had conducted themselves superbly, operating from hides in stifling heat and humidity, with minimal protection from the elements and mosquitos. Everyone acted in the best traditions of the Service, and I was immensely proud of them.

Whilst all this was going on, the resident army battalion based in Belize camp (the Royal Regiment of Wales), seemed to us to be taking a very low-key approach to events. I do not recall at any time they stood-to to defend against expected air attacks, while No.1 Squadron was at battle stations. I would like to think this was a vote of supreme confidence in the RAF's ability to destroy all raiders before they reached the camp.

However, we got on with them very well, despite the competition for "local talent" at the "Big C" bar downtown. Colonel John Head, the garrison commander, was hugely supportive in helping the Squadron's operations. As time moved on, we dug in, and with the arrival of portakabins in remarkably quick time, we made life as comfortable as the situation allowed. Nothing will erase the memory of the tensions and pressures of that first week when we expected to go to war, but didn't.

Towards the end of March 1978, we arranged, with the connivance of the garrison quartermaster, to have the following inserted into garrison orders: "On 1 April, following decimalisation of national currencies, NATO will be adopting metric time, starting at 1200 hours. There will be 100 new minutes to the hour, and ten new hours to the day. All personnel are to report to the quartemaster's store at 1000 hours to be issued with metric watches." Needless to say, there was a long queue of April Fools!'

During the detachment, individual aircraft had names written on the tailplanes. Wing Commander Saye's read: *Jeremy's Jungle Jumper*. The RAF and particularly 1 Squadron had received a tremendous welcome yet again, with people dancing in the streets as the Harriers flew in. In a local magazine someone recorded that: "*Calling out the Harriers, they say in Belize, is like calling on James Bond.*" In the same magazine, Flight Lieutenant John West, being asked about the Harrier, was quoted as saying: "*We have a tremendous engine. It has ten tons of thrust, the acceleration is tremendous. I'd be very happy to go to war in it. It has enough combat potential to keep you alive. After all, no Mig pilot can put the brakes on in the air. We can stop dead in seconds. And we get through 12 sorties a day where a Phantom would do two and a Mirage four if its lucky.*"

As the detachment went on, it was obvious that other Harrier units and pilots would have to be fed into the Belize situation, so the two German-based squadrons took turns to fly in. By June the Squadron no longer took sole responsibility and so their people were finally returned to home base. Just as this was accomplished, Jeremy Saye handed over command to Wing Commander R B Duckett, a former leader with the Red Arrows display team.

* * *

Exercise 'Northern Wedding' was carried out in the Orkney and Shetland islands in the late summer, and with it came some severe weather, then snow at Wittering heralded a deployment to Norway. This was followed by a trip to Sardinia – in the warm – which prepared everyone for another spell on Belize in July 1979. Once again Guatemalan aircraft seemed to be preparing for action but everything died down again.

The CO and Flight Lieutenant C J Gowers collided in mid-air on 21 September during an air combat sortie over Wisbech. Both men ejected, the CO whilst his Harrier was in a spin, Chris Gowers after an attempt to get his damaged machine back home. A wing finally came off and so it was time to go. The aircraft fell onto a house and unfortunately three civilians were killed. A couple of months later Flight Lieutenant A R Boyens crashed on Holbeach Range following a cannon ricochet, but Ross Boyens got away with it, ejecting safely.

There was no let-up in training for the first half of 1980. White-washed Harriers flew over Norway during exercise 'Anorak Express' [who thinks up these names?] competing against US, RCAF, Danish and Norwegian air defence fighters, then it was off to Alberta, Canada, the Harriers again using Victor tankers to cross the 'pond'.

Taceval at Gütersloh in September again helped with the 'duty free', followed by a NATO exchange to Montijo, in sunny Portugal. Then it was time for Dickie Duckett to hand over to Wing Commander P T Squire AFC in March 1981, following yet another trip to Tromso. Peter Squire was an experienced pilot having been with 20 Squadron in Singapore with Hunters, then with the Red Arrows when they had Gnats. Then he had been a flight commander on 3 Squadron, Germany, before going off to do a ground course, Staff College and then, on promotion, was given 1 Squadron. "Cometh the hour, cometh the man." Peter Squire was suddenly at the right place at the right time.

Chapter Nineteen

THE FALKLANDS BATTLE

Sir Peter Squire:

'I had hoped to get a squadron commander's job, and go to No.1(F) Squadron, which at that stage was significantly different in its operational role to the two Harrier squadrons in Germany, which were committed to the central European theatre of potential conflict. They operated in support of the 1st British Corps on the German border.

No.1 Squadron had quite a different role. It no longer operated from the austere rural field sites but tended to operate from airfields, albeit austere or even bare-based airfields anywhere from north Norway to south-east Turkey. Indeed, when I took over we had nine different potential deployment options in places like Norway, Denmark, Germany, Greece and Turkey. Many had never been visited and were little more than a map reference on a secret file, but Norway and Denmark were our most common deployment areas.

The other significant difference was that it was the only Harrier squadron which carried out in-flight refuelling. The crews were all trained up to do that for overseas deployments, such as Belize, so this tanking role again separated them from the German-based squadrons. This meant that, if ever aircraft had to be ferried a long way, regardless of who was going to operate them, my Squadron tended to take them there because we had acquired that particular skill.

Early in 1982 the Harrier Force as a whole were all due to take part in a Canadian exercise called "Maple Flag", from Cold Lake. To get aeroplanes there we had to fly with in-flight refuelling to Goose Bay, although we were not going to be the first ones to use them. Landing at Goose Bay we handed them over to our Germany-based colleagues and they flew them on to Cold Lake.

This took place just before the Falklands operation; in fact we knew we would be going to the Falklands but still flew the aircraft to Canada. At the time it rather surprised us. We thought it would be cancelled but, in the event, for some of us who hadn't done six or seven hour legs before, it was a very useful rehearsal, for the sorties which took us from UK to Ascension Island, or for others from Ascension down to the carriers in the South Atlantic and the Total Exclusion Zone.

Although at home base our establishment was about 18 officers and 90 or more ground crew, if we went away on deployment we were reinforced substantially to give us the operational capability on a rugged airfield. We would take a lot of additional engineers from the second line engineering organisation and a detachment of Royal Engineer sappers, mobile caterers, signals people, either from the army or the Tactical Communications Wing. We also took fuel supply specialists from the Tactical Supply Wing. This increased our numbers from 110 to something in excess of 450 bodies. The thing about the Harrier Force is that you never, ever, fight from your own base airfield.

The invasion of the Falkland Islands came as a complete surprise. I often say that on the morning of 2 April 1982, many of us said where on earth are they. Once we discovered where, we thought it very unlikely anybody was going to get involved down there, but did think it might be nice to be deployed to Rio de Janeiro, or somewhere of that nature to be held in reserve.

Not a great deal happened initially except for a few signals from MoD about a possible deployment, but if anything it would be as attrition replacements for Sea Harriers embarked in the two carriers. Operational analysis had estimated that the Navy would lose, perhaps, one aircraft a day and we should plan on that sort of rate. Therefore No.1 Squadron was increasingly put on stand-by to go down as replacements.

Because of this, and because with the size of the carriers there was little spare accommodation, we were told not to take too many people – just enough pilots for the aeroplanes – but not too many ground crew because the matelots would be there and our aircraft were not so different from their Sea Harriers. As things developed I was eventually ordered to deploy with six aircraft, eight pilots and only 19 ground crew. As the operational employment was likely to be predominantly in the air defence role, it seemed to me that we needed the ability to carry and fire air-to-air missiles, which had not been done with the RAF Harrier. Sidewinders were available to the Navy but not us. So we pushed very hard for that and remarkably we actually had Sidewinders fitted to the aircraft, test-fired and proven, all within three weeks of suggesting it.

There was a lot of work to do. We had to "navalise" the aircraft, put shackles on them so as to tie them down on a deck, seal all panels against salt water; the engine was going to be particularly difficult because of the amount of magnesium alloy in RAF Harriers, not in Sea Harriers. We needed to put in I-band transponders so when doing carrier-controlled approaches, perhaps at night, we could actually act as a beacon so they would see us better on radar – again standard on Sea Harriers, not on ours. Later we fitted and trialed the Shrike, anti-radiation missile, and laser-guided bombs (LGBs); all were improvements for us.

During the initial three weeks therefore, the engineers worked extremely hard to modify our Harriers. We borrowed extra aeroplanes from the Germany squadrons and did some very operational training, including air-to-air combat against French aircraft which were typical of ones we might meet, such as the Mirage and Etendard. We also did a lot of low level flying and weapon delivery using live weapons, the constraints in using these being suddenly lifted.

I also had to choose a team to take with me. I was offered carte blanche to choose anybody from the Harrier Force but I took the view that I wasn't going to take anybody who wasn't on the Squadron. So basically I chose eight pilots from those on the Squadron at the time and the first and second reserves, as it were, were pilots who had just literally left to go back to the OCU but were pilots I knew well, rather than taking relatively unknown chaps from Germany.

Eventually came the decision to deploy the aircraft, so at the beginning of May we took eight aeroplanes down to Ascension Island in waves – fairly long sorties of 8-9 hours – using in-flight refuelling. I had a very long day getting to the Island because the tankers, going south, had problems of their own and didn't actually have enough fuel to get the first three Harriers there in one hop. So I sent two of them on with one tanker. I went back with the other to Banjul, in the Gambia. There we turned both aeroplanes round and went on again together. So I did about 11 hours flying that day, and was ready for a beer when I got down on Ascension.

After a couple of days there, waiting for the amphibious group of ships to assemble off Ascension, which included the "Atlantic Conveyor" – a five-deck car ferry – quickly modified to act as an enormous carrier of military equipment. All sorts of weapons and equipment were loaded on the car decks and containers put on either side of the fore-deck to provide a sort of hangar for our aircraft. In all we loaded our six Harriers and eight Sea Harriers [809 Sqd], alongside something like a dozen helicopters – Chinooks and Wessex – loaded in the UK. The Harriers were bagged to protect them from the elements and we sailed in company with the LSLs, Sir Galahad, Sir Tristram and a number of other amphibious craft, joining the Task Force in the Exclusion Zone, some 11 days later.

With no peace deal by the 18th we transferred all the Harriers to the two carriers, "Hermes" and "Invincible". All 1 Squadron aircraft went to "Hermes", the eight Sea Harriers being divided between the two. Not long afterwards the "Atlantic Conveyor" was sunk with a lot of equipment still aboard, but at least all the Harriers were off. We soon found that the Navy had not lost anything like one aircraft a day – they'd lost about four all together – mostly accidents, so instead of being used as replacements we were used as reinforcements and allocated to the offensive support role. The Sea Harriers were retained for the air defence role which was exactly the right decision.'

Chief Technician Fred Welsh was nearing the end of his RAF career and had been asked if he had a last choice. Liking Canada he asked to go there – Maple Flag 9 – and so found himself on his way with the Squadron, knowing that by June he would be finished. In early April 1982, on the 3rd, Fred was orderly sergeant and was starting to get lots of funny 'phone calls from Navy officers from Portsmouth and Plymouth. He then rang the orderly officer about them and asking if there was something going on he should know about. The OO told him the Falklands had been invaded. Fred recalls:

'All I could think about was losing my Canadian trip but of course, only our pilots and ground crews could do the in-flight refuelling but the available tankers could only get us to Goose Bay. So from there we had to hop across to Montreal and then on to Cold Lake, Alberta. 36 hours later all the Harrier blokes from Wittering had to return, leaving 3 and IV Squadrons there. We had this notorious Hercules that never seemed to get 1 Squadron to a place on time, it always went u/s en-route. When it turned up for us we all thought there was no way this aircraft is going to get us home on time. For the first and only occasion the Herk flew two legs – to Gander and Wittering – without breaking down. Everyone knew I was due out, but I made it clear that if I had been dragged back from Canada, and didn't go to the Falklands, I'd be very annoyed. But I was going.

We were back about 12 days, modifying our Harriers for naval tasks, and we cleared 12 Harriers in ten days, fixing Sidewinders, fittings to tie down the jets on ship, etc. It was a lash-up but we got it done. We also had to make wills, something which made us all think a bit.

We set off on 1 May to Ascension Island, feeling quite gung-ho until news came that HMS "Sheffield" had been sunk. This made us realise that perhaps it was not going to be as easy as we imagined. We left Ascension in a Chinook and landed on the "Atlantic Conveyor", then got the aircraft on. By the 21st we were on the "Hermes". When the "Atlantic Conveyor" was sunk, it was Carolyn Squire who got word to wives back at Wittering that we had not been on it.

On the carrier we worked eight hours on and eight off, and because we were at sea, had to keep our clothes on at all times, even when we slept. Our main problem was that we had no relevant Air Publications – they'd all gone down with our transport ship. Everybody was servicing aircraft with what they had in their heads and major problems had to have a brain-storming session to overcome them. When you consider some of the new aircraft which arrived to replace losses, they came with equipment we had never seen. They looked like they had two guns but only one was a gun, the other was a pod that had been turned into a chaff dispenser, photo-recce unit, and so on. And then we got Paveway bombs and that was all new to us.

The engineering done aboard ship was phenomenal, just to get aircraft serviceable and back into the air. Everyone worked hard and some problems with the Navy guys were quickly resolved once they began to understand we were all doing the same job and literally all in the same boat.'

Operation 'Corporate'

The first three Harriers had flown from St Mawgan in company with Victor tankers from Marham and given Search and Rescue (SAR) cover by a 42 Squadron Nimrod from Freetown. The CO, diverting to Banjul, left Tony Harper and Mark Hare to carry on, reaching Ascension with a new record – nine hours, 15 minutes. Another first was the CO's night-tanking prior to his belated arrival. The second wave set off from St Mawgan the next day, although one Harrier – John Rochfort's – had to divert to Madeira with a fault. He later flew on in a C-130 while the faulty aircraft was flown back to the Squadron. The third wave also had problems, Ross Boyens having to divert to Banjul following a fuel transfer problem where he stayed over-night.

As the aircraft went aboard *Atlantic Conveyor*, (plus Flight Lieutenant B Mason and 18 ground crew) Flight Lieutenant P W 'Bomber' Harris talked the CO into taking him in place of the missing Boyens, which upset the latter no end, and when he arrived at Ascension, found he and Tim Smith had been given the job of defending the island. Meantime, the Squadron knew their interests were being looked after, for back at MoD, Air Vice-Marshal Ken Hayr was Assistant Chief of the Air Staff (Operations), and thus a key staff officer. More than that, Wing Commander Joe Sim, another former 1 Squadron pilot, was his assistant. The pilots now in the South Atlantic were:

Wing Commander P T Squire AFC

Squadron Leader T R C Smith	Squadron Leader R D Iveson
Squadron Leader J J Pook	Squadron Leader P W Harris
Flight Lieutenant A R Boyens	Flight Lieutenant J W Glover
Flight Lieutenant M W J Hare	Flight Lieutenant A Harper
Flight Lieutenant J R Rochfort	

Aboard the *Atlantic Conveyor* was the CO, Bob Iveson and the ground crews, with Jerry Pook and the five other pilots sailing aboard the North Sea ferry *Norland*. During the trip the ground crew worked with the FINRAE team (Ferranti Inertial Navigation Reference and Attitude Equipment) to enable the INAS (Inertial Navigation-Attack System) to be aligned properly from a moving ship. It was designed to compensate for a ship's movement, at least enough to give reliable HUD, weapon aiming and instrument information, as well as a degree of navigational accuracy. Joe Sim had organised this, enquiring of Ferranti how long the company would take to bring this on line, bearing in mind it had not been used since the deployment on *Ark Royal*! They thought six months. Joe said he wanted it much sooner; they got it less than three weeks later.

On the afternoon of 18 May, Wing Commander Squire landed on *Hermes*, followed by Jerry Pook, Bob Iveson, Peter Harris and John Rochfort, and were welcomed by its Skipper, Captain L E Middleton. He, the CO and others then went into a huddle, briefing Peter Squire how his Squadron would be expected to operate. The first order was for three aircraft to fly a dusk training mission, which was going to be a problem as the FINRAE equipment had yet to come aboard, but sense finally prevailed and this was cancelled. In the event the first sorties were flown on the 19th.

Wednesday 19 May 1982
The CO with Jeff Glover took off at 1145[1] on a routine ACT sortie but once airborne were re-tasked to intercept a possible Argentinian recce plane – a Boeing 707 of the Argentinian Grupo 1 – 180 miles north-east of the Task Force. They were carrying AIM-9G Sidewinders and climbing to 30,000 feet they were vectored towards the 'bogey' but the interception proved unsuccessful. The two pilots were out of radio range at 150 miles but they returned safely.

Thursday 20 May
Pre-planned attack against POL (Petrol, Oil, Lubricants) fuel storage area at Fox Bay settlement. The CO led Bob Iveson and Jerry Pook off at 1430 (1030) carrying nine CBU (cluster bomb units) between them. The attack was carried out in escort formation following a run-in at low level from the north. The target area was easily identified and attacked as briefed. The CO's weapons were seen to fall and cause several secondary explosions, but explosions from the other's bombs were not seen. There was no ground fire although search radar was heard on the RWR (radar warning receivers, fitted to divert missile and fighter aircraft fire control radars) from Argentinian positions in Stanley and on Pebble Island.

Friday 21 May
This was D-Day at San Carlos, British marines and paratroopers landing on the beaches while it was still dark to begin the invasion of the Falklands. Squadron Leader Pook and Mark Hare took off at 1100 (0700 and therefore 20 minutes before sunrise at this time of year) for their first ever night launch, carrying four CBUs. FINRAE had also arrived so the pilots finally had head-up displays (HUD). Their target was a reported helicopter FOB on the slopes of Mount Kent, spotted by SAS troops. On his first run, Jerry Pook spotted one Chinook and one Puma on the ground and a Bell Huey with its rotors turning. Mark Hare was unable to carry out an attack as the light was poor. Using terrain screening, Pook ran back in for an attack but missed the Chinook due to an overshoot, and Hare's bombs hung-up. On a second pass, Mark Hare strafed the Chinook which caught fire and on a third run, both pilots strafed and set on fire two individual Puma helicopters. The Huey had been seen to land a short distance away, but this could not be found in the poor light.

In fact one Puma (AE501) of the Batallon de Aviacion de Combate 601 was damaged, while the Chinook (AE521) from the same unit was burnt out. The Huey had a slight damaging hit on one of its rotors.

During the attack, Jerry Pook's aircraft had been illuminated by Super Fledermaus radar but he had considered himself to be out of range of the only known AAA (anti-aircraft artillery – triple-A) position in that area. Mark Hare had seen but not reported, troops on the ground firing at the aircraft. In the attack his Harrier was hit in the intake and port wing. Another (dubious) first for the Squadron. Returning to the carrier, Hare jettisoned his hang-ups and experienced a port fuel transfer failure but landed with some 400 lbs total usable fuel left.

At 1155 (0755), the CO and Jeff Glover were sent off on a CAP (combat air patrol) for possible tasking in support of the ground assault. After launch the CO's Harrier became u/s and he was forced to land back on board. Glover was detached as a singleton. Later he was seen by ships over the beach-head and was believed to have been shot down in the area of Port Howard. It seems that the Harrier was hit by a Blowpipe SAM (Surface to Air Missile) fired by a soldier from the Argentine Special Forces (Compania de Comandos 601) deployed at Port Howard. Jeff Glover was later to report:

> 'I was flying over the sea going as low as I could. I was just about to coast in and pick the nose up when I was hit. There were three bangs in very close succession. After the third bang the aircraft rolled hard to starboard; I tried to correct the roll but the stick did not move – it was right in the central position. As I went through 30° I looked down and saw my hand pull the ejector seat handle. I heard the bang and then passed out. *[He regained his senses four feet under water.]*
>
> I was swallowing water like crazy. I could not see out of my right eye and I'd lost my helmet. I was in shock and trying to find my dinghy, looking around the water for it and could not see my parachute. I then realised my dinghy was still attached to my backside.'

Then a rowing boat arrived and unfortunately for him the chaps on board were Argentinians. Glover was taken to Port Howard and treated at the social club building being used as a medical centre, then

---

[1] All times quoted are GMT (zulu), and not local Falklands time. Thus 1145z would really be 0745 hours in the South Atlantic, which was four hours behind GMT. Falklands time will be shown in brackets.

to Port Darwin by helicopter, and finally to Port Stanley. From there he was flown to the Argentinian base at Commodoro Rivedavia, and from there went to La Rioja, in north-west Argentina, spending the next five weeks in solitary confinement. Peter Squire:

> 'We lost our first aeroplane early on (XZ972), really on the first day of amphibious landings. Jeff Glover and I had been teamed up but my aircraft became unserviceable so he went off on his own. I should have told Jeff to return too, but he was tasked just to go over the area of operations and provide top cover and to only be used if necessary. The tactical situation to me seemed to indicate that he was most unlikely to be used and would probably just stooge around for a while and come home.
>
> When he got there, he wasn't required for support, so he was handed to another ship which was controlling a different bit of air space, and asked him to go across from the San Carlos area to West Falkland, to the Port Howard area and do some recce, having had a report of troops there. So he suddenly ended up doing a singleton recce of an area he knew nothing about. Whilst doing two or three passes over there he was shot down, probably by Blowpipe, and we had no idea where he'd been and nobody else seemed to know either.
>
> The fact that he had been shot down brought us all a bit of a jolt. Like most people we hadn't actually thought we'd have aircraft shot down – certainly not quite so early. About a day later we were pretty sure he was alright because we got a signal intercept which talked about his name and about transferring him to Port Stanley, then to Argentina. The Command put an embargo on shooting helicopters down for a period of about 36 hours to make sure we didn't shoot him down while he was in transit. Sadly we couldn't let his family know he appeared safe because of the way we had found out, but luckily the Red Cross made contact in Argentina. However, it was a sharp reminder that we might not all get through entirely unscathed.'

Peter Harris and John Rochfort flew a CAP which began at 1340 (0940) and because of hostile air activity in the area of activity (AOA) they were kept clear, then tasked to fly an armed recce from Cape Dolphin to Bombilla Hill to Bodie Peak, but they saw no ground activity. Landing back, Rochfort's aircraft ended up with its port out-rigger in the catwalk but it was lifted back without damage.

At 1845 (1445) Pook and Tony Harper carried out an armed recce of Dunnose Head airstrip but again nothing could be observed and there was no evidence of recent use.

Saturday 22 May

With hills covered in low cloud, four Harriers took off at 1700 (1300) with eight CBUs to bomb tented positions and possible dispersed Pucara aircraft at Goose Green. It would be a simultaneous attack from the east on four UTMs (grid reference target location). Low cloud did not help and Jerry Pook missed the IP forcing him to make an orbit. Easing up to 200 feet he dropped chaff as briefed. Seeing nothing at the assigned UTM, he attacked a camouflaged box-bodied vehicle on the rear edge of the airstrip. Bob Iveson attacked a line of fox-holes on the northern edge and also saw Pook's bombs cause some secondary explosions. There was considerable triple-A.

On his run-in, Pete Harris was locked-up by Super Fledermaus radar but this was broken by a hard jink and a chaff drop. Despite considerable ground fire he continued his attack but his CBUs failed to release. Rochfort dropped his weapons on his briefed UTM and all four Harriers ran out to the west and returned to the *Hermes*.

The CO, with Tony Harper, went off at 1915 (1515) to fly an armed recce of the airstrip at Weddell Island, but nothing of interest was seen. They landed back after dusk.

Sunday 23 May

Peter Harris led a four-man mission at noon (0800), with Hare as his No.2, the CO and Harper as the other pair. They carried 4 x CBUs and 6 x 1,000 lb retard bombs, the section leaders taking the CBUs, the wingmen the bombs. They headed for the airstrip at Dunnose Head coming in low over Elephant Point, Roy Cove settlement and the 'Narrows' in order to approach the target out of the sun from the east. At the Narrows they split into two elements in order to achieve the required 30-second spacing between the bomb-droppers.

All aircraft dropped weapons as briefed although it was thought that Mark Hare's third bomb fell close to the settlement. During his attack, Hare picked up some debris from the leader's CBU 'furniture' or bomblet explosions. Mark Hare's bomb had indeed fallen closer to the settlement than planned, as Peter Squire relates:

'Mark Hare was hit by the CBU furniture of his leader and dropped his bombs late. Sadly this caused some damage to the local settlement and injury to Mr Tim Miller, who lost an eye. Subsequently Mark and Tim became firm friends, after Mark later went ashore with some ground crew to help repair the damage.'

Pook and Rochfort took off at 1645 (1245) for an armed recce around Port Howard, ingressing from the south in order to be screened by a long ridge which ran all the way to the target. Abeam of the target both pilots popped up to take long-range oblique F-95 photos but no targets or AAA were seen. A second pass was then flown north directly over the settlement and while there were plenty of defensive positions observed, there were no troops or vehicles. Later examination of the film revealed many positions and tents plus some activity in the settlement itself.

The last operation of the day was a three-man mission led by the CO, with Pook and Rochfort again, taking off at 1855 (1455), one hour and ten minutes after the latter two had landed, and using the same refuelled aircraft. Each carried two CBUs with which to attack Pebble Island airfield and then make a recce of Chartres airfield. The bombs went down on the target and the recce revealed nothing of the enemy there.

Monday 24 May
Peter Squire:

'As expected we were tasked to attack the runway at Stanley with 1,000 lb bombs. The Sea Harriers were to loft-bomb at the airfield for defence supression during our run-in. Some RN pilots had over-emphasised the dangers of attacking the airfield at low level and as a result I altered the composition of the formation to include myself. All four aircraft returned safely despite the ground fire. We hit the runway three or four times but the bombs had been fused with 40-second delayed action fuses and so they would have skipped and the damage was not significant. Due to debris damage to one of the aircraft together with the lack of effective penetration of the runway, Command decided that future bombing efforts would be high angle.'

The four pilots were Bob Iveson, Tony Harper, the CO and Mark Hare, and each carried three 1,000 pounders. Ingress by the four RAF and two FAA Harriers was over MacBride Head where the Sea Harriers went off to the south-east while the GR3s went west. Splitting into two elements, the 1 Squadron aircraft came in individually. As they pulled away after the attack the pilots estimated that one Pucara and a helicopter on the airfield would have been damaged. Mark Hare's machine was again hit by debris but got back safely. Radar locked up a Sea Harrier but the pilot evaded and some AAA and some small arms fire was encountered by the GR3s. Peter Squire:

'What we didn't know was that the naval armourers had set up a slight delay on the fuses of the bombs so that they weren't absolutely impact bombs. While we hit the runway, I think they all skipped, so were marginally off the ground when they exploded. This meant that we didn't do a great deal of damage, but did pot-mark the place a bit. We found later that the runway was pitted in lots of places and one would have been hard pressed to employ high pressure tyres on that sort of surface, so between us and the Sea Harrier's cluster bombs, we had done quite a lot of damage.'

Tuesday 25 May
It was back to Stanley airfield on the 25th – Pook, Harris, Squire and Rochfort, taking off at 1415 (1015) carrying in all 12 x 1,000 lb freefall bombs with, despite the previous day's lesson, a variety of time delay fuses. Each pair of Harriers was led by a Sea Harrier.

The attack was carried out as planned, with the GR3s formating on a Sea Harrier in loose vic formation for simultaneous release of bombs. Following the release of his weapons, Jerry Pook climbed overhead to observe the fall, and he saw that the bombs from the first three impacted on the west end of the airfield whilst those of the second trio fell some 100 yards north of the eastern threshhold. Whilst overhead, Pook was locked-up by Roland radar and saw the missile in flight. It peaked at almost 15,000 feet some distance below him. He also saw a Tiger Cat launched against the second vic, but this also fell short.

At 1730 (1330) Peter Harris and Mark Hare returned to Stanley airfield each carrying three 1,000 lb free fall bombs, dropping them from 20,000 feet. Triple-A and Roland missiles were fired during these attacks, in which the bombs were dropped singly, but at the height they were flying the Harrier pilots remained out of range. Harris went back to Stanley later that afternoon, taking off at 1925 (1525) with three 1,000 pounders but all three fell short. The CO also flew an armed recce to west Falklands.

Aboard the *Hermes* this day were some anxious sailors and airmen. HMS *Coventry* was sunk and later it was known that 'Exocet' missiles were on their way in. Chaff was fired from the ship and then one of *Invincible*'s "Sea Dart" missiles was fired which hit some chaff and expoded mightily above *Hermes*' deck! This day too saw the loss of *Atlantic Conveyor*, together with her skipper, Captain North, who had been quite a friend to the pilots on their way out.

Wednesday 26 May

Two Harriers, piloted by Bob Iveson and Tony Harper, were off at 1240 (0840) each carrying two CBUs with which to attack hostile positions at Port Howard, identified from film from a previous sortie. Weather caused some problem with the route in but both pilots attacked a line of tents plus a command post/HQ vehicle. Sea Harriers overhead confirmed the effectiveness of the attack, but no defensive fire was seen. Pook and Rochfort were the next off, away at 1500 (1100) on an armed recce looking for Argentinian artillery but nothing was observed.

Two hours later Peter Squire took three 1,000 pounders to Port Stanley airfield on his own. He flew to the pull-up point at low level and lobbed the bombs from a 30° loft angle. The central bomb did not drop and this had to be jettisoned later. The Harrier was locked up on RWR on pull up and an escape manoeuvre was made to break it. Forty minutes after the CO had left to attack, Jerry Pook and Mark Hare lifted away (1740/1340) as a pair for an armed recce from Teal Inlet settlement to Port Stanley. This was a large area in which there were known to be many hostile defensive positions and a number of observation posts (OPs) manned by British Special Forces. Positive identification of Argentine targets would therefore be essential before any attack was carried out.

Little was seen on the first run through the area from west to east although both aircraft were locked up by Super Fledermaus radar in the Two Sisters area. Some five kilometres from Stanley the aircraft turned to make a re-run. On the northern slopes of Mount Kent, Pook spotted what appeared to be a damaged helicopter and, supposing it to have been one of those attacked on the 21st, he flew past to take a photograph. Mark Hare reported some small arms fire and also that the helicopter appeared to him to be undamaged.

Pook elected to carry out a further looksee, which confirmed the Puma was indeed undamaged but during this run a Blowpipe SAM was fired and exploded above his aircraft. Hare was unable to attack the Puma and so both aircraft departed from the immediate target area, and, using terrain screening, Pook manoeuvred for a further pass, which he carried out with his CBU. The Puma was bracketed in mid-pattern and several secondary explosions were seen. (This was indeed the Puma damaged by the Squadron on 21 May and had now been destroyed before it could be taken away.) In the meantime, Hare saw further evidence of triple-A and small arms fire so both aircraft headed north. On recovery, a hole was found in Jerry Pook's starboard drop tank.

Thursday 27 May

The Battle of Goose Green was fought on this day. Harris and Harper were away at 1345 (0945) each carrying three 1,000 lb free fall bombs with which to loft-bomb Stanley airport. Harris' bomb explosions were not seen although smoke later came up and Harper's landed in the water to the south. At 1400 (1000), Iveson and Hare were tasked with a support mission for the ground forces at Goose Green.

Poor communication with the FAC (Foward Air Controller) forced the pair to hold at 8,000 feet over the IP, and the FAC was also having trouble confirming where British troops had got to. A target of a 105 mm gun was finally confirmed and an attack made. On the first run neither pilot saw any sign of the gun emplacement, and further observations failed to find it. Finally all four CBUs went down on a line of six foxholes, despite ground fire.

At 1600 (1200) Iveson and Hare took off again for a second support mission. This time contact with the FAC was better but they were still held at 8,000 feet which lost any element of surprise. Finally a target field gun was called in, with four alternate targets. Again it was impossible to locate the gun so attacks were made on an alternate. Bob Iveson then volunteered to the FAC that they still had some cannon left, and so they were given another target. Iveson later thought he had been a bit over-confident, and no doubt Mark Hare was wishing he were somewhere else.

They were told to strafe some troop movements near where they had bombed earlier; the first attempt was unsuccessful but a second run saw both pilots strafing the foxholes. It appears that well dug-in troops here were pinning down British forces. Throughout the attack there was considerable ground fire and triple-A. Bob Iveson's Harrier was hit by triple-A (35 mm Oerlikon) from Goose Green airfield. The fire warning light came on, his controls froze, and as he crossed out the Harrier caught fire. He continued away to the west for some 40 seconds before ejecting from 100 feet. The jet (XZ988) crunched into the ground and blew up, seven miles west of Goose Green settlement.

'Heavy calibre tracer started coming up. There was an enormous thump and bang, the aircraft lifted in the air and the controls started to go soft. I could see fire in my mirror and the nose had started to drop. Two large shells had hit the aeroplane and moved it sideways and things started to go wrong pretty quickly.

I was trying to keep it airborne to get it out of the Goose Green area. I managed to do that and then the cockpit filled with flame and I ejected. It was not a very controlled ejection. I had no time to set up for it and it was a high speed ejection.

Once on the ground, which I hit with a hell of a thump, I must have knocked myself scatty and couldn't see properly. I then saw what appeared to be men approaching, so I pushed off in the opposite direction. When my vision began to come back I realised that they must have been sheep.'

Landing safely, Bob Iveson made his way to a lone building, Paragon House, (farmhouse). Despite an Argentinian helicopter crew looking for him, he kept out of sight, remaining under cover for the next two days, complete with food and a bed. A Search and Rescue sortie was flown over the area by Jerry Pook in an attempt to locate him via Bob's SARBE (Search & Rescue Beacon Equipment). Heavy AA fire forced him away. The 2nd Paras effectively removed the Argentine troops from their positions during 28-29 May and Iveson was then rescued and picked up by a Gazelle helicopter flown by Lieutenant William Scott, 45 Commando Army Air Corps at 1800 (1400) on the 29th.

Friday 28 May

Today saw a pre-planned attack on a storage area south-east of Mount Kent by the CO, Harper and Harris. Taking off at 1300 (0900) they carried 42 rockets in pods. Peter Squire was later to write:

'The day starts with sea fog and even when this clears the weather is pretty foul with a strong sea. On the first mission of the day we fly in atrocious weather at low level and it takes some time positively to identify our position on the coast of Fonia. However, I am pleased that we succeed in putting our weapons into the target area – it was quite a challenge.

On the way in, at high level, I hear a transmission on Guard using Iveson's call-sign of the previous day. Back on board I try to persuade the captain to support a helicopter recce but he is not interested and suggests that it might be a spoof.

That evening, Peter Harris leads a most successful attack on Goose Green. For once the targets are easily acquired and the Paras are left in no doubt that the results were instrumental in achieving the cease-fire.'

In the first attack Harper was unable to release his weapons, and the CO's attack produced secondary explosions. All three Harriers broke out in a climbing turn and headed for the ship. All had been locked up by radar and chaff had been used to break the lock until above maximum height for triple-A.

An armed recce at 1610 (1210) over the Douglas settlement area by Pook and Rochfort, was followed by the raid led by Peter Harris, in company with Tony Harper and Jerry Pook. They left the ship at 1905 (1505) with four CBUs and two pods of 2" rockets. They were tasked to support 2nd Para's assault on Goose Green. Harris and Harper each dropped their CBUs while Pook fired rockets, and all were seen to impact on the target. Afterwards a recce run was flown over the position where Bob Iveson was seen to eject. Radio transmission was made but nothing seen or heard.

On the ground at this time, 2nd Para had been held up by direct fire from 35 mm Oerlikons by the airstrip, the guns that had shot down Iveson. Their CO, Colonel 'H' Jones had been killed shortly before (posthumous VC) and the second in command had called for an air strike against the gun positions.

The strike came at dusk and not long afterwards the Paras were able to negotiate a surrender by the Argentinians. The second in command later signalled the Squadron to confirm this attack had made a significant contribution to the outcome.

Saturday 29 May

Only one strike made this date, due to poor weather, by the CO and Mark Hare. They took off at 1545 (1145) each with two rocket pods, in order to attack a hostile OP on the west face and dug-in defensive positions on the northern slopes of Mount Kent. The attack was carried out, although results could not be seen, but at least there was no ground fire; both pilots picked up RWR indications of search radar.

Sunday 30 May

The CO and Mark Hare were off at 1150 (0750) to support the ground forces, each carrying two rocket pods. FAC contact gave them enemy positions on the northern slopes of Mount Kent and an attack was satisfactorily carried out. Pook and Harper followed this up at the same time, carrying six retard bombs, their target a possible radar position on Mount Round and Mount Low. Targets were not seen on the first pass on Mount Round so Pook strafed a target on Mount Low then re-attacked the position given on Mount Round. Harper bombed the Mount Low UTM. Both Harriers were illuminated by Super Fledermaus radar from Stanley but met no AA-fire.

Harper and Harris headed out at 1430 (1030) to see if the GR3 could use LRMTS (Laser Ranges and Marked Target Seeker) to designate for LGBs – laser guided bombs. The weapons were dropped from a 60° dive initiated from 35,000 feet using a release depression of 150 MR. The designating aircraft, flying chase, attempted to illuminate the aiming point using the Rev Sight set at 100 mls. Each LGB released was matched with one 1,000 free fall bomb to prevent asymmetry on recovery. No impacts were seen – which was a disappointment.

The LRMTS was part of the weapon delivery system. The laser ranger could be used to give very accurate range to the target. The Seeker facility was used in conjunction with hand held Laser Target Markers for target identification. This was the first time 1 Squadron had used LGBs in action. Air Vice-Marshal Ken Hayr, back in UK, had started the trials which proved the Harrier could operate LGBs. Once this had happened, bombs were parachuted to the Task Force by C-130s, with full instructions how to fit and use them.

At 1435 (1035) Pook and Rochfort had been sent off as a pair against artillery seen on Mount Wall, but this target was subsequently changed to helicopters on the ground some 14 km further east. Ingress was from the south, crossing the main road to Stanley. As Jerry Pook's aircraft crossed this road it was hit by small arms fire from some troops and SSVs parked on it.

Pook felt the impact and was told by Rochfort that he appeared to be leaking fuel, but carried on. They saw no sign of the helicopters but Rochfort clearly saw some artillery, which he immediately attacked with rockets. Pook, who had pulled wide from his search, saw Rochfort's fall of shot, which landed in the middle of the guns and SSVs, and now attacked the same target with his rockets, which also impacted the position. By now Pook's Harrier (XZ963) was streaming fuel and so both aircraft ran out to the south-east with Rochfort strafing the road in an attempt to keep Argentinian heads down.

Once clear of the target area, both aircraft climbed and headed for the ship. At this stage Pook saw his fuel gauges indicated 4,000 lbs of fuel remaining which was well in excess of that required to get him home. However, he then suffered a total radio failure and noticed that the fuel was rapidly decreasing. He jettisoned the empty fuel tanks and rocket pods and climbed to 25,000 feet. In this climb he also experienced partial hydraulic failure.

At height, Pook was joined by his wingman and they flew as fast as possible towards the carrier with Rochfort alerting the SAR facilities of an imminent ejection. Finally Pook's engine flamed out as the last of his fuel drained away and he continued to glide towards home, then at 10,000 feet and at 250 kts he ejected. Rochfort's timely call for assistance meant that a SAR Sea King helicopter from 826 Squadron FAA was on the spot straight away. Pook was rescued from the water in less than ten minutes.

Final mission of the day came at 1750 (1350), the CO and Mark Hare going off with rockets to attack the troops reported by Rochfort on the road south of Mount Challenger. They came in from the north but the troops had gone, so instead they attacked known enemy dug-in positions on the northern slopes of Mount Kent.

Monday 31 May

Further ground troop support sorties came on the morning of the 31st, Harper, Harris and Rochfort taking off at 1130 (0730), carrying two LBGs and two 1,000 free fall bombs. Once again the attempt was being made to designate for the LGBs, released at 25,000 feet. No weapon impacts were seen and during this time RWR locked up the aircraft. The sortie ended with a low level recce of the high ground from Mount Low to Long Island and although nothing was seen, the film indicated one 30 mm AA gun position.

The CO and Mark Hare were Scrambled and set out at 1440 (1040). They were armed with rocket pods to support troops but this had suddenly changed to an attack on Stanley airfield in co-ordination with Sea Harriers (800 Sqn), which had also been diverted from a mission. The FAA boys would toss

VT 1,000 lb bombs for flak supression as 1 Squadron went for the target.

The target was the sudden appearance of swept wing aircraft, thought to be Etendards, parked adjacent to the eastern threshold. This caused some panic hence the immediate switching of targets to all Harriers in the air.

The CO headed in at low level, led by the Sea Harriers. The Navy boys allowed themselves to be illuminated by climbing in order to check radar position, which removed any hope of a surprise arrival. The pair split at MacBride Head and the CO and Hare attacked individually. Rockets were fired from level delivery at targets which appeared to be straight-winged aircraft (later proving to be Aeromacchis). Considerable small arms fire came up and both Harriers suffered cracked front canopy screens. The CO also had both external fuel tanks holed while Hare suffered a bird strike. Later, Peter Harris made a lone attack on Stanley airfield too. Peter Squire:

'I and my No.2 were sitting on deck waiting to be launched at short notice. A Sea Harrier on its way back from a CAP reported seeing what he thought were Etendards sitting on the end of the runway, so the Captain decided it was sufficient to go and we were launched.

It so happened that my No.2 was Mark Hare who had been my wingman on the original sortie against the Stanley runway and, therefore, we remembered how we'd got there previously, not having the proper maps with us. We flew below the air traffic control tower and what we found on the end of the runway turned out to be Aeromacchis. We fired our rockets and both Harriers picked up some debris but got through and out.

What the Argentinians had done, quite skilfully, was to lay some metal planking in the shape of swept-wing aircraft and put these Aeromacchis on top, so to the naked eye it did look like they were swept-wing aircraft. They had clearly set these up as a decoy.'

Tuesday 1 June

The CO went off at 1705 (1305) in the only serviceable GR3, with Lieutenant Edward Ball of 800 Naval Squadron, to carry out a line search from Bluff Cove to Goose Green for military activity followed by an attack on a suspected radar unit on Mount Usborne. The search was carried out with photos taken of four selected sites. This later showed hostile positions by Fitzroy Bridge. Peter Squire then attacked the radar site but without seeing results.

A period of atrocious weather ended all hope of further operations between 2 and 5 June, but it gave the Squadron time to work on the aircraft. Two new pilots arrived, Flight Lieutenant M M Macleod and M Beech, both from 3 Squadron, who landed on the carrier following a 3,500-mile trip, aided by eight Victor tankers. They had left them with still two hours to go, so it was with some skill the two single-seaters found the ships with approaching bad weather.

Meantime, ashore, the REs at Port San Carlos had built a rough landing strip where Harriers could land. Squadron Leader B S Morris AFC, who had flown Harriers with the Squadron in the 1970s, commanded this forward airstrip which was called 'Sid's Strip'. Both RAF and FAA Harriers would soon be able to refuel here and be on close alert for operations during the day. (The Navy called it HMS *Sheathbill*.) If aircraft had flown patrols and not fired their guns or dropped weapons, they could now refuel at the ALG (advanced landing ground) rather than go back to the carrier each time.

Saturday 5 June

First to use the strip were Bob Iveson and Tony Harper. They had been sent off at 1200 (0800) to support troops, but, with thick fog about knew they would have to land at San Carlos. One of the Harriers had no IFF so there was some apprehension about getting through the Rapier and Sea Wolf missile screens. They landed safely but were not used for any operations. Later that afternoon Harris and Rochfort flew in, then taking the first pair of Harriers off to attack the airfield at Two Sisters with rockets.

Pook and Hare took off at 1650 (1250) for a low-level photo-recce from Bluff Cove to Hooker Point, looking for land-launched Exocet missiles. Jerry Pook thought this a bit dangerous and sent his wingman ahead out of range of triple-A to act as a 'spoof', using chaff, whilst Pook ran in at low level. However, nothing significant was seen and there was no SAM/AAA radar in evidence.

Two hours later Squire and Mike Beech went on an armed recce of Pebble Island, Keppel Island, Rat Castle Shanty, Dunnose Head and Spring Point, for signs of the enemy. At Pebble Bay they found what they took for two new Pucara aircraft which they attacked with rockets. Later SBS reports indicated that both aircraft were already damaged. This attack forced an early return due to fuel.

Sunday 6 June
Despite rain and low cloud over the islands, the CO and Beech were off again at 1310 (0930) to make a recce of those land-launched Exocet sites around Hooker Point, and took CBUs with them to drop on troop positions south of Stanley. The recce revealed nothing either visually or on film. The CO dropped his CBUs on enemy positions as planned but Beech failed to pick out a target.

Monday 7 June
An hour after dawn (1200 [0800]) Jerry Pook and John Rochfort took rocket pods to attack a 155 mm artillery position located on Sapper Hill. Originally Pook and Macleod were going, while Harris and Rochfort were tasked with another target, but both Macleod and Harris had their aircraft go u/s, so Pook and Rochfort teamed up. They headed in from the south-west keeping low to stay out of SAM radar but this imposed an approach through early morning low sun which made target acquisition impossible. Both aircraft fired their rockets at the briefed UTMs and ran out to the south. They saw no ground fire but on landing Pook's Harrier was found to have been hit by small arms fire on the nose cone. A Sea Harrier observed the attack, and reported seeing a SAM fired at the two RAF aircraft as they headed south, but it exploded before reaching them.

Tuesday 8 June
No operations flown but the CO and three others did land at San Carlos in case they were needed. The CO suffered an engine wind-down, as he explains:

> 'Mark Hare and I were programmed to mount Ground Alert at our FOB, and I had aircraft XZ989 which was carrying a number of known defects. At the FOB I misjudged the height going across the side of the pad and lifted some metal. I overshot in order to see what damage had been done and at about 30 knots there was a marked drop in thrust which I could not correct. As a result, and the fact that I was pointing directly at a Rapier FU, I elected not to eject and the aircraft hit the ground very hard. The undercarriage was broken as well as the canopy. The aircraft, still under power, came to rest at the far end of the strip where I shut the engine down and vacated the cockpit. Mark orbitted until the pad was clear of flying metal then landed, refuelled and returned to the ship.'

The Harrier became beyond economic repair but it did serve as a 'parts shop'. As Fred Welsh relates, each time a bit was needed that was no longer in store on the ship, pilots going to the landing ground would be given a shopping list, and asked to bring back this or that bit from the wreck. As it was never certain who might get to land at the ALG, each pilot flying missions needed a duplicate shopping list so that hopefully at least one pilot would be able to bring back the piece required. Fred was one of the ground crew who received a commendation after the campaign.

Two more pilots arrived – Nick Gilchrist and Ross Boyens, the latter finally released from duty on Ascension. They had flown 3,900 miles with no diversions available had they run into trouble. They brought two aircraft fitted with ALE 40 (chaff and flare dispensers), which gave the Squadron four such equipped machines, together with an ingenious I-band jammer (to use against triple-A radars) and one aircraft capable of firing Shrike armament.

Wednesday 9 June
Peter Squire noted:

> 'The first thing I do in the morning is to get a helicopter ride to the FOB to fly one of the ground alert GR3s. Tony Harper is the unfortunate one who loses his seat, and I lead Ross Boyens on his first mission.'

Armed with rocket pods they were off at 1200 (0800) to attack hostile artillery positions on the northern slopes of Mount Longdon. They headed in at low level from the north-west and both fired into the target although nothing was seen. Some small arms fire was met from the area of Wireless Ridge on the run out but neither were hit.

Harris and Murdo Macleod took off from the ship at 1340 (0940), again with rockets, going for a 155 mm gun near Sapper Hill. No gun could be seen but the target area was blasted. Moderate triple-A was encountered and Macleod's aircraft was hit by shrapnel on the way out, causing a hydraulic failure on lowering the undercarriage for landing, so he had to blow his wheels down with the emergency system.

Thursday 10 June

Wing Commander Squire and Mark Hare left the carrier at 1300 (0900) for a recce of Mount Harriet to Mount Tumbledown and Wireless Ridge, then over Mount Two Sisters and Mount Longdon. During the first part the CO dropped two CBUs on likely target positions on the eastern slopes of Tumbledown. Later, film revealed six heavy artillery positions in this area and a large number of troop concentrations in the Moody Brook area. Hare went over the second recce area and dropped his CBUs on to positions on Mount Longdon. Film revealed the presence of troops armed with Blowpipe and SAM missiles.

Pook and Ross Boyens flew off at 1630 (1230), tasked initially for a Scramble at FOB but the mission was re-tasked to the ship for attack support of Special Forces in the Port Howard area. No contact was made with the FAC so an armed recce was carried out but nothing of interest was seen.

At the same time, Harper and Rochfort had flown off for a LGB trial. Again the FAC was not in position, owing to communications failure, so weapons were jettisoned on the return flight to the ship.

Finally, the CO and Murdo Macleod went off at 1855 (1455) with CBUs to attack the positions spotted at Moody Brook road. Search radar was heard on the RWR during the run-in but was ignored as far as was possible! The target was easily identified although individual targets proved more difficult to spot in the failing light. The UTM was hit which caused several secondary explosions. Coming out through Ull to the north considerable triple-A was encountered by both pilots. Macleod's front canopy screen was hit badly and cracked by small arms fire – his second damaging hit in two missions.

Friday 11 June

First up this day were Tony Harper and Flight Lieutenant Nick Gilchrist at 1120 (0720) with LGBs. Some SAS troops had found an enemy force and were being stopped opposite Port Stanley. Calling up the Harriers the FAO's LTM had run down so he was no longer able to guide the bombs. The FAO suggested an attack anyway but Harper was not keen so dropped the bombs in a manual 30° loft profile into an area of Tumbledown Mountain. Impact results were not observed. Ross Boyens and John Rochfort were launched at 1425 (1025), taking CBUs and cannon to Argentine positions on Two Sisters Mount. However, on take-off the wind speed over the deck proved lower than stated and Rochfort began to sink after lift-off from the ski-jump and he had to quickly jettison his bombs and tanks, missing the water by just a few feet. Nevertheless he escorted Boyens who bombed positions on Mount Longdon, the CBUs seen to explode amongst troops and camp fires. This was the first operational use of ALE 40 chaff and flare dispenser. Boyens was locked-up by TWS/I but on release of chaff immediately became un-locked.

Shortly after these two had left the ship, Pook and Beech took CBUs against artillery and possible motor transport on Mount Harriet. They came in from the south unopposed and their target positions were attacked with no radar lock-up although an I-band search radar was heard on RWR during run-in, indicating a potential SAM attack.

Harris and Gilchrist were off at 1810 (1410) with CBUs for troops and gun positions on Mount Longdon. They ran in from the north and split up, one bombing to the west the other to the east, passing through some ground fire that came up from the south.

At 1820 (1420) the CO and Hare were tasked against artillery and a HQ position on the eastern slopes of Tumbledown, armed with 4 x 1,000 lb retard bombs with delay fuses. The selection of weapons was aimed at negating the use of prepared positions only occupied at dusk. The Squadron thought this questionable as retard bombs, if not instantaneous, usually bounced then rolled beyond a target (as had happened at Stanley airport). In the event the bombs were dropped as free fall as the retard tails had not been properly set. Luckily for the two pilots they did not have time to arm and so fell as UXBs (unexploded bombs). They flew in from the south with minimum exposure to radar but on approaching the area, the CO's aircraft was hit by small arms fire and the cockpit holed. His bombs fell into an area of Argentine barracks, and Hare's bombs were also long owing to tail parachute and fusing problems.

On coming out, three Blowpipe SAMs were fired at both aircraft. That aimed at the CO fell short but Hare had to take evasive action towards his and it exploded harmlessly – but un-nervingly – 100 feet above his canopy. That night the barracks had to be evacuated due to an unexploded bomb found stuck in a wall.

Saturday 12 June

Ross Boyens with Mike Beech took off at 1145 (0745) with CBUs and attacked a gun position by Sapper Hill. Triple-A came up from the Moody Brook area and on the way out full use was made of chaff and flares which certainly seemed to confuse the triple-A.

At 1405 (1005) two pairs were sent off. The first, Harper and Gilchrist, were Scrambled following an alert by ASOC for an armed recce of the road east of Sapper Hill. They flew in from the south-west at low level and attacked troops in the open with CBUs and cannon during a single pass. Harper's Harrier was hit by two small arms rounds and triple-A splinters, causing superficial damage to the port wing leading edge and air brake.

Harris and Macleod were sent against a 155 mm gun position on Sapper Hill. They came in low through the hills to the west, approaching the Hill close abeam of Mount Harriet and Mount William. Smoke could be seen rising south-east of the target UTM and an attack was made on this position. During the attack, Macleod's aircraft (XW919) was hit by shrapnel which penetrated the rear equipment bay area and fractured the aft reaction control pipe. On later decelerating to the hover, this caused a fire to start in the bay and smoke was seen coming from the aircraft. Fuel indications suggested a considerable fuel leak at the same time. Murdo Macleod executed a very quick and professional landing in worrying circumstances, and on landing the fire was quickly extinguished by deck crews, which was just as well for his control runs were beginning to melt. It also made Macleod's hit total three out of three! Chief Tech Fred Welsh remembers this incident:

> 'One of the aircraft had a fire. It had been hit through one of the reaction ducts. The pilot had no problems as he flew back but he found he had one when he came alongside the carrier and put his nozzles down to land. All the hot air came through the holes and began melting everything. The pilot later said the lights which came on in the cockpit were like the Blackpool illuminations! He landed alright, switched off and hopped out.
>
> When we opened the back hatch most of the stuff there just came out in liquid form. We tried to repair the damage but for the INAS stuff, for example, we had no spare cables so the INAS blokes actually took the cables out of the test kits and threaded them into the machine. The only thing then was we had no test kits if we were faced with another problem.'

Sunday 13 June

Peter Squire and Mark Hare went out at 1430 (1030), again to try the Paveway LGB concept. This was the time of the land troops' final assault on Stanley, and using the FAC with LTM for guidance. Hare carried CBUs for support. The attack profile was a 30° loft, using an IP behind the FLOT (forward line of troops). The CO's first bomb fell short by 400 yards because the FAC illuminated the target immediately on weapon release (too soon). The second bomb was guided perfectly causing a direct hit on Argentine positions.

In the afternoon (1850/1450) Pook and Beech followed up with another LGB attack to Tumbledown. Pook ran in from Bluff Cove and his first bomb was a direct hit on an enemy 105 mm gun position. The second bomb fell short by 400 yards. During the attack Mike Beech gave cross-over to his leader to confuse ground gunners, but no triple-A or SAMs were seen, although Super Fledermaus audio was heard. Danger, however, came from elements of the Scots Guards, for on seeing a bomb dropping they thought they were under attack and opened up. They scored no hits!

Monday 14 June

It fell to Peter Harris and Nick Gilchrist to make the final operational sortie over the Falklands. British forces began their final assault on Port Stanley before dawn and the pair were deployed to the ALG to await targets. On the carrier, Harris and Gilchrist had been bombed-up with LGBs for the leader, CBUs for the wingman, and took off at 1500 (1100). They were held overhead behind the front line for 30 minutes but as the Argentinians in the target area of Sapper Hill then surrendered, and cease fire negotiations were under way in Port Stanley, the mission was aborted and the Harriers returned to the ship. The war was over.

Chapter Twenty

APRÈS LA GUERRE

Wing Commander Peter Squire jotted down his final comments as the Falkland War came to an end.

'11 June. A day of good weather is spent softening up the defence positions prior to the assault on Stanley. Despite the use of air defence call-signs our purpose is compromised and we note a significant increase in ground fire including small arms, AAA and SAMS. During the run-in to a target my aircraft is holed through the cockpit but fortunately the damage is miniscule. Tony Harper and Nick Gilchrist attempt to co-ordinate LGB delivery with LTM but the latter u/s.

12 June. The push towards Stanley begins. The first day's objectives of Mounts Longdon, Two Sisters and Harriet are achieved. Our aircraft are used for CAS. Again a number of aircraft are damaged by small arms, notably Murdo Macleod, whose aircraft is hit in the rear equipment bay, severing a reaction control duct. A fire on landing required swift reaction.

13 June. Ground forces consolidate before the final push. At last we mount two successful LGB sorties with LTMs, achieving direct hits against pin-point targets. The ship's crew present me with a plaque commemorating the battle damage to my aircraft.

14 June. Surrender.'

As word of the cease-fire came in, the Harriers aboard the Hermes were re-armed with Sidewinders and joined the Sea Harriers on a CAP just in case of a reaction to the surrender triggered something big from mainland Argentina. But nothing happened and it soon became apparent that it wouldn't. However, the Navy wanted shot of the Squadron as Peter Squire recalls:

'At the end of the conflict the carriers were clearly keen to get back to the UK, certainly "Hermes" and her captain were, and so equally keen that we went ashore. It was planned that we should go to Stanley and look after the air defence of the islands. The airfield was in a bit of a mess and wasn't ready for operational use, which I told the captain and eventually he sent his number two to see me, Commander John Locke – a very pleasant man – and he said they had a good deal for me. He could let me have, at cost price, a case of whisky if we went in the next few days. I told him we would go the day after next but I'd like four cases – free! And so I got four cases – of New Zealand whisky – thereby allowing them to return to England.

I think the Squadron personnel were pretty pleased to get ashore. We had had a rough time on the carrier, with people sleeping on the floor and not having proper beds and so on. That said, at first we only had tents at Stanley, and it was pretty cold there too.'

The RAF Harriers were flown ashore on 4 July to take up air defence operations from Port Stanley, with two aircraft on QRA (quick reaction alert) with pilots in the cockpits. The original pilots and ground crew were quickly released and replaced, at first with crews in from Germany. As soon as practical they were flown home by Hercules and VC10s to receive a grand welcome at RAF Brize Norton. Last home was Jeff Glover, released from captivity – complete with boater and a laugh on his face!

On 5 August, Gerry Honey (OC Operations Wing at Wittering) arrived on the Falklands to take over from Peter Squire and later the CO took off in a C-130 for Ascension. However, a fuel transfer problem forced a diversion to Montevideo, but after refuelling they made Ascension. Transferring to a VC10 he landed at Brize then went on to Wittering in a 115 Squadron Andover. His wife, Carolyn, and two sons awaited him and there followed an impromptu party with most of the Squadron personnel.

Meantime the ground personnel had arrived home by VC10 too, via Senegal. As Fred Welsh recalls, they were then diverted to Anglesey due to fog, but nobody could see any fog. As they finally flew into Wittering all became clear. They had been delayed in order for TV camera crews to set up their equipment to record the welcome home.

Wing Commander Squire and Squadron Leader Jeremy Pook were later awarded the DFC, with Bob Iveson and Mark Hare being Mentioned in Despatches. Peter Harris and Mike Beech later received AFCs while Sid Morris (ALG CO) became an Officer of the Order of the British Empire and Flight Lieutenant Brian Mason, who had led the ground crew, a Member of the Order. Group Captain

Pat King, Wittering's Station Commander was later made a Commander of the OBE, having master-minded the support, organisation and despatch of the Harrier Squadron in the Falklands. There were also six commendations – see appendix.

Back now at Wittering the Squadron had something of a rest but Peter Squire returned to Stanley in October for two months, before being relieved by the CO of IV Squadron. Later 23 Squadron took over responsibility for the islands' air defence. On Peter Squire's first sortie on 6 November, he had to eject following an engine failure and was picked out of Stanley harbour by a SAR Sea King helicopter.

Meantime the Squadron lost Flight Sergeant Ray Cowburn, who had seen service on the Falklands. This highly respected SNCO died from a heart attack while on home leave in November.

Fred Welsh, who, had the war continued for a few more weeks, might have been fighting it as a civilian, in fact signed on for another period of service. Not long after the war, he was sent on a battle damage course, along with a mate of his. Each time the officer talked of something about battle damage, this pal would chirp up from the back of the room, and say to Fred who was down the front, 'Is that right, Fred?' and Fred would nod. After a while the exasperated officer asked why he kept asking Fred, to which he responded, 'Well, Fred's seen all this battle damage during the Falklands do!' The officer's obvious retort was why then was Fred doing the course?

* * *

Peter Squire left just before Christmas 1983, the new CO being Wing Commander J D L Feesey AFC. John Feesey was no new-boy, for this was his third tour on the Squadron. He had been with it from November 1966 to June 1969 (Hunters), and again from July 1969 to October 1971 (Harriers).

> 'I took the reins from Peter Squire less than 18 months after he and the Squadron had returned from the South Atlantic and as such he was something of a hard act to follow! My time in command was very much one of peacetime normality after the excitements of the previous period, although throughout my tour we normally had at least one Squadron pilot on detachment to both RAF Stanley and RAF Belize in support of the Harrier flights still helping to keep the peace in those places.
>
> The principal remit given to me on taking over by the AOC, Air Vice-Marshal John Thomson, was to bring the Squadron up to Readiness for NATO Taceval, something that had naturally been put on the back burner during and immediately after the South Atlantic war, and to develop a proper secondary shipborne role for the Squadron, using the lessons learned from the emergency deployment aboard HMS "Hermes" as a starting point.
>
> I took over quite a battle-hardened Squadron. Most of the pilots and ground crew had taken part in the war the previous year, and the Falklands and Belize were still semi-operational theatres. It was a challenge to motivate people to take a serious interest in such relatively mundane things as Taceval, much less an annual AOC's inspection.
>
> Another important task was to develop further the Squadron's field deployment role more on the lines of the RAF Germany Harrier squadrons. In Germany at that time the concept was to deploy the Harriers away from vulnerable airfields and into well hidden urban sites, in flights of 6-8 aircraft with full logistic support. No. 1 Squadron's wartime deployment options included Norway and Denmark, and while the Squadron would always be tied to their main operating base (MOB) for logistic support, the aim was to identify a number of sites on, or very close to, the MOB from which the Harriers could operate relatively covertly. Lacking the extensive transport, communications, engineering, weapons and ground defence capabilities of the Germany Harrier Wing, this was certainly a challenge for us, and especially for my SENGO, Squadron Leader Graham Collins, and his excellent band of engineers, as well as for my small but professional RAF Regiment Flight under Flying Officer Ian "Pebble" Rees.
>
> Taceval was due to take place just eight months after I took command. Not long to carry out all the necessary preparations but long enough to know exactly where the axe would fall if it didn't go reasonably well! In those days the Cold War was at its height and Taceval was taken extremely seriously. The test would start at Wittering, where the whole base would be put on an alert footing and be evaluated alongside the Squadron, and then the Taceval team would follow the Squadron to its deployment sites at Vandel, Denmark. From there the Squadron would fly under simulated wartime conditions for a further three days until the evaluation was over. It was impossible to do a full dress rehearsal because there were no deployments to Vandel planned in the time available. Instead, we had to carry out mini-deployments to dispersals on the other side of Wittering airfield and try to pretend we were really in Denmark. This stretched the imagination to the limit, but it was

the only way to practise bringing the many disparate elements together.

For Taceval the Squadron effectively quadrupled in size to around 450 people. Reinforcements included detachments from the Tactical Communications Wing, the Tactical Supply Wing, the Mobile Catering Support Unit, as well as numerous additional engineers, armourers, etc., from our parent Station. I was fortunate that the Wittering OC Operations Wing, Wing Commander Peter Jevons, acted as overall site commander, leaving me free to worry about the flying side of the operation.

In the event the Taceval, part of exercise Bold Gannet, from 9 to 12 September 1984, went well enough, although there were inevitably difficulties in co-ordinating the activities of so many people who had little opportunity to practise together before. Many useful lessons were learned, not least the need for the Squadron to have a full practice deployment each year in the UK under simulated Taceval/wartime conditions, in order to keep fully up to speed with field operations. From this was developed the exercise Mayfly series of deployments at RAF Hullavington, with the first being a Maxeval (a Group level evaluation) from 10 to 18 July 1985. Hullavington proved ideal for practising Harrier deployments, being a large airfield with three runways, lots of grass for strip landings, plenty of redundant hangars and other useful buildings. And above all, a Station Commander and station staff who were extremely helpful and keen to see their airfield once again operating "real" aircraft like the Harrier.'

Flight Lieutenant C Huckstep arrived in 1984, and remembers that there was constant activity on the Squadron:

'We were always deploying somewhere. The year was always mapped out in advance so one knew exactly what exercises were coming up. Norway, Deci, a boat for two weeks, or Hullavington on a field exercise. Our four main roles were being able to deploy to "Northern Flank" (Norway), Denmark, reinforce Germany, "Southern Flank", Turkey or Cyprus.

It was all day visual attacks; the aircraft were much simpler then, and the planning was light on maps, a lot of visual map reading, stop watch – the navigation equipment wasn't brilliant, not as good as the Jaguars had for example. So there was a lot more charging around, working out where you were the whole time, but still very professional.

The biggest change on the aircraft types is the capability to be much more precise in one's planning so you can begin to work out all the "way points" and put them into the aircraft. With the GR3 it was around 6,600 lbs of fuel with external tanks. On later tours we would have 7,600 lbs and with tanks it went up to 11,700 lbs. So whereas in 1984 we used to fly 45 minutes at low level, half an hour sometimes, by the late 1990s we would be up to 90 minutes at low level.'

Aircraft Carriers
John Feesey:

'Deploying into a RN aircraft carrier should have been a relatively easy task, given the quite recent experience that so many squadron personnel had of doing it in anger. It proved to be anything but straighforward! For a start, the Squadron now had to learn to operate from an Invincible-class of "through-deck cruisers" (as the RN euphemistically called them), rather than the more traditional and considerably larger HMS "Hermes". Not only was space at an absolute premium on "Invincible", but she was also configured only for helicopter activity and Sea Harrier air defence operations, with no capability for the tasking communications nets, weapons storage, planning and briefing facilities or anything else necessary to conduct offensive air operations in support from afloat. Much of the RN's experience and expertise in these matters seemed to have gone with the sale of "Hermes" and the earlier large carriers.

Secondly, on the RAF's side, virtually all the special "Releases to Service", which had been granted as emergency measures to get the Squadron afloat for the Falklands, had since been withdrawn, and it proved a very long drawn out affair to persuade the "powers" that equipment which had operated perfectly well on board for weeks during the conflict could not be cleared for regular use at sea without at least three years of testing at Boscombe Down!

Eventually, enough clearances were granted to enable the Squadron to undertake a small scale trial deployment, of I think four aircraft, on board "Invincible" off north-east England under the splendidly titled "Exercise Hardy Crab 84". The Harriers were aboard from 30 October until 1 November (the ground crew a lot longer as they were at pains to point out!!) and targets were attacked on Otterburn Range. As expected the most difficult part of the operation at sea was not the flying, but rather the problem of communicating with the Air Support Operations Centre ashore. This gave my Ground Liaison Officer, Major John Hickey, many a headache but he was indefatigable in chasing the ship's communicators and the RAF Tactical Comms Wing team that we had on board, until eventually the system was made to work – after a fashion.

The other major difficulty was with aligning the Harrier's Intertial Navigation and Attack System (INAS). Because of the ship's movement during the alignment process it was not possible during the Falklands war to achieve anything but a very coarse INAS alignment. Thus the Harriers were flown during the conflict with no inertially derived navigation information and no instrument flying. Not the ideal state of affairs if deck-borne operations were to become a regular thing! Ferranti subsequently worked very hard to overcome these severe limitations and produced a better piece of FINRAE kit. However, despite the best efforts of the Ferranti team and the Squadron engineers, the equipment proved temperamental, rarely achieving anything better than a 10 to 15 mile navigation error after a 50-minute sortie. This made finding the ship rather an interesting exercise in poor visibility!

Next year, the Squadron deployed again on the "Invincible" for exercise "Hardy Crab 85", from 16 to 22 May. This was a bigger deployment with, I think, six Harriers taking part in an offensive air support exercise in south-west England. The carrier was in the south-west Approaches, notorious for fog at that time of year, and sure enough we spent a lot of time steaming around trying to avoid large fog banks. Nonetheless, we achieved a lot of useful flying and increased our experience of "through deck carrier" operations considerably. The Captain and Air Group of "Invincible" were extremely helpful – and forgiving of the landlubberly ways of the Squadron – and we were fortunate to have as a flight commander, Squadron Leader Ian "Morts" Mortimer, who had flown the Sea Harrier with the FAA from "Invincible" during the Falklands conflict. *[This included a shoot down by a Roland SAM and an ejection into the sea whilst with 801 Sqn FAA. Ed.]*

Life on board was not all work. The Squadron officers participated in a "Saturday Night at Sea", which was basically a dining-in night followed by the usual post-dinner games. As these traditionally took the form of the fixed wing element of the Air Group versus the helicopter crews, the Sea Harrier folk, normally greatly outnumbered, were only too happy to enlist the support of the 1 Squadron officers and the result was a resounding victory for the combined Harrier force. I still have the tug-of-war carpet burns on my elbows to remind me of the occasion.

The other highlights of my tour in command were the two detachments to Tromsø from 7 to 28 March 1986, and exercise "Maple Flag" at CFB Cold Lake in Alberta, from 10 to 27 May. The former were the biennial deployments exercising our ACE Mobile Force role, flying from snow-covered runways in temperatures down to minus 20° Celsius, and in weather that changed from Blue to Red in minutes as snowstorms came rolling in from the Arctic, equally challenging air and ground crews. The social programme, too, could be challenging in Tromsø; not for nothing is it known as the Paris of the North! Accommodation for most people was fairly basic, the ground crew, for instance, being quartered in an underground bunker in very cramped conditions; there was, therefore, every incentive to spend as little time as possible in bed at night, and every reason to enjoy the clubs and pubs downtown instead. Most people also took advantage of the ski-ing opportunities available as well. My abiding memory, though, is of a visit by COMNON, a Norwegian two-star general, during the 1984 exercise. Entertained by the Squadron officers to dinner at a local restaurant, the general was amazed to see, when the first course was slow in arriving, the potted flowers being passed around the table and eaten instead. The general duly took his turn in nibbling the flowers only to be caught in the act by the manageress, who had been called by her staff to sort out these troublesome air force types. It took a lot of fluent Norwegian on the part of the general before dinner was eventually served – and a handsome tip afterwards.

The Harrier Force took part in exercise Maple Flag, as I remember, only one year in three, making it very much a high point of anyone's tour. As well as offering the opportunity of an interesting trans-Atlantic ferry flight, a stay in a fascinating part of Canada near the Rockies, and flying in multi-national composite formations in a very realistic threat environment, the detachment also required proficiency in Operational Low Flying (OLF) – and provided ideal terrain over which to put the skills into practice. Before deploying to Canada selected pilots undertook an intensive and progressive work-up, with particular emphasis on OLF, achieving the ability to operate and navigate at heights down to 100 feet and speeds of up to 550 knots. Training started in the Welsh low flying areas with evasion from attacks by our own Harriers and first run attacks against Pembrey Range, culminating with a deployment to RAF Kinloss (13-14 Jan) to use the remote areas of Scotland for OLF. Tain Range for bombing and the Electronic Warfare Range at

Spadeadam. Evasion was also conducted against Air Defence Phantoms.

For the actual detachment at Cold Lake the Squadron took over six Harriers already in situ, one of which had suffered "bird damage", losing a training Sidewinder missile as a result of the impact. Closer investigation revealed the "bird" too strongly resembled a small Canadian pine. In the otherwise featureless Alberta landscape it was never easy to judge height, especially at high speed, and many a pilot was surprised to find that his height, assessed visually as 100 feet by reference to the tall pines, was more like 20 feet over little saplings. The Maple Flag exercise was successful and enjoyable with many Squadron personnel being able to appreciate a wonderful weekend in the Rockies. The Squadron pilots also acquitted themselves well at "crud", the game much beloved of Canadian aircrew, played on a billiard table but otherwise having no connection with that sedate activity.

On our return from Canada, the Squadron was host to our families and to Squadron Association members at an Open Day at Wittering on 7 June, which included a flying display which would have done credit to any station Battle of Britain day, and which included a four-ship Harrier formation demonstration which I led as my "swan song". On 12 June, I led an eight-ship mission which culminated in the famous "Flying One" formation over the airfield and my handover to Wing Commander Ian Stewart.

In summary my time at the helm was intensely busy, but relatively uneventful. Thankfully we lost no aircraft although there were a few incidents. One pilot managed to land "wheels-up" on the northern taxi-way at Wittering. I was spared having to give him much in the way of a b......ing as his father, who was an air chief marshal, got to him first! Another undercarriage incident took place at Bodø in northern Norway. The Norwegian ground crew, in an effort to be helpful, decided to tow a Harrier back into the hangar as heavy snow stated to fall. The aircrew, on a Ranger flight, had gone back into operations to review the weather, omitting to remind the Norwegians that Harriers must not be moved without the outrigger locks in place. Inevitably the outriggers collapsed and I, who had only assumed command three weeks earlier, spent an uncomfortable twenty minutes having a very one-sided 'phone conversation with the SASO as a result.

Another pilot, who shall also remain nameless, achieved a near-miss with a practice bomb on a bridge near Ross-on-Wye due to a minor mistake in his switchery! Fortunately the event was not witnessed and the media was not alerted, so a damage limitation exercise was very successful. Needless to say, however, Group were not exactly amused by the incident. On a happier note, the Squadron was honoured by a visit from Diana, Princess of Wales on 28 September 1985 as part of an inaugural visit to the Station in her new role as Honorary Air Commodore of RAF Wittering. She was particularly interested in the Squadron's Spitfire and in the Squadron museum, including two Argentinian anti-aircraft guns brought back three years previously.'

***

Wing Commander I M Stewart took command on 13 June 1986. Training, APCs, detachments, all continued as before.

Exercise Bold Guard came in September, the Squadron's Part II Battle Phase of the Taceval at Vandel, which involved land, sea and air forces over Schleswig-Holstein. The advance party went to Vandel on the 17th, the air party over the 19-21st, the exercise being flown between the 22nd and 26th.

Exercise Hot Rod at Deci between 19 November and 10 December saw eight aircraft and the T4 involved, using Capo Frasca Range on the west coast of Sardinia. Squadron Leader Harper won the Hilly Brown Trophy.

The New Year hockey match against the OCU was played out in which the opposition claimed a 2-1 win but one goal was rejected on the grounds that it had been scored with a cricket bat, so 1-1.

In February came exercise Snow Falcon at Bardufoss, with air-to-air refuelling from tanker aircraft. A rude awakening came on landing, the Norwegian weather temperature was 25° below! Back to Deci (to thaw out?) in April – Hot Rod 87 – and this year the ground crew flew by 10 Squadron VC10 from Brize Norton, arriving non-stop after AAR by 101 Squadron VC10s. Squadron Leader Mortimer suffered radio failure and handed over to Flight Lieutenant Cheal. Flight Lieutenant Tracy had pressurisation failure and needed to transit over France. Without the benefit of cabin conditioning, a rather cold and ill-humoured Tracy had to be chipped out of his cockpit on arriving at Deci.

July and exercise Hill Lodger, with 11 aircraft flying to Gütersloh to practise the Squadron's Central Region Option in Hardened Aircraft Shelter (HAS) Operations, following 3 and IV Squadrons there. FAC, SAP and recce sorties were flown plus some ACT missions, using 100-gallon tanks on the outboard pylons which have a reduced fuel load consistent with the short range tasks being flown over

Germany. The Squadron had not operated HAS since 1981. High temperatures and lack of ventilation produced a hot, noxious working environment which was particularly unpleasant during cockpit turn rounds. In August exercise Accord Express in Denmark saw poor weather which caused problems on the site with all the hides collapsing under the weight of rain water and wind.

* * *

The GR5 arrives

Vandel was revisited at the beginning of September 1988. After this the Squadron began to re-equip with the Harrier GR5 and the CO led a seven-ship formation to 'attack' (flypasts) North Coates, Cranwell and Wittering to celebrate the last day of solely GR3 flying. (The last GR3 sorties were eventually flown by Group Captain Peter Day, and Wing Commander Tony Harper, both former 1 Squadron pilots.)

As the GR5 simulator at Wittering was still a long way from completion, Flight Lieutenant 'Slim' Whitman, the QFI, was sent to Rota in Spain, for an introductory course on the GR5 simulator. He would be followed by other pilots. This heralded the arrival of the first GR5s and in October the first pilots started a conversion course at the OCU. This began with 1½ weeks of ground school then 4½ weeks of programmed sorties designed to familiarise everyone with the radically improved navigational and weapon aiming systems, as well as the slightly different handling qualities. Squadron Leader G 'Bones' Jones, OC A Flight, was the first Squadron pilot to fly the GR5. (Gareth Jones was later the Exec and later still OC Operations Wing at Wittering, having, except for a short period behind a desk, flown Harriers since 1981.)

Wing Commander I R Harvey MBE BSc arrived to take command on 3 October 1988, Stewart leaving to become OC RAF Gütersloh. There was a dining out for the old CO at the Haycock in Wansford. Because of the terrorist threat at the time the management were asked not to make this known, so they publicised it as the AGM of a local hang-gliding club.

A cut-down Squadron of just six GR3s went to Decimomannu during the month to fly with Tornado F3s from 229 OCU and the Tornado Operational Evaluation Unit. The F3, billed as NATO's most advanced interceptor and *the wonder of the western world* had considerable problems with its radar and in consequence was *creamed* by the Squadron's vintage, non-radar equipped Harriers! The ground crews soon cottoned on to this and began painting kills on the sides of the aircraft. In the end the Squadron began to feel decidedly sorry for the F3 'target drone' pilots.

Norway came around again in November. Due to tanker problems the deployment took some time to get there and only two arrived in Tromsø, the others having to go to Bodø. Overall it became a disaster flying-wise but socially an overwhelming success.

After this, Squadron Leader C R Benn arrived as the new OC B Flight, Squadron Leader Gowers becoming the Squadron Exec from 'Morts' Mortimer, pending planned retirement. GR5s were now arriving in numbers, 11 being on strength by Christmas, but it was a difficult time with pilots in Spain and the OCU, while others tried to continue with Squadron commitments.

The New Year began with the annual hockey match versus the OCU, and as always the result was a draw although the Squadron scored the most goals! A visit by the West German Minister of State in early January saw a discussion about low level flying over Germany, where civilians were beginning to feel more threatened by low flying RAF aircraft than fear of aggression from the East!

Norway in February was no more successful than it had been in November, the weather proving the greatest problem and only 13 sorties were flown. Also this month saw the last GR3 sorties flown, and a planned show for the local press was scuppered by fog and only one lone VSTOL demonstration was possible.

The Harrier in service – 20 years

Improved weather in March and April saw more flying, but it also heralded a long line of press and VIPs all wanting to see the new GR5s at work. There was also a 'do' to celebrate the 20th anniversary of the Harrier in service, and a dinner was organised to which a large number of guests were invited. Unfortunately nobody from British Aerospace was invited so they hosted their own dinner on the same evening in Stamford offering complimentary tickets to any Harrier pilot who wished to go. Their dinner was poorly attended.

There were some problems with the GR5 beginning to rear their heads in April and then a major glitch with the ejection seat firing mechanism grounded them all. The Martin Baker Company quickly sorted this out and within a week or so, aircraft were flying again. There followed the first GR5 detachment, a Squadron exchange to Albacete, Spain, home of the Spanish 14th Air Wing. The chance to show-off their new aircraft ended prematurely and the Squadron were sent home in some disgrace.

From all accounts – several being published in local and then British newspapers – some airmen had been involved in an incident at their hotel. What began as a normal Squadron briefing the next morning, ended abruptly with the arrival of the CO who told everyone that they were all being sent home. Within a few hours the aircraft were heading for the UK and then a Hercules arrived to collect ground crew and their equipment. In the end no further action was taken by the Spanish and despite a lot of questions no airmen could shed any light on the problem, or who had caused costly damage to the Hotel Europa. The damage was later paid for and an apology sent. In the end one junior tech. was fined and a SNCO posted out. It was not one of the Squadron's finest hours.

Putting this behind them they prepared for the coming Taceval and a local field exercise. The field operation saw aircraft operating from hardcore and a total of 67 tyres were changed either through bursts or wear; each tyre cost over one thousand pounds – quite an expense.

A detachment to Valley in June was a success during which some AIM-9G missiles were fired, Flying Officer 'Spike' Jepson firing the first Sidewinder from a GR5. July saw the Squadron at RAF Leeming as their forward base during a tactics operation, part of which was with Canadian F-18 Hornets from the 4th Canadian Wing. One example of a sortie flown was eight Harriers, with tanker support, escorted by six F-18s and two Hawks, fighting through eight F-3 Tornado aircraft in order to attack a convoy in the Scottish Highlands.

On 21 August the new GR5s were taken to Deci and it was here that the Squadron found just how good their new machines were in air combat. They were pitted against American, French and Dutch as well as F-3s. Number One more than held their own against US F-15 Eagles, F-16 Falcons and F-18s and French Mirage F1s. A lot of vino Rosso/Deci was consumed and the Squadron semi-pro tennis team took on all-comers.

At the end of September came part two of the Taceval, during which 120 sorties had been flown. Later that year came another visit by Princess Diana. November saw trips to Italy, Sardinia (Deci) and Norway, followed by a trip to Gütersloh in December. The detachment to Deci resulted in the Squadron 'monstering' 229 OCU, and by the end of the second week the OCU people became rather depressed. Gütersloh came on 11 December and was a chance for the Jackboot Johnnies/Hitler Youth (pilots who have done a tour in Germany) to show the Winstonians (pilots whose first tour was on 1 Squadron in UK) the ins-and-outs of flying over the Fatherland. Unfortunately the weather was not very good but at least the Winstonians could now join in the: 'When I was in Germany ...' line-shoots.

January 1990

The annual New Year hockey match against the OCU, ostensibly ended in a draw, but this time, the 'student filth' at the OCU decided, for some reason best known to themselves, to take it seriously. They had twice the number of players 1 Squadron fielded and were soon 2-nil up. Flying Officer Sean Perret got upset by this so threw down his stick, picked up the ball, and running past all OCU players, dived into their net. The Ref (Station Commander) said: 'Good goal 1 Squadron, but we won't be having any more of that, will we Sean?' Halfway into the second period, after some refreshing gluwein, the CO took out the OCU's JENGO. With a sickening crunch he went down, bleeding profusely with a three-inch gash between his eyes. The Doc took one look at him and seeing his need for stitches had him Casevac'd off the field and into hospital. The final score remained 2-1 but the Squadron declared that the loss of the OCU's junior engineering officer should count as a goal and thus it became 2-2.

In the spring, the Squadron's US exchange officer, Pitt Merryman left and was dined-out, but he turned up with some rattlesnake and alligator meat as threatened for everyone to sample. Four days beforehand, he, together with Squadron Leader Benn, Flight Lieutenant Ellison and Sean Perrett flew a four-ship flypast at Berry-au-Bac on 25 May, a former 1 Squadron base in 1940 during the French campaign. The four had lunch in Reims then flew over Veules-les-Roses to commemorate the fallen of Dunkirk.

Most of June saw the pilots at Vandel and in July the CO led some of the pilots in practising the 'Flying 1'. Of the 11 pilots needed, all flew well except the two out of position at the back – both Squadron's QFIs!

Farnborough 1990

Farnborough came in August/September, the pilots swanking around in smart navy blue flying overalls supplied by British Aerospace. As the Squadron was one of the main attractions it was never difficult for the non-flying chaps to get lunch and 'orange squash' in the various VIP tents, although they had to show many people round the static aircraft display. So it wasn't all fun and one can only eat so much smoked salmon, and drink so much champa ... sorry, squash.

The Harrier GR5 had made its first appearance at Farnborough in 1986 but in 1990 1 Squadron deployed nine operational GR5s, six of which took part in a pageant reminiscent of pre-WW2 days with pyrotechnics and mock bombing runs.

Four Harriers mounted a mock raid upon the airfield, a fifth leapt through the smoke from the taxi-way to hover over the smoke, while the sixth taxied out for a more conventional take-off. The finalé had five aircraft hovering in a line, then bowing, as the sixth machine zoomed in behind them to soar upwards in the non-afterburning vertical climb that has set the Harrier apart from thirstier jets.

The CO was part of the bombing run, and much of the planning came from Squadron Leader Gareth Jones, while Les Garside-Beattie mapped out the demonstration. Others in the team were Squadron Leader Ashley Stevenson, Flight Lieutenants Tim Ellison, Dave Poole, Spike Jepson, Jim Marden and Andy Studdards. Simon Meade was also part of the set up, a former Hawk display pilot, and he had several contacts on the flying display circuit which were vital for holding the whole show together. Warrant Officer (then F/Sgt) Dave Ellis relates:

> 'We were based at Farnborough for nearly two weeks covering the rehearsals plus the trade and public days. For this we displayed six GR5s which were supported by a party of approx 40 ground staff. We rotated the party so that the majority of Squadron personnel were able to participate, of these the Senior Engineering Officer, Squadron Leader John Piggott, Chief Technician Dennis Horseman and myself were there for the whole period.
>
> It was a unique occasion seldom seen since the 1930s, which has not been repeated since and in these days of austerity it is doubtful if it will be seen again. It is interesting to note that Squadron Leader Les Garside-Beattie went on to be the team manager for the Red Arrows and Flight Lieutenant Spike Jepson a team member. Flight Lieutenant Simon Meade after his spell on the team was later a team leader (S/Ldr).'

This year saw the 50th Anniversary of the Battle of Britain and a flypast over Buckingham Palace came on 15 September. It was led by a Spitfire and with 168 aircraft, was the largest since the Queen's Coronation. 16 Harriers took part, four each from 1 and 4 Squadrons, four from the OCU, plus four Sea Harriers.

First Harrier loss since the Falklands

The Squadron was back in Denmark in October, for air defence exercises with the Royal Danish Air Force. On the 17th Squadron Leader Ashley Stevenson ejected from the boss's jet '01' (ZD355) near Karup. Its engine stopped at 23,500 feet whilst in a climb out of a Danish base, with a very loud bang, loss of thrust and very high JPT. As he lost height, Ash tried a number of re-lights but with no result. Finally he pointed the Harrier out to sea and ejected at 2,000 feet. He landed shortly afterwards with only cuts and bruises. The un-manned jet turned back on its own and crashed into a field about 400 yards short of the coast. The accident was caused by fatigue failure of a second stage LP compressor blade.

* * *

Over the winter the Squadron were in Norway, with two jets stuck in Bergen due to them being temporaily u/s. The British Aerospace film crew went too in order to make a video of the GR5.

In the spring of 1991 it was back to Deci for the ACMI range, but it wasn't working very well so some of the pilots and all the jets had to fly to Majorca. One poor pilot had a sick aircraft and was forced to 'rough it' in a hotel there for a week. Then it was off to Crete for an exchange with the 340 MB Squadron of the Greek Air Force, flying A7s. They said their lower height limit was 300 feet but it didn't stop some of them going lower. The CO professionally 'side-stepped' the chance of a ride in the back seat of one and the Squadron's JP went instead and he recalls going down Rhodes High Street with the tops of buildings above him so wasn't over keen on another ride!

Names quickly change sometimes, so the Squadron's nominal roll as at the first day of 1991 was:

W/C I Harvey	(Iain)	S/L C R Benn (Exec)	(Chris)
S/L L Garside-Beattie (OCA)	(Les)	S/L A Stevenson (OCB)	(Ashley)
F/L B Bryson	(Brick)	F/L D Court	(Dave)
Capt P Fulton USAF	(Paul)	F/L C R Huckstep	(Chris)
F/L Spike Newbery	(Spike)	F/L A Norris	(Tony)

| F/L S Perrett | (Sean) | F/L A Pinner | (Al) |
| F/L M Taberham | (Mark) | F/L S Turner | (Simon) |

W/C J Piggott (SEngO)	(John)	F/L P Higgs (JEngO)	(Pete)
Maj M M Howes (GLO)	(Mike)	F/L M Bird (RegO)	(Mike)
F/L C Glaze (Squintess)	(Chris)		

'Clingons' were:

| S/L G A Humphreys | (Gerry) | S/L G Jones | (Gareth) |

RAF Lossiemouth for exercise Splash II in January, then exercise 'Battle Griffin' at Bardufoss in February prepared everyone for Red Flag in April and while this detachment was on everyone became glued to SkyTV as 'Operation Desert Storm' began. There was obvious interest and concern, hearing of mates going missing and others, as prisoners, turning up on Iraqi TV. On the lighter side, it was noted that the Exec had managed to be dragged away from his paper work to reluctantly fly club class to the USA and during a recce of Las Vegas had to go through the hell of staying in a 5-star hotel room at Caesar's Palace.

Iain Harvey left in May 1991, and the new CO, Wing Commander C C N Burwell MBE took over on the 17th. Chris Burwell relates:

'I took command of the Squadron immediately after their return from Red Flag 91-X at Nellis AFB, USA. After a short detachment to Denmark in June for exercise Central Enterprise, the first major event during my tour was the grounding of all RAF Harrier GR5/7 aircraft on 30 July following three aircraft fires in short succession. These were attributed to electrical problems following chaffing and the breakdown of Kapton wiring which led to arcing and the subsequent fires.

Since the grounding was unlikely to be resolved quickly, with the concurrence of Wittering's CO, Group Captain 'Syd' Morris, I borrowed two Harrier GR3s and a T4 (to add to the one we already had) and set about back-converting the pilots. Both Squadron Leader Mark Green, one of the flight commanders, and myself were both current T4 QFIs. It took about ten weeks before we were flying the GR5 again and not until November that the Squadron returned to a useful daily number of available airframes.

During this period all the pilots were converted back to the GR3. Some pilots had limited prior GR3 experience, including Captain Paul Fulton, our USAF exchange officer, and Flight Lieutenant Al Pinner, a first-tour GR5 pilot who made the unfortunate mistake of thinking that INAS on the GR3 was reliable, but he did eventually arrive back at the right airfield! The Squadron also participated in a detachment to the ACMI at Decimonannu in October, flying against RAF F-4s and Jaguars. This was dubbed the vintage aircraft ACMI – but what a detachment!

However, on 25 September, Squadron Leader Ashley Stevenson, the Exec, in a T4 had a serious accident while giving Cadet Kate Saunders, a Cambridge UAS undergraduate an air experience sortie. The aircraft suffered a birdstrike whilst flying at 420 knots at low level over the Yorkshire Wolds. The bird hit the canopy quarterlight, the remains entering the cockpit, smashing into Ashley's visor and oxygen mask, rearranging his teeth in the process. Pieces of perspex from the canopy entered the engine causing the Pegasus to lock in a surge. Kate was flying the aircraft at the time but with Ashley unable to see or communicate with her, and aware that the engine was in surge but unable to sort out the situation, he wisely decided that ejection was the only option.

Kate soon got the idea as she saw Ashley's seat leave the aircraft just in front of her and, only just in time, she followed suit. Unfortunately her ejection was so late that she landed close to the wreckage, in a field of stubble that had been set alight by burning fuel from the T4. Kate suffered multiple injuries and was badly burned before she was rescued by Ashley, who was subsequently awarded the Queen's Commendation for Brave Conduct for his role in saving her life despite his own painful injuries.'

Kate was reading classics at Queen's College and was 22. While Ashley came down in a corn field beside a country road near Driffield, she drifted down into another which had been set on fire by burning fuel and it set her clothes alight. Hitting the ground she broke a leg and her pelvis. Ashley pulled her from the flames and beat out her burning clothing with his gloved hands. An oblique claim to fame for her and the Squadron was that she was the first woman in RAF history to eject from an aeroplane. (Yet another first!) Kate later returned to flying until stopped on medical grounds, taking on married life instead.

Another first was that Ashley Stevenson, later CO of 3 Squadron, was the first RAF pilot to eject twice from a Harrier. His nearest rival was Chuck Coulcher, who had been on Hunters with the Squadron, but his two ejections had been from USAF Phantoms while on attachment with the Americans. Chris Burwell continues:

'Once into 1992 the Squadron was fully back into the swing with its reworked GR5s and enjoyed a most successful APC at RAF Valley, firing off the year's full allocation of AIM-G9s in just 24 hours, before deploying to Macrihanish in February for exercise "Hardcore" – a consolidated operational training phase including ultra low level (100 feet) flying, live weapons delivery on the Scottish air weapons ranges and a very successful evasion exercise against the Tornado F-3 Wing at Leeming, employing the Harrier GR5's Zeus EW system. The next few months of the year were taken up with a series of major exercises and deployments: exercise "Teamwork" (Bardufoss) in March; a training field deployment to Vigo Wood on Wittering airfield in April – memorable for the rain and the number of bog-ins!; and exercise "Mayfly", the Squadron's operational evaluation (Opeval) at RAF Kemble in May. This latter exercise was a major undertaking since the Squadron had to plan the whole enterprise itself, deploy 350 personnel including various support units into the woods on Kemble airfield for two weeks, and undergo a searching evaluation by a national Taceval team from HQ Strike Command.

In June the Squadron received the first Harrier GR7, the night capable version of the GR5, fitted with FLIR (Forward Looking Infra Red), cockpit lighting compatible with NVGs (Night Vision Goggles) and a digital moving map display, ready for the Squadron to undertake a two-season night trial. For some time the Strike Attack Operational Evaluation Unit (SAOEU) at Boscombe Down had been developing night operations for the Tornado and Harrier Forces; the time had now come for a trial to be undertaken to determine the feasibility of converting a frontline Harrier squadron to night operations and No.1 Squadron was selected for the task. The RAF Germany squadrons at Laarbruch would then follow on from the start made by us – "In omnibus princeps".

In the same month we celebrated the Squadron's 80th birthday with a weekend at Wittering that was blessed with excellent weather and an outstanding turnout of former members. At Happy Hour on the Friday night, Ned Crowley (Hurricanes in 1941), then aged 73, performed his party trick of drinking a half pint of beer whilst standing on his head! On the Saturday, the Squadron Commander led a Flying One; a Spitfire, a Harrier and the Red Arrows all displayed; and there was a sunset ceremony and buffet supper in the evening. On Sunday there was a church service in the Wittering Parish Church followed by a jazz lunch in the garden of the Officer's Mess. The whole weekend was organised with a great deal of style and panache by our GLO, Major Mike Howes.

In July the Squadron went back to Deci for a two-week detachment on the instrumented combat range, while in August, Flight Lieutenant Chris Huckstep parted company from his aircraft immediately after take-off at Wittering following an engine failure. In October we were privileged to invite back one of the most illustrious squadron commanders – Air Marshal Sir Ken Hayr – to dine him out on his retirement from the RAF. Sir Ken spent the day with the Squadron and enjoyed a final Harrier trip in our T4, with Mark Green, before the Squadron dinner that evening.'

Low-level ejection

Flight Lieutenant Chris Huckstep was gaining much experience on the Harrier. This was not his first tour with Number One – that was in 1984-87 – nor would it be his last, and interspersed by a period with 3 Squadron and the OCU. On the Friday he departed from his Harrier (ZD350) – 8 August 1992 – the moment of truth came at 0925 in the morning:

'I had come in that morning and wasn't down to fly but then came a slot in the program so I went. I was leading Roly Sharman, one of the JPs, off to the range at Holbeach. It was a nice sunny day, light south-west breeze, and a few white fluffy clouds.

On the pan I was held for a couple of minutes as someone had seen a single spark come from the engine and he had called the line walker but after both had watched and seen nothing else happen, we were allowed to taxi out to take off.

I was nozzling out and accelerating away normally. Mark Zanker was hovering to the north in the back of the T4 and looking across at us he saw sparks coming from my engine just as I was climbing away. He called up: "Harrier Lead taking off, sparks from your engine!" I heard this and

Top left: Chuck Coulcher in the dyed overalls that came out more maroon than red. *(C P Coulcher)*

Top right: Harriers aboard *Atlantic Conveyor*, on their way to the Falklands. *(P T Squire)*

Middle left: Mark Hare on Ascension Island, May 1982. *(P T Squire)*

Bottom: Harriers All! Top to bottom: GR3 20 Sqn, T4 1 Sqn, FRS1 899 Sqn Fleet Air Arm, GR5 20 Sqn, GR7 1 Sqn. Over King's Lynn, near Holbeach Range.

(Br Aerospace)

Top: 1 Squadron Harriers at Nellis AF Base, Nevada, for Red Flag, August 1994.

(Cpl J Cassidy, RAF Official)

Bottom left: Harrier GR7 in colour scheme for Operation Warden, Iraq. Carrying a black recce pod,

Sidewinder missiles and a PHIMAT pod for chaff dispensing.

(Br Aerospac

Bottom right: Dave Walker and Brig Gen Robin Olds swap hats during a visit to Wittering in September 199

(Sgt D Whitema

Top: A 1,000 lb bomb drops away from a Harrier GR7.

Middle: W/Cdr Dave Walker (left) and pilots October 1995. From left: Andy Tagg, Warren Ward, Steve Underwood, Steve Hunt, unknown, Scott Adey, Mark Wootten, Sqn JENGO. The Harrier – ZD323 – was in action over Kosovo in 1999. Steve Hunt became a flight commander in 1999.

Left: From left, Myles Garland, Ian Cameron, W/Cdr Mark Leakey, Jim Provost, Pete Kosogorin, and Steve Jessott in front.

(Mark Rowe)

Top left: 1 Squadron Harrier taking off from HMS *Illustrious*, 1997.

Top right: Mark Leakey on *Illustrious*. LA Tate's open hand is to tell the pilot to release brakes as the tow bar is now secured. Mark's fist confirms the brakes are on – important to be understood on a pitching deck.

Bottom: S/Ldr Chris Huckstep and the Squadron arrive back from Kosovo, June 1999.

thought, he's talking about my aircraft and in that split second I was able to adjust my mind to a possible danger.

What happened next was that one of the spacer blades in the compressor, which had come loose, twisted, and rubbing against the set of the whirling blades, caused sparks to pour out. At that moment it broke away and chewed its way down into the turbine, wrecked it and fuel began to pour out, followed immediately by fire. The thrust dropped off and there was an enormous noise and vibration, and without flying speed the aircraft just dropped from my gained height of about 50 feet. That call from Mark just gave me that split second of mental preparation that not all was well. So, when it went, I just reached down and pulled the ejection handle. As I found out later, I went out at just 16 feet above the ground and three to four seconds later I hit the deck. Believe me it is a very dramatic way to leave an aeroplane.

There was a huge crash and the whole thing feels like its brewing up around you as the seat fires and ejects you out, with one's eyes tightly shut, followed by a jerk as the seat falls away. I just had time to get my legs together and hunker down a bit, then I was on the concrete like a sack of potatoes. Suddenly it was completely quiet, so I sat up, looked round, could not feel any damage so stood up. The aircraft had gone in on fire on the army pan at the end of the runway, and I could see the smoke rising.

Birds were singing, it was still sunny, all quiet, but I thought I bet it's not all quiet in the tower! Then sirens were going off, a wagon raced out, the fire engine pitched up, the Squadron Commander arrived, Station Commander, then some of the boys. All very un-real and it had all happened in just a few seconds.'

Night vision trials and Iraq
Chris Burwell continues:

'With various technical problems associated with night operations in the GR7 finally resolved – most importantly a system to automatically "blow off" the NVGs from the pilot's helmet in the event of an ejection – the Squadron undertook its first night electro-optical (EO) sorties on 17 November 1992. (This milestone event is commemorated by the Mike Rondot painting which now hangs in the Squadron, commissioned by the Squadron executives.) Prior to this, the pilots had undertaken a fair amount of weapons training, to increase their limited night flying experience. Squadron Leader M J Harwood was posted onto the Squadron as OC Night, but was more usually known as POD (Prince of Darkness) due to his previous experience of night trials with the SAOEU at Boscombe Down. Due to the limited number of aircraft available for night work initially, it was decided that the CO and QWI – Flight Lieutenant Rob Adlam – would run at the front of the night syllabus devised by Mike Harwood. The night task focused on the work of the Squadron over the next 18 months, with all the pilots working through a comprehensive and demanding training programme.

In January 1993 we detached to RAF Leuchars to carry out the annual OLF (100 feet) training and took the opportunity to fly night low level sorties in Scotland and to carry out live weapon deliveries (1,000 lb HE bombs) on Garvie Island at night, despite a ferocious depression off the north of Scotland which gave winds of around 60 knots at 500 feet (and the turbulence to go with it) on the run-in to Garvie! At the end of the first night session, the Squadron deployed to Yuma, Arizona, in April 1993 to expand their experience of night operations in a totally different climate and environment, these factors having a marked impact both on FLIR and NVG performance.

At the end of the Yuma detachment the Squadron was given one RAF Tristar to meet its transport and air-to-air refuelling (AAR) requirements for the return to Wittering. Consequently, three of our GR7s had to return without AAR. Led by Squadron Leader Gerry Humphreys, Flight Lieutenants Tom Lyons and Roly Sharman staged back through Goose Bay but got caught out by the weather at Keflavik in Iceland. Without a suitable diversion, and the situation compounded by Gerry Humphreys suffering a generator failure on the recovery into Keflavik which necessitated him carrying out a pairs approach in the foulest of weather, the three were fortunate to get safely back on the ground.

The early part of the summer provided a return to a more normal existence after the winter's night flying, but in August we relieved 3 Squadron on Operation "Warden", policing the no-fly zone in Northern Iraq, for two months. This provided an interesting new departure for the Squadron, with sorties lasting typically, two hours, 45 minutes and involving AAR outbound and 30-45 minutes carrying out recce tasks in Iraq airspace. Pilots taking part in this operation were awarded the General Service Medal (Air Ops Iraq). On return to Wittering in October, it was time to resume the Night Trial.'

Hitting a cable over a fjord

In November (the 15th), Flight Lieutenant C R Soffe had a lucky escape during a sortie over northern Norway in ZD469. Clive Soffe was on his first detachment. The exercise was for two pairs to operate and with the winter weather the pilots only had a 2½-3 hour window of usable daylight. A briefing was held but it went on a bit longer than usual so in order to get the sortie in, there was a route change, and things got a bit rushed.

One of the aircraft then went u/s, so a three-ship was flown in arrow formation, Clive being the No.2 on the right-hand side. The aircraft flew off and were heading down a fjord at 330 feet in loose formation, but unseen across the fjord stretched a high tension cable. The leader and the No.3 were very lucky, as they went by the cable, the leader missing it and the No.3 just glimpsing it pass underneath him. Clive Soffe hit it.

At first he thought he'd suffered a bird strike; the aircraft decelerated rapidly and he pulled up and called the leader to say he had a problem. The No.3 then called to say Clive's Harrier was venting fuel from both external tanks. Upon closer inspection, the No.3 reported that as far as he could see, the Harrier had lost all its aerials, all under-wing equipment and he could see lots of damage. It also appeared there was a piece of cable wrapped around one fuel pylon.

Soffe had lost all his instruments so after giving a Mayday, he decided to divert to nearby Tromsø. The leader called out the vital airspeed and heights as he flew alongside. Gradually losing height he made it safely into Tromsø. Climbing down from the Harrier, Clive was amazed to see, as he looked into the air intakes, that virtually all the blades were bent, buckled and torn, but at least the engines had kept going. Later the engineers found they couldn't turn the turbine – it had seized up solid after landing.

Clive Soffe had been extremely lucky. Just a few inches lower and the wire would have sliced into the canopy and decapitated him. He went on to complete his three-year tour with the Squadron followed by three years on the teaching unit – 20 Squadron – before joining BA. Chris Burwell:

'In early 1994 we were back at Leuchars, but this time for OLF and weapons training, since a detachment to Bardufoss the following month provided an ideal opportunity for the Squadron to practise night operations in the Arctic Circle in the depths of winter. This was an outstanding experience for all who flew at night during this detachment, not least was the chance to view the Northern Lights through NVGs!

In addition, whilst the Squadron had up until now restricted night formations to a maximum of two aircraft, whilst in Norway Gerry Humphreys, Flight Lieutenant Chris Norton and myself flew the Squadron's first night three-ship. Back at Wittering, on 28 April, Gerry, Mike Harwood, Flight Lieutenant "Jack" Frost and I flew the Harrier Force's first night four-ship.'

This was Chris Burwell's last sortie with 1 Squadron. Although he had been promoted to Group Captain back in July '93, he had remained with the Squadron to see the night trials through to a successful conclusion and, as a consequence, commanded the Squadron for two years, 11 months. The following day, 29 April 1994, he handed over to Wing Commander D Walker AFC BSc.

Chapter Twenty One

TURKEY, BOSNIA, IRAQ AND *INVINCIBLE*

Operation Warden

Prior to taking command of the Squadron, Dave Walker had been Squadron Leader Tactics at the Central Tactics Organisation which covered the OEU, having returned from the USA where he had been working on night attack development flying F-18s and the AV8-B Harrier. After a spell at Staff College, he was given No.1 (F) Squadron. The Squadron Exec was Squadron Leader M J Harwood, with Squadron Leaders J G Richardson OCA, M J M Jenkins OCB, and I A MacDonald OCN Flights; SEngO was Squadron Leader P R Ewen. David Walker relates:

'I took over at the point at which the Squadron had just finished the night phase of tactics development for the Harrier Force. Up until this time the Squadron had effectively been protected from other activities, as it was conducting the proof concept work in relation to night flying in the Harrier.

We had just started to deploy to Incirlik Air Base, Turkey – half there, half in the UK. We continued with the night attack work-up, taking it from a tactics trial into being routine training, so that it stopped being a special task and then routine.

There was the operational deployment side which was initially to Turkey, then to go to Bosnia after the Dayton Agreement and IFOR forces into Bosnia. On top of this was the work for positive extraction of friendly forces from within the enclaves that were developing inside Bosnia. This involved a lot of night attack work with Special Forces and other Army and Navy units, to go in and pull folk out, especially from Gorazda where British armed forces were deployed. This took from September 1994 to the end of the summer of 1995. It was quite a significant operational tempo with the changes of state in Bosnia, while still working in Turkey.'

Operation Warden was the UK contribution to the American-led Operation Provide Comfort, designed to protect the Kurdish peoples of northern Iraq from Iraqi harassment. A UN safe haven had been set up in July 1991 with RAF support helicopters, transport aircraft and RM commandos. Once Operation Warden was set up the Harriers of 1, 3 and IV Squadrons became responsible for providing the UK offensive support, primarily tactical air reconnaissance (TAR) within the Area of Responsibility (AOR).

No.1 Squadron began deploying to Incirlik on rotation with the other two Harrier units armed with recce pods (Vinten Vicon Pod) and CRV7 rockets. The rockets gave an excellent stand-off capability combined with great accuracy, especially if engaging targets where small arms fire might preclude short-range area or overflight weapons systems, and specifically where collateral damage must be minimized. Meantime, the areas covered were also being patrolled by AWACs aircraft, US F-4s and F-111s, plus F-15 and F-16 fighters.

Pilots were always on the look-out for Iraqi SAMs, the Harriers using their ZEUS system – the integral electronic warfare suite, while visually searching for the tell-tale plume of smoke. Most Harrier sorties needed two hours of planning and the recce film was rapidly down-loaded and given to the photo interpretation people within ten minutes of touchdown. The terrain was rugged, from mountains of over 8,000 feet in the far north to the flat desert-like plains to the south, around Mosul. The thought of a pilot coming down in any part of the No-Fly Zone is not a happy one, although one pilot, who did eject following an engine problem in November 1993 (not 1 Sqn), did return safely with help from Kurdish tribesmen; in return they were given a generous reward of cattle and supplies. Dave Walker:

'On the normal routine training side there were all the usual deployments to Norway, the Med. and so on. In August 1994 we did lead the Harrier Force out to America to take part in exercise "Air Warrior". Nothing special but it was the first time we had actually deployed as a three-squadron force for a whole exercise. Overall this was the work-up for the Taceval in September '95 which was at Chivenor. During this time IV Squadron were over Bosnia, so we had the rather bizarre situation where half the Harrier Force was being tested to see whether or not we could go to war, while the other half was in Bosnia going to war, but not fit to go to take part in the practice!

During January-February 1995, while we were having our turn at Incirlik, I was hit on 2 February. We were on patrol along the Iraqi border flying at about 250 feet, keeping an eye on the various Kurdish factions there. It was the classic PKK, the Iranian-backed Kurdish separatists, and the KVP, the Iraqi-Turkish, more moderate bunch, who were constantly fighting. We were going down to see what was going on as part of the marshalling force. We had spotted some small-arms gunfire below and had turned to come back for another look and a photo run. They seemed to take an exception to this and someone took a pot-shot at us.

After some lucky shot with a Kalashnikov, the bullet hit the front edge of the sliding canopy of my Harrier (ZD405) on the left side. The impact set off the MDC and this lot went "boom"! My immediate, classic, pilot response was, what have I done wrong? I was thinking that I do not want to jump out here, because this is where the Iranian-Kurdish gentlemen live and they don't like me. Then I wondered if the engine was still going, which it was. The canopy plastic had all but gone. Some pieces had clattered into the cockpit around me, I later found out some had gone into the air intake, slightly damaging some of the turbine blades. Some damage had also been inflicted to the tailplane.

Having been showered with plastic bits myself, I found I had also been peppered around the neck and the first thing I did was to raise my hand to the canopy to find out what had happened. This was immediately whipped back in the slipstream. Pulling my arm back, I then felt my neck only to discover my white glove had turned a sort of reddy colour. I thought, this is not good! So added to my other problems I thought I am going to bleed to death, as there was a reasonably-sized piece of plastic sticking out of my neck. It didn't seem too deeply embedded, but I knew there were a lot of important veins going up and down here!

I was also flying in the wrong direction, roughly towards Baghdad, so thought it would be good to turn soon. This I did and transmitted a Mayday on the AWACs frequency and suddenly the air turned dark with American fighters, which began escorting me out. Meantime, Flight Lieutenant Paul Wharmby, one of my pilots, was taking photos of me with his recce pod. To add to my discomfort it started to rain on the way back and although I was hunkered down in the cockpit, rain, at that speed, hurts!

By the time I landed at Diyarbakir, flying an hour in an open cockpit, soaked by rain, with blood everywhere, it really made me look the part, as I stood up – without of course, sliding back what was left of the canopy. This impressed the Turks and I became an absolute hero to them. They were in conflict with Kurdish separatists in whatever form they happened to appear, so here was a member of the British armed forces who had taken them on!!'

David Walker, as this is written, is Station Commander of RAF Cottesmore. Sitting on a cabinet near his desk is a mounted piece of perspex plastic from his smashed canopy. It is inscribed to W/C Walker on the occasion of his first Harrier cabriolet flight!

One of David Walker's pilots was Flight Lieutenant E S Hunt, who only a few years later would become the Squadron's A Flight commander. Steve Hunt remembers:

'Steve Underwood and I were doing our slot in the area. At that stage we were allowed to low fly over Kurdistan, so at the end of every AOR, we'd drop into low level flying. We were called up by the AWACs that the Iraqis had moved some artillery up over-night, right up to the banks of the Tigris, and were shelling across the river into Kurdistan. They tasked us to go and stop the shelling, although we were not cleared to release anything, which was a bit bizarre.

So we dropped onto the Tigris itself, right down on the water, below the banks, and flew down until we could actually see the muzzle flashes and the smoke. We pulled up over the guns at the last second, which must have given them a hell of a shock, then went round again and did it again. The shelling stopped immediately and they pulled the guns away. It was exciting, heading down the river at around 15 feet, not wanting to show ourselves too early but to give them a fright as we flashed over them.

Apart from that there were strange missions, such as being tasked to find out what was in the hardened aircraft shelters on Mosul airfield. The only way we could do that was to fly down the runway at 20 feet and look through the doors! They'd been hiding equipment there so it was really low level, slightly banked over while filming with the old GR3 camera pod turned on. Filming inside hangars etc, with another Harrier at higher level spotting for hostile missles or ground fire, was an exciting recce pastime.

We flew really low sorties, or very high, never anything in the middle, as we knew there were Roland missiles about. One day we were tasked to go and see if one Roland site was manned because there hadn't been any emissions from it for a long time. We found the vehicle, so again one Harrier went high, at around 15,000 feet on the edge of the threat ring, while I went down low right across the truck, with all the cameras on, but it was deserted. In addition, of course, we had been a visual deterrent too.

These were similar to our missions over Bosnia, where most of the time we were at 10,000 feet, but if a border fracas, cross-road/checkpoint problem arose where people started shooting, we'd go down and disperse them. We came in low and fast in a dive over their heads to scare them away.'

* * *

At around the time Dave Walker took command, Squadron Leader Mike Jenkins also arrived:

'It was an interesting time, for as a QFI I was posted in as the Attack Flight Commander, which is normally a weapons instructor. With the job came a lot of responsibility in the deployment role. Consequently I ended up being the detachment commander for all the field deployments with the joint Harrier Force concept deployments, which came in at around the same time.

The concept had moved from being single squadron assignments with different responsibilities, to one whereby the Force was being considered as a whole and would work together. All this had happened basically because of the changes in the Cold War.

The interesting thing was that 1 Squadron had never been a field deployment outfit but I had done my time in Germany, which had field deployment squadrons. So the first one we did was to Bentwaters, near Woodbridge, when it was still part of the RAF's real estate. Each squadron set up a site. By hook or by crook it was decided that 1 Squadron would have a bare field site and I was sent as detachment commander. In some respects this was an amusing mistake because I had a brand new regiment officer. Between us we basically prepared to beat the other squadrons at their own game – so we did.

We set up an incredibly tactical field site in some woods and operated in the old way, whereas other units were operating from built-up sites. There were two amusing anecdotes about these deployments.

The first is that because we were slightly isolated as a site, we employed the standard operating procedures for letting in and out of the site – guards, check-posts, etc. We'd been criticised one day because we'd not employed it to the extent it should have been. Then we had a VIP visitor and I said, OK, everything by the book. So we held up the VIP's convoy at the gate whilst we checked every single I/D. This led to me in particular, getting a dressing down for being over-zealous!

The second story was that each Saturday we used to fly during the morning in order to fly air combat, as we couldn't do normal tactical flying at the weekends. The other two squadrons began and we were the second wave, doing air combat against No.IV Squadron. We dropped off all the fuel tanks very quickly – in a matter of an hour or so – in order to give ourselves a tactical advantage over them. They were most dis-chuffed because they hadn't thought this up themselves and we had waxed them! So overall a very successful deployment.

The next most interesting time was Incirlik, flying with the Americans in large combined missions, sometimes as many as eighty aircraft. We'd refuel in south-eastern Turkey, doing recce missions into northern Iraq in order to verify the surface-to-air missile situation and make sure a war wasn't going on. What was more interesting was the fact that most of the fighting going on there was between two factions of Kurds. This resulted in the frequent change-over of the ownership of Erbil, which is a small but historic town in the south-east corner of the No-Fly Zone. The fact was that 1 Squadron had been doing the exact opposite thing in the 1920s, when it had been based at Hinaidi, a level of irony that did not escape us. One of the key events there was that Mike Harwood received an MBE *[for his work with the GR5 on night flying development. Ed.]* and he flew his last flight on the Squadron over Iraq.

Dave Walker usually only came out towards the end of detachments to be there at change-overs, as he liked to leave flight commanders in control. On one of his visits he was hit over Iraq and his canopy was shattered. On his flight back he was asked by the AWACs guys if there was anything they could do for him, to which he replied: "I don't suppose you've got a jumper!"

When we came back from Turkey, we were still night training. Our next task was to go to Gioia del Colle, Italy, in support of Bosnia. I went out to do the recce, and to set up the Harrier take-over from the Jaguars; we were the second squadron out there. This coincided with the BBC documentary "Defence of the Realm", so we had film crews all over the place. We also went to Chivenor for an exercise. To cock-a-snoop at the other squadrons we went fully tactical from the start. For some reason they had forgotten their large camouflage nets, so we had a small 1 Squadron site, which was quite beautifully tarted up, right next to rows and rows of very un-protected tents!

We were literally falling over these BBC people. One classic remark from one of our armourers stands out. A pilot, not in a good mood, had upset him; he was complaining his flares hadn't worked. The armourer turned round and retorted: "Well, if I was one of your f...... flares, I wouldn't have worked for you either!"'

David Walker recalls the BBC programme and a long flight he made in June 1995:

'On 21/22 June I flew into Wales at 2100 hours in broad daylight, spent all night tanking and doing close air support around Sennybridge with other members of the Squadron. I was off first and landed last – once more in broad daylight – having been airborne for seven hours. This was all about training in day and night, proving that 'night' is not necessarily in darkness.

Also during this period, roughly from April 1995 to March 1996, we were involved with the TV people in the "Defence of the Realm" Harrier Force programme. As it ended, I handed over to Mark Leakey.'

Mike Jenkins continues his own recollections:

'When we went out to Gioia we had various problems, especially between Christmas and New Year. So I instigated a dining-in night series with both the SNCOs and the officers in their hotels. We made a whole lot of Squadron silver out of silver-paper and flare cases and made a "deployment standard", on which we listed various horrible hotels that we had stayed in. These went down so well we continued them during other deployments.

On a Burns Night do, I arranged for the CO to fly out a haggis, whisky and neeps, and invited the Americans over. We went down to a local tailor and had kilts made for all the officers, with leopard-skin dress shirts, bow ties, etc. We made sporrons out of various things. The Yanks just did not know how to cope with men dressed in skirts. We ended up in the bar with their women folk trying to look up our kilts. Then we moved into the dining room, and Flight Lieutenant Stuart Ather "addressed" the haggis in correct form. Using a blown-up rubber glove and a pillow case, a set of golf clubs and a sporron which was a mini-CD player to pipe music, we marched in the haggis on the unsuspecting Americans. Stuart then addressed the haggis before splitting it open with a good bayonet we'd found. We went through the whole ritual. The image of Hornby, with a few golf clubs over his shoulder, glove, pillow and the two CD extension players hanging from his shoulders with pipe music blaring, marching in, was epic.

On 19 February 1996, Simon Jessett was on his way back from Cyprus and had his engine pack up on final approach into Wittering. It was amazing because everyone knew very quickly that he'd ejected but no one could work out where he was. The fire engines, ambulances, and so on, rushed to the main gate, then roared off up the A1, hoping someone would tell them where exactly to go, or hoped they'd spot a rising column of smoke. They got to the first roundabout, then began to come back again, then turned once more at the main gate and headed north once more.

I was watching all this with some vague amusement as well as being worried about Simon, but then the Ops 'phone rang. I answered it and said who I was. A voice said: "Hi, Sir, it's Si!" I replied: "Si, you're supposed to be in an aeroplane, what are you doing?" "Well, I'm in a farm house actually." I asked where, and then he described where he was. I then spoke to the farmer and told him to sit our man down and give him a cup of tea and to make sure he didn't move around too much, as help was on the way. Meantime the "help" convoy was still shooting up and down the A1. As we didn't have a link with them, only the Air Traffic guys could, in the end, send out in a vehicle to head for the farm house with the convoy in tow.

We set up a managerial style in operating the Squadron. If we had, say, eight jets available in the morning we'd program six. Hitherto if eight jets were available and one went u/s the program fell apart. Doug Gale and I set up meetings with the SNCOs where we could discuss problems. We started monitoring days away for ground crews, especially key ground crew, otherwise courses, etc., meant people were away all the time. Our set up was, the CO, and two flight commanders – one attack, one training. The attack flight commander was usually a QWI, who would be responsible for weaponeering, deployments etc., while the training guy would be responsible for the professionalism of the Squadron. The engineers would be in A and B shifts under the SEngO.

One job I got was overseeing the knocking down of our old 1930s building and its replacement. Because we were moving out of the building before demolition, we had a Christmas party, and we'd got permission to wield a sledgehammer. We started with a huge lunchtime thrash, then began to swing the sledgehammer, knocking down the first of the walls. Then it suddenly became a jolly good jape to loose off some fireworks about the place, which sadly set fire to a bush outside, next to which was parked Flight Sergeant O'Reilly's brand new Mercedes. We had rapidly to try and move this car and put out the fire, which ended up with some interesting exchanges with police and firemen, as to how the fire had started.

Some of the boys also made a bazooka from empty catering-size baked bean tins, which one filled with lighter fuel at one end, shook it about a bit, then ignited it through a small hole, and out came a missile – a cabbage or whatever else seemed handy and appropriate. Its power was under-estimated. Having loaded it with a ball made with masking tape, it sadly hit the boss at the back of the head and knocked him over!

We decamped during the actual re-building, to a set of portakabins erected on the flying pad. This was a horrendous existence, and one which taxed the health and safety at work act. Regiment Officer Karl Harding was the H & S officer and it soon became evident that the main risk was in dodging the various hanging signs which began to appear everywhere – such as "this is a trip hazard", or "this is a bang hazard", to "this is a low ceiling hazard" and so on. It eventually became something of an obstacle course of H & S and completely removed half of the place's functionality.'

Wing Commander (Air Commodore!) Walker also recalls this latter episode:

'We had the most magnificent party when we vacated our old building knowing the wreckers were coming in on the Monday morning. So on the Friday we had an absolute ball! It also really cemented the Squadron together.

We became far too over-refreshed and certainly did not want to let the National Audit Office take too close a look. To help things along we painted some bulls-eyes on the wall as we had some sledgehammers on call. As I took the first swing, Steve Hunt and Scott Ady, having built a mess cannon, fired this thing, missed what they were aiming at. As I turned round with a big grin on my face – 'donk' – this thing clouted me, and I thought, this is very good! I looked up and saw these two JPs the other side of a hatch and in typical childlike fashion, both ducked down out of sight, hoping I hadn't seen who they were!!

Never again will we be in such a position to do such things. Outside someone climbed the flagpole and then somebody else cut it down – pure hooliganism. It seemed to recreate a 1940's squadron thrash and those who missed it wished they hadn't. I won't even mention the fire!'

The two JPs were indeed Steve Hunt and Scott Ady. Steve recalls the cannon they made and seeing their first missile crash into the CO's head which then banged against the wall before he toppled over. Another missile was aimed at a window, and fired a split second before a regiment officer's face appeared, trying to see what all the noise was about. Just in time he saw the missile heading his way and he dropped down, only to be showered by broken glass which caused a few cuts.

Steve also recalls it was himself who first scaled the flag-pole, followed by the Jengo. As the pole was then attacked he attempted to jump down but caught his leg in the rope, which arrested his fall but caused him to bang his head on the ground; off to hospital.

As it was Christmas time, there followed the usual drive round the married quarters, singing carols and banging on doors to raise money for local charities. By this time the party mood had overtaken events and the RAF police had to disperse the mob, as the carols had turned to something far less agreeable from the 'choir'.

David Walker ended his tour with the Squadron in March 1996, handing over to Wing Commander M A Leakey MA BSc on the 18th. Mark Leakey's first operational tour had been with 3 Squadron in Germany in 1981, seeing duty in Belize and the Falklands. At the latter place in March 1983 he ejected from a stricken GR3 into Port Stanley harbour following engine failure. He was then a QWI on Hawks with 79 Squadron and in 1986 he moved to the USA to fly F-16s in Florida. A second tour with 3 Squadron followed as a flight commander, after which he undertook the Advanced Staff course at Bracknell (including taking an MA in Defence Studies), and finally a spell at MoD. 1993 found him as a wing commander (Offensive Support), HQ 2 Group, Germany, responsible for staffing Harrier and helicopter matters before taking over 1 Squadron. While in Germany he also had responsibility for 1 Group, so his career had covered pretty much the whole Harrier Force in both Germany and the UK.

'The posting wasn't a total surprise but certainly pleasant. There were probably so few of us then who could fill the right rank and experience criteria, but it was a huge honour. After a refresher at the OCU, I took over in March 1996. Dave Walker had arranged a hand-over ceremony. We had both been on exchange tours to the States so we'd seen how the Americans hand-over, which was a lot better than the way we did it. Traditionally in the RAF there would be a chap with a lot of stripes on, saying he was the new boss, with no ceremony or anything to mark the occasion. We had a parade in the hangar and quite a ceremony.

I also took the opportunity for the padre to come and pray for us. Then I stated my aims publicly. These were, firstly, that I expected everybody to be totally professional in everything we did but secondly we would be a team and that it would involve everybody. I wasn't going to be a white knight on a charger, yelling: "We're over here!" all the time; there might be times I was going to have to do that but I expected team work from everybody – all 180 people. Thirdly, in spite of all that we were going to have fun, a quality of life, whatever the circumstances.

Straight away we were off into Operation "Decisive Edge". It was the Squadron's second such, the first having taken place the previous Christmas. My Exec was Mike Jenkins, and I also had Squadron Leaders Dave Eakins and Ian Cameron, with Benny Ball joining us a little later, as did Squadron Leader Chris Huckstep. We had a nominal 17 Harriers of which one at that time was declared to the OEU (Strike Attack, Operational Evaluation Unit), and one was in reserve. One was also a T10, so effectively we had 14 as our AE (Aircraft Establishment). Generally, in reality, it was much lower, with various problems, so we never had our full quota. It was a struggle to get the flying hours we were tasked to fly every month. I had about 120 ground personnel and was supposed to have 19 pilots, but at that time it was slightly over with 21 or 22.

There were several exercises in the first half of 1996. Some pilots flew out aircraft to the US eastern seaboard ready for deployment in Alaska with 3 and IV Squadrons. The rest went by Tristar. This was a very successful exercise which involved deploying into the Alaskan training areas with operational flying down to 100 feet. For those who had not been there before it was a lot of fun. The terrain was different; we were there in June, so the daylight hours were pretty extraordinary; socially it was pretty good too. Then, of course, we had to bring the jets back, being the last deployment and that was quite a memorable "trail", through Canada to Goose Bay, then across the Atlantic to the UK, using tankers.

The next event was Wittering's 80th birthday in July. We held an airfield attack and a flypast. We also attended the IAT [International Air Tattoo] at Fairford that month, and we had ten jets for a display to mark the 30th anniversary of VSTOL flight. In December we went to the CFS for the annual flying assessments. After that the next major event and really what coloured the whole of the tour as far as I was concerned, was the deployment to HMS "Illustrious" as part of an on-going and long-standing desire to deploy GR7s onto aircraft carriers. The GR3s had been doing this on and off since "Hermes" and the Falklands, so the expertise was there but problems with the GR5 and GR7 excluded them from some tasks, including "Desert Storm". It took a long time and a lot of work by the OEU before our deployment, as the first operational GR7 squadron on a carrier, not least on the inertial navigation system.

Off we went in February 1997 to join "Illustrious" after a lot of uncertainty as to when we'd actually do it. However, the decision was made and we deployed to exercise "Ocean Wave 97" – the biggest RN deployment east of Suez for many years. Lots of ships, with 'Illustrious' the flagship, which eventually went off to Hong Kong for the hand-over ceremonies there, and then to Fremantle in Australia, before returning in August.

We were tasked for about a five-week period and there was lots to do, for example to incorporate the GPS – General Positional System – one of the major stumbling blocks in getting effective performance from the aircraft. At the end of February we took four aircraft to Muscat, via Cyprus, and then on to "Illustrious" as she sailed up the coast of Amman. It was the first time any of us had landed on a carrier although I had taken off from one in the early 1980s. It was a great moment as we all got down safely.

We docked in Muscat and collected our men and equipment, then we sailed round the Gulf, as the ship was tasked for operation "Southern Watch", which involved Sea Harriers in operational flying while we were just doing our basic syllabus flying as well as learning to land on the carrier safely. There was a stop at Abu Dhabi for a defence export sales show, then the ship went to Goa on the west coast of India and we had a couple of pleasant days there on a stop-over, fraternising with the Indian Navy. After exploring a bit of India we pressed on south and then east towards Malaysia.

After five weeks, we disembarked to land at the Malaysian air base at Butterworth where we had an exercise with the MAF and their Hawk F-5s. There we were finally able to do some over-land flying which was above some impressive terrain. The ship had sailed on and then it was time for us to trail back with our tanker support, Tristar and so on, via Colombo, Sri Lanka, Muscat, Cyprus to UK – a memorable trip all-round.

Harriers on carriers made a lot of sense especially where the only way to get to an area of interest was by sea. The GR7 being so much more stable than the GR3 it leant itself towards the role. Its increased aerodynamic performance meant that it could actually take-off either from much shorter lengths or with much greater weight than the Sea Harrier. So we felt we were actually lending the Navy or MoD a huge enhancement in capability.'

RAF Harriers are slightly larger than the Sea Harrier FA2, (five feet in both wingspan and length) and are slightly heavier, although the FA2 is faster. The Navy pilots also have a different technique for landing on carrier decks, which the RAF pilots needed to learn. They tend to drop their FA2s down the last eight feet on their moving base whereas RAF pilots generally try a more gentle landing on a pad that is static. Mark Leakey continues:

'The downside to all this was a combination of ship-board living conditions, the RN generally, the lack of low-flying over land and the overall life-style on the carrier. I'm afraid overall their life did not meet our aspirations. There was a general feeling that this was not our cup of tea at all. RAF traditions and life-style did not lend themselves to their environment. *["If I had wanted to go to sea I'd have joined the Navy!" was a repeated comment.]*

We arrived back in April and got straight back to work, going to Honiton on deployment with all three squadrons. Just prior to this we had an accident and one of my pilots unfortunately got himself into an awkward position doing some VSTOL at the end of a sortie. He was preparing for VSTOL "in the field", trying to perfect his hover and then take off again. Electing to do a mini-circuit after that, he taxied off, took off at slow speed but allowed the aircraft to run out of performance. As it sank down, he ejected and the aircraft crashed. These things happen but at least the pilot was OK.

We were soon building for our next sea deployment. This time we took six jets and joined the carrier just after it had sailed from Portsmouth on 1 September. We had just about the whole of the month on HMS "Invincible", and the plan was to take forward the lessons learnt on the earlier deployment and to start night flying. Our aim was to be able to declare ourselves as truly day and night capable from a carrier by the end of our trip – which we did.

We began with a lot of low flying over Cornwall, then we sailed across the Bay of Biscay to the south-west of Gibraltar where we operated with the Spanish Navy and Sea Harriers, so we had a sort of tri-lateral exercise – a NATO exercise under NATO format. We had a good deal of overland flying across Spain, limited of course, but at least we were flying from the ship. Our learning curve certainly accelerated upwards during that period, as well as our qualifying some half a dozen pilots for night work as well.

The culmination was a combined attack sortie, launched pre-dawn on an airfield deep in Spain. Sea Harriers provided escort (top cover) and the Spanish Navy Harriers went in first over our GR7s. We all came back to the ships just as it was getting light – a memorable occasion which I felt put the seal on our day and night capability.

It wasn't long after this that Iraq began a bit of sabre-rattling over the weapons inspections and created some tension. "Invincible" was called into the Med, and we deployed to her in the middle of November.'

'Operation Bolton' proved a hectic time. No one knew for certain if another Gulf War effort was about to start but in the end things fizzled out. However, on 25 November 1997, Wing Commander Leakey, while operating off Sardinia, was attempting a night landing on the carrier. He had levelled off a little too high and was letting down further prior to moving sideways onto the deck when the aircraft sank. Before he was able to correct, the Harrier hit the sea and flipped over.

The ejector seat fired, sending the CO into and under the water. As far as those on board could see, the Harrier had gone down, taking its pilot with it, but 20 minutes later, Mark Leakey was spotted in the water and rescued by Sea King helicopter, much to the relief of everyone. With its wing fuel tanks empty the aircraft did not immediately sink and flotation bags were quickly fixed to it and it was then raised from the sea by crane.

However, this was the end of the CO's tenure due to medical grounds. In May 1998 he took an appointment as a deputy director of Operational Requirements at MoD and promoted to Group Captain.

* * *

The new CO was Wing Commander A Golledge BSc, who officially took over on 9 January 1998. He had been OC of 20(R) Squadron/HOCU at Wittering.[1] The deployment with *Invincible* in the end lasted 4½ months and having 'lost' a good CO, the Squadron was not that happy about being on a carrier. They had been aboard for a long time and not doing an awful lot. Life had become difficult.

It was nevertheless, the first GR7 deployment and the Squadron had started work with TIALD (Thermal Imaging Airborne Laser Designator) which had been rushed into service, never having been used on a carrier, but within days the Squadron had ended up being able to self-designate its laser guided bombs. For the pilots the flying had been pretty good and all round them were Royal Navy, US Navy and USAF aircraft operating in really big packages.

There was also an incident in January. One of the jets from the carrier was on a temporary detachment to Italy as part of a familiarisation programme and two 1,000 lb bombs were accidentally dropped while approaching Giola del Colle airbase. They were not fused and did not go off but landed about 150 metres from a farmhouse.

The Gulf situation was again reaching fever pitch but then it all died down as agreement was reached with the Iraqi dictator, and being due to change over with 3 Squadron on *Illustrious* it was hoped that a return to Wittering was on the way. In the event there came another political decision for the Squadron to remain on board for another two weeks. Andy Golledge remembers this period so soon after his tenure of command had begun.

> 'We came back in April 1998, and the Squadron needed a period of consolidation and some better deals. The AOC 1 Group promised us a good deal. This had been the Squadron's third time on a ship, something no other RAF squadron had done, so we were due for, and given, some good deployments.
>
> We started off by going to Scotland for operational low flying for a week. Then came a squadron exchange to the Greek Islands followed in September by a trip to Goose Bay, Canada, taking ten jets there. Another good deal, tacked on, was to go down to Oceana on the US eastern seaboard. We flew down and for two weeks had some nice flying in a splendid area. In November we had a week in Norway, then a week to RAF Valley in December to fire live Sidewinder missiles. Over Christmas we prepared for Red Flag, beginning the trip out on 2 January 1999.
>
> Red Flag proved excellent for us. It was the first night tactics Red Flag to be flown by the RAF using FLIR and NVGs; very exciting. 1 Squadron started off followed by a combination of 3 and IV Squadrons. Back from there we started to plan for a 4½ month stint over Bosnia, but, of course, we didn't know that Kosovo was going to rear its head.'

Flight Lieutenant D Killeen joined the Squadron in September 1997 and as the Squadron deployed to the carrier he was about to start his three-month work up, so he and another pilot moved across to the OCU. By the time they had finished, the Squadron was coming back from the Med and being combat ready they had then to begin to integrate themselves with their fellow members. Damien Killeen recalls:

> 'We went out to Greece in July on a squadron exchange, flying around the Greek Islands from a place called Larissa. Incredibly hot and on some days the base commander stopped flying due to the heat. We worked with GR3 recce pods, which, because we did not have any of our people there, were developed by the Greeks. They went all through the film to decide which parts of their country we were allowed to have pictures of. There was also a bit of flying up by the Turkish border. One of the boys had something click on his RWR from the Turkish side and mentioned it to the Greeks who went ballistic thinking that the Turks were looking at us.
>
> Then we went out to Goose Bay for low flying – where it rained a lot – then down to Oceana for combat training against F-14s, which was outrageous. Fighting against F-14s is amazing; they're so manoeuvrable for their size. We did quite well; on one sortie with Squadron Leader Chris Norton (OC 'B' Flight) we were up against a couple of them trying to stop us bombing their aircraft carrier and we managed to get round them, so they were really upset. Obviously they caught up with us afterwards, and although we "got" one of them, they "got" both of us.

---

[1] The Harrier OCU at Wittering, previously known as 233 OCU had become 20 (Reserve) Squadron/Harrier Operational Conversion Unit following the disbandment of 20 Squadron at Laarbruch, in September 1992.

Norway at the end of '98, then just after Christmas, off to Red Flag, for which I pitched up eight days late! I launched from Wittering on 2 January just to fly after the Christmas break, then left a couple of days later. The plan was, first day to the Azores and from there to Maguire Air Force Base in New Jersey, just north of Philadelphia, then across to Nellis Air Force Base, Las Vegas. However, due to weather we didn't get airborne to the Azores on time and when we did we decided on a quick turn-round then off to Maguire. We stayed the night at Maguire, having left three aircraft on the Azores – two with problems. At Maguire I had an undercarriage problem. The wheels came up but didn't show they were up and locked properly, so the others all went off while I had to circle to burn off all the fuel; the Americans wouldn't let me dump it.

Then the three jets on the Azores got stuck due to tanker problems. Next, a huge snowstorm hit Maguire and one of the support Hercules aircraft had to divert to St Johns, Newfoundland, with an engine problem. Overnight there, a storm hit with enough force to move the Herk 15°. As the wheels were frozen to the ground, this actually snapped one of the main wheel axles.

The Azores boys eventually went via Bermuda to avoid all the snowstorms but halfway across, their diversion point was St Johns, so if their tanker support had a problem they had nowhere to go to reach land, so they had an interesting day!

When they did land at Bermuda, the Herk, which was finally serviceable went down to Bermuda and, with the other C-130 that had come out to help, had to off-load some kit to sort out my jet. Finally the three jets got off and arrived at Nellis on the Sunday, just making it for Red Flag.

Meantime, the engineers got to work on my Harrier but couldn't find the problem at first but eventually got it fixed. With no support tankers available I was left to hop across the States on my own, which was fun. My first stop was due to be Illinois, but next morning four States had been taken out by a huge thunderstorm from Canada, so I had to re-plan the whole trip. Eventually I went to Fort Campbell in Kentucky, quick refuel, then off to Sheppard Air Force Base, Texas – huge great place. Next day was the final leg, arriving at Nellis eight days late. The boys later worked out that, if I had been able to bicycle out on the first day, I would have got to Vegas faster than by jet!

Getting back from Red Flag we were obviously at a peak for Kosovo. At first we were assigned to the peace-keeping duties over Bosnia – "Deliberate Forge" – in February. Within the first three weeks we had everybody qualified down there for close air support etc. At this time I got my hands on TIALD, a rare piece of kit, and learnt how to use it. Therefore we were soon all qualified on this too.

I returned to UK, and when the conflict started I was at Wittering, getting all the info on Cefax and Sky TV. Very weird feeling to know most of the boys were operating and me being stuck at home.'

Damien's US 'tour' embraced, Wittering to Lajes (VC10), MaGuire, MaGuire to Fort Campbell, Fort Campbell to Sheppard, and Sheppard to Nellis. It took four hours in the VC10 and almost eight hours in the Harrier.

Squadron Leader Chris Huckstep, now on his third tour with 1 Squadron, recalls Red Flag:

'It's a very good training exercise because of the facilities. You have an excellent range so we can plan big missions. The value too is that these big Ops are with AWAC, SEAD (Suppression Enemy Air Defences), EW (Electronic Warfare – the jammers) and SAM systems. Our Harriers were just part of the whole scenario going in, and we did very well. We only got "shot down" a few times by air and by SAMs. We were also the only people at Red Flag who did night low-level Ops and the Americans were very impressed.

Our low-level training is good. At the end of the Kosovo show, we were the only NATO Squadron prepared to send in aircraft at low level – especially at low level – to support the troops by day or by night. The Americans just don't train as we do.'

All this was just as well, for Kosovo was just around the corner.

Chapter Twenty Two

KOSOVO:
THE RIGHT PLACE AT THE RIGHT TIME

Turmoil in the Balkans continued to pre-occupy the world's attention. By the spring of 1999 it was clear to many that hostilities would again be a major issue. Serbia was making it more and more difficult for the ethnic Albanians in Kosovo to live anything like a normal existence. Finally Serbian police and soldiers began moving into Kosovo and imposing a totally unacceptable oppressive regime upon them.

The world soon began to hear of the massive killings of civilians. Men were being segregated from their families and either shot out of hand or taken away and never seen again. Meanwhile, the women and children were being herded away from their towns and villages and forced to flee towards the borders. As the UN and NATO tried desperately to bring these oppressive actions to an end, it soon became clear that the pleadings and then the warnings were going unheeded and that more direct action would have to follow.

The Western alliances of course were mindful of the consequences. While these countries were keen to see the killings – now more familiarly referred to as *ethnic cleansing* – cease and the refugees be able to return to their homes, they knew that any action against the Serbs would result in losses of Allied troops. Body-bags would not be an acceptable price to pay but it seemed inevitable that this was the way it would have to be.

Any ground action would, of course, have to be preceded and then maintained by an air assault. Just as in the Gulf War, the Western Allies were beginning to build up their air, land and sea forces for what seemed the inevitable. Ground troops would move into Kosovo and then, who could say how far that road would lead. Initially, however, once the Serbian leadership had failed to pull out its forces – indeed, their actions seemed to be stepped up a notch – the moment of truth quickly approached. Air actions were suddenly approved and implemented.

Back in the UK the plan to move the Harrier Force to RAF Cottesmore had been agreed. No.1 Squadron and the two German-based units, 3 and IV Squadrons at Laarbruch, would begin to deploy to Cottesmore during 1999-2000. This being the case, the three main Harrier squadrons were taking it in turns to be on operational stand-by on the Adriatic coast at Gioia Del Colle, Southern Italy, for peace-keeping work over Bosnia.

At the moment diplomatic negotiations broke down, No.1 Squadron was in situ at Gioia, and they knew that they were going to be immediately in the firing line and in the forefront of operations. Operation 'Noble Anvil' was about to begin.

* * *

Once again by the very nature of things, none of the 1 Squadron pilots had even flown in combat. The senior pilots all had a vast amount of experience, not only of flying in general but in more recent times, on the Harrier in particular. Some had anything from 1,500 to 3,000 flying hours on the Harrier alone. Others of course – the JPs – while fully competent to fly the Harrier, were still comparative novices. But it would take the skilled and the semi-skilled to see this emergency through. It would, like any other conflict, test their training to the full. Only in actual combat would their tactics be put to the test for real. Several of the pilots were married and had children. One of the flight commanders had five children but there was no flinching. All were keen to see it through however long it took. Many previous emergencies had, in the event, failed to materialise, others had become watered down to little more than police actions. Little did 1 Squadron's modern 'few' know that there stretched before them 79 days of continuous action. The boss – Andy Golledge – recalls the moment and the first sorties:

> 'The reason we were out in Italy during the Bosnian episode was to cover for 3 and IV Squadrons moving to Cottesmore, so we agreed to take a large chunk of the year, which is why we were going for 4½ months. We had eight aircraft and 12 pilots, and no sooner had we got there the political situation in Kosovo deteriorated, so we quickly got ready for action. There were still a couple of weeks before the action started and we flew with other NATO air forces over Bosnia, with large packages being put together.

Then it was just a case of waiting while the Rambouillet talks were on, then it was time to go in. One day we were on the roof of our hotel and we were enjoying a bit of bronzing, and the Squadron Exec went into work to see if anything was happening. We had a little code word to use on the mobile 'phone if anything started and sure enough he called me up and used the code word, saying that it was on tonight! We all immediately went to the airfield and started our planning. I shall never forget it.

Personally I like to fly and to lead, and having canvassed around, it was an interesting task to choose who was going to lead the various sorties and who was going to fly in the formations on that first night. There was a lot of sensitivity around as can be imagined. Who was going to lead, and who was going to fly the next night, and so on.

It was decided that I would lead the first night, which I felt was how it should be. The Exec would lead the second night and "Snorts", the B Flight commander, would lead the third night. We only planned for three nights as nobody was sure just how long the campaign would last.'

First missions

Planning took seven hours that first afternoon. There was a vast amount of things to do and get right, and the Harriers would only be one part of a huge air effort against specific targets in Serbia. These were all military; airfields, radar, SAMs, ammo dumps, fuel dumps, barracks, and so on. The Serbs were known to have a number of Mig 29s and any number of SAM sites, so other NATO units would be seeking out the Migs and watching for SAMs, while the whole force would be going for their assigned targets. All this would be backed up with AWACs and refuelling aircraft, so it was going to be a big night. Andy Golledge continues:

'It was an amazing night. I recall flying towards Kosovo and everyone was on the same radio frequency, so we heard there were Mig fighters airborne, then the combats between them and the NATO fighters, we were all listening to that. Then the NATO guys shot down the Migs, so to us it was all for real as we were heading in. There was also massive jamming on the frequency as we went over the border and suddenly we couldn't speak to anyone – it was all very interesting!

As it turned out we ourselves did not have a very successful night for various reasons; smoke, not being able to identify the target, another pilot was evading a possible SAM threat – it was so confusing out there but we were all pleased to get back.

That first night we flew six aircraft, although one aborted. Generally we flew four bombers escorted by two "spotter" aircraft that didn't carry weapons. Their job was to watch out for SAM launches and warn the four bombers, so they really looked after the others. On night two I didn't fly, and because we'd missed on night one, the pressure was on, due in no small way to the press coverage. The Squadron felt enormous pressure to hit something and hit it well. The heat was on.'

The A Flight commander, Squadron Leader Chris Huckstep, remembers:

'As the Rambouillet talks finished, we took over from IV Squadron out in Italy. As the war seemed inevitable we began planning for a two or three night mission package. After a poor first night the pressure was really on.

The first operational sortie always sticks in your memory. You take off and hold, then you push in and there's the border. After years of training you're suddenly on a war mission, trying to get a bomb on a target and people are going to try and shoot you down.

We were the middle pair of six and I was the bomber. The first pair didn't drop due to an aircraft problem and as we went in we could see over the countryside little fires burning, villages on fire. My designator called "capture" which meant he had his part sorted out and I had to put the weapons in the right place to see the laser energy. Then it was "stores away". Then climbing off target and looking back, our bombs taking about 30-40 seconds to hit; the ammo storage went up with a huge explosion. When we reached the border 40 miles away we could look back and see the target still burning. This was the first ever Harrier-Harrier TIALD/LGB combat drop, and the first Harrier bombs of the campaign to hit the target. The third pair had scored hits too.'

Andy Golledge:

'I personally went out on the airfield and met the boys as they landed back that second night, and asked them if they had hit targets. We decided we would all go into a room – strictly pilots only – and look at the video tapes first to assess what we'd done, and only then report back. But that didn't work out that night for everybody was anxious to see, so this tiny room was packed with about fifty people!

When we watched those tapes and saw we'd actually destroyed the targets, there was a massive cheer and immediately the pressure just fell away. We desperately needed that, and this was only night two.'

With the Squadron at this time was Flight Lieutenant Chris Averty. He was one of the young JPs having only recently joined following completion of his flight training. Originally from the Birmingham University Air Squadron he had trained via Cranwell and the US. He relates:

'We were going out to Italy as part of operation "Deliberate Forge", the peace-keeping flights over Bosnia, although we knew the situation in Kosovo was deteriorating. But we certainly didn't think it was going to kick-off as it did. I expected there to be a political solution, even up to the last night.

Not being a night-combat-ready pilot, I knew it would be the night-ready guys who were initially going to fly using PGM (precision guided munitions) which were the laser guided 1,000 pounders. Those initial Ops were the worst ones for the whole Squadron because everyone had at the back of their mind that we were going to lose a person or two during the conflict but we were all hoping nobody got hurt.

The first night, during which I was only helping on the planning side, we were most apprehensive. Suddenly they were off and we were then just sitting there waiting for them to return. We were all very anxious, desperately wanting everyone to come back and when they did it was great. We had cracked the initial nut in that we could get people airborne, and get them back without losing anyone.

The hardest part however, was we didn't hit any targets on the first night because of smoke in the target area. Although we got a good reception from the press they really wanted us to hit targets and the fact we didn't was a disappointment. This put a lot of pressure on the Squadron on the second night, but it really is a situation where the weather has to be good to drop a LGB, you just can't drop it through cloud, you have to be able to see the target for a certain length of time so you can lase the target and the bomb can travel from the aircraft to the ground. This takes about 30-40 seconds so all that time you have to see the target.

There are other factors which also enhance or degrade the performance of the system due to the atmosphere, etc. Fortunately on the second night we were successful and that was just such a relief for the boss and everyone.

Other nights were also completely filled up with cloud in the middle air space – 10-20,000 feet – and impossible to organise a package of 200-300 aircraft, so all had to come back. But trying to explain this to the press was very difficult.

We had a bunch of about 30-40 press people at our hotel the whole time we were in action, but over a period we managed to get them on our side. In the bar we got to know each other very well, which gave us time to explain our problems in detail.'

Once the press people understood the problems, and later on when attacking moving targets in Kosovo as opposed to static targets in Serbia, the NATO airmen were supported, especially when pilots brought their bombs home rather than risk dropping them on a target that didn't seem quite right at the crucial moment of dropping. With so many civilians about, with Serbian forces close by or even intermingling themselves with refugee columns, there was no stigma to anyone who decided against releasing weapons if there was any chance of endangering non-Serbs, or even wasting ordnance.

***

Warrant Officer John McMath BEM, the engineering senior NCO on the Squadron, together with the engineering team under Squadron Leader Simon Moss (Sengo), Flight Lieutenants Tim Casey and Dougie Bye (Jengos), kept the aircraft on the line during the campaign. John McMath remembers:

'This was the culmination of what we were about and while we were in a fairly safe situation in southern Italy there was always that concern that you were going to send guys across on live missions, and that this was for real. When orders came through that we were going to start bombing, we endeavoured to make everything as much a normal day as possible, just another exercise.

The first night missions were particularly tense and when the boys landed back there was a great deal of relief all round. But during that interim period – the time we took over until we actually started bombing – we were still updating some of the systems within the aircraft to improve the serviceability aspects.

The operations then just grew like topsy; it was six aircraft, then eight, twelve and finally sixteen. Having started with a plan to support just six jets we soon had to start making infrastructure that would support more. One problem was where to actually park more aircraft. We had some REs there laying metal surfacing platforms and meantime the weather was getting warmer and warmer, so each aircraft needed a shelter-like hangar to use as a sunshade. When we left in July we were really beginning to struggle with the heat.

Starting ops the boys were pretty well up for it. Most of us had seen news footage on CNN and Sky News and we could see what was happening in Kosovo. You really didn't have to focus on it and everyone felt they were helping with the humanitarian problems. So what started as a small operation built into a big operation, with about 150 engineering staff in Italy, covering 24-hour periods, working two 12-hour shifts. The critical part was the weapons guys, where we needed enough of them at the right time to re-load the aircraft. Most of this came under Chief Technician Chas Chambers, and all the armourers were out there the full four months.

Eventually it all became second nature. Serviceability was very good but it was essential we had chaps there 24 hours a day. Spares were not a major problem; we were well supported from home and had priority for any spares we required, but at the same time we were still developing and improving aircraft systems.

The site we operated on was barely enough to support the small number of men we took initially, so it had to grow. Storage space, the erection of a mobile servicing hangar on the site, Thermal Imaging Pod was deployed with us – not many of us had worked that before, as the early missions were all TIALD-type sorties. These were precision bombing sorties for the big thing was to avoid collateral damage, so the learning curve on thermal imaging was particularly high.

We certainly thought it would be over in seven days, never imagined it would be 79 days in all. The guys didn't have a break for the first 30-odd days, 30 days, 12 hour shifts – just work, eat, sleep – and soon became very tired. Then we began rotating them, getting fresh guys in, and those sent back to UK were only back about ten days before the size of the operation increased again so we needed to bring them back out again.'

Flight Lieutenant MOU (call-sign) had joined the Squadron in June 1998, having started his career via Northumberland UAS, then RAF Cranwell, the US and then Valley. He remembers:

'I was at Wittering with KIL (call-sign), Dave and Rob. At this stage the war hadn't started so we only had a certain number of people out there. Later, once things began to happen, they all got sent out, so I became No.1 Squadron in the UK! However, after a few days I got the "heads-up" that I was going too.

At first we started just flying over Bosnia, but then things began to get tense. Once it began only the night boys were flying and all the young guys got called in to help with the planning. Once the night guys went in it was quite tense because we all knew it was high threat and we had the unknown to contend with but it was good when they all came back – a big relief.'

Another JP was Flight Lieutenant Dave Kane, who had been on the Squadron since September 1997, another to come through Cranwell.

'When I got the 'phone call I was on my way to Ireland on leave and was only about 20 minutes from the ferry as the mobile went off. So I turned round, left my fiancée to carry on, and four of us were off the next morning. I had been out to Italy already, flying sorties over Bosnia prior to this leave, but was soon back. I was still on my night work-up so I would only be on day missions.'

Flight Lieutenant KIL (call sign) was at Wittering and finally got the call:

'When the conflict started I was at Wittering getting all the info. from Ceefax and Sky TV! Very weird feeling to know most of the boys were operating while I was stuck at home. A few days later another four jets were called in and I took one of them down, along with Dave, plus Jocky and Mark from the OCU. Being only day-combat ready I helped out with the night planning until the day Ops began.'

Andy Golledge:

'One morning that first week, we were in Met Brief, someone rushed in to tell me that the PM was on the telephone, so I went out and Tony Blair was there talking, which was very nice. We had loads of visitors dropping in at odd times, press people arriving too, all making it difficult for the night pilots to sleep, and our long planning sessions were interrupted, all of which did not help our increasing tiredness. Nonetheless, the support and encouragement from the military hierarchy back in UK was fantastic. I must say also that the press in due course were awesome and we got a good rapport going with them.

After a couple of weeks, and we only had a dozen night qualified pilots, while the day boys killed the administration, the night chaps were getting tired. Then we started a wave of night and then a wave of day sorties. The night boys were still going against targets such as bridges, barracks, petrol dumps – all fixed targets, while the day boys were specifically against the Serb army, dug-in in Kosovo.

That went on for another couple of weeks and after that they dispensed with the night Ops, and CAOC (Command and Operations Control Centre) wanted us with our good avionics to concentrate on close air support against the Serb army. Our total number of aircraft soon went up from eight to 12, to 16, and with 24 pilots, 150 ground crew and 30 armourers. By then we were flying about 20 sorties a day, pilots flying once a day, just about.

Everyone wanted to be in on the action, nobody wanted a day off and if given a day off, he'd still stick around. Nobody wanted to go off and sleep, or play golf on his own. We had some poor weather days when we couldn't fly which gave us a small breather but this was not very often. And we were, in the early days, definitely split into two teams, the night team and the day team.

The night team had it all and they loved it. They usually got up at lunch time had a late breakfast in the hotel, followed by a bit of bronzing on the roof, then drive to the airfield early afternoon, plan their mission, fly off about 10 pm, return, debrief, drive back to the hotel for a couple of beers at 3 or 4 o'clock in the morning, relax and go to bed.

The day team had an awful schedule. Get up was at 2 am, no hotel breakfast at that hour of course, so they had to have an RAF breakfast on camp – big cholesterol – plan then fly a mission am, return and finish de-brief about mid-afternoon, then back to the hotel and bed around 7 o'clock. The local Italian restaurants did not open till around 8 or 9 pm, so nowhere to eat in the early evening. In consequence they all felt hard done by – quality of life issues.

Something else I found interesting in theatre, flying every day, etc., Wittering would 'phone up asking how long could we do this for, weren't we getting tired? *[Other Harrier pilots wanted to join in the campaign, and eventually a few extra pilots went out, four from the OCU, four from the two Germany squadrons and a couple of instructors. Ed.]* It was, however, pretty obvious that we needed a break of some sort. A plan was devised that after a month, everybody would return to Wittering for a five-day break. So as we sent five guys home, Wittering supplied five people from 20 Squadron or other units. So around about April/May, everybody got home for five days. Very interestingly, trying to sell this to the boys, especially the night team, who were not the least bit interested because of their happy routine, couldn't see how this would help them! I found this extremely fascinating. In the end they all went but then, in any event the night Ops finished and we all went on to days. However, the many and varied excuses put up by the pilots as to why they should not go home for a break was amazing. (My wife won't like me under her feet! or It'll upset the kid's schooling!)'

Shortly before night Ops ended, it was becoming evident that there was a definite split between the night and day boys, which was not going to be healthy in the long term. In the Squadron *Line Book* there is the story of one pilot meeting on the evening of 16 April:

Boss:	'Because we've been working in two waves, it seems we have split into two teams and the banter is starting to get a bit harsh. So, from now on, we are one team. Everyone happy?'
Pilots:	'Yes Boss.'
Boss:	'Right then, moving on; the Day Team has found that ....'
Pilots:	'Boss!!!'
Boss:	'Oh, *@#$&*!!'

As the night sorties came to an end, the night experienced pilots were becoming a little apprehensive about flying in daylight. Meantime, the youngsters, who were only day combat ready, and who had been flying day missions for the previous 2-3 weeks, were completely happy. Flight Lieutenant Averty:

'As only a day ready pilot I personally didn't fly for two weeks till after the campaign started. Everyone had expected the Serbs to capitulate but as things continued it became necessary to hit them during the day too.

As regards tactics, in theory the day is a lot more dangerous than at night, so we became known as the "Twenty Minuters" from the Blackadder TV sketch, where they had said that the average life of a RFC pilot was 20 minutes. So all the junior pilots, who didn't have very long on the Harrier anyway, got the brunt of the usual inter-team banter that we day people were all going to get shot down!

It took a while to get co-ordinated so finally we were working with the American A-10 tank-busters. We were hitting army-style targets, so we were going for tanks, trucks, mortar and artillery positions, check points, etc., which were all mobile.

We would get airborne and once over the "Sausage Side", the A-10 guys would find targets and call us forward, and then they'd talk us onto the target and we'd hit it with cluster bombs or 1,000 pounders. These Ops generally took about 20 minutes too so that was another reason for our new name.

What we found in reality was that the day Ops were better in some ways, for at night you could see all the missile launches and triple-A (anti-aircraft artillery [flak to the older generations]) even if it was a long way off. Gradually we became aware that all this was survivable; we could get back.

My first time across the border and where I dropped a weapon I was with the Exec, and we were talked onto a target and I knew Benny, with all his flying experience, had never flown on a live day mission either, so we were even in those terms. I could tell from the banter that he was as excited as I was. He hit the target first time round and I had problems getting the weapons off, something to do with the TV lock, so had to go round again. We'd always been told not to re-attack a target but here I was doing just that. Benny was calling, "Get on with it; get on with it!"

Despite all the dangers it was exciting and exhilarating as our training kicked in. All our work was for this moment and it had all worked and we had achieved our aim.'

Other JPs had started to arrive at Gioia as it became obvious the campaign was not going to be over quickly. They helped out with the night planning but once day sorties began to be flown, they too got their chances. Flight Lieutenant MOU (call-sign):

'Once we got to go ourselves it was total excitement but very nervous that you'd screw up. Initially we had bad weather so it was pretty certain we would not be called in but flew to the hold points and then came back, so it was a slow introduction.

The first time I went "sausage side", and given a target, we punched off north and seeing the border – a big red line on the cockpit map – and as you cross it, say to yourself, OK, this is for real!

The junior guys were flying No.2s, our job being to make sure that our leader didn't get shot down, but obviously giving each other cross-cover as we flew to the target, but over the target, spinning, your primary aim is to make sure the leader doesn't get hit, so you're really looking out for SAMs and so on.

We were generally working air support with the A-10s and occasionally with the F-16s. They'd talk us onto the target, and obviously they're bombing themselves as well. There is a huge pressure to get the bombs off; you don't want to be the guy who doesn't drop, but you have to be professional and I think everyone was.

I will always remember the first time I went over. It was amazing. Typically the training prepares you, but there were a couple of A-10s below us and they would mark the target with rockets or bombs and talk us onto it. Then it is a case of tipping over and pickle your bombs off.

Another time we went out against a SAM-6 on a position we were given but it was overcast and as we were running in, I was with Stewy. He got indications of early warning radar which could have been used to key in the SAMs. I got "looked at" by a SAM-6 on one sortie and it certainly gets your attention!

On another mission the A-10s brought us into a target and we were asking for its elevation, and they called for us to stand-by, they were sorting out a SAM, so we spun back. They said they'd be just two minutes while taking care of the SAM launch site. So they went in with their horrendous Gattling guns, then they were back with us. Those A-10 guys were very good at their jobs.'

Flight Lieutenant Dave Kane:

'One mission we'd started as a four-ship but ended up as a pair having sent the other two home after about two hours because we couldn't get enough tanker time. We eventually tanked up several times and in all it became a four-hour mission.

We went for a bridge but we were not completely happy because of broken cloud and we were using LGBs. It was early, about 6 or 7 am. We had been over two or three times but then came out, feeling it was going to clear in an hour or two, and rather than fly home, if they could get us a tanker, we'd refuel and go back and take the bridge down.

Once the other two left us we went all the way up the Adriatic to get a tanker by which time we were somewhat short of gas. Then back down into Kosovo about an hour and a half later and dropped on the first attack. The bridge was definitely standing before we got there and had definitely dropped afterwards. Some of the boys went later with a recce. pod and took photos of it. They showed bombs on – direct hits – and taken out. In all we'd made three refuels, taking as much fuel from each tanker as they could spare.

A CBU (cluster bomb unit) attack against five revetments just north of the Macedonian border I remember. Some A-10s who were working as our FAC (foreword air controllers) had already attacked and they cleared for us to take out these targets being so near to the border. In each revetment were three self-propelled artillery pieces, and a couple of trucks and mortars.

We had a four-ship, each with four CBUs and we got four of the five revetments. It was one of the first CBU drops where we actually had the TIALD (thermal imaging and laser designator) looking into the area as well, so the infra-red picked up every single bomb going off, showing the ripples going through the target. It was on TV soon afterwards, although they dubbed out my commentary!

Height at which one dropped CBUs depended on whether or not you'd got easy acquisition of the target and if you could, you'd lock your own TV on at quite a distance and stay level; you don't want to put your nose into the threat if you can help it. In the early days you would literally have to dive down into the target to get the TV on and locked. The TV gives a good picture, six times magnification and it's also a contrast tracker so the logic will follow that, or track the contrast of your target against the background.

We saw several missile launches, most of them were ballistic or radar guided. Plenty of triple-A, and of course, the air was generally full of aircraft. I flew over 40 missions, and got shot at every day.'

On the Squadron at this time was a USAF captain on an exchange tour, Bob Cockrell. He had been an F-16 pilot and had flown operations earlier in the area with the USAF out of Aviano. After gaining permission from the Pentagon to fly ops with the RAF he was in the unique situation of being the first American air force officer to fly combat with an RAF Harrier squadron. He recalls:

'When we were deployed to Italy I thought it was going to be another Bosnia, standard thing, hopefully not getting too bored. When things started, and not being night cleared, I went to the Tower for the first couple of weeks, and I was experienced working with the TIALD ops having been stationed there earlier. Watching them take off, thinking, this is for real – hope they all come back.

Then day ops began and at first we were pretty tense. I'd been on some ops before with the USAF back in 1995 flying F-16s over Iraq. After a couple of missions you'd get your confidence up, so then you just had to pace yourself to make sure you didn't burn yourself out, not knowing how long this stuff was going to go on. I'd try to relax and only get tense when I was ready to go "feet dry" *[heading into hostile territory, going in over the Adriatic coast. Ed]*'.

Captain Bob Cockrell flew on 39 missions during the Kosovo campaign, none more important than the occasion he recognised a tasked convoy was civilian:

'KIL and I were holding over Albania waiting to get moved forward to a target area and when I switched over to CAS frequency to listen to what was happening, we heard them calling aircraft in on targets. We looked over to the area and KIL saw a couple of bombs exploding on the ground near a convoy.

I went over to talk to the FAC and heard about a 100 vehicle convoy being looked at by some F-16s. They passed us the co-ordinates and we went to look at it. I peered down from high altitude through binoculars and it just didn't look right, just not military. So I went round for another look and definitely saw coloured vehicles, nothing military as far as I could make out. So I called the FAC but then some F-16s bombed another smaller convoy. The FAC then told the other aircraft in the area not to bomb the large convoy, so it was nice to know it was not attacked.

I recall another mission which gave me a scare. Some American A-10s were operating near us in a target area close by – about five miles away – so I began drifting in that direction. I looked away for a second to check something in the jet, then looked out and saw this huge smoke trail and immediately thought it was a SAM. I yelled at my leader about missiles, then heard an American voice of an A-10 pilot, saying, "Hey, that's us, we're firing Mavericks!" I hadn't spotted that the trail was going down, not up, but it sure was a shock at first.'

Squadron Leader Huckstep:

'We actually did 32 days of continuous Ops, firstly at night, then on days. I remember one night we were going for a SAM storage facility and there was a lot of triple-A coming up which all seemed to be aimed at us. I moved away from it although it never got that near to us, and it began to follow me, so it was an interesting time.

As we ran in my "spiker" hadn't called "capture" as I was coming up to my release point. We had to drop in the correct spot or the bomb would overshoot. Two seconds later he called "capture" at which time had I dropped I would have missed. So I put the nose down about 25 degrees, which meant going into the triple-A area, and released, but the weapons hit the target lased. Unfortunately, what appeared to be a bunker on "his" display was a point a little way off among the trees.

Day Ops put us against tanks, mortars, artillery positions, convoys and so on, but we needed to be careful with the convoys because the Serbs were mixing themselves in with the civilians.

Luckily we didn't encounter the SAMs in the number we expected. Some of our air controllers in A-10s did, SAM-7s or SAM-14s, but often it was a case of them having a quick look at you on radar then switching off again. We suspected they were afraid of being located themselves and they wanted to keep their missiles for later. Obviously we didn't hang around to see what they decided once we got radar indications!

There were a lot of aircraft around and over the holding areas at night we'd all have our nav. lights on and one could see all these lights buzzing around at various heights. Then as soon as we pushed off to the war zone, all the lights went out, so it got very dark very quickly, but you knew the aircraft were still all there.

I remember once going in through Albania and into Kosovo from west to east. The NATO targets were often close together and some American F-15s were late attacking one way as we came in the opposite direction. As we were coming out, the F-15s' bombs were exploding below us; in fact they were actually bombing through us which was a bit disconcerting. Fortunately we all got through to fight another day! I also had a near miss with a French Mirage.

We were circling round being talked onto a target by an A-10 pilot, which was difficult to locate. I was looking down trying to pick it out through binoculars, and this Mirage went right past me about 30-40 metres away. The co-ordination keeping the strike package away from our CAS area had broken down.'

Flight Lieutenant MOU also recalls other aircraft:

'It was a problem that there were so many other aircraft in the air, all at various altitudes. It is quite dangerous unless controlled and it was well controlled by the airborne controllers.

I think most guys wanted to help get the Serbs out, for it was nasty what they were doing. We could see it. One day you'd see a village and the next day you'd find all the roofs were off the houses and everything would be smoking where the Serbs had gone through and razed the place to the ground. You also knew that not everyone had got out unscathed. The mass graves were evidence, so most of us were pleased to be helping.

We usually dropped our bombs at medium level, flying higher than normal to keep out of the small arms fire and most of the SAM ranges. We could really do this accurately. The adrenaline kept you going because you are so aware of every threat.

In all I think I flew 38 or 39 trips.'

Flight Lieutenant Averty:

'We all met triple-A, people got looked at by SAM systems – we carry sensors that tell us what kind of system is looking at us so we know that we've been "illuminated" by a SAM – which necessitated a quick reaction in order to break the lock. You knew it could be just seconds before a SAM was launched at you so one didn't hang around.

I flew 35 missions, not always dropping bombs. We'd also fly as spotter aircraft, looking out for our No.1s, trying to spot SAMs and so on. The leader would be very busy in the cockpit with all the things one had to do, which prevented being able to look out, so the No.2 would be "riding shotgun" as a safety net. In all I probably dropped about 20 times.

We needed about 25 pilots in the end and as we had only 16 we had guys in from other squadrons. Some came from 3 and IV Squadrons, plus some of those who had recently left our Squadron to go to training jobs. Others came from the OCU.

Generally a mission would take about 1hr 20 minutes. Tactically it was useful for us being where we were, just a short distance across the Adriatic, with our COAC at Vicenza.'

Flight Lieutenant KIL (call sign):

'There is a lot of apprehension knowing you're going into a live situation. It's the unknown more than anything; how good their SAM systems and operators are going to be, how good my training had been, how good the American suppression systems are, etc, etc. So one really prepares for the worst case scenario.

Finally I am walking out to my aircraft with all these live weapons on board, including live Sidewinder missiles, to go to war. A huge change of attitude and really pedantic checks on the equipment. Once airborne a lot of the apprehension disappears and the training kicks-in; one begins to concentrate on getting the jet to the target.

We would fly to the holding area, check the systems, then check them again; I must have checked things 15 times on that first mission. Once on "hold" one begins to wonder if we were going to be called in, will they find targets for us?

Once I'd flown a few missions and had been into the badlands a few times things got better but you never knew if this time they'd shoot you down; this time their SAMs would be up and ready. But as things got more familiar and we got more experienced we were less apprehensive and less nervous about things.

The first time I had a radar system illuminate me on the RWR (radar warning receiver), which also tells you if a missile is on the way, I had wondered how I would react. We were in a pair and just went into our defensive manoeuvre and told my wingman, and then he also got illuminated and that was it. We shook it and headed out. It surprised me how calm I had been.

I did 40 Ops. One I recall I was with Stewy and we were called in by the FAC A-10s to some emplacement and as they were marking we saw some triple-A below but assessed it would not trouble us. It was all very matter of fact and we just got on with the job.'

Squadron Leader Huckstep:

'Our aircraft could only "see" radar missiles on the RWR, not infra-red ones, which is why we needed our wingmen to watch for these, so we could get off flares and so on.

We got the impression that eventually the Serbs were not doing very much by day, they were all hunkered down and only moving at night. Gradually, as time went on it became harder and harder to find targets on the ground. We also used our recce. capability and gave the developed film to the A-10 chaps who'd go out and look for the targets and then talk us onto them again.

It was all very tiring but with only flying one mission a day it was sustainable. Day Ops tended to be launched at 5 am so we were up soon after midnight to get the planning organised. We felt it was a worthwhile cause to be involved in, so it was high morale all the time. We saw the TV news of the refugees so this gave us a focus.

The pilots were very motivated and very courageous. It was our first conflict and everyone was tremendous, whether they were an experienced flight commander or a new junior pilot. We worked well as a team, you had to trust other people and if you were a TIALD operator on night Ops and you were "heads-down" for two or three minutes, you had to rely on another guy to watch out for you. Overall I flew 34 missions of which I led 19.

The ground crews were great. They worked 12-hour shifts without a break for the first 30 days. It was very hard work but their morale was excellent. They were very involved in what we were doing and would always wish you luck before you went off. The armourers particularly were tremendous, working very long hours in weapon prep, and changing weapon loads as the task or weather changed. We wouldn't have done it without the enormous effort by the ground crews.'

Wing Commander Golledge:

'I remember the support from the UK was outstanding but it was inevitable one would have a bit of friction with someone. I had this with the taskers and felt there was a bit of interfering going on. To such an extent, I was getting really worked up about it, and this built up just before my five-day leave. It came to a head; I went up on a sortie and maybe I wasn't as sharp or in the right frame of mind.

Our target was a bridge in daylight and I put the wrong laser code, which must tie-up with the bomb. Both aircraft and bomb must be coded the same and we tell the TIALD pod the code, so the bomb was set correctly but I dialled in the aircraft code wrong by one digit. I was locked onto the target and the bombs went in short because the bombs didn't see the laser energy. I was furious at my error. The next day I was due to go to the UK and at that point I felt stressed.

The main thing overall, of course, was that we didn't lose a pilot or an aircraft. The pilots were all very professional. If anyone didn't like a target, any doubt about it, thought it was, or could be civilian, we brought the bombs back. It was frustrating but no disgrace was ever attached to it.

Some pilots were lucky and got lots of targets allocated to them, some were unlucky. One youngster on the Squadron dropped many bombs. I think we all averaged around 35-40 missions – I flew 38 – so we were all in that sort of bracket.

The ground crews were pretty happy. It was sunny, they were outdoors, they got lots of positive press coverage and lots of VIPs visiting, so knew they were doing a good job. The armourers did have some difficulties, for when they load up they want to see the bombs gone, but on the occasions when bombs were brought back they knew it was extra work taking them off and then putting them back on again.

We carried four types of ordnance; Paveway 2 LGBs, Paveway 3, freefall cluster bombs and 1,000 lb freefall bombs. We generally used the unguided weapons against Serb army targets and the LGBs against fixed targets which we needed to hit directly.

As yet we are still awaiting a precision guided weapon that we can use through cloud. It's being procured but it was the biggest deficiency I saw during the campaign. We could drop freefall bombs through cloud using GPS (global precision system) which while pretty accurate was not a precision weapon. These were only dropped on targets where there was no risk of collateral damage.

After approximately ten weeks of intense action the end appeared to be in sight. The Squadron organised a party at the hotel – in fact a peace party – on the Friday evening. It was a trifle premature as the CO and MOU both recall:

'After the bombing stopped (we thought) we took the opportunity to have a peace party, a Bar-B-Q on the hotel roof, but two days later we were bombing again so we were a tad premature.'

'The peace party was great; we drank the war back on! We knew the peace was there but I'm not sure everyone was convinced. You can't let an opportunity pass by for as soon as it stopped for real we knew everybody would be spinning off so we wanted everyone together. However, next day we were off bombing again for a short while.'

Once the bombing finally came to a halt there was a period of calm but not of freedom from active duty. The allied forces needed to ensure the Serbs were really retreating back home and would not suddenly come back again. There was no immediate return to Wittering for the Squadron. Work had still to be done. Andy Golledge:

'At the end we stayed at Gioia for two weeks on alert to be there to provide support for KFOR troops. There was no flying and it gave us time to get up to date with all the paper work.

To show how good our training is, we were the only unit in the whole of NATO to declare a low-level role to support KFOR. Because, if KFOR suddenly needed support and there was low cloud around, we took on the low-level commitment, night and day. This is because for years we have trained for just this sort of thing.

Many countries do not allow low-level flying but in the UK we do. It does create nuisance but it proves its worth, and was proving it now. KFOR was made up with a good percentage of UK soldiers. If they asked for our support we would be there. This shows the value of the RAF training methods.'

John McMath:

'The Squadron worked very well but were worked very hard, and of course, needed to have everything checked and double checked. There was a lot of pride associated with it and we wanted the bombing to finish while we were still at Gioia; we were not keen to have another squadron come in and finish the job. And when it did end, it was no gradual wind down, it was like switching the light off.

There was a good deal learnt, such as how long it took from an aircraft landing to it being ready to go off again. The lads also had to deal with VIPs and the press. Some times I could watch on Sky News at our hotel, see our aircraft taking off, and I'd know how many were going out before I left for the airfield! There was a huge mix in personnel too. Some of our new boys had been filling supermarket shelves 18 months earlier and couldn't believe they were in a war situation. While others, who had been in the Service for 15-16 years, were seeing active duty for the first time.'

Achievements and coming home

In total No.1 Squadron had flown 870 missions during the campaign, 77 at night and 793 in daylight, covering 1,250 operational flying hours. They had dropped 894 bombs of all types.

In mid-June 1999 they finally got orders to return to their UK base. Not surprisingly there was going to be something of a reception for them. Not quite a New York ticker-tape parade, but good enough for British traditionalists to be proud of. The boys were coming home.

It should have been a proud moment for the CO but fate's fickle finger rose into the air in 'the bird' like fashion. Andy Golledge:

'On the day we came home I thought it important we came into Wittering in a big formation. So we planned to fly in with ten aircraft – leaving six in Italy – supported by VC-10 tankers. The press, VIPs and families would all be waiting and we'd get good publicity out of it.

Unfortunately that morning the ligaments in my back went, and I couldn't walk, let along fly. So I had to hand over lead to my A Flight commander, and was left behind. I was carried to my hotel room and had to watch it all on Sky TV.

A week later the ground crew went home – in a VC-10 so we had another big press day, making sure they also got a good pat on the back too. As they came in some of our Harriers flew out, met them and escorted them home. A great moment.'

Squadron Leader Huckstep:

'I was due to stay for another week but the boss, poor chap, put his back out right in front of me so I had to pack and get ready to lead the aircraft home.

We arrived near base and formed up, orbiting below cloud 15 miles away then ran in in V-formation and the guys back in Gioia were watching it all on Sky at the hotel.

Having landed with all the press and VIPs, plus families, was quite a moment and I had to say a few good words to everyone. My children ran out and were all standing around the aircraft. The press liked all that! All in all we had done 79 days of continuous operations, with a total of five days in UK and four days off spread throughout the time in theatre. I was tremendously proud of what the Squadron had achieved.'

* * *

Flight Lieutenant MOU, like some of the other JPs on the Squadron, had been fortunate, and even the 'old hands' had been lucky too. MOU relates:

'I was lucky that at the beginning of my career I had got to go and do the job for real which not very many people do at all. It never got routine but it certainly gets a bit "ground hog day'ish", flying, dropping, maybe not dropping, getting home, back to the hotel, exactly the same thing seven days a week all the time.

Everyone was happy it was over, but some of the guys who came out in the latter days obviously hoped it would go on for a few more days so they could have a go.'

Some weeks later the authors of this book were visiting the Squadron and were being looked after by Flight Lieutenant Chris Averty. He said he would probably not see us much the next day as he had to fly a training sortie over the Wash, to drop bombs. A comment was made as to why, having recently flown almost 20 bombing sorties over the former Yugoslavia. The answer was simple, as far as the annual training syllabus was concerned, the box on his record sheet did not as yet have the appropriate tick in it to show he could actually do it!

* * *

In June 1999 the Squadron received a message of congratulations from Air Force Commander, Kosovo, Lieutenant-General Mike Short:

1. As the Combined Forces Air Component Commander I would like to express my deepest thanks to the Squadron for a job well done. Success would not have been possible without your discipline, professionalism and courage. Your individual and collective dedication to duty was critical to enable NATO air power to meet all its objectives.

2. Throughout the air campaign I asked you to operate against a highly capable enemy, with exacting rules of engagement, in challenging weather and under a very high operations tempo. Despite these many challenges, day after day, you delivered your ordnance on target on time. You never failed me. Aircrews, maintainers and support personnel should take great pride in the unparalleled achievements of this air campaign.

3. It has been the high point of my career to have served as your combined forces air component commander. Rarely does a commander have the privilege to lead such a professional and dedicated military force. As we enter into what, I hope, is a lasting peace, I wish you the best in every future endeavor.

* * *

Returning from Kosovo the Squadron had no sooner celebrated everyone's safe return than it was back to training. Obviously experience now included actual combat in a combat zone. Most things had worked as advertised, and if anything needed to be even slightly adjusted, the Squadron knew how to fix it.

As the summer came everyone was back in the old routine. One or two pilots left as tours ended, new pilots arrived, no doubt thinking how near they had been to seeing action, yet how far.

For the CO too his period of leadership was coming to an end. His flying tour had started with 20 Squadron, so his actual time with Number One was less than normal. He handed over command to Wing Commander Sean Bell on 26 October 1999. Sean Bell had joined the RAF in 1980 with the University of London Air Squadron, then Cranwell in 1983. By 1990 he was on 3 Squadron in Germany, then OS 3, HQ 2 Group, a squadron leader appointment in support of Germany-based Harrier squadrons. In 1995 he had a four-month tour with AOCC Sarajevo supporting NATO/UN efforts before becoming a flight commander and then Exec back on 3 Squadron. Prior to joining 1 Squadron he attended the Advanced Staff Course in Toronto, Canada.

Awards

Then, shortly after Andy Golledge left came the proud announcement that four pilots had been decorated for operations over Kosovo. To Andy Golledge went the Distinguished Service Order – the first to be awarded to a member of 1 Squadron since 1942, and only the fifth in its history. Distinguished Flying Crosses went to Squadron Leaders Martin 'Benny' Ball (a former member of the Red Arrows Team), Chris Huckstep and Christopher Norton. Added to these prestigious awards came four Mentions in Despatches: Flight Lieutenants Andy McKeown, Mark Zanker, Myles Garland and Dave Kane.

As the year 2000 began plans were afoot to change the make-up of the RAF. In April the RAF comprised three Groups. No.3 Group – the Harrier force (inc Sea Harriers) – plus maritime aircraft and helicopters. 1 Group the Tornado force. 2 Group everything else, including training. Over the years many former 1 Squadron personnel have risen to high rank within the Service. The new Chief of the Air Staff from 21 April 2000 was Air Chief Marshal Sir Peter Squire, former CO of No.1 Squadron and more recently AOC-in-C Strike Command and Commander Allied Air Forces NW Europe.

Both he and No.1 Squadron will help take the Royal Air Force into the new millennium beginning with a four-aircraft detachment at Gioia, which started on 28 December and went through till the end of January 2000 (Operation Deliberate Forge). For pilots who had been in action over the same areas, it was strange to fly over Kosovo without the threat of triple-A and SAM missiles.

Exercise 'Snow Falcon' came in February, training pilots and ground crews in arctic conditions at Bardufoss, Norway. A period at RAF Leuchars in March on a night Tactical Leaders Training (TLT) and day Operational Low Flying (OLF) will be followed by more intensive work. Another detachment to Gioia in May/June, the Squadron move to RAF Cottesmore in August, then a long 3-4 weeks at sea in September before they have to send men and aircraft once more to Gioia in mid-October till the end of the year.

At the end of June came some changes. Chris Huckstep left to go to 3 Group at High Wycombe, and Chris Norton took over as Exec. Steve Hunt was A Flight commander and Gary Waterfall came in from the Red Arrows to command B Flight. The Squadron's history is on-going.

Appendix One

COMMANDING OFFICERS

Major E M Maitland	13 May 1912
Major C A H Longcroft (MiD)	1 May 1914
Major W G H Salmond	28 Jan 1915
Major P B Joubert de la Ferté	19 Aug 1915
Major G F Pretyman DSO	24 Nov 1915
Major G C St.P de Dombasle	24 Dec 1916
Major A Barton Adams (MiD)	20 Jun 1917
Major W E Young DFC	3 Aug 1918
S/Ldr J O Andrews DSO MC & Bar	21 Jan 1920
S/Ldr J B Graham MC AFC	18 Sep 1920
S/Ldr G G A Williams	10 Nov 1922
S/Ldr E O Grenfell MC DFC AFC	8 Oct 1923
S/Ldr E D Atkinson DFC AFC	25 May 1924
S/Ldr C N Lowe MC DFC	19 Apr 1926
S/Ldr E D Atkinson DFC AFC	11 Apr 1927
S/Ldr E O Grenfell MC DFC AFC	19 Mar 1928
S/Ldr C B S Spackman DFC & Bar	27 Jul 1931
S/Ldr R W Chappell MC	21 Nov 1933
S/Ldr C W Hill	1 Oct 1934
F/Lt T R McEvoy (acting)	31 Jan 1936
S/Ldr C W Hill	1 Dec 1936
S/Ldr F R D Swain AFC	12 Apr 1937
S/Ldr I A Bertram	15 Jan 1938
S/Ldr P J H Halahan DFC	17 Apr 1939
S/Ldr D A Pemberton DFC	24 May 1940
S/Ldr M H Brown DFC & Bar	10 Nov 1940
S/Ldr R E P Brooker DFC	23 Apr 1941
S/Ldr J A F MacLachlan DSO DFC & Bar	3 Nov 1941
S/Ldr R C Wilkinson OBE DFM & Bar	31 Jul 1942
S/Ldr A Zweigbergh	30 May 1943
S/Ldr J Checketts DSO DFC	3 Apr 1944
S/Ldr H P Lardner Burke DFC & Bar	29 Apr 1944
S/Ldr D G S R Cox DFC & Bar	11 Jan 1945
S/Ldr R S Nash DFC	21 Apr 1945
S/Ldr H R Allen DFC	9 Jan 1946
S/Ldr C H MacFie DFC	26 Oct 1946
F/Lt N H D Ramsey DFC (acting)	7 May 1947
S/Ldr T R Burne DSO AFC	15 Jul 1947
Major R Olds USAF	4 Feb 1949
S/Ldr T R Burne DSO AFC	1 Oct 1949
Major D F Smith USAF	10 Jan 1950
S/Ldr J L W Ellacombe DFC & Bar	18 Aug 1950
S/Ldr R B Morison DFC	21 Nov 1952
S/Ldr D I Smith	27 Jul 1953
S/Ldr F W Lister DSO DFC	1 Dec 1953
F/Lt H Irving (acting)	1 Jun 1955
S/Ldr R S Kingsford	8 Aug 1956
S/Ldr L de Garis AFC	5 Jul 1958
S/Ldr J J Phipps	1 Dec 1958
S/Ldr P V Pledger	1 Jan 1961
S/Ldr F L Travers-Smith	1 Jan 1963
S/Ldr D C G Brook	28 Dec 1964
S/Ldr G Jones	1 Nov 1966
S/Ldr L A B Baker	20 Sep 1968
W/Cdr J A Mansell	10 Apr 1969
S/Ldr L A B Baker	21 May 1969
W/Cdr D Allison	4 Aug 1969
S/Ldr L A B Baker (acting)	17 Oct 1969
W/Cdr K W Hayr AFC	1 Jan 1970
W/Cdr E J E Smith OBE	6 Jan 1972
W/Cdr P P W Taylor AFC	3 Dec 1973
W/Cdr G Saye	9 Jul 1976
W/Cdr R B Duckett AFC	17 Jul 1978
W/Cdr P T Squire DFC AFC	26 Mar 1981
W/Cdr J D L Feesey AFC	23 Dec 1983
W/Cdr I M Stewart	13 Jun 1986
W/Cdr I R Harvey MBE BSc	3 Oct 1988
W/Cdr C C N Burwell MBE	17 May 1991
W/Cdr D Walker AFC BSc	29 Apr 1994
W/Cdr M A Leakey BSc	18 Mar 1996
S/Ldr I Cameron (acting)	26 Nov 1997
W/Cdr A Golledge DSO BSc	9 Jan 1998
W/Cdr S M Bell BSc	26 Oct 1999

Appendix Two

DECORATIONS & AWARDS
WWI

Distinguished Service Order

Captain M McB Bell-Irving	January 1916
Captain W C Campbell MC	September 1917
Captain P F Fullard MC	November 1917

Military Cross

Lieutenant O D Filley	July 1915
Captain R A Saunders	January 1916
Lieutenant E O Grenfell	March 1916
Lieutenant W V Strugnell	June 1916
Captain M McB Bell-Irving DSO	July 1916
Lieutenant J D Latta	July 1916
Captain B J W M Moore	July 1916
Captain R Balcombe Browne	July 1916
Captain C J Q Brand	April 1917
Lieutenant E S T Cole	May 1917
Captain T F Hazell	July 1917
Captain W C Campbell	August 1917
Captain P F Fullard	September 1917
Captain L F Jenkin	August 1917
Captain W W Rogers	February 1918
Captain G B Moore	May 1918
Captain P J Clayson	June 1918
Lieutenant F P Magoun	June 1918
Lieutenant H A Rigby	June 1918
Lieutenant E M Forsyth	July 1918
Captain H J Hamilton	July 1918
Lieutenant L W Mawbey	July 1918

Bar to Military Cross

Captain W C Campbell MC	August 1917
Captain L F Jenkin MC	August 1917
Captain P F Fullard MC	September 1917

Distinguished Flying Cross

Captain R A Birkbeck	June 1918
Captain P J Clayson MC	July 1918
Lieutenant H A Kullberg USAS	November 1918
Captain C S T Lavers	February 1919

Distinguished Conduct Medal

Corporal S C Griggs 354	June 1915
Sergeant Major H McKenna 1776	June 1916
Corporal C J French 11559	April 1918

Military Medal

Flight Sergeant T F B Carlisle	February 1917
Sergeant G P Olley	July 1917

Meritorious Service Medal

Corporal A J Copplestone 1484	January 1919
Sergeant J B Thomas 2167	June 1919

Mention in Despatches

Captain E R Ludlow-Hewitt	June 1915
Sergeant Major J Mead	June 1915
Sergeant Major W J Waddington	June 1915
Lieutenant E O Grenfell	November 1915
Captain R A Saunders	November 1915
Captain M McB Bell-Irving DSO	January 1916
Lieutenant O D Filley MC	January 1916
Captain E O Grenfell	January 1916
Lieutenant E P Plenty	April 1916
Sergeant M B Fitzgerald 1705	June 1916
Lieutenant T McK Hughes	June 1916
Captain M McB Bell-Irving DSO	June 1916
Captain A J Capel	May 1917
Sergeant Major M B Fitzgerald 1705	May 1917
Major A B Adams	December 1917
Lieutenant D E Cameron	June 1919

French Croix de Guerre

Lieutenant W Watts	September 1915
Lieutenant V W B Castle	May 1917

1919 to 1939

Distinguished Flying Cross

Flight Lieutenant F J Vincent	June 1924
Flying Officer D F Anderson	June 1924
Flight Lieutenant F L Luxmoore	December 1924

Bar to Distinguished Flying Cross

Flight Lieutenant F O Soden DFC	December 1922

Air Force Cross

Flight Lieutenant O E Carter	December 1933
Flight Lieutenant E G H Russell-Stracey	December 1935

British Empire Medal

Warrant Officer W J L Brown 159383	October 1927

WWII

George Medal

Corporal N Gouldin BEM	January 1944

Distinguished Service Order

Squadron Leader J A F MacLachlan DFC	May 1942

Distinguished Flying Cross

Squadron Leader P J H Halahan	June 1940
Flight Lieutenant P R Walker	June 1940
Flight Lieutenant P P Hanks	June 1940
Flying Officer P M H Richey	June 1940
Flying Officer M H Brown	June 1940
Flying Officer L R Clisby	June 1940
Flying Officer J I Kilmartin	June 1940
Flying Officer P W O Mould	June 1940
Flying Officer C D Palmer	June 1940
Pilot Officer W H Stratton	June 1940
Pilot Officer P V Boot	September 1940
Flight Lieutenant P G H Matthews	April 1941
Pilot Officer A V Clowes DFM	April 1941
Squadron Leader R E P Brooker	May 1941
Flight Lieutenant K M Kuttelwascher	May 1942
Flight Lieutenant L S B Scott	August 1943
Flight Lieutenant D P Perrin RNZAF	October 1943
Flying Officer H T Mossip RCAF	October 1943
Flight Lieutenant I P J Maskill RNZAF	March 1945

Bar to Distinguished Flying Cross

Squadron Leader M H Brown DFC	April 1941
Flight Lieutenant C F Gray DFC	September 1941
Flight Lieutenant K M Kuttelwascher DFC	June 1942
Squadron Leader H P Lardner Burke DFC	December 1944

Distinguished Flying Medal

Flight Sergeant F J Soper	June 1940
Sergeant A V Clowes	June 1940
Sergeant G F Berry	June 1940
Flight Sergeant J D Dygryn-Ligoticky	May 1941

Member of the Order of the British Empire (MBE)

Flying Officer E D Hills	January 1941

Mention in Despatches

P/O A V Clowes DFM	July 1940
Flight Lieutenant B H I Hillcoat	January 1941
Flight Lieutenant P E Warcup	January 1941
Flight Sergeant R E Fuller	January 1941
Flight Sergeant H W P Regnard	January 1941
Corporal J Maloney	January 1941
Corporal H S Dimmer	January 1941
Corporal J W Trim	January 1941
Flight Lieutenant J S Chown	
Flight Lieutenant D H Davy	January 1946
Flight Lieutenant N S Brown	January 1946
Flight Lieutenant P W D Stewart	January 1946
Flight Lieutenant R Brown	January 1946
Flying Officer J W McKenzie	January 1946

French Croix de Guerre
Flying Officer M H Brown	May 1940*
Lt J-F Demozay FFAF	May 1941

* not received due to the collapse in France

Czech War Cross
Flight Sergeant J D Dygryn-Ligoticky	May 1941
Squadron Leader M H Brown DFC	1942
Flight Lieutenant K M Kuttelwascher	1942

POST WWII

Distinguished Service Order
Wing Commander A Golledge BSc	November 1999

Distinguished Flying Cross
Wing Commander P T Squire AFC	September 1982
Squadron Leader J J Pook	September 1982
Squadron Leader M Ball	November 1999
Squadron Leader C R Huckstep	November 1999
Squadron Leader C H Norton	November 1999

Air Force Cross
Squadron Leader D J Willis	January 1973
Squadron Leader M A P Pugh	1973
Flight Lieutenant P Harris	1982
Flight Lieutenant M Beech	1982

Mention in Despatches
Squadron Leader R D Iveson	September 1982
Flight Lieutenant M W J Hare	September 1982
Squadron Leader P W Harris	1982
Flight Lieutenant J R Rochfort	1982
Flight Lieutenant A Harper	1982
Flight Lieutenant J W Glover	1982
Flight Lieutenant M Beech	1982
Flight Lieutenant A McKeown	November 1999
Flight Lieutenant M Zanker	November 1999
Flight Lieutenant M Garland	November 1999
Flight Lieutenant D Kane	November 1999

Member of the Order of the British Empire (MBE)
Flight Lieutenant B T Mason	1982
Squadron Leader M J Harwood	1995

Commander Task Force 317 Commendation
Chief Technician F L Ridge	1982
Corporal D M Kellaway	1982

Air Commander Task Force 317 Commendation
Chief Technician F W Welsh	1982
Sergeant D G Stinchcombe	1982
SAC T R John-Lewis	1982

Queen's Commendation for Valuable Service in the Air
Flight Lieutenant M M Macleod (attached)	1982
Flight Lieutenant N Gilchrist	1982
Flight Lieutenant A R Boyens	1982

Queen's Commendation for Brave Conduct
Squadron Leader A Stevenson	1991

Appendix Three

SQUADRON BASES

Farnborough	13 May 1912	Brooklands	1 May 1914
Netheravon	13 Nov 1914	St Omer	7 Mar 1915
Bailleul	29 Mar 1915	St Marie Cappel	29 Mar 1918
Clairmarais	13 Apr 1918	Fienvillers	5 Aug 1918
Senlis-le-Sec	6 Oct 1918	Bouvincourt	26 Oct 1918
Le Hameau	18 Nov 1918	London Colney	3 Mar 1919
Uxbridge	19 Sep 1919	Risalpur	21 Jan 1920
Bangalore	11 May 1920	Hinaidi	20 Apr1921
Tangmere	1 Feb 1927	Octeville	9 Sep 1939
Norrent-Fontes	29 Sep 1939	Vassincourt	9 Oct 1939
Berry-au-Bac	11 Apr 1940	Condé/Vraux	17 May 1940
Anglure	18 May 1940	Châteaudun	3 Jun 1940
Rouen/Boos	14 Jun 1940	Angers	16 Jun 1940
Nantes	17 Jun 1940	Northolt	18 Jun 1940
Tangmere	23 Jul 1940	Northolt	1 Aug 1940
Wittering	9 Sep 1940	Northolt	15 Dec 1940
Kenley	5 Jan 1941	Croydon	7 Apr 1941
Redhill	1 May 1941	Kenley	1 Jun 1941
Redhill	14 Jun 1941	Tangmere	1 Jul 1941
Acklington	8 Jul 1942	Biggin Hill	9 Feb 1943
Lympne	15 Mar 1943	Martlesham Hth	15 Feb 1944
North Weald	3 Apr 1944	Ayr	20 Apr 1944
Predannack	29 Apr 1944	Harrowbeer	20 Jun 1944
Detling	22 Jun 1944	Lympne	11 Jul 1944
Detling	10 Aug 1944	Manston	18 Dec 1944
Coltishall	8 Apr 1945	Ludham	14 May 1945
Hutton Cranswick	23 Jul 1945	Hawkinge	24 Sep 1945
Hutton Cranswick	22 Oct 1945	Tangmere	30 Apr 1946
Acklington	17 Jun 1946	Tangmere	22 Jul 1946
Acklington	24 Feb 1947	Tangmere	1 Apr 1947
Lübeck	29 Apr 1947	Tangmere	26 Jun 1947
Nicosia	1 Sep 1956	Tangmere	24 Dec 1956
Stradishall	2 Jul 1958	Waterbeach	8 Nov 1961
West Raynham	13 Aug 1963	Wittering	18 Jul 1969
Cottesmore	Jul 2000-		

Appendix Four

1 SQUADRON ROLL OF HONOUR

1912-1919

Lt H F Boles	24 May 1915	Lt L Playfair	6 Jul 1915
2/Lt D C Cleaver	29 Dec 1915	Capt J D G Sanders	5 Jan 1916
2/Lt R Barton	12 Jan 1916	Lt E S Wilkinson	12 Jan 1916
Lt W Watts	17 Jan 1916	Lt C O Hayward	17 Jan 1916
2/Lt H A Johnston	4 Mar 1916	2/Lt R P Turner	9 Mar 1916
Capt R A Saunders	14 Mar 1916	F/Sgt T F B Carlisle MM	8 Jul 1916
2 A/M J Simpson	13 Jul 1916	2/Lt T G G Sturrock	16 Oct 1916
2/Lt C C Godwin	17 Oct 1916	Lt P C Ellis	17 Oct 1916
Lt T A Tillard	6 Dec 1916	1 A/M T Foye	22 Dec 1916
Cpl G Dinnage	24 Dec 1916	Capt J M E Shepherd	15 Feb1917
2/Lt A I Gilson	17 Mar 1917	Lt H Welch	28 Mar 1917
Lt M G Cole	18 May 1917	Lt L Drummond	18 May 1917
Capt J R Anthony	25 May 1917	2/Lt J A O'Sullivan	27 May 1917
2/Lt W G Milliship	7 Jun 1917	Lt R W L Anderson	12 Jun 1917
2/Lt R S Lloyd	18 Jun 1917	2/Lt T M McFerran	21 Jun 1917
Lt C Street	26 Jun 1917	2/Lt T Littler	3 Jul 1917
2/Lt J M S G Stevens	14 Jul 1917	2/Lt G B Buxton	28 Jul 1917
Capt A B Jarvis	10 Aug 1917	2/Lt F M McLaren	12 Aug 1917
2/Lt C A Moody	21 Aug 1917	2/Lt C Pickstone	3 Sep 1917
Capt L F Jenkin MC*	11 Sep 1917	2/Lt W S Mansell	11 Sep 1917
2/Lt E D Tyzack	15 Sep 1917	2/Lt F J Chowne	20 Sep 1917
2/Lt R H Garratt	20 Sep 1917	Capt W V T Rooper	9 Oct 1917
Lt A W MacLaughlin	29 Oct 1917	2/Lt E D Scott	30 Oct 1917
2/Lt C S Fuller MC	11 Nov 1917	2/Lt W D G Murray	3 Jan 1918
Lt E K Skelton	9 Jan 1918	Lt R C Sotham	9 Jan 1918
Capt H G Reeves	24 Jan 1918	2/Lt W C Smith	8 Feb 1918
Lt A H Fitzmaurice	12 Mar 1918	2/Lt A McN Denovan	26 Mar 1918
Capt G B Moore MC	7 Apr 1918	Lt H B Winton	21 Apr 1918
Lt C A Pelletier	11 May 1918	Capt K S Henderson	2 Jun 1918
Lt H S Hennessy	5 Jun 1918	Lt E T S Kelly	15 Jun 1918
Lt H B Bradley	25 Jun 1918	Capt K C Mills	8 Aug 1918
2/Lt W Joffe DSO	1 Oct 1918	2/Lt H H Hunt	26 Oct 1918
Lt W Newby	29 Oct 1918		

1919-1939

F/L J M McAlery	4 Jan 1924	F/O S A Young	14 May 1926
F/O N H Jackson	26 May 1932	F/L R Brown	23 Apr 1934
F/O W E S Tanner	23 Apr 1934	Sgt J J Tanfield	29 May 1937
F/L H H Peck	17 Dec 1937	Sgt R E Pattern	17 Dec 1937
P/O M V Baxter	22 Feb 1938	F/O A C Douglas	14 Jan 1939
Sgt A V Hancock	7 Feb 1939	Sgt W A Cuthbert	13 Mar 1939
F/L W O C Hemmings	26 Jun 1939		

1939-1945

P/O J S Mitchell	2 Mar 1940	F/O L R Clisby DFC	13 May 1940
F/O L R Lorimer	13 May 1940	P/O J A J Davey	11 Aug 1940
P/O D O M Browne	15 Aug 1940	Sgt M M Shannon	15 Aug 1940
F/Sgt F G Berry DFM	1 Sep 1940	P/O R H Shaw	3 Sep 1940
F/L H B L Hillcoat	3 Sep 1940	S/L D A Pemberton DFC	3 Nov 1940
P/O A Kershaw	19 Mar 1941	Sgt G M Stocker	22 Apr 1941
Sgt F Behal	11 May 1941	F/O J C E Robinson	21 May 1941
Sgt A Nasswetter	16 Jun 1941	P/O B Horak	29 Jun 1941
F/L A Velebnovsky	16 Jul 1941	Sgt E Bloor	27 Aug 1941
Sgt E Ruppel RCAF	18 Nov 1941	Sgt L J Travis	22 Nov 1941
Sgt E G Parsons	11 Feb 1942	Sgt E F G Blair	12 Feb 1942
P/O E S G Sweeting	16 Feb 1942	F/S J Vlk	10 Apr 1942
Sgt V Machacek	24 Apr 1942	F/S G C English	3 Jun 1942
Sgt J Dygryn-Ligoticky DFM	4 Jun 1942	W/O G Scott RCAF	26 Jun 1942
P/O P N Dobie	21 Oct 1942	P/O G C Whitmore RCAF	6 Mar 1943
Sgt H R Fraser RAAF	6 Mar 1943	F/O C L Bolster RCAF	29 Mar 1943
P/O J M Chalfour	15 Jul 1943	F/O L G Wood	16 Aug 1943
P/O P L Gray	23 Aug 1943	F/O J W Wiley RCAF	25 Nov 1943
W/O J D Fairbairn	7 Dec 1943	F/Sgt S D Cunningham	21 Dec 1943
F/O H T Jackson	23 Mar 1944	F/O R G Ward	20 Apr 1944
Sgt E F Jacobson	22 May 1944	F/Sgt G Tate	30 Jul 1944
F/O T Wylie RNZAF	27 Sep 1944	W/O E R Andrews	27 Sep 1944
F/S T Jeffrey	3 Aug 1945	F/O T Glaser	27 Sep 1945

1946-2000

F/L J Burls	24 Sep 1948	PII G E T Forest	28 Feb 1949
F/L P W Speller	19 Apr 1950	P/O R W M Dixon	26 May 1950
F/O J M Gisborne	16 Aug 1953	F/O C H P Anthonisz	16 Aug 1953
F/O J J Turner	5 May 1958	F/L M J Paxton	5 May 1958
F/O B J Dimmock	1 Mar 1961	Capt F A Matthews USAF	24 Apr 1963
F/L D J Page	15 Jan 1969	W/C J A Mansell	21 May 1969
Capt L V Distelweg USAF	3 Aug 1971	F/L J E Downey	19 Jan 1976
F/L J K Roberts	19 Jan 1976		

Appendix Five

SQUADRON COMBAT VICTORIES WWI

Date	Pilot	Destroyed	OOC	Driven Down	Aircraft
1915					
13 Sep	Lt E O Grenfell			1 Alb	5056
19 Dec	Capt M McB Bell-Irving			1 C type	
1916					
17 Jan	Capt E O Grenfell			3 Fokker	5068
	Capt E O Grenfell			1 Alb C	5068
5 Feb	Lt W V Strugnell			1 C type	5068
29 Feb	Capt R A Saunders ⎱	1 HA			5119
	2/Lt C A B Joske ⎰				
19 Mar	F/Sgt T F B Carlisle ⎱		1 Alb		5089
	Lt J McElvie ⎰				
27 Apr	2/Lt C E Foggin	1			A118
18 May	F/Sgt T F B Carlisle		1 Aviatik		A116
25 June	Lt B J W M Moore	1 KB			A116
	Lt J D Latta	1 KB			A130
26 June	Lt B J W M Moore	1 KB			A116
	Lt J D Latta	1 KB			A130
	Capt R Balcombe Brown	1 KB			A125
3 Jul	Lt T A Oliver ⎱	1 HA			5170
	Sgt R B Mumford ⎰				
6 Aug	Lt T A Oliver			1 HA	A125
8 Aug	Lt B J W M Moore	1 Alb			A136
9 Sep	Lt W H Dore ⎱			1 Fokker	
	Lt R M Collingwood ⎰			1 LVG	A132
	2/Lt T M B Newton ⎱			1 Fokker	5184
	1 A/M O'Lieff ⎰				
16 Oct	Lt C C Godwin ⎱		1 HA		A190
	Lt P C Ellis ⎰				
2 Nov	Lt J M E Shepherd ⎱				
	Lt G F Bishop ⎰	1 Roland			
27 Nov	Lt V W B Castle ⎱	1 HA			
	1 A/M O'Lieff ⎰				
1917					
15 Feb	2/Lt J A Slater		1 Alb C		A6613
	2/Lt V H Collins	1 Alb D			A6610
4 Mar	2/Lt C J Q Brand ⎱	1 C type			A6668
	2/Lt V G A Bush ⎰				A6670
	2/Lt E S T Cole	1 LVG C			A6619
	Lt T F Hazell		1C type		A6604
11 Mar	2/Lt V W B Castle	1 Alb C			A6644
15 Mar	Capt C J Q Brand	1 Alb C			A6668
	2/Lt C C Clark	1 Alb D			A6672
	Capt C J Q Brand ⎱				A6668
	2/Lt C C Clark	1 Alb C	2 Alb C		A6672
	2/Lt R H Cronyn ⎰				A6619
17 Mar	2/Lt C C Clark ⎱		1 Alb D		A6672
	2/Lt J A Slater ⎰				A6624
25 Mar	Capt E D Atkinson	1 KB			A6624
28 Mar	2/Lt E S T Cole			1 Alb D	A6603
	2/Lt C C Clark			1 Halb D	A6672
8 Apr	Capt C J Q Brand	1 KB			A6668
	2/Lt E S T Cole	1 KB			A6603
22 Apr	2/Lt E M Wright		1 Alb D		A6644
	Capt E D Atkinson		1 Alb D		A6624
	2/Lt E S T Cole	1 KB			A6790
24 Apr	Lt T F Hazell	1 Alb C			A6738
26 Apr	Lt A V Burbury	1 KB			A6671
	2/Lt E S T Cole		1 Alb D		B1508
29 Apr	2/Lt E S T Cole			1 Alb D	B1508
30 Apr	Capt C J Q Brand	1 DFW			A6668
	2/Lt E S T Cole		1 D type		B1508
	Capt C J Q Brand		1 D type		A6668
	2/Lt E S T Cole		1 D type		B1508
1 May	Capt C J Q Brand	1 Alb C			A6668
	2/Lt L M Mansbridge	1 Alb C			A6670
	Capt E D Atkinson		1 Alb D		A6678
	2/Lt E S T Cole	1 Alb D			B1508
9 May	Lt T F Hazell		1 Alb C		B1632

Date	Pilot	Destroyed	OOC	Driven Down	Aircraft
12 May	Lt C Street		1 Alb D		B1554
	Capt F W Honnet		1 Alb D		B1635
13 May	Lt L Drummond		1 Alb D		B1635
14 May	2/Lt W C Campbell	1 C type			B1635
18 May	Lt H J Duncan	1 KB			B1543
	2/Lt T H Lines	1 KB			A6644
19 May	2/Lt W C Campbell	1 KB			A6670
21 May	2/Lt W C Campbell	1 Alb D			A6670
23 May	2/Lt W J Mussared	1 Alb C			B1641
	Lt L F Jenkin		1 Alb C		B1554
24 May	2/Lt L M Mansbridge		1 Alb D		A6670
25 May	Lt L F Jenkin		1 Alb D		B1638
26 May	Capt R H Cronyn		1 Alb D		B1689
	Lt F Sharpe		1 Alb D		B1550
	2/Lt P F Fullard		1 Alb D		B1559
	2/Lt W J Mussared		1 Alb D		B1641
1 June	Sgt G P Olley		1 C type		B1681
2 June	Lt L F Jenkin		1 Alb D		B1690
	2/Lt L M Mansbridge		1 Alb D		B1639
	2/Lt W C Campbell	1C type			B1700
4 June	Lt T F Hazell	2 Alb D			B1649
	Lt T F Hazell			2 Alb D	B1649
	2/Lt P F Fullard		1 Alb D		B1553
	2/Lt P F Fullard	1 Alb D			B1553
	2/Lt W C Campbell		1 C type		B1700
	Lt F Sharpe	1 C type			B1550
	2/Lt W J Mussared		1 C type		B1641
5 June	Lt T F Hazell		1 Alb D		B1649
	Lt T F Hazell		1 C type		B1649
7 June	2/Lt R W L Anderson		1 C type		B1638
	Lt F Sharpe ⎫				B3481
	Lt L F Jenkin ⎭	1 Alb D			B1547
	Lt F Sharpe	1 KB			B3481
8 June	2/Lt P F Fullard	1 Alb D			B1553
	Lt T F Hazell		1 Alb D		B1649
	Lt L F Jenkin		1 Alb D		B1547
	Lt W J Mussared	1 Alb D			B1550
9 June	2/Lt W C Campbell	2 Alb D			B1700
	2/Lt W C Campbell		1 Alb D		B1700
	Lt L F Jenkin	2 Alb D			B1547
	2/Lt J M Stevens		1 Alb D		B1689
	Lt T F Hazell		1 Alb D		B1649
12 June	Sgt W J Beadle	1 Alb C			B1680
14 June	2/Lt P F Fullard		1 Alb D		B3486
	Lt L F Jenkin	1 Alb D			B1547
15 June	2/Lt W C Campbell		1 C type		B1700
	2/Lt P F Fullard		1 Alb D		B3486
16 June	2/Lt W C Campbell	2 Alb C			B1700
	2/Lt W C Campbell	1 C type			B1700
	2/Lt T Littler		1 C type		B1638
17 June	Lt L F Jenkin		1 Alb D		B1649
18 June	Lt L F Jenkin ⎫				B1681
	Lt C S T Lavers ⎬	1 Alb D			B3495
	2/Lt H G Reeves ⎭				B1630
20 June	Lt L F Jenkin		1 Alb C		B1547
21 June	2/Lt W C Campbell ⎫		1 Alb D		B1700
	2/Lt T M McFerran ⎭				B3495
23 June	2/Lt W C Campbell ⎫		1 LVG		B1700
	Sgt G P Olley ⎭				B1681
26 June	2/Lt H G Reeves		1 Alb D		B1630
	Sgt G P Olley		1 Alb D		B1681
2 July	Lt L F Jenkin	1 C type			B1547
	Sgt W J Beadle		1 Alb D		B1700
7 July	Lt L F Jenkin		1 Alb D		B1547
	Lt C S T Lavers		1 Alb D		B3485
	2/Lt P F Fullard		1 Alb D		B1666
	2/Lt F M McLaren		1 Alb D		B1648
	Sgt W J Beadle		1 Alb D		B1675
11 July	2/Lt P F Fullard		2 Alb D		B1666
	Lt C S T Lavers		1 Alb D		B3485
12 July	Capt T F Hazell		1 Alb D		B3456
	Lt L F Jenkin		1 Alb D		B1547
	Capt T F Hazell ⎫				B3456
	Lt L F Jenkin ⎪				B1547
	2/Lt W W Rogers ⎬	2 Alb D			B3463
	2/Lt R S Davies ⎪				B1659
	2/Lt R E Money-Kyrle ⎭				B3484

Date	Pilot	Destroyed	OOC	Driven Down	Aircraft
13 July	Lt L F Jenkin	1 DFW			B1547
	2/Lt P F Fullard		1 Alb D		B1666
16 July	Capt W C Campbell	2 Alb D			B3463
	Capt W C Campbell		1 Alb D		B3463
	Sgt G P Olley	1 Alb D			B1681
	Lt L F Jenkin	1 Alb D			B1547
17 July	2/Lt P F Fullard		1 D type		B3459
21 July	Capt W C Campbell	1 KB			B3474
	Capt W C Campbell		1 Alb D		B3474
	2/Lt W S Mansell		1 Alb D		A6680
22 July	Capt T F Hazell	1 C type			B3455
	Capt P F Fullard	1 Alb D			B3459
	Capt P F Fullard		1 Alb D		B3459
	Capt W C Campbell	1 KB			B3474
	Lt L F Jenkin	2 Alb D			B1547
	Capt T F Hazell	1 Alb D			B1547
	Capt T F Hazell		1 Alb D		B1547
	2/Lt R A Birkbeck		1 Alb D		B1582
24 July	Capt W C Campbell		1 Alb D		B3474
28 July	Capt P F Fullard	1 Alb C			B3459
	Lt L F Jenkin	1 Alb D			B1547
	Lt L F Jenkin	1 C type			B1547
	Capt W C Campbell	2 KB			B3474
	2/Lt W V T Rooper		1 Alb D		B1675
31 July	2/Lt H G Reeves	1 Alb D			B1547
	Capt P F Fullard	1 KB			B3459
9 Aug	Capt P F Fullard ⎫	1 C type			B3459
	2/Lt W V T Rooper ⎭				B1675
	Capt P F Fullard		1 Alb D		B3459
	2/Lt F M McLaren		1 Alb D		B1692
10 Aug	Capt T F Hazell		1 Alb D		B3455
	2/Lt R A Birkbeck		1 Alb D		B1582
	Capt P F Fullard	1 C type			B3459
12 Aug	Capt P F Fullard		1 C type		B3459
	Sgt G P Olley		1 C type		B1681
13 Aug	Capt T F Hazell	1 C type			B3455
	Capt T F Hazell ⎫		1 C type		B3455
	2/Lt H G Reeves ⎭				B1672
14 Aug	Capt T F Hazell	1 Alb D			B3455
	Capt T F Hazell		1 Alb D		B3455
	Lt C S T Lavers		1 Alb D		B1692
	2/Lt H G Reeves		1 Alb D		B3558
15 Aug	Capt P F Fullard	1 Alb D			B3459
	Capt P F Fullard		1 Alb D		B3459
16 Aug	Capt P F Fullard	2 Alb D			B3459
	2/Lt R A Birkbeck		1 Alb D		B1582
	Capt P F Fullard		1 Alb D		B3459
	Capt T F Hazell		1 Alb D		B3455
17 Aug	Lt C S T Lavers		1 DFW		B1692
19 Aug	Capt P F Fullard	1 Alb D			B3459
21 Aug	Capt P F Fullard		1 Alb D		B3459
	2/Lt H G Reeves		1 Alb D		B1672
	2/Lt W S Mansell		1 Alb D		B3558
22 Aug	Capt P F Fullard	1 C type			B3459
3 Sept	2/Lt W S Mansell	1 Alb D			B3558
4 Sept	Capt L F Jenkin		1 C type		B3474
9 Sept	2/Lt H G Reeves		1 C type		B1672
	2/Lt W S Mansell		1 Alb D		B3648
11 Sept	Capt L F Jenkin		1 Alb D		B3635
	Lt W V T Rooper		1 Alb D		B3632
	2/Lt H G Reeves		1 Alb D		B3630
	Sgt G P Olley		1 Alb D		B3628
19 Sept	Capt W V T Rooper	1 Alb D			B6767
20 Sept	2/Lt L Cummings	1 C type			B3631
21 Sept	Sgt G P Olley	1 C type			B3628
23 Sept	2/Lt P Wilson	1 Alb D			B3629
25 Sept	Capt W V T Rooper		1 Alb D		B6767
1 Oct	2/Lt L Cummings ⎫	1 C type			B6790
	2/Lt L Cummings ⎬	1 C type			B6790
	Capt W V T Rooper ⎭				B6767
	2/Lt R A Birkbeck				B6753
	2/Lt F G Baker ⎫				B3630
2 Oct	2/Lt G B Moore ⎬				B1508
	2/Lt H J Hamilton ⎪		1 C type		B6774
	2/Lt R C Sotham ⎭				B3589
	Sgt G P Olley		1 C type		B3628

Date	Pilot	Destroyed	OOC	Driven Down	Aircraft
5 Oct	Capt W V T Rooper	1 Alb D			B6767
	Sgt G P Olley	1 C type			B6768
	Capt P F Fullard	1 C type			B6789
	2/Lt G B Moore	1 C type			B1508
	2/Lt J Baalman		1 C type		B3627
7 Oct	Capt P F Fullard		1 C type		B6789
	2/Lt M A Peacock		1 Alb D		B3577
	2/Lt W W Rogers		1 Alb D		B6754
	2/Lt G B Moore		1 Alb D		B1508
8 Oct	Capt P F Fullard		1 C type		B6789
	2/Lt G B Moore		1 Alb D		B1508
	2/Lt W W Rogers		1 Alb D		B6754
	2/Lt P Wilson		1 Alb D		B6769
9 Oct	2/Lt W W Rogers		1 Alb D		B3629
	2/Lt G B Moore	1 Alb D			B1508
	2/Lt H G Reeves	1 Alb D			B6774
	2/Lt R A Birkbeck	1 Alb D			B6753
	2/Lt R A Birkbeck		1 Alb D		B6753
	2/Lt F G Baker		1 Alb D		B3630
12 Oct	2/Lt R A Birkbeck	1 C type			B6753
14 Oct	Capt P F Fullard		1 C type		B6789
	Sgt G P Olley		1 C type		B3628
15 Oct	2/Lt H G Reeves		1 C type		B6774
17 Oct	Capt P F Fullard	1 C type			B6789
	Capt P F Fullard		1 C type		B6789
	Capt P F Fullard		1 Alb D		B6789
	2/Lt H G Reeves		1 Alb D		B6774
20 Oct	2/Lt W W Rogers		1 Alb D		B3629
24 Oct	Capt P F Fullard		1 C type		B6789
27 Oct	Capt P F Fullard	2 C type			B6789
30 Oct	Capt P F Fullard	1 Alb D			B6789
31 Oct	2/Lt R A Birkbeck	1 C type			B6753
9 Nov	2/Lt P G Kelsey		1 C type		B6754
	2/Lt R A Birkbeck		1 C type		B6825
15 Nov	Capt P F Fullard	2 Alb D			B6789
	2/Lt L Cummings		1 Alb D		B6815
18 Nov	Capt H G Reeves		1 C type		B6774
29 Nov	Capt W W Rogers		1 C type		B6789
12 Dec	Capt W W Rogers	1 Gotha			B6825
17 Dec	Capt W W Rogers		1 Alb D		B6789
	2/Lt G B Moore		1 Alb D		B3629
	2/Lt P G Kelsey	1 Alb D			B6818
18 Dec	Capt W W Rogers		1 Alb D		B6789
	2/Lt W D Patrick	1 Alb D			B6830
1918					
4 Jan	2/Lt G B Moore	1 Alb D			B3629
16 Feb	2/Lt P J Clayson	1 Alb D			B4881
28 Feb	Capt W D Patrick				B641
	Lt F P Magoun		1 Alb D		A8904
	2/Lt P J Clayson		1 Alb D		A8930
9 Mar	Capt H J Hamilton	1 KB			B32
10 Mar	2/Lt F P Magoun		1 KB		C5306
	Capt G B Moore				B34
	2/Lt A E Sweeting		1 KB		A8932
	2/Lt H A Rigby				B511
	2/Lt J C Bateman		1 KB		B641
11 Mar	Capt H J Hamilton				B32
	2/Lt P J Clayson		1 C type		A8908
12 Mar	2/Lt A McN Denovan		1 C type		B34
13 Mar	Capt W D Patrick				B641
	Capt G B Moore				B511
	Capt H J Hamilton	1 Pfalz			B32
	2/Lt A Hollis				B520
	Lt H A Rigby				C9624
15 Mar	Capt W D Patrick	1 Alb D			B520
	2/Lt F P Magoun				A8904
	2/Lt M W Mawbey	1 DFW			B632
26 Mar	Lt H A Rigby	1 Alb D			B4851
27 Mar	2/Lt P J Clayson	1 Alb D			A8908
28 Mar	Capt G B Moore	1 LVG			C1083
11 Apr	Capt W L Harrison	1 Pfalz			C6405
	Lt F R Knapp	1 Pfalz			B532
21 Apr	Capt C C Clark				B8410
	Lt K C Mills	1 Pfalz			C5374
23 Apr	Capt C C Clark	1 Triplane			B8410
25 Apr	Lt K C Mills	1 Triplane			C5374
	Capt C C Clark		1 Pfalz		B8410

Date	Pilot	Destroyed	OOC	Driven Down	Aircraft
29 Apr	Capt H A Rigby		1 Alb C		C1113
	Capt C C Clark	1 Pfalz			B8410
2 May	Capt H A Rigby	1 Pfalz			C1113
	Lt P J Clayson		1 Pfalz		C1095
7 May	Lt K C Mills	1 C type			C1849
14 May	Capt P J Clayson	1 Alb D			C1102
21 May	Lt E M Forsyth	1 C type			B733
27 May	Lt E F S Kelly	1 LVG			B8508
	Capt P J Clayson	1 Alb D			C1114
28 May	Capt K S Henderson				C113
	Lt D Knight				C6479
	Capt P J Clayson				C1849
	Lt H A Kullberg	1 DFW			B8254
	Lt E E Owen				B8512
	Lt A F Scroggs				C6416
29 May	Capt P J Clayson				C1114
	Lt A F Scroggs	1 C type			C6416
	Patrol	1 Pfalz			
2 Jun	Capt P J Clayson	1 Alb D			C1114
6 Jun	Capt P J Clayson	1 Pfalz			C1114
	Capt P J Clayson	1 Alb D			C1114
	Lt E E Owen	1 Pfalz			B8512
	Lt C B Henderson	1 D type			C1106
9 Jun	C Flight	1 Triplane			
13 Jun	Capt P J Clayson	1 Pfalz			C1114
15 Jun	Capt P J Clayson	1 KB			C1114
27 Jun	Capt P J Clayson				C1114
	Lt D Knight	1 LVG			C1894
	Lt H A Kullberg				C1835
30 Jun	Capt P J Clayson	1 Fokker			C1114
1 Jul	Lt J C Bateman				C1835
	Lt H A Kullberg	1 C type			B8254
	Lt W A Smart				C1092
2 Jul	Capt P J Clayson	1 C type			C1114
9 Jul	Lt H A Kullberg	1 Fokker			C1835
29 Jul	Lt H A Kullberg	1 Alb C			C1835
8 Aug	Lt E E Owen	1 Alb D			C8846
	Lt C G Pegg	1 D type			C8841
9 Aug	Lt H A Kullberg	1 Fokker			C1835
22 Aug	Lt D Knight	1 Fokker			C1812
	Lt C G Pegg	1 LVG			C8841
30 Aug	Lt H A Kullberg	2 Fokkers			B8427
3 Sep	Lt H A Kullberg	1 Fokker			B8427
15 Sep	Capt W Pallister	1 D type			C8846
	Lt C G Pegg	1 Fokker			C8841
	Lt D E Cameron	1 Pfalz			F6429
16 Sep	Lt H A Kullberg	1 Fokker			B8427
27 Sep	Lt B H Moody	1 Fokker			B8501
28 Oct	Lt D E Cameron				H7257
	Lt B H Moody	1 Fokker			B8501
29 Oct	Lt W A Smart	1 Fokker			D6973
	Capt R T C Hoidge	1 Fokker			E5799

Appendix Six

SQUADRON COMBAT VICTORIES WWII

Date	Pilot	Destroyed	Probable	Damaged	Aircraft
1939					
30 Oct	PO P W O Mould	1 Do17P			L1842
23 Nov	Sgt F J Soper ⎫				L1681
	F/O C D Palmer ⎬	1 Do17P			L1925
	F/O J I Kilmartin ⎭				L1971
23 Nov	S/L P J H Halahan ⎫	1 Do17			L1905
	F/O M H Brown ⎭				L1971
23 Nov	F/L G H F Plinston ⎫	1 He111K			L1960
	F/Sgt A V Clowes ⎭				L1842
1940					
22 Feb	P/O P W O Mould			1 He111K	N2341?
2 Mar	Sgt F J Soper ⎫	1 Do17P			L1843
	P/O J S Mitchell ⎭				L1671
3 Mar	F/O M H Brown ⎫				L1843
	Sgt F J Soper ⎭	1 He111			L1679
29 Mar	F/O P H M Richey	1 Me109E			N2382
29 Mar	F/L P R Walker ⎫	1 Me110			N2382
	F/O W H Stratton ⎭				N2334
	F/Sgt A V Clowes	2 Me110s			L1969
1 Apr	P/O P W O Mould	1 Me110			L1681
	F/O L R Clisby	1 Me110			L1856
	F/L P P Hanks	1 Me110			N2381
2 Apr	F/O L R Clisby ⎫	1 Me109E			L1297
	F/O J I Kilmartin ⎭				L1685
20 Apr	F/L P R Walker	1 Me109E			N2383
	F/L P P Hanks	1 He111			N2380
	P/O P W O Mould	1 Me109E u/c			P2469
	F/Sgt F G Berry	1 Me109E u/c			P2541
	P/O B Drake	1 Me109E			L1590
	P/O B Drake	1 Me109E u/c			L1590
	F/O M H Brown	1 Me109E			P2678
	Sgt R A Albonico		1 Me109E		L1927
	F/O J I Kilmartin	1 Ju88			L1843
10 May	F/L P R Walker ⎫				N2382
	F/O J I Kilmartin ⎪				
	F/O P H M Richey ⎬	1 Do17			L1679
	F/O H M Brown ⎪				
	Sgt F J Soper ⎭				L1905
	F/L P P Hanks ⎫	1 He111			
	P/O R G Lewis ⎭				
	P/O B Drake	1 He111			
	P/O P W O Mould			1 Do17	
	P/O P W O Mould	1 He111			
	F/O M H Brown ⎫				
	F/L P P Hanks ⎬	1 Do17			N2380
	P/O R G Lewis ⎭				
	F/O L R Clisby	2 Do17s			
11 May	F/O P H M Richey	1 Do17 u/c			L1679
	F/O L R Clisby ⎫	1 Me110			N2380
	F/L P P Hanks ⎭				
	F/O L R Clisby ⎫	1 Me110			
	P/O C M Stavert ⎭				
	P/O P W O Mould ⎫				
	F/L P P Hanks ⎬	1 Me110			
	F/O L R Clisby ⎭				
	F/O P H M Richey	2 Me110s			L1685
	F/L P R Walker	1 Me110			
	F/L P R Walker	1 Me110 u/c			
	F/O M H Brown	2 Me110s			
	F/O J I Kilmartin	2 Me110s			
	Sgt F J Soper	2 Me110s			L1905
12 May	Sgt F J Soper	1 Me109E			L1686
	Sgt F J Soper ⎫	1 Me109E u/c			L1686
	F/O R L Lorimer ⎭				
	F/O J I Kilmartin	1 Me109E u/c			
	P/O P V Boot	1 Me109E			
	P/O R G Lewis	1 Me109E	1 Me109E		L1688
	S/L P J H Halahan	1 Me109E			L1671
	S/L P J H Halahan		1 Hs126		
	F/O L R Clisby	1 Me109E			

Date	Pilot	Destroyed	Probable	Damaged	Aircraft
	F/O L R Clisby	2 Hs126s			
	F/O L H Lorimer	1 Me109E			
13 May	P/O B Drake	1 Do17			
	P/O P W O Mould	1 He111			
	F/L P P Hanks ⎫				N2380
	F/O L H Lorimer ⎬	1 He111			L1681
	P/O G E Goodman ⎭				
	P/O P W O Mould	1 Me110			
	F/O L R Clisby	1 Me110			N2326
	F/O L R Clisby	2 He111			
14 May	F/L P P Hanks	2 Me110s			
	F/O P G H Matthews	1 Me110	1 Me110		
	F/O M H Brown	1 Me109E			
	F/O M H Brown	1 Ju87			
	F/O W H Stratton	1 Ju87			
	P/O P W O Mould ⎫	1 Me110			P2649
	P/O P V Boot ⎬				
	P/O P W O Mould	1 Me110			
	F/O J I Kilmartin	2 Ju87s			
	F/Sgt F J Soper	1 Me109E			
	F/Sgt A V Clowes	1 Me109E			
	F/Sgt A V Clowes	1 Ju87			
	F/O C D Palmer	1 Me109E			
15 May	P/O P W O Mould	1 Me110			
	F/O M H Brown	1 Me110			
	F/L P R Walker	1 Me110			L1681
	F/O W H Stratton	1 Me110			
	F/O P H M Richey	2 Me110s			L1943
	F/O J I Kilmartin	1 Me110			
	P/O R G Lewis	1 Me110			
	Sgt F J Soper	1 Me110			
	Sgt A V Clowes	1 Me110			
17 May	F/O J I Kilmartin	1 Me110			
	F/O J I Kilmartin	1 Me110 u/c			
	F/Sgt F J Soper	2 Me110s			L1905
	F/L P R Walker	1 Me1101		1 He111	
	F/O C D Palmer	1 Me110 u/c			P2820
	F/O M H Brown	1 Me110			
	F/O M H Brown	1 He111			
18 May	P/O C M Stavert	1 Do17			N2353
	P/O C M Stavert	1 He111			”
	F/O M H Brown	1 Hs126			
19 May	P/O P W O Mould			1 He111	
	F/Sgt F J Soper			1 He111	L1925
	F/Sgt F J Soper	2 He111s			L1925
	F/O P H M Richey	3 He111s			P2805
	F/O C D Palmer ⎫	1 He111			
	F/O P W O Mould ⎭				
	F/O M H Brown	1 He111			
	F/O M H Brown	1 He111 u/c			
	F/L P R Walker	1 He111 u/c			
	F/O W H Stratton		1 He111		
	P/O R G Lewis			1 He111	
	F/O J I Kilmartin			1 He111	
	P/O C M Stavert			1 He111	
21 May	F/O M H Brown	1 He111			
23 May	F/Sgt A V Clowes ⎫				
	F/L R H Warcup ⎬	1 He111 u/c			
	F/O D S Thom ⎭				
	P/O R H Dibnah	1 Do17			
1 Jun	F/L M H Brown	1 Me109E *			

(* originally only damaged but wreckage later found)

Date	Pilot	Destroyed	Probable	Damaged	Aircraft
5 Jun	F/L M H Brown		1 Do17		
	P/O H B L Hillcoat		1 He111		
	F/O G P H Matthews	1 He111			
	F/O G P H Matthews	1 He111 u/c			
	P/O P V Boot	1 He111			
	P/O P V Boot	1 Do17			
14 Jun	F/L M H Brown	1 Me109E			P3652
	F/L M H Brown	1 He111			P3652
	F/Sgt A V Clowes	1 He111			
17 Jun	P/O G E Goodman	1 He111			
	F/Sgt F G Berry	1 He111			

(dates unknown – F/Sgt Berry 4 others destroyed in France)

Date	Pilot	Destroyed	Probable	Damaged	Aircraft
18 Jun	F/O G P H Matthews ⎫	1 He111			
	? ⎭				

Date	Pilot	Destroyed	Probable	Damaged	Aircraft
19 Jul	S/L D A Pemberton				P2951
	F/O G P H Matthews			1 He111*	P3042
	P/O D O M Browne				P3471
	(*He111 finished off by 43 Squadron)				
25 Jul	P/O G E Goodman	1 Me109E			P2686
	F/O H N E Salmon			1 Me109E	P3684
31 Jul	F/O G P H Matthews				P3042
	P/O J A Davey			1 Do17	P3172
	Sgt H J Merchant				P3047
11 Aug	F/L M H Brown	1 Me110			P3047
	P/O C E C Chetham	1 Me110			P2548
	P/O G E Goodman				P2686
	P/O D O M Browne	1 Me110			R4075
15 Aug	F/O G P H Matthews		1 Ju88		P2980
	P/O H J Mann		1 Me109		EP3395
	P/O J F Elkington		1 Me109		EP3678
16 Aug	S/L D A Pemberton	1 He111			P2751
	F/Sgt A V Clowes	1 He111			P3169
	F/Sgt A V Clowes	1 Ju88			P3169
	F/O G E Goodman	1 He111*			P2686
	(* EA attacked by Spitfires and it crashed, although Goodman did not agree they hit it)				
	F/O G P H Matthews	1 Me110			P3042
	F/Sgt F G Berry	1 He111			P3276?
	F/O H N E Salmon		1 Me110		P3678
	P/O C M Stavert		1 He111		P3782
18 Aug	S/L D A Pemberton	1 Me109E			V7301
	F/O H B L Hillcoat				
	P/O G E Goodman	1 Do17			P3396
	P/O C M Stavert				
	P/O G E Goodman	1 Me110			P3678
28 Aug	Squadron	2 Do215s			
30 Aug	F/Sgt A V Clowes			1 Me110	P3395
	F/Sgt A V Clowes			1 He111	P3395
	F/O G P H Matthews			1 He111 *	P3042
	(* finished off by 56 Squadron)				
	Sgt H J Merchant		1 He111		V7375
	P/O N P W Hancock		1 He111		P3390
	P/O C N Birch			1 He111	V7376
	P/O H J Mann			2 Me110s	V7302
31 Aug	F/Sgt A V Clowes		2 Do17s		P3395
	F/Sgt A V Clowes		1 Me110		P3395
	P/O P V Boot		1 Me110		V7258
	Sgt H J Merchant	1 Me110		1 Me110	V7375
	S/L D A Pemberton			1 Ju88	P2751
	P/O R H Dibnah			1 Me110	P2548
	P/O H J Mann			1 Me110	V7302
1 Sep	P/O P V Boot	1 Me109E			P3169
	F/O H B L Hillcoat	1 Me109E			P3044
	P/O C N Birch	1 Me109E			V7376
	P/O C E C Chetham	1 Me109E			P2548
	F/O H B L Hillcoat		1 Me109E		P3044
	P/O C E C Chetham			1 Me109E	P2548
6 Sep	F/L M H Brown			1 Ju88	L1934
	P/O C M Stavert	1 Ju88			P3042
	P/O R H Dibnah	1 Me110			P3169
	P/O G E Goodman	1 Me110			P2686
	P/O C M Stavert			1 He111	P3042
7 Sep	P/O A V Clowes	1 Me110			P3395
	F/L J B Holderness	1 Do215			V7301
	F/L J F F Finnis			1 Do215	P3406
	P/O M G Homer			1 Do215	V7256
8 Oct	P/O G E Goodman			1 Ju88	V7372
9 Oct	P/O J F Elkington		1 Ju88		P3318
	Sgt M P Davies				
24 Oct	F/L M H Brown				V7379
	P/O A V Clowes	1 Do17			P3595
	P/O A Kershaw				P3169
27 Oct	P/O G E Goodman		1 Do17		P3318
29 Oct	Sgt W T Page				P3318
	P/O J C E Robinson	1 Do17			P2877
	Sgt V Jicha				P2618
30 Oct	F/O R G Lewis	1 Ju88			P3229
	Sgt V Jicha				P5199
8 Nov	2/Lt J-F Demozay			1 Ju88	?
1941					
2 Feb	Sgt K M Kuttelwascher		1 Me109E		W9151
	P/O N P W Hancock			1 Me109E	P3396

Date	Pilot	Destroyed	Probable	Damaged	Aircraft
8 Feb	S/L M H Brown			1 Me109E	V6933
24 Mar	2/Lt J-F Demozay	1 Me109E			Z2484
8 Apr	Sgt K M Kuttelwascher	1 Me109E			Z2464
21 Apr	F/O J C E Robinson			1 Me109E	Z3072
	Sgt J Prihoda		1 Me109E		Z2909
28 Apr	Sgt J Prihoda	1 Me109E			Z2690
10/11 May	S/L R E P Brooker	1 He111			Z2625
	Lt J-F Demozay	1 He111			Z2909
	Sgt J D Dygryn-Ligoticky	1 He111			Z2687
	Sgt B Kratkoruky			1 bomber	Z2490?
	Sgt J D Drygryn-Ligoticky	1 He111			Z2687
	F/L K C Jackman	1 He111			Z3240
	P/O J C E Robinson		1 He111		Z2457
	P/O W Raymond	1 bomber			Z2482
	Sgt J D Drygryn-Ligoticky	1 Ju88			Z2687
16 May	Sgt J D Drygryn-Ligoticky	1 Me109			Z2628
21 May	P/O W Raymond			1 Me109F	Z2687
	F/O A Volebnovsky			1 Me109F	Z3241
	Sgt J D Drygryn-Ligoticky			1 Me109F	Z2628
	Sgt K M Kuttelwascher	1 Me109F			Z3160
	Sgt B Kratkoruky	1 Me109F			Z3165
	Sgt A Nasswetter			1 Me109F	Z2390
25 May	Lt J-F Demozay	1 Me110			Z3241
16 Jun	F/L C F Gray				Z3072
	P/O R N G Allen				Z3504
	P/O Kopecky	1 He59			Z3241
	P/O Liska				Z3240
	Sgt J Novak				Z3461
	Sgt J Prihoda	1 Me109F			Z3449
17 Jun	W/O J D Drygryn-Ligoticky	1 Me109E			Z3263
21 Jun	S/L R E P Brooker	1 Me109F			Z3448
	P/O B G Collyns	1 Me109F			Z3165
	Sgt J Prihoda		1 Me109F	1 Me109F	Z3251
	Sgt Stefan			1 Me109F	Z3497
	P/O Kopecky		1 Me109F		Z2909
	Sgt B Kratkoruky	1 Me109F			?
	P/O R Marcinkus	1 Me109F			Z3486
	Sgt Plasil		1 Me109F		Z3489
27 Jun	F/Sgt K M Kuttelwascher	1 Me109F			Z3449
22 Aug	F/L C F Gray	1 Me109 *			P6463

(* Flying Op with 41 Squadron, but possibly in R7223)

1942					
2 Apr	F/L K M Kuttelwascher	1 Ju881		Ju88	BE581
16 Apr	F/L K M Kuttelwascher	1 Do217?			BE581
26 Apr	S/L J A F MacLachlan	1 Do217		1 Do217	BE215
27 Apr	F/L K M Kuttelwascher	1 Do217		1 Ju88	BE581
1 May	F/L K M Kuttelwascher	1 Do217			BE581
	F/L K M Kuttelwascher	1 He111			BE581
4 May	S/L J A F MacLachlan	1 Do217			BD983
	S/L J A F MacLachlan	1 He111			BD983
	F/L K M Kuttelwascher	3 He111s			BE581
31 May	W/O G Scott			1 Ju88	BN232
1 Jun	F/Sgt G S M Pearson	1 Ju88C-4			BD872
2 Jun	P/O H Connolly			1 Ju88	BD946
	F/Sgt G C English	1 Do217			BD770
3 Jun	F/L K M Kuttelwascher	1 Do217			BE581
4 Jun	S/L J A F MacLachlan	2 Do217s		2 Do217s	BD983
	F/L K M Kuttelwascher	1 He111		1 Do217	BE581
	F/L K M Kuttelwascher	1 Do217			BE581
22 Jun	F/L K M Kuttelwascher	1 Ju88		1 Ju88	BE581
	F/Sgt G S M Pearson		1 bomber		BE150
29 Jun	F/L K M Kuttelwascher	1 Do217			BE581
2 Jul	F/L K M Kuttelwascher	2 Do217s		1 Do217	BE581
	Sgt J R Campbell			1 Do217	BD983
	F/Sgt G S M Pearson			1 Do217	BE150
6 Sep	P/O D P Perrin	1 Me210			R7922
	P/O T G Bridges	1 Me210			R7923

1943					
13 Mar	F/L L S B Scott	1 FW190			DN585
	Sgt R W Hornell	1 FW190			R7922
9 Apr	Sgt R W Hornell	1 FW190			R7919
23 May	F/Sgt W H Ramsey	1 FW190			R8752
16 Jun	F/O S P Dennis RAAF			1 FW190	DN585
21 Oct	F/O J W Wiley	1 FW190 (234th)			JP961
	F/Sgt J D Fairbairn				JP795

Date	Pilot	Destroyed	Probable	Damaged	Aircraft
1Nov	P/O R W Hornall			1 Me109F	EJ983
1944					
27 Jun	F/O R Bridgeman ⎫				MK997?
	F/Sgt K C Weller ⎬	1 V1			'L'
	F/Sgt I Hastings ⎭				?
	F/O W J Batchelor	1 V1			?
28 Jun	F/O D McIntosh	1 V1			MK901
	F/O E G Hutchin	1 V1			MJ422
	F/Sgt I Hastings	1 V1			MK846
	F/L T D Williams	1 V1			ML118
	F/O E N W Marsh	1 V1			MK988
30 Jun	F/O N E Brown	1 V1			MK644
	F/O D R Wallace	1 V1			MJ481
	F/O N E Brown	1 V1			MK644
	P/O K R Foskett	1 V1			MK986
	F/O H L Stuart	1 V1			NH246
	W/O J W McKenzie	1 V1(sh)			MK997
4 Jul	F/O D H Davy	1 V1			MK846
	F/L T D Williams ⎫	1 V1			
	F/O D R Wallace ⎭				
	F/O D McIntosh ⎫	1 V1			MK644
	F/Sgt K Weller ⎭				ML258?
5 Jul	F/L P W Stewart	1 V1			NH253?
	F/Sgt I Hastings	1 V1			MK997
	W/C R P R Powell*	2 V1s			MK846
	(* flying a 1 Squadron Spitfire)				
7 Jul	F/L H L Stuart	1 V1			NH253
	F/Sgt H J Vessie	1 V1			MK987
	F/O E N W Marsh	1 V1			MK986?
10 Jul	F/O T Wyllie	1 V1			MK867
	F/Sgt G Tate	1 V1			MK744
11 Jul	F/S I Hastings	2 V1s			NH466
	F/O F W Town	1 V1			MK726
	F/Sgt G Tate	1 V1			NH246
14 Jul	F/L P W Stewart	1 V1			NH253
	F/O E N W Marsh	1 V1			MK423
15 Jul	F/Sgt H J Vessie	1 V1			MJ422
16 Jul	F/L T D Williams	1 V1			ML423
22 Jul	F/O J O Dalley	1 V1			MJ422
	F/O D H Davy	1 V1			ML117
23 Jul	F/Sgt H J Vessie	1 V1			MJ481
	F/O D H Davy	1 V1			MK986
	F/O D H Davy	2 V1s			ML423
24 Jul	F/O F W Town	1 V1			MK926
	F/O K R Foskett	1 V1			MK986
26 Jul	F/L I P Maskill	1 V1			NH466
	F/O D H Davy	1 V1			ML117
	F/O D H Davy ⎫				ML117
	F/Sgt G Tate ⎭	1 V1			MK987
28 Jul	F/O J O Dalley	1 V1			MK987
	F/O F W Town	1 V1			MK919
	F/O F W Town	1 V1 sh			MK919
3 Aug	F/O D R Wallace	1 V1			MK919
4 Aug	F/O W J Batchelor	1 V1			MJ481
9 Aug	F/L J J Jarman	1 V1			MK659

Appendix Seven

AIRCRAFT SERIALS

Boxkite
640   SOS 29 Sep 1914.
718   Erected 7 Nov 1914.

Blériot
297   Taken on charge 7 Oct 1914.
298   From 6 Sq 15 Sep 1914.
323   Taken on charge 7 Oct 1914.
630   From 6 Sq 15 Sep 1914;to Netheravon 4 Dec 1914, back 21 Jan 1915.
635   From 6 Sq 29 Sep 1914.
706   From RAS 31 Oct 1914.
723   SOC and reduced to spares 10 Feb 1915.
732   From AP 27 Nov 1914.

Henri Farman
367   Taken on charge 14 Oct 1914.
653   From 6 Sq 22 Sep 1914; to 6 Sq 10 Oct 1914.
680   From AID 1 Oct 1914; to 6 Sq 10 Oct 1914.
689   Taken on charge 16 Oct 1914; SOC and reduced to spares 28 Oct 1914.

Maurice Farman
478   To Netheravon 5 Nov 1914.
500   Taken on charge 26 Oct 1914.

Martinsyde
482   Taken on charge 7 Oct 1914.
629   Taken on charge 7 Oct 1914.
696   Taken on charge 12 Oct 1914; to CFS 23 Feb 1915.
702   Taken on charge 26 Oct 1914; to CFS 23 Feb 1915.
710   To 12 Sq 23 Feb 1915.
717   To 12 Sq 23 Feb 1915.
724   Taken on charge and to A Flt 10 Nov 1914.
730   SOS 22 Feb 1915.
748   From AP 15 Mar 1915; to AP 25 Jul 1915.

BE8
399   From England 7 Mar 1915; to AP 27 Mar 1915.
639   From AP 22 Nov 1914.
645   W/O and reduced to spares 1 Mar 1915.
656   Taken on charge 12 Oct 1914; W/O and reduced to spares 1 Mar 1915.
663   Taken on charge 14 Oct 1914; to 12 Sq 1 Mar 1915.
670   Taken on charge 20 Oct 1914; to AP 14 Nov 1914.
693   To 12 Sq 1 Mar 1915.
727   To 12 Sq 1 Mar 1915.
740   From St Omer by Lt V A Barrington-Kennet 3 Jun 1915; to 8 Sq 8 Jun 1915.
2130   From England 7 Mar 1915; to 8 Sq by Lt E O Grenfell 9 Jun 1915.
2131   From England 7 Mar 1915; SOC 10 May 1915.
2132   From England 7 Mar 1915, Lt O M Moullin MIA 12 Mar 1915.

BE2a
267   Taken on charge 14 Oct 1914.

Vickers Boxkite
639   SOC and reduced to spares 16 Oct 1914.
641   SOC and reduced to spares 14 Oct 1914.
642   SOC and reduced to spares 16 Oct 1914.
657   SOC and reduced to spares 16 Oct 1914.

Sopwith Tabloid
326   To CFS 8 Dec 1914.

Avro
430   From CFS 19 Jan 1914; to 12 Sq 23 Feb 1915.
715   To overseas by Lt A B Ford 9 Nov 1914.
752   From UK 7 Mar 1915; to AP 11 Aug 1915.
753   From England 7 Mar 1915; SOC 23 Mar 1915.
754   From England 7 Mar 1915; SOC 24 Apr 1915.
755   From England 7 Mar 1915; to 5 Sq 10 Mar 1915.
756   From England 21 Mar 1915; to 1AP 21 Apr 1915.
757   From England 14 Mar 1915; SOC 15 Apr 1915.
758   From St Omer by Lt L Parker 9 Jun 1915; to AP 12 Oct 1915.
769   From AP 20 May 1915; to AP 12 Oct 1915.
773   From AP 29 May 1915; to AP 2 Oct 1915.
774   From 1 AP 22 May 1915; SOC 9 Jun 1915.
784   From St Omer by Lt E P Plenty 20 Sep 1915; to AP 12 Oct 1915.
1005   From England 7 Mar 1915; rtd 23 Mar 1915.

1006	From England 7 Mar 1915; to 5 Sq 10 Mar 1915.
1007	From England 7 Mar 1915.
1008	From England 7 Mar 1915.
2857	From England 7 Mar 1915, rtd 23 Mar 1915.
2858	From England 7 Mar 1915; to 5 Sq 10 Mar 1915; rtd AP 12 Oct 1915.
2859	From England 7 Mar 1915; to AP wrecked 16 Jul 1915.
2860	From England 7 Mar 1915; SOC 5 Apr 1915.
4223	From England 24 May 1915; to AP 20 Sep 1915.

Caudron

1884	From Paris 27 Mar 1915; SOC 9 Sep 1915.
1885	From Paris 27 Mar 1915; SOC 2 Oct 1915.
1891	From Paris 10 Apr 1915; to AP wrecked 20 Jul 1915.
1895	From Paris 14 Apr 1915; SOC wrecked 31 May 1915.

Bristol Scout

1601	From St Omer by Lt E O Grenfell 13 Sep1915; to AP19 Sep 1915.
1602	From England 15 May 1915; to AP wrecked 9 Aug 1915.
4672	From 1 AP 1 Oct 1915; to 1 AP 26 Oct 1915.

Morane

1855	From 3 Sq 10 Apr 1915; to AP 3 Aug 1915.
1892	Taken on charge 18 Apr 1915; SOC 2 May 1915.
1894	From AP 14 Apr 1915; to AP 7 Oct 1915.
1897	From AP 23 Apr 1915; to AP 10 Sep 1915.
5006	From AP 10 May 1915; to AP 13 Nov 1915.
5046	From AP 12 Aug 1915; to AP 5 Nov 1915.
5048	From Paris 8 Aug 1915; to AP 5 Nov 1915.
5051	From AP 21 Aug 1915; to 1 AD 28 Dec 1915.
5052	From AP 22 Aug 1915; to 1 AD 27 Dec 1915.
5056	From AP by E L Gossage 5 Sep 1915; to 1 AD dismantled 23 Dec 1915.
5060	From St Omer by Lt B Brown 17 Sep 1915; wrecked 15 Dec1915.
5068	From 1 AD 8 Jan 1916; crshd by Lt W V Strugnell 19 Mar 1916; to 1 AD 22 Sep 1916.
5069	From 3 AP 8 Oct 1915; Lt R P Turner KIA 9 Mar 1916.
5076	From AP 12 Oct 1915; to 1 AD 2 Feb 1916.
5080	From AP 7 Oct 1915; wrecked 18 Nov 1915.
5082	From AP 12 Oct 1915; to St Omer by Lt A M Walters 6 May 1916.
5085	From AP 12 Oct 1915; to 1 AD dismantled 18 Mar 1916.
5086	From AP 12 Oct 1915; SOC wrecked 10 Nov 1915.
5089	From AP 5 Nov 1915; to St Omer by Lt J D Latta 6 May 1916.
5090	From AP 14 Nov 1915; to 1 AD 1 Jan 1916.
5091	From AP 5 Nov 1915; Lt J G McEwan and Lt F Adams MIA 10 Jan 1916.
5100	From AP 14 Nov 1915; Lt R Barton and Lt E S Wilkinson KIA 12 Jan 1916.
5101	From AP 16 Nov 1915; crashed by Lt W G Pender 25 Mar 1916.
5105	From St Omer by Lt W Watts 14 Dec 1915; Lt D C Cleaver KIAcc 29 Dec 1915.
5107	From 1 AD 28 Dec 1915; Capt R A Saunders KIA 14 Mar 1916.
5108	From 1 AD 28 Dec 1915; crshd by Lt W G Pender and Lt G B Crole 13 Mar 1916.
5109	From 1 AD 28 Dec 1915; crashed on take-off Lt E M Smith 21 Jun 1916.
5113	From St Omer 2 Jan 1916, Lt W Watts and Lt C O Hayward KIA 17 Jan 1916.
5115	From 1 AD 8 Jan 1916; to St Omer by Lt W V Strugnell 9 Mar 1916.
5118	From 1 AD 16 Jan 1916; to St Omer by Maj G F Pretyman 30 Apr 1916.
5119	From 1 AD 15 Jan 1916; to St Omer by Lt E L M L Gower 30 May 1916.
5124	From St Omer 19 Jan 1916; to 1 AD after crash landing 24 May 1916.
5126	Taken on charge 6 Jan 1916; Capt J D G Sanders killed on test fight 5 Jan 1916.
5130	To St Omer by Lt W V Strugnell 5 Feb 1916.
5132	From 1 AD 19 Mar 1916; L/Col D S Lewis and Capt A W Gale KIA 10 Apr 1916.
5134	From St Omer by Lt W V Strugnell 9 Apr 1916; to 1 AD damaged 20 May 1916.
5138	From 1 AD 14 Apr 1916; to 1 AD by Capt T A Oliver 5 Nov 1916.
5139	From St Omer 6 May 1916; crshd landing by Lt L B Williams 8 Aug 1916.
5142	From St Omer 5 Feb 1916; Lt S E Parker and Lt D Carruthers crash 9 Apr 1916.
5144	From St Omer 9 Mar 1916,crashed by Lt W H Dore 5 May 1916.
5145	From 1 AD 1 Apr 1916; crashed by Lt C E Foggin 8 Apr 1916.
5147	From 1 AD 24 May 1916; to 1 AD worn out after 123 flying hours 15 Dec 1916.
5150	From St Omer 7 Jun 1916; crashed by Maj G F Pretyman 11 Aug 1916.
5151	From 1 AD 7 Jun 1916; crashed on take-off Lt G D F Keddie 9 Jul 1916.
5152	From St Omer by Lt J D Latta 22 May 1916; crashed on take off 16 Aug 1916.
5154	From St Omer by E L M L Gower 30 May 1916; SOC 18 Jul 1916.
5155	From St Omer 24 Jun 1916; crashed on landing by Lt E M Smith 26 Jun 1916.
5157	From 1 AD 15 Mar 1916; crashed on landing by Lt A W Walters 17 Jun 1916.
5159	From St Omer 6 May 1916; to 1 AD after engine failure 24 May 1916.
5160	From 1 AD 18 Mar 1916; to 1 AD 29 Jun 1916.
5163	From St Omer 10 Apr 1916; to 1 AD damaged by AA fire19 May 1916.
5164	From St Omer 6 May 1916; Capt M McB Bell-Irving WIA; to 1 AD 19 Jun 1916.
5166	From St Omer 19 May 1916; to 1 AD after crash landing 24 May 1916.
5168	From 1 AD 24 May 1916; crashed landing by Lt W H Dore 1 Aug 1916.
5169	From 1 AD 2 Aug 1916; crashed landing 28 Nov 1916.
5170	From St Omer by Lt S E Parker 24 May 1916; crashed 28 Jul 1916.
5174	From 1 AD 19 Jul 1916; to 1 AD 23 Jan 1917.
5175	From 1 AD 22 Jul 1916; Capt T A Tillard killed in accident 6 Dec 1916.
5183	From St Omer 30 Apr 1916; to 1 AD after crash landing 2 Jun 1916.

5184	From 1 AD 2 Jun 1916; crashed on landing by Lt C J Q Brand 10 Nov 1916.
5186	From 1 AD 18 Aug 1916; to 1 AD in need of overhaul 15 Dec 1916.
5188	From 1 AD 9 Aug 1916; crashed on landing by Lt F G Garratt 5 Nov 1916.
A132	From 1 AD 2 Aug 1916; crashed on aerodrome by Lt D J Macdonald 5 Jan 1917.
A137	From 60 Sq 18 Aug 1916; Lt C M Kelly and Lt T G G Sturrock MIA 16 Oct 1916.
A138	From 1 AD 29 Jul 1916; wrecked on landing by Lt J A Slater 21 Sep 1916.
A151	From St Omer by Lt T A Oliver 19 Jun 1916; crashed landing 27 Jan 1917.
A152	From1 AD 10 Jul 1916; crashed on landing by Lt J B Fitzsimons 21 Jul 1916.
A153	From St Omer 28 Jun 1916; crashed on take off 8 Sep 1916.
A154	From 1 AD by Maj G F Pretyman 24 Jun 1916; to 46 Sq 4 Jan 1917.
A155	From St Omer 21 Jun 1916; crashed by Lt J B Fitzsimons 1 Aug 1916.
A157	From 1 AD 12 Aug 1916; crashed on landing by Lt T A Oliver 30 Sep 1916.
A158	From 1 AD 3 Oct 1916; crashed by Lt J A Slater 27 Dec 1916.
A159	From 1 AD 11 Sep 1916 by Capt B J W M Moore; to 1 AD 23 Jan 1917.
A163	From 1 AD by P M Le Gallais 12 Nov 1916.
A189	From 60 Sq 18 Aug 1916; crashed on landing by Lt G D F Keddie 10 Nov 1916.
A190	From 60 Sq 18 Aug 1916; to 1 AD 29 Jan 1917.
A226	To 1 AD 29 Jan 1917.
A227	To 1 AD 29 Jan 1917.
A228	From 1 AD by Lt W H Dore and A/M Scragg 6 Nov 1916; to 1 AD 4 Jan 1917.
A229	From 1 AD 18 Oct 1916 by B J W M Moore; to 1 AD 4 Jan 1917.
A242	From 1 AD by Lt C J Q Brand 12 Nov 1916; to 1 AD 29 Jan 1917.
A251	From 1 AD 7 Jan 1917; crashed on landing by Lt D J Macdonald 25 Jan 1917.
A291	From 1 AD by Lt T A Oliver 6 Nov 1916; to 46 Sq 4 Jan 1917.
A297	From 1 AD 11 Dec 1916; to 1 AD 23 Jan 1917.
A298	From 1 AD 4 Jan 1917; to 1 AD 23 Jan 1917.
A6601	From 1 AD 16 Dec 1916; to 1 AD 23 Jan 1917.
A6629	From 1 AD 16 Dec 1916; to 1 AD 23 Jan 1917.

Nieuport Two-Seater

A154	From St Omer by Maj G F Pretyman 24 Jun 1916; to 46 Sq 4 Jan 1917.
A156	From 1 AD 29 Jun 1916; to 46 Sq 4 Jan 1917.
A185	From 1 AD 28 Jul 1916; to 2 AD 11 Aug 1916.
A258	From 1 AD 22 Sep 1916 by Capt B J W M Moore; to 1 AD 4 Jan 1917.
A259	From 1 AD 23 Sep 1916; Lt C C Godwin and Lt P C Ellis KIA 17 Oct 1916.

Nieuport Scout

5171	From St Omer by Lt W V Strugnell 24 Mar 1916.
5172	From 1 AD 4 Jul 16; crashed on landing by Lt J D Latta 5 Aug 1916.
A116	From St Omer 23 Apr 1916; F/Sgt T F B Carlisle killed in accident 6 Jul 1916.
A118	From 2 AD 23 Apr 1916; crashed on landing by F/Sgt T F B Carlisle 1 Jun 1916.
A125	From St Omer by 24 Jun 1916; crashed on landing by Lt T A Oliver 6 Aug 1916.
A130	From St Omer 26 Apr 1916,crashed on landing by Lt T A Oliver 3 Jul 1916.
A131	From St Omer by Capt M B J W Moore 2 Jun 1916; to 2 AD on 24 Jun 1916.
A313	From 1 AD by Lt V W B Castle 4 Jan 1917,Lt A W Wood POW 22 Apr 1917.
A6603	From 1 AD 5 Jan 1917; crashed on landing by J C C Piggott 12 May 1917.
A6604	From 1 AD 5 Jan 1917; crashed by Lt V W B Castle after AA hit 13 Mar 1917.
A6605	From 1 AD by Capt A J Capel 4 Jan 1917; Lt R J Bevington POW 7 Apr 1917.
A6610	From 1 AD 29 Jan 1917; Lt J B Maudsley WIA and crashed 22 Jul 1917.
A6611	From 1 AD 5 Jan 1917; Lt R S Watt crashed on landing 14 Apr 1917.
A6613	1 Sq 29 Jan 1917 to 7 May 1917 and 13 Jul 1917 to 16 Jul 1917.
A6614	From 1 AD 4 Jan 1917; Lt B S Cole injured in crash 28 Jan 1917.
A6615	From 1 AD 23 Jan 1917; Lt H Welch KIA 28 Mar 1917.
A6616	From 1 AD 23 Jan 1917; crashed on take-off by Lt J R Anthony 23 Apr 1917.
A6617	From 1 AD by J M E Shepherd 23 Jan 1917; Lt A I Gilson KIA 17 Mar 1917.
A6618	1Sqn 23 Jan 1917; J F Henderson POW 10 Aug 1917.
A6619	From 1 AD 29 Jan 1917; crashed on landing by Lt L F Jenkin 26 May 1917.
A6620	From 1 AD 22 Aug 1917; to 2 AD by Maj A B Adams 7 Sep 1917.
A6621	From 1 AD by J A Slater 23 Jan 1917; crashed by Lt V G A Bush 14 Feb 1917.
A6622	From 1 AD 23 Jan 1917; Capt M E Shepherd KIA 15 Feb 1917.
A6623	From 1 AD 31 Jan 1917; Lt S McKercher seriously injured landing 23 Apr 1917.
A6624	From 1 ASD 29 Jan 1917; destroyed in mid air collision 25 Apr 1917.
A6644	From 1 AD by Lt V W B Castle 28 Jan 1917; Lt T H Lines POW 18 May 1917.
A6668	From 1 ASD 29 Jan 1917; crashed landing by Capt W C Campbell 4 May 1917.
B1541	From 1 AD 7 Aug 1917; crashed landing by Lt H S Preston 16 Aug 1917.
B1543	From 1 AD 18 Apr 1917; crashed landing by Lt H E Waters 20 May 1917.
B1546	From 1 AD 24 Apr 1917; crashed on landing by Lt C S T Lavers 4 Jun 1917.
B1547	From 1 AD 4 Jun 1917; to 1 AD, damaged in ground accident 10 Aug 1917.
B1550	From 1 AD by Lt J A Slater 24 Apr 1917; Lt W J Mussared POW 9 Jun 1917.
B1551	From 1 AD 25 Apr 1917; crashed on take-off by Lt H J Duncan 1 May 1917.
B1553	From 1 AD by Lt C Street 2 May 1917; crashed by Lt R S Lloyd 11 Jun 1917.
B1554	From 1 AD 22 Apr 1917; crashed on landing by Lt L F Jenkin 23 May 1917.
B1555	From 1 AD by Lt L Drummond 25 Apr 1917; Lt M G Cole KIA 18 May 1917.
B1559	From 1 AD 27 Apr 1917; damaged taxiing Lt J M S G Stevens 2 Jun 1917.
B1566	From 1 AD 15 Aug 1917; crashed on landing by Lt W S Mansell 17 Aug 1917.
B1582	From 1 AD by F W Honnet 11 Jun 1917; Lt C Pickstone KIA 3 Sep 1917.
B1613	From 1 AD by Capt T F Hazell 11 Aug 1917; Lt C A Moody KIA 21 Aug 1917.
B1630	From 1 AD 9 Jun 1917; crashed by Lt G A Wood in forced landing 26 Jul 1917.
B1632	From 1 AD by 28 Apr 1917; crashed landing by Lt T F Hazell 24 May 1917.
B1635	From 1 AD 4 May 1917; crashed by Lt G C Atkins 4 Jun 1917.

B1636	From 1 AD by Lt C Street 8 May 1917; Lt L Drummond KIA 18 May 1917.
B1638	From 1 AD by Lt P F Fullard 11 May 1917; Lt R S Lloyd KIA 18 Jun 1917.
B1639	From 1 AD by Lt F Sharpe 4 May 1917; Lt L M Mansbridge WIA 3 Jun 1917.
B1641	From 1 AD 6 May 1917; crashed by Lt E G Nuding 8 Jun 1917.
B1643	1 Sq 1 Jun 17 to 7 Jun 1917 and14 Jan 1918 to 19 Jan 1918.
B1644	From 1 AD by Lt W C Campbell 19 May 1917; Lt R S L Boote POW 8 Jun 1917.
B1645	From 1 AD 25 May 1917; crashed by Lt W V T Rooper 4 Jun 1917.
B1646	From 1 AD by Lt F Sharpe 28 May 1917; crashed by Lt W W Rogers 5 Jun 1917.
B1648	1 Sq 3 Jun 1917 ; Lt F M McLaren KIA on 12 Aug 1917.
B1649	From 1 AD by Lt P F Fullard 25 May 1917, Lt C Street KIA 26 Jun 1917.
B1656	From 1 AD by Lt E G Nuding 5 Jun 1917; Lt F D Slee POW 8 Jun 1917.
B1659	From 1 AD 22 Jun 1917; to 1 AD by Lt W W Rogers 7 Sep 1917.
B1662	From 1 AD 4 Jun 1917; crashed by Lt J H C Nixon 30 Jul 1917.
B1666	From 1 AD 4 Jul 1917; crashed in shell hole by Lt P F Fullard 13 Jul 1917.
B1672	From 1 AD by Sgt G P Olley 17 Jul 1917; Lt E D Tyzack KIA 15 Sep 1917.
B1675	From 1 AD 5 Jun 1917; crashed by Lt A W McLaughlin on landing 16 Oct 1917.
B1676	1 Sqn 8 Jun 1917 and 12 Jun 1917 to 11 Jul 1917 when crashed on landing.
B1680	From 1 AD by Capt F W Honnet 9 Jun 1917; Lt G C Atkins POW 19 Jun 1917.
B1681	From 1 AD 26 May 1917; to 2 AD by Sgt G P Olley 7 Sep 1917.
B1683	From 1 AD 17 Aug 1917; Lt H E A Waring POW 19 Aug 1917.
B1685	From 1 AD by Lt P F Fullard 12 May 1917; Lt R R MacIntosh POW 26 May 1917.
B1687	From 1 AD 8 Jun 1917; crashed by Lt E G Nuding forced landing 4 Jul 1917.
B1689	From 1 AD 19 May 1917; Lt R W L Anderson KIA by AA fire 11 Jun 1917.
B1690	1 Sq 24 May 1917 ; Lt C Pickstone crashed 18 Aug 1917.
B1691	From 1 AD by Capt R H Cronyn 21 May 1917; Lt H E Waters POW 2 Jun 1917.
B1692	1 Sq 19 May 1917; crashed by Lt G A Wood 6 Sep 1917.
B1700	From 1 AD 24 May 1917; crashed by Sgt W J Beadle 15 Jul 1917.
B3455	From 1 AD 27 Jun 1917; crashed by Lt W H Robinson 24 Sep 1917.
B3459	From 1 AD 14 Jul 1917; crashed on landing by Lt G B Moore 11 Sep 1917.
B3461	From 1 AD 24 Jul 1917; crashed by Lt W H Robinson landing 25 Sep 1917.
B3463	1 Sq 4 Jul/17 to 23 Jul 1917; Lt W D Murray killed in accident 3 Jan 1918.
B3466	From 1 AD 16 Jul 1917; crashed landing by Lt C S T Lavers 26 Jul 1917.
B3474	From 1 AD 16 Jul 1917; crashed landing by Lt V F S Dunton 6 Nov 1917.
B3481	From 1 AD by Sgt G P Olley 5 Jun 1917, Lt F Sharpe POW 9 Jun 1917.
B3482	From 1 AD by Lt G C Atkins 5 Jun 1917; Lt L Read POW 12 Aug 1917.
B3483	From 1 AD by Capt Waller 8 Jun 1917; Lt W C Smith POW 13 Jul 1917.
B3484	From 1 AD 4 Jul 1917; crashed landing by Lt R E Money-Kyrle 12 Jul 1917.
B3485	From 1 AD 22 Jun 1917; Lt C S T Lavers force lands 15 Jul 1917.
B3486	From 1 AD 11 Jun 1917; Lt T Littler killed by friendly fire 3 Jul 1917.
B3487	From 1 AD 8 Jun 1917; crashed landing by Lt E G Nuding 13 Jun 1917.
B3495	From 1 AD 12 Jun 1917; Lt T M McFerran POW 21 Jun 1917.
B3496	From 1 AD 5 Jul 1917; crashed on landing by Lt J B Maudsley 12 Jul 1917.
B3500	1 Sq 28 Jul 1917 to 14 Aug 1917 and 11 Nov 1917 to 20 Nov 1917.
B3540	From 1 AD 23 Jul 1917; crashed in forced landing by Lt H S Preston 5 Aug 1917.
B3555	From 1 Issue Section 18 Nov 1917; Lt J Brydone POW 28 Dec 1917.
B3558	From 1 AD 13 Aug 1917, Lt W E le B Diamond POW 9 Sep 1917.
B3577	From 1 AD by Lt P G Kelsey 24 Sep 1917; Lt M A Peacock POW 9 Oct 1917.
B3580	From 29 Sq, L/Col van Ryneveld's machine, to 1 Issue Section 19 Jan 1918.
B3589	From 1 AD 23 Sep 1917; crashed on landing by Lt H T Matthews 7 Nov 1917.
B3607	From 1 Issue Section 7 Nov 1917; Lt E K Skelton KIA 9 Jan 1918.
B3608	From 1 Issue Section 7 Nov 1917; Lt V F S Dunton crashed 13 Nov 1917.
B3609	From 29 Sq 14 Jan 1918; to1 Issue Section by Lt J C Bateman 24 Jan 1918.
B3612	From 1 Issue Section 7 Nov 1917; to 1 Issue Section 12 Jan 1918.
B3613	From 29 Sq by Lt P A de Fontenay 14 Jan 1918; to 1 Issue Section 19 Jan 1918.
B3614	From 1 Issue Section 18 Dec 1917; to 1 ASD by Maj AB Adams 12 Jan 1918.
B3617	From 1 Issue Section 8 Dec 1917; crashed by Lt V F S Dunton 17 Dec 1917.
B3621	From 1 AD 10 Sep 1917; crashed by Lt F J Chown 16 Sep 1917.
B3622	From 1 AD 12 Sep 1917; crashed landing by Lt C S T Lavers 27 Sep 1917.
B3627	From 1 AD by Lt J Baalman 9 Sep 1917; Lt E D Scott KIA 30 Oct 1917.
B3628	From 2 AD by Sgt G P Olley 7 Sep 1917; crashed by Lt R C Sotham 5 Nov 1917.
B3629	From 2 AD 7 Sep 1917; to 1 Issue Section by G B Moore 24 Jan 1918.
B3630	From 2 AD by Maj A B Adams 7 Sep 1917; Lt A W McLaughlin KIA 29 Oct 1917.
B3631	From 1 AD 11 Sep 1917; hit by Sopwith Triplane on landing 28 Sep 1917.
B3632	From 2 AD by Lt H J Hamilton 7 Sep 1917; Lt R H Garratt KIA 20 Sep 1917.
B3635	From 2 AD by Capt L F Jenkin 7 Sep 1917; Capt L F Jenkin KIA 11 Sep 1917.
B3636	From 1 AD 4 Sep 1917; crashed by Lt F G Baker on take off 11 Sep 1917.
B3648	From 2 AD 7 Sep 1917, Lt W S Mansell KIA by AA 11 Sep 1917.
B3650	1 Sq 16 Sep 1917 to crashed 23 Sep 1917 and 29 Nov 1917 to 12 Jan 1918.
B6752	From1 AD 12 Sep 1917; damaged on ground by Capt C L Bath 21 Sep 1917.
B6753	From 1 AD by Lt F E Bond 21 Sep 1917; Lt C E Ogden POW 5 Dec 1917.
B6754	From 1 AD 21 Sep 1917; Lt H T Matthews crashes from spin 10 Nov 1917.
B6755	From 1 AD by Maj A B Adams 11 Sep 1917; Lt F J Chown KIA 20 Sep 1917.
B6766	1 Sq 20 Sep 1917 to 24 Jan 1918; to 1 Issue Section.
B6767	From 1 AD by Lt H G Reeves 17 Sep 1917; Capt W V T Rooper KIA 9 Oct 1917.
B6768	From 1 AD 21 Sep 1917; Lt R C Sotham KIA mid-collision 9 Jan 1918.
B6769	From 1 AD 26 Sep 1917; crashed forced landing Lt C H Holcombe 6 Dec 1917.
B6770	From 1 AD 21 Sep 1917; crashed by Lt J F Bremner 22 Sep 1917.
B6774	From 1 AD 24 Sep 1917; Capt H G Reeves killed in accident 24 Jan 1918.
B6785	From 1 Issue Section 11 Nov 1917; crashed Lt F P Magoun 18 Nov 1917.

B6788	From 1 Issue Section 3 Dec 1917; to 1 ASD by Capt R A Birkbeck 12 Jan 1918.
B6789	From 1 AD 28 Sep 1917; to 29 Sq by Lt P A de Fontenay 14 Jan 1918.
B6790	1 Sq 28 Sep 1917 to 20 Oct 1917 and 5 Jan 1918 to 29 Sq 14 Jan 1918.
B6798	From 1 AD 11 Oct 1917; Lt C S Fuller killed in accident 11 Nov 1917.
B6809	From 1 AD 10 Oct 1917; crashed by Lt F E Bond 27 Oct 1917.
B6810	From 1 Issue Section 25 Dec 1917; to 29 Sq by Capt H J Hamilton 14 Jan 1918.
B6815	From 1 AD 21 Oct 1917; to 1 Issue Section by Maj A B Adams 24 Jan 1918.
B6818	From 1 AD by 17 Oct 1917, to 1 AD by L/Col H A Van Ryneveld 1 Jun 1918.
B6819	1 Sq 29 Oct 1917 to 15 Nov 1917 and 10 Jan 1918 to 12 Jan 1918.
B6824	From 1 Issue Section 31 Oct 1917; Lt R O Phillips crashes 18 Dec 1917.
B6825	From 1 Issue 31 Oct 1917; to 1 Issue Section Capt R A Birkbeck 24 Jan 1918.
B6830	From 1 Issue Section 9 Nov 1917; to 1 Issue Section 19 Jan 1918.
B6836	From 1 Issue Section 6 Dec 1917; to 1 Issue Section 19 Jan 1918.
B6837	From 1 Issue Section 22 Dec 1917; to 1 Issue Section 19 Jan 1918.

SE5a

A8904	From 1 ASD by Lt GB Moore 12 Jan 1918; u/c collapsed 26 Mar 1918.
A8908	From 1 Issues Section 24 Jan 1918; crashed by Lt W A Smart 20 Apr 1918.
A8929	From 1 Issues Section 24 Jan 1918; Lt R B Donald shot about 18 Apr 1918.
A8930	From 1 Issues Section 21 Jan 1918; crashed by Lt J C Bateman 13 Apr 1918.
A8932	From 1 Issues Section 19 Jan 1918; Lt A E Sweeting crashes 22 Mar 1918.
A8933	From 1 Issues Section 28 Mar 1918; Lt G A Mercer POW ground-fire 9 Apr 1918.
B32	From 1 Issues Section 26 Feb 1918; Capt HJ Hamilton shot about 26 Mar 1918.
B34	From 1 Issues Section 19 Jan 1918; to 1 ASD by Lt Stemp 22 Apr 1918.
B72	From 1 Issues Section 24 Mar 1918; Lt A E Sweeting WIA 30 Mar 1918.
B130	From 1 Issues Section 31 Mar 1918, Lt B H Moody shot about 8 Jun 1918.
B511	From 1 Issues Section 24 Jan 1918; Lt A McN Denovan KIA 26 Mar 1918.
B518	From 1 Issues Section 24 Jan 1918; Lt V F S Dunton crashes 30 Jan 1918.
B520	From 1 Issues Section 24 Jan 1918; Lt A Hollis crashes 25 Mar 1918.
B531	From 1 Issues Section 11 Mar 1918, Lt W M R Gray crashes 15 Mar 1918.
B532	From 1 Issues Section 27 Mar 1918; Lt F R Knapp POW 16 Apr 1918.
B543	From 1 Issues Section 26 Mar 1918; Lt E M Forsyth crashes 31 Mar 1918.
B570	From 1 Issues Section 16 Apr 1918; crashed by Lt E E Owen 21 Apr 1918.
B576	From 1 Issues Section 19 Jan 1918; crashed by Sgt H F O'Hara 9 Mar 1918.
B597	From 1 Issues Section 13 Jan 1918; Lt E M Forsyth crashes 1 Apr 1918.
B632	From 1 Issues Section 28 Jan 1918; Lt B H Moody crashes 30 Apr 1918.
B641	From 1 Issues Section 28 Jan 1918; Lt W M R Gray POW 26 Mar 1918.
B643	From 1 Issues Section 4 Jan18; Lt A Hollis POW groundfire 26 Mar 1918.
B733	From 1 Issues Section 9 May 1918; to 1 Issues time expired 3 Aug 1918.
B4851	From 1 Issues Section 19 Jan 1918, Lt R B Donald crashes 22 Apr 1918.
B4881	From 1 Issues Section 19 Jan 1918; Lt D M Bisset crashes 1 Apr 1918.
B4884	From 1 Issues Section 2 Feb 1918, Lt I O Chantler crashes 28 Feb 1918.
B4889	From 1 Issues Section 13 Jan 1918; Lt A H Fitzmaurice KIA 12 Mar 1918
B7881	From 1 Issues Section 9 Jun 1918; to 2 ASD by Lt F P Magoun 15 Oct 1918.
B7909	From 1 IS by Lt H H Hunt 6 Oct 1918; Lt H H Hunt KIA 26 Oct 1918.
B7920	From 2 IS by Lt F C Bowler 1 Nov 1918; to Marquise by Lt Heenan 28 Jan 1919.
B8254	From 1 IS by Lt Hiscock 15 Apr 1918; to AD unfit for service 18 Jul 1918.
B8258	From 1 ASD 13 Jan 1918; crashed by Lt P J Clayson 24 Feb 1918.
B8265	From 1 IS 13 Mar 1918; abandoned after forced landing 26 Mar 1918.
B8371	From 1 IS by Lt F R Knapp 3 Apr 1918; Capt W D Patrick POW 10 Apr 1918.
B8410	From 1 IS by Lt Hiscock 18 Apr 1918; Capt C C Clark POW 8 May 1918.
B8426	From 1 IS 10 Aug 1918; crashed in shell-hole by Lt W A Smart 10 Apr 1918.
B8427	To 1 Sq 22 Aug 1918; Lt W Joffe KIA 1 Oct 1918.
B8501	From IS by Lt L H Phinney 26 Aug 1918; crashed by Lt F P Magoun 1 Jan 1919.
B8504	From 1 IS 29 Apr 1918; to 1 IS by Lt H B Parkinson 9 Jun 1918.
B8506	From 1 IS 1 May 1918; crashed into on ground by RE8 7 May 1918.
B8508	From 1 IS by Lt W A Smart 7 May 1918; Lt E F S Kelly KIA 13 Jun 1918.
B8512	From 1 IS 20 May 1918; overstressed in flight by Lt E E Owen 12 Jun 1918.
C1074	From 1 IS by Lt E M Forsyth 28 Mar 1918; crashed by Lt B D Clark 5 May 1918.
C1083	From 1 IS by Lt A E Sweeting 27 Mar 1918; Capt G B Moore KIA 7 Apr 1918.
C1092	From 1 ASD 22 Apr 1918; badly damaged by AA fire, to 2 ASD 10 Aug 1918.
C1095	From 1 IS 6 Apr 1918; Lt P J Clayson shot about, to 1 AD 8 May 1918.
C1101	From 1 IS 21 Apr 1918; F/L due A A damage Lt E M Newman 19 Jun 1918.
C1102	From 1 IS by Lt Stemp 23 Apr 1918; Lt H B Bradley KIA 25 Jun 1918.
C1103	From 1 IS 20 Apr 1918, bad landing by Lt C S T Lavers, to 1 AD 19 May 1918.
C1104	From 1 IS 15 Apr 1918; Lt F A S Nesbitt shot about, pilot wounded 25 Apr 1918.
C1106	From 1 IS 15 Apr 1918; forced landing by Lt G W Bellin 21 Aug 1918.
C1107	From 1 IS 12 Apr 1918; Lt D W Hughes crashes due engine failure 3 May 1918.
C1110	From 1 Repair Park 25 Apr 1918; to 1 IS by Lt E M Newman 30 Jul 1918.
C1113	From 1 IS by Lt Futcher 23 Apr 1918; Capt K S Henderson KIA 2 Jun 1918.
C1114	From 1 IS 8 May 1918; to 2 IS by Lt D Knight needing overhaul 19 Aug 1918.
C1145	From 1 IS 25 Oct 1918; to Marquise by Capt L W Jarvis 6 Feb 1919.
C1812	From 1 IS 20 Jul 1918; forced landed by Lt D M Bissett 23 Oct 1918.
C1816	From 1 IS 8 Jun 1918; Lt W M Chowne force lands injured 15 Jul 1918.
C1835	To 1 Sq 12 Jun 1918; to IS by Lt F M Squires 1 Sep 1918.
C1849	From 1 IS 5 May 1918; heavy landing by Lt C W Arning 21 Jul 1918.
C1853	From 1 IS 9 May 1918; Lt K J P Laing force lands, pilot OK 29 May 1918.
C1875	From 2 ASD 1 Sep 1918; Lt W Newby force lands, engine shot 15 Sep 1918.
C1894	From 1 IS by Lt J C Bateman 2 Jun 1918; Lt G R Touchstone POW 8 Aug 1918.

C1898	From 1 IS 30 May 1918; Lt E E Owen crashes into mess hut 16 Jun 1918.
C1943	From 1 IS by Lt C G Pegg 5 Jul 1918; heavy landing by Lt C R Boyd 1 Aug 1918.
C5306	From 1 ASD 12 Jan 1918; crashed by Lt K C Mills 3 Apr 1918.
C5374	From 1 IS 6 Apr 1918; Lt K C Mills shot about by AA fire 6 May 1918.
C6384	From 1 IS by Lt Blight 15 Apr 1918; crashed by Lt A H J How 23 Apr 1918.
C6405	From 1 IS 8 Apr 1918; Capt W L Harrison crashes landing in dark 13 Apr 1918.
C6408	From 1 IS by Lt K J P Laing 22 Apr 1918; Lt J C Wood POW 8 May 1918.
C6411	From 1 IS 1 Apr 1918; crashed on landing by Lt B D Clark 11 Apr 1918.
C6416	From 1 IS 1 Apr 1918; Lt A F Scroggs wounded, machine wrecked 5 Jun 1918.
C6441	From 1 IS 14 May 1918; crashed on landing by Lt H A Kullberg 11 Jun 1918.
C6444	From 1 IS 6 May 1918; Lt C A Pelletier shot down in flames KIA 11 May 1918.
C6458	From 1 IS 3 Jun 1918; to 2 ASD, engine unserviceable 6 Sep 1918.
C6479	From 1 IS 22 May 1918; Lt D Knight shot down, pilot OK 31 May 1918.
C8841	From 1 IS by Lt W A Smart 26 Jun 1918; Lt L M Elworthy POW 29 Sep 1918.
C8842	From 1 IS 6 Jun 1918; crashed by Lt H B Parkinson 16 Jun 1918.
C8843	From 1 IS by Lt N T Trembath 6 Jul 1918; to 2 ASD 8 Aug 1918.
C8846	From 1 IS 16 Jun 1918; Lt L H Phinney shot about, pilot OK 30 Oct 1918.
C8847	From 1 IS 17 Jun 1918; Lt N T Trembath shot about, pilot OK 5 Jul 1918.
C8902	From 2 ASD by Lt G W Bellin 4 Jan 1919; to 110 Sq 28 Feb 1919.
C8909	From 2 ASD 1 Nov 1918; to Marquise by Lt L A Arnold 28 Jan 1919.
C9065	Arrives 11 Aug 1918; to 2 ASD 8 Nov 1918.
C9067	Arrives 11 Aug 1918; crashed in F/L by Lt L Lovatt, pilot OK 23 Oct 1918.
C9292	From 2 ASD 21 Sep 1918; to Marquise by Lt C S Dickinson 14 Feb 1919.
C9299	From 2 IS 3 Nov 1918; to Marquise by Lt C G Pegg 13 Feb 1919.
C9610	From 1 IS 3 Apr 1918; Lt R B Donald shot about, pilot OK 12 Apr 1918.
C9621	From 1 IS 27 Mar 1918; Lt K J P Laing shot about, pilot OK 21 May 1918.
C9624	From 1 IS 5 Mar 1918; crashed by Lt P J Clayson 1 Apr 1918.
D277	From 1 IS 11 Apr 1918; Lt H Towse runs into another SE5a landing 16 Apr 1918.
D280	From 1 IS 17 Apr 1918; Lt H B Winton killed in T/O accident 21 Apr 1918.
D332	From 1 IS 7 May 1918; Lt H S Hennessy force lands 11 May 1918.
D337	From 1 IS by Lt F S Crossley 14 May 1918; Lt H S Hennessy KIA 5 Jun 1918.
D6878	From 1 IS 13 Jun 1918; Lt B H Moody shot about, pilot OK 24 Aug 1918.
D6881	From 1 IS 6 Jun 1918; wrecked on landing by Lt C W Arning 7 Jul 1918.
D6894	From 1 IS 17 Jun 1918; Capt H M Sison shot about by AA, pilot OK 4 Jul 1918.
D6899	From 1 IS 21 Jun 1918; to 2 ASD by Lt E M Newman 21 Sep 1918.
D6930	From 1 IS 17 Jul 1918; crashed in F/L by Lt L Lovatt 24 Jul 1918.
D6946	From IS 20 Aug 1918; crashed on landing by Lt C W Arning 26 Sep 1918.
D6951	From IS by Lt N T Trembath 10 Aug 1918; Lt N T Trembath POW 28 Oct 1918.
D6962	From 1 IS by Lt C R Boyd 3 Aug 1918; Capt K C Mills KIA 8 Aug 1918.
D6970	From 1 IS 6 Aug 1918; Lt R H Ritter KIA 24 Aug 1918.
D6973	From 2 IS 9 Aug 1918; to Marquise by Lt C S Dickinson 28 Jan 1919.
E1353	From 1 IS 7 Jul 1918; to 2 ASD by Lt G W Bellin for overhaul 4 Jan 1919.
E4023	From 2 IS 9 Aug 1918; to Marquise by Lt J J Magill 28 Jan 1919.
E5772	From 5 IS 1 Oct 1918; to Marquise by Maj W E Young 28 Jan 1919.
E5778	From 2 ASD 16 Oct 1918; to Marquise by Lt P Addison 10 Feb 1919.
E5799	From 2 IS 24 Oct 1918; to Marquise by Lt G W Bellin 28 Jan 1919.
E5886	From 2 IS 10 Nov 1918; to Marquise by Lt L A Arnold 10 Feb 1919.
E5969	From 1 IS 30 Jul 1918; to Marquise by Capt C S T Lavers 28 Jan 1919.
E6009	From IS 25 Aug 1918; crashed on landing by Lt C S Dickinson 26 Oct 1918.
F902	From IS by Lt F C Bowler 28 Oct 1918; to Marquise by P Addison 28 Jan 1919.
F908	From 2 ASD 31 Oct 1918; to Marquise by Lt H Blatcher 28 Jan 1919.
F5473	From 2 ASD 29 Sep 1918; crashed into hangar by Lt C G Pegg 29 Oct 1918.
F5476	From IS by Lt W Newby 28 Sep 1918; Lt W Newby KIA 29 Oct 1918.
F5503	From 2 ASD 17 Sep 1918; Lt W Newby F/L due combat damage 27 Sep 1918.
F5661	From IS 27 Oct 1918; crashed on test by Lt H G Freeman 25 Jan 1919.
F5912	From 1 IS 28 Jul 1918, to Marquise by Lt L H Phinney 28 Jan 1919.
F6429	From 2 ASD 5 Sep 1918; to Marquise by Lt E C Mogridge 28 Jan 1919.

Sopwith Snipe

E6655	Jun 1926
E6801	Jun 1926
E6954	
E6960	Collided with E7715 1 Apr 1926
E6965	
E7373	Jan 1925
E7514	
E7565	
E7638	
E7639	Collided with DH9a on landing 2 Feb 1925 – SOS, F/O F G Jennings OK.
E7642	
E7645	Nov 1923.
E7705	Apr 1923.
E7705	Apr 1923.
E7715	Collided with E6960 1 Apr 1926.
E7721	Jun 1926.
E7771	
E8219	Jun 1923.
E8245	
E8248	

E8249	Jun 1926.
E8384	May 1926.
E8801?	
F2345	
F2373	F/L and crashed 18 Apr 1923 by F/O A P Davidson, due engine failure.
F2387	
F2424	
F2435	
F2457	May 1923.
F2466	
F2469	
F2488	
F2499	
H4866	
H4867	Nov 1921; damaged on T/O in collision due dust 11 Jul 1924.
H4872	Forced landed 21 Aug 1923 due engine failure, F/O A P Davidson.
H4879	Nov 1921.
H4883	Jul 1921.
H4884	F/L F O Soden forced lands 1 Nov 1920.
H4885	Apr 1923; SOS 11 Jul 1924 due collision in dust on T/O.
H4886	Jul 1920.
H4893	Mar 1920.
H4894	Mar 1920.
H4896	Oct 1921.
H4900	Risalpur.
H4901	
H4902	Risalpur.
H4905	
H8675	May 1923.
H8676	May 1923, forced landed due engine failure 2 Jun 1923, F/O A P Davidson.
H8692	SOS 11 Jul 1924 due collision in dust on T/O.

Nieuport Nighthawk

| J6925 | Later rebuilt as JR6925. |
| J6927 | Mar 1924. |

Hawker Siskin

J7000	Oct 1927; Mark III dual control.
J7169	ex 41 Sq, 1 Sq c.July 1927; to 43 Sq.
J8049	crashed 23 Feb 1931.
J8058	Oct 1930; to 29 Sq.
J8059	ex 111 Sq, 1 Sq Nov 1927, crashed 23 Feb 1931.
J8060	ex 32 Sq; 1 Sq 5 Feb 1930; to 29 Sq 1931.
J8384	Holt flare ignited petrol night flying 13/14 May 1926; to 41 Sq.
J8396	Oct 1931.
J8626	Dec 1929, turned over in long grass and wrecked 14 Jun 1930, F/O Selway.
J8629	Oct 1927; to 41 Sq Jan 1928.
J8630	ex 56 Sq, 1 Sq Jan 1928; to Duxford.
J8631	Oct 1927, ex 25 Sq.
J8632	ex 43 Sq, 1 Sq 1929-30.
J8634	wef 31 Oct 1927.
J8635	wef 28 Oct 1927; to 56 Sq Nov 1929.
J8637	Nov 1927-Dec 1929 – to 29 Sq.
J8638	wef Nov 1927.
J8639	wef Nov 1927; hit by Woodcock J8292 on ground; to 41 Sq.
J8640	wef Nov 1927; caught fire on ground 16 Aug 1928 and SOC.
J8659	ex 41 Sq, 1 Sq 19 Feb 1933; to SF Duxford Feb 1933.
J8660	ex 32 Sq, 1 Sq – collided with J8961 6 May 1931 and SOC.
J8667	ex 29 Sqn, 1 Sq wef Mar 1932.
J8671	1929-31.
J8826	ex 43 Sq, 1 Sq Jan 1930.
J8834	Aug 1928.
J8859	ex 43 Sq, 1 Sq wef Jan 1929.
J8861	Kenley; 1 Sq 1928; to 32 Sq Sep 1928.
J8939	ex 41 Sq, 1 Sq Sep 1929-Feb 1930.
J8943	Burnt out landing at Tangmere 27 Aug 1929.
J8944	
J8947	ex 41 Sq, 1 Sq wef 25 Oct 1929.
J8959	ex 29 Sq, 1 Sq Sep 1929; to 43 Sq.
J8961	ex 32 Sq, 1 Sq – collided with J8660 6 May 1931.
J9201	ex 43 Sq, 1 Sq May-Oct 1932, dual control.
J9202	May-Sep 1929, dual control.
J9211	ex 32 Sq; 1 Sq Apr 1931, dual control.
J9341	ex 43 Sq.
J9876	1930.
J9877	1930, to 41 Sq.
J9883	Wef May 1930; force landed & blown over 11 Feb 1931; to 41 Sq.
J9887	Feb 1930, damaged in crash.
J9888	1930
J9892	Mar 1930, to 19 Sq.

J9894	Mar 1930.
J9909	(Mk IIIb) 'H' – wef Jul 1931.
J9920	May 1931-32, to 29 Sq.

Hawker Hornet

J9682	Collided with 43 Sq Siskin 11 Apr 1930 – SOC.

Hawker Fury I

K1926	Trials.
K1931	SOC 13 May 1937.
K1940	2 Nov 1932 – to 1 AAS.
K2035	Jan/Feb 1932.
K2036	wef 21 Jan 1932; SOC in collision with K2064 26 May 1932.
K2037	,,
K2038	,, ; SOC in collision with K2044, 5 Apr 1932.
K2039	,, ; u/c collapsed 2 Nov 1937 – SOC.
K2040	,, ; till 5 Aug 1932.
K2041	,, ; to 25 Sq 25 Jan 1932.
K2042	,, ;
K2043	,, ; 'C' – hit by K5675 Tangmere 23 Sep 1937.
K2044	,, ; collided with K2038 5 Apr 1932; collided with K2047 23 Apr 1934, SOC.
K2045	wef 25 Jan 1932; force landed 20 Jul 1936.
K2046	,, ; to 20 Sep 1938.
K2047	,, ; collided with K2044 23 Apr 1934, SOC.
K2048	wef 10 Feb 1932; CO's aircraft; to 25 Sq.
K2049	wef 20 Feb 1932; SOC 10 Aug 1932.
K2050	,, ; to 43 Sq.
K2051	,, ; to 43 Sq.
K2060	ex 25 Sq; SOC 20 Dec 1937.
K2061	,, ; 1 Sq 10 Feb 1932, crashed 22 Feb.
K2062	,, ; 1 Sq 27 Jan 1937; to 87 Sq 15 Mar 1937.
K2063	wef 20 Feb 1932; taxied into Gladiator at Tangmere 24 Mar 1937.
K2064	,, ; collided with K2036 26 May 1932 – SOC.
K2065	,, ; to Hawkers 4 Dec 1934.
K2066	wef 4 Jun 1932; to 25 Sq.
K2067	wef 25 Feb 1932; to 25 Sq.
K2069	,, ; to 25 Sq.
K2073	
K2074	wef 24 Oct 1932; to 43 Sq.
K2075	wef 17 Jan 1933; to 43 Sq 1 Jul 1936.
K2076	ex 25 Sq; 1 Sq wef 11 Dec 1936; SOC in crash 29 May 1937.
K2878	ex 25 Sq; 1 Sq wef 21 Dec 1936; to 87 Sq 15 Mar 1937.
K2881	'E' – wef 3 Feb 1934; hit by K8275 on landing 23 Feb 1938.
K2899	3 Feb 1934 to 7 Dec 1939; to S Africa ITS 7 Oct 1940.
K2900	wef 28 May 1934; SOC in accident 16 Nov 1937.
K2901	,, ; collided with K2902 17 Dec 1937 – SOC.
K2902	wef 26 Jun 1934; collided with K2901 17 Dec 1937 – SOC.
K2903	c.1933, to 2 FTS 6 Oct 1934.
K5673	wef 2 Jun 1936; damaged in crash 23 Feb 1938 – to 3 FTS.

Hawker Fury II

K8247	ex 73 Sq.
K8248	ex 73 Sq.
K8249	ex 73 Sq.
K8255	ex 73 Sq.
K8272	ex 73 Sq.
K8275	wef 10 Feb 1937; damaged swinging into K2881 23 Feb 1938.
K8278	,, ; to 7 FTS.
K8279	,, ; to 24 MU.
K8281	wef 9 Feb 1937; ,,
K8290	,, ; ,,
K8291	,, ; ,,
K8296	wef 19 Feb 1937; ,,
K8303	wef 24 Apr 1937; ,,

Hawker Hurricane I

L1671	S/L Halahan c/landed 12 May 1940 – abandoned.
L1673	Shot down 13 May 1940.
L1676	F/O Lorimer killed 14 May 1940.
L1677	overshot landing Tangmere 24 Nov 1938.
L1678	overshot Tangmere, crashed, 16 Feb 1939.
L1679	JX-G; destroyed on ground, 14 May 1940, Mezières.
L1680	crash landed on beach at Hayling Island 4 Jul 1939.
L1681	F/O Lorimer f/landed 13 May 1940 – abandoned.
L1682	hit ground at night SE Debden 7 Feb 1939.
L1685	1, 43 and 1 Sqs; F/O Richey baled out 11 May 1940.
L1686	lost in France May 1940.
L1687	to 43 Sq.
L1688	F/O Lewis baled out 12 May 1940.
L1689	P/O Lorimer baled out 10 May 1940.

L1690	dived into ground at Tangmere at night 26 Jun 1939, FO Hemmings killed.
L1691	crash landed Tangmere 5 Jan 1939.
L1692	stalled on approach to Tangmere 5 Jan 1939.
L1693	to 73 Sq.
L1694	NA-F; crashed on take off Tangmere 13 Mar 1939; lost 13 May 1940?.
L1731	JX-H; ex1 RCAF, to 56 OTU.
L1813	46, 43, 1, 87 Sqns.
L1842	to 310 Sq 1940.
L1843	Damaged by Do17 2 Mar 1940; shot down 20 Apr 1940.
L1844	to 73 Sq.
L1855	crashed at night, Tangmere 13 Mar 1939.
L1856	shot down by flak 18 May 1940, Sgt Albonico PoW.
L1905	JX-H; damaged 17 May 1940, burnt 18 May.
L1925	Damaged in combat with Do17, 23 Nov 1939; abandoned, France May 1940.
L1927	to 73 Sq.
L1934	JX-D; F/L Brown – Battle of Britain.
L1943	ex 504 Sq; shot down by Me110 15 May 1940.
L1944	ex 504 Sq; lost in France May 1940.
L1959	1, 151, 43, 1 Sqns – to 73 Sq.
L1960	to 73 Sq.
L1961	to 151 Sq.
L1962	1, 151, 1 Sqns – to 73 Sq.
L1963	to 87 Sq.
L1964	to 87 Sq.
L1965	to 87 Sq.
L1966	to 73 Sq.
L1967	to 73 Sq.
L1968	to 73 Sq.
L1969	to 306 Sq.
L1970	to 32 Sq.
L1971	crashed Fentrange France 2 Mar 1940, P/O Mitchell killed.
L1972	to 32 Sq.
L1973	to 111 Sq, 1 Sq, to 1 RCAF Sq.
L1974	43 Sq, 1 Sq – burnt on evacuation May 1940.
L1975	to 56 Sq.
L1976	to 56 Sq.
L1977	to 151 Sq.
L1978	to 85 Sq.
L1979	to 85 Sq.
L2061	to 605 Sq.
N2318	to 73 Sq.
N2319	to 85 Sq.
N2326	ex 85 Sq; shot down 2 Apr 1940.
N2341	crash-landed 29 October 1940, P/O Cizak OK.
N2380	JX-S; ex 501 Sq; F/O Hanks baled out 14 May 1940.
N2381	ex 501 Sq, 1 Sq, to 242 Sq.
N2382	JX-B; F/L Walker crash-landed 10 May 1940 – later SOC.
N2383	to 43 Sq.
N2385	to 43 Sq.
N2388	to 43 Sq.
N2391	to 43 Sq.
N2618	JX-V; ex 6 OTU, to 55 OTU.
P2545	to 73 Sq.
P2546	F/O Clisby killed 14 May 1940.
P2548	JX-A
P2649	JX-T – Ex 73 Sq; lost in France May 1940.
P2686	P/O Goodman baled out 6 Sep 1940.
P2688	to 615 Sq.
P2689	to 73 Sq.
P2694	lost in France May 1940.
P2751	JX-L; S/L Pemberton killed hitting ground 2 Nov 1940.
P2810	burnt 16 May 1940.
P2811	shot down 11 May 1940.
P2820	ex 73 Sq; F/O Palmer baled out 17 May 1940.
P2822	to 6 OTU.
P2860	Ex 17 Sq.
P2877	JX-P; ex 229 Sq; to 59 OTU.
P2880	missing 25 May 1940.
P2901	ex 9 FTS; to 55 OTU.
P2980	force landed and overshot 24 Aug 1940.
P3042	JX-A or F; to 8 FTS.
P3043	JX-G; reported lost 16 Aug 1940.
P3044	lost 3 Sep 1940, F/L Hillcoat.
P3045	burnt at Nantes 18 Jun 1940.
P3047	JX-E; FL Brown's a/c; Sgt Shanahan baled out 15 Aug 1940 – Me109 attack.
P3169	JX-T; damaged by exploding a/c 16 Aug 1940.
P3170	JX-M; P/O Hancock shot-up 16 Aug 1940; to 9 FTS.
P3172	JX-K; damaged by Me110 11 Aug 1940 cr/landed, P/O Davey killed – SOC.
P3173	JX-O; shot down by AA fire 16 Aug 1940 – P/O Elkington baled out.

P3229	JX-T; to 59 OTU.
P3276	shot down by Me109 1 Sep 1940, Sgt Berry.
P3318	JX-W; ex 3 Sq, to 111 Sq.
P3390	
P3395	JX-B – F/L Clowes' a/c; damaged in crash landing 2 Nov 1940; to 55 OTU.
P3396	JX-Y; ex 501 Sq – to 59 OTU.
P3406	JX-Z; to 59 OTU.
P3471	JX-E; damaged and crash-landed 19 Jul 1940 – SOC.
P3590	damaged 5 June 1940 – SOC.
P3652	FL Brown's a/c June 1940; to 111 Sq.
P3653	JX-C; P/O Boot crash-landed after combat 16 Aug 1940; to 501 Sq.
P3672	to 501 Sq.
P3678	JX-R; to 253 Sq.
P3684	JX-V; ex 242 Sq; hit balloon cable 19 Aug 1940.
P3782	crashed 3 Sep 1940, P/O Shaw.
P3886	JX-V; ex 601 Sq, to 59 OTU.
P3897	pilot dazzled by searchlight and baled out 27 Aug 1940.
P3920	ex 238 Sq; shot down by Me109 5 Feb 1941, F/O Lewis lost.
R4075	JX-E; shot down 15 Aug 1940, F/L Brown OK.
V6932	to 59 OTU.
V6933	JX-W; ex 1 RCAF; SL Brown's a/c 1941; to 59 OTU.
V6997	to 79 Sq.
V7025	ex 308 Sq, to 5 FTS.
V7099	to 59 OTU.
V7223	ex 55 OTU, to 55 OTU.
V7256	JX-O; to 59 OTU.
V7258	to 59 OTU.
V7301	JX-H; to 253 Sq.
V7302	JX-G; damaged in crash-landing 29 Oct 1940; converted to MkII.
V7375	Merchant baled out 31 Aug 1940.
V7376	Sgt Warren lost 9 Oct 1940.
V7377	JX-R; to 59 OTU.
V7379	JX-B, then M; to 315 Sq.
W9151	to 79 Sq.
W9181	to 59 OTU.

Miles Magister
T9680

Miles Master
N7684

Hawker Hurricane X (Canadian built, converted to IIb)

AM280	
AM347	
P5197	to 79 Sq.
P5199	to 55 OTU

Hawker Hurricane II

Z2390	to 247 Sq.
Z2457	to 247 Sq.
Z2459	to 238 Sq.
Z2464	JX-T; to 43 Sq.
Z2482	JX-O; to 79 Sq.
Z2484	to 247 Sq.
Z2490	to 247 Sq.
Z2501	SOC 24 Apr 1941.
Z2525	to 615 Sq.
Z2590	ex 238, to 607 Sq.
Z2625	to 79 Sq.
Z2628	to 79 Sq.
Z2687	JX-Z; to 79 Sq.
Z2690	JX-M; to Russia 9 Sep 1941.
Z2759	shot down by Me109 19 Mar 1941, P/O Kershaw killed.
Z2764	shot down by Me109 21 May 1941, F/O Robinson killed.
Z2801	to 43 Sq.
Z2810	SOC after combat with Me109 19 Mar 1941, Sgt Stefan.
Z2828	to 247 Sq.
Z2834	to 79 Sq.
Z2909	shot down 21 Jun 1941, P/O Kopecky OK.
Z2919	crashed in forced landing 9 May 1941.
Z2921	P/O Behal lost on night patrol 11 May 1941.
Z2927	to Russia 12 Jan 1942.
Z3072	to 607 Sq.
Z3160	to 247 Sq.
Z3165	to 302 Sq.
Z3183	ex 257 Sq; lost 4 Jun 1942, W/O Dygryn killed.
Z3234	to 3 Sq.
Z3239	ex 601 Sq, to and from 43 Sq, to 121 Sq.
Z3240	crashed 29 Jun 1941.
Z3241	to 257 Sq.

Z3251	to Russia 31 Jan 1942.
Z3252	to Russia 23 Oct 1941.
Z3263	to 401 Sq.
Z3332	to 302 Sq.
Z3341	to 402 Sq.
Z3448	to 257 Sq.
Z3449	to 607 Sq.
Z3455	JX-T; to 247 Sq.
Z3459	to 121 Sq.
Z3460	lost 16 Jun 1941, Sgt Nasswetter killed.
Z3461	lost 21 Jun 1941, P/O Maranz killed.
Z3489	to 257 Sq.
Z3491	SOC 29 Jun 1941.
Z3496	to 43 Sq.
Z3497	to 257 Sq.
Z3504	to 615 Sq.
Z3595	to 615 Sq.
Z3774	shot down 12 Feb 1942, Sgt Blair lost.
Z3841	to 615 Sq.
Z3842	Sgt Metcalf crash-landed 29 Aug 1941, OK; to 32 Sq.
Z3843	P/O Bloor killed 27 Aug 1941.
Z3844	crashed on landing 2 Oct 1941.
Z3885	to 615 Sq.
Z3897	crashed 3 Jun 1942, F/S English killed.
Z3899	collided with BD940 22 Nov 1941, Sgt Perrin baled out.
Z3902	crashed 16 Jul 1941, F/L Velebnovsky killed.
Z3903	to Russia 29 Jan 1942.
Z3970	crashed 10 Apr 1942 – hit cables – Sgt Vlk killed.

Hawker Hurricane IIc

BD770	to 539 Sq.
BD872	ex 615 Sq; to 539 Sq.
BD935	to Russia 21 May 1943.
BD937	to 615 Sq.
BD940	collided with Z3899 22 Nov 1941, Sgt Travis killed.
BD945	crashed 11 Feb 1942, Sgt Parsons killed.
BD946	JX-H; to 486 Sq.
BD947	P/O Connolly baled out 3 Apr 1942 – OK.
BD948	to Far East.
BD949	lost 12 Feb 1942, P/O Marcinkus PoW.
BD950	ditched off Bognor, 11 Sep 1941, Sgt Smith.
BD983	JX-G; to 539 Sq.
BE150	JX-F; to 457 Sq.
BE215	JX-I; crashed 2 May 1942.
BE572	to 486 Sq.
BE573	Sgt Machacek lost 25 Apr 1942.
BE576	crashed 18 Nov 1941, Sgt Ruppel killed.
BE581	JX-E; F/L Kuttelwascher's aircraft; to 486 Sq.
BE647	crashed 5 Apr 1942, Sgt Bachurek injured.
BN189	to Russia 16 Jun 1942.
BN205	to 539 Sq.
BN232	JX-R; to 486 Sq.
BP668	to 257 Sq.
HL589	lost 26 Jun 1942, W/O Scott killed.
HL603	JX-I; to 539 Sqn.

Miles Magister

T9680	crashed 22 Apr 1941, Sgt Stocken killed.
V1013	crashed 16 Feb 1942, PO Sweeting and Mr Martin killed.

Hawker Typhoon 1b

R7851	
R7856	crashed 23 Aug 1943, P/O Grey killed.
R7861	collided with R7867 21 Oct 1942.
R7862	crashed 21 Nov 1942, F/O Watson OK.
R7863	lost 19 May 1943, P/O Glover PoW.
R7864	crashed 13 Feb 1943, Sgt Hornell OK – SOC.
R7865	
R7867	collided with R7861 21 Oct 1942.
R7868	SOC 19 Nov 1942.
R7876	lost over Channel 29 Mar 1943, F/O Bolster killed.
R7877	
R7919	JX-R; SOC 16 Jun 1943, F/L Scott wounded by FW190.
R7921	SOC 19 Feb 1944.
R7922	SOC 11 Jan 1944.
R7923	SOC 11 Jan 1944.
R8630	SOC 22 Sep 1943.
R8631	P/O Mossip shot up several trains in this a/c.
R8634	crashed 28 Apr 1943, Sgt Bletcher OK.
R8690	crashed 5 Sep 1942, Sgt Pearce OK.

R8708	
R8752	JX-L; hit tree over France 2 Jun 1943, crash landed, F/S Ramsey OK.
R8942	collided with DN615 and crashed 6 Mar 1943, Sgt Fraser killed.
DN241	overshot landing 9 Feb 1943, Sgt Crowley OK – SOC.
DN244	
DN331	to 195 Sq.
DN335	overshot landing 19 Mar 1943, P/O Watson OK.
DN385	SOC 11 Jan 1944.
DN432	to 164 Sq.
DN451	
DN490	
DN502	to 198 Sq.
DN585	lost 16 Jun 1943, F/O Dennis PoW.
DN615	collided with R8942 6 Mar 1943, P/O Whitmore killed.
EJ982	crashed taking off 6 Jul 1943, P/O Watson OK.
EJ983	to 3 TEU.
EK113	crashed into hill 7 Dec 1943, W/O Fairbairn killed.
EK139	ex 198 Sq; F/S Bletcher crashed 26 Jan 1944, OK – SOC.
EK176	JX-K; crashed in forced landing 16 Aug 1943, F/O Wood, DoI.
EK210	to 609 Sq.
EK228	lost tail in dive 15 Jul 1943, P/O Chalifour killed.
EK245	ex 198 Sq; ditched off Suffolk 23 Mar 1944, F/O Jackson died.
EK288	
JP483	force landed 2 Mar 1944, W/O Howard evaded.
JP498	lost 29 Jan 1944, F/S Watson killed.
JP592	lost 25 Nov 1943, F/O Wiley killed.
JP611	ex 198 Sq; crashed 25 Feb 1944, F/O Smith OK.
JP677	JX-C; F/O Mossip carried bombs 15/16 Sep 1943; to 137 Sq.
JP687	to 164 Sq.
JP738	JX-N; to 193 Sq.
JP751	ex 198 Sq.
JP795	fire damaged in accident 12 Dec 1943 – SOC.
JP841	crashed 30 Jan 1944, W/O McKenzie OK.
JP961	JX-U; force landed in France 22 Dec 1943, W/O Wyatt PoW.
JR126	JX-H;
JR144	ditched off Dover 21 Dec 1943, F/S Cunningham lost.
JR147	to 609 Sq.
JR237	lost 22 Dec 1943, P/O Sutherland PoW.
JR380	to 184 Sq.
JR433	to 55 OTU.
JR522	to 3 TEU.
MN115	JX-Q; to 440 Sq.
MN124	JX-F; to 3 TEU.
MN207	
MN242	JX-O; to 3 TEU.
MN266	
MN285	
MN286	
MN435	to 439 Sq.

Supermarine Spitfire IX

EN636	ex 441 Sq.
MJ244	ex 91 Sq.
MJ411	F/S Jeffrey killed in collision, 3 Aug 1945.
MJ422	F/S Tate killed 30 Jul 1944.
MJ481	lost 27 Sep 1944, W O Andrews lost.
MJ627	ex 441 Sq.
MJ796	lost to flak 22 May 1944.
MK242	ex 91 Sq; to 3 APS.
MK423	to 411 Sq.
MK426	JX-V; ex 91 Sq.
MK515	JX-N; ex 91 Sq.
MK583	
MK644	JX-M; S/L Burke's a/c, then S/L Cox; SOC after crash, 2 Mar 1945.
MK659	
MK715	ex 402 Sq.
MK725	JX-N; collided with Spitfire after take off, 20 Apr 1944, F/O Ward killed.
MK726	
MK733	
MK738	to 165 Sq.
MK744	shot down by FW190 17 Aug 1944, W/O McKenzie evaded.
MK796	F/L Vale PoW to flak 22 May 1944
MK798	hit by flak 1 Jun 1944, F/O Cattermoul PoW.
MK846	
MK867	lost 27 Sep 1944, F/O T Wylie lost.
MK890	lost to flak 22 May 1944, Sgt E F Jacobsen killed.
MK901	
MK919	u/c collapsed 12 Sep 1944.
MK926	to 421 Sq.

MK986
MK987
MK988
MK997   JX-F.
ML117
ML119   JX-B; Czech and Israeli airforces, later a/c of Co No.1 Burmese Sq and now
           gate guardian Mingladon aerodrome, Burma (coded UB441).
ML258   force landed 29 Dec 1944, W/O Royds PoW.
ML270   to 602 Sq.
ML313   to 165 Sq.
ML423
NH200
NH201   W/O Wells baled out OK, hit by FW190, 17 Aug 1944.
NH209   JX-V; ex 441 Sq.
NH246
NH253
NH255
NH276   to 12 FU.
NH290   ex 441 Sq.
NH356   crash landed on ops 18 Apr 1945, W/O Vickery OK – SOC.
NH401   ex 91 Sq.
NH466   ex 229 Sq; W/O McKenzie crash landed 4 Aug 1944 – SOC.

Taylorcraft Auster I
LB369   ex 657 Sq.

Supermarine Spitfire 21
LA190   ex RAE; to 3 CAACU.
LA196   ex 91 Sq; to122 Sq.
LA198   JK-C; to 602 Sq.
LA201   ex AFDU; to 91 Sq.
LA202
LA207   JX-G?; ex 91 Sq.
LA219   JX-3; ex Rotol Co.
LA220   JX-2; ex AAEE.
LA251   to 122 Sq.
LA255   JX-U; ex-91 Sq; to 91, 122, 41 and 602 Sqs, then 3 CAACU; now with 1 Sq.
LA260   to 41 Sq.
LA262
LA267   to 602 Sq.
LA268   to 602 Sq.
LA273   to 615 Sq.
LA275   JX-E; to 602 Sq.
LA276
LA277
LA299   wef 26 Mar 1946 (JX-1), damaged 1 Apr; to Station Flt Wittering
LA301
LA303   SOC accident 15 Nov 1945.
LA308   JX-O; SOC 22 Aug 1947.
LA311   wef 25 May 1946; SOC 22 Aug 1947.

Airspeed Oxford I
EB862?
LB530
NM412?

Gloster Meteor F.III
EE247   ex 222 Sq; to 222 Sq.
EE284   ex 245 Sq; to 66 Sq.
EE367   ex 56 Sq; to 226 OCU.
EE368   ex 222 Sq; to 66 Sq.
EE388   JX-C; ex 222 Sq; to 92 Sq.
EE412   ex 222 Sq; to 206 AFS.
EE421   JX-A; ex 222 Sq.
EE424   ex 222 Sq; to 500 Sq.
EE425   ex 222 Sq; to 266 Sq.
EE458   JX-B; ex 222 Sq.
EE461   ex 92 Sq; collided with Tiger Moth at Tangmere 24 Sep 1948.

NA Harvard

Gloster Meteor F.IV
RA371   JX-D; to 63 Sq.
RA387   ex RAE; to 203 Sq.
RA449   JX-A; to 205 Sq.
VT103   ex 43 Sq; to 205 AFS.
VT140   PIII Forest KIFA 28 Feb 1949.
VT146   collided with VT243 Tangmere 19 Apr 1950, FL Speller killed.
VT172   Cat B damage 14 Sep 1948; SOC 27 Jan 1949.
VT173   JX-B; PO Dixon crashed 26 May 1950.
VT178   JX-B; ex Duxford; to CGS.
VT179

VT180   JX-D; undershot landing at Heathrow 4 Oct 1949 – engines flamed out.
VT181   to 203 AFS.
VT182   to 615 Sq.
VT219   ex 222 Sq; to 63 Sq.
VT243   damaged in collision with VT146 19 Apr 1950; to 63 Sq.
VT265   JX-G; to 615 Sq.
VT270   ex SF Tangmere; to 615 Sq.
VT280   JX-D
VT284   JX-E; to 63 Sq.
VT288   to 63 Sq.
VT291   to 43 Sq.
VW270   JX-D; to 615 Sq.
VW294   to 615 Sq.
VZ420   JX-B
VZ424   JX-B
VZ426   JX-E
VZ428   to 615 Sq.
VZ436   JX-E; to 63 Sq.

Gloster Meteor F.VIII
VZ438   JX-E
VZ454
VZ458   JX-B
VZ470   to 63 Sq.
VZ496   'J'
VZ503   ex 222 Sq.
VZ548   JX-C
VZ549   to 613 Sq.
VZ550   to 263 Sq.
VZ551   'J'; to 611 Sq.
VZ552   JX-L
WA842
WA845   JX-E
WA851   JX-C
WA853
WA854
WA855   JX-O
WA856   JX-P, JX-C; lost in mid-air collision 16 Aug 1953.
WA868   JX-D; lost in mid-air collision 16 Aug 1953.
WA872   JX-R
WA873
WA994
WE867
WE947   JX-E
WE955
WF642   JX-T
WF700
WF947   JX-L
WH286   JX-S; damaged by bird strike 12 Dec 1952.
WH307
WH350
WH375   JX-H
WH507
WK856   JX-O
WK908   JX-L
WK916   damaged in belly landing at Wittering.
WK917   JX-V
WK985   JX-C
WK989   JX-V
WL143   'H'
WL165   'K'; wef May 1954.
WL170   'N'; wef Apr 1954, from 81 Gp.
WL175   wef Apr 1954, from 81 Gp.
WL176
WL177   wef Apr 1954, from 81 Gp.
WL190

Gloster Meteor T.7
WL360

DH Vampire T.11
XD428
XH307

Hawker Hunter F2
WN919   May 1955.

Hawker Hunter F5 and F6
WN923   'B'
WN956   'P'

WN974   'H'
WN977   lost in collision 5 May 1958, F/L Paxton killed.
WN988   'A'
WN973   'B'
WN975   'C'
WN977   'P'
WN978   'F'
WP105   'R'
WP113   'Q'
WP118   FO Ginn ejected 5 Dec 1955.
WP119   'T'
WP121   'R' and 'W'
WP137   'S' – lost in collision 5 May 1958, F/O Turner killed.
WP138   'T'
WP146   FL Irving's display a/c 1955-56.
WP147   'G'
WP180   'F'; blown up by terrorists 10 Nov 1956, Cyprus.
WP182   'V'
WP188   'X'
WP190   'K'; a/c being restored late 1990s.
WP191   'Z'
XE267
XE557
XE584   'W'
XE591   'P' and 'A'
XE601
XE604   'D' – hit parked a/c 1 Aug 1958; FO Dimmock KIFA 2 Mar 1961.
XE607
XE614   Cat 3 damage at Duxford, 25 Aug 1958.
XE615   'A'
XE616   'E'
XE619   Hit tree at Honiton and written off, 17 Feb 1959.
XE620
XE622   'Y'
XE623
XE624   'B'
XE625   Cat B damage, Nicosia, 7 Oct 1958.
XE627
XE628   'X' – lost in crash off Libyan coast 24 Apr 1963, Capt Matthews killed.
XE646   'V'
XE650   'U'
XE651   'L'
XF419
XF431   'O'
XF441   'P'
XF445   'Z'
XF462
XF517   FL Page KIFA 15 Jan 1969.
XF519
XG154   'T'
XG172   'B'
XG175
XG188
XG195   'C'; FL Davidson's record flight to Malta 23 Apr 1961.
XG196
XG197
XG201
XG207   'F'
XG238   'F'

Hawker Hunter T.7
WL360
WL595
XL241
XL539
XL596
XL601
XL607

Hawker Hunter FGA9
XE419   XF ? wef May 1963.
XE584   'W'
XE591   'H'
XE597
XE615   JX-A
XE616   WC Mansell KIFA 21 May 1969.
XE622   JX-E; damaged in crash 18 Nov 1960, Cat 4.
XE624   JX-B
XE628   'X' – CO's a/c.
XE646   'V' – FL Curtin crashed 31 Dec 1966, Cat 5.

XE650	'U'
XE651	wef Jul 1963.
XF419	
XF442	'H' FL Pollock flew this machine through Tower Bridge 5 Apr 1968.
XF454	'E'
XF462	'Y'
XF517	
XF519	
XG130	'E'
XG153	
XG194	
XG195	'C'
XG207	'F'
XG228	Cat 3, bird strike, 20 Mar 1966.
XG229	'K'
XG251	
XG252	
XG253	Mk 6 conversion; 'X' – CO's aircraft; FL Scotford ejected, 28 Oct 1962.
XG717	
XJ640	
XJ642	
XJ712	'H'
XJ713	
XK139	'X'
XL620	
XL623	

Hawker Harrier GR1/1A

XV744	
XV745	damaged by fire Cat 4, Oct 1969; lost in mid-air collision 19 Jan 1976.
XV746	
XV747	
XV748	
XV749	usual mount of CO, WC Smith; FL Marshall ejected 26 Apr 1972.
XV750	
XV752	later GR3
XV753	
XV754	later GR3
XV755	later GR3
XV756	
XV757	
XV758	
XV759	
XV760	
XV761	
XV762	
XV776	damaged landing at Paris Air Show, 1969; converted to GR3 and FL Buckler ejected 9 Apr 1975.
XV777	'W' – FO Adams ejected 1 May 1972.
XV778	
XV788	later GR3; FL Scott ejected over Belize 1 Dec 1976.
XV792	damaged in Norway, 24 Nov 1971.
XV795	
XV796	FL Wharton ejected 6 Oct 1970.
XV803	Capt Distelweg USAF killed 3 Aug 1971.
XW923	

Hawker Harrier T2

XW271	wef 20 Jul 1971.

Hawker Harrier GR3 (inc Falklands)

XV739	FL Hulley ejected 24 Sep 1973.
XV740	
XV744	
XV745	lost in collision with XV754 19 Jan 1975, FL Downey killed.
XV746	
XV748	
XV749	
XV751	08 (tail number); FL Sowler turned over 5 Aug 1969.
XV752	04
XV753	
XV754	WC Hayr proving flight to Cyprus, 16 Feb 1970; lost in collision with XV745 19 Jan 1975, FL Roberts killed.
XV755	20
XV756	mid-air collision with XZ128 21 Sep 1979, WC Duckett ejected.
XV757	FL Boyens ejected 21 May 1982.
XV762	37
XV777	
XV778	16 – damaged by ground fire 10 Jun 1982.
XV787	02

XV789	32 – ex IV Sq; damaged over Falklands (WC Squire) 31 May; to IV Sq.
XV792	
XW269	
XW270	
XW271	
XW763	
XW767	06 – WC Squire ejected 6 Nov 1982, a/c lost.
XW769	24
XW919	damaged in crash 28 Jun 1973 – FL Blackford; aircraft repaired to become —
	03 – Ascension Is. defence a/c; later damaged by ground fire 12 Jun 1982.
XW922	damaged rolling over on landing Wittering, 19 Nov 1985.
XW924	35 – ex 233 OCU; Harrier Defence detachment Jul 1982.
XW934	
XZ128	mid-air collision with XV757, 21 Sep 1979, FL Gowers ejected.
XZ129	29 – Ascension Is. defence a/c; later Harriet Det, Jul 1982.
XZ130	27
XZ132	36 – ex 233 OCU; a/c u/s and returned to UK.
XZ133	10 – ex 233 OCU; Cat 4 storm damage on Stanley Jul 1982.
XZ963	14 – SL Pook ejected after combat damage, 30 May 1982.
XZ964	09
XZ968	
XZ972	33 – ex 233 OCU; FL Glover shot down (PoW) 21 May 1982.
XZ988	34 – ex 233 OCU; SL Iveson ejected after 35 mm hits, 27 May 1982.
XZ989	07 – several ops; WC Squire crash landed 8 Jun 1982 – SOC.
XZ992	05 – Harriet Det at Stanley Jul 1982.
XZ993	
XZ997	31 – ex IV Sq; several ops inc 1st LGB attack by WC Squire 13 Jun 1982.

Hawker Harrier T4

XW925	17

Hawker Harrier GR5

ZD350	FL Huckstep ejected Wittering 8 Aug 1992.
ZD355	SL Stevenson ejected over Denmark 17 Oct 1990.
ZD400	02
ZD465	
ZD468	
ZD469	FL Soffe hit cables over Norwegian Fjord, 15 Nov 1993.
ZD470	

Hawker Harrier GR7

ZD232	04
ZD321	02
ZD323	05 – Kosovo ops.
ZD327	Kosovo ops.
ZD329	Kosovo ops.
ZD352	Kosovo ops.
ZD376	24 – Kosovo ops.
ZD401	Kosovo ops.
ZD405	WC Walker hit by ground fire 2 Feb 1995, canopy shattered.
ZD431	Kosovo ops.
ZD435	47
ZD436	Kosovo ops.
ZD438	03
ZD464	54
ZD467	57
ZD468	
ZG472	62
ZG476	FO Jessott ejected near Wittering 19 Feb 1996.
ZG477	Kosovo ops.
ZG502	73
ZG503	74 – Kosovo ops.
ZG505	76 – Kosovo ops.
ZG530	Kosovo ops.
ZG857	Kosovo ops.
ZH659	'O'
ZH665	'S'

Harrier T10

ZH658	106

Index of Personnel